Anything But Mexican

Chicanos in Contemporary Los Angeles

RODOLFO F. ACUÑA

V

VERSO

London • New York

The map on page 4 is from Eugene Turner and James P. Allen. 1991. *An Atlas of Population Patterns in Metropolitan Los Angeles and Orange Counties, 1990*. Department of Geography, California State University, Northridge. It appears by the kind permission of the authors.

First published by Verso 1995
© Rodolfo Acuña 1995
All rights reserved

Verso
UK: 6 Meard Street, London W1F 0EG
USA: 180 Varick Street, New York, NY 10014-4606

Verso is the imprint of New Left Books

ISBN 1-85984-936-9 (hbk)
ISBN 1-85984-031-0 (pbk)

British Library Cataloguing in Publication Data
A catalogue record for this book is available from the British Library.

Library of Congress Cataloging-in-Publication Data
A catalog record for this book is available from the Library of Congress.

7 9 10 8 6

Typeset in Dante by NorthStar,
San Francisco, California
Printed and bound in the UK by
The Cromwell Press

Anything But Mexican

V

THE HAYMARKET SERIES

Editors: Mike Davis and Michael Sprinker

The Haymarket Series offers original studies in politics, history and culture, with a focus on North America. Representing views across the American left on a wide range of subjects, the series will be of interest to socialists both in the USA and throughout the world. A century after the first May Day, the American left remains in the shadow of those martyrs whom the Haymarket Series honors and commemorates. These studies testify to the living legacy of political action and commitment for which they gave their lives.

Contents

v

Preface

In the course of the twentieth century we have seen the United States shift from that prejudice against the foreign-born called nativism, directed at immigrants from certain European countries, to a full-fledged racism toward Third World immigrants. This racist form of nativism is not new; in the nineteenth century, for example, anti-Chinese hysteria led 94 percent of California's voters to approve a referendum excluding all Chinese, Congress to pass the 1882 Chinese Exclusion Act, and Wyoming settlers to murder in cold blood twenty-eight Chinese workers in 1885. Earlier in this century we saw it in the repeated, mass deportations of Mexican workers, often including US citizens. More recently the anti-immigrant hysteria has reached crescendo levels in place like California with the passage of Proposition 187 under the banner of 'Save Our State'. Past waves of US racist nativism often had economic origins very similar to those of today, with scapegoating immigrants serving to mask the effects of economic crisis on the fortunes of native-born Americans.

But there are certain significant and indeed sinister differences between past and present forms of racist nativism. First, it has become more global than ever before, as recent European history indicates. Dutch professor Teun A. van Dijk writes, 'In late 1991 and early 1992 ... ethnic minorities, immigrants and refugees in North America and especially Europe continued to be confronted with increasing racism, ethnicism and xenophobia.'[1] It is also more 'open to fascism ... directed against all migrants, refugees and asylum-seekers displaced from their own countries by the depredations of international capital.'[2] Here in the United States, racist nativism sees *all* immigrants of color as 'illegal aliens', regardless of their actual legal status. It does not distinguish one Brown person from another, citizen from immigrant, recent immigrant from second generation. It seemingly exempts African Americans because they are citizens and speak English. But racist nativism, as Europe today shows us, ultimately categorizes all people of color as 'immigrants and refugees and all immigrants and refugees as terrorists and drug dealers';[3] in the US, we can add, as welfare recipients, criminals, or other morally inferior creatures – in short, anyone not a 'real American'.

The tensions and excesses of racist nativism are nowhere more evident than in Southern California today. This is a major reason why *Anything But Mexican* focuses on Los Angeles, once a thriving industrial city and now the Third World capital of the United States. The restructuring of L.A.'s economy, which mirrors a global economic restructuring, has unsettled many Euroamericans, nestled in areas formerly protected from the decaying inner city. They now seek to blame Latin American, Asian and other immigrants for the effects of post-industrial capitalism.

I have also focused on Los Angeles because racist nativism promises to have a profound impact on Chicanos/as and other Latinos. It is here that immigration from Latin America, as well as from Asia and the Middle East, has dramatically challenged Euroamerican racial and cultural hegemony. Nearly 4 million of the 16 million persons of Mexican descent in the United States live in Los Angeles and its environs. In 1990, Chicanos and Mexicanos made up some 30 percent of the city; along with other Latinos they comprised 40 percent of the population. And over 40 percent of the undocumented live in L.A.[4] With these characteristics, Los Angeles is the ideal social laboratory for a micro-study of a global phenomenon. In that laboratory, upheaval is the norm.

In Los Angeles, the rest of California, and much of the United States, racist nativism feeds on white fears of losing control over this society as a result of changing demographics. The reality of people of color soon forming the majority population in Los Angeles fuels a vicious antipathy. Along with the issue of control comes that of national identity. Always defined as Euroamerican, the US self-image seems to white people to be seriously threatened for the first time since the birth of the nation. Euroamerican dread of what would be a profound transformation – and one that may well occur – is another reason for the virulence of today's racist nativism. At stake, then, are power and control as well as definition of the individual and collectivity. At stake is history: how it is written and how it is remembered. At stake is culture: how to define US culture, and whose definition shall be dominant?

Not surprisingly, in an era when many Euroamericans fear the surrender of what have been their least challenged, most comfortable assumptions, people of color have been pushing for drastic change of those same assumptions. Again Los Angeles is ideal as a social laboratory for the examination of these forces at work. This book is, in essence, about the struggle of Chicanos and Mexicanos in Los Angeles to affirm their political, economic and cultural presence as peoples during the last fifteen years – the same period in which racist nativism has built to a new crescendo. Key to that Chicano/Mexicano struggle is reconstructing a historical memory of Los Angeles that has been diluted or denied by Eurocentric forces. This requires retelling what happened and redefining the causes of what happened. In these ways the reconstruction of history and affirmation of identity go hand in hand.

The Complexity of Identity

Anything But Mexican grapples with the issue of identity. As we will see, identity has always been problematic among the 'other' in US society – and it is no different among Chicanos, who especially since the 1960s have hotly debated what to call themselves. It was natural, then, that the debate grew even more intense as immigration from Mexico and Central America increased dramatically – and the national origins of the various Latino groups grew more complex. The issue of identity was not confined to nationality, but included class considerations. For example, prominent in this conversation were the aspirations of rising middle-class Latino and Chicano professionals, who sought to package their group in ways furnishing them maximum leverage in economic and political markets. Also important were the voices of nationalists within the various Latino communities. The complexity of identity thus made solutions to common problems difficult.

Issues of identity, immigration, class, and relations with other minorities are often joined in the arena of electoral politics. Thus readers will find that Chapters 3 to 7 are devoted primarily to electoral politics and immigration issues in Los Angeles. Minorities in general, and Chicanos in particular, are obsessed with electoral politics; victories in this arena have become measures of empowerment. The number of office-holders from a particular minority – rather than the quality of their representation – has become the measure of success. In this context, it cannot be denied that Latinos made significant electoral gains during the 1980s and 1990s. By 1994, for the first time in this century, Chicanos had three representatives on the Los Angeles City Council and one on the Los Angeles County Board of Supervisors. Statewide they elected ten state legislators and four members of Congress, and achieved appointment of a host of judges. For the first time, Chicanas and Latinas were political powerbrokers. Moreover, Chicano and Chicana politicos and organizations supposedly had the ear of President Bill Clinton; cabinet secretaries Henry Cisneros and Federico Peña were regular items on the Washington scene. But how much has it really mattered? Chicano Democratic politicos could not persuade their own party to stop immigrant-bashing, or win appointment of one of their own, Sam Paz – an attorney whose life has been dedicated to upholding the US Constitution – to the federal bench.[5] Such limitations stem from society's racism, together with the lack of a clear sense of identity preventing Chicanos from developing a unified and cohesive force for political and social change.

Various reasons exist for that lack of identity. They include the fact that, unlike San Antonio, for example, where overt racial oppression left little doubt in the minds of Chicanos that they were Mexicans, it has been easier for lighter-skinned Mexicans in L.A. to pass – to move and to live where they wanted. Euroamericans made exceptions for them; indeed, intermarriage has always been common in Los Angeles.

The reconstruction of identity in Los Angeles also involves addressing the cultural, generational and class differences that permeate a community. The problems of identity facing my middle-class Chicano students at California State University, Northridge, provide a case in point. These students often pass through a crisis in their first year of college, when they come into contact with a critical mass of barrio students for the first time. Raised in predominately white neighborhoods, they identify with their white neighbors and white classmates to the point that they adopt a white sense of identity. Looking at and listening to barrio Chicanos, who are more often than not from working-class families, the Anglo-oriented students are often ashamed of them. The barrio students are poor, dress differently, and speak differently from Chicanos raised in Euroamerican neighborhoods. Becoming aware of this false identity, many Chicano youth have sought to reject it. Others try to avoid the whole issue, while still others are attempting to identify with their roots.

The Cultural War

Though identity is important to Chicanos, *Anything But Mexican* is not only about identity. Rather it is a political work, one that attempts to define an emerging Chicano/Latino political space. The definition of this political space is difficult because it challenges Eurocentric interests that want to preserve the national identity of the United States as a Western European nation.[6] To this end, Eurocentrists have declared a cultural war against those wanting to define US history in terms of realities not comprehended by Euroamerica, and have attempted to establish their version of reality and their terms of reference as the common sense of US political discourse. For example, Ernest Lefever, a fellow at the ultraconservative Ethics and Public Policy Center, accused the proponents of affirmative action of distorting and corrupting language: 'We should call a quota a quota and a subsidy a subsidy and not sugarcoat it by calling it affirmative action.'[7]

By the late 1980s, right-wing ideologues in alliance with conservative politicians had invented a multiculturist revolution in universities, and portrayed themselves as the last-ditch defenders of civilized standards against 'political correctness'.[8] For them, equality in education was the antithesis of quality education. Massive Third World immigration, according to some of the New Right, stimulated multiculturalism and was changing fundamental Euroamerican traditions. The rise and eventual dominance of a school-aged population of color would ensure the emergence of future generations even more removed from Western civilization. Neoconservative critic Irving Kristol went so far as to claim that multiculturalism was a threat equal to those of Nazism and Stalinism.[9] In this context, history became a battleground.

Today this assault on non-European ethnic identity is led by some of the nation's leading conservative scholars, financed by conservative think-tanks seeking to justify white racial privilege and Euroamerican cultural hegemony. Their strategy requires them to deconstruct newborn Chicano identity and corrupt public political discourse with regard to Chicanos and other people of color. Prime examples of such corruption are Peter Skerry's *Mexican Americans: The Ambivalent Minority,*[10] funded by the American Free Enterprise Institute (critiqued in Chapter 5 of this book), and L.H. Gann and Peter J. Duignan's *Hispanics in the United States: A History* (1986), sponsored by the Hoover Institution.[11] Because of a dearth of scholarly books on Chicanos, these two works have been able to stake out important intellectual space. Written in a Reaganesque style, they feign social concern while dealing in half-truths and coded racist messages. By blaming immigrants (read, Latinos) for US social decay, they conceal the real roots and effects of US de-industrialization.[12] At the same time, such a political/cultural strategy enables a capitalist elite to 'make economic gains without incurring social costs or political dislocation.'[13] They can exploit immigrant and even native-born Chicano workers, while saving themselves the cost of educating those workers' children or caring for their health, as any civilized society would require them to do.

It matters little that the authors of *Hispanics in the United States* are non-Chicano specialists who had never written a book about Chicanos before.[14] If a minority scholar had published a book with as many material errors of fact as are found in Gann and Duignan's book, he or she would have been ridiculed as the product of an affirmative action education.[15] Yet books like Gann and Duignan's are accepted as scholarship, which, according to myth, is nonideological, objective, and based on uncontroverted facts.[16]

In part, *Anything But Mexican* answers the Ganns, Duignans and Skerrys by offering the perspective of a specialist in Chicano Studies. Thus the concept of identity as discussed here is more than a sociological expression: it includes economics and politics, and addresses themes of immigration, labor, women, Chicano–Mexican relations, police–Chicano relations, education, and other topics in relation to Chicano identity and the new racism.

We cannot separate either scholarship or government policy from their consequences. We should remember that the Immigration Acts of 1921 and 1924, which excluded Asians and gave preferences to northern Europeans, provided the intellectual as well as legal framework for the massive repatriations of Mexicans in the 1930, and setting the precedent for putting over 100,000 Japanese Americans into concentration camps in 1942. The consequences of cultural wars can be serious indeed.

The logical next step in the New Right's cultural war is the resurrection of eugenics doctrines that seemed dead after the defeat of Nazi Germany at the end of World War II. In 1994 Charles Murray, a fellow at the American Enterprise Institute, and Richard Herrnstein published *The Bell Curve*. The book provides a theoretical base for reactionary policy-makers and politicians seeking to use hot-button rhetoric about immigration, crime and welfare reform to exploit white fears of Mexicans, Latinos, Asians and African Americans. *The Bell Curve* offers a pseudo-scientific justification for ignoring the real causes of poverty and crime and for dismantling the social safety net. It makes social pathology a function of genes, as supposedly proven by the large numbers of Blacks and Browns in prisons.[17]

The essence of the New Right's strategy was expressed by Florida gubernatorial candidate Jeb Bush in 1994, who, when asked what he would do for the African American community, responded, 'Probably nothing'.[18] Instead, Bush said, he would reduce welfare, fight crime and downsize government, a message tailored to fit white middle-class biases. In California, Governor Pete Wilson mastered the Orwellian game of politics by code word, substituting *criminal* for *Mexican* and putting the blame for the state's budget crisis and the impact of recession and defense cuts on immigrants.[19] The result has been an increase in interracial tensions and the racial polarization of the 1994 California gubernatorial election.

In the past, coded language has usually been a way for the oppressed to disguise their criticism of those in power. Today, it is part of the ideological strategy of Euroamerican elites, serving to justify their domination of communities of color while disguising openly racist sentiments (*criminal* instead of *Mexican*). Related to the current use of code words are other forms of language manipulation that serve ruling-class interests. For example, the Hoover Institution and the American Free Enterprise Institute work hard at deconstructing and then exploiting the language of the civil rights movement as part of an attack on the entire concept of equity. Through access to the media, they control the debate on class and race exploitation by delegitimizing discussion of the struggle of the oppressed for equity, and dismissing it as an effort to impose 'political correctness'.

In summary, the power relationship between Chicanos/Latinos and Euroamericans in Los Angeles affects the interpretation of history and political discourse itself. The social climate of Los Angeles, like other developed cities, has 'been marked by mass narcissism and historical amnesia.'[20] Once again we see the United States and Europe portrayed as the custodians of civilization. The problem for Chicanos and other Latinos is that because of the disparate power relationship between them and the Euroamerican population, their interpretation of social reality tends to be given less value – although it may be more valid – than that of those in power.[21]

A Chicano Perspective

Anything But Mexican by no means pretends to be a definitive work on the New Right's ideological assault on immigration policy, Eurocentric racism, or contemporary Los Angeles. It is a micro-view of Chicanos and Chicanas, and sometimes other Latinos, in Los Angeles, written to inform and redirect the present national and global discourse about diversity and racism in relation to the growing presence of the Third World in one of the First World's premier cities.

This book is divided into twelve chapters. Chapter 1 introduces the Chicano/a and Latino/a in Los Angeles. Its theme is Chicano identity in the context of Euroangeleno racism, and how race, class and gender intersect. The chapter explores the theme of 'anything but Mexican', the book's term for the prevailing Euroangeleno evaluation of Mexicans and Mexicans' view of themselves. It shows where Chicanos live and how they are changing Los Angeles's physical and cultural environment.

Chapter 2, 'Taking Back Chicano History', deals with Chicano history and the Chicano sense of place in Los Angeles in the context of the struggle for identity and human rights in this country. It speaks to struggles within the Chicano community and with forces outside it to control the definition of Chicano history and culture. The fight over Olvera Street and the campaign for a Latino museum symbolize this taking-back of Chicano history. Finally, the chapter discusses the role of the Catholic Church, which remains a colonial institution, although a benevolent one at times.

The work of City Councilman Edward R. Roybal in the 1950s gave birth to modern Chicano politics. Roybal was the last Chicano politician to develop an independent grassroots organization that gave him independence from special-interest groups. Throughout this period, the success and form of Chicano politics were limited by low registration and the politics of the Democratic Party. The dramatic growth of the Latino population forced redistricting after the 1970 and 1980 Censuses that enabled the rise of Assemblyman Richard Alatorre and his election to the Los Angeles City Council in the mid 1980s. These developments are covered in Chapter 3, 'Chicanos in Politics: A Struggle for Existence'.

The dramatic events surrounding the mobilization of the Mothers of East Los Angeles and their fight to keep a prison out of Boyle Heights begin Chapter 4, 'Marching Mothers and the Rise of Gloria Molina', which describes Assemblywoman Molina's election to the City Council and then to the County

Board of Supervisors. Threats of yet another prison, a gas pipeline through Boyle Heights and a toxic waste incinerator mobilized disparate interests, as the Mothers of East L.A. marched through the streets. Molina's ability to exploit these energies put her in a position to challenge the 'old guard' led by Richard Alatorre.

Chapter 5, 'Politics for the Few', covers the backlash against Chicano political successes, which – aside from representation – have meant more city and county jobs, as well as the growing influence of Chicano and Latino developers and other interest groups. Efforts of ultraconservatives to retain their dominance over the unrepresented Latino community resulted in a power struggle over space and resources. This struggle was intensified by Proposition 13 and its clones, which have cut taxes on private property, driven the downsizing of government and closed opportunities for all people of color, for whom civil service employment has always been route into the mainstream economy. Economic restructuring also increased competition between African Americans and Chicanos for jobs in the ever-shrinking labor market. Rounding off the chapter are accounts of the struggle over reapportionment following the 1990 Census and the 1992 presidential election, both marked by immigrant bashing to divert attention from the growing gap between rich and poor.

Chapter 6, 'Immigration: "The Border Crossed Us"', deals with the history of Chicano immigration to Los Angeles; its title comes from the reaction of Chicano youth to conservative attacks on immigrants: 'We didn't cross the border, the border crossed us.' Indeed, the dynamics of immigration and the border drive Euroamerican–Chicano relations. The Great Repatriation during the 1930s political disempowered Chicanos. It also furthered the idea of the Chicano as 'other', as did militarization of the border and professionalization of the border patrol after World War II. Racist nativism increased further after the 1965 Immigration Act opened the gates of the US to the Third World, ushering in an era when the United States joined Europe in creating a racist discourse to justify the exclusion of the 'other'. The chapter then looks at how the immigrant has become the scapegoat for the economic restructuring and its social consequences, which accelerated during the 1970s and 1980s.

Multisided struggles for control of L.A.'s government marked the 1990s and are the theme of Chapter 7, 'The Politicization of the "Other"'. Changing neighborhood demographics led to conflicts over turf and resources among Chicanos, Blacks and Asians – and these tensions were often poorly handled by community leaders. Mexicans and Blacks contested for political control of districts where Latinos were becoming the majority, but remained a minority of voters. Understandably, Black leaders were not ready to give up power, which means badly needed jobs and contracts for Black contractors. In 1992 the City Council created a second Chicano district on the Board of Education cutting into the San Fernando Valley. This unleashed the pent up frustration and anger of Euroamerican San Fernando Valley homeowner associations, which responded by launching a campaign to break up the mammoth Los Angeles Unified School District. The political power of the San Fernando Valley and its white voting majority intimidated politicos such as state Senator David Roberti and progressive state Senator Tom Hayden into supporting this power play. In this context, Richard Riordan, a representative of L.A.'s ruling elite, was elected mayor. In 1994, Governor Pete Wilson resurrected his flagging governorship and was reelected by a using campaign strategy that scapegoated immigrants as the reason for California's recurring budget crises. Californians overwhelmingly passed Proposition 187, whose provisions deny education and basic human services to immigrants, and which badly polarized Los Angeles and the rest of the state.

Chapter 8, 'Mexican/Latino Labor: Working in a Meaner and Leaner World', charts the restructuring and globalization of L.A.'s economy. Although Mexicans and other Latinos have one of the highest labor-force participation rates in the US, they are L.A.'s lowest-paid workers. The elimination of jobs in heavy industry has widened the gap between rich and poor, while the new service economy has failed to produce well-paying jobs. The dismantling of the region's defense industries has intensified competition among workers, often along racial lines. The chapter also focuses on the heroic struggle of the immigrant worker to unionize through the Justice for Janitors campaign and on the leadership of organizers such as María Elena Durazo to empower the most vulnerable workers in L.A.

Chapter 9, 'Chicanas in Los Angeles', addresses the gendered particulars of identity and the political space occupied by Chicanas in Los Angeles. Although they are half the Latino people in Los Angeles, until the gains of Latinas in the 1980s in politics and the professions they have been almost invisible as subjects of their own history. The chapter thus attempts to take them out of the shadow of the Chicano male. The lack of consciousness about Chicanas and Latinas is in part due to the dearth of information and analysis available. To partially fill this gap, the chapter presents a demographic profile of Latinas in L.A., and analyzes the effects of the 'glass ceiling' in education and the workplace on their upward mobility.

It is said that Mexico is always with Chicanos, and that they still feel an emotional attachment to 'México Lindo', even to the third and fourth generations. This love for the motherland strengthens relations between Chicanos and Mexico, as the growth of a Chicano petty bourgeoisie makes that population even more valuable to Mexican elites. Chapter 10, *'México Lindo* and NAFTA', analyzes the intersection of Mexican–Chicano interests. During the presidency of Carlos Salinas de Gortari, the Mexican government increased its efforts to wed Chicano interests to those of Mexico, with the president of Mexico openly courting Chicano business and political leaders. Middle-class Chicanos played an important role in the passage of the North American Free Trade Agreement (NAFTA), while Chicano organizations tried to have it both ways, using NAFTA as a bargaining chip to increase their influence with the Clinton administration.

Chapter 11, 'Troubled Angels', is about Los Angeles's reaction to growing poverty and Third Worldization: with an increase in poverty and a decrease in hope have come more crime and the decay of the family and the social infrastructure. Rather than address these realities, the media draws a portrait of Los Angeles entering a '*Blade Runner*' epoch. The L.A. Police and Sheriff's departments have long envisioned themselves as an occupying army, with people of color as the enemy population. However, the overreaction of police and police brutality in the case of Rodney King led to police reform of sorts.

Education is one of the last avenues of upward mobility open to people of color, enabling Chicanos and other Latinos to rise above the minimum-wage limbo where the working poor live. Chapter 12, 'The Stairway to the Good Life', describes how educational opportunities shrank in the 1980s and 1990s as an undemocratic tax system allowed the state's education system to deteriorate, from one of the top five in the US, to one of the poorest in the country. The business community responded by arguing that the schools did not need money – they only lacked good business management. Corporate America would teach the Los Angeles Unified School District how to manage its resources. The lack of funds led to the dismantling of bilingual education programs, while expensive magnet schools were constructed to serve the children of the middle class, and especially the white middle-class; Latinos were generally relegated to below-average facilities. Colleges and universities also closed the window of opportunity as higher tuition rates excluded minorities, while New Right scholars perpetuated the myth that the presence on campus of Chicanos and Latinos along with Blacks drags down the quality of education. Chicano students have reacted to these attacks with increased militancy and hunger strikes, perhaps most notably in the struggle for a Chicano Studies Department at UCLA.

Acknowledgements

I would like to take this opportunity to thank my friend, Dean of Humanities Jorge García, for the inspiration of the name *Anything But Mexican*. I would also like to acknowledge the CSUN Foundation for funding three units of released time for one semester from my teaching duties so that I could continue to write. The writing of this book has been especially trying, since it was completed during a period when I was suing the University of California, Santa Barbara, for political, race and age discrimination. I learned a great deal about elite institutions from this experience, and about what a scholar should not be. I am grateful to my attorneys for their encouragement and lessons in applied knowledge. Indeed, my universe was expanded through legal research and its application. Mil gracias also, to my close friends in the FOR (Friends of Rudy) Acuña Support Committee, without whose support I could not have finished this book.

I also thank Professors Mary Pardo and Mary Beth Welsh for reading passages of the manuscript. I am especially indebted to Elizabeth Martínez for editing this book. Betita, as we all know her, is a leading intellectual and writer in the Chicano community, combining theory and practice. (Sometimes, however, I wished that she wouldn't ask so many hard questions.) I also want to thank Steven Hiatt for his copyediting, and especially for his patience. Lastly, my two sons, Walter and Frank, were and are always in my heart. The support and inspiration for this book came mainly from my daughter, Angela, and my wife, Lupita, who had to put up with a severe loss of quality time and the stress that comes from writing and struggle.

Notes

1. Teun A. van Dijk, *Elite Discourse and Racism* (Newbury Park, Calif.: Sage, 1993), p. 1.

2. A. Sivanandan, 'The New Racism', *New Statesman & Society*, vol. 1, no. 22 (4 Nov. 1988), p. 8; the existence of anti-immigrant hysteria in Europe, in a perverted fashion, gives legitimacy to the familiar argument that Americans are not alone in this sentiment – as though the existence of zenophobia in Western Europe somehow excused anti-immigrant hysteria in the US.

3. Ibid., p. 9.

4. Samir Amin, '1492, Columbus and the New World Order, 1492–1992', *Monthly Review*, vol. 4, no. 3 (July 1992), p. 10. Amin writes that there is a growing fear of the Asiatic and African demographic revolution. The reaction is an alarmist and racist discourse, which is more hysterical than based on fact. In 1770 the global population was 80 percent Asian and African; however, by 1990 this had fallen to 71 percent. The difference was that in 1770 most of the Third World was controlled by Europe, with the world order changing during and after World War II and rise of national liberation movements.

5. Tony Perry, 'Nominees for 2 Judgeships Withdraw', *Los Angeles Times*, 21 Jan. 1995. Chicanos had been elated when Clinton nominated attorney Sam Paz to a federal judgeship. Paz, a former president of the Southern California Chapter of the American Civil Liberties Union, had devoted his career to the defense of the US Constitution, and had defended many victims of police brutality. However, Clinton asked Paz to withdraw from consideration after the ultraconservative Police Officers Research Association of California and Senate Republicans attacked Paz's nomination. The message from the administration was clear: unless you championed corporations, you had better not aspire to the federal judiciary. Meanwhile, where was the public outcry from the Latino community?

6. Paul Hockenos, 'Making Hate Safe Again in Europe: Right Cultural Revolutionaries', *Nation*, vol. 259, no. 8 (19 Sept. 1994), p. 271. Hockenos points out that the thinkers of the European New Right have adopted the long-term cultural strategy advocated by Antonio Gramsci: 'The New Right strategists insisted that a political revolution could not occur without change in popular political culture, a shift in values that underpinned the existing consensus. If they were to make a comeback, they realized, their illiberal, essentially fascist convictions, off-limits since World War II, had to be made palatable again to a broad segment of the population.' After twenty years the

assumptions of the New Right have become an established part of political discourse throughout Western Europe. Indeed, the same process has taken place in the United States as a result of the incessant attack on liberalism by the New Right. In Germany, the New Right wins 5 to 15 percent of the vote in state elections, and has failed to make it into the federal legislature, whereas in the United States, the Republican Party is controlled by the far right.

7. Betsy Pisik, 'The Semantics of Hate', *Washington Post*, 14 Nov. 1991.

8. The ridiculous nature of this debate is expressed in William Endicott, 'Don't Need PC to Know a Slur', *Sacramento Bee*, 18 July 1993. Endicott claims that the PC cops would have us refer to short people as 'the vertically challenged', the homeless as 'the underhoused', and the poor as 'the economically marginalized'. My own position is that no manner of speech should be limited in the classroom; however, I see the danger of the university degenerating into a street environment, since I cannot condone calling anyone a 'bitch', 'coon', 'chink', 'kike' or 'beaner', which is what groups such as David Horowitz's advocate. There was a lot of open racism in the 1950s when I returned to college as a Korean War veteran. I was one of the few Chicanos at Los Angeles State College. A critical mass of the students, however, were veterans, and in the service they had learned to respect each other's space. Racist words and insults had consequences. Hence, it was not a matter of political correctness not to use these words – it was a matter of survival. Personally, I do not really care what people call me, just as long as I have the right to insult them – but such a tit-for-tat adds little to the learning process.

9. Lawrence Auster, 'The Forbidden Topic', *National Review*, vol. 44, no. 8 (27 April 1992), p. 42. Not all conservatives agreed with this analysis.

10. Peter Skerry, *Mexican Americans: The Ambivalent Minority* (New York: Free Press, 1993).

11. L.H. Gann and Peter J. Duignan, *Hispanics in the United States: A History* (Boulder, Colo. and Stanford, Calif.: Westview Press and Hoover Institution, 1986). The latter book is almost comical with its numerous misspellings and factual errors.

12. Victor Valle and Rodolfo D. Torres, 'Latinos in a "Post-Industrial" Disorder', *Socialist Review*, vol. 23, no. 4 (1994), pp. 1–7.

13. Sivanandan, 'The New Racism', p. 8.

14. Richard Chabrán, 'The Emergence of Neoconservativism in Chicano/Latino Discourses', in Special Issue: 'Chicana/o Cultural Representations: Reframing Alternative Critical Discourse', *Cultural Studies*, vol. 4, no. 3 (October 1990), pp. 221–6.

15. Rodolfo Acuña, 'Book Review of *Hispanics in the United States: A History*', *Pacific Historical Review*, no. 57, vol. 2 (1988), pp. 230–1.

16. Unfortunately, some Spanish-surnamed scholars reviewed Gann and Duignan's book as noted in its preface. If so, they should have had the professionalism to correct the errors that appeared in it.

17. See Salim Muwakkil, 'The Ugly Revival of Genetic Determinism', *San Francisco Examiner*, 6 Dec. 1994. This and other articles point to the intersection of the English-Only Movement, the voucher program, anti-immigrant hysteria, anti–political correctness/multicultural movements, and the Federation for American Immigration Reform, and ties them to right-wing foundations such as the Pioneer Fund. The Pioneer Fund also had links to the Coalition for Freedom, which established the Jesse Helms Institute for Foreign Policy and American Studies. Associated Press, 'Campaign Ads Often Disguise Prejudice, Buzzwords Used to Court Racists', *The Record*, 9 Nov. 1994.

18. Bush said he would work to get mothers off welfare in two years, divert resources from the public schools by instituting a voucher system, and cut back programs in the Dept. of Education and Health and Rehabilitation Services, which at the time employed 15,700 Black people. Peggy Peterman, 'Election '94: Campaign Considerations', *St. Petersburg Times*, Nov. 1994.

19. Teun A. van Dijk, *Communicating Racism: Ethnic Prejudice in Thought and Talk* (Newbury Park, Calif.: Sage, 1987), pp. 31–2.

20. Fred Halliday, 'The World in the 1980s: Notes on the New Political Culture', *Nation*, vol. 249, no. 7 (4 Sept. 1989), p. 234.

21. Van Dijk, *Communicating Racism*, pp. 51 – 9. Van Dijk conducted studies in San Diego and the Netherlands, and drew parallels from the responses. Statements such as, 'They take "our" jobs', and 'They should learn to speak the language of the country' were common to both: van Dijk, *Elite Discourse and Racism*, p. 1.

1

Introducing Chicano L.A.

In June 1993 I visited students on the UCLA campus who were staging a hunger strike to force the university to establish an autonomous Chicano Studies department. On the way home my eight-year-old daughter, Angela, tearfully asked her mother why everyone couldn't be the same. It was hard to be a Mexican; people didn't like her father because he was Mexican; they didn't give him a job because he was Mexican; and now her friends were starving because they were Mexicans. It was too hard to be Mexican! At an early age, Angela was learning that Los Angeles is a great place for Mexicans – so long as they make no claim to the city's history or to a place in its political life.

It has long been an insult to be considered Mexican in this city. Until recently, for example, Mexican food was called 'Spanish', although it is one of the few things Mexican almost universally accepted by Euroamericans. The neon signs at some of the most established Mexican restaurants in L.A., like El Cholo, reputedly L.A.'s oldest, even today advertise 'Spanish' food. This preference for the European reappears in L.A.'s public relations as the city fathers promote a mythical Los Angeles in which cultural borrowing and harmony are the rule. That myth includes the fantasy of a romantic 'Hispanic' – read, European – past of *dons* and *ranchos*. That tradition is acceptable to Euroangelenos; the Mexican reality is not.

So we find Los Angeles welcoming King Juan Carlos I and Queen Sofia of Spain to Los Angeles in October 1987. When I asked Bea Lavery, an aide to then Mayor Tom Bradley, what significance the trip held for Latinos, she replied, 'That's what the trip is all about.' After all, she added, 'Felipe Neve *discovered* Los Angeles.' A statue of King Carlos III, who granted Los Angeles its first charter in 1781, was moved from MacArthur Park to El Pueblo Park for the royal visit. This allowed the king and queen to pay homage to their Bourbon ancestor in the place considered to be the city's original center. While there, they walked Olvera Street – a bit of 'Old Spain' in Los Angeles. If they so desired they could have eaten traditional 'Spanish' food like tacos and tamales and listened to 'Spanish' mariachi music. Totally ignored was the fact that Neve and the Spanish did not 'discover' Southern California any more than Columbus discovered America; they invaded.

Mexican acceptability in Los Angeles varies according to the Mexican's appearance and socio-economic status. Euroangelenos often stumble when asking people if they are Mexican, seeming surprised when the answer is 'yes'. Almost apologetically the questioner responds, with a smile, 'Oh, you don't look Mexican!' – as if that were some kind of compliment. Euroangelenos love French accents (they're sexy), and Central European accents like Henry Kissinger's (they sound so intelligent); on the other hand, they find Mexican and other Latino (or Asian) accents hard to understand. Minerva Pérez, a former KTLA-TV anchor, described how during her tenure at the station she irritated some viewers by simply pronouncing Spanish words properly, including her own name: 'I got resistance to my Mexican ways from viewers and management ... It took me by surprise because I thought I was coming to a place that was mostly Hispanic. There were some very vocal people who told me to go back to Mexico ...'[1]

The Euroangelenos' lack of any sense of local history makes it possible for even the most recent arrivals from the East Coast or Europe to think of themselves as more entitled, more 'native,' than Chicanos or Mexicanos, even though Mexicans have lived in California for generations.[2] It is difficult for Euroangelenos to fathom that they are not the only Americans, and that to call only white people 'American' reflects the imperial pretensions of 'manifest destiny'.[3] Indeed, throughout its history Euroamerican society has almost always claimed for itself the privilege of whether or not to accept 'outsiders', and what to call them.[4] Slowly Anglo-Americans accepted the Irish and immigrants from Southern and Eastern Europe; the only 'unmelted ethnics' remaining in the United States are non-European and dark. Yet Euroangelenos want everyone to believe that they are open-minded, that traditional ethnic and racial biases have been left back East. They want everyone to 'wannabe' Americans, and they are infuriated when people don't 'wannabe', spitting out clichés such as 'America: love it or leave it!'; or smugly telling brown-skinned people to go back where they came from. A 1989 *Los Angeles Times* survey reported that four out of ten Euroangelenos resented seeing foreign-language signs in stores.[5] They seem to want Mexicans to identify not as Mexicans but as Americans, yet at the same time they insist on labeling all Mexicans – whether US-born, legal immigrants, or undocumented – as 'illegal aliens', a term that is today's euphemism for 'wetbacks' or 'greasers'. This hostility has many roots, but Euroangeleno insecurity in the face of continuing Mexican/Latino immigration is a key factor in the social and political life of Los Angeles.

Where and How Chicanos and Latinos Live

Chicanos and Latinos are everywhere in Southern California. The 1990 Census showed a Los Angeles city population of 3,485,398, 39.9 percent of whom were Latino, some 37 percent white, 13 percent Black and 9.2 percent Asian.[6] In Los Angeles County, Latinos comprised 37.8 percent (or 3,351,242) of the 8,863,164 residents. Of that number, those of Mexican extraction were 2,527,160 or 28.5 percent of the total, and 'other Hispanics' 738,113, or 8.3 percent.[7] African Americans numbered 992,974 (11.2 percent), Asians 954,485 (10.8 percent), and Euroamericans 3,318,850 (40.8 percent). Given the usual census undercount, the number of Latinos in the county may very well have surpassed that of Euroamericans.[8]

In Los Angeles and Orange Counties combined, the Latino population grew by 1.5 million during the 1980s, with the new arrivals coming mostly from Mexico and Central America. They were typically young adults (in 1990 nearly seven out of every ten Latinos were younger than thirty-five), and they had a high birth rate. These new Latino immigrants, undocumented and documented, have crowded the traditional Mexican/Chicano barrios like Boyle Heights, East Los Angeles and the Pico-Union district. They also moved north of the southern part of Downtown, into the five cities – Bell Gardens, Cudahy, Huntington Park, South Gate and Maywood – that once comprised the industrial heartland of the county. Bell Gardens and Cudahy have become over 85 percent Latino, and these cities had the lowest per capita incomes in the county. The new immigrants also pushed into South Central Los Angeles where, by the end of the decade, they were almost a majority.[9]

Many Chicanos and Latinos are concentrated in a large, inner-core area dubbed Nuevo Los Angeles. It includes the areas bounded by Hollywood, Boyle Heights, Lincoln Heights and South Central, and is inhabited by over a million people. This solidly Latino area would be the seventh largest city in the United States if it were a separate city. *Daily News* reporters David Parish and Beth Barrett reported that 51.5 percent of this area's residents were not citizens, and that half did not speak English. 'Culture, language, income, opportunity and need' separated them from the mainstream ... Here workers, mostly immigrant women, toil 50 hours a week in garment factories to earn $200.' According to the reporters, these industries survive only because of the availability – and exploitability – of immigrant workers.[10] Some Chicano families have lived in Nuevo Los Angeles for as many as five generations. Some remain because they would feel out of place in other parts of the city: most remain because they like places like Pico-Union.[11]

The Pico-Union district, often called Pequeño Centro América or Nuevo Cuscatlán, lies within Nuevo Los Angeles along with Koreatown, the edge of Downtown, and Westlake. 'Nearly half of the people living in selected tracts of

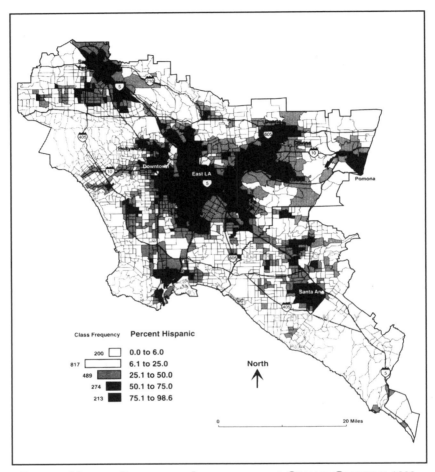

PERCENT HISPANIC POPULATION, LOS ANGELES AND ORANGE COUNTIES, 1990.

Pico-Union came to this country in the 1980s, and slightly more than one in four were born in the United States.' (In Boyle Heights, on the other hand, the ratio of 1980s immigrants to native-born was 32 percent to 40 percent – and 20 to 50 percent in selected census tracts in East Los Angeles.)[12] It is in this area that the Salvadoran and Guatemalan communities are concentrated. The combined Pico-Union and Westlake districts (which includes MacArthur Park) are the most overcrowded in the city, with 147 people per acre, having a density four times that of New York City. Councilman Mike Hernández, who represents the area, describes the problems of the new arrivals:

> What we are dealing with is a population that is almost invisible… because of the lack of documents they cannot participate in our society in any way. The work rules are against them: they can't obtain federal aid … without having documents.

The proportion of Mexicans in the county's Latino population dipped from 80 percent to 75 percent during the 1980s as a result of war and economic dislocation in Central America. In 1993, one in five residents of the Pico-Union district was Salvadoran and one in ten Guatemalan. The Salvadoran population started coming to L.A. en masse in 1981, accelerating during 1983 when Salvadoran death squads and the army were disappearing as many as 30 people a day. Some 136,000 Salvadorans qualified under the Immigration Reform Control Act of 1986, but a majority did not qualify for amnesty, with some 72,000 working as temporary residents in 1993.[13] Despite legal barriers, the 1990 Census counted some 271,301 Salvadorans and 139,372 Guatemalans.[14]

The eastern portion of the San Fernando Valley, once part of the citadel of white power in the city of Los Angeles, also saw phenomenal Latino growth in recent years. In 1980, 234,819 Latinos comprised 18.7 percent of the San Fernando Valley's total population of 1,253,623. Ten years later Latinos made up 30 percent, and their number had almost doubled to 461,269 out of a total of 1,534,267. As the *Los Angeles Times* reported, 'The increase of the ethnic diversity of the San Fernando Valley during the 1980s was remarkably widespread, with minorities moving in greater numbers to virtually every block of every street in every community … [T]he number of Anglo residents dropped in about 240 of roughly 315 census tracts dividing the Valley.'[15] The change was fueled 'by increases in immigration, the aging of Anglo residents compared with other groups, the upward mobility of minorities and the construction of thousands of apartments that drew nonwhites out of traditional enclaves in the northeast Valley.' This did not necessarily increase diversity, since, like Los Angeles as a whole, San Fernando Valley neighborhoods remain segregated along class lines: 'The affluent south Valley areas of Sherman Oaks, Studio City, Encino and Tarzana are still more than 85 percent Anglo.'[16]

Indeed, the Valley represents an interesting case study for Latinos. Historically, the Valley was home to the anti-busing crusades of the 1970s. Much of the 'white flight' from the inner cities had migrated there over the years. The Valley had become the epitome of suburbia, dotted with ranch-style homes and trim green lawns. This utopia, however, changed dramatically in the space of ten years, with Mexican-looking people everywhere throughout the landscape. In addition, Hindus and Asians seemed to be taking over the convenience stores and cleaners. As one observer put it: 'Many of us [whites] are very unhappy with what's going on.'[17] Not surprisingly, the San Fernando Valley has been a cradle of anti-immigrant hysteria in the 1990s.

As must be obvious by now, the location of Latino peoples in Los Angeles is closely linked to economic status. They are hardly uniform in class background; in fact, class differences among Latinos are becoming increasingly important. For example, there is a growing gap between Latino homeowners and renters; increasingly homeowners come from the older and more affluent sectors of the Latino community, although working-class people still own their homes in older barrios such as Boyle Heights, unincorporated East Los Angeles, the San Gabriel Valley and other sections of the county.[18] While working-class Latinos are spread throughout the city, middle-class Chicanos are concentrated (but not exclusively) in the San Gabriel Valley. Some facetiously call Hacienda Heights 'the Mexican Beverly Hills'.

A COMPARISON OF LOS ANGELES–AREA NEIGHBORHOODS

Area	Per Capita Income	Percent of Poor People		Percent of High School Graduates	
		1990	1980	1990	1980
Boyle Heights	$7,996	34	32	20	17
East Los Angeles	$8,877	26	24	26	22
Watts	$7,050	41	36	16	19
Pico-Union	$7,611	34	30	26	27
South Central	$7,697	31	32	25	29
County Total*	$20,759	15	12	70	70
Latinos*	$11,489	23	21	39	40
City Total*	$20,482	19	16	67	69
Latinos*	$10,018	28	14	33	35

*Based on selected census tracts.
source: *Nuestro Tiempo,* 10 September 1992.

Along with differences in class, generational and regional differences also distinguish Latinos in L.A. These can be noted by how they speak English. For instance, the Chicano students from South Central live in close proximity to African Americans and often adopt a Black English dialect. Eastside students adopt the intonation peculiar to most second-generation Mexican Americans. In the San Fernando Valley, speech depends on the affluence of the neighborhood and the size of the barrio. By contrast, in Spanish the Mexicans sound alike, with the Salvadoran and Guatemalan students differing in intonation and cadence.

Work and Class

Most Mexicans have always been workers, performing much of L.A.'s menial labor; their color, however, has set them apart from their fellow workers. For example, it was long common for many of the craft unions to exclude Mexicans from apprenticeship programs; and exclusion was the preferred Euroamerican method of dealing with unemployment. For example, the Depression years saw 600,000 Mexicans (many of them US citizens) deported, with over 11,000 shipped out of Los Angeles in 1932 alone. Few organizations noticed the injustice.[19] Even during World War II, a time when many young Chicanos marched off to war to the beat of *El Soldado Razo*, a popular Mexican *corrido* of the time, the percentage of Mexicans working in war industries remained low.

Not all Mexicans coming to L.A. have been poor, of course. Some Mexicans had come to the United States after the Mexican Revolution of 1910 for political reasons, much as Cubans had in the 1960s, forming a middle- and upper class that did not relate to the interests of the majority, and often living in white neighborhoods such as Los Feliz. There they formed social clubs such as *Las Damitas Católicas*, which once had a religious purpose but evolved into an exclusive social club. Annual *Blanco y Negro* balls (by invitation only) were held where the elite could pretend to preserve a fictitious Mexican culture. This sector accomplished little, even as a broker class, failing to champion the political and economic interests of the Mexican working-class majority. Along with this Mexican elite were the Californios, descendants of the Mexican Californians who had received land grants before the North American invasion of 1846–48, and who often traded on the 'Romance of the *Ranchos*' myth of an idyllic Spanish society.

Class differences became more obvious in the 1980s as a result of sweeping shifts in L.A.'s economic base. As the marketplace became 'freer', workers became more subordinate and unequal. Los Angeles government agencies of the 1980s became more crass in their protection of capital, with special tax funds squandered on the development of downtown L.A. while housing for the poor deteriorated in quantity and quality. With the decline in L.A.'s heavy industries the city's labor market became more segmented. Foreign-born workers became an integral part of the service and sweatshop economy; working within an underground economy, their incomes remained low and their working conditions dangerous. The 1986 Immigration Reform and Control Act enforced employer sanctions to the detriment of the large pool of undocumented labor. Rather than upgrading wages and working conditions for those 'legalized' under the amnesty provisions of the 1986 act, companies further marginalized Latino workers by threats of plant closures and other union-busting tactics. The revolving door of immigration that was for so many years common to California agriculture became a permanent feature of L.A.'s economy. With growing economic insecurity, tensions increased between the various communities of color, and between Latino groups – as well as within the Mexican/Chicano community.

Given these class contradictions, the only thread connecting Mexicans/Latinos in Los Angeles has often been a strong sense of nationalism. This nationalism is continuously fed by both Latino/Chicano self-interest and the anti-immigrant hysteria found in the Euroamerican and other communities. The antithesis to this Chicano/Latino identification is the growing seduction of Euroamerican culture, based on Euroamerican middle-class values and interests. Those influences are eroding the nationalism of Latinos/Chicanos as many more reach middle-class status.

The *Pendejo* Factor

Mexicans themselves internalize the 'Anything But Mexican' mindset. An internalized racism, popularly called a 'colonized mentality' by Chicano movement activists during the 1960s, splinters Latino and even Mexican unity. It is more than a cliché that many Mexicans and Latinos want to be white, or at least consider fairer skin to be better. The innocuous praise of relatives and friends for a newborn child, '*¡Qué bonita pero prietita!*' ('How pretty she is, but a little dark!') thus takes on special meaning: darkness has many connotations, most of them negative.

Some Mexicans, despite their strong indigenous faces, will confide that they have a French grandmother. Latin Americans recently arrived from countries much less developed than Mexico will be offended when asked, 'Are you Mexican?' For some Latin Americans, to be Mexican is *ser indio* – to be Indian; this signifies racial and social inferiority in much of Latin America.

The acceptance and internalization of the dominant society's racism by Mexicans and Latinos is irrational and produces a false consciousness.[20] For instance, it is not uncommon for first-year Chicano university students to talk about reverse racism toward whites or express anti-immigrant sentiments. Or, for that matter, for the second-generation Mexican to look down upon the first-generation Mexican. Even so, after years of being conditioned to think of themselves as white, only 46.9 percent of the foreign-born and 55.4 percent of the native-born Chicanos classified themselves as white in the Latino National Survey of 1992.[21]

As in mainstream US society, where you live and how much you earn determines your social position. Dispersal has weakened the ties between Chicanos living in various parts of Los Angeles and encouraged a 'you're different' mindset often based on economic status. Police and politicos alike foster the development of such false consciousness, which I call 'se hacen pendejo' – which in Spanish refers to those who 'act stupid', even though they should know better. Under its influence some Chicanos and Latinos take comfort in the fact that they are classified as Caucasian.

In related ways, the term 'Hispanic' has been enthusiastically embraced by the emerging Chicano and Latino middle class. Its members, while not gauche enough to call themselves Spanish, readily accept the euphemism *Hispanic*, launched by Nixon administration bureaucrats in the 1970s. In one fell swoop, they lumped together Cubans, Mexicans and Puerto Ricans together into a single package. No mess, easy to deal with, and still easier to manipulate. This change conveniently gave conservative Cubans, to whom Nixon had strong ties, a disproportionate influence. Thus began the Republican strategy of wooing middle-class 'Hispanics' with policies favoring their interests.

Genuine differences exist, of course, among the various Meso-American nationalities, or for that matter between Mexican and US-born Chicanos. Because of these differences, what to call Mexicans and other Latinos becomes problematic. The term *Chicano* is contentious, having been popularized as an expression of identity and pride in the 1960s, and today used also by gang members. Even among activists the term *Chicano* or *Chicana* has different meanings. To some it includes only Mexicans born in the United States, while for others it encompasses those born on either side of the border. The arrival of large numbers of Central Americans has generated a third school, which accepts this new reality by using *Chicano* as a political term rather than one referring to a single nationality.

In the neighborhoods, the various Latino groups just call themselves Mexicans, Salvadorans or Guatemalans. Among working-class people there is no apparent thrust to create a common identity. It is different among the political activists, some of whom (like this author) have *tentatively* accepted the term *Latino* for convenience when working in solidarity.

The recent influx of large numbers of Mexican and Central American immigrants has added to the dilemma of identity during the 1980s, while simultaneously slowing the assimilation process. In the case of working-class Mexicans, this influx has had positive effects, in that Mexicans are now so large a group that they cannot be easily isolated or dismissed. Twenty years ago, the Chicano population was mostly US-born and poor. Today, the foreign-born population is much larger:[22] California in 1980 had 67 percent of the nation's undocumented Mexicans, and Los Angeles County alone had 44 percent of them.[23] Along with L.A.'s proximity to the border and attraction to immigrants, Euroamerican racism has also slowed the 'melting', especially of the darker and poorer Mexicans in California.[24]

Twenty years ago, most L.A. Chicanos were losing their cultural identity. José Angel Gutiérrez – founder of the Mexican American Youth Organization and La Raza Unida Party in Texas – visited my classroom at San Fernando Valley State College (now California State University, Northridge) circa 1970, and asked my students, 'How many of you speak Spanish?' Only a few hands went up. José Angel snapped that we were becoming brown *gringos*. About two years ago, José Angel revisited CSUN. I goaded him into asking the same question. This time almost every hand (including those of some white students) went up, in a reaffirmation of Mexican cultural identity.

Seeing the Barrio Through Women's Eyes

Inseparable from the issues of class and race is gender, an important component of social organization and social identity – and until recently, often neglected. When Latinos speak about ethnicity, they speak as if that identity were genderless, or without a gendered point of view. This marks a point of tension between Chicanos and Chicanas, with Chicanas attempting to make women visible and gender an important issue of identity. It is not at all presumptuous to generalize that most Latinas and Mexicanas recognize that there is a distinct lack of equality between the sexes; it is also true that these differences are much more obvious to Latinas than to men. However, the sense of identity as women varies greatly among Chicanas. It ranges from a shared sense of powerlessness, for example, when walking streets at night, to a consciousness of women's role in the family, to actively participating in women's organizations, or, for that matter, lesbian associations. Yet in all cases, their experiences differ from those of men, not only Euroamerican men but those of their own class and race. At the same time, class and national origin create chasms between Chicanas and Latinas.

Salvadoran women, for example, have a distinct historical memory that incorporates years of civil war in their home country. Mostly working class, their material circumstances govern their choices and their identity as Salvadoran. Unless they are involved in labor organizations, their identity remains Salvadoran. Poor Mexican women, who are emigrating at a higher rate than ever before, are similar with respect to identity; they remain Mexican as long as they are limited to interaction with other Mexicans of the same class. Both Salvadoran and Mexican women do not see a need to incorporate other groups into their respective identities. The poor working-class Latina rarely identifies herself as a Latina or the officially sanctioned 'Hispanic'. Such identification is more popular among professional women, for whom the use of Latina or 'Hispanic' represents either self-interest or a choice based on her position, or among youth, who learn this identity in the school system.

The vulnerability of females in general and Latinas in particular has increased in recent years as economic globalization has intensified competition, restructuring the economy to include more women in the workforce and creating modern-day *maquiladoras* within the urban areas of the Southwest, and most especially Los Angeles. In this pecking order, all immigrants face greater vulnerability, but Mexicanas and Central Americans, along with Chicanas, are left at the bottom of the socioeconomic order.

Vulnerability is not limited to the border, the workplace or the streets. Women are even more vulnerable in the home, within the family, where patriarchy is embedded in the cultural memory of men and women. Spousal abuse is all too common, not only in working-class but also in middle- and upper-class families. Such abuse is often ignored, especially when the victims are poor Latinas and Mexicanas.[25]

In essence, both middle- and working-class Latinas and Chicanas internalize the ideology and values of the oppressor through the experiences of their class. This obstructs the creation of a single, all-inclusive Latina culture that crosses class lines. In the case of middle-class Latinas, not all the opportunities open to white women are available to them. That, however, does not prevent them from often seeing the interests of Latinas in general in terms of their class interests, excluding the needs of working-class women. Even so, many middle-class Chicanas consciously work for Chicana and Chicano working-class interests; having been raised in working-class families, they retain a knowledge of working-class problems, and a sense of loyalty to their working-class roots.

Chicano Urbanism and the Face of L.A.

The recent growth of the Latino presence in Los Angeles has changed the urban landscape in both obvious and more subtle ways. Urban planner James Thomas Rojas has described a uniquely Chicano urbanism that is being shaped not only by Mexican but also by Central American cultural influence. Mexicans use the space around buildings to construct a sense of place, and '[because] people are not architecture, it takes time to understand the place they create ... No space in East Los Angeles is left unused or unmarked.'[26] The barrios are extroverted. They differ from the Anglo neighborhoods whose homes conform but do not connect. 'In East L.A., the house is defined from the property line rather than the floor plan and walls of the home.' *La yarda*, 'the yard', is a Chicano innovation, since Mexican houses don't have front yards.[27] Rojas contrasts the use of the front yard in Mexican neighborhoods to its function in Anglo neighborhoods. 'The green continuous park-like setting that symbolized the American front yard in the suburb has been cut up into individual slices in East Los Angeles. There streets create diversity, and allow individuals and sociability to take place more readily.'[28]

Subtleties abound in definitions of class and place: Rojas quotes a Chicano in Montebello, where many Latinos are second generation and middle class, as saying, 'On that side of the street they live different from us. They speak Spanish more, they fix their cars in the street and play their stereos loud as well as build fences and put things in their front yards.'[29]

Whether during the day or night there are people on the streets. Reminiscent of the way Mexicans congregate around La Placita, Central Americans go to MacArthur Park to learn news about what's happening in their country or *los últimos*, the latest news about jobs. Vendors appear to be everywhere. Writing about East L.A., Rojas notes, 'The vendors are not begging but are people starting economically from the bottom up, in the United States.' There are different kinds of vendors, the *mariachis*, who carry their wares; the 'asphalt vendors', standing on the freeway off-ramps selling oranges; the 'tent vendors', the 'weekend vendors', and the 'auto vendors'. Lastly there are the 'roach coaches', who sell food out of large trucks. These all define place in the barrio, where people have an equal footing with buildings.[30]

A Matter of Control over Interpretative Space

Chicanos and other Latinos are changing L.A.'s urban culture in ways that go beyond the conversion of living space. Steve Loza points out that Chicano music in Los Angeles is different from and more varied than the music found in other cities.[31] It ranges from the current rage for the *quebradita*, which 'combines country-western with cumbia, salsa and occasionally flamenco',[32] to *mariachi* and *jarocho* music, which are still fashionable, especially since the success of Linda Ronstadt.[32] Today we hear about the 'Eastside Renaissance', a barrio music that has influenced musicians throughout the Southwest. Also, of course, there are Los Lobos, who have attained international fame. *Salsa* remains the most popular form of dance in Los Angeles, unlike Mexico.[34] *Conjuntos* like the Alienz, Quetzal and Marcos Loya's group play sets ranging from Latino rock, *salsa* and *cumbias* to *corridos*. The *nueva canción*, the revolutionary folk song, continues in popularity and has influenced Euroamerican folk and rock musicians such as Jackson Browne. These and other musicians are heard every Saturday night over FM 89.3, where 'The Sancho Show' reaches an audience of a quarter-million. Sancho intertwines music, often East L.A. two-step, with political commentary.[35] Barrio music, then, is a fully developed art form and adds to the definition of place.

Live theater is alive and well in Latino Los Angeles. Carmén Zapata's bilingual productions are of professional quality, as is José Luis Valenzuela's work with the Latino Actors' Lab at the Plaza de La Raza in Lincoln Heights. Chicano comedians appear regularly, exploring Chicano and Latino themes: Culture Clash is currently the best known. These and other groups play at Plaza de La Raza, which has become a center for the arts. Poetry readings are also held regularly at La Plaza and other venues, where poets like Helena María Viramontes, Gloria Alvárez, Marisela Norte and Naomi Quniñones recite to packed houses. Las Tres, an all-Chicana trio, plays political music. Active during the late 1980s and early 1990s was Alma Elena Cervantes, whose biting political satire is reminiscent of the Chicano poet José Montoya. Performing visual artists like Guillermo Gómez Peña are integrating both the Mexican and Chicano expressions.

Although Chicano artists were initially influenced by the Mexican muralists, most have developed defined Chicano styles. Among them are John Váladez, Gronk, the late Carlos Almáraz, Patsi Váldez, Leo Limón, Diane Gamboa, Barbara Carrasco, Yolanda González, Chaz Bosorques, Wayne Healy, Kathy Gallegos, José Ramírez, Salamón Huerta and Harry Gamboa. They blossomed after the 1968 East Los Angeles school walkouts.[36] All of the Chicano/Latino genres mentioned have received a warm reception in Mexico, Cuba, and throughout Europe. Latina artists abound in Los Angeles, where SPARC (Social and Public Arts Resource Center) and Self-Help Graphics (which opened in 1983) promote their artists' works. SPARC is headed by Judith Baca, whose central work is *The Great Wall of Los Angeles;* her energy and brilliance have influenced a generation of artists.[37] In sum, although Chicanos have not been able to define their own presence, they have been able to define cultural space, which in turn is being interpreted by cultural commentators such as Max Benavidez and Rubén Guevarra.[38]

The culture rooted in Chicano/Latino barrios did not flourish free from the influence of Euroamerican critics, who practiced a form of cultural imperialism. A classic example is how they compelled changes in Luis Váldez's play *Zoot Suit*, taking it from Chicano theater through a Hispanic phase until, in Váldez's own words, it became part of American theater tradition.

Another example is José Luis Valenzuela's *August 29*, a play about Rubén Salazar and the Chicano Moratorium of 1970, which was universally well received by Chicanos but panned by critics. Despite its vaunted multiculturalism, the work of critics like Sylvie Drake of the *Los Angeles Times* often reflects their cultural biases.[39] *August 29* contained a great deal of social commentary, which may have offended Drake: it also poked fun at Chicanos, often with a humor to which Euroamericans are not privy. It was clear from Drake's review that she wanted her Chicana characters to be like the Torito chain of 'Mexican' restaurants – Euroamerican-friendly. She even found the young Chicana militant and her boyfriend too soft and sweet to be credible, when in fact they were typical of Chicano students.

The question of cultural interpretation continued to be a sore point throughout the 1980s. Institutions such as the Teatro Campesino started to appeal to a wider audience than they had during the 1960s and 1970s. At the same time, there remained a tension between Euroamerican and Chicano critics.[40] Even the most progressive Euroamericans have difficulty conceding that their interpretation is uninformed when it comes to Chicanos. This tension greatly resembles race relations generally in Los Angeles, which loves the myth that it is a multicultural city where cultural interchange is the rule. Nothing, however, could be further from the truth; superficial trappings like Mexican restaurants and a romantic version of the past replace true acculturation, which is a two-way street. This tension over cultural interpretation is not limited, however, to white and brown. An internal tension exists between Chicano and Chicana artists – Chicana poets, writers and musicians explore identity issues without forgetting that they are women. They add issues often considered 'women's concerns' – domestic violence, abortion, sexuality, rape. Women artists cannot talk about being Chicanas without raising issues of sexism, addressing themes in their work that have remained inadequately addressed within the Chicano community. In doing so, Chicana feminists have made the personal political; and Chicana lesbians and other feminists have played a key role in Los Angeles in keeping these gendered viewpoints in the forefront.

Every culture produces its own expressions. In Los Angeles, Mexicans and Chicanos along with Central Americans and a potpourri of Latin American groups have come to form a mass larger than many nations. As part of this process came the production of art, literature and music, which define the cultural and racial mass. The ability to make decisions about its cultural space, and convey itself to the wider society, is a mark of a group's power. Up to now, and despite Mexican/Latino population growth, that cultural production has remained almost solely within the Chicano and Latino communities. Only the future will tell whether Chicano culture as defined by Chicanos will be as successful as the burrito and the taco in invading the Anglo world.[41]

If the arts unify a people, history bonds them. In the case of an ethnic minority, unity helps those less able to fend for themselves. Identification with the dominant society invariably benefits those best able to compete, and not the less fortunate.[42] For instance, the Mexicanization of the indigenous peoples in Mexico during the Age of Reform (1855–75) made the Indians 'equal', but it also opened their communities to unbridled exploitation, and led to the cooptation of indigenous leaders who became legally Mexican, no longer Indian. The same process occurs among those Chicanos who assimilate into Euroamerican society, and who in the process lose a sense of responsibility to the Mexican community.

Notes

1. 'Homeward Bound', *Los Angeles Times*, Calendar Section, 10 Dec. 1991.

2. It is important to emphasize that the Mexican nation is a product of the Spanish conquest and colonization. Mexicans are, for the most part, of mixed ancestry, and most have more indigenous than Spanish blood, so to consider them European would be illogical.

3. Rodolfo Acuña, 'Hispanic Label: The Gringo's Revenge', *Pacific News Service* (Feb. 1988); for a provocative work on Chicano politics, see Juan Gómez-Quiñones, *Chicano Politics: Reality and Promise, 1940–1990* (Albuquerque, N.M.: University of New Mexico Press, 1990), pp. 6–8.

4. Arthur M. Schlesinger, Jr, *Disuniting of America: Reflections on a Multicultural Society* (New York: W.W. Norton, 1992), p. 49. Although Schlesinger makes only two references to so-called Hispanics, by inference he includes them in the generalization that minorities exaggerate 'past glories and purposes', producing what he calls compensatory history. What is grating about these arguments is that Schlesinger knows nothing about Chicano history.

5. Kevin Roderick, 'Toward Equality: Exploring a World of Difference', *Los Angeles Times*, 13 Feb. 1989. The poll offered clues as to the nature of prejudice. 'Nearly a third said minorities have gotten more economically than they deserve and 43 percent said they just do not see what minorities have to be angry about.' These responses suggest an increasing polarization along racial and ethnic lines.

6. Diana Martínez and Andrés Chávez, eds, *Covering L.A.'s Majority* (Los Angeles: Intermedia Task Force, 1991), p. 94.

7. Norma Stolz Chinchilla and Nora Hamilton, 'Seeking Refuge in the City of Angeles: The Central American Community', in Gerry Riposa and Carolyn Dersch, eds, *City of Angeles* (Dubuque, Iowa: Kendall/Hunt, 1992), pp. 84–7. Prior to passage of the 1980 Refugee Act, refugees were defined as those fleeing from communism. The 1980 law separated political asylum and refugee status. One had to establish a well-founded fear of persecution, which was much easier to prove if the refugee came from a communist country. During the 1980s, as conditions worsened in their respective countries, Guatemalans and Salvadorans poured into the United States, undertaking a long and arduous journey. Although larger numerically than in previous decades, immigration during the 1980s followed the pattern set in the 1960s and 1970s: 'As Central America began to undergo important economic changes (the expansion of capitalism in agriculture, the relative decline of small and medium-sized family farming, a greater dependence on a cash consumer market for daily necessities, and the replacement of home-manufactured crafts and consumer goods by manufactured ones) a second wave of Central Americans began to find its way to the United States, a group somewhat less well off than the first but still better educated and having access to more resources than the majority of their compatriots.' By the mid 1970s, political upheaval in Nicaragua, El Salvador and Guatemala accelerated the flow, beginning the third wave.

8. Eugene Turner and James P. Allen, *An Atlas of Population Patterns in Metropolitan Los Angeles and Orange Counties* (Northridge, Calif.: Department of Geography, California State University, Northridge, 1990), n.; also see 'Census Study Reveals Extent of Undercount', *Southwest Voter Research Notes*, July 1991. According to the SVRI, there is an estimated 4.6% undercount, making the L.A. total 9,262,000; 'California's Quiet Revolution', *Los Angeles Times*, 27 Feb. 1991; also see Oswald Johnston, 'Funding Levels May Be Altered Before Census', *Los Angeles Times*, 17 July 1991, and Henrik Rehbinder, 'Censo define Hoy sobre hispanos no contabilzados', *La Opinión*, 15 July 1991, which showed that 5% of Blacks and Latinos were not counted versus 2% of whites; Maribel Hastings, 'Hispanos serán la minoría étnica más grande de EU', *La Opinion*, 8 Dec. 1991; Bureau

of the Census, *Persons of Spanish Origin in the United States: March 1982* (Washington, D.C.: Government Printing Office, 1982).

9. See *The Changing Profile of Mexican America: A Sourcebook for Policy Making* (Claremont, Calif.: The Tomás Rivera Center, October 1985) for a general overview.

10. David Parrish and Beth Barrett, 'Nuevo Los Angeles', *Daily News*, 17 Jan. 1993.

11. Guadalupe Compean, 'The Los Angeles Corporate Center: Its Probable Impact on North East Los Angeles', School of Architecture and Urban Planning, University of California Los Angeles, 6 June 1983. This interprets land-use changes in Northeast Los Angeles caused by land-use patterns in adjacent Monterey Park. Compean makes heavy use of census data along with Los Angeles County property tax records. Among other things she traces a pattern of 'peasant landlord' ownership and heavy bank investment in the census tracts adjoining Monterey Park.

12. Cheryl Brownstein-Santiago, 'Census Data Track Status of Latinos', *Nuestro Tiempo*, 10 Sept. 1992.

13. Roger Lindo, 'Pico-Unión, donde palpita la diáspora Salvadoreña', *La Opinion*, 27 March 1993.

14. Cheryl Brownstein-Santiago, 'Census Data Track Status of Latinos', *Nuestro Tiempo*, 10 Sept. 1992; Roger Lindo, 'La Pequeña Centroamérica de LA, su batalla continua', *La Opinión*, 26 March 1993; Parrish and Barrett, 'Nuevo Los Angeles'.

15. Richard Lee Colvin, 'Anglos Predominate But Majority Status Slipping', *Los Angeles Times*, 31 March 1991.

16. The Department of City Planning drafts community plans for some thirty-five communities within Los Angeles. They are useful in tracing the history of the various communities that form the city.

17. For a brilliant comparison of Euroamerican and Mexican environments in Los Angeles, see James Thomas Rojas, 'The Enacted Environment: The Creation of "Place" by Mexicans and Mexican Americans in East Los Angeles' (Master's Thesis, Dept. of Architecture, Massachusetts Institute of Technology, May 1991).

18. Aaron Curtis, 'Homeowners Dig In to Defend Their Turf', *Los Angeles Times*, 18 Dec. 1993; Joel Kotkin, 'A Multiethnic Middle Class Is Growing in California', *Los Angeles Times*, 14 Nov. 1993.

19. Carey McWilliams, *Southern California: An Island on the Land* (Salt Lake City, Utah: Peregrine Smith Books, 1983), p. 317.

20. Herbert Marcuse, *One Dimensional Man: Studies in the Ideology of Advanced Industrial Society* (Boston: Beacon Press, 1964), p. xiii.

21. Rodolfo O. De la Garza, *Latino Voices: Mexican, Puerto Rican, and Cuban Perspectives on American Politics* (Boulder, Colo.: Westview Press, 1992), pp. 21–3.

22. In 1960 only 20% of the Mexican-origin population in California had been born in Mexico: Leo Grebler, Joan Moore, Ralph C. Guzman et al., *The Mexican-American People: The Nation's Second-Largest Minority* (New York: Free Press, 1970), p. 107. In 1980, 41.9% of Los Angeles's Mexican-ancestry population was Mexican born, Donald J. Bogue, *The Population of the United States: Historical Trends and Future Projections* (New York: Free Press, 1985), p. 372.

23. David M. Heer, *Undocumented Mexicans in the United States* (Cambridge: Cambridge University Press, 1990), p. 58.

24. The dramatic growth of the Latino population will no doubt contribute to increased nationalism among Latinos. Hastings, 'Hispanos serán la minoría étnica más grande de EU'; Frederick W. Hollmann, *US Population Estimates, by Age, Sex, Race, and Hispanic Origin: 1980–1991*, US Department of Commerce, Bureau of the Census, Feb. 1993; Bureau of Census, *Hispanic Americans Today* (Washington D.C.: US Government Printing Office, 1993).

25. Gerda Lerner, *The Creation of Patriarchy* (New York: Oxford University Press, 1986), p. 5, examines into the tension between women's actual historical experience and how they are excluded from interpreting that experience. This is especially critical in the case of Latinas, where even intellectuals of their own race distort working-class points of view.

26. James Thomas Rojas, 'The Enacted Environment', p. 58.

27. Ibid., pp. 62, 80–82.

28. Ibid., pp. 62, 66–7.

29. Ibid., pp. 2, 4, 22, 30–31.

30. Ibid., pp. 52–5.

31. Steve Loza, *Barrio Rhythm: Mexican American Music in Los Angeles* (Urbana, Ill.: University of Illinois, 1993).

32. Michael Quntanilla, 'Awesome!', *Nuestro Tiempo*, 5 Aug. 1993; Rubén Martínez, 'The Shock of the New', *Los Angeles Times Magazine*, 30 Jan. 1994, p. 10.

33. Frank Del Olmo, 'Latino "Decade" Moves into '90s', *Nuestro Tiempo*, 14 Dec. 1989; David Gates, 'A Rocker Reclaims Her Roots', *Newsweek*, 29 Feb. 1988, pp. 66–7; Enrique Lopetegui, 'Mariachi with a Twist', *Los Angeles Times*, 28 June 1993.

34. Leila Cobo, '¡A Bailar Se Dijo!', *Nuestro Tiempo*, 14 Oct. 1993, pp. 24–5.

35. Nancy Matsumoto, 'A Streetwise Latino Beams His Message', *Los Angeles Times*, 19 Feb. 1994; 'Sancho' beams out of Pasadena City College. He is Daniel Casto, Ph.D, an associate dean at East Los Angeles Community College.

36. Max Benavidez, 'Arte de Los Angeles', *L.A. Style* (March 1990): pp. 136–41, 144, 198; Max Benavidez, 'Graphic Expressions', *L.A. Style* (March 1990), pp. 142–3; Bill Tankes, 'Latino Art Exhibition a Colorful Milestone; Artist Chides Museum', *Nuestro Tiempo*, 23 March 1989. The exhibition 'Hispanic Art in the United States: Thirty Contemporary Painters and Sculptors', held at the Los Angeles County Museum, was curated by the late Carlos Almaraz, who had criticized the museum for slighting Chicano artists. This was its first exhibit of Chicano art in fifteen years.

37. Patricia Ward Biederman, 'Artists Shine Critical Light on Columbus', *Los Angeles Times*, 13 Oct. 1991; Max Benavidez, 'The Labyrinth of the North', *Los Angeles Times*, 15 Sept. 1991.

38. Max Benavidez, 'The Labyrinth of the North'.

39. Divina Infusino, 'Latinos: Bound for Glory', *San Diego Union*, 30 June 1991.

40. See Yolanda Broyles Gonzalez, 'What Price "Mainstream"? Luis Váldez' Corridos on Stage and Film', *Cultural Studies*, vol. 4, no. 3 (Oct. 1990), pp. 281–4, for a criticism of Váldez.

41. Rose Apodaca, ''Tis the Season for Variety of Tamales', *Nuestro Tiempo*, 19 Dec. 1991.

42. See Kevin Lynch, *What Time Is This Place?* (Cambridge, Mass.: MIT Press, 1972), for a provocative discussion of time and place. A rash of articles appeared in the late 1980s and early 1990s decrying the quest for an ethnic identity: Joel Kotkin, 'Fear and Reality in the Los Angeles Melting Pot', *Los Angeles Times Magazine*, 5 Nov. 1989, pp. 6–19; Arthur Schlesinger, Jr, 'The Cult of Ethnicity, Good and Bad', *Time*, 8 July 1991, p. 21; Paul Grey, 'Whose America?' *Time*, 8 July 1991, p. 17.

2

Taking Back Chicano History

Los Angeles has little sense of the past or of place. A partial explanation for this is that Euroamericans have devoted little time or energy to learning the history of the region, treating that history much the same as they do learning other languages. The simple equation prevails that if it's not in English, it's not worth learning; and if it's not 'American' history – meaning the experience of Euroamericans – it's not worth reading. Mexicans have never figured in this design.

However, there are other reasons for their lack of visibility in Los Angeles history. Until recently, Mexicans in L.A., unlike their counterparts in San Antonio, did not have sufficient numbers to affect the politics of the city or even the Catholic Church, to which a majority of them belong. In addition, the vastness of the city and lack of cheap transportation have made it imperative for Mexicans, like other working-class Angelenos at the bottom of the wage scale, to live close to work. Since historically many Mexicans have been urban migrants, they have been dispersed throughout the region in agricultural colonies, near brickyards, railway maintenance yards, factories and other employment centers. All this has impeded the growth of a united community.[1]

This lack of a concentrated Mexican presence has in the past made Mexicans seem less threatening to Euroangelenos. Thus racial segregation was never as rigid as in San Antonio, where until recently Mexicans were limited to the Westside and where all socioeconomic classes of Mexicans lived in close proximity. In Los Angeles the lack of rigid segregation allowed upwardly mobile Mexicans to move to more affluent barrios or to move into working-class Euroamerican neighborhoods. The latter did not feel threatened as long as Mexicans remained below 10 percent of the population.

The city's addiction to urban renewal projects has also resulted in the dispersal of Mexicans throughout the city via displacement of working-class renters. Even homeowners were not immune to massive projects, which uprooted entire Mexican neighborhoods to make sure that the suburbs had freeways and that corporate leaders had choice building sites. Mexicans and other poor and working-class people were also moved to give the Dodgers a home in Chávez Ravine and the managerial class a music center, upscale housing and hotels in Bunker Hill.[2] One result of this continuous uprooting has been diminished community consciousness, except for some specific barrios. Without a sense of community, and a sense of their history as a community, people become vulnerable to the plans and whims of the dominant groups, which can not only displace them but control them in other ways as well. There is, for example, very little preservation of anything that has Native American or Mexican roots, with the history of these groups submerged by the presence of other folk. The resulting lack of local history and connectedness has the effect of alienating Chicanos and Native Americans, of discouraging development of a united community. When either group attempts to reconstruct history and regain lost space, the dominant society is offended and claims that the Mexican or Native American is encroaching on *its* past. The preservation of buildings is almost completely limited to those built by Euroamericans, giving the impression that nothing existed before the Anglo invasion. The lack of architectural presence erases historical memory, with newer buildings then defining the past.

This erasure has devastating consequences: an ethnic group unable to define its past is unable to take pride in its accomplishments, learn from past mistakes or assess its current situation. History is more than just an esoteric search for facts; it involves a living community and its common memory. Chicanos are thus denied a sense of their place in the history of Los Angeles. This prevents even the most progressive non-Mexican Angelenos from appreciating the dimensions of the Chicano struggle in this country.[3] Indeed, a sense of historical appreciation, or the lack of it, determines whether Angelenos accept the moral authority of Latino demands to be included in a US civil rights agenda.

Bringing a Hidden History to Light

Across the Southwest tension between Mexicans and Euroamericans stemmed from the two wars in which Euroamericans invaded Mexican territory. Following the invasions of Texas and Mexico proper in the 1830s and 1840s and the Anglo seizure of half of Mexico, the conquerors treated Mexicans like colonials with no citizenship rights, despite a treaty promising respect for those rights. Lynchings of Mexicans were as common in California as in Texas. Uprisings in the form of social banditry occurred across the Southwest throughout the century. In response to discrimination, Mexicans also formed *mutualistas*, mutual aid societies, and other organizations to fight for their rights in what resembled a colonial situation.

At the turn of the century, thousands of Mexicans were brought or came to the Southwest to build its railroads and work in its mines and on its farms, performing the bulk of any hard labor. At the same time, Mexican workers built the infrastructure of modern-day Los Angeles. In a determined effort to combat exploitation, they organized massive strikes and other labor protests all over the Southwest; in Los Angeles, railway workers demanded better wages and working conditions. Mexicans also formed pro-immigrant rights organizations, which combatted repatriation efforts and anti-immigrant hysteria during the first three decades of this century. Indeed, L.A. was the center for the Mexican Liberal Party led by Anarchist leader Ricardo Flores Magón, as well as other groups of political exiles.

In the public schools Chicanos fought against various forms of discrimination, for example, segregation and the abuse of I.Q. tests. As early as 1910, in San Angelo, Texas, Mexican parents refused to send their children to a segregated school. In 1930 in Lemon Grove, California, Mexican parents went to court to enforce their children's right to quality education by ending segregation. In Los Angeles, there were designated Mexican schools until just after World War II, when US District Court Judge Paul J. McCormick in *Méndez* v. *Westminster School District* declared the segregation of Mexican school children unconstitutional. This ruling served as precedent for the historic 1954 US Supreme Court decision against segregation in the better-known *Brown* v. *Topeka Board of Education* case.

These early highlights of the long Chicano struggle can only suggest the rich history that has been hidden from everyone in this country. Anglos (or, for that matter, Chicanos) cannot really understand the current debate about immigration without realizing that white fears of Mexican immigrants go back many years; they are part and parcel of the history of racism and human rights violations. At the core of the Chicano student movement of the 1960s, like the Black civil rights movement, was a call for ethnic studies to bring that hidden experience into the light. It was in the context of this movement that Chicano scholars and students created Chicano Studies, not only to teach students about Chicano society and promote Chicano research but also to empower people. Part of the research mission was to demystify history and establish a history that would be read by everyone – not just educational elites. As stated in the preamble of the call for a National Association for Chicano Studies, founded in 1972:

> The Association has, from the beginning, presupposed a divergence from mainstream academic research. We recognize that mainstream research, based on an integrationist perspective which emphasized consensus, assimilation, and the legitimacy of societal institutions, has obscured and distorted the significant historical role which class conflict and group interests have taken in shaping our experience as a people to the present moment. Our research efforts are aimed at directly

confronting such tenuous images and interpretations and challenging the structures of inequality based on class, racial, and sexist privileges in this society.[4]

But by the 1980s the courts and public pressure had reversed many of the political gains of the 1960s. The window of tolerance for minority scholars closed; they were labeled malcontents and accused of exaggerating their case for political ends.

During the 1980s and 1990s, Presidents Ronald Reagan and George Bush brilliantly mythicized history, celebrating the 1984 Olympics, the bicentennials of the US Constitution and the Bill of Rights, the centennial of the Statue of Liberty and the quincentennial of Christopher Columbus. Myths such as the story of those allegedly freedom-loving Texans who defended the Alamo crept back into circulation. Liberal historians who had once opposed the Vietnam War recanted and became the neo-nativists of the 1980s, defending American institutions with a renewed 'conviction of righteousness'.[5] By the 1980s, Chicano scholars were conforming more and more to Eurocentric criteria. Promotion and tenure had become measures of success in academia. Revisionist history was less popular, with some Chicano scholars even accusing those who questioned mainstream works of creating 'them and us' history. In abandoning their commitment to the community, these scholars have in effect reinforced the Euroamerican 'fantasy heritage' of California, to use the term Carey McWilliams popularized in his 1949 book *North from Mexico*.[6]

Still, within the minority communities this nativist trend was countered by those activists who remembered the lessons of the 1960s. These activists saw it as essential to engage the academic establishment in struggle over the interpretation of history. They knew that national leaders and much of the public are in the habit of manufacturing 'knowledge' to substantiate claims of moral authority and thus justify aggression, exploitation and repression. These activists, among them some scholars, concluded that this mythologizing must be challenged by a committed scholarship that distinguishes right from wrong.[7]

In addition to activists, one of the few groups in the Chicano community that has a sense of place is the gang. However, that sense of territory is not linked to a historical memory, and is often limited to identifying enemies. The sense of community among these youths is based on oral traditions passed along by the gang members themselves. Instinctively, however, many Chicanos yearn for that sense of a historically based community. Lacking that sense of history the gangster or the tagger sprays his or her *placa* on a wall, or defiantly glares at society, saying, '¿Y qué?' ('And what of it?'). This lack of historical memory prevents the group from embracing a politics that asserts a collective entitlement to a better life and organizes to achieve it.[8]

The Fight over Olvera Street

In the context of the struggle of Chicanos to reclaim their history, the fight over the preservation of Los Angeles's Olvera Street takes on important dimensions. Since the Euroamerican occupation, successive waves of Easterners and Midwesterners have buried the city's past architecturally. One of the few remaining centers of the Mexican past has been Olvera Street; it is a reminder that Mexicans were here before Euroamericans. The presence of the Mexican as a non-European, moreover, is evidence of the conquest of native peoples by Europeans: Mexicans are the mixed-race product of that conquest, and this is what sets them apart from Euroamericans.[9]

The plaza area, where Olvera Street is located, has been inhabited by Mexicans since 1781, when a dozen or so peasants of mixed blood – Indians, Africans and Spaniards, mostly from the Mexican states of Sinaloa and Sonora – settled on land populated by the indigenous people of the area as part of Spanish colonial expansion. They thus established what we know as Los Angeles. Since this time, Mexicans have had a continued presence in the area, often sharing the space with other poor people. During the 1880s, Olvera Street formed part of a larger Mexican barrio called Sonora Town and encompassed some of today's Chinatown. Although they competed with newcomers to live there, Mexicans made up a majority of its residents at the turn of the century. But by the mid 1920s Sonora Town had been reduced to Olvera Street and was in its last urban cycle, its residential character had been extinguished, and its buildings were occupied by commercial establishments. When light industry moved in, almost everyone expected Olvera Street to be bulldozed.

Enter Mrs Christine Sterling, who wanted to save the nineteenth-century house of the Avila family and other buildings to preserve a bit of 'Old Mexico'. With the help of the city's elite and convict labor, Olvera Street as we now know it opened in the early 1930s. The area was not only meant to be a tourist attraction: it also was intended to be a showplace of Los Angeles's multi-ethnic heritage, a demonstration of how different races could work and live together in the city. Sterling's 'Ramonaland' was a sort of Mexican fantasyland in which *rancheros* wear oversized sombreros and their wives wear layered petticoats. That fantasy was daily undermined by federal and local police looking for Mexicans, who, during the Depression, were blamed for the shortage of jobs. A mural critical of American capitalism – *América Tropical* by David Siqueiros, the great Mexican muralist – was whitewashed.

In 1953 the state of California established El Pueblo Historic Park, which encompasses Olvera Street. During the 1980s the directors of El Pueblo Park, under the state and later under the city, were non-Mexican, as was Curator Jean Bruce Poole, an amateur historian of British extraction. They did not solicit the advice of Chicano scholars, and they made it clear to the Mexican merchants that the direction of the park was none of their business. Poole's basic position was that the Mexican presence on Olvera Street wrongly eclipsed that of other ethnic groups and that it had to be downplayed. In the name of multicultural-ism she and other civic and political leaders sought to bury the Mexican past. With Poole's support, state bureaucrats insisted on restoring the buildings on Olvera Street constructed by the Italians, the Chinese and other ethnic groups. (The adobes, where Mexicans had lived since 1781 – had been bulldozed ear-lier.)

This is not to negate the merits of other cultures but to point out that on Olvera Street many of the merchants and their families have developed strong ties to the neighborhood. Some have lived there for over fifty years. Mexican traditions such as *Las Posadas* and the Blessing of the Animals are still cele-brated. The rise of Chicano nationalism and the arrival of hundreds and thou-sands of Mexican nationals and Central Americans has significantly affected the character of El Pueblo. On Sundays, up to 13,000 Latinos of various na-tional origins attend mass at La Reina de Los Angeles, Our Lady Queen of the Angels. The plaza is increasingly used to celebrate Latino holidays, as well as to protest continuing injustices. In short, Olvera Street is not just an enclave of Mexican business families. Over the years, it has come to represent a sense of place for the larger Latino community.

The struggle over Olvera Street intensified when massive redevelopment be-gan at the old Terminal Annex and Union Station nearby. That redevelopment upped the political and economic stakes. Outside interests began pushing for the concessions on Olvera Street to go to the highest bidder, thereby removing the Mexican merchants who represented the historical memory of Olvera Street. A 1987 redistricting by the Los Angeles City Council put Olvera Street squarely in City Councilman Richard Alatorre's district as a result of his politi-cal maneuvering. Some of the merchants worried that Alatorre's ties to East L.A. redevelopment corporations might influence him to put developer profit at the top of his priorities. While Alatorre could not be accused of wanting to change the Mexican marketplace character of Olvera Street, the direction and control of its development were at stake.

Two camps were emerging. One was led by Vivién Bonzo, owner of La Golondrina Restaurant on Olvera Street, a tireless woman in her mid thirties. Vivién, whose grandmother, Consuelo Bonzo, had founded the restaurant in the 1920s, rallied merchants by promoting a sense of history and responsibility to the street. She organized the Olvera Street Merchants Association, which represented an overwhelming majority of the merchants. To her credit, she alerted them to the city's development plans. Their fears were fanned by the growing hostility of Jean Bruce Poole.

The merchants, in a counteroffensive, paid $100,000 to Barrio Planners in 1987 for a development plan for Olvera Street. The Barrio Planners study proposed a $25 million, privately financed project that would highlight the contributions of Mexicans to the city. The plan was followed by Bonzo's appointment to the mayor's Office of Economic Development (OED), which intensified the conflict.[10]

The second camp was led by Councilman Alatorre and included Mayor Tom Bradley and the Recreation and Parks Commission, which oversaw the park.[11] Among them they had a formidable array of connections with wealth and power. Alatorre wanted those who would lead and benefit from Olvera Street's development to be from his political cabal: members of the powerful East Los Angeles Community Union (TELACU), including his friend attorney Andy Camacho, an affable mover and shaker in the Los Angeles community.

A Word about TELACU

The shadow of TELACU loomed large over the Olvera Street struggle. Founded in 1968, TELACU is a nonprofit corporation based in East Los Angeles and intended to advance economic development in predominately Latino communities. It serves as an umbrella for twelve subsidiaries, which are for-profit holding companies. In 1993 it grossed over $60 million, and had a portfolio of one-third of a billion dollars.[12] As a community development corporation, it has capitalized on a wide range of federal, state and local grants and Small Business Administration loans. TELACU's strength has been its housing development strategy: building low-cost, first-buyer and senior-citizen housing as well as public housing, such as the Casa Maravilla housing project.

Despite having allegedly created 10,000 jobs and given $500,000 in scholarships over an eight-year period, TELACU's record is questionable. Much of the distrust comes from Chicano activists, who clashed with TELACU during the late 1960s and 1970s over control of the Congress of Mexican American Unity. Many of them had expected TELACU to be a public organization with grassroots input serving as a catalyst for qualitative social change, something it was never intended to be. TELACU was created to reform the system and in the process build a political and economic power base (much like parallel organizations in the African American and Jewish American communities). TELACU and groups like it fundamentally engage in forming a new propertied elite, a brown bourgeoisie.[13]

But distrust of TELACU also flows from a record that includes charges of corruption and bribery, which in turn have led to federal investigations. A 1982 Department of Labor investigation found that a TELACU subsidiary had received SBA loans and invested them in high-yielding certificates instead of redistributing them as expected. Investigators also found that TELACU gave its executives big salaries, fancy cars, personal loans and free worldwide travel. Its 380 bank accounts in the United States and Switzerland made tracing the money difficult.[14]

In 1988 it came to light that Alatorre had lobbied on TELACU's behalf for a $727,500 transportation contract. Earlier, the corporation had flown Alatorre to Lake Tahoe and paid him a $1,000 honorarium for a speech.[15] Councilman Alatorre was fined $2,000 for violating conflict-of-interest laws, although he denied having done so knowingly. But Alatorre was hardly alone in being criticized for questionable TELACU-related dealings. In the early 1980s, the Eastside City Council member Art Snyder rented quarters in TELACU's building and actively lobbied to win contracts for TELACU.[16]

From these and other dealings TELACU acquired a negative image, which its longtime CEO David Lizarraga worked hard to dispel. He succeeded for the most part by making TELACU more fiscally accountable and by forging ties with many of the movers and shakers in Los Angeles – the black-tie set.[17] TELACU could also count on strong links to both Democratic and Republican Party officials, links that would extend on up to President Clinton by 1994.[18] Indeed, by the mid 1990s TELACU's influence extended well beyond Alatorre's circle.

Another major player in Alatorre's camp was the city Recreation and Parks Commission. At the time, attorney Richard Riordan – who became mayor of Los Angeles in 1993 – headed the commission. It also included African American attorney Stan Sanders (who became a candidate for mayor and later endorsed Riordan) and attorney Dominick Rubalcalva, both of whom had strong personal and professional ties with Alatorre and Bradley. From the beginning the commission showed a willingness to do Alatorre's bidding.[19]

Poole on the Offensive

In 1988 full control of the El Pueblo Historic Park began to pass from the state to the city of Los Angeles (the process was completed in 1990). This gave Poole and her gaggle the opportunity to go on a full offensive. They portrayed themselves as the gatekeepers of El Pueblo's past. Poole had even developed a small constituency among liberals with her efforts to restore the Siquieros mural, *América Tropical*. She surreptitiously met with members of other ethnic groups, seeking their approval by telling them that they had a place in the history of the park and that the Mexicans were keeping them out. The curator promised support to the Italians and the Chinese, telling them that they were entitled to public financing for their museums. She also enlisted the aid of the powerful Los Angeles Conservancy, whose leaders had served as paid consultants to her.

Tensions developed between the Mexican community and other minorities as a result of Poole's manipulation. She embraced Olvera Street's dilapidated buildings – mostly stucco and red brick – rather than its traditions and people.

It was no secret that she believed the Mexican presence on Olvera Street overwhelmed the contributions of the Chinese, the Italians and other neighborhood ethnic groups to the city's development. To dilute the Mexican presence, she advocated that the restoration of Olvera Street spotlight the architecture of its buildings. Toward this end, she enlisted the support of architectural historians. Following the advice of these consultants, the Rec and Park commission proposed a plan that called for Olvera Street to be renovated and its history interpreted to conform with the architecture of a 'Prime Historic Period' of 1920–32, when Mexican influence was at its weakest. Historians will tell you that 'Prime Historic Periods' are a convenient device for diluting the influence of unwanted groups: in the case of Olvera Street, 'No Mexicans Wanted'. It is ironic that the buildings Poole wanted to preserve would have been demolished long before if it had not been for the Mexican presence.

Incensed at Poole's plan, middle-class Chicano and barrio activists supported the fight to save Olvera Street. Academics such as Juan Gómez-Quiñones, William Estrada, Marta López-Garza and I joined Vivién Bonzo and the merchants to form the Los Angeles Mexican Conservancy with the goal of saving Olvera Street and the rest of El Pueblo Park. Estrada, then an Occidental College administrator, contributed valuable research to counter Poole's claims that people other than Mexicans and Native Americans had built the street. Under Bonzo's leadership, the Conservancy began to counteract the fantasy heritage manufactured by Poole.

Tensions increased between the members of the Conservancy and the Recreation and Parks Commission. Conservancy members met with Riordan, who in effect told them that he didn't give a damn about history and indicated that the Olvera Street renovation should be awarded to the highest bidder, which would have resulted in the conversion of Olvera Street into a Taco Bell. The commissioners closed ranks with Alatorre and his political allies: Riordan and another member of the commission told the group flatly that they would vote the way the mayor and Alatorre told them to vote.

Los Angeles Mexican Conservancy members knew that they had to do something dramatic. They called a mass mobilization for the Rec and Parks Commission meeting of 11 June 1990, and then went to the community to garner support, making presentations at churches throughout the Eastside. Belmont High School teacher Sal Castro, well known for his support of Chicano student activism in the 1960s, solicited parental consent for students to attend the rally. On that day, several thousand supporters assembled at the park's kiosk and marched to City Hall behind Father Juan Santillán of St Lucy's in City Terrace.[20] Five hundred protestors packed the City Council chambers where the commission was meeting, while the rest waited noisily outside. It was a stormy session: Councilman Richard Alatorre, resplendent in his all-white suit, was even booed. The Italians and the Chinese sat alongside Jean Bruce Poole. Actor

Edward James Olmos, singer Vikki Carr and director Luis Váldez testified.[21]

In response, the commissioners railroaded through a $30 million plan to renovate Olvera Street. Among the objectionable sections was the inclusion of an Italian museum. Mexican Conservancy supporters saw this as part of Poole's plot to dilute the Mexican presence in the park.[22] The proposal would also have put the renovation out to bid, with the developer paying half the cost and the merchants the other half. This would bankrupt the small merchants, some of whose families had been on Olvera Street since the 1920s: they could not afford to split the costs, which would have exceeded $200,000 per merchant. Protestors feared that the result would be a commercial venture like San Diego's Old Town, since it was the small merchants' presence that had previously prevented the commercialization of Olvera Street.

Although Bonzo and the Mexican Conservancy had been highly successful in mobilizing the Chicano community and enlisting the support of a large number of Euroamericans, Alatorre's forces had won the first round of the struggle for Olvera Street. To deal with the need for expensive seismic stabilization of El Pueblo's buildings, the city created two separate projects, Olvera Street and the Pico-Garnier complex, each of which was put out for development bid. Up to this point, the Mexican Conservancy had paid scant attention to the Pico-Garnier contract. Now they began to scrutinize the negotiations. In 1984, the Rec and Parks Commission had granted the Old Los Angeles Corporation a contract to develop Pico-Garnier to provide limited museum space, historic displays and office space.[23] The lease was for a 25-year term, with a binder requiring a minimum of $30 million in gross sales to qualify for a ten-year lease extension.

By 1987, Old Los Angeles Corporation still had not begun work on the development of Pico-Garnier. It asked the Recreation and Parks Commission board to renegotiate the contract, claiming that the revision of the 1984 federal tax code made it impossible for the company to make a profit. The new agreement, negotiated by Riordan, was a sweetheart deal: it did not include the $30 million binder – and the developer would have the sole option to renew for twenty-five years (not ten). While the Olvera Street merchants paid the city annual rents totalling $765,000, Old Los Angeles Corp. would pay $100,000 a year with annual increases of $4,000 in rents for its first twenty years at Pico-Garnier. For the remainder of the term the city would get a percentage. The limited space made available for historical displays in Pico-Garnier would be severely reduced and the amount of office space increased.[24]

Moreover, the Old Los Angeles Corp. would take 100 parking spaces from Olvera Street for $64,200 annually, depriving the street of $210,000 in revenues. Over the next twenty-five years the merchants would pay $24 million in rents, compared with $3.7 million from Old Los Angeles Corp. The merchants resented the fact that money that should have been earmarked for the development of Olvera Street would subsidize the Pico-Garnier complex. To add insult to injury, Old Los Angeles Corp. planned to build its project around a French restaurant. There were no provisions for a Mexican museum.

Mexican Conservancy members were also angry. They had hoped to convert Pico-Garnier into a cultural center that would include theater performances throughout the year, and envisioned a cultural space that would bond all segments of the community – workers, activists, academics, professionals. On 19 June 1990, they again packed the City Council chambers, this time asking the Council to overturn the Recreation and Parks Commission's actions.[25] Testimony pointed out that Poole had bought the support of other groups by committing funds to the preservation of their histories, with the Mexican merchants picking up the tab. A law-and-order museum – but not a Mexican Museum – was planned at the Pico-Garnier Complex. Ample evidence was presented to confirm that history was being sacrificed to the profits of the Pico-Garnier developer.

The Conservancy took special care not to attack the Chinese community. It respected the territorial integrity of the Chinese, and was not demanding the restoration of Sonora Town, which would incorporate some of Chinatown. Nor did it ask for Italian Hall on Broadway or Little Joe's, another Italian-American enclave. Unfortunately, Italian community leaders displayed very little respect for the Chicano community during the entire process.[26]

Bringing further pressure to bear, the Mexican Conservancy announced that it would ask for a congressional investigation of a possible conflict of interest between the Recreation and Parks commissioners, the mayor's office and Alatorre. At that point, Alatorre and Mayor Bradley proposed that a nonprofit corporation manage all El Pueblo Park, both Olvera Street and Pico-Garnier. This reversed the commission's decision of 11 June 1990. In response the Mexican Conservancy ended its call for a congressional investigation, even though it opposed having a nonprofit corporation manage the park because it would not be subject to public scrutiny. The Conservancy insisted on a special commission that would be accountable to the City Council and the mayor. Alatorre resisted but finally settled on a public body to oversee the park.[27]

The concerns of the Mexican Conservancy went beyond the impact of the Bradley-Alatorre development plan on the merchants. Many members began to discuss the implications of the plan for the homeless and for the racial composition of the area. Of special concern was Our Lady Queen of the Angels Church, known as La Placita, the first and oldest Catholic Church in Los Angeles. Historically it has served the Mexican poor and other Latinos, including Salvadoran refugees who come from parishes throughout the county to avoid the bureaucracy and nosiness of local pastors. As many as 200 to 300 baptisms are performed there on weekends. Would the Latinos be forced out to make room for a more upscale clientele?

Conservancy members met with the different developers, including the developer of the county property on the westside of Main Street. He flatly stated that he had problems getting a loan because of the homeless, so he wanted the homeless out of the area. He had an agreement, the county developer said, with the archdiocese that the Church would clean up the homeless problem in exchange for parking space. A sizeable body of the Olvera Street merchants also complained about the homeless (most of them undocumented), the street vendors, and the panhandlers. Some of them, led by Vivién Bonzo, wanted to take a more humane approach.[28]

The developers blamed 'the homeless problem' on Father Luis Olivares, the former pastor of La Placita, who in 1986 declared Our Lady Queen of the Angels a sanctuary for Central American refugees. With Olivares now gone (he had been transferred) they believed that the archdiocese would cooperate in getting rid of 'these people'. What most forgot was that it was logical for Central American Catholics to seek out the Catholic Church for *posada*, refuge. Our Lady Queen of the Angels is in the center of the city; it is the official parish for all Spanish-speaking Catholics and, even without its sanctuary policy, it was a magnet for those who take Christian principles seriously. The undocumented homeless cannot obtain aid from agencies receiving federal assistance, a policy that is aggressively advocated by militant anti-immigrant groups. This policy has worsened the environment on the street, making nativist and racist violence common, with Central Americans often the targets.

In this context, 150 to 200 Central American and Mexican refugees usually congregated around La Placita and set up an underground economy. Unable to afford tourist prices on Olvera Street, they depended on street vendors for their needs. They were able to use the church's toilet facilities, thanks to Father Olivares. The city had purposely not built toilets in downtown Los Angeles, a decision designed to force the homeless to move on. All this meant that the Chicano community had to keep in mind the rights of the homeless and the growing Central American population. La Placita, which shared Olvera Street's space and history, has always been a refuge for the poor. The moral authority for the preservation of Olvera Street rests on people, not bricks.[29] Important though Olvera Street is and has been as a symbol, its preservation is not the ultimate goal.

In the end, Bradley dragged his feet on the installation of the authority that was to oversee the park. During his tenure, it was decided that the members would be innocuous, and include representatives of the Italian and Chinese communities. But Bradley waffled and did not actually constitute the park authority while in office. Only in 1994 did Riordan name the authority's members, including two leading Chicanos with roots in the 1960s movement, as well as Chinese and Italians. The future of Olvera Street remains uncertain, since few decisions of moment were left to the authority's members to make.

Happy Hour for *La Raza*

The war over Olvera Street has been a struggle to reaffirm Mexican place and identity in Los Angeles history. Another struggle, also waged on Olvera Street, has been a fight against distortion and exploitation of that Mexican culture and history. For years Olvera Street merchants out of their own resources promoted traditional Mexican events such as the Blessing of the Animals and the Day of the Dead. The administration of El Pueblo Park has frustrated these community initiatives by turning the celebration of Cinco de Mayo into one big 'happy hour' with beer and tobacco companies handing out free samples. Recreation and Parks Commissioner Riordan, who himself owned five Coors beer distributorships, could see nothing wrong with this commercialization.[30] And the granting of permits for these concessions had to go through the council member in whose district the event was held, so they served as an important source of patronage for Richard Alatorre.

Twenty years ago, Cinco de Mayo was an event largely unknown outside the schools and parks of the Mexican community, a celebration of the victory of Mexican forces led by General Ignacio Zaragosa over a French invasion of Mexico on 5 May 1862. It was a minor holiday among Chicanos in the United States until the 1960s, when a nationwide revival of Chicano nationalism made it better known. Enter the beer companies. Recognizing that Latinos comprised the largest beer-drinking market in California, they developed a plan to expand sales. According to Jim Hernández, director of the California Hispanic Commission on Alcoholism and Drug Abuse, the brewers adopted what is now known as the 'Budweiser strategy': make alcohol a staple of Latino social life.

The beer companies published calendars depicting Chicano heroes and Mexican American yuppies, which they put in restaurants, and reinforced sexism by running ads using women as objects. They became sponsors of Chicano banquets and functions. In 1985 leading Mexican American national organizations – the National Council of La Raza, the American G.I. Forum and later the League of United Latin American Citizens – signed an agreement with Coors Brewing Company. In return for their calling off a long-standing national boycott of Coors, the company promised to give more than $350 million to Latino organizations. Coors suddenly became a good corporate citizen; the deal was known widely among Chicanos as 'Drink a Coors for *La Raza*.' Given the decline of federal and state funding of community-oriented projects, many organizations found themselves increasingly dependent on funds from corporate America. It is also no secret that the Spanish-language media would have been in trouble if they had lost the advertising revenues from beer companies.[31]

The cost of ignoring the alcohol problem, however, has been high. Reports show that nearly one-third of adult Mexican American males can be considered 'heavy' or 'problem' drinkers. The Department of Health and Human Services reports that Mexican-born males in the United States have a 40 percent higher risk of death from alcohol-related cirrhosis of the liver than do white males. Nearly 50 percent of those arrested for drunk driving in Los Angeles County are Latinos. According to Dr Juana Mora, alcohol-related problems are also becoming more common among Chicanas and Mexican women, who once were primarily victims of males' alcoholism but with exposure to US society are themselves more likely to become heavy drinkers.[32]

Alcohol abuse among Mexicans and other Latinos went beyond the stereotype. It was a disease that the alcohol distributors effectively exploited. There are more liquor outlets in Mexican and Latino neighborhoods than in middle-class neighborhoods, and billboards carry their message even on the front lawns of homes. (Corporations have always been able to afford legalized graffiti in poor neighborhoods.) Like the tobacco companies, the liquor industry spreads its poison in both Latino and African American communities with total indifference to human well-being.

In 1990, Proposition 134, better known as the nickel-a-drink tax, was placed on the ballot. It would have imposed an additional tax on alcohol in order to pay for programs designed to reduce consumption, not unlike those conducted against smoking. The programs would also have provided some recovery services. The alcohol industry played hardball and introduced its own Proposition 126. This measure would have raised the tax by only a penny a drink, and contained no program to reduce consumption. The California Teachers Association shortsightedly supported the alcohol lobby because Proposition 134 did not funnel money into teachers' salaries or the schools.

Admittedly, there were problems with Proposition 134. Although Latinos would pay a major portion of the alcohol tax, there were no guarantees that money would be funneled back to programs serving them. In 1990, Latinos were almost 40 percent of the county's population, and had 49 percent of the DUI convictions, but received only 18 percent of alcohol rehabilitation services. In South Central L.A., where more than 50 percent of the population was Latino, no Latino alcoholism programs existed. Ultimately, the alcohol industry's strategy resulted in a public opinion chaos that led to the defeat of both propositions.

Meanwhile, the struggle continues to redeem Cinco de Mayo from its degeneration into a multicultural beer bust and to promote a genuine Mexican identity on Olvera Street and in other parts of Los Angeles, as does the tension between Mexican cultural heritage and the demands of the marketplace. Although Chicano and Latino organizations want to reconstruct history, they are strapped for money, and the brewing industry has become a major source of funds. In the end, the fantasy heritage is often more attractive than the truth – and certainly more profitable.

The Fight for a Mexican Museum

The Mexican integrity of Olvera Street has yet to be guaranteed. In a similar way, the dream of a Mexican historical museum in the Los Angeles area has also remained unfulfilled. By the late 1980s, most major ethnic groups in California had a museum, most with generous state and local subsidies. Even though Latino legislators helped sponsor bills to create museums for other groups, they did not make the same effort to gain a similar institution for their own constituencies. At tremendous personal sacrifice, historian Antonio Ríos-Bustamante and William Estrada incorporated a nonprofit Latino Museum in the early 1980s and held exhibitions, pushing the concept among legislators and almost anyone else who would listen.

After a number of false starts, they convinced then Assemblyman Charles Calderón to carry a bill – AB2798. The Alhambra Democrat's effort, however, became embroiled in politics and he deferred to Councilman Alatorre, who wanted the museum in his own district. Eventually, the Los Angeles City Council appropriated some money for a study, and a blue ribbon committee was formed that included Alatorre and then Councilwoman Gloria Molina. By late 1995, the museum had found a site, but had not yet become a reality.[33]

The need for a Latino/Chicano museum was underscored by the Gene Autry Western Heritage Museum in Griffith Park, which opened in the late 1980s.[34] The museum claims to trace the history of the West from the sixteenth century to the present. When I first visited the museum, it was clearly the Euroamerican cowboy's vision of the West. It lacked any criticism of the genocide against Native Americans. In the big mural *Spirits of the West*, the only identifiable Mexicans – or for that matter, Spaniards – were a missionary and a brown man playing a guitar. A buxom Latina dance-hall girl was described to a group of junior high students as 'one of the girls who kept the boys happy.' Black people were portrayed only as small farmers who had helped settle the West, with nary a mention of slavery or racism.

A sign in one gallery delivered the familiar message of inevitability: 'When people of different cultures meet, they often fight, especially if their way of life or families seem threatened. Sometimes individuals adapt to newcomers, however, and attempt to live in peace. In either case, change is inevitable.' The planned, military elimination of the Indian was explained away with a similar phrase: 'Wind blows change.' As in so many other histories, these messages avoided any thorny issue or any explanation of conflict from the victim's perspective, or any description of struggles for liberation. The whole presentation was slick, and visiting children would accept the museum's portrayal as accurate. Well-meaning teachers, limited in their knowledge of history and by personal biases, would not correct the museum's version of 'how the West was won.'

When I returned to the museum in October 1994, I found few Latino and no Black visitors. There had been small improvements but no change in the museum's basic perspective. In standard 'multicultural' fashion, an altar reminiscent of those displayed on the Day of the Dead had been installed near the main mural, adding a little Mexican spice without altering the museum's dominant spirit. In the mural itself the Native Americans portrayed were all Plains Indians, emphasizing the warrior aspect of indigenous societies. The Mexican presence was limited to the *conquistador*, the cowboy or *vaquero*, and the Mexican woman dressed in a white ballroom gown. A single Black cowboy appeared. A sign said that the first cowboy came from Spain, with no information about the evolution of that profession in the West.

A popular children's museum had been added. Its featured display was modeled on the Ruelas's family ranch in Tucson, which includes some excellent photos. But the Ruelas family is described as European, although visibly mestizo with some members having marked Indian features. The Alianza Hispano-Americana plaque fails to explain that the Alianza was formed because of growing racism toward Mexicans in Tucson in the late nineteenth century – a typical omission. Here and elsewhere you could see the fundamental problem with the museum, unchanged since its opening: the problem of how to interpret history while at the same time avoiding painful truths.[35]

One tidbit offset the museum's general effect. Tucked away in a corner was an exhibit about Modesta Avila, who in 1889 was convicted of trying to wreck a Southern Pacific train. She had hung clothes across the tracks to protest the railroads' preemption of her family's land in Orange County. She was released from San Quentin after serving two and a half years of her three-year sentence. In retrospect, I could see why there were no Black children visiting: there was little there for them. And not much more for Latinos.[36]

Chicanos and the Church as a Source of Community

For people of color, the church has often provided a sense of place, of community – as in the African American community, where leadership has historically come from the churches. Given this pattern, we might expect the Catholic Church to play a community-strengthening role among the Latinos of Los Angeles, where the majority of Mexicans and Central Americans are Catholic. We might hope it would play a strong advocacy role, as it did in defending the rights of Irish and other European immigrants in the nineteenth century.

But in fact the Catholic Church, reflecting its origins as a colonial institution imposed on the Americas by the Spaniards, has been traditionally conservative.[37] It has usually sided with political and economic elites, and rarely produced people like Martin Luther King, Jr, Rev. James Lawson and others in the

Black churches who were moved by the desire to lead their people out of Egypt. This conservatism and the lack of priests from Mexican backgrounds may explain the growth of evangelical Protestantism among Latinos in the 1980s and the fact that only 70 percent of Los Angeles's population was Catholic in 1990, compared with some 85 percent in the 1970s.[38]

The Los Angeles Archdiocese of the Catholic Church includes Los Angeles, Ventura and Santa Barbara counties. Historically it has been dominated by Irish and German Catholics; only recently did it become predominately Latino. Since the appointment of Bishop Thomas Conaty in 1903, Irish prelates have held dominion. During the 1930s, Catholic Action groups supporting Spanish dictator Francisco Franco were favored by Spanish priests. Conditions changed little in later years: in 1965 Cardinal John Francis McIntyre called the Watts rebels 'inhuman, almost bestial' and defended Police Chief William Parker's racist conduct during the Watts Rebellion.[39]

Some improvements began within the Church after Católicos por La Raza, led by Ricardo Cruz, held demonstrations on Christmas Eve of 1969, and Mexican American and Latino priests and nuns themselves became more active.[40] McIntyre was replaced by the more moderate Archbishop Timothy Manning, who eventually became a cardinal. Manning, however, followed many of the policies of his predecessor, catering to the Irish and German elites. In 1985 Roger Mahoney became archbishop of Los Angeles. Many had high hopes when Mahoney accepted the resignation of several church officials, including arch-conservative Monsignor Benjamin G. Hawkes. To many, Hawkes's fondness for expensive suits, gold jewelry and his membership in the Jonathan Club and the Los Angeles Country Club symbolized the distance between the Catholic hierarchy and the worshipper. 'The rich have souls, too' was one of his favorite observations. People were ecstatic when Mahoney reversed the Church's decision to sell Cathedral High School, whose student body is 95 percent Latino, to developers. They also took courage from his support of programs for the poor and the undocumented, which demonstrated a belief that the poor have souls, too.

However, the Latino honeymoon with Mahoney gradually soured. Throughout his tenure Mahoney was criticized for his doctrinaire and unyielding stances on such issues as abortion and AIDS.[41] The AIDS crisis demanded more of the Church, but Mahoney failed to use his moral authority to deal with taboos that resulted from homophobia. Indeed, Church policies reinforced homophobia in the Latino community by tacitly approving it.[42] When Mahoney withdrew the Archdiocese of Los Angeles from participation in a Latino AIDS education program, he said that participation would be 'tantamount to condoning birth control and encouraging promiscuity.' (As of the mid 1980s, 14 percent of the AIDS patients nationally were Latinos – and this proportion was growing.)[43]

Cardinal Roger Mahoney has nevertheless been an improvement over his predecessors: for example, he has forcefully condemned the anti-immigrant hysteria of the 1990s (something that many Chicano politicos have not done as steadfastly as the cardinal). Nevertheless, he can hardly be termed a Latino leader in the same way that the African American ministry has provided leadership in Black communities. For instance, during the Rodney King uprisings, the Church remained almost silent concerning police cooperation with the Immigration and Naturalization Service. Mahoney has supported social action projects modeled after Saul Alinsky's Industrial Areas Foundation (IAF). Parishes furnished funds for citizen-based organizations such as UNO (United Neighborhood Organization), SCOC (South Central Organizing Communities), EVO (East Valley Organizations) and VOICE (Valley Organized in Community Efforts). These Church groups involved members in taking on 'winnable issues' such as the redlining of the Eastside by auto insurance companies. They also pressured politicos on social issues.

The IAF organizations politicized a number of priests and nuns, most notably Father Luis Olivares, who became one of the IAF's early leaders. The IAF-style groups in Los Angeles, however, never acquired the same power or prestige that they have won in Texas. One reason for this was that many of the L.A. leaders have been clergy, whereas in places like San Antonio they came from the ranks of the parish councils. Mexicans had always constituted a majority of the Catholic Church members in San Antonio, and, unlike Los Angeles, they formed a stable community of homeowners. Los Angeles parishes were made up of recently arrived immigrants, whereas San Antonio's base was Chicanos who had long settled in the city and created a stable sense of identity and place.

One often repeated criticism is that the Los Angeles IAF affiliates were more reluctant to take chances, strictly adhering to the Alinskian credo of taking on only 'winnable issues'. UNO, for instance, did not take on the East Los Angeles prison issue (see Chapter 3) until the Mothers of East Los Angeles had mobilized the community.[44] But for all of these criticisms, the Church was better off under Mahoney, who used culture and language like no other Los Angeles prelate had before him. He made an effort to reach out to Latinos; he speaks Spanish and knows Latino culture. Spanish-speaking priests have become more common since his appointment, as has the *mariachi* mass. The problem, however, is not only cultural; it is also a matter of class.[45]

Father Joseph P. Fitzpatrick, S.J., writes, 'When I was a boy, many rectory kitchens served as political clubs. They vibrated with sensitivity to the joys and sorrows, frustrations or satisfactions of their people; because the poor were *their* people there was an identity between them that was deep and strong and spontaneous.'[46] Father Fitzpatrick argues that the lack of real struggle on the part of priests in defending the rights of immigrants today is not 'because of a difference of culture; it is because of a difference of class.' Priests can learn Spanish and understand some of the culture, but 'differences in social class are much more difficult to recognize, and much more difficult for the middle class to respect.'[47] He adds, 'Class in the United States touches the issues of power, wealth and education. The United States, unlike Latin America, is predominantly middle-class, and the church is middle-class within it.'[48]

Affirming a Chicano Presence

Chicanos have had a difficult time sustaining their sense of community for various reasons, with the repression of their community's history playing a major role. The continuing struggle to preserve Olvera Street has been so important precisely because it affirms that history in the face of a Euroamerican presence that sees as alien all things Mexican. The dominant society has been intent on preserving the bricks of *its* past – bricks that cover the Mexican roots of the city. Resistance to the idea of a Mexican museum to preserve and celebrate the Mexican contribution to Los Angeles indicates both this historical bias in favor of the Euroamerican experience and the importance of the struggle to reconstruct Chicano history.

The Olvera Street struggles also show how political opportunism and financial interests can end up calling the tune even when grassroots forces press for recognition of the community. Thus the twin forces of racist exclusion and greed combined to undermine the meaning of Olvera Street and official recognition of the Mexican/Chicano reality of Los Angeles. The almighty power of the dollar is also obvious in the alcohol industry's attempts to exploit Mexican history and culture for profit.

The Catholic Church has offered a minimal contribution to the development of the Latino community, often finding it wisest to side with the Euroamerican elite. In Los Angeles the Church has made a priority of political and financial self-interest, as suggested by the devout Mayor Riordan's gift of a helicopter to Cardinal Mahoney, whom he also serves as an economic adviser. Where a sense of community has developed in a Church context, it is usually thanks to parishioners who initiate grassroots campaigns, sometimes with the assistance of sympathetic priests and/or nuns.

After recounting so many setbacks in the struggle to affirm the Mexican/Chicano presence in Los Angeles, we should close with one success story: the renaming of Brooklyn Avenue Avenida César Chávez soon after the farmworker leader's death. This was one of the few times that the Chicano community prevailed against opposition from shopkeepers, who in cases like these often argue that it would be too expensive to change signs and stationery. Chicanos also prevailed against opposition from Jewish-Americans who had once lived and thrived there.

There was some merit in the arguments of the Jewish community: Brooklyn Avenue was part of their historical memory. Chicanos, however, argued that Jewish people had left Boyle Heights, where Brooklyn Avenue ran, as part of the 'white flight' after World War II. Renaming this important artery, which runs from downtown Los Angeles through Boyle Heights and East Los Angeles, symbolized official recognition of today's Chicano presence in those areas.

Changing the name of Brooklyn Avenue was not meant to show disrespect for the Jewish American past. Instead, it was intended to contribute to the development of a positive self-image among Chicano and Latino children. Not only did it give them a street named for a Chicano/Latino, but a Chicano/Latino who was both contemporary and relevant to their working-class lives – unlike some Spanish explorer, colonizer or *ranchero*. In this spirit the name became Avenida César Chávez in November 1993.

Notes

1. Carlos Navarro and Rodolfo Acuña, 'In Search of Community: A Comparative Essay on Los Angeles and San Antonio', in Norman M. Klein and Martin J. Schiesl, eds, *20th-Century Los Angeles: Power, Promotion and Social Conflict* (Claremont, Calif.: Regina Books, 1990), p.196.

2. For a brilliant analysis, see Donald Craig Parson, 'Urban Politics During the Cold War: Public Housing, Urban Renewal and Suburbanization in Los Angeles', dissertation, UCLA 1985. Chavez Ravine was originally slated to be a large public housing project – the first planned integrated project in the city. These plans were cut short by Cold War anti-communist hysteria.

3. Paulo Freire, *Pedagogy of the Oppressed* (New York: Herder and Herder, 1972), p. 87.

4. Teresa Córdova, ed., *Chicano Studies: Critical Connection Between Research and Community* (Albuquerque, N.M.: The National Association for Chicano Studies, 1992), p. i.

5. Larry Gordon and David Treadwell, 'On Race Relations, Colleges Are Learning Hard Lessons', *Los Angeles Times*, 4 Jan. 1992; Special issue of *Time*, 'California: The Endangered Dream', 18 Nov. 1991; Paul Grey, 'Whose America?' *Time*, 8 July 1991, pp. 13–16; Arthur Schlesinger, Jr, 'The Cult of Ethnicity, Good and Bad', *Time*, 8 July 1991, p 21.

6. Carey McWilliams, *North from Mexico: The Spanish-Speaking People of the United States* (New York: Greenwood Press, 1968), p. 35.

7. See Rodolfo Acuña, 'Inside the Alamo', *Texas Observer*, 26 Jan. 1990, for a discussion of the role of the myth of the Alamo in perpetuating racism. The article concerned a tour of the Alamo in 1989 during a twentieth anniversary of the Chicano movement in Texas; Acuña, 'Alamo Memories', *Texas Observer*, 22 March 1991, is a review of Jeff Long, *Duel of Eagles*, which explodes the myth of the Alamo and its depiction of freedom-loving Americans defending democracy.

8. Arthur Schlesinger, Jr., *The Disunity of America* (New York: W.W. Norton, 1992), p. 60, misrepresents the campaigns to correct ('revise') history by minority scholars. I have never read a Chicano scholar who belittles European accomplishments, only the excesses in their praise.

9. Of course, indigenous people had lived in the Los Angeles basin for thousands of years before the founding of Los Angeles. *Indios*, mestizos, Blacks and mulattoes were brought to the region as part of a colonial process. They mixed with the indigenous peoples of the Los Angeles area, and were used by the Spanish Empire to hold this territory. The process has never been fully understood, and scholars from this side of the Río Bravo have generally analyzed it using a Eurocentric or Afrocentric model. Further confusing the analysis is presentism in the interpretation of

history, which dwells on the concept of borders. Before the coming of the Spaniards there was no Mexico, there was no New Spain. The forging of a Mexican nation was a process of struggle, which culminated in but did not end with the War of Independence. It was a process that the indigenous peoples and those of mixed blood had no control over. The United States was also a product of European invasion; however, as it forged nationhood it excluded anyone other than Europeans: the indigenous peoples had no rights, nor did those of African descent. For a discussion of race mixing in the forging of the Mexican nation, see Eric Wolf, *Sons of the Shaking Earth: The People of Mexico and Guatemala* (Chicago: University of Chicago Press, 1959), pp. 29–33, which says, for example, of the impact of African slaves, 'Roughly 250,000 were imported into Mexico during the three centuries of the slave trade.' Wolf makes the point that only 300,000 Spaniards arrived during this same period. He estimated that more than two-thirds of the indigenous population was lost in the 'holocaust' of Spanish conquest. (Wolf's figures are an undercount.) It is therefore reasonable to celebrate the African influence on Mexico, but at the same time one must remember that this influence in the making of Mexico differs from the experience of Africans in the US. See also Roxanne Dunbar Ortiz, *Roots of Resistance: Land Tenure in New Mexico, 1680–1980* (Los Angeles: UCLA, Chicano Studies Research Center and American Indian Studies Center, 1980). Still useful is Milton M. Gordon, *Assimilation in American Life: The Role of Race, Religion, and National Origins* (New York: Oxford University Press, 1964), pp. 10–57.See also Rupert Costo and Jeanette Henry Costo, eds, *The Missions of California: A Legacy of Genocide* (San Francisco: Indian Historical Press, 1987). Agustín Cue Canovas, *Historia social y economic de Mexico* (México: Editoria F. Trillas, 1969) lists (Chapter 10) the racial/ethnic composition of Mexico's population of 6,122,354 for 1810: Europeans, 15,000; Africans, 10,000; Indians, 3,676,281; Euromestizos, 1,092,367; Afromestizos, 624,461; Indomestizos, 704,245.

10.   One group was led by Bonzo and the other by Camacho and Peter Martínez, who formed the Business Leadership of Olvera Street (BLOS). By late 1988 Bonzo's term had ended, and according to insiders Alatorre blocked her reappointment.

11.   Rubén Martínez and Ron Curran, '¡Se Vende! The Fight over Olvera Street', *L.A. Weekly*, 16 November 1990, pp. 20–28. Alatorre had strong ties with the mayor's office through Bradley's assistant Art Gastelum, who was appointed liaison between the mayor's office and Olvera Street. Gastelum also had ties with Camacho, who gave him half interest in a $375,000 property in upscale San Marino as a so-called 'bona fide gift'. When the *L.A. Business Journal* reported this very questionable deal in March 1990, Gastelum resigned. Up to then, he was a key player in the Olvera Street struggle, giving an edge to the Alatorre forces.

12.   'David Lizarraga: In the Business of Rebuilding the Eastside of Los Angeles', *Los Angeles Times*, 25 Sept. 1994.

13.   Ferdinand Lundberg, *The Rich and the Super Rich: A Study in the Power of Money Today* (New York: Lyle Stuart, 1968), p. 102.

14.   Claire Spiegel, 'Investment Firm Was Target of Lengthy US Probe', *Los Angeles Times*, 18 Aug. 1985; United Press International reports, 16 April 1983, 7 Dec. 1982 and 9 Nov. 1982.

15.   Rick Connel, 'Alatorre Fined $2000 for Conflict of Interest to Steer Pact', *Los Angeles Times*, 3 Feb. 1988.

16.   During the second half of the 1980s, I was under contract to write monthly columns for the *Los Angeles Herald-Examiner*. On several occasions, I was asked to write muckraking articles on Alatorre. I refused to look at the files the newspaper offered me, and confined my criticism to controversies within the community. I also refused to delve into family or personal problems. My position was that unless the *Herald* was willing to write exposés on all the council members (indeed on all politicians), it was not fair to single out a Chicano politico, which has often been the case in L.A. This kind of one-sidedness in effect invites a political pogrom against Chicanos. In the case of the late *Herald* and the *Los Angeles Times*, editorial treatment has not been even. And, although I am often critical of TELACU, it should be pointed out that until recently it received worse press than similar corporations in other racial and ethnic communities.

17.   Mary Lou Loper, 'Governor's Awards to Honor Legends, Patrons', *Los Angeles Times*, 21 Jan 1993.

18.   James Rainey, 'Earthquake: The Road to Recovery', *Los Angeles Times*, 12 Feb. 1994.

19.   Ibid, p. 22. Riordan was a dealer in downtown real estate and a confidant of Archbishop Roger Mahoney. He balanced his conservatism with small-time philanthropy, donating computers

to Mexican schools and heavily courting the United Neighborhood Organization, an Industrial Areas Foundation group with member chapters based throughout Eastside Mexican churches. Indeed, Riordan could be seen regularly on the pages of *The Tidings*, donating computers to Eastside parochial schools. Riordan was extremely active behind the scenes in attempting to privatize Olvera Street. In a meeting with Vivién Bonzo, Juan Gómez-Quiñonez, Diego Vigil and me, he told us that he could get more Mexicans than we could when we threatened to picket a commission meeting. I called UNO and asked them if they were supporting Riordan against the interests of the community to keep Olvera Street a Mexican marketplace. I was told that they had made no such commitment to Riordan but were cooperating with him on the 'Kids First' Campaign, which was designed to restructure the Los Angeles Unified School District. My source, who asked not to identified, added that UNO had the year before lobbied heavily for raising the minimum wage, and that they were aware of Riordan's opposition to the proposal. Rodolfo Acuña, 'History Is People, Not Bricks', *Los Angeles Times*, 2 April 1990.

20. Martínez, p. 24, reports that there were 200 protestors. He was, however, not at the rally. George Ramos, 'Olvera Street Rival Wins Approval of Commission', *Los Angeles Times*, 12 June 1990, reported that there were 500 in the City Council chambers. Over 1,000 supporters waited outside. José Luis Sierra, 'Alatorre reafirma su oposición al establecimiento de un museo italiano en la Plaza Olvera', *La Opinión*, 14 June 1990.

21. The support of the entertainers was important, but members of the group had to compromise to keep their support. Olmos, for instance, insisted that the Italians and the Chinese be given space in the Park. In view of this, some of the members of the Conservancy moderated their public stance, saying if the Italians and the Chinese wanted museums they should at least pay for their construction, development and maintenance. Funds generated from Mexican activities such as the Cinco de Mayo should be used to enhance the Mexican presence and not diverted for other uses.

22. Poole had done little to promote Mexican culture in the park and had shifted funds that should have been used for development of Mexican cultural events to the development of a Chinese museum. The Chinese museum would get $225,000 for the first year's operation from Olvera Street revenue and parking; Poole, according to sources, had promised a like sum to the Italians for a museum. Meanwhile, the park bureaucracy had not allocated a cent of its $2.3 million budget for a Mexican museum.

23. This company was affiliated with Grand American of Santa Monica, which also owned Gladstone's 4 Fish and RJ's Ribs. It owned a share of Camacho's El Paseo on Olvera Street and TELACU's Tamayo Restaurant. Martínez and Curran, p. 21.

24. A confidential source working as a consultant for the Old Los Angeles Corp. told me that historical preservation was the furthest thing from the minds of the developers.

25. Rodolfo F. Acuña, Testimony before the Los Angeles City Council, 19 June 1990: 'Since we entered the fray, we have been insulted, called dupes of greedy merchants – a ridiculous charge when you consider that the scholars earn more than the average merchant. Moreover, the charge becomes ludicrous when you consider that Jeane Poole is a wealthy lady, and the Park and Recreation Commissioners themselves are wealthy men.'

26. In response to the Italian leaders, I pointed out at the hearings: 'Mexicans have suffered more than any other group save Native American and Mexican buildings from private and government encroachment, from the beginning to the end of this century. We still remember Bunker Hill and Chavez Ravine. We still remember the Bozzani family tearing down the Santa Cruz adobe to make room for a parking lot for Bozzani Motors. Freeways have displaced tens of thousands of Latinos. And, at this very moment, we are fighting the dumping of toxic dumps and prisons on our community.'

27. 'El Pueblo Logjam Cleared', *Downtown News*, 6 April 1992; José Luis Sierra, 'Los votantes decidieran el futuro de la Calle Olvera, *La Opinión*, 12 Feb. 1992; 'A Big Deal for Olvera Street', *Los Angeles Times*, 30 May 1992.

28. Patt Morrison, 'Crime and Charity: An Uneasy Mixture', *Los Angeles Times*, 18 June 1989; Mary Ballesteros, 'Avanza la lucha por preservar la tradición de la calle Olvera', *La Opinión*, 4 Feb. 1992; Sierra, 'Los votantes decidirán el futuro de la Calle Olvera'.

29. After Father Luis Olivares left, La Placita's mission changed, and, although it served the spiritual needs of the Latino poor, it became less active in the protection of the homeless, whose

presence was 'discouraged'.

30. Coors was controversial because of the company's union-busting and anti-Chicano policies in the 1970s, which resulted in widespread boycotts. The Coors issue remained a point of
contention among Chicano activists throughout the 1980s. However, activists no longer had the
moral authority to threaten the growing number of Latino organizations and politicos who actively cooperated with Coors. This, even though the Coors family has strong ties to right-wing
think tanks and the John Birch society. Bella Stumbo, 'Coors Clan: Doing It Their Way', *Los Angeles
Times*, 18 Sept. 1988.

31. See Rodolfo Acuña, 'Latinos' Worst Enemy', *Los Angeles Herald-Examiner*, 1 Sept. 1989; and
Rodolfo Acuña and Juana Mora, 'Afterword', in Bruce Maxwell and Michael Jacobson, *Marketing
Disease to Hispanics* (Washington, D.C.: Center for Science in the Public Interest, 1990), pp. 2, 58,
81–3.

32. Juana Mora, 'Running Ahead: Learning to Drink and Early Drinking', unpublished MS,
California State University, Northridge.

33. Cheryl Wittenaur, 'The Economics of Culture: L.A.'s Most Successful Plaza de la Raza',
Hispanic Business, Jan. 1983, pp. 12–13, 29. Plaza de La Raza, founded in 1970 by Mexican actress
Margo Albert, wife of actor Eddie Albert and a social activist in her own right, served as a cultural
center that was very important for the preservation of the arts.

34. Bob Sipchen, 'The Only Question at the Gene Autry Museum Is Will It Be Interpreted',
Los Angeles Times, 20 Dec. 1987; Rodolfo Acuña, 'No Way to Celebrate Cinco de Mayo', *Los Angeles
Herald-Examiner*, 5 May 1989.

35. The tragedy of this distortion of the past by museums like the Autry is that most Americans believe them. A recent survey by historians Roy Rosenzweig and David Thelen, *How Americans Learn from and Use the Past* (Bloomington, Ind.: University of Indiana Press, forthcoming),
found that most Americans, including Mexican Americans, found museums the most trustworthy
source of information about the past, scoring markedly higher than high school and college history teachers.

36. Terry Pristin, '"Taming" of the Wild West Is Rewritten by Scholars', *Los Angeles Times*, 14
Nov. 1990. Some Euroamerican scholars are also challenging the interpretations of older historians: 'Turning their backs on the heroic frontier story as told in countless movies, a new generation
of scholars has rejected the notion that the West was "tamed" through an unbroken series of triumphs and acts of individual courage.' These revisionist historians were led by Patricia Limerick
of the University of Colorado in seeking to 'explore the settler's failures – economic and moral –
the environmental consequences, the role of the federal government, the resilience of native peoples and other ethnic groups and the part played by women.'

37. Despite the declining influence of the church and the challenge of evangelical churches,
the Los Angeles Catholic Church is a powerful force in the lives of Latinos. On his papal tour in
1987 Pope John Paul II targeted Los Angeles, and his visit to the city was the occasion of an emotional outpouring on the part of Latinos. 'The irony in all this is that if the Catholic Church is to
achieve its goal of regenerating the family, it must preserve communities'; see Rodolfo Acuña, 'The
Latino L.A. Juan Pablo Won't See', *Los Angeles Herald-Examiner*, 11 Sept. 1987. During the 1980s,
the American Catholic Church hierarchy lobbied the Vatican to grant sainthood to Father Junipero
Serra. They seemed to believe that Mexicans would automatically identify with this affirmative
action saint. It never dawned on them that Serra was part of the colonial structure that oppressed
the indigenous populations in Mexico, Central America and California. Native American historians
and Chicano activists naturally questioned this process. 'Father Serra Beatified by Pope', *Daily
News*, 26 Sept. 1988.

38. Nationally, in 1979 the Church had 56,000 priests, of whom 585 were Latino, even though
25% of the nation's Catholics are Latino, Lucy Norman de Sánchez and Pablo Sánchez, 'Latinos
in Parochial Schools: Divine Neglect?' *Nuestro Magazine*, Sept. 1979, p. 42; 193 of L.A.'s 1,340 priests
are Latino, Martínez and Davis, p. 22. Lyn Smith and Russell Chandler, 'Evangelicals Gain Followers', *Nuestro Tiempo*, 8 Feb. 1990. There is a growing Protestant fundamentalist movement among
Mexicans and Central Americans. Father Ricardo Chávez, director of the Hispanic division of the
California Catholic Conference in the 1980s, excuses the Catholic Church: 'Most of the people
leaving have never been truly evangelized in the Catholic faith. From where they've come the
whole culture has supported the Catholic faith and they've known no other alternative ...' Accord-

ing to him, US culture no longer supports the faith, and Latinos have not had the religious instruction necessary to defend their faith against Protestant evangelizing. Interestingly, Chávez and other Church figures blamed the Mexican experience of the newcomers rather than the Euroamerican Church itself, Julie Sly, 'Protestants Gaining Numbers in Hispanic Community', *The Tidings*, 8 Feb. 1985. Storefront churches attract many Latinos, who are often clustered in small communities with poorly trained ministers (who nevertheless were from the same race and class as the adherents). Assemblies of God and pentecostal and evangelical churches spread because the Church took Chicanos/Latinos for granted. Only recently has the Catholic Church put priests of US-Mexican background in Chicano parishes. In the past it had sent them to Latin America as missionaries, Sly, 'Protestants Gaining Numbers'; Steve Goldstein, 'Conservative Blacks, Latinos Targeted by Christian Coalition', *Daily News*, 10 Sept. 1993.

 39. Rubén Martinez and Mike Davis, 'The Church', *L.A. Weekly*, 22 Dec. 1989, p. 16.

 40. Julie Sly, 'Laity, Pastors', *The Tidings*, 1 March 1985.

 41. Dean Murphy, 'All Business in Doing God's Work', *Los Angeles Times*, 14 June 1992; Teresa Puente, 'El aborto y los hispanos', *La Opinion*, 18 June 1991; Francisco Robles, 'El Cardenal Roger Mahoney promete protección a desanparados e inmigrantes', *La Opinion*, 8 July 1991.

 42. María Del Pilar Marrero, 'El machismo también causa el SIDA', *La Opinion*, 2 June 1991; Eric Jones, 'Escasan estudios de importancia sobre electo del SIDA entre hispanos', *La Opinión*, 9 Dec. 1991.

 43. See Rodolfo Acuña, 'Keep Mahoney's AIDS Decision in Perspective', *Los Angeles Herald-Examiner*, 19 Dec. 1986.

 44. Louis Negrete, 'Another Way', *Los Angeles Times*, 21 Sept. 1992.

 45. Mahoney has often been criticized for closing parochial schools, heavily impacting the Chicano/Latino community. In 1986 there were 82,695 elementary students in parochial schools, and 35,377 in high schools; by 1992 there were only 70,016 in parochial grade schools, and 31,947 in Church high schools. Murphy, 'All Business in Doing God's Work'.

 46. Joseph P. Fitzpatrick, 'The Hispanic Poor in a Middle-Class Church', *America*, 2 July 1988, p. 11.

 47. Ibid., p. 12.

 48. Marc Lacey, 'Word on the Street', *Los Angeles Times*, 14 Sept. 1993; George Ramos, 'A New Name Can't Change a Street's History', *Los Angeles Times*, 20 Sept. 1993.

3

Chicanos in Politics:

A Struggle for Existence

For over a century, Mexicans were for the most part excluded from Los Angeles politics. During the nineteenth century, according to historian Robert Fogelson, 'Not everyone shared in the town's community life. Maladjusted Mexicans, uprooted Chinese, and transient Americans all remained separate from the larger society. Few in number, these people were conspicuous by their differences. They lacked entrepreneurial and professional skills, placed a low priority on material achievement and held modest expectations of future accomplishments.'[1] From the 1880s, a conglomerate of conservative downtown commercial interests spearheaded by the *Los Angeles Times* controlled the electoral process,[2] and they designed the political structure of Los Angeles to keep these unassimilated folk in their place.

Like other big cities in the US, L.A. was and is controlled by economic elites. Unlike its Eastern and Midwestern counterparts, however, neither party machines nor labor unions played a role in the political process until the end of World War II. The City Council, the major instrument of local power, was not structured around an ethnic-based ward system like Chicago's. It was limited to fifteen large council districts (CDs) encompassing several communities and designed to frustrate the development of neighborhood ethnic political clubs. Moreover, the city charter provided for a weak mayor system; a hidden government of middle-class/professional commissioners ran the city, answering only to the political and economic players familiar with that hidden bureaucracy.[3]

Within this structure, workers and immigrants had no voice. From the turn of the century, Los Angeles was an open shop–city that was primarily white, and the *Los Angeles Times* and the Chamber of Commerce worked assiduously to keep it that way. During this same era, Eastern political machines depended on the immigrant vote, and many foreign-born workers voted in local elections the day after they got off the boat. The machines and the ward bosses provided a measure of protection for workers and recent immigrants, and political participation offered rewards through political patronage jobs and city contracts.[4]

In Los Angeles, even the Mexican elite had no influence on the city's politics. Other than an occasional radio personality or reformer, few voices championed the rights of Chicanos. But changes were under way: during the New Deal, Mexican youth on the Eastside began to join local Democratic Party clubs. Interest in politics grew, and a core of youth and other activists recognized the discrimination against Chicanos and their lack of political power. World War II crystallized this new political consciousness, especially with the return of Chicano war veterans. This generation, still smarting from the forced repatriation to Mexico of the 1930s and the anti-Mexican Zoot-Suit Riots by military personnel, was not as willing to accept segregated swimming pools, schools and even cemeteries. To achieve equal rights for Mexican Americans, they formed organizations such as the Asociación Nacional México-Americana, the American G.I. Forum and the Community Service Organization (CSO).

At the same time, a radicalization was taking place among a small sector of Chicanos. Some had joined unions and been politicized by the growing industrialization of the city during the 1930s. The growth of the Congress of Industrial Organizations (CIO) gave Chicanos some political space in which to operate, and also politicized their historical memory. Many Chicanos, influenced by Jewish radicals who lived among them in Boyle Heights and City Terrace, joined Henry Wallace's Progressive Party and similar groups, sometimes becoming candidates for office. Politics became part of their collective vision for ending the second-class status of Mexican Americans.

After World War II the downtown elite gradually lost its hegemony. The dramatic growth of L.A. spawned a new developer class and the growth of the Westside commercial elite; these new groups contributed to the corruption of government, offering middle-class city officials incentives to introduce zoning and other business-friendly changes. Members of the City Council and the mayor were also eager to please, and the political *piñata* became filled with prizes like fat campaign contributions, free trips and other perquisites.

Los Angeles, like the rest of the country, grew meaner in the 1950s. The Cold War and its witch hunts created an anti-labor, anti-progressive climate nationwide, and progressives of all colors within the ranks of labor were purged via the Taft-Hartley Act and the McCarran Acts of 1950 and 1952. Unions and other organizations became less willing to advocate social change for fear of being labelled as Communist fellow travellers. This turn to the right had a devastating effect on Chicanos in Los Angeles, and political opportunities for even conservative Mexican Americans became rarer.

Despite the impact of McCarthyism, other forces continued to undermine the political isolation of the barrios. First, returning Chicano ex-servicemen and a corps of working women moved beyond the boundaries of the barrio. Second, the construction of freeways and the bulldozing of homes incorporated the barrios into the rest of the city. Finally, Mexican living space was targeted by brigades of social workers, news reporters, urban developers, and even Saul Alinsky's Industrial Areas Foundation. Chicanos were spreading throughout the city, and the automobile gave them, and especially youth, more mobility.

But constructing a Chicano political agenda was difficult. The late political scientist Ralph Guzmán wrote: '[I]n 1934 there were 3,607 precincts in Los Angeles County. In this total only 46 precincts had enough Spanish surname registrations for them to be classified as "Mexican" precincts.'[5] Most of the 500,000 to 600,000 people forcibly sent to Mexico during the 1930s, some 80,000 of them from Los Angeles itself, were US citizens and would have had voting rights had they remained in the United States. Their loss made it more difficult to build the necessary political base, because one-third of the Mexican population was foreign-born and its median age was under twenty.

The Rise of Eddie Roybal

The most successful and respected political figure in the history of Chicano Los Angeles has been Edward R. Roybal, who became widely known as 'Eddie' during his City Council years. Like so many of the early Chicano leaders, Roybal was a *manito*, a nickname for Mexicans from New Mexico. In 1947, at the age of thirty-one, he first ran for City Council and lost. With only 22,000 Spanish-surnamed registered voters in the whole of the Eastside, his defeat came as no surprise. In 1948 the Community Service Organization, headed by Roybal, launched a massive registration drive that led to his landslide victory the following year. Roybal thus became the first Mexican American to serve on the City Council since 1881. Roybal remained the sole Chicano voice in L.A. politics during the next decade. However, his constituency reached well beyond Mexicans or his 9th Council District. While not a radical, Roybal had a gut-level grasp of working-class issues, and immediately earned the ire of the downtown powers by championing fair employment practices legislation and rent control. Although he supported the Korean War, Roybal opposed the overwhelming majority of the council when it voted in 1951 to require Communists to register with the police and to forbid them the right to own guns. Roybal termed the measure 'thought control' and called its sponsors 'biased crackpots'.

Re-elected by a three-to-one margin in 1951, Roybal found himself increasingly at odds with the *Los Angeles Times*, not only over the issues of rent control, the scapegoating of Mexican youth and police brutality, but also over freeway construction, urban renewal and public housing. It was a measure of Roybal's popularity that he represented a district in which only 16,000 of the 87,000 voters were Mexican American. In 1954, Roybal ran for lieutenant governor in the

Democratic primary, bumping heads again with the *Los Angeles Times* by opposing the Central Valley Project, a boondoggle for grower interests including the Chandler family who ran the *Times*. Although Roybal won the primary, he lost in the general election.

It was clear that Roybal represented a new kind of Mexican American leadership. Many were encouraged by his successes and believed that they would ignite the community with a fervor for political action. Roybal's style put him at odds with the city's powerbrokers, and his reluctance to make backroom deals made them certain that they could not trust him. In 1958, Roybal ran for a vacancy on the Los Angeles County Board of Supervisors; he was opposed by Councilman Ernest Debs, who had headed the City Planning Committee since 1947. This seat was important not only to Mexicans in the city but also to those living in unincorporated areas of the county like East L.A., who had no other representation. In response, reactionary forces within the Los Angeles metro area coalesced to work for Roybal's defeat, while liberal Democrats stood by cutting their own deals. After the votes were counted, Roybal had won by 393 votes, 139,800 to 139,407. The county registrar's office announced, however, that it had made 'clerical errors' in counting 12,000 votes. After four counts, Debs was declared the winner, 141,011 to 128,994.[6]

Roybal's defeat in the supervisorial election, and the defeat of Hank López for California Secretary of State, diminished Chicano faith in the Democratic Party, but these races also showed the community's political potential and encouraged formation of the Mexican American Political Association (MAPA) in the late 1950s. Chicanos worked hard in the Víva Kennedy Clubs of 1960, hoping to contribute to Kennedy's victory and thereby stake a claim on the new administration. In spite of these efforts, the community was still not taken seriously by the Democratic Party, which made promises during election years only to be break them when in office.

The Jewish-Black Alliance

As the city spread out in the 1950s, new poles of political power developed, one of which centered on the Westside Jewish community. At first this sector vied with the Downtown establishment for control. In time, however, the Downtown crowd made an alliance with Westside liberals, who then cooperated with the conservatives to create a developer-friendly climate – for example, giving away public land to the Brooklyn Dodgers baseball team to lure it to Los Angeles.

In 1962 Eddie Roybal resigned from the L.A. City Council to run for Congress, winning a House seat in the fall elections. Roybal's move to Washington, together with a redistricting of City Council seats, resulted in removing Mexicans from the local political map.[7] Chicanos were not prepared to deal with this transition, lacking unity, a well-defined middle-class leadership and a historical memory, reinforced by the fervor of the civil rights movement, comparable to that of the African American community. The Mexican population had grown; by the early 1960s the L.A. metropolitan area had a population of 629,000 Mexican Americans. But for all the talk about the 'Sleeping Giant' awakening, Mexicans were still not part of the Democratic Party's political universe. Chicano voter registration drives were a family affair: a study of fourteen selected Census tracts in the county by political scientist Ralph Guzmán found that registration stood at 15,948 voters in 1958, 18,588 in 1960, 18,187 in 1962, and 13,989 in 1963.[8]

L.A.'s African Americans, on the other hand, had begun to mobilize politically, the result of both the national civil rights movement and the rapid growth of the Black community in Los Angeles: '[B]y 1960 Los Angeles Blacks had reason to hope for political change. The 1960 census, released in March 1961, revealed a big jump in African-American population, to nearly half a million. Blacks now comprised 13.7 percent of the city's people, compared to 8.9 percent in 1950 and 4.2 percent in 1940.'[9] The 1962 City Council redistricting favored Blacks in the 9th Council District (Roybal's former seat), making it 39.8 percent Black to 33.5 percent Latino. The 8th CD was 54 percent Black and the 10th 34.4 percent, and Black candidates won in all three districts. This gave them 20 percent of the seats on the L.A. City Council, a proportion that became a source of future tension between Blacks and Chicanos.[10] The latter shortsightedly viewed the three victories as denying them proper political representation, since 20 percent exceeded the African American share of L.A.'s population.

According to political scientist Raphael J. Sonenshein, Blacks were helped in winning those council seats by Jewish community leaders Rosalind and Eugene Wyman, powers in the Democratic Party, who can thus be credited for building a Jewish–Black alliance.[11] During this same period, the relationship between Mexicans and Jews was tenuous. When Mexicans and Jews shared Boyle Heights and City Terrace during the 1930s and 1940s, they had discovered and acted on common interests. However, there was less contact between the two groups after the Jewish community left for the Westside. Furthermore, over the years large numbers of Jews had arrived in Southern California from the eastern US who had no knowledge of Mexicans but some knowledge of and sympathy for African Americans.[12]

The problem ran deeper than ethnic relations, however. The Jewish-Black alliance was not between working-class groups but between elites from the two groups. Housing discrimination against Blacks had led to the creation of Black middle-class neighborhoods such as Baldwin Hills and Leimert Park, which became enclaves for Black liberal Democratic clubs; these clubs facilitated the alliance between Westside Jewish liberals and the Black middle class. The alliance with Blacks was invaluable to Westside Jewish American interests in their power struggle with the Downtown establishment. Indeed, that alliance eventually benefited the Jewish community more than it did the Black community.

Black ties to Jewish liberals and the liberal California Democratic Council (CDC) grew during the 1963 election and the rise of Tom Bradley. This coalition opposed the more working class–oriented Black political leadership of Mervyn Dymally, who was allied to California Assembly Speaker Jesse Unruh. (Dymally also had close ties with many of the moderate Chicano activists during this period.) The distance between Chicanos and Blacks widened during the 1960s, as a result of competition over War on Poverty funding. These tensions increased as bureaucrats of all races used the race card, with white administrators often playing Blacks off against Mexicans and vice versa.

During the 1960s, Jewish organizations played the role of political brokers. Tensions arose when they favored a Black candidate, the Rev. James Jones, over a Chicano candidate, Ralph Poblano (who had ties to Mervyn Dymally), for the Board of Education in 1965.[13] Two years later the Jewish community supported Dr Julian Nava, a historian at San Fernando Valley State College, for another board seat, but, according to sources close to the campaign, 'not as enthusiastically'. In 1970, Westside forces backed an African American, Dr Wilson Riles of Oakland, for state superintendent of schools over Nava.[14] The possibility of any multiethnic coalition was a casualty of this inter-ethnic political competition.

Chicano frustration at their lack of political influence grew during the late 1960s as the Chicano population in Los Angeles County grew to 1,228,593, a 113 percent increase over the previous decade, while the African American population stabilized and the number of Euroamericans fell. Given those numbers, the paucity of Chicano representation compared with the influence of the Black community caused resentment and sometimes jealousy – and made it easy for other groups to solve problems of resource allocation and budgeting at the expense of Chicanos.[15]

The 1960s molded the future of L.A. politics for people of color in general. Nava and Roybal were the only successful Chicano politicos of the decade. Two Chicanos, Phil Soto and John Moreno, briefly held seats in the state Assembly. According to Loyola-Marymount political scientist Fernando Guerra, 'In 1960, ethnic minorities had five percent of the most significant electoral positions in Los Angeles County. By 1986, the ethnic communities of Los Angeles (Latino, Black, Jewish and Asian) provided fifty-four percent.' But if we look at the actual numbers and how they changed over the years, the lack of progress for people of color is glaring. In 1960, minorities held three 'significant' posts countywide, while in 1967 that number had climbed to sixteen. Of these, Latinos held two (Roybal and Nava); Blacks held nine; and Jews, five. By 1979, the total number of significant posts had risen to forty-six, with Jewish Americans holding two-thirds of the twenty-six new positions.[16] If we focus on the fifteen-member City Council as a weathervane of how political winds are blowing in Los Angeles County, we find that in 1994, Blacks with 13 percent of the population held three seats, or one-fifth; Latinos, with 40 percent of the population, held three; and Jewish Americans, with 14.4 percent of the city's population, held seven – almost half. (Asian Americans, who comprised 9.8 percent of the city, had no representation at all.) This is the growth pattern that was set in motion during the 1960s.[17]

According to Sonenshein, 'History might have been different had Edward Roybal, so similar to Bradley in style and political base, stayed in city politics.'[18] When Roybal moved to Congress, elite ties between minority politicos weakened, with African American leaders allying themselves more closely with their white counterparts. But the reason multiethnic coalitions have failed in Los Angeles is more basic than lack of collaboration between elites. The political structure of the city and county promotes established interests. Huge resources are needed to gain a piece of the City Council pie. Had the districts been small and defined along ethnic lines, as in Chicago, there would be an incentive to form coalitions for citywide elections. Jews, African Americans and Chicanos are no different from other groups in US history: they have acted politically to gain resources for their communities, and to defend those gains once made.

Today, only remnants remain of the Black–Jewish alliance. The Jewish community turned to the right as it became more affluent and as many youth lost a sense of its progressive historical memory. Its interests now often collide with those of the Black political leadership, which has in turn become more nationalistic and often more entrepreneurial.

How Chicanos Achieved Representation

Throughout the 1960s the California state legislature saw a number of struggles over reapportionment as a result of court cases stemming from the US Supreme Court's 'one-man, one-vote' ruling of 1962. However, reapportionment plans usually disregarded Mexican/Chicano interests. The original 1970 state Assembly reapportionment was no different, according to Jorge García, who wrote, 'Gerrymandering had been synonymous with partisanship for so long as this country had existed. Thus it was no surprise [in 1971] that the districts were drawn to favor the Democrats who controlled the Assembly at the time.' Ironically, Chicanos found an ally in Governor Ronald Reagan, who vetoed the Democrats' 1971 reapportionment legislation, citing among other reasons the exclusion of Chicanos. That veto generated a lawsuit that went to the state Supreme Court; in its decision the court ordered the drawing of a new set of districts, which did benefit Chicanos.[19]

Partly as a result of redistricting, three L.A.-based Chicanos – Richard Alatorre, the most prominent Chicano politician after Roybal; Alex García; and Art Torres served in the legislature during the 1970s.[20] However, their success came in spite of the Democratic Party, rather than reflecting a decision by the party leadership to favor Latino candidates. The Chicano population of Los Angeles had doubled from 1960 to 1970.[21] Democratic leaders did take note that this population had become increasingly dissatisfied during the 1960s, as shown by the massive East Los Angeles school walkouts of 1968 and the Chicano Moratorium of 1970. The party had no choice but to change its approach and support Latino candidates for state offices.

At the city level, Chicano political unrest focused on the City Council redistricting process. On the eve of the 1972 redistricting (based on the 1970 Census), Chicanos formed Chicanos for Fair Representation. Members attended numerous hearings of the City Council and worked closely with the Mexican American Legal Defense and Education Fund (MALDEF), which proposed an alternative plan. The outcome was the creation of one supposedly sure Chicano City Council district, the 14th CD, and another district that seemed likely to elect a Chicano in the near future.[22]

But there was a catch: although the newly drawn 14th Council District was 68 percent Mexican American; 45 percent of them were under the age of eighteen, and 40 percent were noncitizens. Boyle Heights had a population of 81,159, while Eagle Rock, which is mostly Euroamerican, had only 28,545. Even so, Boyle Heights had only 13,618 registered voters at the time of the 1969 mayoral race, and recorded only a 34 percent turnout. In contrast, Eagle Rock had 16,584 registered voters and a 77 percent turnout.

In spite of the apparent setback, gains were made. *Calderón* v. *City of Los Angeles* (1971), a suit brought by longtime activist Richard Calderón, resulted in a ruling that the city must base apportionment strictly on the basis of population in a given area, and not on the number of registered voters.[23] This was an important case, since the number of children and the undocumented could be used for the purpose of configuring a district.

The kind of Chicano representation won during the 1970s and 1980s rested in great part on the city's history and structure. When it became evident that the Chicano population was too large to ignore, the Democratic Party decided to create its own Chicano brokers rather than support development of organic political institutions within the Mexican community. The Democratic Party in L.A. had long discouraged the development of neighborhood political organizations, making it impossible to forge community-based political clubs. The largest Democratic Party organization, the California Democratic Council, had not given Chicanos (or Blacks) space within the organization, denying them control even of voter registration drives in their own communities. Democrats worked with individual Chicanos and Chicanas, discouraging the political education of the Mexican community as well as the training of organic leadership.[24] Like other white liberals they had little idea of Mexican/Chicano problems, stereotyping Mexicans as conservative and fanatically Roman Catholic, or reacting negatively to what they called 'Chicano separatism' during the 1970s.[25]

At the same time, the absence of organic neighborhood political organizations resulted in individuals and groups who represented special interests acquiring undue influence with the newly elected officials. Simply put, rank-and-file community residents lacked the opportunity to 'play the game'. Thus, in Chicago it was possible to elect a grassroots activist like Jesús 'Jesse' García, who had been a member of the Centro de Acción Autonoma (CASA), based on the work of volunteers from neighborhood organizations. Chicago's City Council is elected from fifty wards of 50,000 to 75,000 residents each, versus 200,000 to 300,000 in Los Angeles, thus encouraging alliances across communities and more intense political involvement.[26] The L.A. situation makes it impossible for someone to be elected who doesn't have money for direct mailers. Nor is it possible for anyone except an incumbent with patronage to organize door-to-door campaigning on a regular basis.

This structure has greatly determined the character and style of Chicano political leaders like Alatorre. The rise of the Community Service Organization had allowed Eddie Roybal to take on the bad guys when he served on the City Council. The CSO, a nonpolitical and nonpartisan organization based on the ideas of Saul Alinksy and his Industrial Areas Foundation, was concerned with community relations and civic improvement. It partly grew out of the model of the United League, which had been formed by longtime activist Ignacio López during World War II. Founded in 1947, many of its leaders were Roybal partisans. After Roybal's election, CSO spread throughout California. Aside from organizing registration drives, it conducted citizenship English-language classes and get-out-the-vote drives in the Chicano community. It also served as an advocate for Chicano civil rights.[27]

The CSO's work thus gave Roybal a progressive base, whereas an Alatorre, Torres or García would not have been elected without the cooperation of the bad guys, since the prerequisite for winning was the amassing of a large political warchest. Richard Alatorre became the prototype for the modern Chicano politico. To lessen his dependence on the Euroamerican power brokers – and he was able to do this to some extent – Alatorre built his own close-knit groups of financial supporters, and he in turn served their interests. By the end of the 1970s, his support groups revolved more and more around The East Los Angeles Community Union (TELACU: see Chapter 2), which he increasingly considered family. It is no surprise that politicos like Alatorre played the political game as they did. Dependent on the political brokers at both the state and local levels, Alatorre and other Latinos built their power the Los Angeles way: by accumulating money. It was also beyond the capability of barrio residents to monitor elected officials in Washington and Sacramento. Thus, politicians came to care much more about which committee he or she would be assigned to than what Mr González thought.

When Art Torres joined Alatorre in the state Assembly, the two became inseparable, eventually becoming formal *compadres*. Survival and influence meant compromise and deal-making; it also meant moving from a position of strength. In the case of Alatorre, his backup was Torres and others in his close circle of friends. It was a style of leadership that could be better understood in a gang context – but which in reality is very compatible with how government operates.[28]

There is a danger, however, in judging Chicano politicos by higher standards than we do other politicians. Alatorre and Torres both promoted liberal agendas, and not everything they did can be reduced to 'let's make a deal'. Both were staunch supporters of bilingual education, workers' rights, social programs and other programs in the interest of the community. During the 1970s they championed the cause of the farmworkers and spoke out against immigrant bashing. Even their harshest critics could not accuse them of being conservative, and their deal-making was well within the parameters acceptable to the liberal wing of the Democratic Party. Within the context of American politics, the fairest criticism of Alatorre and Torres would be that they privatized the political process instead of extending the participation of the public.

The Historic 1980 Census

The legal basis for greater Chicano representation was laid as a result of the Voting Rights Acts of 1965, 1975 and 1982. The 1965 act gave the attorney general the power to determine a history of racial discrimination. A political jurisdiction found to have a history of discrimination had to get preclearance for any structural changes, which meant that it had to demonstrate to the Justice Department or the US District Court of the District of Columbia 'that the proposed electoral system change had neither the purpose nor effect of discrimination against protected minorities.'[29]

The 1975 act gave this protection to language-minority groups such as Latinos (section 5 of the 1965 Voting Rights Act applied only to 'racial' minorities). The 1982 Voting Rights Act clarified the intent of the law and stated that the plaintiff did not have the burden to prove discriminatory *purpose* – merely discriminatory results.[30] Significantly, the courts also gave individual plaintiffs the right to initiate the preclearance process in the event that neither the Justice Department nor the federal courts acted.

The full impact of the Voting Rights Acts was felt in the 1980s. At the beginning of the decade, Latinos comprised more than 2 million of Los Angeles County's population of some 7.5 million. The number of Latinos in the county's public schools had zoomed, from 30 percent in 1977/78 to 45 percent in 1986/87. By the end of the decade, just under two out of three students in the Los Angeles Unified School District were Latino.[31] This Mexican-Latino presence mirrored the view on the street, where the browning of the city and county was visibly taking place. Indeed, the 1980 Census and publicity about it helped advertise what many nativists termed a 'Mexican invasion'. That census recorded a 61 percent Latino population increase nationwide, including an even more dramatic 87 percent increase in California.[32]

LATINOS IN LOS ANGELES COUNTY

Year	Total County Population	Number of Latinos	Percent Latino
1920[a]	936,455	166,579	17.7
1930[a]	2,208,492	199,165	9.0
1940[a,e]	2,785,643	134,312	4.8
1950[b]	4,151,687	287,614	6.9
1960[b]	6,038,771	576,716	9.5
1970[c]	7,041,980	1,045,958	14.8
1980[c]	7,447,503	2,065,503	27.6
1990 (projected)[d,f]	8,987,757	3,325,274	36.9
2000 (projected)[d,f]	9,899,898	3,993,656	40.3

a Spanish spoken at home.
b Spanish-surname in population.
c Spanish-origin population (self-identification).
d Estimate from Los Angeles County.
e This decrease occurred largely because of the mass expatriation and departure of Mexican nationals during the Great Depression.
f These estimates are widely regarded as flawed.
SOURCE: US Census Bureau; Los Angeles County for projections, quoted in Marita Hernandez, '1990 Census Holds Promise for Latino Political Activists', *Nuestro Tiempo*, 23 March 1989.

University of California at Los Angeles demographer Leo Estrada recalls that in preparing for the 1970 Census it had been hard to convince East Coast Census officials that Mexicans mattered. For 1980, Estrada and other 1970 Latino Census takers convinced the bureaucrats – with difficulty – to make innovations in the counting of Latinos. According to Estrada, 'The 1980 census gave us a visibility we never had before on a national level',[33] and thus registered beyond any doubt the need for reapportionment based on Latino population growth. As a result of the 1980 Census–based reapportionment of congressional, state and local districts, during the 1980s the number of Latinos in Congress doubled, and hundreds of Latino officials were elected throughout the country. Other changes were also taking place locally. As California State University, Los Angeles political scientist James A. Regalado noted, the *Los Angeles Times*, a historically conservative, anti-labor newspaper, was becoming more sensitive to minority issues by 1982. Thanks to the presence of Frank del Olmo as a columnist and larger numbers of Latino reporters, its coverage of the community improved, making politicos more aware of the large presence of the Chicano/Latino.[34]

Much more weight was given to the 1980 Census than the 1970 count because it was not overshadowed by other Chicano political activities.[35] A growing number of Chicano professionals had graduated from college, thanks to educational opportunities programs. Political successes in Texas also encouraged California Chicanos, and activists who had once shunned electoral politics now participated in greater numbers. Although many of them were cynical about the value of fighting for political representation, they nevertheless realized that it was important for Chicanos to hold office.

Republicans, inspired by the fact that Richard Nixon received 30 percent of the Latino vote nationally in 1972, began to compete with Democrats for Latino votes. This competition led the Republican-supported Rose Institute of State and Local Government at the Claremont Colleges to lend Latinos valuable computer time. According to political scientist Richard Santillán, 'The purpose of this GOP strategy was to increase the number of minority districts, in hopes that the Republican Party would then have a better chance to defeat Democrats who depended on Latino and black voters to stay in office.'[36] Access to computer technology also allowed Chicanos to develop their own redistricting plans.

The 1981 Reapportionment and Its Aftermath

That was the situation when Californios for Fair Representation (CFR) was formed, a statewide coalition of Latino groups that aimed to intervene in the California state and congressional reapportionment process. In 1982, Latinos – although then nearly 20 percent of the state's population – held only one of California's forty-three US congressional seats, only three state Senate seats, and only four Assembly positions.[37] Californios, along with Proyecto Participar (a group that encouraged Chicano participation in the redistricting process) and MALDEF, kept up pressure on the state legislature, where Richard Alatorre chaired the Assembly Committee on Reapportionment. Californios complemented MALDEF, since the latter is not a mass-based organization. On the other hand, Californios, a single-issue organization, would last only through the life of the reapportionment process, although the activists involved acquired skills that would last them a lifetime.[38]

The Democratic Party remained antagonistic. Assembly Speaker Willie Brown, an African American politico with a reputation for being liberal, told a *Los Angeles Times* reporter in April 1981 that, while an effort would be made to meet Latino demands, new Latino Assembly districts would not be created at the expense of the Democratic Party: 'I don't think the house will support dismembering any incumbent just to achieve a racial minority district.' Brown added, 'They're fine people [Mexicans], but if they're not registered to vote, they can't help you very much.' Brown cited Census figures showing tracts that were '85 percent Chicano and 5 percent registered to vote. It is absolutely outrageous.' According to Brown, if they did not vote, Mexicans were not entitled to more seats.[39]

At a press conference Chicano attorney Miguel García, chair of Californios, challenged Willie Brown to specify the Census tract he was referring to.[40] Tensions reached a peak when a group of Californios stormed out of a joint Senate and Assembly Reelection and Reapportionment Committee hearing in Sacramento. Activists led by attorney Antonio Rodríguez took over Brown's office and were arrested. Californios for Fair Representation was so disgusted with the reapportionment process that the group pressed Governor Jerry Brown to veto the Senate district reapportionment plan. Leticia Quezada, a Californio activist later elected to the L.A. School Board, charged that state Sen. Daniel Boatwright (D-Concord), chair of the Senate Committee on Reapportionment, had promised to create a new Latino district. Instead, the Senate pitted Blacks and Latinos against each other by putting equal numbers of them into districts proposed for Democratic state Senators Bill Greene and Ralph Dills. For the moment, Chicanos had gained no seats in the state legislature, and this defeat left a bitter taste. Moreover, these confrontations over reapportionment hurt Alatorre, doing some damage to his image as a political broker.[41] Alatorre's enemies capitalized on his relationship with Brown, whom they called his 'big daddy'. (Brown had named Alatorre to head the Assembly Reelection and Reapportionment Committee.) They felt that they had tested Alatorre's loyalty to Chicanos, and that he had failed the test.

The reapportionment based on the 1980 Census was not a complete bust. California gained two new seats in Congress, and because of rapid growth in the Los Angeles area, these new seats would go to Chicanos as representatives of the newly redrawn 30th and 34th Congressional Districts.[42] Matthew 'Marty' Martínez, a state Assemblyman from Monterey Park, won the 30th in a special election in June 1982. Martínez, a Republican turned Democrat, was adopted by the Berman-Waxman Westside machine. The 34th District seat went to Esteban Torres, a former White House official under President Jimmy Carter and a US representative to UNESCO.[43] Torres's support came from organized labor, national Chicano organizations and national Democratic leaders. In time, Torres became a congressional leader and one of the most independent Chicano politicos.[44] These two victories were significant, because both districts were considered conservative and had never before been represented by Chicanos. In order to win, both candidates broke away from ethnic issues and concentrated on 'pocketbook issues'.[45] With the re-election of Roybal, three Chicanos from California sat in the US Congress as of 1982.

The 1981 reapportionment also gave birth to the Gloria Molina–Richard Alatorre feud in the City Council, a feud that would rage throughout the decade. It began in 1982 when Assemblyman Art Torres vacated the 56th Assembly District to challenge state Senator Alex García. The 56th was a so-called jewel because it was 80 percent Democratic and its electors usually voted the party line.[46] To avoid a bloodbath, the Chicano candidates held a closed-door meeting in November 1982 and decided that Richard Polanco should be designated for the 56th District. Assemblyman Martínez would run for the 30th Congressional District, and Esteban Torres would opt for the 34th. Art Torres would challenge García for his state Senate seat. Alatorre attended the meeting; Gloria Molina was not invited.[47] After these matters had been arranged to the satisfaction of everyone present, they informed Gloria Molina that she should not run against Polanco, who was a close associate of Alatorre and a TELACU partisan.

Molina, then thirty-three, was a former aide to Art Torres and Willie Brown who had worked for President Carter. She decided to challenge the all-boys network, as she called it, and run in the 56th District. Polanco and Molina seemed identical politically, with both supporting pro-choice measures and the death penalty (an odd but not unusual combination), and agreeing that crime was the district's most serious problem. According to the Mexican American Bar Association, the only difference was that 'one's a man and one's a woman'. Indeed, both had come up through the ranks of the Alatorre-Torres cabal. Molina had even worked for TELACU for a short time; however, she was not an insider. Polanco was a former vice president of the Community Research Group, a TELACU subsidiary and think-tank.[48]

The campaign turned bitter. 'From the very beginning I didn't like the idea of both people running', Alatorre said. 'I just don't think it's very productive. It drains away resources.' Alatorre took a neutral stand in public by not endorsing either candidate; everyone knew, however, that he favored Polanco. The election became a test of his power in the wake of the state reapportionment fiasco. Polanco received $5,000 from TELACU and led Molina in raising funds. Favored by Speaker Willie Brown, who committed resources to his campaign,

Polanco was also endorsed by county Supervisor Ed Edleman and Matthew Martínez. Molina, supported by Art Torres and women's groups, had raised only $20,000 to Polanco's $43,000 as of early April 1982.

For Molina, the decision to run against Polanco meant that there was no going back; after this, her relationship with the state Eastside politicos, including even Torres, deteriorated. What Alatorre and his loyalists did not realize was that the time of the Chicana had come and that Eastside politics would never be the same. Molina won the election, proving that Chicanas were tough enough, but more important, that they could raise money in their own right, both inside the Latino community and outside it, and that Latinos would vote for them.[49]

Meanwhile, the City Council still had no Chicano members, Roybal having been the only exception. But the challenge of Steve Rodríguez, a 34-year-old progressive urban planner, to Art Snyder in the 14th Council District in 1983, showed that it could be done, laying the groundwork for the election of another Chicano to the council by attracting many divergent Chicano activists who had dropped out of electoral politics. Rodríguez was energetically backed by the United Farm Workers and Alex García.

Art Snyder seemed unbeatable, having held court in the district for sixteen years – but Rodríguez missed putting Snyder into a runoff by a mere four votes, in spite of getting little help from Eastside politicos. Torres and Roybal endorsed Snyder;[50] with both Roybal and Alatorre refusing to support Rodríguez because he lacked Democratic Party credentials (he had once registered with La Raza Unida Party).[51] According to Los Angeles Times columnist Frank del Olmo, Snyder's victory became a symbol of Latino weakness, since the failure of local Latino leaders to support Rodríguez surely cost him the victory. Moreover, Rodríguez's supporters were disillusioned with politicos who claimed a commitment to Latino empowerment and then supported Euroamericans.[52]

In the summer of 1984, Rodríguez led another challenge to Snyder, this time a recall campaign. It failed, perhaps because the Chicano community was split during this campaign, running several candidates. Alatorre himself supported a close ally, spending tens of thousands of dollars on the election. Although unsuccessful, the recall election put tremendous pressure on Snyder, and shortly after his victory he announced his retirement.[53]

Meanwhile, the importance of reapportionment became even more evident. Without doubt, one of the biggest obstacles in the struggle for empowerment was the self-interest of the city's Democratic Party incumbents, who gave lip service to Latino participation but support only when their own power base was not threatened. For example, the City Council approved a Californio-sponsored reapportionment plan that moved the city of South Gate out of the 5th District. Larry González subsequently challenged fourteen-year incumbent Richard Ferraro in the 1983 School Board election, who without his South Gate stronghold lost by 5,000 votes. Chicanos were thus able to regain a seat on the Board of Education, where they had been unrepresented since Julian Nava resigned in 1979. The council was thus willing to make concessions to Latinos in redistricting the School Board, but resisted approving a reapportionment plan that would change the council itself.

In 1986 Alatorre ran for City Council. He poured $300,000 into the campaign and won, becoming the only Latino to be an elected local official in the second largest city of the nation. The importance of Alatorre's victory cannot be minimized: it ended a long drought and marked the first time in two decades that a Chicano sat on the council. Alatorre's swearing-in ceremony took on the dimensions of a coronation, with leading politicians of all races attending. Few questioned the structural imperfections of a system that had denied Mexican Americans representation for twenty years, or the inordinate amount of resources that it took to finally elect another Chicano to the council. Instead, they celebrated the event as an awakening of the Latin population, and/or proof that the system worked. Indeed, the struggle by activists such as Steve Rodríguez was forgotten – for the time.

Alatorre became the heir apparent to Congressman Edward R. Roybal. He seemed to be the undisputed king of the Chicano mountain, the spokesman for all Latinos in Los Angeles. Political reporter Bill Boyarsky contributed a more penetrating analysis in 1986:

> In his years in the Assembly, Alatorre proved himself a reliable member of Speaker Willie L. Brown's fund-raising political machine that milks the business community for money needed to elect Democrats. He will feel at home in City Hall, where developers, promoters of refuse-disposal schemes, cable television operators, municipal bond selling firms and other businesses contribute to council campaigns in return for sympathetic consideration of their project. Nothing in the new councilman's record or in his campaign statements indicates a desire to change things.

Boyarsky added, 'Alatorre is a player. He likes the game. He knows how to push in public and private. He knows how to deal.'[54] The councilman would live up to that rating, as we saw in the Olvera Street struggle and in many other key moments in recent L.A. history. However, a new political power was rising in the Chicano community, as Alatorre and other L.A. politicos would soon see.

Change was also facilitated by the Reagan administration, which, prodded by Chicano interests and eager to embarrass Democratic Mayor Tom Bradley, brought suit against Los Angeles in federal court for violation of the Fourteenth and Fifteenth Amendments and an array of voting rights acts. The Department of Justice maintained in US v. City of Los Angeles that the city's purpose was to deny the expansion of Latino representation, and it pressed for creation of an additional seat. In an effort to outflank the Justice Department, the city agreed to submit a new plan to the court by 31 July 1986, and appointed newly elected councilman Richard Alatorre to chair the apportionment committee. MALDEF then submitted a plan that would give the Latino community two additional seats. Alatorre drew a new Latino district, largely at the expense of 13th CD representative Michael Woo. Bradley vetoed this plan, and the impasse was resolved only with the unexpected death of Howard Finn in August 1986. Finn's 1st CD lay in the heavily Latino Northeast San Fernando Valley, prompting Woo and John Ferraro to create a new 1st CD that would become the new Chicano district. In addition, a newly redrawn 7th CD would give Chicanos the possibility of winning a seat in 1989.

Notes

1. Robert M. Fogelson, *The Fragmented Metropolis: Los Angeles, 1850–1930* (Cambridge, Mass.: Harvard University Press, 1967), pp. 187–8.

2. The best history of the political role of the *Los Angeles Times* is Robert Gottlieb and Irene Wolt, *Thinking Big: The Story of the Los Angeles Times, Its Publishers and Their Influence on Southern California* (New York: Putnam's, 1977); see also Mike Davis, *City of Quartz: Excavating the Future in Los Angeles* (London: Verso, 1990).

3. Fogelson, p. 211: 'The strong mayor, a large council, and appointive administrators [in the 1910s] all derived their authority from city-wide rather than ward constituencies. Reform destroyed the traditional devices for organizing politics too. With the parties defunct and the machine dismantled, the bosses had no way to reach the voters and no means to influence government. Progressivism also compelled the candidates to appeal to the entire electorate, placing priority on publicity rather than familiarity and on finances instead of favors. Hence it weakened the position of local groups such as neighborhood associations, ethnic minorities, and radical activists and increased the importance of metropolitan institutions such as daily newspapers, civic clubs, business interests, and commercial organizations.'

In the 1920s Los Angeles returned to councilmanic districts and later the powers of the mayor were weakened; however, the commission form of government, nonpartisan politics, and its large, unwieldy council districts kept control in the hands of 'the metropolis' native-American, middle-class majority ...' As a result, Mexicans were unable, unlike Irish immigrants in the nineteenth century, to form political machines to protect themselves from competitive forces, nor even create space within a machine that could lobby for their interests.

Although I do not want to romanticize ward politics based on community representation, the lack of this support structure facilitated the gerrymandering of council districts to keep Mexicans off the City Council as well as the Board of Supervisors and the School Board (whose members ran at large until 1980s). The size of the CDs allowed a circle of incumbents to effectively write Mexicans off the political map.

4. Bill Boyarsky, 'Alatorre: A Power Comes Back Home', *Los Angeles Times*, 15 Dec. 1985.

5. Ralph C. Guzmán, *The Political Socialization of the Mexican American People* (New York: Arno Press, 1976), p. 211.

6. See Rodolfo Acuña, *A Community Under Siege* (Los Angeles: Chicano Studies Resource Center, UCLA, 1984), p. 63; Robert Gottlieb and Irene Wolt, *Thinking Big*, p. 269.

7. Jorge García, 'Forjando Ciudad: The Development of a Chicano Political Community in East Los Angeles' (Ph.D. Dissertation, University of California Riverside, December 1986), p. 140. Roybal was opposed by the AFL/CIO's COPE because of racism; according to García, p. 145, unincorporated East Los Angeles was divided among the 45th, 48th and 51st Assembly Districts and the 19th, 20th and 30th Congressional Districts. For an excellent overview, see James A. Regalado,

'Latino Representation in Los Angeles', in Roberto Villarreal, Norma Hernandez and Howard D. Neighbor, eds, *Latino Empowerment: Progress, Problems, and Prospects* (New York: Greenwood Press, 1988), pp. 91–104. According to Regalado, 'Through boundary manipulation, East Los Angeles became roughly halved into county and city sections, thereby dividing Latino political strength. It also deprived Latinos of genuine communities of interest which could serve as bases for representation. Greater Los Angeles was split among "nine different Assembly Districts, seven different state Senate Districts, and six different Congressional Districts" in the early state reapportionment.' See also Leo Grebler, Joan Moore and Ralph C. Guzmán, *The Mexican-American People* (New York: Free Press, 1970), p. 562.

8. Guzmán, pp. 212–13.

9. Raphael J. Sonenshein, *Politics in Black and White: Race and Power in Los Angeles* (Princeton, N.J.: Princeton University Press, 1993), p. 36. In 1961 there were uprisings by African Americans in Griffith Park and Compton. The Mexican community was unprepared when Gilbert Lindsay, an African American and a former aide to Kenneth Hahn, made a bid for the so-called Latino 9th CD. Yorty favored Richard Tafoya, a Roybal cousin who was the leading Chicano candidate – an endorsement that was a kiss of death, given the council members' animosity toward the mayor. The Black community in turn was politically starved, and '[s]ome Black activists speculated that it would be easier for the council to appoint a Black to replace an Hispanic in the Ninth than to replace a white in the Tenth', Sonenshein, pp. 40–42, 43. The council leadership had promised Roybal that they would let the voters decide, a promise that the council then broke. Councilman Joe Hollingworth, a Republican who had been appointed by the council to represent the 10th CD, nominated Lindsay, who was appointed on 28 January 1963. The truth is that some Chicano activists (mostly liberal) supported this appointment because they were bitterly opposed to Tafoya.

10. The representation of African Americans was not high in proportion to their numbers, especially considering the high concentration of the African American population because of segregation. In L.A. the source of the problem was the drawing of district boundaries pitting the two groups against each other. Gottlieb, pp. 310–12. The Jewish community had increased its influence in L.A. politics and society, with Dorothy Chandler bringing in new Jewish money to the Center for Performing Arts Council in order to finance the Music Center. This initiative was interwoven with Rosalind Wyman's leadership in the development of Bunker Hill and Chavez Ravine at the expense of the Mexican community. Roybal had opposed both these projects.

12. Acuña, *Community*, pp. 25–31. There had been heavy involvement of Jewish progressives in the 1940s with the organization of the Progressive Party and the Mexican Civil Rights Congress. Joe Kovner, publisher of the *Eastside Sun*, was very active in Chicano affairs. They represented elements who were raised with Mexicans, having lived in the city for some time, Sonenshein, p. 48. A large portion of the Jewish community arrived in Los Angeles after 1930. There were an estimated 168,000 Jews in Los Angeles in 1946; between 1945 and 1948, 60,000 arrived. According to Sonenshein they were less working class than their New York counterparts.

13. See Acuña, *Community*, p. 129; Sonenshein, p. 75.

14. Acuña, *Community*, p. 207; I was at a meeting in which Dr Nava was told that he should not run against Riles, and that if he insisted on running the liberal coalition would dry up his campaign funds.

15. Ibid., p. 153. Take the use of Hazard Park, for example, which was in a heavily Chicano area. Parts of it were traded in 1966 by the city for Rose Hill for property in the affluent Westside to make tennis courts for Councilwoman Rosalind Wyman's constituents. Mayor Yorty, Councilwoman Wyman, Councilman Ed Edelman, and Supervisor Ernest Debs were part of this deal, which deprived Mexicans of needed park space. A Save Hazard Park Committee was formed, which did include many Jewish Americans. Any discussion of Mexican–Jewish relations must always be qualified, since both communities are highly heterogeneous.

16. Fernando J. Guerra, 'Ethnic Officeholders in Los Angeles County', *SSR*, vol. 71, no. 2 (January 1987), galley proofs; see also Guerra, 'The Career Paths of Minority Elected Politicians: Resemblances and Differences', in Shirley Williams and Edward L. Lascher, Jr, eds, *Ambition & Beyond: Career Paths of American Politicians* (Berkeley, Calif.: Institute of Governmental Studies Press, 1993), pp. 231–51; Guerra, 'The Emergence of Ethnic Officeholders in California', in Bryan O. Jackson and Michael B. Preston, eds, *Racial and Ethnic Politics in California* (Berkeley: Institute

of Governmental Studies, 1991), pp. 117–30.

17. Guerra, 'Career Paths', pp. 234–5. Guerra's critique of 'significant' positions is important, especially with regard to county offices: 'Los Angeles County has 13 congressional districts completely within its boundaries and shares five others with neighboring counties. Los Angeles County has more than three times the number of state Senate and state Assembly districts of any of California's 57 other counties. In total, including special district, judicial, and political party positions, there are over 2,000 electoral opportunities available in Los Angeles', p. 233.

18. Sonenshein, p. 65.

19. Ibid.

20. Assemblyman Alex García won re-election to the Assembly in 1972 running against Art Torres, who was endorsed by César Chávez; that same year Alatorre was elected to the Assembly. García was a former aide to Congressman Edward R. Roybal, García, pp. 217–18; Acuña, *Occupied America*, p. 318, John Moreno and Phil Soto had been elected to the Assembly in 1962. Moreno served until 1964 and Soto until 1966. They had been the victims of gerrymandering in the reapportionments of 1961, 1965 and 1967. Ironically, the liberal California Democratic Council was a force – but it never occurred to these liberal Democrats to question the process, thus supporting an 'anything but Mexican' mind-set.

21. Joan Moore, *Mexican Americans* (Englewood Cliffs, N.J.: 1976), pp. 55, 58; Rodolfo Acuña, *Community Under Siege*, p. 184. Latinos in 1970 were 18.4% of the population in the city of Los Angeles and 18.3% of the county.

22. The classic radical argument that electoral politics are bad, and that it doesn't matter if you have Chicano or other minority representation, is flawed. Radicals are usually middle-class activists who have the luxury of not participating in the system. In minority communities, jobs and services are the prime issues. Take the fact that by the late 1980s the Latino population was some 35% of the county but held only 18% of the jobs. Moreover, if progressive or even liberal Latino candidates don't run, this political space is left to Euroamericans or right-of-center Chicanos.

23. Regalado, p. 96.

24. One of the irritating aspects of working with white progressives is that they in general seem more critical of flaws within the Chicano political community than of those in other groups. Perhaps this attitude stems from the fact that Chicanos were never part of the liberal agenda, and have always been seen as foreigners.

25. During the 1960s I had extensive contact with the CDC and was also active in the Mexican American Political Association. I found that the Democratic Party discouraged the formation of independent Mexican American groups, and used them only around election time. Early on, Chicanos should have been given the resources to form an organization such as the Texas-based Southwest Voter Registration and Education Project, which was founded in the 1970s. Instead, the attitude was that Mexicans don't vote and when they do, they vote for the Trinity – Roosevelt, Kennedy and the Virgin of Guadalupe. This was so even in the face of the success of the Community Service Organization, which conducted extensive voter registration drives during the late 1940s and 1950s. The Democratic Party in the last analysis wanted total control over Chicano political organizations. Political scientist Ralph Guzmán made the point that both the Democrats and the Republicans felt threatened by the CSO and attacked it. See Guzman, *Political Socialization of the Mexican American People*, pp. 137–43.

26. Sonenshein, p. 146. While I recognize the pitfalls of the ward system and its corruption in places like Chicago, Los Angeles politics are in fact just as corrupt – and much more deceptive. It was my experience that race and class politics in the Bradley years were swept under the table, whereas the political situation in Chicago was at least more clearly readable to the average citizen. Los Angeles is a seductive city, with many minorities still claiming that there is no racism – which may seem to be true if you never get off the freeways.

27. Matt S. Meier and Feliciano, *Dictionary of Mexican American History* (Westport, Conn.: Greenwood Press, 1981), pp. 97–8.

28. Alatorre and Torres received high marks on civil rights and on immigrant and labor issues. Alatorre, for example, could always be counted on to support Chicano Studies, having formerly taught at California State University, Long Beach. In spite of not liking one of the members of the Chicano studies department at California State University, Northridge, he supported the depart-

ment in a conflict with the Migrant Mini Corps. He sent a strong letter when I personally was under attack by ultraconservatives. The principal criticism during the 1970s seems to be his association with TELACU and his favoring of a small circle of friends. On another level, it was a matter of style and the fact that he was not a radical. Yet Alatorre was effective in getting his legislation through; he played the 'game' by the rules of American politics. See 'The Buying of the President', *Harper's* (August 1992), p. 18, for a view of American politics.

29. Howard D. Neighbor, 'New Rules in Voting Rights Cases Demand New Strategies for Chicano Empowerment', in Villarreal et al., eds, *Latino Empowerment*, p. 106.

30. Ibid, pp. 115–16. Exceedingly important was the ruling in *Thornburg* v. *Gingles*, 1986, which strengthened the 1982 law and held that there is a single set of rules governing all jurisdictions.

31. 'Latinos in Los Angeles County: An Update', *Tomás Rivera Center Report*, vol. 2, no. 1 (Fall 1988), p. 1.

32. Marita Hernández, '1990 Census Holds Promise for Latino Political Activists', *Nuestro Tiempo*, 23 March 1989.

33. Ibid.

34. Regalado, 'Latino Representation', in Villareal et al., p. 97. By 1992 the *Los Angeles Times* had returned to a neoconservative policy. For a discussion, see James Sterngold, 'A Family Struggle for the Soul of the *Times Mirror*', *New York Times*, 27 Nov. 1995.

35. Richard Santillán, 'The Latino Community in State and Congressional Redistricting: 1961–1985'; statistics in F. Chris Garcia, ed., *Latinos and the Political System* (Notre Dame, Ind.: University of Notre Dame Press, 1988),p. 333.

36. Santillán, p. 338.

37. Ibid., p. 340; Maurilio E. Vigil, 'Hispanics Gain Seats in the 98th Congress After Reapportionment', in Garcia, ed., *Latinos and the Political System*, p. 279.

38. Regalado, 'Latino Representation', in Villareal et al., eds, *Latino Empowerment*, pp. 102–4; a weakness is the comparatively paltry body of literature derived from this experience.

39. Claudia Luther, 'Latinos May Get Little in Redistricting', *Los Angeles Times*, 30 April 1981.

40. Ibid. Brown's freewheeling discussion with the *Times* reporter showed little respect for the Latino community. He made his point by showing that Assemblyman Art Torres had the fewest votes of any Assembly winner in the state. He also pointed to the Chicano community's inability to unseat Art Snyder.

41. Frank del Olmo, 'Will Gloria Molina Lead Us into Decade of the Hispanic?', *Los Angeles Times*, 11 Nov. 1982.

42. Vigil, pp. 279–80.

43. Critics accused Torres of being part of the East Los Angeles 'Taco Mafia' and The East Los Angeles Community Union (TELACU), which he had founded in the late 1960s.

44. Vigil, pp. 280–81.

45. Fernando Torres-Gil and Tony Zamora, 'Woo Victory Raises Issues But Bodes Well for Latinos', *Los Angeles Times*, 24 July 1985.

46. Kevin Roderick, '2 Latino Candidates Fight over a Jewel – L.A.'s 56th District', *Los Angeles Times*, 11 April 1982.

47. Del Olmo, 'Will Gloria Molina Lead Us into Decade of the Hispanic?'

48. Roderick, '2 Latino Candidates Fight'.

49. Even more bitter was the García-Torres campaign for the 56th Senate District, which took in northeast Los Angeles, south through unincorporated East Los Angeles to small cities such as Vernon, Maywood and Bell Gardens. It was a campaign noted more for its mud-slinging than for its issues. García charged that Torres was a Baptist in a heavily Catholic area, lived in a Sacramento mansion and didn't speak Spanish. Torres called García a liar. Frank del Olmo, 'Garcia, Torres Talk Trivia – Too Bad for Latinos', *Los Angeles Times*, 20 May 1982; the United Farm Workers supported García against Torres, a one-time protégé of César Chávez. Relations between the two had soured after Torres and Alatorre backed Willie Brown against Howard Berman in a fight for the speakership of the Assembly, while Chávez had committed himself to Berman. Torres won the race.

50. Frank del Olmo, 'Snyder's Narrow Victory Gives Latino Political Activists a Rude Awakening', *Los Angeles Times*, 28 April 1983.

51. Janet Clayton, 'Latino Endorsements Split in 14th District', *Los Angeles Times*, 31 March 1983.

52. Frank del Olmo, 'Snyder's Narrow Victory'; Clayton, 'Latino Endorsements'.

53. Frank del Olmo, '14th District Is No Place for Shifty Politics', *Los Angeles Times*, 26 Sept. 1985.

54. Bill Boyarsky, 'Alatorre: A Power Comes Back Home', *Los Angeles Times*, 15 Dec. 1985; Boyarsky, 'Redrawing Los Angeles to New Reality', *Los Angeles Times*, 14 Sept. 1986.

4

Marching Mothers and the

Rise of Gloria Molina

Boyle Heights was a crowded Eastside neighborhood of 89,000, half of whose residents were under twenty-five.[1] Half were foreign-born, and almost 90 percent spoke a language other than English at home.[2] Most were blue-collar or service workers. In May 1985, the California State Department of Corrections publicly announced its choice of a site for the first state prison on the doorstep of East Los Angeles; it would be five-minute walk from Boyle Heights. Eastsiders opposed the prison because Los Angeles County had a history of dumping unwanted facilities there. Their area already housed the Los Angeles County Men's Central Jail, one of the largest facilities in the nation, and the Sybil Brand Institute, a women's prison. The Eastside had a total of five prisons; the state prison would make six. Indeed, roughly 75 percent of the L.A. prison population was warehoused on the Eastside, and other plans existed to expand these existing facilities.

Because Gloria Molina had won election to the state Assembly in 1982 without owing favors to any politicos in L.A.'s Chicano or Democratic Party establishment, she could act independently to oppose the project, which was being pushed by both conservatives and liberals. A core of middle-class Mexican American women professionals and government workers, as well as white feminists, provided her with contributions that allowed her a degree of political independence.[3] In September 1985 the bill authorizing the prison passed the California state Senate with no opposition. The Los Angeles Times endorsed it, and many local leaders saw the prison only as a source of jobs for construction workers and prison guards. Molina seemed alone among L.A. politicians in her objections to the project, and KNX radio editorialized, 'Gloria Molina likens herself to a drum major in a march against the East L.A. Prison. Few have fallen in line behind her.'[4]

The Mothers of East Los Angeles did not start out as an organization but a movement.[5] It was like a river without a single source: individuals and groups with a variety of organizational experiences and constituencies converged and marched behind Molina's public leadership. They included Juana Gutiérrez, who with her husband Ricardo had been active for some twenty years in the local Parent Teacher Association, the Neighborhood Watch and various other community activities, and who had a strong sense of place. They owned their own home in Boyle Heights and did not plan to leave. In May 1986 the Gutiérrezes along with Erlinda Robles, whose mother had been active in Boyle Heights as one of the founders of the CSO in the 1950s, and other activists from St Isabel Parish heard about the prison from Martha Molina, field representative for Gloria Molina (no relation).[6] They organized in St Isabel Parish, collecting 900 signatures on a petition against the project.[7]

Simultaneously Molina's field representatives, themselves products of the Chicano student movement, spread the word to other groups in the community, who immediately saw the threat. Among them were the Lincoln Heights Chamber of Commerce; the Lions Club; and businessmen Steven Kasten, José Luis García and Frank Villalobos of Barrio Planners, whose technical knowledge and enthusiasm would play a major role in the fight against the prison. The entrance of Father John Moretta of Resurrection Parish into the struggle against the prison was instrumental in turning these different sectors of the community into a movement. Resurrection Parish served as the base for this coalition, which, with support from Molina's office, as well as from other communities, pressured the Department of Corrections to hold a public information meeting in the spring of 1986.[8] Over 700 residents attended. By the summer, women were marching over the bridge to the site of the prison. Father Moretta dubbed the group 'the Mothers of East Los Angeles', inspired by *The Official Story*, a film about 'Las Madres de la Plaza de Mayo' in Argentina, who mobilized against the repressive machinery of the state to find out what had happened to their disappeared children.[9] As a result of these marches and the publicity they generated, the Mothers of East L.A. forced the Department of Corrections to conduct an environmental impact study on the proposed prison, a requirement that the department had previously waived. It is significant that up to this point, no major Chicano organization had joined Molina and the community activists.

Even so, Molina's popularity grew at the expense of newly elected Assemblyman Richard Polanco, whom Alatorre had supported for his former Assembly seat. Polanco defeated Molina's choice, Mike Hernández, by only 328 votes in a special election. In June 1986, he again defeated Hernández in the Democratic Party primary, this time with the support of Assembly Speaker Willie Brown. Beholden to Brown for this support, Polanco voted to take the prison bill out of the Assembly Public Safety Committee, where it had languished and almost died, thus reviving the fight over the prison. This act, which Molina skillfully exploited, generated a good deal of moral indignation and revived the Stop the East L.A. Prison Coalition.[10]

Members of the group travelled to Sacramento to lobby legislators. Frank Villalobos was invaluable in this aspect of the campaign because of his knowledge of the community, environmental regulations, land use and the political process, as well as his contacts in the business community.[11] Father Moretta furnished transportation and the moral authority of the Church, while Juana Gutiérrez and others extended the network of supporters by making presentations to Chicano students and other organizations throughout the L.A. area.[12] The pressure of these women attracted national attention.

Leading the forces for the prison was Republican Governor George Deukmejian, who fancied himself a political John Wayne and called himself 'the Duke'. Deukmejian had a long history of viewing Chicanos solely as cheap, temporary farm labor. The San Joaquin growers contributed heavily to his campaigns, and he returned the favor by destroying the California Agricultural Labor Relations Board, thus crippling the United Farm Workers. 'The Duke' also attempted to scuttle the state's bilingual education program. The governor cared little that the prison would cause further deterioration in the surrounding communities or that it would further weaken the area's declining industrial zone. He was supported by County Supervisor Mike Antonovich, who had promised white Republican voters in Newhall-Saugus that a prison would not be built there. Deukmejian acted like an obsessed man in pursuit of his prison, pressuring the Department of Corrections to buy the property without a full environmental impact report (EIR), although there was evidence of toxic pollution on the site. Moreover, the cost of the property was about $500,000 an acre versus $6,000 an acre at other possible sites.

Throughout this controversy, the California Correctional Peace Officers Association played an important role. The salaries of California's prison officers are higher than those in other public safety agencies, and observers invariably mention the political clout of their union and its generous campaign contributions.[13] Both Deukmejian and Brown benefitted from this generosity, as did elected officials of all colors. Meanwhile, a bill authorizing the prison cleared the Assembly. Most observers had expected the bill to pass the Senate as well, but it fell short by two votes with the help of Senate President Pro Tem David Roberti. Senator Art Torres, who had originally voted for the bill, repented and worked vigorously to defeat its final passage.

In September 1986, some 3,000 East L.A. residents gathered at Olympic Boulevard and Santa Fe to rally against the prison. There had been various marches to the prison site since the beginning of the summer, attracting hundreds and then thousands of supporters. Mothers of East Los Angeles, community business leaders, the powerful United Neighborhood Organization and the South Central Organizing Committee participated. Archbishop Roger Mahoney also supported the stop-the-prison drive. It was a display of collective moral outrage infrequently seen in the Chicano community. Meanwhile, Deukmejian grew furious and called a special session of the state Senate to pass the prison authorization bill. He accused two Democratic senators, Roberti and Torres, of reneging on previous agreements and leading the anti-prison opposition. He also warned of a major prison riot if the East L.A. site was not approved.[14] Deukmejian ignored estimates of $15 million needed to clean up toxic wastes at the proposed site, and acted as if the choice of the site had been a divine revelation. Deukmejian told a group of reporters that he had seen the site while flying over it when he was a legislator and it suddenly came to him that the location would be ideal for a prison.[15]

Molina Goes to City Hall

Gloria Molina's popularity had grown as a result of the fight against the prison, guaranteeing her a cadre of East Side business people and grassroots Catholic activists. For the moment, she had taken over the leadership of left-of-center Latinos. Before the prison campaign, the latter had distrusted her, accusing her of fence-sitting on important issues and of belonging to the Alatorre machine. By 1987, however, many of them hoped that Molina would take up the Roybal tradition in the City Council.[16] When the newly created First District seat became open as a result of Howard Finn's death in 1986, Molina decided to run for the council. Alatorre immediately backed school board member Larry González.[17] The 1st CD was 69 percent Latino and had only about 36,000 registered voters, 40 percent of them Latino. Since the special election, set for November 1987, would draw only about 10,000 voters, Euroamericans were expected to be a higher proportion of actual voters than usual.[18]

Alatorre steered contributors to González's campaign, including major developers such as Goldrich & Kiest and Alexander Haagen. The United Southern California PAC, a clone of TELACU, was active in González's campaign organization. Former Councilman Art Snyder, also closely connected with Los Angeles developers, worked behind the scenes for González. But despite Alatorre's superior political and economic network, Molina won the race handily, with many Chicano activists supporting the idea that the time had come for a Latina to have a seat on the council. Molina's election permanently laid to rest the idea that a woman could not be elected in East Los Angeles. (As in her Assembly race, Molina received financial support from white women's groups, strengthening her base.) Latinos now made up 13 percent of the council seats, though their proportion of the population was around 40 percent. The quality of representation remained an issue as well. Chicano elected officials assumed leadership in a community without neighborhood organizations serving as checks on them. Individually or collectively, these officials seemed to lack a vision of where the community should go. Personal careers were often put ahead of community interests, and, as usual in US politics, the ability to raise money provided the keys to the Chicano political kingdom.

The scramble to fill Molina's Assembly seat began immediately after her election to the City Council.[19] Eastside politicos ultimately reached a consensus that they would support Lucille Roybal-Allard, Congressman Roybal's daughter, for Molina's former seat. The choice was not a bad one. However, many people had supported Molina in order to break the monopoly of the Eastside machine in naming candidates, and they resented the need to go to a godfather or godmother and get his or her blessing. They were disappointed that Chicano politics was business as usual, and that Molina seemed to be building her own machine. Many activists still smarted over the loss of Steve Rodríguez, the last of the independent candidates.[20] Moreover, Roybal-Allard did not have her father's history of political involvement; he had come out of an organic movement, while she simply accepted the nod from the machine.

Roybal-Allard herself could not be blamed for playing by the rules of the political marketplace, where the winner was usually known beforehand. A candidate merely had to go to the brokers, assert her or his intention to raise $100,000 to $150,000 and other potential candidates would drop out. Her victory was thus a foregone conclusion and strengthened the Molina clan. Once in the Assembly, Lucille Roybal-Allard found herself operating in a world very different from that of her father. She had to deal with Speaker Willie Brown, who had the reputation of assigning broom closets as offices to those who did not do his bidding. Roybal-Allard's style was also less confrontational than Molina's; generally she stayed on good terms with most of the Latino caucus in the legislature and felt much more comfortable negotiating an issue than crusading. After all, she was the daughter of a congressman, coming from a background different from Molina's.

Meanwhile, Gloria Molina represented the poorest of council districts, a fact that perhaps defined her streetfighting political style.[21] She was prone to step on the toes of other members of the council in the defense of Latinos, and often used the council to take on and even bait Alatorre.[22] This approach made her popular with the public, but given the clubby rules of the political game on the City Council, it limited her effectiveness in passing legislation. After the election, Roybal-Allard and Molina teamed up in taking on the prison issue. Their staffs worked tirelessly, not only in the legislature but also with the Environmental Protection Agency, the Correction Peace Officers Association, the governor and a host of others who wanted the prison in East Los Angeles.[23]

As the struggle proceeded the community activists, and especially the women, became more politically conscious and willing to take on other environmental issues. At one hearing they asked an oil representative why Boyle Heights had been chosen for the route of a company pipeline.[24] Chicano Studies professor Mary Pardo has reconstructed the scene:

'Is [the pipeline] going through Cielito Lindo [Reagan's Ranch]?' The oil representative answered, 'No.' Another woman stood up and asked, 'Why not place it along the coastline?' Without thinking of the implications, the representative responded, 'Oh, no! If it burst, it would endanger the marine life.' The woman retorted, 'You value the marine life more than human beings?' Unaccustomed to being questioned by Mexican women, his face reddened with anger and the hearing disintegrated into angry chanting.'[25]

As in the case of the pipeline, Eastsiders were incensed by the lack of concern about hazardous waste dumping. In 1988 a chemical fire threatened to explode 26,000 gallons of lethal chemicals (among them cyanide) in Lincoln Heights. Thousands of residents were hurriedly evacuated, raising nightmarish visions of another Bhopal. Builders Hardware Finishers was located in a residential neighborhood, like thousands of other metal-plating companies surrounding the Eastside. The danger of an explosion was not solely the fault of Builders but reflected the haphazard state and federal regulation of toxic chemicals. It was almost impossible to monitor the estimated 8,000 companies handling toxic materials in Los Angeles. According to *Los Angeles Times* reporter Maura Dolan, the Builders Hardware Finishers fire did not make the front page of the city's largest newspaper. Within three days, the media, with some notable exceptions, considered the 'mishap' yesterday's news.[26]

The Mothers of East L.A. also fought the installation of a $29 million hazardous-waste incinerator in Vernon in 1988, charging that it would lead the city to an ecological Armageddon. Vernon was surrounded by one of the most densely populated areas in the Los Angeles basin, and the incinerator would burn up to 22,500 tons of hazardous waste annually in a city that was already notorious for its pollution. However, the Southern California Air Quality Management District ruled that the incinerator would have no significant environmental impact; thus, the owner, California Thermal Treatment Services, didn't even have to file an environmental impact report.

Roybal-Allard's staff took the lead in organizing community opposition, supported by Molina's people. The Mothers of East L.A. and their supporters provided the shock troops. After marches and rallies and petitions calling attention to the incinerator, the Air Quality Management District refused to extend California Thermal's incinerator permits. Nevertheless, the US Environmental Protection Agency issued the company permits without requiring an EIR. California Thermal took the AQMD to court, where Superior Court Judge Kurt Lewin ordered the district to issue the incinerator company permits without a full EIR.

Lewin's ruling seemed to go out of its way to insult the Mexican community. The incinerator, said the judge, was like the Mexican pyramids: it represented progress. The AQMD appealed the ruling and the Mothers this time joined forces with Black activists from South Central Los Angeles who were fighting against a Lancer waste-disposal incinerator in that area.[27] This coalition was successful in holding up the project by insisting on a full environmental impact report. Finally, primarily thanks to the efforts of the Mothers, installation of the Vernon incinerator was halted.[28]

Meanwhile, the prison fight continued to simmer. In 1989 the EIR Certification Panel rejected the environmental impact report for the proposed prison, with Deukmejian's appointee abstaining. However, this vote did not end the controversy because the Department of Corrections had already bought the land at a cost of $14.6 million. Critics pointed out that the DOC had spent $500,000 to $600,000 on two worthless EIRs and would probably spend $500,000 more for yet another report. At the same time, Deukmejian's FY1990 state budget proposed cuts in funding for county probation camps from $67.3 million to $30.4 million. If enacted, 1,660 boys and 110 girls would be shipped to more draconian California Youth Authority camps, making rehabilitation almost impossible. It was this very lack of vision and these wrongheaded policies that made more prisons necessary.[29]

As the struggle against the Eastside prison dragged on it was clear that the Mothers of East L.A. would not go away. Political leaders failed to understand that the Chicanas were fighting for more than property values: they were primarily struggling to preserve an endangered species – their community. Because of their race and class backgrounds, they saw so-called gender issues much more intensely than did their Westside counterparts. In 1990 Democrats and Republicans in the state legislature made a new effort to circumvent the community's wishes and passed what was called a 'pain for pain' law. They proposed that another new prison be built in largely white, Republican Lancaster, thus hoping to undermine the Latinos' contention that they were being discriminated against. This 'exchange of pain' was, however, transparently lopsided. A full EIR was required for Lancaster, while only a requirement for a partial report was approved for the Eastside.[30] The battle against the East L.A. prison lasted well into the summer of 1992, when all legal remedies had been exhausted. By this time the Mothers of East Los Angeles had split into two camps, one centered on Resurrection church and the other on St Isabel's, as the result of clashes over control and personalities.[31] In the end, legislative leaders cut a deal and the plan to build the East Los Angeles prison was abandoned; Willie Brown and Richard Polanco played key roles in this settlement. In late September, Governor Pete Wilson signed a bill that also abandoned the 'pain for pain' compromise. The victory was marred by the animosity between the two Eastside camps, which by this time reflected not only polarization of the community but also factionalism within the Chicano political establishment. Gloria Molina refused to go to the victory celebration, not wanting to share the podium with Polanco,[32] and the Mothers from St Isabel were not invited to the festivities, a slight that left enduring scars.

In the end, the victory over Deukmejian's prison project left a strong memory of a time when the community had fought back – and won. It proved that the residents cared about having a decent quality of life and were prepared to fight for it, building a struggle that included many sectors of the community. The people participating in the struggle brought with them their own history of struggle, and in the process created a new chapter in that history.[33]

A Chicana Joins the Board of Supervisors

The election of Gloria Molina to the Los Angeles City Council brought about important changes. Foremost among them was her breaking of the gender barrier. This, however, did not mean that the electoral process was now open to Mr or Ms Everyperson. In the end, two Eastside camps emerged, both of which privatized the political process rather than collectivizing it. If you wanted to run and win, you had to join the Molina camp or the Alatorre camp. The two camps were close ideologically, nestled just left of the center of the political spectrum.

Much of Molina's attraction was her style. She appeared willing to rock the boat and take on established interests at City Hall – a stance that appealed to voters who wanted heroes where few were to be found. Moreover, she was helped by the growing political awareness of middle-class Chicana feminists.[34] Councilman Richard Alatorre represented the old machine politics of logrolling, which helped him build good relations with prominent white and Black politicos and made him very effective within this environment. Alatorre was pro-labor, and he always had strong backing from this sector. However, Alatorre's style seemed increasingly out of step; like smoking, it had become gauche during the 1980s.[35]

The final showdown between the Molina and Alatorre forces came in the fight over Chicano representation on the county Board of Supervisors, a body that controls a budget of over $13 billion and serves 8.5 million people – a population greater than that of forty-two states. The five county supervisors who control this kingdom are known as the five little kings. Mexicans had been excluded from this body for 115 years.[36]

In June 1990, US District Judge David V. Kenyon, after a lengthy and costly trial,[37] ruled in *Garza v. County of Los Angeles* that the supervisors had violated the federal Voting Rights Act by intentionally denying Latinos an equal opportunity to elect candidates of their choice to the county Board of Supervisors.[38] During the course of the trial MALDEF attorney Richard Fajardo and ACLU attorney Mark Rosenbaum exposed a closed-door meeting of the board during which the 1981 redistricting plan had been discussed.[39] To circumvent state law requiring that discussions among three or more supervisors be public, only two supervisors at a time attended the meeting. The *Los Angeles Times* noted: ' ... after the supervisors appointed a commission to draft a redistricting plan and invested money in a sophisticated computer redistricting operation, they ended up in a private meeting, drawing their own plan with one clerk calculating population changes on an adding machine and another clerk tracing lines on a map made by hand.' The *Times*'s article revealed that the conservative Republican majority on the board spent $18,000 in campaign funds for a political consultant to protect their interests. In the end, liberal Democrats Kenny Hahn and Ed Edelman voted for a plan to protect the districts of white male conservatives on the board. This was an act of self-preservation in which the board 'secretly fashioned a redistricting plan that diluted Latino voting strength in order to protect their own political bases ...'[40]

Almost up to the last moment conservative Supervisor Pete Schabarum attempted to torpedo a settlement in the Garza suit. Schabarum, who had held office since 1972, announced in December 1989 that he would have no problem running in a largely Latino district, 'being a Hispanic such as I am.' He even claimed that his paternal grandmother was Mexican.[41] This bit of bravado was, not surprisingly, unsuccessful. Even after he finally decided not to run, Schabarum still sought to determine his eventual successor. The other two conservative supervisors, believing that the election of a Latina would deter Judge Kenyon from implementing his decision, supported Sarah Flores for Schabarum's former seat in the spring of 1990, and Flores won the June primary against Schabarum's opposition.[42] Despite this maneuver, in November 1990 Kenyon set aside the election in favor of a new redistricting plan.[43]

The Garza case revealed much about Euroangelenos and their attitude toward Mexicans. Suffering from historical amnesia, many of them continued to view Latinos as foreigners and questioned the suit against the Board of Supervisors: 'Why should Mexicans have representation on the board?' Whites – and often Blacks – seemed to think that civil rights was not a Latino issue.[44] Breaking through this historical and institutional ignorance was a major challenge in preparing a brief in the case. While judges presume discrimination against African Americans, they tend to see Chicanos and other Latinos as latecomers without a history of discrimination or civil rights struggle, and efforts to raise the history of the Chicano struggle for civil rights are often met with hostility. Perhaps the key political point is that numbers alone do not automatically bring political strength or influence. In fact, they usually intensify nativism toward Latinos among Euroamericans.[45]

Eventually, Judge Kenyon's ruling ordering an end to the white male monopoly on the Los Angeles County Board of Supervisors was sustained on appeal. After 115 years, Latinos would have a fair chance to elect one of their own to one of the most powerful governmental bodies in the county. The new 1st

District was the brainchild of UCLA demographer Leo Estrada and was 71 percent Latino and 12 percent Anglo. It included the Eastside, El Sereno, the south San Gabriel Valley, Pico Rivera, La Puente and Santa Fe Springs. The price tag for representing the new district was estimated at a half-million dollars; non-incumbents without existing volunteer networks need not apply.[46] The district had 1.78 million residents. Fifty-one percent of the registered voters were Latino, 66.5 percent of whom were Democrats and 23.3 percent Republicans.[47] However, a split along class lines existed between the Eastside and the San Gabriel Valley. And, fragmented by years of intentional political separation, the area lacked a sense of community. The real voting strength rested in the San Gabriel Valley, which included mostly middle-class townships like Hacienda Heights – 284,000 registered voters, of whom 100,435, or 35 percent, were Latino. By contrast, the Eastside had only 44,600 registered voters, some 80 percent of them Latino.[48]

Los Angeles Times reporter Edmund Newton wrote in January 1990: 'In the old days, Anglo politicians went after Latino voters by staging photo opportunities in East Los Angeles, posing in Belvedere in mariachi sombreros or downing tacos on Brooklyn Avenue.'[49] But over the years many newly middle-class Latinos had moved along the Pomona and San Bernardino Freeway belt into the San Gabriel Valley and adjacent areas. It had become an area where a critical mass of eligible Latino voters lived.

In all probability, Congressman Esteban Torres could have had the nomination for the new seat for the asking. Molina would have surely deferred to Torres, who was respected in the community and had strong bases in the Eastside and the San Gabriel Valley. Perhaps overly cautious because he had not won reelection to Congress by the landslide he had hoped for, Torres decided not to run. Along with Congressman Ed Roybal, he threw his support to Molina. Alatorre, who had been expected to announce his candidacy, did not run because 'running for two offices at the same time seems selfish and is not fair to my constituents.' (There was doubt as to whether he could legally run for the Board of Supervisors and City Council at the same time.)[50] State Senator Art Torres threw his hat in the ring at what seemed the eleventh hour,[51] setting up yet another confrontation between Molina and the Eastside cabal.[52]

Four Latino candidates ran for the new seat: Sarah Flores, Charles Calderón, Art Torres and Gloria Molina. Leading up to the 22 January 1991 primary, their campaigns focused mostly on personalities rather than differences in program or philosophy, reflecting the posture of restraint adopted by the four. Their supporters, however, engaged in character attacks, including a whispering telephone campaign. As a result, progressives lost another chance to assemble a coalition that could hold the winner accountable to the community. Unfortunately, supporters seemed all too willing to pay the price of asking little from their candidate. How to secure public safety was an issue high on everybody's list in the district, yet the four principal candidates largely sidestepped it. Safety *from* law enforcement was another neglected issue. The Republican-dominated Board of Supervisors had long given Sheriff Sherman Block virtual carte blanche. Police brutality was as common as it had been twenty years ago, when journalist Rubén Salazar was cut down by an L.A. County sheriff's deputy. From 1985 to mid 1990, 202 deputies were involved in shootings countywide. At least 56 people were shot under highly questionable circumstances, 49 of them minorities.[53] Building more prisons for the young and poor, the favorite advice of former Governor Deukmejian and Supervisor Pete Schabarum, was the fashionable way to deal with the district's gang problem, and the four Chicano candidates apparently saw no reason to question that strategy.

The candidates also failed to discuss Metro Rail, the high costs of its routes, or the low percentage of contracts received by Latino contractors. They did not talk about jobs, the homeless, or environmental racism. All of the candidates played it safe and took pains not to alienate the white vote, realizing that the election of a Latino was not a sure thing, even though the district was largely Latino.[54]

Many pundits had predicted that Flores would be in the run-off election because of her middle-class base and the supposed conservatism of the area. However, the election led to a surprise run-off between Molina and Torres on 22 February 1991. Molina's base of support went beyond the Eastside and included Westside women's groups: she raised some $500,000 from women's organizations, including the Fund for a Feminist Majority.[55] Though she was a liberal on many social issues, Molina had refrained from criticizing L.A. Police Chief Daryl Gates, and she had championed the controversial Central City West Project, a commercial and low-income housing development. Nor did Molina automatically support Chicano Movement issues. While it cannot be said that she was anti-immigrant, she was reluctant to champion the civil rights of immigrants suspected of illegal activities.

Torres, one of the most articulate Latino politicos, was an attorney who had worked as a volunteer for the United Farm Workers; he had historically championed liberal positions on labor, immigrant rights and education issues. Torres's most immediate problem was that the public perceived him as a *jefe* in the so-called Alatorre-Torres machine and as a partisan of TELACU. This hurt his image, as did his break with César Chávez over Torres's switching political loyalty from Howard Berman to Willie Brown when those two struggled for speakership of the Assembly.

This race split the progressive Latino community. Molina enjoyed the support of many on the left. Some critics feared that Torres owed too much to Local 660, which represented county workers and was white-controlled at the time, to advocate strongly for the interests of Chicanos in their struggle to win a more equitable distribution of county jobs.[56] Other critics feared that he was tied to developer interests, and that Molina was therefore supposedly the more independent of the two. In contrast, some Chicano progressives criticized Molina because of her failure to aggressively champion immigrant rights and trade unions. Just before the run-off election, activist lawyer Antonio Rodríguez attacked Molina in an op-ed column for her criticism of the overwhelming support of the service workers' union for Torres.[57]

The campaign itself was bitter, with personal attacks on both sides leaving scars. Molina, whose father was a janitor, was stung by accusations that she was anti-union. She vehemently denied that she was anti-immigrant and believed that the Torres camp had purposely lied about her position. The other side accused Molina of playing the gender card and conducting a whispering campaign against Torres. Worst of all, progressive factions within the two camps encouraged this level of attack, and continued to push their candidate on a personal basis rather than advocating a progressive agenda.

On election day, Molina won a decisive victory. Endorsed by the *Los Angeles Times* and buffered by an army of volunteers, she overcame Torres's better-financed campaign. Her camp was not gracious in victory, openly displaying a 'We kicked their ass!' attitude.[58]

The Molina forces drew strength from their victory. In 1990, Assemblyman Charles Calderón (D-Whittier) vacated his seat to run for the seat left open at the resignation of state Senator Joseph Montoya. This left Calderón's old seat vacant, and Xavier Becerra, a former aide to Senator Art Torres and a former state deputy attorney general, was a surprise challenger. Everyone believed that Becerra would automatically look to Torres for aid, but instead Becerra turned to a cadre of recent Chicano graduates from Ivy League schools and local universities. Rather than coming home to the Eastside expecting to be annointed leaders simply because of their degrees, they worked to develop reputations as activists on community issues, such as fighting alongside the Mothers of East L.A.[59]

Polanco, George Pla (president of Cordova Corp., a TELACU clone) and Calderón met and named Marta Maestas, a Calderón aide for seven years, as their candidate for the Assembly seat. Diane Martínez, daughter of Rep. Matthew Martínez (D-Monterey Park), also ran. Esteban Torres backed his longtime friend, Bill Hernández, a Rio Hondo College trustee. All these campaigns were well-financed: Maestas, for example, sent out 30,000 potholders with her logo on them.

Becerra and his volunteers went door-to-door in the San Gabriel Valley as well as among the Eastside poor, countering the big money his competitors had available. Becerra also reached out to Molina partisans for support, a necessary move since most of the young Chicanas and Chicanos who were alienated from what they perceived as the Eastside machine, and who wanted to become players in Eastside politics themselves had gravitated to Molina during the struggle against the Eastside prison. Calderón had strong ties to the Alatorre camp. Angered that Becerra had the audacity to challenge his right to name his successor, Calderón baited Becerra, making an issue of what he referred to as Becerra's Ivy League background (Becerra had actually gone to Stanford) and charging that Becerra had not 'paid his dues'. Despite this attack, Becerra won, and his victory undoubtedly strengthened Gloria Molina.

LATINO ELECTED OFFICIALS IN CALIFORNIA

	1974	1976	1980	1984	1988	1989
US representatives	1	1	1	3	4	3
State executive officers	0	0	0	0	0	0
State legislators	5	6	7	7	7	7
County officials	7	12	10	10	7	15
City officials	131	159	167	168	155	180
Judges	19	26	36	52	43	53
School board members	-	-	-	222	247	293
Special district board members	-	-	-	-	-	29

SOURCE: *California Fact Sheet*, Southwest Voter Registration Institute, 1990.

The Gloria Molina Factor

When Gloria Molina took her oath as a county supervisor, she stepped into one of the most powerful positions in California politics. According to Professors Victor Valle and Rudy Torres, the basis of this power went far beyond the demographic game that lulled many Chicanos. In politics, the moral authority that a politician can command matters little if it is not bolstered by money and by mobilized registered voters – in that order. In any reconfiguration of districts, clusters of business executives, industries and corporate centers are vital. (Molina's predecessor, Pete Schabarum, knew this, which made him for a time the most powerful politico in Southern California.)[60] According to Valle and Torres, 'it was fear of losing strategic political and economic resources, rather than ideological differences, that inspired the Board of Supervisors' conservative majority to oppose the court-mandated redistricting plan' that had resulted from the Garza suit.[61] Molina inherited this legacy, along with the support from the district's high-tech, light manufacturing, warehousing and distributions industries. For a Richard Alatorre, this opportunity for political juice would have been like being in a candy store. For Molina, with a political style that *supposedly* rejected the 'good old boys' approach, this created a problem: could she fully exploit these resources and simultaneously maintain her political reputation as an outsider?

Molina's tenure on the Board of Supervisors saw efforts to make several changes in its structure, which had remained remained essentially unchanged since 1885. Proposition B was put on the November 1992 ballot: it called for an elected county executive. Proposition C on the same ballot proposed expanding the board to nine members. MALDEF opposed measure B and supported C, but both measures lost.[62]

During this time County CAO Richard Dixon came under fire from Molina.[63] Following standard Reaganite doctrine, Dixon attempted to privatize many county services, consolidate departments and weaken public employee unions. Under his direction the budget grew while the county's workforce and the services it provided shrank. He created megadepartments headed by his cronies, which were too large to be accountable. In 1988 Dixon had been voted the authority to approve contracts without board approval. What finally brought him down were the millions of dollars spent on remodeling his offices.[64] A grand jury report not only revealed the $6.1 remodeling expenditure, but also that Dixon had destroyed documents in an effort to conceal the amount that he had spent.[65] When Dixon finally resigned people cheered in the halls of the county courthouse, according to Gil Cedillo, general manager of Local 660.[66] Molina took the opportunity not only to get rid of Dixon but to reduce the power of the CAO's office by bringing it under closer scrutiny on the grounds that the board had delegated too much power to a nonelected official.[67]

While Dixon was still CAO, the county's finances suffered a major blow when the state voted to shift $299 million in county property tax revenue to Sacramento so that the state could balance its budget. After the shift Los Angeles County had a $2.2 billion deficit. Dixon's response to this budget crisis in the summer of 1992 was a series of anti-labor proposals such as requiring the county's workforce of 86,000 to give up two days a month without pay.[68] The unions representing the county workers began to rebel, and a coalition of unions, among them Local 660, publicly attacked Dixon's proposed cuts and his personal spending excesses.[69] Also at risk was the county hospital, one of the nation's premier medical training facilities.[70]

In 1993, the supervisors once more had to cut hundreds of millions out of its proposed $13.1 billion budget. The new budget called for the closing of libraries, public assistance and public health facilities.[71] Naturally, the heaviest burden fell on the poor. Even the *Los Angeles Times* asked editorially: 'How many poor families will become homeless while they wait for that government lifeline?'[72] On 31 August 1993, some 5,000 county workers assembled in front of the Board of Supervisors' headquarters to protest the cutbacks. Jesse Jackson addressed the throng, and the workers vowed to take back their government. That evening they voted to strike if the cutbacks went into effect.[73] A crisis was averted when the county found a $125 million surplus, a 'discovery' that compromised the integrity of acting CAO Harry Hufford and the county administrators. This occurred in late August only after some 500 employees had been laid off in the summer and after the emasculation of the welfare system and cutbacks in services, and just as forty-three of the eighty-one county libraries were being shut and twenty health clinics were closing.[74]

Meanwhile, Molina continued her muckraking ways, questioning Hufford closely about budget details, and her contribution to exposing the machinations of county government was extremely important. It continues to irritate county bureaucrats when she puts them on the spot. She flaunts the fact that she runs a tight ship, spending considerably less than Supervisor Antonovich, who employs thirty-seven staffers at a cost of $1.9 million.[75]

Molina is clearly a populist, but she is by no means radical, having taken centrist stands on issues such as police brutality. As a supervisor, she has clashed in public with Sheriff Sherman Block but takes care to remain on good terms with him. At least one reporter has called her angry, and she is often abrasive. She can be criticized for carrying grudges to the extreme, often hurting a community that needs leadership, not vendettas. She can also be faulted for a narrow interpretation of what is legal, as in her reluctance to champion the rights of street vendors. As an unidentified close associate of Molina put it, 'Gloria respects authority, whether it is a priest, or the chief of police. It is hard for her to question established authority.' With all that said, she has shaken up county government. Molina has been successful in raising funds for her own campaigns but has not been as successful in building warchests for Schabarum-like political patronage, although she has gone to great lengths to maintain a high visibility within the Democratic Party.[76]

Nevertheless, the Molina factor has not been sufficient to move Los Angeles County in a fundamentally different direction. In the fall of 1993, Sally Reed, formerly Santa Clara County CEO for twelve years, took over as L.A. County CAO at a salary of $174,000 a year.[77] The county's finances were in a shambles, and the liberal majority had neither a long-term strategy nor a plan to deal with the impending budget crisis.

Regional Differences: California versus Texas

Los Angeles, although it was the Chicano capitol of the US, lagged far behind Texas in Chicano electoral gains during the 1980s.[78] Aside from differences in stability, size of the native-born population and the proportion of citizens to non-citizens, the California and Texas Chicano communities differed organizationally. The lack of a tradition of mass-based movements is evident in the failure of La Raza Unida Party to take root in California during the 1970s, while during these years the Texas LRUP won small but significant victories. After the demise of LRUP in Texas, the Southwest Voter Registration Project (SVREP) embarked on massive voter registration drives that led to the election of Chicanos in Texas. During this same period, attempts to increase voter registration among Latinos in California became an endangered species. Indeed, there has not been a well-organized voter registration drive in the state since the efforts of the Community Service Organization (CSO) in the late 1940s and 1950s.

By the mid 1980s, the SVREP was attempting to perform the same miracle in California.[79] California, however, is not Texas, and the SVREP leadership was not able to deliver the resources needed to set the process in motion.[80] With limited staff and local resources, the organization was also greatly handicapped by the death of its charismatic founder, Willie Velásquez.[81] Velásquez, a visionary, had died in 1988 at the age of forty-three from cancer. It had been his goal to set up an independent Chicano organization, so that Chicanos would not be taken for granted by either the Democratic or Republican parties; to influence them, Chicanos had to have an independent source of power. It was his aim to empower Chicanos by setting up an organization that would systematically register them to vote. 'Campaigns were not won by luck. They were won by being ever mindful of their concrete and specific goals.' Velásquez grew up in San Antonio, and during the 1960s worked as a volunteer for the United Farm Workers in the Rio Grande River Valley. Later he worked with La Raza Unida Party. In 1973, Texas had 565 Chicano elected officials; fourteen years later, they numbered 1,572.[82]

SVREP was also hurt by the scandal that overtook US Senator Alan Cranston of California and his L.A.-based Center for Participatory Democracy. The latter received $400,000 from Charles Keating, Jr, the conservative financier whose Lincoln Savings and Loan personified the S&L scandal. Worried about winning reelection in 1986, Cranston poured money into his own voter organization, and on election day won by about 100,000 votes. Indeed, the Latino vote took him over the top, although he did not give Latinos credit for his victory. According to Willie Velásquez, Cranston had agreed to cooperate with SVREP and to solicit funds for its California campaign, so that his center would not cut into the SVREP's funding base. Allegedly Cranston went back on his word, monopolizing sources of funding to such a degree that SVREP's finances were shaken. (At the time of Willie's death he had not made health or life insurance payments, leaving his family destitute.) Other Chicanos were infuriated by Cranston's organization when it ran its own slate in Salinas. Once again, the Democratic Party seemed reluctant to allow Latinos to control the political process in their own communities.[83]

Presidential Politics

On the national level during the 1980s, the Nixon strategy of wooing middle-class 'Hispanics', especially business owners and executives, paid off. Chicano organizations saw conservatives challenging liberals and progressives for control.[84] Organizations like the 140,000-member League of United Latin American Citizens (LULAC) became the targets of these business people, who had the flexible calendars and money necessary to attend national conventions. Conservative corporations such as Coors sponsored friends by paying for their rooms and transportation, and by hosting receptions. Although a small minority, Republican Latinos wielded considerable influence within these national organizations. Moreover, because Republicans held the presidency they became gatekeepers to the political kingdom and the world of patronage. As might be expected, Orange County was the stronghold of the Latino conservative network.[85]

The challenge from the right revealed a longstanding problem: the lack of a cohesive Latino organizational agenda. The separatist political stance of Chicano activists during the late 1960s and early 1970s had left a vacuum as activists abandoned mainstream Chicano organizations to conservatives. In a city the size of Los Angeles, it was impossible for Latinos to forge a political agenda in the absence of political organizations. The political process was therefore limited to catering to the minority who voted and to those who contributed money to campaigns. Without an alternative agenda, Chicanos across the country were often unduly influenced by national organizations and the 'Hispanic' hype, which was based on the dramatic growth of Spanish-speaking people nationally, but with little discussion of real issues lest they offend Cubans and splinter what amounted to a fragile coalition.

In the 1980 presidential election, Mexican Americans remained loyal to the Democratic Party. In East L.A., the vote was 68 percent for Carter versus 27 percent for Reagan.[86] Yet Latinos in general and Chicanos in particular were again ignored by the Democrats during this campaign. Why did this happen? Although the number of Latinos of voting age had increased by 77 percent during the 1970s, compared with 11 percent for the population as a whole, a large number of them were foreign-born and could not vote.[87] The 1980 Census estimated that only 74 percent of Latino adults were citizens.[88] Moreover, the median age of Latinos was almost ten years younger than that of the Euroamerican population, contributing a large number of young people who were ineligible to vote.[89] Those figures made the Latino vote seem unimportant; at best the Democrats took Latinos for granted.

In 1984 the Democratic Party ran Walter Mondale; Reagan won by a landslide. A SVREP exit poll revealed that in Los Angeles 72 percent of Mexicans had voted for Mondale.[90] During this election, the Rainbow Coalition made some inroads among L.A. Chicano activists. Generally, however, and despite minimal attention from the Democratic Party, Latinos, and Mexican Americans in particular, remained loyal to the party of Roosevelt and Kennedy.[91]

Surprisingly, under the Reagan administration the Republican Party made few efforts to exploit its foothold in the Latino community. Except for conservatives, especially Cubans, few Latinos received appointments. Programs for the poor were gutted. In 1988, George Bush took up the Reagan mantle, and skillfully manipulated the presence of a growing number of Latino conservatives within the GOP. The Democrats, in turn, offered reheated leftover promises. To many Chicanos the Dukakis-Bentsen presidential campaign against Bush and Quayle brought to mind an old Texas-Mexican saying about politicians: Never trust a Mexican who smokes a cigar or a gringo who speaks Spanish. Latino supporters of Michael Dukakis invariably stressed his fluency in Spanish, implying that this made him mindful of Latino interests. Lloyd Bentsen's Spanish, they say, was so good that English could be his second language. But his family came from the Lower Rio Grande Valley, where they made their money buying land and working Mexicans cheap.[92] Jim Hightower, once Texas agriculture commissioner, wrote that 'Lloyd Bentsen was raised rich, and it shows.' Bentsen also voted rich. Without a historical memory, Latinos were lulled by the fact that they had a Spanish-speaking ticket.

The Democrats tried to out-Republican the Republicans during the 1988 presidential race. For the first time in many years, the Democratic candidate did not court César Chávez, ignoring his fast for life. Indeed, the Dukakis camp directed its appeal to the middle class and ignored the working class in general.[93] At the same time, the Bush-Quayle campaign invented a new reality in which Bush was a man who had always cared about the little guy. In doing so, the vice-president was as adept as his mentor in the White House.

Many Latino Republicans could be found in the George Bush Show, but the star attraction was Jaime Escalante, the Bolivian-born Garfield High School calculus teacher. The vice-president appointed him National Honorary Chairman of Hispanics for Bush and frequently invoked his name in campaign speeches. Escalante's real-life teaching feats at Garfield had been made the subject of a movie, *Stand and Deliver*, released in March 1988. It showed, Republicans claimed, that problems in education could be solved by superteachers, not by increased funding. Bush went to Garfield to rub up against Escalante's fame, but he insulted Garfield students by telling them, '[You] don't have to go to college to achieve success. We need those people who build our buildings, who send them soaring to the sky.' In spite of this insult Escalante endorsed Bush, saying that 'If I ask him to help me out, he's going to do it.'[94] But SVRI exit polls showed that Michael Dukakis won 79 percent of the Mexican American vote, with George Bush getting only 21 percent; in California, Dukakis won 75 percent of the Latino vote.[95]

Notes

1. George Ramos, 'American Dream Lives in Barrio', *Los Angeles Times*, 27 July 1983; Louis Sahagun, 'Boyle Heights Couple Found Their Dream House Right Down the Street', *Los Angeles Times*, 31 July 1983; Louis Sahagun, 'Boyle Heights: Problems, Pride and Promise', *Los Angeles Times*, 31 July 1983; Virginia Escalante, Nancy Rivera and Victor Valle, 'Inside the World of Latinos', *Los Angles Times*, 30 July 1983. The articles are part of a Pulitzer Prize–winning series, *Southern California's Latino Community*, a series of articles reprinted from the *Times* (Los Angeles: Los Angeles Times, 1983), pp. 82–91.

2. Mary Santoli Pardo, 'Identity and Resistance: Mexican American Women and Grassroots Activism in Two Los Angeles Communities' (Ph.D. dissertation, University of California, Los Angeles, 1990), pp. 98–101. The figures quoted are for 1990, but they were roughly the same in 1985.

3. Ibid.

4. Ibid., pp. 129, 132–4.

5. See Rodolfo Acuña, 'Forming the Debate: The Present Interprets the Past', Renato Rosaldo Lecture Monograph (Tucson, Az.: Mexican American Studies & Research Center, University of Arizona, 1992), pp. 55–82.

6. Erlinda's mother was one of the founders of the Community Service Organization, in which she was also active.

7. Raymundo Reynoso, 'La incansable lucha de una activista comunitaria', *La Opinión*, 6 Aug. 1989.

8. Resurrection Parish was itself a community under seige, with parishioners from the Estrada Courts Housing Project, and neighborhood renters and homeowners. No doubt the presence of Fr Moretta brought with it the moral authority of the Church, and parishioners who would not ordinarily have participated in marches.

9. Pardo, 'Identity and Resistance', p. 149.

10. See Rodolfo Acuña, 'Richard Polanco: The Assemblyman Who's King of the 55th', *Los Angeles Herald-Examiner*, 1 April 1988.

11. Villalobos had been a political player for some time, raising funds for various Chicano politicos. He had good relations with state Senator Pro Tem David Roberti, Art Torres and other politicos.

12. The crusade against the prison gained momentum in the summer of 1986 when newly elected Democratic Assemblyman Richard Polanco of Los Angeles angered Eastsiders by voting in the Assembly Public Safety Committee for a bill that resurrected the construction of a 1,500-bed medium-security prison in downtown Los Angeles. During his campaign, Polanco had repeatedly promised to vote against the downtown site – and without his vote, the bill would have died in committee. Weeks earlier, the same committee had voted against the downtown site, favoring instead a location near Magic Mountain. Shortly after the Eastside Democrat took office, however, Assembly Speaker Willie Brown removed Richmond Democrat Robert J. Campbell, who had voted against the downtown site, and replaced him with Polanco. That same day Polanco voted against locating prisons near Magic Mountain and Disneyland before supporting the East Los Angeles site.

A major reason for Polanco's reversal involved personal politics. Brown may have wanted to discipline Assemblywoman Gloria Molina, who had angered Brown by not being a 'team player'. The story went that Molina had backed Hernández against Polanco during the previous election, costing Brown a bundle to get Polanco elected. Polanco in turn needed to repay Brown, whom he feared more than he did the Chicano community; communities have short memories compared with Brown, who never forgot who had crossed him. Ultimately, the prison project involved Brown's paying his debts to the state Correctional Officers' Association, which was a major campaign contributor, and a deal made with Deukmejian. By contrast, the Mothers movement was in its early stage, and no one had expected it to grow to the proportions that it did. To a seasoned politico the threats by the Mothers of East Los Angeles to run a candidate against Polanco were just that, threats. Ultimately, Polanco ran unopposed for re-election. Moreover, he did not support the prison bill once out of committee.

13. The California Correctional Peace Officers Association gave $921,000 to Pete Wilson in 1990 and $533,000 in 1994. Mary Lynne Vellinga, 'Guards Hit Jackpot with Overtime Pay', *Sacra-*

mento Bee, 23 April 1995.

14. A 1982 law required approval of the downtown site before new prisons nearing completion in San Diego and Stockton could be opened. In the case of these sites, Deukmejian had insisted on a full environmental impact report. Rodolfo Acuña, 'Another Prison No Reward for Latino Unity', *Los Angeles Herald-Examiner*, 11 Sept. 1986.

15. See Rodolfo Acuña, 'Governor Must Curb L.A. Prison Obsession', *Los Angeles Herald-Examiner*, 12 June 1987.

16. Rodolfo Acuña, 'L.A. Latinos Need a New Ed Roybal', *Los Angeles Herald-Examiner*, 23 Jan. 1987.

17. Rodolfo Acuña, 'The Coming Battle in the New Latino District', *Los Angeles Herald-Examiner*, 31 Oct. 1986.

18. Rodolfo Acuña, 'The New Latino District Needs a Risk Taker', *Los Angeles Herald-Examiner*, 1 Feb. 1987.

19. Bill Boyarsky, 'Unopposed Molina's 1989 Campaign: Hike the Voter Registration in 1st District', *Los Angeles Times*, 12 March 1989.

20. Rodolfo Acuña, 'How Not to Choose Latino Candidates', *Los Angeles Herald-Examiner*, 17 April 1987.

21. Rodolfo Acuña, 'Taking the Measure of Gloria Molina', *Los Angeles Herald-Examiner*, 5 Feb. 1988.

22. Rodolfo Acuña, 'The Latinas Make Their Mark', *Los Angeles Herald-Examiner*, 5 Aug. 1988.

23. To Roybal-Allard's credit, she chose a cadre of young aides such as Marta Molina, Miguel Méndivil and Martín Gutiérrez in her Los Angeles office and María Ochoa in Sacramento. These aides pushed community issues around the theme of environmental racism, playing a leading role in the prison issue and the fight against the Vernon incinerator.

24. Eric Mann with the Watchdog Organizing Committee, a pioneering study of the politics of L.A.'s air pollution: *L.A.'s Lethal Air. New Strategies for Policy, Organizing, and Action* (Los Angeles: A Labor/Community Strategy Center Book, 1991); also during this period there was a fight over the siting of toxic waste dumps, Amy Pyle, 'Lopez Canyon to Stay Open, State Rules After Tests', *Los Angeles Times*, 21 March 1989.

25. As reconstructed by Juana Gutiérrez, Ricardo Gutiérrez and Aurora Castillo, quoted in Mary Santoli Pardo, 'Mexican American Women Grassroots Community Activists: Mothers of East Los Angeles', *Frontiers*, vol. 11, no. 1 (1990), p. 4.

26. Rodolfo Acuña, 'The Fire That Too Many Are Willing to Forget', *Los Angeles Herald-Examiner*, 3 June 1988.

27. According to a report by the United Church of Christ's Commission on Racial Justice, 'Toxic Wastes and Race in the United States', 15 million Blacks and 8 million Latinos lived in communities with one or more licensed toxic-waste sites, numbers far out of proportion to their percentage of the population and clearly justifying charges of environmental racism. During the struggle against the prison, and the subsequent fight against the incinerator, Roybal-Allard successfully sponsored AB58, which protected all Californians by requiring an environmental impact report before the construction of hazardous waste incinerators, Pardo, *Frontiers*, p. 2.

28. Rodolfo Acuña, 'The Armageddon in Our Backyard', *Los Angeles Times*, 7 June 1989.

29. See Rodolfo Acuña, 'The Fate of East L.A.: One Big Jail', *Los Angeles Herald-Examiner*, 28 April 1989.

30. Rodolfo Acuña, 'Latinos Are Fighting for Community, Not Just for Property Values', *Los Angeles Times*, 22 Jan. 1990.

31. Pardo, 'Mexican American Women Grassroots Community Activists', pp. 18; Pardo, 'Identity and Resistance', p. 190.

32. Mark Gladstone, 'L.A. Prison Scuttled, Lancaster's Will Open in February', *Los Angeles Times*, 15 Sept. 1992.

33. Ron Russell, 'Latino Leaders Protest Plans to Build Prison on Eastside', *Los Angeles Times*, 21 July 1992; Alejandro Balotta, 'Se conjura amenaza de la carcel en ELA', *La Opinión*, 15 Sept. 1992; Louis Sahagun, 'Mothers of Conviction', *Los Angeles Times*, 16 Sept. 1992.

34. Within the Chicano community, gender issues never proved to be as contentious as many pundits forecast. Most candidates were pro-choice on abortion rights, and although the community is heavily Catholic, abortion did not become an issue. For example, Father Moretta was a

major anti-abortion leader within the archdiocese, but he worked closely with Molina, who as pro-choice. Thus the fact that Molina received money from the Fund for a Feminist Majority never became an issue, since her views appeared to be compatible with those of her constituents.

35. Louis Freedberg, 'Latinos: Building Power from the Ground Up', *California Journal* (Jan. 1987), p. 14; Alatorre's style was perhaps more effective in Sacramento, where deals could be made without the intense public scrutiny of the local media. Local exposure was invaluable for the ambitious politician because of the critical mass of voters and press in the Los Angeles area. The downside was that the politico was constantly under a microscope. In the case of Alatorre and other Chicano politicians there was also the buzzsaw of conflicting agendas. For instance, many Chicano activists criticized Alatorre when he voted against an ordinance allowing Occidental Petroleum to drill for oil in the Pacific Palisades. Alatorre's logic was probably that the lease brought money to the city and projects that benefited the Eastside, a reason that, although not ideologically correct, was a way of thumbing his nose at the Westside: see Rodolfo Acuña, 'The West Side's Unfair Shot at Richard Alatorre', *Los Angeles Herald-Examiner*, 13 March 1988.

36. Richard Simon, '$6 Million Spent by County in Voting Case', *Los Angeles Times*, 22 Jan. 1991; Philip Hager, 'How Panel Redrew the Political Map', *Los Angeles Times*, 8 Dec. 1991. Chicano empowerment did not come without a fight. To defend their 1981 redistricting, the supervisors hired John McDermott, a pricey Century City lawyer who had helped Pomona defeat a voting-rights suit. He argued that it was impossible to create a Latino district, and that such forms of racism as lynchings, vigilantism and 'greaser' laws were all in the distant past. It was up to the plaintiffs to prove a current pattern of racism and its malicious effects. See Rodolfo Acuña, 'Diluting Latino Power, Pride Has to Be Stopped', *Los Angeles Herald-Examiner*, 3 Feb. 1989.

37. *Yolanda Garza, et al. v. County of Los Angeles, et al.*, Case 88-Aug. 24, 1988; also *Dolores Cruz Gomez v. The City of Watsonville*, 852 F. 2d. 1186 (9th Cir. 1988). Lisbeth Lipari wrote in the *Texas Observer*, 'The practice of gerrymandering – drawing political boundaries to favor certain political interests – traces its dishonorable provenance to the earliest days of this country. The word is derived from the name Elbridge Gerry, a signer of the Declaration of Independence who was trying to use cartography to give him what democracy would not: a safe return to office. In contemporary times gerrymandering has, on occasion, been used for something far more insidious than mere partisan bickering; namely, as a mask for racism.' Lisbeth Lipari, 'Shapes of Things to Come', *Texas Observer*, 4 Oct. 1991, p. 5.

38. Richard Simon and Frederick M. Muir, 'L.A. Supervisor Districts Illegal', *Los Angeles Times*, 14 June 1990. Kenyon wrote, 'During the 1981 redistricting process, the supervisors' primary objective was to protect their incumbencies and that of their allies. This objective, however, was inescapably linked to the continued fragmentation of the Hispanic population core.' The county's legal expenses would eventually cost taxpayers some $12 million.

39. 'Board: A Look at Closed-Door Politics', *Los Angeles Times*, 5 Jan. 1990.

40. Richard Simon, 'County Bias Alleged in Remap Case', *Los Angeles Times*, 4 Jan. 1990; Nancy D. Kates, 'New Kingdoms for the Five Kings: Discrimination, Redistricting and the Los Angeles County Board of Supervisors', President Fellow of Harvard College, Case Program, Kennedy School of Government, 1991, C 16-91-1042-0.

41. Richard Simon and Frederick M. Muir, 'Board Votes to Shift Schabarum in Redistricting', *Los Angeles Times*, 13 Dec. 1989; Joe Scott, 'Schabarum Needs More Than a Latino Grandmother', *Los Angeles Times*, 17 Dec. 1989. The Justice Department suit was brought in 1988. In order to avoid a lawsuit the supervisors attempted to sacrifice Schabarum. It was speculated at this point that Richard Alatorre would run for the new seat, which would have been 63% Latino.

42. Richard Simon, 'Judge Kenyon Enlivened Case with a Gentle Wit', *Los Angeles Times*, 5 June 1990.

43. Edward J. Boyer and Richard Simon, 'Racing to Be Century's 1st Latino Supervisor', *Nuestro Tiempo*, 20 Dec. 1990; Ricardo Romo, 'Southern California and the Origins of Latino Civil Rights Activism', *Western Legal History*, vol. 3, no. 2 (Summer/Fall 1990), pp. 379–406.

44. Rodolfo Acuña, 'Shut Out by Historical Amnesia', *Los Angeles Times*, 25 Feb. 1990.

45. Cited in Tracy Wilkinson, 'Political Power Is Key to Progress for Latinos, L.A. County', *Los Angeles Times*, 7 Sept. 1989; Maribel Hastings, 'El Poder es vital para realizar mejorar', *La Opinión*, 10 Dec. 1991.

46. Rep. Edward R. Roybal hinted at one point that he would run to prevent the political

bloodletting that would surely result if more than one Latino candidate declared. As the respected dean of local Latino politicians, Roybal had in effect the first right of refusal: the belief in Latino political circles that Roybal's victory in the 1958 Board of Supervisors race had been stolen from him would further preempt a challenger. The names of Molina and Alatorre were also mentioned. Rodolfo Acuña, 'Now, the Fight for the Spoils', *Los Angeles Times*, 12 Aug. 1990.

47. Boyer and Simon, 'Racing to Be Century's 1st Latino Supervisor'.

48. Edmund Newton, 'San Gabriel Valley Becomes the New Power Base of Latino Votes', *Los Angeles Times*, 21 January 1990.

49. Ibid.

50. Richard Simon, '1st District Race Comes into Focus', *Los Angeles Times*, 14 Nov. 1990; Boyer and Simon, 'Racing to Be Century's 1st Latino Supervisor', *Nuestro Tiempo*, 20 Dec. 1990.

51. Torres had been elected to the state Assembly in 1974 and to the Senate in 1982. He was backed by Alatorre and Supervisor Kenny Hahn.

52. Molina's main problem in making up her mind was money. Her supporters estimated that she would have to raise a million dollars. Molina had previously relied more on volunteers, which gave her independence from the Eastside brokers. As of August 1990, the evaluation was that Alatorre would not run, since he had a higher risk factor than Molina. He did have the advantage of support from labor, the Community Redevelopment Administration and Downtown developers – all good sources of money. He also had an extended network of middle-class Chicano professionals who contributed to his campaigns, altogether giving him a warchest of $600,000. Alatorre would, however, have to run for supervisor concurrently with his re-election bid for the council. He had also recently faced an unsuccessful recall staged by disidents in El Sereno, and had had to spend $270,000 to defeat that effort.

Part of the new supervisorial district, on the other hand, fell in Molina's council district and her old Assembly district, which was now held by her ally Lucille Roybal-Allard. The new district was 71% Latino and 12% Anglo. Moreover, Molina had a strong ally in Congressman Ed Roybal. According to sources who chose not to be identified, Roybal told Alatorre that he was running for the seat because he wanted to stop Alatorre from announcing, thus giving Molina more time to organize. Jill Stewart and Hector Tobar, 'District Feedback, Residents Savor Chance to Pick a Latino Supervisor', *Los Angeles Times*, 14 Nov. 1990; Stewart and Tobar reported a political rift in which Reps. Roybal and Esteban Torres backed Molina at a secret meeting while Alatorre demurred.

53. Based on the investigative articles by Beth Barrett and David Parish in the *Daily News*, 7 Oct. 1990. This series is the most inclusive collection on the L.A. County Sheriff's Department.

54. Rodolfo Acuña, 'Where Did All the Vital Issues Go in the 1st District?', *Los Angeles Times*, 13 Jan. 1991.

55. Hector Tobar, 'The Politics of Anger', *Los Angeles Times Magazine*, 3 Jan. 1993, p. 13.

56. At the time Local 660 was in the throes of an internal battle, with a leadership made up of whites and Blacks that seemed to ignore growing Latino aspirations to share in the leadership.

57. 'Molina's Anti-union Attack Is Pure Reagan', *Los Angeles Times*, 15 Feb. 1991.

58. Bill Boyarsky, 'In 30 Years History Came Full Circle, from Roybal to Molina', *Los Angeles Times*, 23 Feb. 1991; 'An Election Day to Make History', *Los Angeles Times*, 19 Feb. 1991.

59. Rodolfo Acuña, 'The Candidate Who Upset Latino Politics', *Los Angeles Times*, 8 June 1990.

60. He was able to amass a war chest that made it possible for him to put his cronies into elected offices in the small incorporated cities within his district. In addition, he had the power to make political appointments. From 1981 to 1987, Schabarum contributed at least $850,000 to other candidates, including $213,000 to Dana. He spent another $440,000 in passing Proposition 140, a proposition limiting the number of terms state legislators can serve. Schabarum forgave another $1 million in loans, making sizeable contributions to conservative causes.

61. Victor Valle and Rodolfo Torres, 'There's More Power Than Votes: Latinos Should Ask Pete Schabarum', *Los Angeles Times*, 23 June 1991.

62. Richard Simon, '2 Measures Would Shift Power of County Operation', *Los Angeles Times*, 12 Oct. 1992. Bill Boyarsky called the changes that took place during this period 'a county revolution', Boyarsky, 'A County Revolution in the Making', *Los Angeles Times*, 26 Aug. 1992.

63. Tom Chorneau, 'Winds of Change Blow in County', *Daily News*, 26 July 1992.

64. This figure was later revised to $8.8 million, Cheryl Thompson, 'Dixon Spent 8.8 Million on Offices', *Daily News*, 9 Sept. 1992.

65. Frederick Muir, 'Supervisor Dana Urges Dixon to Quit County Post', *Los Angeles Times*, 17 July 1992. Dixon was arrogant: in the midst of the 1992 budget crisis he gave 70 employees 8% raises. While he was earning $174,610, he gave himself a 3% raise. His pension would be $137,595 annually, an increase of $22,159 as a result of controversial pension changes that he recommended. Cheryl W. Thompson, 'Dixon Gives Office Staff Raises', *Daily News*, 20 Aug. 1992.

66. Hector Tobar, 'County Hall Became Temple Street Circus', *Los Angeles Times*, 22 July 1992.

67. Richard Simon and Frederick M. Muir, 'Supervisors Propose Further Reductions in Powers of CAO', *Los Angeles Times*, 23 July 1992.

68. Hector Tobar, 'County Plan Urges Unpaid Workdays', *Los Angeles Times*, 28 July 1992.

69. Cheryl W. Thompson, 'County Unions Resist Proposed Salary Cuts', *Daily News*, 28 July 1992.

70. Bill Boyarsky, 'It's So Bad, L.A. County Might Have to Shape Up', *Los Angeles Times*, 6 July 1992.

71. Bill Boyarsky, 'County Workers' Loss of Traditional Job Security Will Hurt Public', *Los Angeles Times*, 15 Aug. 1993.

72. 'The Economics of the Underclass', *Los Angeles Times*, 17 July 1993; Frederick M. Muir, 'Revised Budget Slashes Benefits, Aid to Poor', *Los Angeles Times*, 10 July 1993. The county received $134 million in sales tax revenues for public safety, which could not be diverted to other uses. Hufford recommended cutting relief benefits by 27% to the state-mandated minimum of $212, closing four of the six comprehensive health clinics, devastating children's services and cutting the libraries and parks to the bone; David Bloom and Mark Katches, 'County Outlines Revised Budget Plan', *Daily News*, 10 July 1993.

73. In a parallel struggle, 10,000 Department of Water and Power workers walked out the next day because of stalled negotiations. Los Angeles city officials had to secure a court order requiring most of them to return to work. Mark Lacey and Richard Simon, '10,000 in DWP Strike; Most Are Ordered Back', *Los Angeles Times*, 2 Sept. 1993.

74. Clara Rivera, 'County Finds Anger Not Joy Over Its Big Windfall', *Los Angeles Times*, 19 Sept. 1993.

75. Frederick M. Muir, 'L.A. Supervisors Vary Widely in Office Expenses', *Los Angeles Times*, 26 July 1993.

76. Hector Tobar, 'Gloria Molina and the Politics of Anger', *Los Angeles Times Magazine*, 3 Jan. 1993, pp. 10–13, 32.

77. Bill Boyarsky, 'The Tasks Facing Outsider Reed as County's New CAO', *Los Angeles Times*, 20 Oct. 1993.

78. See Carlos Navarro and Rodolfo Acuña, 'In Search of Community: A Comparative Essay on Mexicans in Los Angeles and San Antonio', in Norman M. Klein and Martin J. Schiesl, eds, *20th-Century Los Angeles: Power, Promotion, and Social Conflict* (Claremont, Calif.: Regina Books, 1990), pp. 195–226, for a discussion of the structural differences between the two cities and the varying fortunes of struggles for Chicano political empowerment.

79. Robert R. Brishetto, *The Hispanic Electorate* (San Antonio, Tex.: Hispanic Policy Development Project, 1984); see also *Southwest Voter Research Notes*, Nov. 1986, on the Texas gubernatorial elections and the role of Chicano voters.

80. 'SVREP Board Declares California Top Priority', *California RPC Report*, Southwest Voter Registration, Oct. 1986, a special issue on California.

81. Juan Vásquez, 'Watch Out for Willie Velásquez', *Nuestro Tiempo*, March 1979, pp. 20–24. Velásquez was an exceptional Chicano leader who was completely loyal to the cause of popular empowerment through voter registration. As a leader, he was generous and did not allow himself to be pulled into the petty gossip and rivalries that are so common in the world of politics. More than registering Chicanos to vote, Willie was out to realize an idea, creating a winning attitude in Mexicans. Willie was tireless, and drew motivation from remarks like those of conservative Texas Republican Bill Clements, who, when asked what he had to offer Mexican Americans, replied, 'I'm not running for governor of Mexico, you know' (p. 22). Velásquez was one of the first to point out that the 1980s might be a decade of frustration (p. 23).

82. Rodolfo Acuña, 'The Young Chicano Who Made Latinos into Kingmakers', *Los Angeles Herald-Examiner*, 1 July 1988.

83. Rodolfo Acuña, 'Don't Count Cranston Among Latinos' Friends', *Los Angeles Herald-Exam-*

iner, 4 Aug. 1989.

84. Freedberg, 'Latinos: Building Power from the Ground Up', pp. 12–13. Latinos suffered setbacks with the defeat of Cruz Reynoso for reselection to the state Supreme Court and the passage of Proposition 63, the English-only initiative. That year 41% of Latinos supported Proposition 63, and 46% voted for George Deukmejian.

85. Rodolfo Acuña, 'A Steady Rise for the Brown Republicans', *Los Angeles Times*, 20 Nov. 1989.

86. Robert R. Brischetto and Rodolfo O. de la Garza, 'The Mexican American Electorate: Political Participation and Ideology', *The Mexican American Electorate Series, Hispanic Population Studies Program*, Occasional Paper No. 3, Southwest Voter Registration Education Project, San Antonio, p. 6; Robert R. Brischetto, 'Latino Political Participation: 1972–1984', Presented at the League of Women Voters Educational Fund, Conference on Electoral Participation, Washington, D.C., 18 July 1985, p. 1.

87. A SVREP poll showed that 33% of its respondents in San Antonio said that both parents were foreign-born, compared to 75% in East Los Angeles, Brischetto and de la Garza, 'Mexican American Electorate', p. 5.

88. Ibid, p. 2.

89. Also see Robert R. Brischetto and Willie Velásquez, *The Hispanic Electorates* (Washington, D.C.: Hispanic Policy Development Project, 1984); see Frank A. Bean, Elizabeth H. Stephen and Wolfgang Opitz, 'The Mexican Origin Population in the United States: A Demographic Overview', in Rodolfo O. de la Garza, ed., *The Mexican American Experience* (Austin, Tex.: University of Texas Press, 1985), pp. 58–69.

90. Brischetto, 'Latino Political Participation: 1972–1984', p. 13.

91. James McCrory, 'Hispanic Ballot Impact Detailed', *San Antonio Express*, 29 Nov. 1984. Willie Velásquez pointed out that Mexican American voter participation went up 22% from 1980, with the greatest support for Reagan coming from Mexican Americans earning $50,000 or more. 'Eighty-six percent of Mexican-Americans 65 or older label themselves Democrats, while only 57 percent of Mexican-American voters 35 or younger identify as Democrats.' What is amazing is that the Democratic Party did not take note of these cracks in Mexican American support and attempt to win back their loyalty. Instead, they continued a neocolonial policy of attempting to control them politically. Liberals and radicals were no less shallow in attempting to explain these cracks by saying that Mexican Americans were culturally conservative. 'Poll Shows Hispanics Not Part of GOP Landslide', *Houston Chronicle*, 19 Nov. 1984; Javier Rodriguez, 'Hispanic Reagan Vote Downplayed', *San Antonio Light*, 29 Nov. 1984.

92. Rodolfo Acuña, 'Latinos Must Beware of Those Spanish-speaking Candidates', *Los Angeles Herald-Examiner*, 7 Oct. 1988.

93. Ibid.

94. 'Bush Won't Stand and Deliver for Latinos', *Los Angeles Herald-Examiner*, 4 Nov. 1988.

95. Ibid, p. 2.

5

Politics for the Few

The success of Chicanos and African Americans in local politics has threatened conservatives, and they in turn have responded by resurrecting the idea that redistricting to increase the political representation of minorities was undemocratic. In June 1993, the US Supreme Court ruled in *Shaw* v. *Reno* that the Constitution does not permit 'racial gerrymandering', citing Justice Sandra Day O'Connor: 'Racial gerrymandering, even for remedial purposes, may Balkanize us into competing racial factions ... It threatens to carry us further from the goal of a political system in which race no longer matters.'[1] The court's five–four decision came in a North Carolina case brought by five white southerners who claimed that a congressional district deliberately drawn to allow Blacks a chance of election was unconstitutional. The Supreme Court directed the US District Court in North Carolina to examine those charges. Fortunately, in August 1994 the North Carolina court upheld the constitutionality of the challenged district. More such legal challenges are expected, however, as conservatives press their legal campaign.[2] ACLU attorney Mark Rosenbaum has pointed out the irony of the conservatives' legal argument: 'What is disturbing is that, in the past, bizarrely drawn districts were approved for white incumbents. The only time the court has lifted its eyes is when districts like this are drawn for the benefit of minorities who have been pushed around by the political process.' Indeed, what is so offensive about the ruling is not that the court chose to protect the privilege of white voters but the absurdity of claiming that US politics has ever been colorblind. In any case, *Shaw* v. *Reno* has had a chilling effect on hopes for electing more Latinos as well as African Americans.

Along with its legal strategy to reverse Latino and African American political gains, the right has also responded with attacks on the ideological front. Peter Skerry, a former fellow at the Brookings Institution and the ultraconservative American Enterprise Institute, became director of UCLA's Center for American Politics and Public Policy in Washington, D.C. While at the American Enterprise Institute, he published *Mexican Americans: The Ambivalent Minor-*

ity (1993), a tract that became a *Los Angeles Times* Book Award winner. It is the product of a dozen years of well-funded research, which unfortunately reflects Skerry's Eurocentric biases rather than a knowledge of the Chicano community.[3] Skerry anticipates Justice O'Connor's reference to the 'Balkanization' of American politics – a common theme of conservatives – and argues that what he calls 'race politics' on the part of Mexican Americans in California has been counterproductive. He was especially critical of redistricting to achieve Chicano representation, ignoring the fact that electoral district boundaries in the US have always incorporated political considerations based on race. Skerry offers instead an ahistorical and condescending analysis:

> Mexican Americans emerge in California as not just any interest group, but – in keeping with the dynamics of our new American political system – as one organized around an idea. That idea is that, like blacks, Mexican Americans comprise a racial minority group. This abstraction poses no problems for the ideologically oriented Chicano activists who see the world in such terms.[4]

As proof of Mexican American ambivalence, Skerry points out that over half designate themselves as white. Considering that Mexicans were for many years officially classified as Caucasian, this is not surprising.[5] Of course, it is one thing to be officially classified as Caucasian and another to be thought of and treated as one.

Skerry blamed the media for the invention of Mexican American racial politics in California, which according to him generated an unrealistic 'revolution of expectations'. As a result, Skerry argues, Mexican Americans erroneously chose the strategy of Black Americans instead of the more assimilationist, entrepreneurial one pursued by European ethnics. Instead of militance, Mexican Americans should exercise 'a degree of patience and a sense of proportion lacking among the media as well as among many Mexican American leaders.'[6] In his scenario the Industrial Areas Foundation organizations provide the proper model for Chicano advancement, while MALDEF has misled the Chicano community by following the Black example.

Although Skerry's analysis has received considerable attention, key points of it are in fact absurd. First, Mexican Americans did not need the media to instill a sense of race in their community's consciousness. Concepts like *La Raza* predated the Chicano movement or the media's sudden interest in Chicanos. Second, Southwestern history is replete with examples of racial politics. Third, though *some* Texas IAF activists may say that the concepts of race and culture are not important, race is an important element in Chicano lives and Chicano culture. IAF leaders and rank-and-file members communicate among themselves on a unique, ethnic basis.

Skerry's main obsession is the Voting Rights Act, which, he emphasizes, applied only to African Americans until amended in 1975. But federal courts have in fact consistently held that Mexicans have suffered the 'systematic racial discrimination experienced by blacks.'[7] In attacking the Voting Rights Act, Skerry falsely implies that a Mexican American could have won a seat on the Los Angeles County Board of Supervisors without redistricting,[8] and chooses to ignore the evidence of collusion to exclude Chicanos by the supervisors when they drew council district boundaries in 1981.

Skerry charges that in pursuit of redistricting, Chicanos are in effect creating rotten boroughs,[9] and calls for limiting Mexican American representation to those who are eligible to vote – a position that is in direct opposition to the Supreme Court's 1962 'one-man, one-vote' ruling. Skerry's proposal would have the effect of penalizing young communities in favor of older populations and would discriminate against residents versus citizens, flying in the face of legal precedent. According to Skerry,

> [t]he term [rotten boroughs] could not be more appropriate, since it harkens back to an era when standards of voter participation and officeholder accountability were far less rigorous than today. The irony, of course, is that these rotten boroughs follow from today's more demanding standards. The result is that we have increased Mexican-American representation, but only in the most formal and delimited sense.

Skerry strongly advocates that Mexican Americans use the model of the European ethnics to pursue assimilation. But he ignores the fact that discrimination against immigrants from southern and eastern Europe did not last as long and was not as intense as discrimination against Mexicans. Ironically, in making this argument he would deny the Mexican American community the very political and economic tools that were used by European immigrant groups. Representation, far from exclusively benefiting elites, translates into role models, stepping stones and jobs for the entire population, helping to reduce the gap between rich and poor based on race/class segmentation.

Proposition 13: Tight Budgets and Mean Streets

The attack on redistricting and the work of ideologues like Skerry exemplify the rise of rightwing forces in California, as elsewhere in the United States, from the late 1970s to the early 1990s. In California, severe economic recession further frustrated the aspirations of Latinos. So did the state's tax structure, especially after 1978. That year saw the passage of Proposition 13, a ballot initiative that slashed city and county revenue by reducing property taxes. Prop. 13 helps explain the nasty politics and the rightist political mood in Los Angeles, for the state of the city's political climate is directly tied to the level of government funding.

Prop. 13 slashed an average of 57 percent of each city's tax revenue, a total of $6.6 billion statewide in the first year the measure was in effect. The measure thus created governmental gridlock, by design tying the hands of government, which could not increase taxes without a two-thirds popular vote. Before Proposition 13 (1977-78) property taxes had provided 46.1 percent of government revenue; sales taxes, 32.4 percent; and other taxes, 21 percent. After Prop. 13 went into effect (1990-91), property taxes accounted for 27 percent, sales and use taxes 32.4 percent and other taxes, 40.6 percent.[10] Despite the conservative arguments in favor of Prop. 13, which emphasized local initiative and control of government, the measure actually resulted in a massive power shift from city councils and county boards of supervisors to state government – the one remaining source of new revenue. In addition, the new property tax system encouraged cities and counties to adopt zoning and other inducements to attract retail stores rather than high-wage industries or housing.[11]

Schools, hospitals and clinics, libraries, indeed, state and local government functions of all types began to shrink after Prop. 13 passed, and they continue to do so. California's infrastructure, once the envy of the nation, has been crumbling.[12] The inequities inherent in Prop. 13 were also becoming obvious. Limits on property taxes benefited older, mostly white, Californians who had been subsidized by the G.I. Bill, the FHA loans, federal aid to education and other government programs, and who now had decent jobs as well as their own homes. Under Prop. 13, access to these same benefits was denied to a younger generation, a larger proportion of whom were people of color.

PROPOSITION 13's IMPACT ON TAX EQUITY

Area	Market Value (Dollars)	Assessment (Dollars)	Taxes (Dollars)	Home Size (Square Feet)	Lot Size (Square Feet)
Palos Verdes	1,400,000	169,897	1,700	3,890	17,000
Venice	214,000	214,000	2,140	690	1,695
Belair Estates	9,000,000	785,000	7,850	10,196	69,260
West L.A.	875,999	885,000	8,850	2,100	6,750

SOURCE: 'High Court Hearing Poses Prop. 13's Stiffest Challenge', *Los Angeles Times*, 24 Feb. 1992.

The unfairness of Prop. 13 lies in its basing property taxes on assessed value, rather than on market value. Moreover, assessed value is based on a property's 1975 value, and a new assessment is made only when the property is sold. As a result, new buyers in poor sections of Los Angeles pay more than wealthy homeowners who purchased their houses before 1978: for example, a person buying a 1,700-square-foot home for $214,000 may pay the same taxes as a wealthy suburbanite with a home worth $1.4 million. Because of the youth of the Latino community, the effects of Proposition 13 fell disproportionately on it.[13] New buyers paid five times and even more in taxes than neighbors who had lived in their homes since 1978. According to *Los Angeles Times* reporter David Savage, 'A new buyer in Santa Monica found himself paying $4,650, almost 17 times more than his neighbor whose property tax was $270.'

Prop. 13 had another economic impact on Latinos: it reduced the number of available jobs. As marginalized groups in American politics achieve some political representation, their numbers in public sector jobs increase: historically, civil service jobs have been a stepping stone for newcomers. With economic restructuring wiping out jobs in heavy industry, public sector jobs are some of the few left paying above the minimum wage and including health insurance. Throughout the 1980s, local governments struggled to hold on to their job base. The state legislature did not have the two-thirds vote necessary to increase taxes, and so it shifted the burden to local governments. The losers were health, human and welfare services, libraries and civil service jobs.[14] For Mexicans and other working-class people, the civil service route into mainstream employment became much harder to pursue.

Unfortunately, most politicians, including the new Chicano officeholders, were unwilling to risk the wrath of Prop. 13 supporters. Proposition 13 remained part of state law, not because it was fair, but as because of the greed of old California homeowners and the gutlessness of politicians,[15] who together kept in place a 'distasteful and unwise' tax system.[16]

Newly elected Latino politicos did not always act collectively, nor did they always represent the interests of their community. They failed too often to exercise the leadership needed by an oppressed minority. This hesitancy was not limited to Proposition 13; it ranged from police brutality to proposals to break up the Los Angeles schools.[17] From the politician's vantage point, such compromises were necessary to get elected and to stay in office. If Latino officials strayed too far from the norm, regardless of how regressive it actually was for the Latino community and for all working-class people, party sources withheld support and backed candidates who were more acquiescent. Getting elected had become an end in itself.

Musical Chairs: 'Don't Cry for Me, Angelinos'

The musical *Evita* contains a scene in which the colonels play musical chairs, with each of the colonels scrambling for a chair as the music stops.[18] To a great extent Chicano politics has resembled this dance of the colonels. Molina's election to the Board of Supervisors in 1990 opened her council seat, touching off another dance of the colonels. When the music stopped Molina blessed Mike Hernández over the objections of some of her staff, who thought that her seat should go to a Chicana. The Alatorre camp did not challenge Hernández, who took office in August 1991.

Hernández, a longtime political activist, had run a strong race for the Assembly in the mid 1980s, losing to Richard Polanco. Hernández was expected to nestle easily in the Molina camp. However, a rift developed in 1992 when Hernández unilaterally endorsed a candidate for an Assembly seat. Molina saw this move as a sign of disloyalty, and the rift became permanent though not open. Meanwhile, Hernández developed a reputation as a sincere and hardworking council member with a dedicated staff that worked the district, especially the Pico-Union area.[19] He forcefully advocated the interests of his district to the point of alienating some of his colleagues. They advised Hernández to 'narrow his focus'. To his credit, Hernández was the only local Latino politician to consistently speak out on police abuse issues, and was generally supportive of immigrant rights. Notable among Latinos for his visibility during the Rodney King uprisings, Hernández demanded that the INS stop its mass deportations during that period.

What unsettled many of the council members about Hernández was that he seriously tried to argue that the wealthier neighborhoods took the resources that should be used in the inner city.[20] His colleagues preferred the 'let's make a deal' approach of Councilman Richard Alatorre, who, despite criticisms, has been the most effective local Latino politico at playing the game of the colonels.[21]

The 1990 Census and Reapportionment

Reapportionment time arrived again in 1991. If the electoral system had been democratic with a small 'd', there would have been no question about the creation of more Latino districts. The growth of the Latino population during the 1980s had been substantial. According to the 1990 Census, California had a population of 29,760,021 (an undercount), 25 percent of whom were Latinos, an increase from 4,544,331 (19.1 percent of the population) in 1980 to 7,687,938 (25.8 percent) ten years later.[22] This population was heavily concentrated in ten of the state Assembly's eighty districts. Yet at the time only four of these districts were represented by Latinos. At stake in any redistricting were seats in both houses of the state legislature and in Congress.[23]

Ironically, the Chicano/Latino drive for fair redistricting did not have the same momentum as it had in 1980. Early on, the Mexican American Legal Defense and Education Fund (MALDEF) and the Southwest Voter Registration and Education Project (SVREP) assumed leadership on the Census/reapportionment issue and held a conference on redistricting. The two groups competed for leadership, but in the end SVREP did not have sufficient resources to fully implement an ambitious plan to influence the outcome of state reapportionment plans, while MALDEF already occupied this political space.

CALIFORNIA STATE ASSEMBLY DISTRICTS WITH LATINO MAJORITIES, 1990

Assembly District	Representative	Percent Latinos in District
39th	Richard Katz	53
46th	Vacant	59
47th	Teresa Hughes	70
48th	Margarite Archie-Hudson	61
55th	Richard Polanco	65
56th	Lucille Roybal-Allard	85
59th	Javier Becerra	57
60th	Sally Tanner	64
72d	Tom Umberg	57
80th	Steve Peace	53

SOURCE: Jaime Olivares, 'Mayoría hispana en 10 distritos de la Asemblea estatal', *La Opinón*, 15 April 1991.

The basic problem once again lay in the number of Latinos who actually voted. In 1990, only 844,000 Latinos voted out of a population of some 2,301,000 Latino adult citizens, 1,218,000 of whom were registered to vote.[24] In the end, Democrats at both the state and local levels acted no differently than they had in 1981, cutting Latinos out of the game. This gave Governor Pete Wilson the opening to veto three proposed reapportionment bills with the excuse that the Democratic majority was seeking an 'unfair partisan advantage'.[25] Ironically, Wilson was right; Democrats had historically used Latinos to stay in office, while drawing district boundaries in such a way as to prevent actual Latino representation.

Assembly Speaker Willie Brown urged Republican legislators to join Democrats to override Wilson's veto of the final remapping bill, but in this instance it was fortunate for Latinos that Brown could not garner sufficient votes to do so. Other groups were dissatisfied with the legislature's reapportionment process. African Americans and Asians joined Latinos in opposing the proposed state senate districts as favoring (Euroamerican) incumbents at the expense of minorities.[26] The controversy was far from exclusively a Los Angeles affair, extending the length of California.[27] Finally, a panel of three jurists headed by 74-year-old retired appellate judge George A. Brown was appointed by the chief justice of the California Supreme Court to remap districts in the state legislature and the US House of Representatives. Their plan, issued in December 1991, although favoring Republicans, did displace incumbents from both parties.[28]

The districts devised by the court made it possible for Latinos to increase their representation by 40 percent in the state legislature. However, this hardly reflected the 70 percent increase in Latino population during the 1980s.[29] If Latinos won election in all these newly drawn districts, they would still constitute only 7.5 percent of the state Assembly, even though they were 25.8 percent of the state's population. The new reapportionment plan gave Latinos the potential to elect 10 percent of the Senate and 7.7 percent of the California House delegation. Again, those numbers fell far below the Latino share of the population. Despite disappointment in the redistricting plan, the 1992 election did bring some changes. Latinos did not gain much ground in the state Senate; Charles Calderón won the 26th Senate District vacated by Joseph Montoya, Art Torres continued as senator in the 20th SD, and Ruben Ayala continued in the 34th. Demographics favored additional Chicano seats in the senate.

LOS ANGELES COUNTY SENATE SEATS, 1992 REDISTRICTING PLAN

District	Percent Democratic	Percent Republican	Percent Anglo	Percent Latino	Percent Black	Percent Asian
17th	36	53	75	16	5	3
19th	40	49	66	24	3	7
20th	57	33	42	56	5	7
21st	43	47	59	22	7	11
22d	63	24	12	67	5	16
23d	54	35	80	10	3	7
24th	58	31	18	59	2	20
25th	74	17	16	42	36	7
26th	80	12	16	37	43	5
27th	46	44	61	20	6	12
28th	53	36	47	27	13	14
29th	41	49	56	26	6	13
30th	65	27	18	75	2	4

SOURCE: 'Proposed Redistricting in Los Angeles County', *Los Angeles Times*, 3 Jan. 1992.

Because of population trends in districts such as the 20th SD in the San Fernando Valley, Latino majorities and/or pluralities will grow. If the Democratic Party were interested in the good of the Latino community, it would make the effort to groom a Latino candidate for that seat. Instead, David Roberti, whose career is based on running in heavily Latino districts, called in his political debts and became a candidate.[30]

Latinos made more gains in the Assembly, where seven won election; they became known as 'Los Siete'. They included five Assembly members from Los Angeles, of whom four were Alatorre-Willie Brown partisans; four were women.[31] The one *veterano* among them was Richard Polanco, who by now was second only to Willie Brown and Jack O'Connell of Santa Barbara in Assembly influence; his links with the Willie Brown machine had made him a major player.[32] Only Hilda Solis was clearly in the Molina camp. The Alatorre candidates were screened solely for personal loyalty. This was clearly the most ideologically diverse group of Latinos/Chicanos to be elected. Louis Caldera, Martha Escutia and Grace Napolitano were all considered conservative,[33] and all three campaigned heavily on a law-and-order platform. Caldera, a West Point graduate and a Harvard-trained attorney, flatly stated that he would have to consider whether to support bilingual education, since he considered learning English a key to success. At the opposite end, Baca supported bilingual education, as did Diane Martínez. Martínez, daughter of a congressman affiliated with the Berman-Waxman machine, fell on the left of center, although only slightly.[34] Joe Baca,[35] Richard Polanco[36] and Hilda Solis,[37] although not in the same camp, emerged as the most liberal of the group, and all won election by substantial margins.[38]

Ideologically, the diversity of *Los Siete* prevented them from forming the critical mass necessary to carry bills and programs to benefit the Latino community.[39] Polanco became chair of the Latino Caucus, but this lack of political cohesiveness means that the Latino Caucus continues to lack the influence of the Black Caucus in the state legislature.

Latinos did not do as well outside Los Angeles in the redistricting process.[40] For instance, in the 69th Assembly District, which includes parts of Santa Ana, Anaheim and Garden Grove, 65 percent of the population was Latino, but only one of ten registered voters. Incumbent Tom Umberg was not challenged, because the actual voters were older white conservatives, mostly Reagan Democrats. Latinos in Orange County, the San Fernando Valley, the Inland Empire, San Diego and San Jose were still unprepared to take advantage of the political opportunities provided by reapportionment.[41]

Latino leaders believed that they were entitled to at least ten California seats in the US House of Representatives. Dr Harry Pachón, director of the National Association of Latino Elected Officials (NALEO) pointed out that thirty of California's forty congressional districts had more than 100,000 Latino inhabitants.[42]

LOS ANGELES CONGRESSIONAL DISTRICTS IN 1992

District	Percent Democratic	Percent Republican	Percent Anglo	Percent Latino	Percent Black	Percent Asian
24th	45	45	78	13	2	6
25th	37	53	72	16	4	6
26th	58	31	34	53	6	7
27th	42	45	61	21	8	10
28th	41	49	57	24	6	13
29th	57	31	76	13	3	7
30th	61	26	15	61	4	20
31st	59	30	17	59	2	22
32d	76	15	24	30	40	7
33d	66	23	8	84	4	4
34th	61	30	27	62	2	9
35th	80	13	10	43	43	6
36th	42	46	69	15	3	12
37th	77	14	12	45	34	10
38th	49	42	58	26	8	9
39th	39	51	61	23	3	13
41st	40	50	52	31	7	10

SOURCE: 'Datos demográficos', *La Opinión*, 7 March 1992; 'Proposed Redistricting in Los Angeles County', *Los Angeles Times*, 3 Jan. 1992.

In September 1991, congressional Democrats, mindful of criticism, unveiled their own reapportionment plan.[43] It included a new Latino seat in the northeastern San Fernando Valley, extending roughly from North Hollywood to Pacoima. This district would be over 50 percent Latino, 54.5 percent Democrat and 35.5 percent Republican. The bill was carried by Rep. Howard Berman (D-Panorama), whose own district included substantial numbers of Latinos.[44] However, the ink was not dry on the bill before Assemblyman Burt Margolin (D-Los Angeles), a Berman ally, staked out his own claim to the proposed district.

The final congressional reapportionment plan led to a dash for empty or safe seats.[45] The three incumbent Latino congressmen were Edward R. Roybal (D-25th CD), Matthew Martínez (D-30th CD) and Esteban Torres (D-34th CD). The number of Latinos in their districts had grown significantly during the 1980s; however, the new congressional districts were significantly changed, and Roybal's 25th District was cannibalized. Had he chosen to run for re-election, he would have represented the new 30th CD. Even so, there was little doubt he would win handily, but Roybal shocked his supporters by resigning. At the age of seventy-six, after thirty years in Congress, Roybal announced that he wanted to devote his time to helping build the Gerontology Center at California State University, Los Angeles, which had been named after him.[46] His only regret after thirty years' service was that he hadn't been able to complete the job of passing universal health care legislation.[47] Indeed, Roybal set a standard that no other Chicano or officeholder of any color in Los Angeles has been able to reach.[48]

The newly drawn 30th District took in parts of Lincoln Heights, Highland Park, Hollywood, Silver Lake and Echo Park. MALDEF had strenuously protested these district boundaries, because although the district was 61.5 percent Latino, only 34 percent of the Latinos living there were registered voters. Assemblyman Xavier Becerra announced his candidacy for the new seat.[49] Supported by Councilman Richard Alatorre, Leticia Quezada, a member of the Board of Education running the gigantic Los Angeles Unified School District, challenged Becerra, but Becerra won the hotly contested primary. Roybal's daughter, Assemblywoman Lucille Roybal-Allard, had already declared her candidacy for the newly created Eastside district, the 33rd CD.[50]

In the November 1992 election, Becerra won with 59 percent of the vote, Martínez with 63 percent, Lucille Roybal-Allard with 63 percent, and Torres with 62 percent:[51] Roybal-Allard thus became the first Mexican American woman to enter Congress.[52] The election resulted in seventeen new Latino representatives in Congress. The leader of the California Latino delegation was clearly Rep. Esteban Torres.[53] An estimated one million Latinos voted in California alone.[54]

Latinos also made significant gains in dozens of small incorporated cities in Los Angeles County. The most dramatic of these came in Bell Gardens, part of the 'rust bowl' that was once the industrial heartland of Los Angeles, housing automobile, tire and steel plants. The 'rust bowl' included a cluster of cities – Bell, Bell Garden, Cudahy, Maywood, Huntington Park and South Gate – that were 80 to 90 percent Latino, had household incomes averaging around $23,000, and little Latino representation in local government. Plant shutdowns had sent the area into economic decline, and over a fifteen-year period the once-thriving area had become poverty-stricken. It had an overwhelmingly Latino majority, many of whom were undocumented immigrants. Yet a white minority controlled the city council, which consisted of four Anglos and one recently elected Chicana. The Euroamerican bloc was intent on driving Latinos out of Bell Gardens by passing a zoning plan that would control how many homes could be built, eventually forcing rents and home prices beyond the range of most residents.[55]

The arrogance reflected in these plans resulted in a Latino drive to gain control, and in Bell Gardens, 62.8 percent voted to recall the four Anglo councilmembers in 1992.[56] The election was a major victory, since only 45 percent of the Latino population was registered to vote.[57] State Sen. Art Torres played a large role in the recall election, which turned into a bitter campaign with racial overtones. Slow-growth advocates and the Anglo power structure played the environmental card by charging that developers were financing the recall effort.[58] In March the recall leaders, Josefina Macías, Frank B. Durán, Rodolfo García and George T. Deitch, were elected to the council. They spent more than $50,000 on an election that in the previously cosy world of Bell Gardens politics had normally cost $1,000 a candidate.[59]

By no means did victories in these small cities bring about major changes; nor did they end the internecine battles within the Mexican and Latino communities. First, Chicanos had to learn how to win. Second, few had governmental experience and the Democratic Party had not routinely provided it. In fact, some activists were angry with the Democratic Party for not supporting or contributing to their victories; even more, they were angry about the lack of technical support for victorious Chicano candidates once elected. Third, each of the cities had severe budget problems, a legacy of Euroamerican rule and structural economic decline. In Bell Gardens, for example, unemployment stood at 12 percent, and $10 million of its $19 million budget came from the Bicycle Club, a poker parlor. In addition, there was tremendous pressure on the new city council members to hire friends.

The 1992 Presidential Race

Chicanos braced themselves for the 1992 presidential campaign, believing that George Bush would make immigration the Willie Horton issue of the 1992 elections, since in the past Bush had demonstrated that he would do almost anything to be elected, and the Republican party has long exploited racial polarization. Nixon strategist John Mitchell put into effect a 'Southern strategy', while Ronald Reagan recounted anecdotes about 'welfare queens' and Bush ran ads featuring convicted murderer Willie Horton, all aimed at playing on the fears of white America. Republicans covered their tracks with references to 'unity' and 'bringing us together' (when in reality they meant the unity of white people). According to Bush, his purpose was 'Uniting Our Family, Our World'. In the end, they all pitted Black against white, white against Black, as well as both against Latinos.[60] Surprisingly, then, Bush himself did not exploit the immigration issue very much during the campaign. Perhaps it was because of his son Jeb's marriage to Columba, a Mexican, and their three children, whom Bush billed in 1988 as the 'little brown ones'.[61] More to the point, the

Bushes had close ties to Mexican elites, and during the campaign Bush continuously touted the North American Free Trade Agreement, passage of which could have been jeopardized by 'Mexican bashing'.

Democratic candidate Bill Clinton did his best to avoid anything to do with race. Veteran journalist Tad Szulc wrote after the Democratic convention of 1992: 'Latinos were not heard in a meaningful way at the convention. Their problems went unmentioned by the party's standard-bearers in their acceptance speeches.'[62] Aside from Dennis Rivera of the New York City Hospital Workers' Union, who cautioned Democrats that Latinos might not vote, no one seemed to want to rock the boat. Not a single leading Latino spoke on the first night of the convention. Like Jesse Jackson, the Latino leadership was hidden from the public. In spite of this, Latinos rallied behind Clinton. None of them wanted to jeopardize Clinton's chances of defeating Bush, so they accepted seats in the back of the bus while hoping that a Clinton victory would lead to Latino gains when the Democrats took office.

Clinton did name Gloria Molina a co-chair of the presidential campaign, with Mickey Kantor, chair of the campaign, announcing: 'The naming of Molina demonstrates the commitment of the campaign to take the message to everyone and include everyone.' On 5 May Clinton promised to deliver a government that 'looks like America'. At the Democratic convention itself, 7.7 percent (330) of the delegates were Latino, and 71 percent of the Latinos were for Clinton. Jack Otero, an official of the AFL-CIO and a member of the National Democratic Committee, summed up the sentiment: 'The important thing is to take out Bush and Quayle.' Frederick Cuenca, of the National Hispanic Leadership Agency, added that the Democratic Party's ideological shift to the center had been accomplished without hurting the interests of Latinos.[63] In reality, the convention revealed a general drift to the right, which was intended to appeal to the middle-class, while excluding the poor.

The Republican Party's convention also ignored the poor and the working class, although some Republicans called for a change in the party's image and the Republicans generally continued, somewhat half-heartedly, to appeal to the Latino middle class.[64] California Latinos had previously demanded more delegates and initiated Proyecto MOVE to increase their share. Tirso del Junco, vice president of the California Republican Party, announced: 'I am living proof that there is no discrimination [in the Republican Party].' He then rhetorically asked how many Latino vice-presidents could be found in the Democratic Party. (Del Junco had also defended Governor Wilson's immigrant baiting, saying that the governor held immigrants in the highest esteem – he just didn't like illegal immigration.) In all, 233 Latino delegates out of a total of 1,500 attended the Republican convention. Gaddi Vásquez spoke in Spanish, giving his '¡Víva Bush!' salute. Catalina Villapando, the US Treasurer, also spoke, with the brief of accusing Clinton and Henry Cisneros of being womanizers.[65]

Despite these and other criticisms of the Republicans, the Bush record on affirmative action with regard to Latinos did not compare badly with those of the Democratic administrations. Bush was the first president to appoint two Latino cabinet members, as well as naming Villapando treasurer and Antonia Novello surgeon general. However, the issue in 1992 for most Latino activists, and for that matter most Americans, was the economy, and on this point the Republican record of the Reagan/Bush years was hard to sell.

The 1992 presidential campaign had little to offer Chicanos. By the end of the campaign, even Raúl Yzaguirre of the National Council of La Raza had criticized both candidates, charging that neither Clinton nor Bush nor Perot had a vision for the Latino community. Clinton was the least of the three evils because he *might* help the poor.[66] On election day, Clinton took 43 percent of the California vote; Bush, 38 percent; and Perot, 19 percent. The Latino vote (mostly Mexican American) went 67 percent for Clinton, 15 percent for Bush and 15 percent for Perot.[67]

The 1992 races for California's two US Senate seats by contrast saw plenty of discussion of Latinos – most of it negative. Marin County Congresswoman Barbara Boxer opened her bid for Alan Cranston's old seat with a 22-point advantage in the opinion polls over Bruce Herschensohn, a conservative who opposed bilingual education. Neither candidate rose above the clamor of the anti-immigrant mob, with both calling for more border patrol guards. Herschensohn closed the gap late in the campaign, and the Latino vote became pivotal to Boxer's victory. In the general election, over a million California Latinos voted, giving Boxer 68 percent of their votes versus 22 percent for the conservative Republican.[68]

The contest between former San Francisco mayor Dianne Feinstein and Senator John Seymour degenerated into an immigrant-bashing affair. An undistinguished candidate who was well behind in the polls, Seymour attempted to catch up at the expense of the undocumented by charging that 20 percent of the inmates in Los Angeles and San Diego jails were illegals. Seymour's television ads were especially offensive. He appeared, looking forceful and yelling to viewers, 'I say: Deport them!' Then he struck another forceful pose and continued: 'Let them serve their time in the country where they came from.' In another ad he stood in front of the gates of Terminal Island federal prison reciting these lines: 'It's incredible. There are more police protecting members of Congress than protecting our borders from illegals.' Feinstein, who had a healthy lead, responded with the same anti-Mexican rhetoric: 'Our borders have to mean something!' and adding, 'They can't continue to be like Swiss cheese like they are [now]. California has double-digit unemployment, [deteriorating] infrastructure that is not replenished … We need to control our borders.' Feinstein went a step further than any of the other candidates by advocating peacetime deployment of retrained soldiers to make the border illegal-proof.

Despite this position, Feinstein sought the endorsement of the Mexican American Political Association (MAPA). When asked about employer sanctions as an existing, allegedly less repressive way to limit the undocumented, she seemed mystified.[69] Feinstein won the election handily.

Nationally, minorities increased their representation as a result of the 1992 elections.[70] According to NALEO, the number of Latino elected officials reached 4,994, of whom 800 were newly elected. In California Latinos held 688 or about 8 percent of elected positions in the state, although they were 26 percent of the population, in contrast to Texas, where 1,995 held office. Among Latino elected officials, 29.6 percent or 1,478 were women, most of whom served on boards of education.

Clinton's New Democrats

After the election came the usual competition to secure political appointments. Former San Antonio Mayor Henry Cisneros was nominated and confirmed as Secretary of Housing and Urban Development, a significant appointment since HUD administered a $24 billion budget. Through Congressman Henry González, San Antonio had benefited greatly from Model Cities Program grants, which the city used to build and repair schools, streets and sidewalks on the Westside.[71] Federico Peña, former mayor of Denver, became Secretary of Transportation; Fernando Torres-Gill from Los Angeles became Assistant Secretary of Health and Human Services; and Jim Baca was named to head the Bureau of Land Management. All in all, however, Latinos in general and Chicanos in particular did not do well in the competition for Clinton administration jobs. Clinton did not live up to his Cinco de Mayo pledge, 'If you vote for me, I will give you an Administration that looks like America.'[72] As for Latinas, they were so neglected that one person commented that the only Latina being mentioned by the press in connection with appointments was Lillian Cordero, Attorney General nominee Zoe Baird's nanny.[73] For Latinos, then, the first six months of the Clinton administration seemed a replay of the previous twelve years.

Notes

1. David G. Savage, 'High Court Rules Against "Racial Gerrymandering"', *Los Angeles Times*, 29 June 1993; David Dante Troutt, 'When Restoring Black Rights Is Discriminatory', *Los Angeles Times*, 4 July 1993. Troutt ridicules the US Supreme Court decision in the North Carolina case, pointing out that Justice Sandra Day O'Connor had formulated her argument in the terms of aesthetics, using words like 'snake-like', 'bizarre', 'contiguity and compactness'. Troutt continued: 'This constitutional quandary is a legacy of the Reagan Revolution that began in 1980 and contin-

ues through the federal courts for the foreseeable future. Given that nearly half the federal judges were appointed according to the ideological dictates of Edwin Meese III and others, this judicial legacy is a birthday gift to those yet unborn.' According to Troutt, the case signals that the Supreme Court is impatient with efforts to protect the constitutional rights of minorities, reflecting the Republican campaigns of '1980, '84 and '88, [which] fed on the fears of bigots. After Willie Horton and David Duke, we've lost our right to wonder why the voice of a Jesse Jackson was hushed by Democrats last year.' Troutt points out that North Carolina officially discriminated against Blacks from 1900 to 1970. When it tried to end this discrimination, the Supreme Court intervened.

    2. Ronald Smothers, 'US District Court Upholds "Gerrymander" for Blacks', *New York Times*, 3 Aug. 1994.

    3. Peter Skerry, *Mexican Americans: The Ambivalent Minority* (New York: The Free Press, 1993).

    4. Ibid., p. 319.

    5. Again Skerry's analysis is ahistorical; my own birth certificate lists me racially as Mexican. Mexicans were long classified as white in order to circumvent immigration laws; Census classifications have since changed several times to reflect political requirements, from 'Spanish surname' to the current 'Hispanic'. Because Euroamericans themselves have historically displayed an ambivalence toward race, it is no surprise that many Mexican Americans are confused, Skerry, p. 319. David E. Hayes-Bautista and Gregory Rodriguez, 'Latinos Are Redefining Notions of Racial Identity', *Los Angeles Times*, 13 Jan. 1993, makes the point that in the 1990 Census 51 percent of California Latinos classified themselves as 'other'. The US does not recognize hybridity, whereas the concept of *mestizaje* is common in Latin America.

    6. Skerry, *Mexican Americans*, pp. 320–21.

    7. Ibid., p. 331.

    8. 'Sarah Flores won the primary in the First Supervisorial District with 35 percent of the total vote, including 60 percent of the Hispanic and 31 percent of the non-Hispanic vote. Moreover, with the second place finisher, a male Anglo, winning only 20 percent of the total vote, Flores was favored to win the seat', Skerry, p. 333. This is an assumption that Skerry cannot substantiate. Thirty-five percent is a long way from 50 percent.

    9. Ibid., pp. 336–46.

    10. Bill Stall, 'State Still Staggering from Prop. 13 Earthquake', *Los Angeles Times*, 14 Oct. 1993.

    11. Ibid.

    12. Ralph Frammolino, 'Bill Coming Due on Prop. 13 Tax Revolt', *Los Angeles Times*, 8 Sept. 1992. The immediate impact of Prop. 13 was not felt by Californians because the state propped up local government services. By 1992, however, recession and declining state tax revenues forced cuts in that subsidy of 45%. Los Angeles County alone took a $259 million hit; the county also lost $328 million because of state budget cuts.

    13. 'Blacks' Earnings Up in '80s, Lag Other Groups' Income', *Los Angeles Times*, 25 July 1992. The 1990 Census showed that the incomes of Latino households increased to $24,156, up 77 percent. But this figure included Cuban Americans, whose incomes were generally much higher than those of Mexicans and Central Americans. One-third of Latino children under five lived in poverty.

    14. Joel Fox, 'State Moves to Devour Local Governments', *Daily News*, 27 June 1993.

    15. Bill Stall, 'Fear of Voter Backlash Stymies All Attempts at Reform', *Los Angeles Times*, 15 Oct. 1993.

    16. John Jacobs, 'Prop. 13 Filled with Troublesome Inequities', *Daily News*, 4 Apr. 1993: 'As far as the Legislature is concerned, Proposition 13 is still Holy Writ. Residents who have owned their homes for at least 10 years – a majority of the state's homeowners – enjoy their low property taxes and would certainly and understandably fight hard to preserve them.' Jacobs notes that the law discourages new businesses and that it is therefore a growth killer, distorting the market and rewarding old business at the expense of new. It especially aids the elderly, 82% of whom have not moved since 1978, and who are overwhelmingly white.

    17. Frank Clifford, 'Long Slump Poses New Political Risks in L.A.', *Los Angeles Times*, 21 Jan. 1992. There were telltale signs that the long recession, combined with loss of revenue directly attributed to Proposition 13, had accelerated an 'era of political uncertainty, presenting risks and challenges for a generation of leaders with little recent experience handling a financial crisis.' Prosperity had lightened the impact of Prop. 13 during the 1980s. The 1990s were another matter. In

1992 the city's anticipated budget shortfall was $150 million. A hiring freeze eliminated 2,000 jobs, many of which would have gone to Latinos.

18. *Angelenos* with an 'e' is the English-language spelling; *Angelinos* with an 'i' is the Spanish-language spelling.

19. James Rainey, 'Mixed Reviews for Council's Newest Voices', *Los Angeles Times*, 1 March 1993.

20. Patrick Greevy, 'Councilman Calls for Funding Shift', *Daily News*, 14 Oct. 1992, Hernández called for a shift in city spending to help long-neglected areas. 'We're subsidizing the haves ... This city is practicing de facto segregation. We are saying it is OK for the haves to live one way and the have-nots and worse than have-nots to live another.'

21. Alatorre won re-election in spring 1991. Urban planner David Díaz, one of the most knowledgeable Latinos in municipal government, John Lucero of El Sereno, who was angry with Alatorre over the councilman's support of a low-cost housing project in El Sereno, and Martin Gutierrez, joined forces and challenged Alatorre. Their goal was to force the councilman into a runoff by preventing him from garnering 50 percent of the vote, with the losers supporting the survivor. They counted on discontent with Alatorre over Olvera Street. They also relied on the support of Gloria Molina; she had reached a temporary armistice with Alatorre, who did not support a candidate against Hernández. In the end, Alatorre won handily. Bill Boyarsky, 'Barrio's New Generation Comes Home', *Los Angeles Times*, 3 April 1991.

22. Jaime Olivares, 'Latinos estudian planes pare ganar asientos en el Congreso', *La Opinión*, 3 June 1991; Jaime Olivares, 'Areas hispanas perderían representantes en la Asamblea', *La Opinión*, 19 April 1991; María del Pilar Marero, 'Gobierno de LA irá a juicio si no es rectifcado el censo', *La Opinión*, 21 June 1991. The City of Los Angeles stated officially that it was undercounted by 200,000. Nationwide, the figure was 2.1% or an undercount of some 5 million. An estimated 1,237,000 Latinos were not counted. Maribel Hastings, 'Análisis revela que el censo contó a más latinas que latinos', *La Opinión*, 10 June 1991, reports a 5.1% undercount of Latinos in Los Angeles, or 186,000 persons. In Inglewood, 11% were not counted; Henrik Rehbinder, 'Censo define hoy sobre hispanos no contabilizados', *La Opinión*, 15 July 1991. It would be interesting to study the amount of space given to the Census undercount in the Spanish-language print media and in the *Los Angeles Times*, where the topic merited what amounted to a footnote; Richard Lee Colvin, 'Census Shows High Desert a Melting Pot', *Los Angeles Times*, 27 Feb. 1991.

23. Even with the apparent undercount, the national numbers were equally impressive: the Census counted 22,354,059 Latinos nationally. Of these 13,495,938 were of Mexican origin, 2,727,754 were Puerto Rican and 1,043,932 Cuban; 5,086,435 others were mostly Central American. Jaime Olivares, 'Mexicanos, el grupo hispano más grande y con mayor crecimiento', *La Opinión*, 23 June 1991. Cheryl Brownstein-Santiago, 'Census Data Track Status of Latinos', *Nuestro Tiempo*, 10 Sept. 1992, shows just how concerned Chicanos were about the picture of their community painted by the 1990 Census: 'Even before the recession hit, working-age Latinos in Los Angeles County were feeling the pinch in 1989 because their per capita income of $11,489 was a little more than half that of the rest of the working-age population.' The Census showed that 39% of Latinos 25 years of age or older had a high school diploma compared with 70% for the rest of the county. Poor educational attainment and the decline of the high-wage manufacturing sector would, he predicted, worsen the situation. Some 60.1% of the Latinos nationally, and in California 79.6%, were of Mexican descent.

24. 'Latino Voters in California', *Nuestro Tiempo*, 30 April 1992.

25. 'Grupos latinos denucían las polítícas raciales', *La Opinión*, 27 Nov. 1991.

26. Antonia Hernández, 'La redistribución de los distritos electorales y el voto latino', *La Opinión*, 14 Oct. 1992.

27. Daniel M. Weintraub, 'Minority Groups Say Remap Plan Leaves Them Split', *Los Angeles Times*, 10 Sept. 1991.

28. Jaime Olivares, 'La Supreme Corte estatal aprobó ayer mapas electorales', *La Opinión*, 28 Jan. 1992; Sherry Bebitch Jeffe, 'Why Republicans May Rue Their Heartfelt Support for Term Limits', *Los Angeles Times*, 8 Dec. 1991. The plan was bad news for Democrats, but many observers pointed out that term limits might not be so attractive to Republicans, even though they were eagerly endorsed by Wilson. By 1998 the first incumbents elected under Proposition 140 would be leaving office, and Democratic power would be expected to lessen. However, reapportionment,

from the Republican view, may make term limits unnecessary and in the end limit Republican power because the term-limit sword had two edges, Sherry Bebitch Jeffe, 'Requiem for an Institution: California's Legislature', *Los Angeles Times*, 12 Jan. 1992; Maria del Pilar Marrero, 'Elogios y críticas para plan de redistribución distrital', *La Opinión*, 4 Dec. 1991.

29. Jaime Olivares, 'Mapas electorales no eliminan subrepresentación latina', *La Opinión*, 3 Feb. 1992.

30. Mary Ballesteros, 'Roberti será candidato al Senado estatal por Distrito 20', *La Opinión*, 6 Feb. 1992; the district included San Fernando, Pacoima, Sun Valley, Van Nuys, Encino, Reseda and parts of Sylmar, North Hollywood and Burbank. Daniel M. Weintraub and Jack Cheevers, 'Renumbering Plan Would Keep Roberti in Senate Seat', *Los Angeles Times*, 14 Jan. 1992.

31. Manuel Jiménez, 'Latinos May Gain Impact in Assembly', *Nuestro Tiempo*, 8 Oct. 1992. Richard Polanco held the 45th Assembly District; Louis Caldera, the 46th; Diane Martínez, the 49th; Martha Escutia, the 50th; Hilda Solis, the 57th; and Grace Napolitano, the 58th.

32. George Ramos and Patt Morrison, 'L.A. County Latinos Headed for 6 Seats in Assembly, 4 in House', *Los Angeles Times*, 4 June 1992. Brown's influence was visible in the Assembly races: Grace Napolitano and Louis Caldera, for instance, turned over their campaigns to Ross Richie, a Brown political strategist.

33. Jiménez, 'Latinos May Gain Impact'. Caldera was born in El Paso. His district includes Boyle Heights, Bunker Hill, Central City, Koreatown, Mid-Wilshire, Pico-Union, Westlake and parts of East and South Central Los Angeles: 70% of his district was Latino, but only 35% of the registered voters. Escutia lives in Huntington Park. She earned a law degree from Georgetown University, then worked in the public sector for 10 years in Washington, D.C. Her district includes Bell, Bell Gardens, City of Commerce, Cudahy, Huntington Park, Maywood, South Gate and Vernon: 89% of the residents in her district are Latinos, with 55% of the registered voters listed as Latino. Napolitano was originally from Brownsville, Texas, and lives in Norwalk, where she had been on the city council. Her district includes Montebello, Pico Rivera, Whittier, South Whittier, Santa Fe Springs, Norwalk, parts of South El Monte and unincorporated areas of East Los Angeles: 44% of the voters in this district are Latino.

34. Jaime Olivares, 'Anuncian foro público pare elaborar agenda latina', *La Opinión*, 31 Dec. 1992; Jaime Olivares, 'Asambleistas discuten temas latinos prioritarios', *La Opinión*, 31 Dec. 1992. Maribel Hastings', Asamblea estatal - Distrito 49', *La Opinión*, 29 Sept. 1992.

35. Jiménez, 'Latinos May Gain Impact'. Baca is a small businessman from Rialto; his district includes San Bernardino, Rialto, Fontana, Colton, Loma Linda and Bloomington.

36. Ibid. Polanco was born in East Los Angeles. His district includes Northeast Los Angeles and South Pasadena.

37. Ibid. Solis was born and raised in the San Gabriel Valley. He was the former president of the Rio Hondo Community College District. His district covers La Puente, El Monte, Hacienda Heights, Irwindale, Azusa, Valinda, Basset, Baldwin Park and parts of South El Monte, 'Asamblea Estatal - Distrito 57', *La Opinión*, 16 Oct. 1992; her district was 64% Latino, and 40% of the registered voters were Latino.

38. Manuel Jiménez, 'Political Change in the Wind', *Nuestro Tiempo*, 19 Nov. 1992.

39. 'Asambleístas latinos discuten sus prioridades', *La Opinión*, 7 Dec. 1992; Jaime Olivares, 'Alto número de legisladores latinos será electo hoy', *La Opinión*, 3 Dec. 1992.

40. Ramos and Morrison, 'L.A. County Latinos Headed for 6 Seats'.

41. Dave Lesher, 'Effort to Boost Latino Political Clout Falters', *Los Angeles Times*, 12 May 1992.

42. Frederick Muir, 'Reapportionment Shuffles the Political Deck', *Los Angeles Times*, 3 Jan. 1992. The 1990 Census undercount concerned Latinos since congressional seats and federal funding formulas are based on the numbers of residents, not on their status or the number of actual voters. Commerce Secretary Robert Mosbacher refused to adjust the Census to compensate for the undercount, and thus cities were stuck with the official results until the 2000 Census. Blacks and Latinos were the groups most affected. Cities such as New York, Los Angeles, Chicago, Houston, San Diego, Detroit, Dallas, Phoenix and San Antonio, all with large Latino populations, suffered. Oswald Johnston, 'Funding Levels May Be Altered Before Census', *Los Angeles Times*, 17 July 1991; Maribel Hastings, 'Tribunal de la Apelaciones suspende orden de juez para actualizar ek Censo', *La Opinión*, 17 Aug. 1991.

43. The 24th District included Canoga Park, Reseda, Encino, Hidden Hills, Thousand Oaks;

the 45th, Northridge, Granada Hills, Santa Clarita, Canyon Country, Acton, Lancaster, Palmdale, Littlerock, Lake Los Angeles; the 26th, Pacoima, Van Nuys, San Fernando; the 27th, Sunland, Burbank, La Cañada, Flintridge, Altadena, Glendale, Pasadena; the 28th, Temple City, Monrovia, Glendora, Covina, West Covina, San Dimas, La Verne, Walnut; the 29th, Hollywood, Beverly Hills, Santa Monica; the 30th, Civic Center; the 31st, Alhambra, Monterey Park, El Monte, Azusa; the 32d, Culver City; the 33d, Civic Center of L.A. and Huntington Park; the 34th, Pico Rivera, Whittier, Hacienda Heights, Santa Fe Springs; the 35th, Inglewood, Hawthorne; the 36th, Torrance, Rancho Palos Verde, El Segundo, Manhattan Beach, Redondo; the 37th, Lynwood, Compton, Carson, Wilmington; the 38th, Lakewood, Downey, Long Beach; the 39th, Brea, Buena Park, Cypress, Fullerton, La Habra, Las Palmas, Placentia, Rossmoor; and the 41st, Diamond Bar, Pomona, Chino, Montclair, Ontario and Upland.

44. Mark Gladstone and Alan Miller, 'Congressional Latino District Gains Support', *Los Angeles Times*, 12 Sept. 1991.

45. Frederick M. Muir, 'Reapportionment Shuffles the Political Deck', *Los Angeles Times*, Jan. 3, 1992.

46. Glenn F. Bunting, 'Roybal Project Voted Down amid Pork Barrel Charges', *Los Angeles Times*, 9 July 1992.

47. Jaime Olivares, 'Retiro de Roybal desata conjecturas sobre su sucesor', *La Opinión*, 2 Feb. 1992.

48. It was a great loss. My own memories of Roybal go back to the late 1950s, when I was a student at Los Angeles State College and he came to speak at the makeshift campus. A councilman at the time, Roybal was the only elected official of Mexican descent in Los Angeles, and I was in awe of him. Roybal was never a radical; but his strong sense of justice was ahead of his times. Roybal's popularity thus went well beyond the Chicano community. The 9th Council District had only 16,000 Mexican Americans out of 87,000 voters, but he won the hearts of his constituents with his battle against freeway expansion and urban renewal, which threatened Boyle Heights and other poor neighborhoods.

49. 'Asamblieísta Becerra será candidato en nuevo distrito', *La Opinión*, 3 Feb. 1992.

50. Arnold, *Nuestro Tiempo*, 6 June 1992; David Díaz, 'Eastside Outcomes: Molina's Up, Alatorre's Down and the Big Winner Is *Willie Brown* (Willie Brown?)', *LA Weekly*, 19 June 1992; Díaz provides an excellent analysis contradicting the popular notion that the Alatorre camp was the victor during this campaign.

51. Manuel Jiménez, 'Political Change in the Wind', *Nuestro Tiempo*, 19 Nov. 1992.

52. George Ramos, 'Roybal's Daughter Expected to Sweep In', *Los Angeles Times*, 27 May 1992.

53. See 'Cámara de Representantes - Distrito 34', and Jaime Olivares, 'Plataformas electorales', *La Opinión*, 2 Oct. 1992.

54. Jaime Olivares, 'Alto número de legisladores latinos será elect hoy', *La Opinión*, 3 Dec. 1992; Roger E. Hernández, 'Latinos in Congress to Reach Record High', *Daily News*, 26 Oct. 1992; Roger Lindo, '17 Latinos elegidoes a la Cámara de Representantes', *La Opinión*, 5 Nov. 1992.

55. Tina Griego, '4 Recalled in Bell Gardens Balloting', *Los Angeles Times*, 11 Dec. 1991.

56. Xavier Hermosillo, 'The End of "Go Along, Get Along" for Chicanos', *Los Angeles Times*, 18 Dec. 1991; Hermosillo, a Republican, emerged as a militant voice for Chicano nationalism. He was criticized because much of his critique seemed to be directed at other groups rather than the system itself. The consistent theme was that Latino numbers entitled them to a large share of the pie. Hermosillo was a moving force behind NEWS for America, which is described in Frank Clifford and George Ramos, 'Group Muscles Its Way to Front of Latino Activism', *Los Angeles Times*, 16 March 1992; the article also discusses the tensions at the Martin Luther King Medical Center between African Americans and Latinos. Essentially, this group of middle-class, middle-aged activists, who were on the right of center, adopted 1960s rhetoric. They rejected bridge-building between Latinos and other groups: Lawyer Manuel Hidalgo, a cofounder is quoted, 'Mexican-Americans have to stop being, quote, "fair" to blacks and fair to the whites and start thinking about the 40% of the population that is ours. We can afford to be fair to others after we have assumed the reins of power in a few places.' Dr Julian Nava and Raúl Nuñez, head of the Los Angeles County Employees, were also active. The group characterized Bell Gardens and its six sister cities as the Seven Cities of Aztlán. They were also heavily involved in promoting Sheriff Lee Baca for chief of the Los Angeles Police.

57. Tina Griego and George Ramos, 'Recall Vote Seen as Birth of a Movement', *Los Angeles Times*, 12 Dec. 1991.

58. Pablo Comesaña Amado, 'Ediles destituidos en Bell Gardens se presentarán en elección de abril', *La Opinión*, 28 Jan. 1992.

59. Tina Griego and Jill Gottesman, 'Bell Gardens Elects Recall Leaders to Council', *Los Angeles Times*, 11 March 1992.

60. Robert S. McElvaine, 'GOP "Values"?' *Los Angeles Times*, 12 Oct. 1992; Roberto Rodríguez, 'La verdad de las cuotas', *La Opinión*, 30 June 1991, notes that Bush had convinced the white population that it was the new victim of the civil rights laws.

61. Maribel Hastings, 'Nuera mexicana de Bush dice que el aborto es asunto privado', *La Opinión*, 20 Aug. 1992.

62. Tad Szulc, 'How Can 29 Million People Be Politically Invisible to Democrats?', *Los Angeles Times*, 26 July 1992.

63. 'Los Latinos democráticos y las elecciones presidenciales', *La Opinión*, 29 July 1992.

64. Joel Kotkin, 'By Ignoring Ethnic Minorities, GOP Leaders Undercut Party's Future', *Los Angeles Times*, 16 Aug. 1992; Kotkin also notes that Governor Pete Wilson missed a golden opportunity by not naming Orange County Supervision Gaddi Vásquez to the US Senate instead of the lackluster John Seymour.

65. Jaime Olivares, 'Los latinos republicanos piden su lugar en todos los niveles del partido', *La Opinión*, 1 March 1992; Henrik Rehbinder, 'Oradores latinos destacan los valores tradicionales', *La Opinión*, 19 Aug. 1992; Dave Leshu, 'Targeting the Middle-Class', *Los Angeles Times Magazine*, 6 Nov. 1992, p. 25. In 1988 Bush had made a play for Latino votes, playing 'La Bamba' at the convention. Twenty percent of California Latino voters were registered as Republicans that year. Latinos had also voted to re-elect conservative California Governor George Deukmejian, an indication that more middle-class than working-class Latinos were voting. Moreover, according to Bruce Cain, as Latinos moved out of the barrio to places like the San Fernando Valley, half of them switched to the Republican Party. The 1992 election showed other trends, suggesting that political generalizations about Latinos in general and Chicanos in particular were risky.

66. Jesús Hernández Cuellar, 'MALDEF pide a Bush que firme el Acta de Registro de Votantes', *La Opinión*, 17 June 1992. Bush had not even signed the new Voting Rights Act; John M. Broder, 'Immigration Delicate Issue for Clinton', *Los Angeles Times*, 7 Sept. 1993.

67. 'Voto Latino de California para presidente', *La Opinión*, 5 Nov. 1992.

68. Jaime Olivares, 'Afirman que el voto latino decidió la eleccion de Bárbara Boxer al Senado', *La Opinión*, Nov. 9, 1992.

69. Jaime Olivares, 'Votos latinos serán decision en elección senatorial', *La Opinión*, 11 Feb. 1993. Feinstein at the time led Seymour 58% to 27%; Tracy Wilkinson, 'Candidates Tough on Illegal Immigration', *Los Angeles Times*, 9 Oct. 1992; Bill Stall, 'Seymour Proposes Battle on Crime by Illegal Immigrants', *Los Angeles Times*, 4 Aug. 1992.

70. William J. Eaton, 'For Blacks and Latinos, Elections May Make '92 Year of the Minority', *Los Angeles Times*, 28 July 1992. The prediction came true; see Jaime Olivares, 'Récord de funcionarios latinos en 1992 en EU', *La Opinión*, 17 Dec. 1992.

71. Gary Martin and Bruce Davidson, '2 Henrys from S.A. to forge HUD policy', *San Antonio Express News*, 20 Dec. 1992; while it is easy to be cynical about the electoral process, it must be emphasized that jobs are allocated as a result of these appointments, with the bureaucracy responding to political changes. In the case of Cisneros, during his tenure as mayor $230 million in HUD funds were spent in economically depressed San Antonio.

72. Gene Martinez, 'Activists Frustrated by Number of Latinos in Administration', *Los Angeles Times*, 4 March 1993. Raúl Yzaguirre of the National Council of La Raza, Andy Hernández of the Southwest Voter Registration and Education Project, Jack Otero, vice-president of the AFL/CIO and Congressman Esteban Torres met with the Clinton transition team and demanded an assistant secretary in each federal agency. This demand was not met. In fact, Clinton did not perform as well as Reagan, who appointed 15 Latinos among 587 top-level positions, and Bush, who appointed 22 Latinos out of 659.

73. Millie Santillanes, 'La mujer latina, la gran ausente en el Gobierno de Clinton', *La Opinión*, 25 Feb. 1993; Paul Richter and David Lauter, 'Women, Latinos See Ideal of Diverse Cabinet Fading', *Los Angeles Times*, 19 Dec. 1992.

6

Immigration:

'The Border Crossed Us'

Most people suffer from historical amnesia about the dark passages of their country's past. It is not surprising, then, that Euroamericans usually don't know much about the forced repatriation of Mexicans and other immigrants during the Great Depression or the imprisonment of Japanese-Americans in concentration camps during World War II. This amnesia leads to a failure to perceive linkages between past events and the present anti-immigrant hysteria in Los Angeles and the rest of California. That is why such hysteria is so frightening: it indicates that nothing has been learned about past injustices or their consequences. The 'brown scare' has been, and remains, an organic part of Los Angeles history.

'A Mongrel Population'

Even scholars find it hard to accept such simple truths as the fact that the American Southwest once belonged to Mexico, and that the United States took it by force of arms. After this conquest, the region was integrated economically with the rest of the US. When labor was needed to develop this conquered territory, Asian, especially Chinese, workers were used for a time until Euroamerican racial fears led to their exclusion, leaving Mexicans as the most logical source of labor. What many Euroamericans regarded as the 'Great American Desert' was thus transformed by Mexican labor (although Euroamericans remember only the role played by North American irrigation and drainage technology).[1]

Migrant Mexican workers arrived in the Southwest by the thousands beginning around 1900. The industrialization of the United States and Mexico resulted in uprooting Mexicans, who were simultaneously pushed by economic conditions in their own country and pulled by the availability of jobs in the United States. These newly arrived Mexican workers were confronted by a

deep-rooted legacy of violence and racism. Nativism towards Mexicans differed in its essence from that toward new groups of Euroamericans, since
Mexicans were not only foreigners with an alien culture but also darker than
Euroamericans and often had Indian features. Mexicans were therefore easily
scapegoated during times of economic hardship. During the 1913 recession,
the Commissioner of Immigration, for instance, publicly announced his fear
that Mexicans might become public charges, since according to these authorities, Mexicans came to the United States only to receive public relief. This
theme was to become a key part of the folklore surrounding Mexican immigration.[2]

This unbridled racism encouraged vigilante violence against Mexicans. In
Rock Springs, Texas, for example, in November 1910 a mob seized twenty-year-
old Antonio Rodríguez while he was awaiting trial and burned him at the stake.
In June 1911, Antonio Gómez, charged with killing an adult with a knife, was
taken from jail by a mob, which tied him to the rear of a buggy and dragged
him around town, killing him.[3] Gómez was fourteen. From July 1915 to July
1916, a virtual state of war existed between Mexicans and Anglos in Texas: 'US
authorities admitted shooting, killing, or beating up to 300 "suspected" Mexicans, while rebels killed 21 Euroamericans during this same period.'[4] Texas historian Walter Prescott Webb wrote that

> the number [of Mexicans] killed in the entire valley [between 1915 and 1920] has
> been estimated at five hundred and at five thousand, but the actual number can
> never be known. The situation can be summed up by saying that after the troubles
> developed the Americans instituted a reign of terror against Mexicans and that
> many innocent Mexicans were made to suffer.[5]

According to Chicano historian Ricardo Romo, 'During the depression of
1913–1914, California nativists found immigrants a prime economic scapegoat.' The *Los Angeles Times*, for example, warned that providing care for 'unin-
vited guests' would prove costly. Romo wrote of the anti-Mexican crusade
during World War I: 'During the period 1913–1918, a Brown hysteria fully as
great as that aimed at Communists and other radicals elsewhere, was directed
at Mexicans living in Los Angeles.'[6] The arrival of large numbers of Mexicans
who were attracted to the region by wartime labor shortages helped increase
the hysteria. In March 1916, Los Angeles County supervisors requested the federal government to deport 'cholos likely to become public charges.'[7]

Change in previously liberal US immigration policies began in 1917, with
the passage of a literacy test requirement for new immigrants (this provision
was not enforced against Mexicans because Western growers depended on
Mexican labor). This was followed by the 1921 and 1924 immigration acts,
which imposed quotas on European immigration and completely excluded

Asians. In essence, these quotas aimed to keep the population of the United States mostly northern European by giving higher quotas to 'preferred' nationalities.[8] This policy was based on what John Higham has called racial nativism, 'the concept that the United States belongs in some special sense to the Anglo-Saxon "race"', whose domination supposedly explains the nation's greatness.[9] Part of this tradition was to define aliens not only as different, but as the 'enemy'. Indeed, the concept of 'race suicide' is very much part of the long history of debate as to who should be admitted to the United States.

The 1920s saw intensified debate as to whether Mexicans should be assigned a quota, and renewed efforts were made to repatriate Mexicans. *El Universal* of Mexico City reported on 5 March 1921 that Mexican workers in the Phoenix area were being put into concentration-like camps. During congressional debates over the 1921 and 1924 immigration acts, Rep. Martin Madden of Chicago put this argument plainly: 'The bill opens the doors for perhaps the worst element that comes into the United States – the Mexican *peon* ...'[10] The headline in the *Los Angeles Times* after the passage of the 1924 Immigration Act read, 'Nordic Victory Is Seen in Drastic Restrictions'; and President Calvin Coolidge proclaimed his approval: 'America must be kept American.'[11] Despite such racial preferences, Mexicans were exempted from the quotas because of lobbying by Western growers.

In 1926, the Commissioner of Immigration wrote: 'It is safe to say that over a million Mexicans entered [into] the United States ....' Commissioners consistently argued that Mexicans were less desirable as immigrants than Europeans; therefore, it was not good policy to limit European immigration with quotas while giving Mexicans preferential treatment. Organized labor supported this position, asking rhetorically in 1928, 'Do you want a mongrel population, consisting largely of Mexicans?'[12] The issue of race was raised repeatedly. The US Department of Labor funded Professor Robert A. Foerester, a Princeton University economist, to investigate the racial derivation of Mexicans. Foerester concluded that the blood of Mexicans and of other Latin Americans was 'mainly Asiatic' (meaning Indian) 'or African' (meaning Black). On the basis of this finding, Foerester wrote that whereas the US 'can properly require of its immigrants that they at least equal, if not excel, the average of its own citizens in the fitness of government, including self-government, and industry, ... no good ground exists for supposing that the immigrants of countries south of the United States would meet the requirements of this criterion.'[13] (Mexicans were classified as Caucasian to circumvent immigration policies that excluded Asians.) Open racism played a role in arguments in favor of continued Mexican immigration. The racist dehumanization of Mexicans resonates in the statement of a prominent Pasadena doctor who testified before Congress in favor of keeping Mexicans quota-free: 'The Mexican is a quiet, inoffensive necessity in that he performs the big majority of our rough work, agriculture, building, and street labor. They have no effect on the American standard of living be-cause they are not much more than a group of fairly intelligent collie dogs.'[14]

Sending Them Back to Mexico

The Depression of the 1930s intensified nativism, and politicians seized the op-portunity to blame Mexicans for massive unemployment. Herbert Hoover's Secretary of Labor, William Doak, stated in 1931: 'My conviction is that by strict limitation and a wise selection of immigration, we can make America stronger in every way, hastening the day when our population shall be more homogeneous.'[15] This encouraged C.P. Visel, Los Angeles's local coordinator of unemployment relief, to spearhead a drive to send Mexicans back to Mex-ico. Visel attacked Mexicans in the cooperative local press, building public hys-teria. On 26 February 1931, immigration authorities aided by local police surrounded the *placita* Olvera, detaining over 400 people for an hour, and ar-resting 11 Mexicans and 9 Chinese. In the next few months 3,000 to 4,000 Mexi-cans were rounded up and held without benefit of counsel. From 1931 to 1934, Los Angeles County shipped some 13,000 'Mexicans' to Mexico.[16] Nationally, 500,000 to 600,000 Mexican Americans were 'repatriated', the majority of them US-born citizens.

The war propaganda conducted during the Mexican 'repatriation' campaign reinforced in the minds of many Euroamericans the idea of Mexicans as 'aliens' and 'the other'. Thus the mass expulsion of Mexicans during the 1930s helped to create the climate for the mass incarceration of over 100,000 Japanese Americans in concentration camps during World War II.

Racism toward Mexicans was rampant during World War II. The infamous Sleepy Lagoon case of 1942 – in which some two dozen Mexican youth were tried for an alleged gang murder – typified the era. This case, later dramatized by Chicano playwright and film director Luis Váldez, remains a symbol of the injustice toward Mexicans during the period. Throughout the trial the judge allowed prosecutors to make racist references toward Mexicans, and the youths were not surprisingly convicted and sent to prison. The convictions were later overturned, however, because of the judge's prejudicial conduct. The next year servicemen, cheered on by police, local authorities and the press, attacked Mexican youth on the streets of the City of Angels in what have been called the Zoot Suit Riots.

At the same time, the World War II period offers a prime example of the contradictions in US immigration policy toward Mexicans and in the attitudes of many Euroamericans. Hostility towards Mexicans was fierce, but the war-time need for labor led to establishment of the Bracero Program, devised by the US and Mexican governments to bring workers across the border to alleviate the wartime labor shortage. Such contradictions continued after the war, as growers continued to use braceros and undocumented workers, even in the face of anti-Mexican hysteria. In Portland, Oregon, for example, an INS officer admitted that the Federal Employment Service had asked him in 1949 not to send inspectors into the field to apprehend 'wet' Mexicans until after harvesting had been completed.[17] Indeed, Democratic and Republican administrations cooperated with growers to keep farmworkers from organizing by ensuring a surplus of labor that was isolated from resident workers.

During the 1950s, the 'other' – including Mexicans – became the target of US anti-communism, taking the form of fear that American traditions and the nation itself were threatened, in part by people who looked 'different'. In October 1953, Ralph Guzmán, later an eminent Chicano political scientist, wrote in the *Eastside Sun* of Los Angeles: 'A few weeks ago Herbert Brownell, the US Attorney General, wanted to shoot wetbacks crossing into the U.S., but farmers fearing the loss of a cheap labor market ... complained bitterly and Brownell changes [sic] his mind.'[18] In May 1954, William P. Allen, publisher of the *Laredo Times*, wrote to President Eisenhower that Brownell had asked for the support of labor leaders in the event that the Border Patrol shot 'wetbacks' in cold blood.[19] Allen added that shooting illegals and beating them up was nothing new, representing a 'vulgar page that is already smeared with blood.'[20]

Eisenhower appointed a former classmate, General Joseph Swing, to head the Immigration and Naturalization Service. (Swing was perhaps considered qualified because he had ridden with General Pershing in pursuit of Pancho Villa.) Under Swing the INS became more militaristic, carrying out 'Operation Wetback', in which over a million Mexicans were deported annually from 1953 through 1955. The 1952 McCarran-Walter Act reaffirmed US commitment to the principle of 'national origins' in immigration law, which included the preservation of the 'American way' (today often referred to as 'family values'). The act allowed small quotas for Asians and Pacific Islanders and made it possible for them to become citizens. It also gave special immigration status to those with certain skills and education. It further empowered the Justice Department to deport politically undesirable aliens and naturalized citizens. President Truman vetoed the bill, but Congress overrode his veto. The McCarran-Walter Act was used to deport many Mexican immigrants active in labor organizing.[21]

The Fourth Wave and the New Scapegoating

The 1960s saw the beginning of the Fourth Wave of immigration to the United States. It was a decade of growing US job opportunities, overpopulation in the sender countries and low travel costs, and saw passage of the 1965 Immigration Act. All these developments swelled total US immigration to 3.3

million, the highest total since the 1920s.[22] Los Angeles was the preferred destination of Mexicans, both from Mexico and internal immigrants from other US states. The county's Mexican population zoomed from 576,716 in 1960 to 1,228,593 ten years later, a leap of 113 percent. This growth took Mexicans outside traditional barrios, and the increase in the native-born, Chicano, population made the community more visible. Some Chicanos joined the civil rights and antiwar movements of the time, further increasing their visibility outside the Mexican community. The realization that this population would become a permanent part of the nation unsettled many Euroamericans.

In this context the Immigration Act of 1965, proposed by Senator Edward Kennedy, was passed. Originally designed to correct discrimination against Asians, it also abolished country-specific immigration quotas.[23] The act changed the policy of exempting people from the Western Hemisphere from quotas, specifying that 120,000 immigrants could enter annually from the Americas and 170,000 from the Eastern Hemisphere. Thus it opened up immigration from the rest of the world, especially Asia, Africa and the Middle East. But it also put a cap of 40,000 on immigration from any one country, a limitation that was considered a direct affront to Mexico.

To replace the country quotas, the post-1965 selection system gave highest priority to family reunification and occupational and skill preferences. Those who framed the act did not intend to open the gates to Third World people; indeed, most believed that Europeans would continue to dominate immigration to the United States. They did not anticipate declining applications by Europeans, who enjoyed better economic conditions in the late 1950s and 1960s. Still, there was little reaction at first, since the 1965 act attracted highly educated Asians and Latin Americans – a factor that changed in the 1980s, when racism was compounded by class prejudice. (By 1988, 43 percent of documented immigrants came from Latin America and 41 percent from Asia.)[24]

A new wave of anti-immigrant hysteria developed even before the 1973–74 post–Vietnam War recession. In 1971, the INS apprehended 348,178 undocumented workers, the next year 430,213, and in 1973, 609,573. By 1976 the number of apprehended undocumented workers had jumped to 870,000 (90 percent of whom were Mexican). Prior to 1970 undocumented workers labored primarily in agriculture, but during the 1970s many shifted to urban occupations – hence their increased visibility.[25] At the same time, structural changes in the US economy, which erased many of labor's gains during the post–World War II period, unsettled many Anglos. Citing job competition from illegal immigrants, the California legislature passed the Dixon-Arnett Act in 1971; it provided fines for employers who hired undocumented workers. The state Supreme Court declared the act unconstitutional, however, because it infringed on federal powers. The next year Congressman Peter Rodino (D-N.J.) proposed a bill that would make it a felony to knowingly employ undocumented workers. Kennedy proposed a similar bill, which also granted amnesty to anyone who had been in the country for three years. These moves launched what became a twenty-year war over immigration legislation.[26]

Meanwhile, President Gerald Ford scapegoated Mexicans for the economic slowdown, saying on 22 April 1976, 'The main problem is how to get rid of those 6 to 8 million aliens who are interfering with our economic prosperity.' That same year, Congressman Joshua Eilberg (D-Penn.) proposed a bill reducing the immigration cap for Mexico from 40,000 to 20,000, with preference to be given to professionals and scientists. The proposal passed. The new law also enabled the government to deport US-born children along with their undocumented parents, allowing them to return to the US only when they reached eighteen.[27]

In the late 1970s the media energetically sensationalized what it termed 'an invasion'. In May 1977, *Time* magazine ran two articles, 'Getting Their Slice of Paradise', and 'On the Track of the Invader'. *Time* sermonized: 'The US is being invaded so silently and surreptitiously that most Americans are not even aware of it. In 1978, ex-CIA director William Colby called Mexican immigration a greater threat to the United States than the Soviet Union, saying that there would be 20 million unauthorized immigrants in the United States by the year 2000.'[28]

An estimated 1,782,000 foreign-born persons lived in California in 1970, a number that jumped to 3,580,000 in 1980 – 7.9 percent of California's 23,668,000 residents.[29] Latino visibility increased in the 1980s as hundreds of thousands of Central Americans joined Mexicans in Los Angeles. This growth increased Euroangelenos' feelings of loss of control over their city.[30] As one observer put it, prior to the 1970s many Angelenos were accustomed to seeing Mexicans only at amusement parks. Yet the threat to Anglo control was hardly serious; more true to life was the opportunistic use of concern about 'illegal aliens' to justify increased budget requests for law enforcement.[31] The Los Angeles Police Department emulated the INS in this way, as did other agencies. In recent years, studies reporting the immigrant 'threat' have often appeared when the INS was under attack or during budget hearings, a practice that found its way into the LAPD and the Sheriff's Department.

By the mid 1980s the campaign known as 'English-Only' was also gaining ground. In 1986, California voters passed a proposition officially called 'U.S. English', declaring English to be the official state language, and its supporters called for efforts to pass such a law in every state. It was a thinly veiled attack on bilingualism and respect for other cultures; bilingual education itself became a favorite whipping boy of the Eurocentrists.[32]

As in the past, politicians exploited the racist mood. In 1985, immigration as a threat to public safety was a key theme in the Republican primary for the US Senate. Los Angeles Supervisor Mike Antonovich, a candidate for the Republican nomination, ran a commercial filmed at the Otay Mesa border linking nightly crossings of a thousand or more undocumented persons to drug trafficking and terrorism. Antonovich called for the use of the military to guard the border, and advocated deportation of US-born children of the undocumented, accusing them of costing the county $130 million. His commercial was so outrageous that Catholic Archbishop Roger Mahoney called it offensive and demanded an apology; Mahoney was also enraged by the remark of an Antonovich aide that the situation was so bad he wished he had a Smith & Wesson.[33]

Reports of INS abuse were common throughout the 1980s and have continued into the 1990s. According to a two-year American Friends Service Committee study of the Border Patrol, between May 1988 and May 1989, there were 814 complainants, many of them from amnesty clients with temporary cards.[34] The frequent misconduct of Border Patrol agents was excused by the War on Drugs and the resulting atrocities remained difficult to prosecute.

The Army Corps of Engineers announced plans to place scores of floodlights along a thirteen-mile strip of border near San Diego to 'deter drug smugglers and illegal aliens.' It would supplement an eleven-mile fence built in 1990 when Bush enlisted the Defense Department in the so-called War on Drugs.[35] This buildup continued into the Clinton administration, with Attorney General Janet Reno approving blockades and roundups in the El Paso and San Diego areas – the latter as an entry point for people heading for Los Angeles.[36] That sense of loss of control led to calls to seal the border completely, which could only be done through an enormous outlay of resources or the application of state-authorized violence. As a 1992 *Atlantic* article suggested, 'It would not require much killing: the Soviets sealed their borders for decades without an excessive expenditure of ammunition.' Such a systematic policy of shooting illegal immigrants would deter most Mexicans, the author observed. But, he added, 'adopting such a policy is not a choice most Americans would make. And, of course, there would be no question of free trade.'[37]

The Immigration Reform and Control Act

The anti-immigrant propaganda war continues to rage. The Washington, D.C.–based Urban Institute issued a report in 1984 on immigration in California, entitled *The Fourth Wave*. It made the point that each wave of immigrants into the United States had distinctive characteristics, describing the Fourth Wave as that of Hispanics and Asians. According to the report, most of the Latino immigrants were working-class with a grade school education, so they would not be able to compete with Euroamericans for white-collar jobs.[38] Statistically, immigrants stood at the bottom of the employment ladder. According.to the report, immigrants were heavily concentrated in manufacturing, where they made up 54.8 percent, 73.7 percent, 89.4 percent, 59.2 percent and 73.6 percent of food, textiles, apparel, lumber and furniture/fixture workers, respectively.[39] Recent immigrants took more than two-thirds of the 645,000 jobs added to the Los Angeles County economy during the 1970s, but most of the jobs were low-paying, low-skill, blue-collar and service jobs – jobs that were not normally attractive to the native-born.

By 1982, the report continued, unemployment in southern California hit 10 percent, with unemployment among blue-collar workers exceeding 15 percent.[40] This was the sector most concerned about job security, and, as L.A.'s heavy industry moved out, displaced workers were most susceptible to the myths of scapegoating. Contrary to those myths, however, immigrants generated economic expansion during the 1970s, which resulted in new jobs and the preservation of old ones.[41]

The Mexican American Defense and Education Fund (MALDEF) was also active in studying these issues, and the work of Linda Wong, MALDEF's former immigration specialist, has been exceptional. MALDEF tracked the different immigration bills, which called for employer sanctions, a guest worker program, a national identification card and greater border enforcement. A combination of Speaker Thomas P. O'Neill, Jr and the Latino Caucus derailed such bills.[42] Aside from employer sanctions, Chicanos most strongly opposed an expansion of the H-2 guest worker program.

After twenty years of struggle, the Immigration Reform and Control Act passed in 1986, in a compromise that combined employer sanctions and amnesty. The bill passed because of the defection of California liberal legislators. It was a major defeat for Chicano activists, who saw employer sanctions as a way to starve out undocumented workers. The act listed two ways that applicants could ask for amnesty: 1) provable, continuous residence since 1 January 1982; or 2) provable farm work for ninety days between 1 May 1985 to 1 May 1986. By January 1989 some 2.96 million had applied, about 70 percent of them Mexican.[43]

IRCA allocated $1 billion dollars a year for four years via the State Legislation Impact Assistance Grant programs to pay for classes in English, US history and government, which were mandatory for all amnesty applicants. Organizations such as Hermandad Mexicana Nacional and One Stop Immigration provided these and other services. But various interest groups were soon chipping away at the IRCA funds. In March 1989, Sen. Edward Kennedy introduced an emergency funding bill to assist in the resettlement of an unanticipated surge of 25,000 refugees from the Soviet Union. To pay for this program, Kennedy proposed to take $200 million away from the funds allocated by Congress for the amnesty program for immigrants. Kennedy was supported by Rep. Howard Berman, despite the fact that many of the Latino amnesty immigrants lived in Berman's district. President Bush had already sought to rescind a $600 million installment destined for IRCA applicants.[44]

In the fall of 1992, Congress cut $812 million from health and education programs for amnesty clients. This was a blow to California, since it would have received half the money, and it intensified immigrant bashing because of Californians' resentment at paying a larger share. In response, Governor Pete Wilson charged that 'Congress has reneged on a promise to fully fund the cost associated with newly legalized residents.'[45]

Clearly, IRCA has not stemmed the flow of immigrants. Even with the recession, there was a demand for workers to provide labor-intensive services. On the other side, the wage differential pushed Mexicans into the United States. Some 55 percent of Mexican wage earners made about $7.50 a day, or under $1 an hour.[46] Meanwhile, US immigration policies were returning to the pattern of preferential quotas for Europeans. For instance, in 1994 a visa lottery was held as a regular component of the immigration selection system. It was referred to as DV-1, and it had a 'diversity' provision, which amounted to giving Europeans a preferred status. Under a complicated formula, 55,000 visa numbers were assigned to this category, which favored nations that did not do well under family preferences. A high school diploma was mandatory, and the purpose was to encourage 'new seed' by favoring 'low admission states' – countries that had fared badly in the past five years.

Under this formula Mexico and Canada were ineligible, and the rest of Latin America received a small fraction of the 'diversity' admits. Europe got the largest numbers, followed by Africa. The purpose, according to Congress, was to help those 'adversely affected' by the 1965 Immigration Act. Critics called the diversity lottery an 'affirmative action' program for Europeans, and charged that the legislation already favored skills-based immigration, cutting into the number of visas reserved for family reunification. The argument for occupational and skill preferences was that Canada and Australia were actively competing for these immigrants, getting an edge over the United States.

Central Americans at Risk

Many Salvadorans and Guatemalans in Los Angeles had arrived after 1982, the cut-off date for qualifying under the 1986 IRCA amnesty program. Large numbers of them were fleeing oppressive conditions imposed by murderous dictatorships actively supported by the US government, only to have their applications to be considered political refugees rejected. US immigration officials created the fiction that there was a difference between political and economic refugees. In essence, if the refugee came from a dictatorship that was friendly to the United States, the worker was an economic refugee, whereas if the refugee came from a country considered unfriendly to the US, he or she was a political refugee.

It is estimated that between 250,000 and 500,000 Salvadorans live in Los Angeles. Many are scattered in the numerous Mexican *colonias*, but heavy concentrations of Salvadorans exist in the Pico-Union, Westlake-MacArthur Park area, Hollywood, and also in South Central Los Angeles, where there are also concentrations of Guatemalans and Mexicans. Most are of working-class background. Many have applied for political asylum, but only 3 percent of Salvadorans and 2 percent of Guatemalans have been granted asylum, in contrast to 70 percent of the Nicaraguans who left during democratic Sandinista rule and 80 percent of the Soviet Jews who applied. Because of the pressure applied by church and human rights groups, these Central Americans were granted work rights or Temporary Protected Status (TPS) while awaiting a ruling on asylum by the courts.[47]

For the Central American refugee in Los Angeles, deportation from the US back home often meant death or imprisonment. Today, while hostilities still continue in Guatemala, a tenuous peace in El Salvador has turned the attention of Salvadoran immigrants to their daily problems in the United States. Realistically, many of the Salvadoran and other Central American children have been Americanized, and the probability that they will return to their homelands is now remote.[48] The conditions Salvadorans face worsened as the Clinton administration and Congress moved to deny them special refugee status. The TPS program had shielded 187,000 Salvadorans from deportation because of the long civil war in the region. Now the rationale was that since the war had ended, it was safe for them to return. The only alternative for many of these refugees was to apply for regular asylum, which is very difficult to obtain.

The Centroamericanos in Los Angeles were mostly poor and did not have the resources to influence elected officials. They did form their own organizations, building an impressive array of solidarity groups and refugee support groups that were helped by white progressives. In the face of these life-threatening dilemmas, some Chicanos in Los Angeles stood shoulder-to-shoulder with Central Americans. Their solidarity work included travel to Central America to support the movements there (also, in the early 1980s, Chicanos actively opposed support for the contras seeking to overthrow the Sandinista government in Nicaragua).

Notable among the Chicanas doing solidarity work was Angela Sanbrano, as executive director of the Committee in Solidarity with the People of El Salvador (CISPES) the highest-ranking Chicana in the US peace movement. Sanbrano came to Los Angeles from El Paso wanting something better than a factory job. In Pomona, she went to junior college because she wanted to get away from a sales clerk job; secretaries sat down. On scholarship at the Claremont Colleges, she majored in psychology. While studying at the Peoples College of Law, she helped found *Inquilinos Unidos* (United Renters) where she came into contact with Salvadoran refugees. Seeing the impact of US policy in Central America, she then became active in the peace movement, to become a CISPES leader. A fiery speaker, she crisscrossed the country calling for an end to US intervention in El Salvador. Because of her views, Sanbrano received threats from the underground Salvadoran death squad in this country.

Chicano students were also heavily involved in the sanctuary movement. Lisa Durán, for instance, headed one of the most active groups, at the University of California, Riverside, offering sanctuary to the undocumented. The Justice Department generally kept these groups under surveillance. Throughout the Southwest Chicanos worked with sanctuary organizations.

Locally, Father Luis Olivares, a Claretian, symbolized the sanctuary movement:[49] Olivares was an early supporter of César Chávez and the farmworkers. As pastor at Our Lady of Soledad in unincorporated East Los Angeles, he helped organize the United Neighborhood Organization (UNO), a grassroots group seeking to expand Latino influence. In 1981 Olivares became pastor of Our Lady Queen of the Angels, the city's oldest Catholic church. Once a symbol of Spanish colonial domination, La Placita, as it was known, later became a refuge for poor Mexicans who were unwelcome in English-speaking parishes like St Viviana and St Vincent. Olivares arrived at the church when waves of Mexican and Central American pilgrims, in a modern-day Christmas tale, were seeking sanctuary in this twentieth-century Belén. Mindful of La Placita's historical significance and the importance of giving people hope, Olivares opened the church's doors to the refugees. His message was clear: How can you show love for a God that you cannot see if you show no love for your fellow human beings?

During his eight years at La Placita, Olivares became the symbol of the Christ who kicked the Pharisees out of the temple rather than the Jesus who ate at their table. An adamant critic of US involvement in El Salvador, he declared his church a sanctuary in 1985, and as a result was threatened by Salvadoran death squads based in Los Angeles. He forged strong links with labor and community organizations, reinforcing their commitment to peace with justice. The impending transfer of Olivares to Fort Worth, Texas caused an uproar. It was interpreted by Latinos as a weakening of the Church's commitment to the cause of social justice. Olivares never went to Fort Worth, dying of AIDS in 1993, contracted in El Salvador during treatment for his chronic diabetes. After he left, more than 200 refugees were removed from Our Lady Queen of the Angels, many of whom were left with few alternatives.[50]

Unfortunately, cooperation between Chicanos and Central Americans is not always a given. In the struggle for space in Los Angeles, Chicanos have not always been generous to other Latino groups. Competition for survival has resulted in tensions between youth and even adults, with some Chicanos blaming

Mexican and Central American immigrants for their lack of access to jobs, housing and other resources. Mirroring these tensions have been tensions between immigrants themselves, with each group asserting its own claims. Indeed, these internal tensions often take on the characteristics of the racism of the dominant society.

It is also important to add that despite the involvement of Chicanos and others in the solidarity movement for peace and justice in Central America, Central Americans themselves led this movement. They were especially successful in winning support to end the war in El Salvador, but the aftermath of that war has brought new problems, with many of the solidarity leaders challenged by the work of offering assistance to refugees and other immigrants. Organizations like the Central American Refugee Center (CARECEN), which was founded in 1983, offer social services and are engaged in economic development. In Los Angeles, CARECEN is led by Roberto Lovato, a Salvadoran American who has effectively worked with Chicanos and others to educate immigrants and protect their rights in the face of assaults such as Proposition 187.

The Central American organizations suffer from the lack of a middle-class base, such as that developing among Chicanos. Much of the support they organized during the 1980s has dwindled. Many progressive Euroangelenos who worked for peace in Central America have failed to recognize that a war is raging in the streets of L.A. In the meantime, the increasing numbers of Central Americans add to the political mass that is making the election of Chicanos possible.

The increasing diversity of Latino groups is testing the moral authority of the Chicano middle class to lead. After years of political struggle, Chicanos have achieved a degree of political power. Almost all Latino elected officials, with exception of Hilda Solis, are of Mexican descent. This is also true of most Latino professionals. Fate and US policy have thrown these groups together, and together they are forging a common culture shaped by their experiences in the City of the Angels.

'Too Many Brown Babies'

Around 2 million persons received amnesty under the 1986 Immigration Reform and Control Act (IRCA), and at least 800,000 of them lived in Los Angeles County: 90 percent were either Mexican or Central American. This did not include many of the children who were already US citizens by birth. Of the 3 million applying for citizenship, 80 percent were Latinos, and more than 50 percent of them were from Los Angeles.[51]

The Euroamerican response has often been hysteria. For example, Ben Wattenberg, a fellow with the conservative American Enterprise Institute, argued in his book *Birth Dearth* that falling US birthrates would lead to a decline of the West: 'Will America remain a nation that can continue to be characterized as one that is predominately white?' he asked. Wattenberg noted that the US was now 80 percent white, but by the year 2080 whites would form only 60 percent of the population. He suggested that the white middle class be paid to have babies – suggesting, in other words, that there were too many brown babies.[52]

The influential *Time* magazine also helped fan this kind of fire. A 1991 article painted a bleak picture of California, pointing out the obvious fact that Los Angeles was a Third World city. In the same issue Jordan Bonfante wrote, in 'The Endangered Dream', 'The main problem underlying California's malaise is simple: the state is attracting far more people than it can cope with.'[53] The underlying message – California was being invaded by dark-skinned people. *Time* cited nativist groups such as the Federation of American Immigration Reform (FAIR) to claim that the influx of newcomers exceeded the flood during the first decade of the century. This was not quite true: during the early 1900s the average annual percentage of immigrants in the population was 10.4 per thousand compared to 2.7 in the 1980s.[54] What made this wave of immigration different was the skin color of the newcomers and the rise of the drug traffic, which Eurocentric racists saw as a single phenomenon.[55]

Meanwhile, selective enforcement of IRCA led to discrimination against Chicanos and other Latinos. A report of the California Fair Employment and Housing Commission revealed that INS enforcement of employer sanctions under IRCA was encouraging US employers to turn away anyone who looked brown.[56] *Los Angeles Times* political commentator Bill Boyarsky warned in August 1993 of the dangers of the campaigns against illegal immigration being waged by Republican Governor Pete Wilson, Democratic Senators Dianne Feinstein and Barbara Boxer and many other politicians. Wilson was then proposing a tough package that included refusing citizenship to US-born children of illegal immigrants, plus 'ending the requirement that the state provide emergency health care to illegal immigrants; denying public education to their children; issuing tamper-proof identity cards to illegal immigrants and using negotiations over the North American Free Trade Agreement as a lever to force Mexico to control its border ...' Although he concluded that illegal immigration was a problem, Boyarsky wrote, 'I've read enough California history to know how attacks on immigrants, backed by new laws, seem to ignite the fires of racism, hurting both legal and illegal immigrants.'[57]

An August 1993 Field Poll showed that 74 percent of Californians believed that illegal immigration had a negative impact on the state, and 76 percent agreed that it was a serious problem. Among Latinos, 58 percent responded that immigration negatively impacted the state, while 64 percent said that it was a serious problem.[58] The poll revealed that 77 percent of the public supported Wilson's opposition to undocumented immigrants receiving welfare via the Aid to Families with Dependent Children program; 72 percent wanted a tamper-proof residency card. Californians were split on the issue of citizenship for children born in the US of undocumented parents.[59] Latinos, however, differed significantly from Euroamericans on whose jobs the undocumented immigrants were taking, with 65 percent saying that they were taking jobs others didn't want, compared with 41 percent of whites.

Mark DiCamillo, associate director of the Field Poll, suggested that the reasons for white fears went beyond the recession and unemployment; perhaps they were stimulated by 'politicians spotlighting the issue' with a view to the 1994 election. Wilson, lingering at a 15 percent approval rating, continued to exploit white economic resentment as well as the mostly unspoken fear that the US would become a non-white nation. Extremist groups like the Federation for American Immigration Reform spent millions of dollars to perpetuate the myth of the 'Mexican invasion'. In this climate, it came as no great surprise that Eddie Cortez, the first Latino mayor of Pomona and a Republican, was stopped while driving home by INS agents who threatened him with arrest and deportation.[60]

Meanwhile, Wilson made a 1991 Los Angeles County report the cornerstone of his anti-immigrant campaign. His message was simple: stop offering illegal immigrants government services, and we'll save state and federal taxpayers $2.9 billion a year. The problem was that Wilson exaggerated the number of undocumented, estimating that there were 4 million in the state.[61] He also advocated the deportation of felons who were illegal immigrants. Critics suggested that Wilson had opportunistic political motives in raising this point, since state law already authorized the deportation of felons. Even Commander Alan Chancellor, a contributor to the L.A. County study, questioned Wilson's claims about saving money if prisoners were shipped back to Mexico. Chancellor, who oversaw the Los Angeles County jails, pointed out that there was no guarantee that the felons, once deported, would not find their way back to the United States.[62] Wilson's claim that California was overcrowded was also bogus: California's population grew by 85.5 percent from 1950 to 1970, but by only 49.6 percent from 1970 to 1990.

A similar report from San Diego County alleged that undocumented immigrants cost San Diego County $146 million. Claudia Smith, an attorney with the Southern California Rural Legal Assistance program, countered the report, emphasizing the benefits of immigration: in particular, 'that this young, cheap, flexible labor pool stimulates the creation of new businesses and helps preserve labor-intensive ones.'[63] Other observers pointed out that the Euroamerican population was getting older and would ultimately depend on the much younger Latino population for social security and other entitlements.[64] A *New York Times* Poll revealed 'that anti-immigrant feelings also are colored by a perception – which is not supported by facts – that most immigrants are in the

United States illegally.'[65]

FAIR regularly sent speakers, such as University of California, Santa Barbara Professor Otis Graham, Jr, to the border to address anti-immigration groups. The White Aryan Resistance (WAR) was also active. *Los Angeles Times* reporters summed up their line: 'Hitler was a saint. The Holocaust never happened. Jews are the children of Satan and are destroying the United States along with other "mud people" African Americans, Asians, Latinos – anyone not descended from Anglo-Saxon stock.'[66]

In March 1991, 800 Latino families of pupils at Santa Monica High School were mailed an unauthorized flyer commending the principal for closing the campus after two Mexican youths fired five rounds near the school:

> Protect innocent, law respecting students from these brown animals. Mexicans [sic] students are inferior and dumb. If these animals can't even learn to be responsible citizens, then they can't be treated in a civilized way. Mexicans are the most lazy and ignorant race in the world ... They don't want to be responsible citizens, they just want to steal. We are dealing with cruel and violent animals with no self control. Look at Rodney King. He'll think twice before robbing another store.[67]

The 'open-season on Mexicans' climate of hate encouraged INS agents to adopt an arrogance of power, especially towards Latinas; many were raped by agents when crossing the border. The journey to the border caused serious post-traumatic disorders; of 200 Latinas studied, 20 percent were found to be suffering from some such disorder.[68]

At the highest levels of government, little was done to curb the hysteria. According to Attorney General Janet Reno, 'In this decade, [immigration] will be the single most difficult problem we face together.' President Clinton was afraid to exercise any moral authority, mindful that he had been defeated in his re-election for governor of Arkansas because of a widespread belief that he did not act quickly enough to put down a riot of Cuban inmates at Fort Chafee.[69] Clinton had also been embarrassed during the confirmation hearings of Zoe Baird and Kimba Wood for attorney general by revelations that they had hired undocumented workers.

In Los Angeles politics, it became clear that a strong shift to the right had occurred on immigration and other issues. Congressman Elton Gallegly's (R-Simi Valley) proposal of a constitutional amendment to deny citizenship to US-born children of undocumented immigrants was in line with the proposals that Antonovich and Fielder had made during the mid 1980s. But Gallegly had been considered a moderate Republican; now he had fallen in line with the extremist groups. He was joined by Rep. Anthony Bielenson of the San Fernando Valley, who had at one time been considered a progressive Democrat, but who had opportunistically exploited the anti-immigrant hysteria in his district.[70]

The response of Latino politicos to the anti-immigration drive lacked commitment. During the 1993 L.A. mayoral race, Latinos supporting Michael Woo were reluctant to censure him for his anti-immigrant stance. During the governor's race, seven Latino lawmakers supported Kathleen Brown despite her failure to defend immigrant rights. This lessened the moral authority of the equation that immigrant-bashing equals racism – a view that the Pope and Cardinal Mahoney had put forward.[71] Latinos were in part to blame for the rightist climate that has developed in recent years, which encouraged the attack on immigrants. Twelve years of Reagan and Bush had made Chicano leaders tolerant of conservative Latino gatekeepers and more 'objective', as it was termed, about defending immigrants. In a naturalization ceremony for 7,000 new citizens, many Latinos called for a crackdown on 'illegals', and the news media widely publicized that sentiment.[72] Limited access to the media also made it hard for Chicanos to develop a unified response to the hysteria.

The campaign against the undocumented was incessant. In the aftermath of the 1994 L.A. earthquake, which left some 20,000 people homeless, sleeping in parks,[73] many Republican congressmen tried to use the tragedy for their own political ends by seeking to deny humanitarian services to undocumented residents. Rep. Dana Rohrbacher (R-Huntington Park) and Assemblyman Pat Nolan led the charge. Nolan shrilled: 'They [Latino earthquake victims] should be relocated back to their home country – that's a humanitarian thing.' Rohrbacher agreed: 'I want the people of California to understand that hundreds of millions [of dollars] that should be going to them is [sic] instead going to illegal aliens, and it's absolutely outrageous.' They held a press conference at which they produced a Black, a Korean and a Spaniard to second their position. Other members of Congress took up the cry, including Rep. Ron Packard (R-Carlsbad), for a ban on medical assistance except in emergency situations. Funding for the $7.8 billion earthquake relief program was held up by these racists in order to tighten the noose around the necks of the undocumented.

Newspaper editors were equally humane. *Daily News* columnist Debra J. Saunders wrote, 'When FEMA [the Federal Emergency Management Agency] gives checks to illegal aliens, it is paying them to stay in America and break the law.' This rhetoric diverted attention from the fact that Gov. Wilson did not commit state funds to help the victims of the Northridge earthquake and refused to support a temporary sales tax, which had been done to help the victims of the Loma Prieta earthquake in 1989. Officials of FEMA denied these allegations and others by Saunders, who claimed that it was passing out $2,000 checks to 'illegals' renting damaged homes,[74] and noted that the law already prohibited undocumented residents from receiving aid. Rep. Esteban Torres, attempting to head off more stringent measures, offered a modified version of the funding bill that FEMA would cut long-term aid such as SBA loans or housing vouchers.[75] Charles Wheeler, executive director of the National Immigration Law Center said, 'I think it is cruel and bizarre to link immigration to a natural disaster of this magnitude.' Even Mayor Riordan stated that it would be a bureaucratic nightmare to cut aid to the undocumented.[76]

Leticia A.: Students Losing Out on a Dream

A major battleground of the struggle for immigrant rights was on the university campuses, where extremist groups like FAIR campaigned in the late 1980s to deny an education to undocumented students. This drive intensified during the early 1990s, when a Los Angeles Superior Court judge overturned the ruling known as Leticia A., a 1985 decision by an Alameda County court that counted undocumented students as residents for tuition purposes. Now *Bradford v. The Regents of the University of California* ended Leticia A., a state policy that indirectly encouraged undocumented students to learn English and be law-abiding residents. Euroangelenos and Californians were reluctant to make this investment.

A coalition of college admissions counselors and administrators formed the Leticia A. Network to keep the doors open to undocumented students. This effort was led by counselors such as the late Arnulfo Casillas of Glendale College; Hilda Solis, now a state senator; Alfredo Figueroa of the University of California Riverside; Alfred Herrera of UCLA; and Ramón Muñiz of CSUN.[77]

The Bradford ruling itself was meanspirited and shortsighted. It shut the door on the dream of going to the University of California to thousands of undocumented students. Then Superior Court Judge Robert O'Brien took occasion to expand the Bradford ruling to the state university system and the community colleges, attempting to totally destroy any hope of a higher education for those students. State Assemblyman Richard Polanco attempted to restore Leticia A. by introducing AB 592. It passed both houses, but Governor Wilson returned the Polanco bill unsigned. Wilson said that federal law classified undocumented students as illegal, so that it would be inconsistent 'to confer upon them a tuition benefit that is based upon legal residence.' He added that the state 'has a legitimate interest in not subsidizing the education of those who may be deported.' Naturally, Wilson's public approval rating rose on announcement of this action.

The impact of Bradford will be felt for years to come. In the fall of 1993, out-of-state university tuition was scheduled to increase to $10,584 versus $2,885 for residents. Out-of-state community college tuition was $103 per unit versus $6 for in-state students. The UC and the community colleges went along with the decision, and students without documents had to pay the higher out-of-state fees. The state universities appealed the decision. In January 1995, the 2nd District Court of Appeals ordered the CSU system to start to collect out-of-state tuition from undocumented students – which, on the heels of Proposition 187, represented a tremendous victory for the forces of reaction in California. The words of Angela Mihelson, a 21-year-old university student, had gone unheeded: 'If more educated Hispanics go back into the Hispanic community, the [Caucasian and Latino] communities as a whole reap the benefits.'[78]

The Bradford decision epitomized the racist, anti-immigrant attitudes of the late twentieth century. Since the passage of IRCA, Congress has approved a series of amendments and acts excluding the poor while favoring immigrants who were rich or highly skilled. The Immigration Act of 1990 authorized a brain-drain immigration from poor countries, robbing them of their most educated sectors, to save US taxpayers the expense of educating their own children. The 1990 act authorized entry of 140,000 scientists (good news for laid-off US aerospace engineers) – and made available 10,000 visas for rich investors.[79]

Immigration and Black–Brown Relations

In the assault on immigrant rights, no tactic was uglier than the efforts to play upon and aggravate tensions between African Americans and Latinos. Ultraright groups like FAIR, for example, broadcast messages to the Black community that its dire economic straits should be blamed on immigrants taking jobs. It's important to understand this aspect of immigrant-bashing in the general context of Black–Latino relations in recent Los Angeles history.

It should come as no surprise that Black–Latino tensions exist in Los Angeles, paralleling friction between Blacks and Asians, Blacks and Jewish-Americans, and the emerging friction between Latinos and Armenians. As part of this society, Chicanos, like other people of color, have internalized its racism, adopting 'the racial prejudices and misperceptions of whites', to use the words of Pitzer College Afro-American studies professor Halford Fairchild.[80] At the same time, Blacks have often considered Latinos whites, and adopted Anglo stereotypes about them.

The sources of these tensions are complex. They include, first, dissimilarities in language, customs and historical experiences. African Americans and Latinos often come from separate universes, and the resulting lack of understanding between them can be a source of conflict. This type of tension is more prevalent among working-class Chicanos and African Americans, whose cross-cultural experiences are more limited than those of middle-class professionals. Language conflict, which frustrates communication between the groups, is not as much a factor among middle-class Latinos and Blacks, who both speak primarily English. Moreover, they are less apt to compete for living space.

A second source of tension that can be found among Latinos is a pattern of racist attitudes toward Blacks, no doubt a legacy of Spanish colonialism and the internalization of US values. Historically, the state has often played one group against the other – for example, by stationing African American soldiers at bases close to Mexican *colonias*, as in south Texas and southern Arizona. At the same time, Blacks have sometimes internalized the nativist attitudes of Euroamericans toward the foreign-born as well as the Euroamerican habit of 'pecking down'. And, as one longtime resident of South Central L.A. put it, '[African Americans] feel threatened by the emerging Hispanic majority. They feel swept aside and squeezed.'[81]

For working-class Latinos and Blacks, economic problems have been a crucial source of conflict. The economic downturn of the late 1980s ended an era of upward mobility via blue-collar work for Blacks. Between 1970 and 1982, L.A. Blacks – especially teenagers – had held their own in the labor market, making gains that were above the average for African Americans nationwide. Even during the 1982 recession, they exceeded the national norm for African Americans, and they seemed to be moving more rapidly into white-collar occupations. In 1980 seven of ten Black women held white-collar jobs in Los Angeles, whereas one out of ten immigrant women worked in white-collar occupations.[82] With the deindustrialization of Los Angeles, that ratio changed for Black women, although not for immigrants.

During the 1980s, many Latino immigrants flocked to service and garment industry jobs, which Blacks and US-born Latinos had long shunned. When the restructuring of the economy eliminated jobs in heavy industry, however, those once-unattractive service jobs became the only alternatives for Blacks. Because a significant number of undocumented workers now held these jobs, desperate Black workers believed that the immigrants had taken jobs that belonged to them. At the same time, Mexican and Latino service workers guarded hard-won gains from their struggles to unionize, which had brought higher wages and benefits.[83] The exact degree of job competition between African Americans and immigrants (meaning primarily Mexicans and other Latinos) continues to be controversial. Some scholars maintain that such competition is real (in the 1980s, if not the 1970s), but must be measured in a context that includes the role of racism in traditionally denying jobs to African Americans, the disastrous effects of California's economic restructuring on the job market, and the increased job opportunities created by immigrants as a result of their increasing the population of an area.[84]

The struggle over political spoils also contributed to Black–Brown tensions. The civil rights movement saw dramatic gains for African Americans, with Blacks making major inroads into government jobs. By 1990, although they represented less than 10 percent of the workforce, African Americans held over 20 percent of the public-sector positions.[85] As long as the Black and Chicano populations remained equal in size, tensions were minimal. But as Chicano/Latino numbers grew during the 1960s, 1970s and 1980s, the expectations of second-generation Chicanos and Latinos also increased. Based on their numbers, they believed that they were entitled to a bigger piece of the political and economic pie, in terms of electoral posts and patronage opportunities.

Both Chicano and Black powerbrokers derive their strength from playing the race card. In this sense Chicanos/Latinos and Blacks are competitors for services, living space and access to government and even the drug trade turf. In the process of this competition, it's tempting for leaders of both groups to rally troops around their community. Competition between middle-class Blacks and Latinos over the division of the political pie is likely to continue to escalate, as we will see. Latinos are becoming a majority in African American council districts such as the 9th CD. The retirement of Mayor Tom Bradley dealt a blow to Black middle-class economic interests in Los Angeles; it threatened their access to public and private sector funds. (There was considerable discontent with Bradley among working-class Blacks, who felt that he did not address their concerns, and that he slighted South Central, for example, in the allocation of city funds.) Meanwhile, the Chicano/Latino bourgeoisie positioned itself to challenge Blacks for what many considered the 'minority' share.

Another source of tension between Black and Brown was the lack of a well-defined vision on the part of both Chicano and Black leaders for a multiracial Los Angeles. They usually advocated programs with a narrow focus and constituency. Neither Chicano nor Black leaders, or, for that matter, whites and Asians, designed goals and programs that took the needs of a multiracial city into account. This lack of vision will surely be another source of growing tension as the number of Chicano and Latino registered voters surpasses that of African Americans.

The basic political structure of the city makes conflict almost inevitable. Latino, Black and Jewish-American politicos hold thirteen of the fifteen council seats; each serves the interests of a race-specific constituency. Power-sharing is difficult in this environment, since there is no tradition or practice of it in L.A. Political questions in Los Angeles tend to be reduced to racial terms – 'Black issues' or 'Latino issues'.[86]

Within this context, historical memories are a source of friction. Many Blacks believe that other minorities, including Latinos, benefit from 'their' civil rights struggle. The historical memory of African Americans is rooted in a national reality and is part of mainstream US history, whereas Mexican American history is considered 'foreign'. Few African Americans know much about the Southwest or the history of Chicanos in this part of the country, a historical illiteracy shared by most Euroamericans. Even advocacy of teaching about Chicano civil rights struggles can increase tensions between Black and Brown.

For their part, Chicano intellectuals and Chicanos in general have failed to explain the experiences of their people in racial terms that might help develop

Black–Brown understanding and solidarity. This is partly due to the lack of research and publication on Chicanos, with the result that the rich literature of African American scholars on the subject simply eclipses that available on other groups. Hence the race question in the US has become synonymous with African Americans to the exclusion of other people of color.

Further, most US literature on racism is laden with terms and paradigms that have little meaning to those outside of academia or the Left. Thus knowledge does not filter down to those most directly affected by intercommunal friction. Ideological struggle in the United States is thus elitist, with little application to working-class practice. It further loses in translation when applied outside the white–Black model.

The reality is that for someone from the Chicano, Black, Asian, or, for that matter, the Jewish communities to be a player in Los Angeles, he or she must maintain some sort of legitimacy within the group, accepting definite parameters within which one must operate. This makes coalition-building very difficult, since one either becomes a professional participant in race-encounter groups – in which case you are seen as pandering to other ethnic groups – or you 'defend' your group, right or wrong.

A meshing of interests is made even more difficult by the inability of Chicano activists to explain what they want and why they deserve it, which should go beyond saying that the land was once Aztlán. Chicanos must talk in terms of a vision of society. For the most part, there is no environment or political culture in Los Angeles that allows for such discussion. The mass media and so-called scholars have often aggravated this problem.

For example, Roy Beck, editor of the conservative quarterly journal *Social Contract*, together with Otis Graham, Jr, a U.C. Santa Barbara history professor and FAIR board member, blamed undocumented immigrants for the 'Rodney King riots': 'We should not have to rediscover that massive immigration widens the divide between wealth and poverty, storing up social dynamite, especially diminishing life, for African Americans.' Graham and Beck singled out the 1965 Immigration Act as the cause of tight labor markets and the end of Black American prosperity, totally ignoring how the restructuring of the L.A. economy had a devastating impact on African Americans along with Latinos and working-class Asians and Euroangelenos.[87]

Jack Miles, a former Catholic priest and one-time editor of the book review pages of the *Los Angeles Times* who drifted onto its Op-Ed pages as a copy editor in 1992, wrote an article entitled 'The Struggle for the Bottom Rung, Blacks vs. Browns' in which he shamelessly pitted Blacks and Browns against one another. Miles went on to make rhetorical statements with no intellectual comprehension of the problems of race in L.A.: 'African Americans seem to me to be competing more directly with Latin Americans than with any other group.' (Who else would they be 'competing' with – white Americans from

Brentwood?) He also wrote that Black men were shadowed by suspicious shop-keepers, inferring that Latinos are trusted, an assumption that is simply not true.[88]

Asian–Chicano Relations

While constituting less than 11 percent of the population, Asian Americans and Asians are very visible in Los Angeles, having more than doubled their numbers during the 1980s. In almost every case, Asians have settled in close proximity to Chicanos and Latinos, with whom they competed for space. Their diversity and economic resources have facilitated movement even into what were exclusively upper-income white neighborhoods. They spread both east and west throughout Los Angeles County and have moved heavily into Orange County. In 1960, 8,000 Chinese Americans lived in Los Angeles, with the number growing to 19,000 in 1970, and 44,000 in 1980.[89] During the 1980s Monterey Park became 57 percent Asian. Nearby Alhambra, San Gabriel and Rosemead became about a third Asian. Asians also expanded north of the traditional Chinatown (where 4,600 people already lived) into Lincoln Heights and Echo Park (where another 25,000 resided).

Filipinos were clustered in the Temple/Alvarado area, where they comprised about one-third of the population. They also had concentrations east of Hacienda Heights and in Long Beach. The Japanese had the oldest community and seemingly the largest percentage of third-generation members. They were fairly well-integrated except for enclaves in Sawtelle, the Crenshaw area, and Gardena. Koreans were situated in Koreatown next to Pico-Union.[90] (Koreatown was actually only 30 percent Asian; a large percentage of this area was Latino.) The major concentration of Vietnamese was in Orange County.[91]

During the 1990s Asians have had to live down the stereotype of being the 'model minority', the image that they were hard-working, intelligent people who have made it in the US. Not all of them, however, were entrepreneurs, professionals or students. Many Asians, especially the refugees from Southeast Asia, lived in poverty. In 1989, median household income in L.A. was $39,352 for Asian Americans, compared with $26,027 for Blacks, $27,803 for Latinos, and $39,106 for Euroamericans. However, as in the case of Latinos, Asians did not rank as high when per capita income was taken into account. A 1993 study by the Leadership Education for Asian Pacific Inc., 'Beyond Asian American Poverty', showed that one out of five Asians lived in poverty, and that about 18,000 were on welfare.[92] Although in need, the image of the 'model minority' hindered them when it came to social services. For example, Angelenos were shocked when 34-year-old Chinese immigrant Ophilia Yip from Sepulveda drowned herself and her four young children in Los Angeles Harbor. A lack of outreach and proper counseling in her language drove her to the edge.[93]

Asian Americans embrace a rich variety of cultures. But we can safely generalize that, as with Chicano–Black relations, most of the communication between Asian Americans and Chicanos has been via their respective elites, meaning politicians and activists, who had a critical mass of second- and third-generation leaders. Chicano–Asian tensions have not been as fraught as Black–Asian relations. Whatever tensions that exist have usually remained under the surface, ranging from complaints of day laborers being gouged by individual Asian employers to nativist reactions toward Asians by second- and third-generation Chicanos, as in Monterey Park, where Chicanos complained about Chinese-language signs. There has also been friction between youth when gangs have found themselves sharing the same territory.[94]

Nationwide, 44 percent of Asians hold college degrees and well-educated Asians have rapidly established themselves in the top scientific and medical professions, outdistancing Blacks and Latinos. The explanation for this success is not cultural. A significant sector of Asian immigrants who have arrived in the United States since 1968 have been better educated or belonged to a higher social class than Blacks and Latinos. Those who did not have money or some sort of position in their home country have had more difficult times.[95]

Because of residential proximity, it is also natural that Asian Americans and Latinos would increasingly become political competitors. With the 1990 redistricting, Councilwoman Judy Chu of Monterey Park led a campaign to create an Assembly district where an Asian could get elected. Asians were 57 percent of Monterey Park, outnumbering Latinos, and 39 percent of the voters. Creation of such a district would have meant cutting into the districts of then Assemblyman Xavier Becerra and Assemblywoman Sally Tanner of El Monte. Chu also planned to run for Diane Martínez's seat in 1994 if Martínez left it to run for Art Torres's state Senate seat, since Asians made up a sizeable chunk of the 49th Assembly District.[96]

After Michael Woo ran unsuccessfully for mayor, there was also a push to create a City Council district extending from Chinatown to Koreatown, and including some Filipino enclaves.[97] Statewide, March Fong Eu, a Chinese American, was elected secretary of state in 1974; before that she had been elected to the Assembly in 1965. Asians had some political success in statewide elections, and since 1970 the number of Asians on city councils in California has doubled to 48. However, that number is tiny compared with the total of council members in California. In 1994, only 29 cities had populations that were more than one-fifth Asian, contrasted with 67 cities having Latino majorities, and an additional 244 with more than one-fifth of the population Latino.[98]

Part of the alienation between groups comes again from the failure to appreciate each other's history. Discriminatory laws prevented Asian immigrants from becoming citizens until 1952.[99] And, like Mexicans and Central Americans, Asians have shared a running battle with the INS, which has regularly rounded up undocumented Chinese workers.[100] And contrary to the stereotype of Asians Americans as satisfied, they have a long history of struggle in California, especially as workers. This history has included alliances with Mexicans and Chicano workers, ranging from the Japanese–Mexican Labor Association formed in Oxnard in 1903 to the Filipino–Mexican grape workers' strike of 1965. They have also filed numerous discrimination suits and most recently have been active in the fight against Proposition 187 (although Asians statewide voted against the initiative by only a small majority). The Asian Pacific American Legal Center has led the fight not only for justice for Asians but for other groups.[101] Despite areas of disagreement, Latinos, Asians and Blacks share a collective sense of been robbed of opportunity by the white majority, according to a 1994 survey. Latinos and Asians also shared the backlash of Prop. 187.[102]

The goodwill between Asians and Latinos will be tested in 1996 if the so-called California Civil Rights Initiative appears on the state ballot. The CCRI is driven by rightwing groups and calls for the abolition of state affirmative action programs. The friction here will be similar to that between Black and Jews, and Jews and Latinos, over the issue of quotas. The challenge will be to convince Asians that democracy goes beyond economic mobility and is based on equality of opportunity.

Notes

1. See Rodolfo Acuña, *Occupied America: A History of Chicanos*, 3d edn (New York: Harper & Row, 1988), p. 141.

2. US Department of Labor, 'Report of the Commissioner General of Immigration', *Report of the Department of Labor* (Washington, D.C.: Government Printing Office, 1913), p. 337.

3. José Limón, 'El Primer Congreso Mexicanista de 1911: A Precursor to Conteı..porary Chicanismo', *Aztlán* (Spring/Fall 1974): pp. 80, 88, 89; *Regeneración*, 5 Aug. 1911; 'La Victima de los "Civilizados"', *Regeneración*, 26 Aug. 1911; Ricardo Flores Magón, 'A Salvar a un Inocente', *Regeneración*, 9 Sept. 1911; 'En defensa de los Mexicanos', *Regeneración*, 17 Aug. 1912.

4. Don M. Coever and Linda B. Hall, *Texas and the Mexican Revolution: A Study in State and National Border Policy, 1910–1920* (San Antonio, Tex.: Trinity University Press, 1984), pp. 85–108.

5. *The Texas Rangers: A Century of Frontier Defense*, 2d edn (Austin, Tex.: University of Texas Press, 1965), p. 478.

6. Ricardo Romo, *East Los Angeles. History of a Barrio* (Austin, Tex.: University of Texas Press, 1983), pp. 90, 91.

7. Ibid., pp. 102–3. In this context, *cholo* is a pejorative term referring to Mexicans.

8. Thomas Miller and Thomas J. Espenshade, *The Fourth Wave: California's Newest Immigrants* (Washington, D.C.: Urban Institute Press, 1985), p. 29.

9. John Higham, *Strangers in the Land: Patterns of American Nativism, 1860–1925* (New York: Athaneum, 1965), p. 9.

10. US Department of Labor, *Annual Report of the Commissioner General of Immigration* (Washington, D.C.: Government Printing Office, 1923), p. 16; Mark Reisler, *By the Sweat of Their Brow: Mexican Immigrant Labor in the United States, 1900–1940* (Westport, Conn.: Greenwood Press, 1976), pp. 55, 66–9; Job West Neal, 'The Policy of the United States Toward Immigration from Mexico' (Master's thesis, University of Texas, 1941), pp. 106, 107–8.

11. Stanley Mailman, 'Upcoming Visa Lottery', *New York Law Journal* (28 Feb. 1994), p. 3.

12. US Department of Labor, *Annual Report of the Commissioner of Immigration* (Washington, D.C.: Government Printing Office, 1926), p. 10; quoted in Robert J. Lipshultz, 'American Attitudes Toward Mexican Immigration, 1924–1952' (Master's thesis, University of Chicago, 1962).

13. In Miller and Espenshade, *Fourth Wave*, pp. 32–3.

14. Quoted in Cletus E. Daniel, *Bitter Harvest: A History of California Farmworkers, 1870–1941* (Berkeley, Calif.: University of California Press, 1981), p. 105.

15. In January 1931 Doak asked Congress to appropriate funds for the deportation of Mexicans, stating that 400,000 aliens had evaded immigration laws. In doing so, Doak encouraged local governments to begin the largest mass deportation of immigrants in the nation's history. Abraham Hoffman, 'Stimulus to Repatriation: The 1931 Federal Deportation Drive and the Los Angeles Mexican Community', in Norris Hundley, ed., *The Chicano* (Santa Barbara, Calif.: Clio, 1975), p. 110; Ronald López, 'Los Repatriados' (Seminar paper, History Department, University of California, Los Angeles, 1968), p. 63. Abraham Hoffman, *Unwanted Mexicans in the Great Depression* (Tucson, Az.: University of Arizona Press, 1974), is a seminal work on the repatriation.

16. López, p. 58; Hoffman, 'Stimulus to Repatriation', pp. 113, 116, 118.

17. John Phillip Carney, 'Postwar Mexican Migration: 1945–1950, with Particular Reference to the Policies and Practices of the United States Concerning Its Control' (Ph.D. dissertation, University of Southern California, 1957), p. 122.

18. Ralph Guzmán, 'Ojinaga, Chihuahua and Wetbacks', *Eastside Sun*, 15 Oct. 1953.

19. Juan Ramón García, 'Operation Wetback' (Ph.D. dissertation, University of Notre Dame, 1977), p. 214.

20. García, 'Operation Wetback', p. 214; what irked Allen was that Brownell had allegedly asked the labor leaders for support. Allen's communiqué was referred to James Haggerty; but there is no record that anything was done.

21. Because of the human rights violations against Mexicans in the US during the decade, a petition was presented in 1959 to the United Nations charging violation of the Universal Declaration of Human Rights, which had been adopted by the UN in 1948. San Antonio Archbishop Robert Lucey wrote the preface, charging that mistreatment of braceros was a national disgrace. Racism toward them was rampant, with many kept in concentration camps and their access to town limited. *Our Badge of Infamy: A Petition to the United Nations on the Treatment of the Mexican Immigrant*, American Committee for the Protection of the Foreign Born, April 1959, pp. iii–v.

22. Miller and Espenshade, *Fourth Wave*, p. 13.

23. James Shenfield, 'Economic Consequences of Immigration', *National Review*, vol. 42, no. 17 (3 Sept. 1990), p. 42. Years later Historian Theodore White wrote that the act was 'Noble, revolutionary – and probably the most thoughtless of the many acts of the Great Society.' White believed it a thoughtless act because Congress did not take into account the consequences of opening the gates to the Third World. James Fallows, 'Immigration: How It's Affecting us', *Atlantic* (Nov. 1983), quote on p. 45; review of Theodore White, *America in Search of Itself: The Making of the President 1956–80* (New York: Harper & Row, 1982), by Susan Bolotin, *New York Times*, 1 June 1982. Bolotin writes, 'One has to give Mr White credit for calling the shots as he sees them; for a respected public figure, himself the descendant of Jewish immigrants, to suggest that the State of Liberty was meant to beckon only to Europe is, at the least, bold.'

24. Scott McConnell, 'The New Battle Over Immigration', *Fortune*, 9 May 1988, p. 89. The 1965 act radically changed traditional European patterns of immigration. Attorney General Robert Kennedy told the Senate that 5,000 Asians might come during the new law's first year. Supporters in Congress thought it would favor the Greek Americans and the Italians.

25. F. Ray Marshall, 'Economic Factors Influencing the International Migration of Workers', in Stanley R. Ross, ed., *Views Across the Border* (Albuquerque, Tex.: University of New Mexico Press, 1978), p. 165. The shift of undocumented workers to urban areas had begun after World War II.

26. By June 1974, 54 persons had been indicted in some 228 cases, including high-ranking INS officials. News media reports even implicated key members of the House Judiciary Committee in corrupt activities; they included Congressman Peter Rodino. In order to divert attention from this corruption, it was alleged that INS commissioner General Leonard Chapman, Jr, had manufactured statistics and selectively offered falsified data, which the press uncritically reported. In 1975, a *Washington Post* investigative reporter found that Chapman's figures varied from 1.5 million to 12 million. It was also learned that the INS did not have a research department, so that the 'data'

amounted to estimates by the commissioner: see Acuña, *Occupied America*, 2nd edn, pp. 168–81.

27. Emilio García Capote, 'The Brain Drain in Latin America', *Granma* (Havana), 5 June 1999. Previously, applicants had been let in on a first-come, first-served basis.

28. William Langwiesche, 'The Border', *Atlantic* (May 1992), p. 68.

29. Miller and Espenshade, *Fourth Wave*, 1985, p. 37.

30. In 1940 only one in eight Californians was foreign-born; by 1960 one in nine was Latino and one in 100 Asian. This changed dramatically in the 1980s, 'The New Ellis Island', *Time*, 13 June 1983, p. 19.

31. Roger Rouse, 'Mexican Migration and the Social Space of Postmodernism', *Diaspora*, vol. 1 no. 1 (1991), pp. 8–23.

32. 'Is English Only Language for Government?' *New York Times*, 26 Oct. 1986; Robert Reinhold, 'Resentment Against New Immigrants', *New York Times*, 26 Oct. 1986. Professor John Higham, the leading expert on immigration, saw 'the new nativism as relatively benign "ethnocentricism," not militant nationalism.' One of the problems with Higham's analysis is that he did not live in California, where nativism was not so benign. Indeed, New York historian David Reimers did not see it as benign: 'The present hostility to bilingualism is veiled hostility toward Hispanics', Robert Pear, 'What Alien Law Will Mean: Some Questions and Answers', *New York Times*, 26 Oct. 1986.

33. 'Letter', Roger Mahoney, *Los Angeles Times*, 18 May 1986; Kevin Roderick, 'On Border: US Senate Candidates Focus on Policy to Combat Illegal Immigration', *Los Angeles Times*, 30 May 1986.

34. Sebastian Rotella, 'Border Abuses Continue 2 Years Study Says', *Los Angeles Times*, 26 Feb. 1992; Rotella, 'INS Agents Abuse Immigrants, Study Says', *Los Angeles Times*, 31 May 1992. A study by Americas Watch documented human rights abuses in the Americas; Jorge Bustamante, 'Aumenta el tránsito de indocumentadoes hacia EU', *La Opinión*, 17 Feb. 1992; Bustamante, 'La justicia abre una puerta a los inmigrantes', *La Opinión*, 23 Feb. 1992.

35. John H. Lee, 'Bank of Lights Planned to Deter Border Activity', *Los Angeles Times*, 10 Sept. 1992.

36. Mexicans responded by calling boycotts of the US market: 'Some Sales Drop-off Seen in Mexicans' Boycott of San Diego Firms', *Daily News*, 21 Nov. 1993.

37. William Langwiesche, 'The Border', *Atlantic* (May 1992), p. 69.

38. Thomas Miller, *The Fouth Wave: California's Newest Immigrants* (Washington, D.C., 1985). The report showed that two-thirds of recent Mexican immigrants in Los Angeles had no more than a grade school education, while three-quarters of all Latinos in Los Angeles had attended at least one year of high school. Only 3% of Mexican immigrants held professional or managerial employment, contrasted to 13% of the Mexican Americans, and 20% of Blacks.

39. Miller, *Fourth Wave*, pp. 45, 58; also see David M. Heer, *Undocumented Mexicans in the United States* (Cambridge: Cambridge University Press, 1990), which has an excellent analysis of studies on immigrants conducted during the 1980s.

40. Miller, *Fourth Wave*, p. 91.

41. Ibid., pp. 92–3, 45–107. In reality the problem was not jobs. It was predicted that by the end of the century there would be 21 million new jobs, many requiring a high level of literacy. Because of the educational level of immigrants, these jobs would not go to them. The problem was that capital did not want to pay for the education of even the native-born. See Scott McConnell, 'The New Battle over Immigration', *Fortune*, 9 May 1988.

42. Linda J. Wong, 'Immigration Crackdown', *Los Angeles Lawyer* (July/Aug. 1984), p. 28.

43. Carey McWilliams, *North from Mexico* (New York: Praeger, 1990), p. 328–30.

44. Margo De Ley, 'Taking From Latinos to Assist Soviet Immigrants: An Affront to Fairness', *Los Angeles Times*, 19 March 1989. What frustrated Latino activists was what they perceived this as a power play by the Jewish community to serve 25,000 Soviet Jews who were still in Rome. They believed that Jewish leaders and politicians should be more sensitive. Stephen Moore, 'A Pro-Family, Pro-Growth Legal Immigration Policy for America', *Background: The Heritage Foundation*, No. 735, 6 Nov. 1989, pp. 1–7. Moore saw the Kennedy bill as an improvement over previous legislation because it put greater emphasis on admitting people with skills. Moore also made the point that President Bush had said that the United States would admit 50,000 to 150,000 Soviet Jews. According to Moore, Bush was reluctant to keep his pledge because each refugee would be entitled to $5,000 apiece in federal assistance, which would worsen the deficit. Moore noted that immigration

had a 'very favorable effect on the nation's economic growth.' In a later but related article, Carlos Alberto Montaner, 'Robando Cerebros', *La Opinión*, 4 Jan. 1992, pointed out that there was a brain drain from Russia, with the US getting technological know-how transferred to it at no cost. According to Montaner, a similar brain drain has been devastating to Latin America.

45. Glenn F. Bunting, 'Congress Cuts Aid Proposed for Immigration Care', *Los Angeles Times*, 2 Oct. 1992.

46. Jorge G. Castañeda and Rafael Alarcón, 'Workers Are a Commodity, Too', *Los Angeles Times*, 22 April 1991.

47. In order to have a reasonable chance of political asylum, they could apply for Temporary Protected Status, part of the Immigration Act of 1990, or ABC status (from *American Baptist Church v. Thornburgh*, filed in 1985), which gave them authorization to work while waiting for their asylum case to be heard. Congress passed TPS in 1990, and nearly 180,000 refugees applied by October 1991.The TPS program closed in 1991. Teresa Puente, 'La madeja que atrapa a los refugiados salvadoreños', *La Opinión*, 12 June 1991, puts the figure at 60,000; organizations such as CARE-CEN, the Central American Refugee Center, were very involved in the process. The article put the number of Salvadoran asylum cases at about 100,000. CARECEN estimated that another 200,000 Salvadorans lived in the Washington, D.C. area. Bush responded to political pressure by signing the Deferred Enforcement Departure, which was open to Salvadorans covered under TPS. They could apply for deferred departure for a fee of $60 to extend time under TPS. If not, the petitioner would be covered under ABC. Edward J. Flynn, 'ABCs of a Complex Immigration Policy', *Nuestro Tiempo*, 19 Nov. 1992; Somini Sengupta, 'INS Extends Work Permits for 200,000 Salvadorans by 120 Days', *Los Angeles Times*, 28 June 1992; Claudia Dorrington, Ruth E. Zambrana, and Deirges Sabagh, 'Salvadorans in the United States: Immigrants and Refugees, Demographic and Socio-Economic Profiles', in Marta López-Garza, ed., 'Immigration and Economic Restructuring: The Metamorphosis of Southern California', *California Sociologist*, vol. 22, no. 2 (Summer 1989), pp. 137–70.

48. Paul Richter and Ronald J. Ostrow, 'Salvadoran Asylum Program May End', *Los Angeles Times*, 2 Dec. 1994.

49. Mary Ballesteros, 'Fallece el padre Luis Olivares', *La Opinión*, 20 March 1993. Father Olivares had been in La Placita from 1981 to 1990. Born in San Antonio, he was a member of the Claretian Order.

50. George Ramos, 'Salvadorans' Eviction from Church Stirs Debate', *Los Angeles Times*, 5 Dec. 1990.

51. *Tranquada*, 16 May 1993; Cheryl Brownstein-Santiago, 'Census Data Track Status of Latinos', *Nuestro Tiempo*, 19 Sept. 1992, reported that there were 4,839,351 Latinos in Los Angeles County: 79.5% were of Mexican extraction (3,848,33); 272,301 were Salvadoran and 139,397 were Guatemalan. Latino per capita income was $11,489 in 1989, slightly over half of what the rest of the working-age population earned. In Los Angeles a total of 803,863 applied for citizenship, of whom 76% were Mexicans, 11% Salvadoran, 2% Guatemalans, 2% South Americans, 4% Asians, and 1% others.

52. Fern Schumer Chapman, 'Where Have All the Babies Gone?' *Fortune*, 6 July 1987, pp. 114–15. Five years later nativists like Princeton Physicist Harry Kendall and Garret Hardin, emeritus professor at the University of California Santa Barbara, along with the arch-Mexican bashers, the Federation for American Immigration Reform, were sounding the alarm. Kendall pointed out that Mexico's population was 88 million and would be 125 million in 15 years. Naturally, according to Kendall, they would be clamoring to come across. Michael D'Antonio, 'Apocalypse Soon', *Los Angeles Times Magazine*, 29 Aug. 1993.

53. 'California. The Endangered Dream', *Time*, 18 Nov. 1991, pp. 33–9.

54. Langewiesche, 'The Border', p. 69.

55. See Sam Fulwood III, 'Children of New Arrivals Avoid Melting into the Mainstream', *Los Angeles Times*, 7 Sept. 1993; Fulwood quotes from a study by Alejandro Portes and Ruben G. Rumbaut suggesting that racism slowed assimilation.

56. George Ramos, 'Report Claims Immigration Reform Act Has Led to Bias', *Los Angeles Times*, 11 Jan. 1990. A corps of young lawyers such as Peter Schey, originally from South Africa, Linda Wong, Antonio Rodríguez and others led the fight to protect the rights of immigrants. Schey headed the National Center for Immigration Rights Inc. Bert Corona's work was exceptional in defense of the foreign-born. His Hermandad Mexicana expanded to include offices in the San

Fernando Valley, Santa Ana, Chicago, Washington, D.C. and New York. His tactic of taking immigrants en masse to Washington and Sacramento to lobby representatives was very effective.

57. Bill Boyarsky, 'A Thin Line Border Between Security and Prejudice', *Los Angeles Times*, 18 Aug. 1993.

58. The idea that immigrants were a liability was popularized by Alan C. Nelson, 'The Merits of Wilson's Immigration Plan', *Daily News*, 24 Aug. 1993. Nelson was a commissioner of the Immigration and Naturalization Service from 1982 to 1989, and consultant to the Federation for American Immigration Reform. This campaign was well financed. George Skelton, 'Scrambling for Just the Right Words', *Los Angeles Times*, 23 Sept. 1993. Wilson benefited politically from his Mexican bashing. His job approval rating increased to 37%, a jump of 7 points.

59. Mike Commeaux, 'Worry Grows over Illegal Immigration', *Daily News*, 19 Aug. 1993.

60. Christine Spolar, 'Anti-Immigrant Mood Worries California Latinos', *Washington Post*, 5 June 1994.

61. 'Impact of California's Immigrants', *Los Angeles Times*, 6 Jan. 1992.

62. What was amazing about the entire debate was the uncritical reporting that took place during the first phases: Cheryl W. Thompson, 'Jailed Aliens Costing County Millions', *Daily News*, 12 Aug. 1992.

63. Len Hall, 'Study of Illegal Immigrants' Fiscal Impact Called Flawed', *Los Angeles Times*, 19 Aug. 1992.

64. Jaime Olivares, 'Latinos fortalecen la base social y económica de California revela estudio', *La Opinión*, 12 May 1992; David E. Hayes-Bautista and Gregory Rodríguez.

65. Seth Mydans, 'Opposition to Immigration Mounting', *Daily News*, 27 June 1993; David M Heer's, *Undocumented Mexicans in the United States* (Cambridge: Cambridge University Press, 1990), offers an excellent analysis of studies on the undocumented residents during the 1980s.

66. Michael Connelly, Davis Freed and Sonia Nazario, 'Southland Is Ripe for White Hate Groups', *Los Angeles Times*, 25 July 1993.

67. 'SAMHO ASSOCIATION FOR THE ADVANCEMENT OF CONSERVATIVE WHITE AMERICANS', Leaflet, 18 March 1991; Pablo Comesaña Amado, 'Distribuyen carta racista e insultante hacia mexicanos', *La Opinión*, 24 May 1991.

68. Nora Zamichow, 'Latina Immigrants Suffer Post-Traumatic Disorders', *Los Angeles Times*, 8 Feb. 1992.

69. Alan C. Miller and Ronald J. Ostrow, 'Immigration Policy Failures Invite Overhaul', *Los Angeles Times*, 11 July 1993; Commissioner Doris Meissner, in cooperation with Janet Reno, took measures to improve fencing and lighting. It was clear that the Clinton administration was reacting to Wilson's pressure; Sebastian Rotella, 'Will Border Buildup Be Effective?' *Los Angeles Times*, 7 Feb. 1994. Three-quarters of the agents were stationed at San Diego and El Paso, which was referred to as 'The Line'. Janet Reno sent reinforcements to San Diego, where 40% of the Border Patrol agents were located.

70. Elton Gallegly, 'Just How Many Aliens Are Here Illegally?' *Los Angeles Times*, 13 March 1994; Mike Comeaux, 'Immigration: The Political Tide Turns', *Daily News*, 27 March 1994.

71. Rick Orlov, 'Seven Latino Lawmakers Back Brown in Race', *Daily News*, 1 April 1994; the seven were Polanco, Cruz Bustamante, Joe Baca, Martha Escutia, Diane Martínez, Grace Napolitano and Luis Caldera.

72. Keith Stone, '7,000 Become US Citizens', *Daily News*, 1 April 1994; *The National Latino Immigrant Survey*, NALEO Educational Fund, 1989. Chicano organizations like NALEO worked hard to naturalize Latinos; 38% of Latinos in California were non-citizens in 1980; Peter H. King, 'Immigration Versus the Immigrants', *Los Angeles Times*, 9 Feb. 1994.

73. Betsy Bates, Meg Sullivan and Janet Weeks, 'Seeking Shelter', *Daily News*, 23 Jan. 1994; 20,000 refugees from the quake flocked to parks, 75% of whom were Latino.

74. Debra J. Saunders, 'FEMA Paying Aliens to Break Law', *Daily News*, 1 Feb. 1994.

75. Herbert A. Sample, 'Alien Issue Key to Quake Recovery Bill', *Daily News*, 3 Feb. 1994.

76. Miguel Bustillo and Marc Lacey, 'US Plan to Cut Aid to Illegal Immigrants Jolts Many', *Los Angeles Times*, 2 Feb. 1994.

77. Larry Gordon, 'Cal State Held to In-State Fees for Immigrants', *Los Angeles Times*, 21 May 1992. Alameda Superior Court Judge Ken M. Kawaichi found in 1985 that under the state's constitutional guarantees of equal protection state universities were forbidden to use immigration status

to deny lower fees to students who had lived in California for more than one year. In May 1990, Los Angeles Superior Court Judge David P. Yaffee ruled in favor of Bradford, Jean Merl, 'Community College Fee Hike Hits Illegal Immigrants', *Los Angeles Times*, 14 May 1992. Community college fees went from $60 a semester to $1,320 per semester.

78. Gary Libman, 'Losing Out on a Dream', *Los Angeles Times*, 23 Jan. 1992.

79. Former Western Regional Director of the INS, Harold Ezell, set up shop in Taiwan, and sold Wienerschnitzel restaurant and Windmill car-wash franchises to potential investors. Instead of rounding up 'illegals', his new motto was, 'Let's bring them [the millionaires] to America'; Fran Valmaña, 'Indocumentados pagarán en Cal State colegiaturas como residentes foréanos', *La Opinión*, 9 Sept. 1992.

80. Gary Lee and Roberto Suro, 'Latino–Black Rivalry Grows: Los Angeles Reflects Tensions Between Minorities', *Washington Post*, 13 Oct. 1993.

81. Ibid.

82. Miller, *Fourth Wave*, pp. 96–7, 101.

83. Cathleen Decker, 'Reality Clouds Optimism on Racial Coalitions', *Los Angeles Times*, 4 Oct. 1989.

84. Paul Ong and Abel Valenzuela, Jr, 'Job Competition Between Immigrants and African Americans', *Poverty & Race* (March/April 1995), pp. 9–10, 12.

85. *Washington Post*, 13 Oct. 1993.

86. Louis Sahagun, 'Latino Campaign Eludes 2 Camps in Charter Vote', *Los Angeles Times*, 23 April 1992.

87. Jorge Bustamante, 'Mentiras oficials que satisfacen prejuicios públicos', *La Opinión*, 21 May 1992.

88. Miles, 'Immigration and the American Dilemma: Blacks vs. Browns', *Atlantic* (October 1992), pp. 45, 52–4.

89. Roseanne Keyan, '1990s: The Golden Decade', *Los Angeles Times*, 15 Jan. 1990.

90. Ivan Light and Edna Bonacich, *Immigrant Entrepreneurs: Koreans in Los Angeles, 1965–1982* (Berkeley, Calif.: University of California Press, 1988).

91. Eugene Turner and James P. Allen, *An Atlas of Population Patterns in Metropolitan Los Angeles and Orange Counties*, 1990 (Northridge, Calif.: Geography Department, California State University Northridge, 1991).

92. Shawn Hubler, 'Regional Report: '80s Failed to End Economic Disparity Census Shows', *Los Angeles Times*, 17 Aug. 1992; K. Connie Kang, 'Study Finds Neglect of Asian Poor', *Los Angeles Times*, 2 Dec. 1993.

93. Barbara Bronson Gray, 'Struggling to Help Troubled Immigrants', *Los Angeles Times*, 17 Feb. 1991.

94. Richard Lee Colvin, 'Music Was the Thing for Victim of Gang', *Los Angeles Times*, 18 May 1994.

95. William J. Holstein, 'The Asian Invasion: A Blessing for the U.S.?' *Business Week*, 26 Sept. 1988; see Donald J. Bogue, *The Population of the United States. Historical Trends and Future Projections* (New York: The Free Press, 1985), pp. 405, 611.

96. Bill Boyarsky, 'Redistricting Drama in the Back Rooms', *Los Angeles Times*, 14 Dec. 1990; Frank Clifford, 'News Analysis: Latinos, Asians Gain in Numbers, Not Power', *Los Angeles Times*, 5 March 1991. Richard Winton, 'Chu Plans to Join Race for State Assembly', *Los Angeles Times*, 21 Oct. 1993.

97. Bruce Stokes, 'Learning the Game', *National Journal*, vol. 20, no. 43 (22 Oct. 1988), p. 2649.

98. Roy Christman and James S. Fay, 'Growing Clout of Asians in California', *Sacramento Bee*, 29 June 1994.

99. Special Report, 'In America, Faces of Asia', *Christian Science Monitor*, 27 July 1993.

100. Lee Romney, 'Plight of Children Held by INS Stirs Chinese', *Los Angeles Times*, 27 June 1993.

101. K. Connie Kwang, 'Column One: Building Bridges to Equality', *Los Angeles Times*, 7 Jan. 1995.

102. Lynne Duke, 'Blacks, Asians, Latinos Cite Prejudice by Whites for Limited Opportunity', *Washington Post*, 3 March 1994; Suzanne Espinosa and Benjamin Pimentel, 'Backlash Against Asians, Latinos', *San Francisco Chronicle*, 27 Aug. 1993.

7

The Politicization

of the 'Other'

The citadel of L.A. nativism and anti-immigrant hysteria is the San Fernando Valley, located almost entirely in the city of Los Angeles except for a few cities like San Fernando and Burbank. The Valley was the home of Bus-Stop, a movement of white middle-class activists who, during the 1970s, fought the busing of white children from the Valley to inner-city schools.[1] During the 1980s, however, the inner city seemed to move to the Valley as the number of its Latino residents doubled. There were 385,000 Latinos in the Valley with a median age of 26 versus a median age of 37 for white Americans. By the 1990s, 38 percent of the Valley's adults were foreign-born, and 30 percent spoke a language other than English at home. In Pacoima/Arleta, some 60 percent were foreign-born, with places like Sun Valley, Mission Hills-Panorama City, and North Hills (formerly Sepulveda) following the same trend.[2]

In fact, by 1990 Brown people could be found everywhere in the Valley – even in upscale neighborhoods like Northridge, where hundreds of Mexicans lined the intersection of Parthenia and Reseda boulevards waiting for day-labor work. Just two blocks to the west on Parthenia was a gated project housing Latino laborers and their families. Reseda, Canoga Park, Granada Hills and Chatsworth all had enclaves of working-class Mexicans and Central Americans. Within the white areas were also sizeable numbers of middle-class Latino professionals and business people, who sometimes became Republicans.[3] Yet working-class Mexicans and Central Americans for the most part remained outside the life of the Valley. Brown people with accents were assumed to be foreigners. Although notable class differences existed among Latinos, few middle-class Chicanos sat on the boards of homeowners associations or the Chamber of Commerce outside areas where they formed the vast majority.

Those areas included Pacoima and Latino enclaves in the Northeast Valley where Mexicans formed the majority; many of these had been there since the turn of the century, when the Valley was a top agricultural producer. Communities such as North Hollywood and Van Nuys were polarized between white homeowners and Latino renters.[4] Canoga Park proper in the West Valley, excluding West Hills and Woodland Hills, also had a large, core Chicano population. Latinos also lived in apartment complexes in Granada Hills, Northridge and Reseda, among other areas.

Anglo anxiety in face of demographic change was rampant. A 1993 article by *L.A. Times* reporter Sam Enríquez seemed to sum up the problem: 'Middle Class Despairs Over Its Paradise Lost'. In 1960 the Valley had been 92 percent white; in 1980, 75 percent; and by 1990 the proportion of whites had declined to 58 percent. However, Euroamericans still controlled elections, with 72 percent of the vote in the 1993 mayoral election being cast by white voters (Latinos cast 10 percent; Blacks, 12 percent; and Asians, 4 percent).

The Valley was not homogeneous in terms of household income, which according to a *Los Angeles Times* survey (11 July 1993) ranged from $86,548 in Encino/Tarzana (89 percent above the citywide average) to $43,764 in Reseda/Van Nuys (4.4 percent below average), and to $39,018 in mostly Latino Arleta/Pacoima (14.4 percent below average). Barry Smedberg, executive director of the San Fernando Valley Interfaith Council, commented on the income gaps: 'Perhaps the disparity of income shows why someone at $86,000 doesn't relate well to someone else in the Valley at $39,000 because their expectations are different.'[5] Citywide the lowest average household income was Westlake (the MacArthur Park area) with $21,204, and the highest was Bel-Air Beverly Crest with $195,119. Six out of the fourteen so-called Valley communities fell below the citywide average, with two others, Sylmar and Tujunga, just above it. The other six were at least 30 percent above the citywide average.

It is therefore no wonder that recent anti-immigrant campaigns have derived much of their strength from the San Fernando Valley. According to *Los Angeles Times* reporter Alan C. Miller, 'The Valley has been in the vanguard of a rising backlash throughout California and elsewhere against the tide of newcomers, *particularly those crossing the Mexican border*' [italics mine].[6] Miller adds, 'Residents of the San Fernando Valley are increasingly outraged about illegal immigration – if not immigration generally – in the face of economic hard times, growing congestion, widespread crime and a dramatic influx of Latinos ...' According to Richard H. Close, president of the Sherman Oaks Homeowner Association, 'There is the perception that the Valley is being overrun by illegal immigrants who are causing most of the crime, who are causing most of the graffiti and who are causing the physical decline.'

An important reason for this hostility was a plunge in Los Angeles–area real estate values, which hit the Valley especially hard. In 1989, a modest three-bedroom home sold for $300,000; by 1993 it sold for only $190,000. In familiar scapegoating style, the Valley's elected officials, Reps. Carlos J. Moorehead (R-Glendale), Elton Gallegly (R-Simi) and Anthony Beilenson (D-Woodland Hills) all proposed anti-immigrant legislation long before Governor Pete Wilson jumped on the bandwagon.[7] Local sentiment was summed up by signs seen at Los Angeles Valley College when President Bill Clinton visited the campus: 'L.A. Is a Third World Cesspool', and 'Deport Illegal Aliens Now'.[8]

Valley Schools: The Fight for Equality

Valleyites had long resented the large number of minority students bused into its schools. On one hand, the schools would have been shut because of declines in local (meaning white) enrollment; on the other, students from the inner city were being transported to their very doorstep. (Until the early 1980s, the Los Angeles Unified School District had been under court order not to build more schools in minority neighborhoods. This led to massive busing of Black and Brown children to Valley schools.) Residents saw this busing as an invasion of their neighborhood schools and blamed the incoming children for crime, the delinquency of their own children, and the urbanization of what was once thought to be a suburban community.[9]

Many Valley residents were also upset with the ruling of retired Superior Court Judge Ralph Nutter in *Rodriguez* v. *LAUSD*, which mandated that the district equalize its funding of individual schools. The suit, brought by the Mexican American Legal Defense and Education Fund (MALDEF), called for the district to factor teacher salaries into the budgets of individual schools. For years Valley schools had employed more educated and experienced teachers whose salary totals were much higher than those of teachers at inner-city schools. It therefore cost the LAUSD more money to run Valley schools than their inner-city counterparts.[10]

The redistricting of the Los Angeles Board of Education, which also resulted from the 1990 Census, fell to City Council members, who had just denied Latinos a fourth seat on the council.[11] In the case of the school district, the council members had nothing to lose, and they approved creation of a second Latino Board of Education district. The new district would be represented by incumbent Leticia Quezada. This district, extending from Boyle Heights to the northeast Valley, took in Quezada's old district and included the Rust Bowl cities (Huntington Park, Bell, etc.) just south of East Los Angeles. It was 80 percent Latino, though only 47 percent of the registered voters were Latinos.[12] The plan received preliminary approval in June 1992 by a nine-to-six vote. Of the four school board members representing the Valley, only one would be required to live there.[13] (The old Board of Education had seven seats, but only one seat went to a Latino although enrollment was over 64 percent Latino).

Valley leaders charged that additional Latino representation was at their expense.[14] 'This plan splinters the Valley', charged Councilwoman Joy Picus. Councilman Joel Wachs complained that race and ethnicity had dominated the redistricting process.[15] Some Black leaders made unsupportive remarks – for example, that the new district should not be 'hooked up with Tijuana.'[16] The plan was also opposed by the Parent Teacher and Student Association (PTSA), United Chambers of Commerce of the San Fernando Valley, Valley Organized in Community Efforts, the Valley Chapter of the National Council of Negro Women and the Black American Political Association.[17]

ETHNIC COMPOSITION OF STUDENTS IN PROPOSED LAUSD DISTRICTS

District	Population	American Indian	Asian	Black	Filipino	Latino	Pacific Islander	Anglo
1	73,476	.05	.7	39.7	0.23	58.4	.09	.7
2	100,646	.20	2.7	1.3	1.26	93.2	.10	1.7
3	65,613	.17	9.1	5.5	2.82	63.6	.19	18.6
4	67,166	.40	8.3	15.9	1.29	39.3	.33	34.4
5	107,408	.20	4.7	1.8	1.66	87.8	.12	3.6
6	77,634	.35	6.9	8.1	1.95	55.6	.27	26.7
7	111,384	.24	2.6	25.8	3.35	59.4	1.40	7.1

SOURCE: Sandy Banks and Stephanie Chavez, 'L.A. Unified Breakup Drive Stirs Minorities' Suspicions', *Los Angeles Times*, 18 May 1993.

A clear polarization took place along racial and class lines. The Valley board of the Parent Teacher and Student Association did not have one Latino or Latina member. Even so, Cecilia Mansfield, vice president of the 31st district PTSA, while conceding that the PTSA Board had no Latinos members, accused 'Eastside interests' of sponsoring the school redistricting plan.[18]

West Los Angeles Councilman Zeb Yaroslavsky held the key vote. Yaroslavsky was vehemently criticized by the 31st district PTSA for supporting the school board redistricting plan.[19] City Council President John Ferraro backed the plan – it was payback time and Ferraro paid a political debt to Richard Alatorre, who had sponsored the plan. Passage of the redistricting plan was a tribute to Alatorre's political savvy.[20] Victoria Castro, a principal at Belvedere Middle School, and a long-time activist, ran for the newly drawn Board of Education district that encompassed Huntington Park, Vernon, Walnut, Cudahy, Florence, Commerce and parts of Northwest Los Angeles. She defeated former Board of Education member Larry Gonzales to become the second Latina board member. Valley forces immediately sponsored a state initiative to change the outcome and formed The Coalition Against Unfair School Elections (CAUSE), calling for the breakup of the LAUSD.[21]

By October 1992 CAUSE and the breakup movement were well under way. Sen. David Roberti (D-Van Nuys) took over the leadership in the breakup movement, knowing that his political future depended on the Valley.[22] Chicanos felt especially betrayed by Roberti, whom they had helped eke out a narrow victory in June 1992. Roberti was joined in the fight by ultra conservative Paula Boland.[23] Disappointingly, State Senator Tom Hayden, whose district cut into the Valley, supported the breakup: 'It [the breakup] is no longer an escapist fantasy [of the Valley]', thus taking the side of racists.[24]

Sen. Diane Watson led the opposition: 'Once you start breaking off pieces of the district, the end result is de facto segregation.'[25] On this issue, progressive Chicanos and Blacks were in agreement.[26] African American, Latino and Asian students made up 87 percent of enrollment districtwide, while whites accounted for only about 13 percent of the students. In a separate district the Valley would be about 27 percent white, and the Anglo student population outside the Valley would drop to 7 percent.[27] By July the breakup movement was on the fast track. It was state Assembly Speaker Willie Brown who stopped the train: 'I have forty-seven votes to manage the House and to avoid any hijacking [meaning the school breakup bill] wherever it happens', said Brown.[28]

The breakup would have undermined the Supreme Court's historic decision in *Brown* v. *Board of Education*, which prohibited segregation of students by race. It would have meant increased segregation in Los Angeles schools. A Valley district would have 190,000 students, with close to 27 percent or 50,000 of them white. The total number of students would include the 18,000 already bused. In the remaining system of 460,000 students, the white proportion would decline from 13 percent to 7.4 percent, or from 84,000 to 33,800. Most would be concentrated on the Westside. According to ACLU attorney Mark Rosenbaum: 'When you go from 13 percent to 27 percent you are doubling the number of whites in that district ... you are bleaching the district.'[29]

After losing the breakup fight, Valleyites turned to Proposition 174, which provided for vouchers – a logical extension of the politics of the breakup movement. A Woodland Hills parent who had pulled her children out of the public schools expressed the now-prevalent hysteria about inner-city students: 'I don't feel safe [from inner-city children?], and no one wants to be accountable.'[30] The voucher system was attacked by almost every state politico because of its potential cost. The powerful California Teachers' Association (CTA) mobilized its political base against the initiative. Money used for the public schools would be diverted to religious schools, CTA argued, since 75 percent of private schools were religious.[31]

It was estimated that the passage of Prop. 174 would drain $1 billion to $1.6 billion annually from the state treasury. The initiative proposed giving a $2,600 voucher to all parents, who could then use it for private education if they wished. Only 62 percent of the private schools were willing to take that amount as full payment, however.[32] In the end, Proposition 174 went down in defeat. However, the idea was not dead, and extremism had gained respectability during the Prop. 174 campaign.[33]

A Chicano Council District in the Valley

Chicanos did take one step forward in the Valley. A potential Latino City Council district, the 7th CD, had been carved out in the mid 1980s by agreement between Los Angeles and the US Justice Department. It was a poor district: a fifth of the people lived below the poverty line, and a third earned less than $20,000 a year, while only 7 percent earned more than $75,000. The population was just under 70 percent Latino, while 17 percent were white, 8 percent African American and 6 percent Asian. Only 31 percent of registered voters were Latino, with Euroamericans accounting for 48 percent. Still, everyone knew it was just a matter of time before a Chicano would represent the 7th CD.[34]

The opportunity came in 1992 when Ernani Bernardi, who had been elected to represent the 7th CD in 1989, stepped down. The top contender for the job was Lyle Hall, a former president of the Firefighters Union who had previously lost a runoff election to Bernardi. The two main Chicano candidates were attorney Ray Magaña, an aide to Bernardi, and Richard Alarcón, a deputy to Mayor Bradley; both were graduates of nearby California State University, Northridge. The Black candidate, Leroy Chase, was assumed to have the African American vote locked up.[35] Alarcón, known as Mr Network, had connections with many charitable agencies and sat on the boards of two major nonprofit agencies, Valley Interfaith and United Way. Like all the other candidates, he tiptoed around the topic of race.

Alarcón and Hall gathered sufficient support to make the runoff election. Hall was the obvious favorite and had the endorsement of the county Federation of Labor, as well as many Black and Chicano leaders. The bulk of the white vote was also expected to go to Hall. Many of the Latino and Black leaders were reluctant to support Alarcón because they were accustomed to working through white politicians who could deliver patronage in the form of grants and contracts.

Alarcón campaigned door-to-door to overcome this disadvantage. He picked up solid support from the Latino community and got a large enough white crossover vote to win the runoff by less than 1 percent of nearly 18,000 votes cast. At least one observer attributed this to the fact that Alarcón refused to be painted as strictly a Latino candidate.[36] But the fact remains that 80 percent of Latino voters backed Alarcón in the runoff, with Hall and Alarcón splitting the Black vote and Hall getting two-thirds of the white vote.[37]

The 1993 Mayoral Race and the San Fernando Valley

The San Fernando Valley School breakup movement and anti-immigrant hysteria played important roles in Los Angeles' 1993 mayoral election. In large part

part Republican and Democratic Party leaders were intimidated by the San Fernando Valley, whose power went well beyond the number of its voters.[38] They knew that like the Westside and the Downtown corporate community, much of the Valley's clout rested on the size of its financial contributions. The 1993 election campaign also marked the end of the Tom Bradley era. Even if it could be said that Bradley served corporate interests more than those of his own Black community, symbolically the end of his era meant the end of Black power within the city.[39]

Whether a Latino candidate would emerge was unclear.[40] Gloria Molina declared that she would not be a candidate, although she had the support of Peg Yorkin of the Fund for Feminist Majority. Molina wisely concluded that she had been in office only twenty months and that Latinos had fought too hard for her seat, which Governor Pete Wilson would fill with his own choice in the event that Molina ran for mayor. When asked whether she would support Richard Alatorre, Molina scoffed: 'We need an assertive, hands-on leader. We don't need anyone who enjoys the political game.'[41] Despite Molina's sarcasm, Alatorre would have been a formidable candidate. Although only 11 percent of voters citywide were Latino, Alatorre had a base beyond the community. He had played the game and in the process had accumulated a considerable number of chips with other politicians and with developers; he surely could have amassed a considerable election warchest.[42]

Ultimately, the only Chicano candidates were Julian Nava, former LAUSD Board member (1967–79) and ambassador to Mexico under Jimmy Carter; and Linda Griego, a deputy mayor under Bradley and now a restaurant owner. Nava noted, 'It's about time that we have someone in the Pueblo de Los Angeles who can speak Spanish and be the mayor.' Nava had not been active in electoral politics since 1979 and did not have a base of support in either of the two major Chicano political cliques.[43] Within the political community the most frequently mentioned reason for not supporting Nava was that he had not been in politics for over fourteen years. A whispering campaign charged that he was not qualified, a ridiculous claim in light of the lack of executive experience of most of the other candidates; most had never held an elected office. Some Chicano elected officials supported Linda Griego, who, although intelligent and capable, did not have a long history of political activism. In general the mayoral candidates avoided Latino enclaves and many did not even bother to attend candidate forums in heavily Latino neighborhoods.[44]

Los Angeles Times writers Frank Clifford and John Schawada reported in January 1993, 'With an emotional power reminiscent of the 1970s furor over school busing, the movement to break up the Los Angeles Unified School District is muscling its way into the 1993 mayor's race.'[45] Nearly 40 percent of the city's voters lived in the San Fernando Valley; they were mostly white and anti-inner city. It mattered little to them what the mayor could or could not do about the schools. Indeed, most of the candidates supported the breakup, including Councilman Nate Holden, a Black, and Julian Nava. Even Michael Woo, the Asian American candidate preferred by many liberals, had refused to dismiss the idea.

Dovetailing with the breakup movement was anti-immigrant hysteria, which former deputy mayor Tom Houston exploited by blaming 'illegal aliens' for the city's fiscal woes, attacking the foreign-born and the street vendors and advocating that the LAPD notify the INS when illegal aliens were arrested.[46] At a candidates' forum, Houston was loudly applauded when he brought up the 'illegal alien'menace. Julian Nava was then booed when he supported the vendors and a proposal by school board member Quezada that immigrant parents be given limited voting rights in school board elections.[47] Meanwhile, the mayoral candidates exploited L.A.'s fear of violence as the Rodney King verdict and the uprising that followed it still hung over the city. Riordan: 'Our city is considered a war zone throughout the world.' Woo: 'The L.A. dream has turned sour. We are losing many families.' Riordan called for 3,000 new police officers; Woo called for an additional 1,000.[48]

THE 1993 MAYORAL PRIMARY RESULTS

	Percent of Total Vote	Richard Riordan	Michael Woo	Richard Wachs	Richard Katz	Linda Griego
Anglo	68	45	13	14	12	7
Black	18	4	52	3	2	7
Latino	8	20	30	11	8	12
Asian	4	21	60	5	6	4
Income						
Under $20,000	17	17	33	10	7	7
$20,000–39,999	25	26	30	11	10	9
$40,000–59,999	24	36	21	15	10	7
$60,000+	34	46	17	10	12	7
Household						
Homeowners	64	41	18	11	11	7
Renters	33	19	34	11	7	8
Region						
Westside	16	39	24	9	7	12
San Fernando Valley	43	42	12	15	16	6
Central L.A.	20	27	30	11	7	9
South L.A.	21	15	45	5	2	5

SOURCE: 'How They Voted', Los Angeles Times, 22 April 1993.

On election day Riordan received 144,690 votes (32.88 percent) to Woo's 106,596 (24.22 percent). Poorer Angelenos were more likely to vote for someone other than Riordan, while homeowners tended to favor him. Riordan supporters were also more likely to be white. As in no other election, the power of the San Fernando Valley hung over the city like a pall. Council Districts 2, 3, 7 and 12, all located in the Valley and containing 75 percent of the Valley's residents, gave Riordan 42.4 percent of their vote. In the heavily Latino 1st and 14th CDs, 26.6 percent voted for him, not far behind Woo's 29.5 percent. Riordan ran strongly in Jewish precincts, and only in Black districts did he take a beating.[49] How well the major candidates ran was strongly correlated to the amount of money they spent: Riordan spent $3,309,500 to get 144,690 votes, for $22.87 per vote, while Woo was able to spend only $20.22 for each of his 106,596 votes, spending a total $2,167,000. By comparison, Linda Griego raised only $593,800, and got only 31,804 votes; Julian Nava spent only $27,600, winning only 6,324 votes.[50]

Since neither Riordan nor Woo received a majority, a runoff election was scheduled for 8 June 1993. Riordan's main qualifications were that he was white and had lots of money. During the runoff campaign Riordan emphasized crime and the economy, while Woo portrayed himself as a reformer and the heir apparent to Bradley's coalition of minority activists and liberals, with added support from gay activists and feminists.[51]

Riordan had strong business ties in Los Angeles, not only in the white community but also with Latinos, Blacks and Asians.[52] One columnist wrote: 'Riordan is late Bradley and the politician who moves easily in the largely Anglo world of downtown business Establishment.'[53] Riordan received the support of Richard Alatorre, whom he had backed in the struggle over Olvera Street. Alatorre, in turn, banked his continued position on the board of the Metropolitan Transit Authority on Riordan's winning the election.[54] In the political game, that position was important because it gave the major players major access to money through contracts the MTA granted. According to journalist Bill Boyarsky, 'The biggest single gathering of business lobbyists in California takes place during the meetings of the Metropolitan Transportation Authority, the agency that runs our bus and train lines ... A total of 1,234 men and women are paid to influence the MTA's decisions, 179 more than those who lobby the Legislature.' The agency had a budget of $3.7 billion at a time when other agencies were severely cutting back. This agency was fueled by money generated from sales tax revenues set aside for transportation. In explaining how contracts were distributed, Boyarsky wrote, 'You may need subcontractors. The MTA has strict rules requiring participation of minority- and female-owned firms in such joint ventures. ... You need one who's qualified and politically acceptable. A firm wouldn't want a Latino subcontractor, for example, who is an enemy of the powerful MTA board chairman, Los Angeles City Councilman Richard Alatorre.'[55] Riordan was also expected to be much friendlier than Woo to Alatorre.[56] Julian Nava supported Riordan,[57] as did African

American attorney Stanley Sanders, himself a candidate for mayor, who had strong business ties to Riordan.

Woo, an upper-middle-class Chinese American businessman, had represented the Hollywood area since the mid 1980s; his father was an owner of the Cathay Bank. Considered a liberal, Woo had earned his reputation as a reformer by confronting the LAPD. During the campaign, however, he vacillated and seemed to believe that he could win by wearing the Bradley mantle and appealing to a coalition of minority groups and Bradley supporters. Supervisor Gloria Molina and Assemblyman Richard Polanco supported him. (Reportedly Molina felt uncomfortable with Riordan because in 1988 he made a comment about 'taking lessons in learning to wave to poor people.')[58]

1993 MAYORAL RUNOFF RESULTS

	Percent of Voters	Riordan	Woo
Westside	18	55	45
San Fernando Valley	44	71	29
Central L.A.	21	40	60
South L.A.	17	27	73
Race/Ethnicity			
Anglo	72	67	33
Black	12	14	86
Latino	10	43	57
Asian	4	31	69
Gender			
Male	50	58	42
Female	50	50	50
Income			
under $20,00	14	42	58
$20–39,999	25	52	48
$40–59,999	22	60	40
$60,000+	39	62	38
Residence			
Homeowner	63	64	36
Renter	33	42	58
Union Member*			
yes	32	49	51
no	68	61	39

* Anyone in household a union member.
SOURCE: Richard Simon, 'The Times Poll: Anglo Vote Carried Riordan to Victory', Los Angeles Times, 10 June 1993.

In the runoff, however, the Valley voted for Riordan and turned the tide in his favor.[59] When it came down to the wire, Angeleno voters were simply tired of Bradley, and they viewed Woo as his surrogate. It also didn't help Woo that, as a member of a minority group, he was associated with the inner city. Finally, Woo alienated many of his supporters by vacillating during the campaign on key issues like immigrant rights and police oversight. This contributed to a low turnout by Blacks and other voters who tended to be generally sympathetic to him. Riordan defeated Woo by a margin of almost 2 to 1 in the Valley.[60] In an article entitled, 'Politicians Who Ignore Valley Voters Pay the Price', *Los Angeles Times* reporter Dan Brennan cited taxation, illegal immigration and an ineffective LAUSD as the Valley's main political concerns – Riordan passed the Valley's litmus test: Woo did not.[61]

The Los Angeles mayoral election satisfied no one outside the white Valley and the business community.[62] In his first days in office, Riordan still talked about privatization. For example, he spearheaded an effort to sell the main library to the Phillip Morris Company, which was met by a barrage of criticism.[63] For all his rhetoric about how 'L.A.'s government has increasingly become the enemy of business. It's like being in a communist country', Riordan was aware that the business community's anti-tax, anti-government policies wouldn't solve urban problems.

Black–Brown Relations and the Appointment of Hermosillo

In his first year Riordan appointed several Latinos to his administration – as expected, mostly rich supporters. Some 59 percent of the commissioners appointed came from comparatively well-to-do neighborhoods, with only 16 percent from lower income areas.[64] But Riordan did not exploit the immigrant issue; in fact, he has been one of the more decent L.A. politicians on that question. He simply stated that the immigrants are here and that the city must do the humanitarian thing to protect their health and safety. At the same time, he did little to combat anti-immigrant hysteria directly.[65]

Mayor Richard Riordan lost his first major battle with the City Council when he nominated as fire commissioner a Latino who was viewed by leaders of the Black community (as well as some Chicanos) as racist and divisive. The controversy over the Xavier Hermosillo nomination is not so simple, however, and needs to be examined in the context of Black political power in Los Angeles in the early 1990s. (See also Chapter 6.)

African Americans had built their political power in council districts south of the central city, and they had voting strength well beyond their numbers. Proud of their political achievements, they were 13 percent of the population and cast 18 percent of the vote in the 1989 mayoral election. In contrast, Latinos constituted just under 40 percent of the city but cast only 8 percent of the vote.[66] During the 1980s Los Angeles had grown by more than 17 percent and much of this growth was among the Latino (and Asian) populations. Neverthe-

less, Latinos were grossly underrepresented, having been locked out of the political game until Alatorre was elected in late 1986 and Molina in 1987 – and
they held only two seats on the City Council.

For Chicano leaders, getting more seats on the City Council signified respect and not being taken for granted. Pouring over the 1990 Census maps,
they found the possibility that a Chicano could be elected in the 7th CD in the
San Fernando Valley and another by shifting the boundaries of Rita Walters's
9th CD. The 9th CD had declined from 56 percent to 36 percent Black during
the 1980s, and its Latino population had increased from 36 percent to 61 percent. However, remapping would mean that Walters's district would lose
Downtown Los Angeles, the commercial and tourist center of the city – and an
important source of patronage and revenue for her district. Walters, as well as
the Black community, was unwilling to give up this plum.[67]

The African American community had slowly lost political ground. During
the 1980s, some 75,000 African Americans had left South Central for the Inland
Empire, where the African American population doubled as a consequence.
South Central Black leaders were aware of this population seepage and
adopted the slogan 'Don't move, improve.' Economic restructuring was the
reason for the 20 percent drop in the Black population in South Central: plant
shutdowns and the resulting loss of blue-collar jobs in the areas just east of
South Central. Moreover, African Americans also paid higher mortgage interest rates in South Central, suffered police repression, and had lower-quality
schools. With a loosening of housing segregation elsewhere, much of South
Central's Black middle-class population moved out.[68] Meanwhile, thousands of
Latinos moved into the abandoned areas, further unsettling Blacks, who depended on South Central as a political power base. More was at stake than just
electoral representation: Blacks had learned that political power and jobs go
hand and hand.

At the same time, Latinos resented the fact that they had made few political
gains under Mayor Tom Bradley. In March 1993, José Luis Sierra reported in *La
Opinión* that less than 30 of the 217 city commissioners were Latinos. Some 45
percent of the elected and appointed positions in L.A. were held by Anglos,
who formed 37.2 percent of the population. African Americans held 22 percent
of the elected and appointed positions, although they made up less than 14
percent of the population, while Latinos held 20 percent of the jobs, but were
39.8 percent of the population.[69]

The city had 44,157 employees, 6,700 of them Latinos. Of the jobs with decision-making power, Anglo-Americans held 62 percent and Latinos less than
10 percent.[70] Latino males held only 7.19 percent of administrative positions,
while Latinas fared even worse with only 1.07 percent. Indeed, Latinas were
only 4.87 percent of all city employees, one-fourth of all Latino employees.
The push for political representation meant that Latinos wanted a greater

piece of the public job pie, as well as more respect and recognition.[71]

Los Angeles Urban League President John Mack, a temperate man, remarked about the redistricting process: 'We have the potential of a political bloodletting along minority lines', which neither he nor anyone else wanted. In this climate, all talk of carving out an additional Latino City Council district went nowhere. Indeed, contrary to the national trend, many Black politicos had second thoughts about using redistricting as a method for correcting imbalances in political representation. Of course, critics of redistricting raised the issue of 'illegal immigrants', alleging that using redistricting could foster electoral segregation, 'pitting one group against another'.[72] African American politicos and leaders argued that 'as long as they [Blacks] cast the lion's share of votes, they should control the fate of the district [the 9th CD].'[73]

Councilman Mike Hernández angrily replied, 'This plan will make sure that the have-nots can [never] become the haves.' Conservative African American Councilman Nate Holden rebutted, 'You know, and I know, that a lot of people in this community are not legal residents, which means they cannot vote.' Therefore, Latinos were told to conduct voter registration drives instead of concentrating on redistricting.[74] In the end, Bradley approved the redistricting plan, which denied Latinos the potential for a fourth seat on the City Council and increased resentment among Latinos and especially among Chicanos.

In retrospect, it was unfortunate that Chicanos fell into the trap of measuring their political success against the achievements of African Americans. At the same time, the decline in African American political power cannot be attributed to Mexicans or Central Americans or, for that matter, Asians. They did not close down the South Gate General Motors plant, the steel mills and other heavy industries. They did not let the city's infrastructure decay, nor did they control the banks that redlined South Central L.A. Nor did they control the Los Angeles police.

Essentially, tensions between African Americans and Latinos over control of Downtown detracted from the struggle for meaningful reform and the redistribution of city revenues. Why should one councilmanic district control Downtown, Century City, and the Warner Center? If the goal was empowerment, splitting up the City Council into thirty-five districts representing a variety of communities would have made more sense, encouraging development of neighborhood political organizations that would have freed the council from precisely those special interests that made the Downtown area so coveted.[75]

Chicanos formed a majority in five City Council districts – the 1st, 7th, 9th, 13th and 14th CDs. In two others, the 10th and 15th, Chicanos numbered over 40 percent. Consequently, during the redistricting debate Chicano leaders privately criticized the Black community for not joining with them to create a Latino–Black majority within the council. Assuredly, African Americans had their own complaints, which were often valid. The differential in the Latino/Chicano communities between population and registered voters cannot be accounted for solely in terms of undocumented immigration.[76] To a great extent the children of the undocumented were citizens; there was also a large amnesty group; and Latinos had a bigger under-eighteen population than both Euroamericans and African Americans.

Tensions led to irresponsible comments on all sides. Latinos and Blacks clashed over jobs, reapportionment, the schools, the Martin Luther King Hospital and 'Rebuild L.A.' Blacks resented Chicano demands such as the proposal of Chicana school board member Leticia Quezada to give the parents of immigrants with children the right to vote in school board elections. On the other hand, Latinos in general could not understand the depth of African American fears of losing the gains made by the civil rights struggle.[77]

Although firm in pressing for another Latino seat, MALDEF's general counsel Antonia Hernández went the extra mile in an effort to be conciliatory. She acknowledged that 'until we get our people to become citizens, and then register and to vote, we don't have an effective voting bloc.' Hernández also pointed out that Councilwoman Rita Walters and Assemblywoman Marta Escutía shared relatively the same-sized area, adding, 'If I were in their [African Americans'] shoes, I would also feel threatened – so from the Latino community there is a certain understanding. Sharing power is not easy.'[78]

Meanwhile, the City Council did little to ameliorate tensions. Los Angeles trailed major Southwest cities in reforming the political structure during the 1970s. It remained a city whose political process had changed minimally since the days of Calvin Coolidge in the 1920s, when the local elites devised a system that allowed the city's 'finest' to rule. The city was controlled by a commission government that was vulnerable to the influence of the 'right' people.[79]

It was against this backdrop of recent tension and resentment between African Americans and Latinos in local politics that Mayor Riordan nominated Xavier Hermosillo, a former reporter turned public relations consultant to the Los Angeles Fire Commission. Hermosillo, a prominent member of the Chicano organization NEWS for America, allegedly rejected the notion that Latinos should form coalitions with other groups. Hermosillo was a Republican who used 1960s Chicano Movement rhetoric, talking about Chicano Power and the return of Aztlán, the legendary ancestral home of the Aztecs, to Chicanos.

Riordan's nomination of Hermosillo to the Fire Commission drew an angry outcry from African Americans, progressive whites, some Latinos, reactionaries and anti-immigrant forces. He was accused of having used the word *mayates*, a Spanish slang term for Black people. (The word literally refers to a black insect found in Mexico's cotton crop.) Over the years the word has taken on an innocuous meaning when referring to African Americans, but unfortunately it is often used in a thoughtless, deprecating manner.[80] Hermosillo was also accused of being divisive during an interview on the CBS program *48*

Hours. He was quoted as saying: 'We [Latinos] are taking it [the city] back, house by house, block by block. Better wake up and smell the refried beans.' On 25 May 1993 in his KCOP-TV commentary he commented: 'Many wonder if leaving four ethnic co-chairs in charge [of Rebuild L.A.] is going to work. Probably not. It hasn't worked with an African American mayor dealing with a Latino majority population in a town where white males control the business community.'[81]

In criticizing the nomination of Hermosillo, Councilwoman Rita Walters said, 'There is a difference between being outspoken and being divisive. Martin Luther King was outspoken but he was always inclusive. Mr. Hermosillo has been outspoken and always divisive.' Joe Hicks, the respected executive director of the Southern Leadership Conference of Greater Los Angeles, called on the council to reject Hermosillo because of 'his documented insensitivity to other groups'.[82] Councilman Mark Ridley Thomas told a columnist that Riordan 'behaved irresponsibly and created unnecessary conflict between African Americans and Latino members in the council.'[83] Indeed, the lines were drawn with Richard Alatorre, Mike Hernández and Richard Alarcón all supporting Hermosillo. Alatorre accused opponents of rejecting Hermosillo because he was an outspoken Chicano.[84] Assemblyman Richard Polanco expressed the mood of many Chicanos by saying that the issue was larger than Xavier Hermosillo.[85]

While many Chicanos opposed Hermosillo, including *La Opinión*, on the street the Hermosillo incident became a Black–Latino confrontation and heightened tensions between the two groups. From the point of view of the Black community, Hermosillo's use of *mayate* was as offensive as Jesse Jackson's use of 'Hymietown' was to Jews. So why then did some Chicano progressives support the candidacy of Hermosillo?

No one excused Hermosillo's use of the term *mayate*. By the same token, many Chicanos felt insulted by the use of the terms *illegal alien* and *wetback*. Councilmembers such as Nate Holden had taken cheap shots bandying those terms. Also, many of those testifying against the Hermosillo appointment represented some of the most racist and anti-immigrant interests in the city. What they objected to was Hermosillo's advocating Chicano Power, to his saying that the Southwest once belonged to Mexico and that the United States had stolen it by force. In criticizing Mayor Bradley and the white power structure Hermosillo expressed sentiments shared by many Angelenos of all racial and ethnic backgrounds.

Ultimately Hermosillo was rejected by a nine-to-five vote. What he should have been criticized for was swept under the rug. Hermosillo interpreted Chicano Power to mean, basically, Mexican or Chicano capitalists getting their share of the economic and political pie. In this pursuit, he erroneously used Blacks as the standard for judging Latino successes and failures, instead of the system itself.[86] On the positive side, he stood against his party on anti-immigrant legislation, criticizing both parties for supporting populist racism. And there was a popular perception that he defended Latino workers who had been kicked off worksites (see Chapter 11). The Hermosillo case showed the need for all groups – white, Brown, Black and Asian – to explore the limits of group advocacy and the need to judge everyone by the same standard.

Immigration and the 1994 State Elections

'Valley fever' dominated the 1994 state elections. Anti-immigrant hysteria had reached moblike proportions by then, allowing Pete Wilson to make the greatest comeback in recent political history. Constantly in the news, his job rating hit 15 percent in May but rose to 22 percent in August as the result of immigrant bashing.[87] Before a business group in the San Fernando Valley, Wilson responded to critics in a truly statesmanlike manner: 'They can kiss my rear end if they can leap that high from the low road where they are dwelling habitually.'[88] Democrats were partly responsible for his success in that they themselves engaged in immigrant bashing, including, to one degree or another, Senators Dianne Feinstein and Barbara Boxer and Congressman Anthony Beilenson, along with Attorney-General Janet Reno and the Democratic contender for governor, State Treasurer Kathleen Brown.[89] Brown even proposed tying a prisoner-transfer pact to the North American Free Trade Agreement, and called for a tamper-proof Social Security card, employer sanctions and military troops on the Mexican border.[90] Throughout, President Bill Clinton as usual sent mixed signals.[91]

Wilson's strategy was to highlight the proposition that 'We Americans' have lost control of our borders and to blame undocumented residents for the state's fiscal problems. He continually distorted the November 1992 Los Angeles County study that alleged that the county spent $946 million in 1991–92 on services to recent immigrants, adding that the county collected only $139 million of the $4.3 billion a year in federal, state and local taxes paid by immigrants.[92] He distorted or ignored such evidence as a July 1993 report by the state Senate Office of Research, which concluded: 'The unfortunate backlash against immigrants, exploited by too many politicians in the past year or so, tends to belittle newcomers to the country as a drag on the economy and an imposition on residents of longer standing. This dismissal of the immensely varied ranks of new and future Americans is unjust to the great majority, and is simply mistaken.' The bottom line was that 'blaming the immigrants won't solve economic woes.'[93]

Simultaneously, the Federation for American Immigration Reform (FAIR) carried on a war of propaganda and misinformation using 'illegal immigration as a convenient excuse to urge drastic cuts in legal immigration, from the current 800,000 a year to nearly 200,000.'[94] Nationally, Pat Buchanan argued that the Republican Party should go further in exploiting the issue of immigration.[95] Pete Wilson's call for immigration control to be part of NAFTA infuriated Mexican Foreign Minister Fernando Solana, who replied that Mexico was not a jail. Solana reminded Wilson of the contributions Mexican labor had made to the development of the richest state in the United States.[96] This issue received considerable attention in the Mexican press.[97]

While many Latinos supported a tougher policy toward illegal immigrants, the intensity of Wilson's attacks began to frighten them. An August 1993 *La Opinión* poll showed that 81 percent of 286 Latinos responded that they disapproved of Wilson's anti-immigrant tactics, which many regarded as racist.[98] Fifteen Latino organizations, led by MALDEF in San Francisco, announced a new coalition called the Latino Civil Rights Coalition to combat anti-immigrant hysteria.[99] In Southern California, Latino leaders including US Rep. Xavier Becerra, Richard Alatorre and Assemblywoman Hilda Solis sent a letter accusing Wilson of stirring up racial tensions.[100]

Cardinal Roger Mahoney urged legislators to continue providing services to undocumented residents, arguing that the long-term social costs of denying education would be paid by all and condemning the anti-immigrant hysteria as 'divisive rhetoric': 'We are witnessing a distressing and growing trend among political leaders, segments of the media and the public at large which capitalizes on prevailing fears and insecurity about the growing number of immigrants in our community.' How could you be pro-life and against a decent life for immigrant children? How could you be a feminist and agree with beefing up the Border Patrol to hunt down women and children?[101] Even so, a *Times* poll showed that 65 percent of Catholics were anti-immigrant.[102]

In February 1994 Latino leaders and politicos formed Proponents for Responsible Immigration Debate in Education (PRIDE) in order to put some sanity into the debate on illegal immigration. PRIDE wanted candidates to support the right of immigrants to medical care, education and citizenship if born in the United States, and to support keeping the INS under civilian control. Kathleen Brown met with PRIDE and said that she opposed direct military border patrols but favored the National Guard assisting the INS. Councilman Mike Hernández was incensed by this stance and threatened to reconsider his endorsement of Brown.[103] All this, however, did not stop some Latino legislators from joining the mob. Assemblyman Louis Caldera even sponsored legislation that required immigrants to show a green card to get a driver's license.[104]

The existence of conflicting attitudes among Chicanos and other Latinos toward immigrants – especially those from Mexico and Central America – has been obvious for several years. The reasons why Latinos, often immigrants or children of immigrants themselves, would support policies to deny immigrant rights are complex. They include class, culture and other factors.[105] Indeed, the right to vote has separated the Latino/Chicano community into voters and nonvoters, with the distinction echoing that between those with, and without, legal residence.

Proposition 187

By May 1994 the campaign to place the draconian SOS (Save Our State) initiative on the ballot had 600,000 signatures, 200,000 more than needed to qualify for the November election.[106] As expected, Governor Wilson endorsed SOS, which became Proposition 187, and stepped up his inflammatory rhetoric about an 'invasion'. 'California simply can't wait any longer. Our borders are a sieve that makes a mockery of our laws and cripples our ability to shape our own identity.'[107] He also filed a suit against the federal government for reimbursement of state costs of providing services to immigrants. (Many Democrats questioned why he had not brought his suit against the Bush administration.)[108]

In reality, an INS survey showed that of those legalized under the Immigration Reform and Control Act of 1986 (IRCA), only 1 percent had received any government assistance. A San Francisco study showed that of the 23 percent of undocumented mothers eligible for welfare because they had US-born children, only 5 percent took advantage of their eligibility.[109] Pro-immigrant studies had little impact on politicians such as Wilson: they had their minds made up, based on their calculation of political advantage. The immigrant was a convenient and politically safe scapegoat, and the only thing they cared about was getting elected.[110]

At the heart of the tension between Latinos and the white community was numbers. By the year 2020, the Latino population in California would increase from 27.3 percent to 36.5 percent, while the Euroamerican population would fall from 52 percent in 1993 to 34 percent.[11] Prop. 187 was based on the color of Latino and Asian skins. No one mentioned the Irish, Polish or Canadian undocumented workers. As one columnist put it, 'The complexion of immigrants is different today. In earlier times [the 1950s] about two-thirds of the legal immigrants came from Europe. Today, only about 15 percent come from Europe, with the rest hailing mostly from Latin America and Asia. In 1900, fully 85 percent of America was "Anglo". Today it's 75 percent. By the year 2040, it will be 59 percent ...'[112]

In other words, Prop. 187 went far beyond scapegoating immigrants for the state's economic woes.[113] It signified a profound resurgence of legalized racism in response to a historic national upheaval. There was a convergence of interests in Prop. 187, bringing together supporters of the school breakup movement in the Valley, the school voucher campaign, the 'Three Strikes and you're out' proposition and homeowner associations of the San Fernando Valley.[114] Although SOS backers maintained that the initiative was not race-specific (as they had claimed during the breakup and the voucher movements), polls suggested otherwise. Prop. 187 was favored 59 percent to 32 percent, with 64 percent of whites supporting the measure while 60 percent of Latinos and a narrow majority of African Americans disapproved.[115]

The June 1994 primaries provided a glimpse of what the November elections would bring. Voters defeated bonds for earthquake-proofing public buildings and building new schools.[116] Over half of those who turned out on election day were over fifty; in past elections only 35 percent were over fifty. They were reluctant to vote for maintenance of the social infrastructure, especially to benefit the young, and they looked for every solution possible so long as it meant not paying taxes.[117]

In July, Diane Feinstein ran an advertisement claiming that 3,000 'illegals' crossed the border each night. She also claimed that her opponent, Rep. Michael Huffington, had voted against hiring 700 new border guards. She proposed charging $1 for every border crossing and hiring 2,000 new border guards. 'I'm Diane Feinstein and I've just begun to fight for California.'[118] Feinstein ignored the fact that about 60 percent of those in the country illegally had entered as tourists and simply overstayed their visas. She also ignored the fact that immigrants consumed goods, which created jobs. In the end, Feinstein, Clinton and most other Democrats opposed Prop. 187. However, they continued to argue that immigration was a problem, and their opposition to the measure rested on arguments that it would cost the Los Angeles School District more than $450 million and California billions in lost federal money.[119] As a result, 10,000 teachers would lose their jobs.[120]

There was some tension between the Black and Latino communities over Prop. 187. According to Deputy District Attorney Kevin Ross, a Black attorney, Latinos should not expect Black support even though the legislation was bad. 'Latino leaders cannot expect African Americans to embrace their struggle while they disrespect ours.' As an example, he called attention to the efforts of some Latino leaders to rename Martin Luther King Hospital after César Chávez. He was incensed that Molina had called fellow supervisor Yvonne Brathwaite Burke a racist for not supporting Molina's measures to resolve the day labor problem.[121] John W. Mack, president of the Los Angeles Urban League and a long-time community leader, struck a very different note: 'Some argue that we need to send a message, but Proposition 187 is not a telegram. It is a real law with real repercussions.' Mack continued, 'My African American brothers and sisters should recognize that the current "close the border hysteria" will be used against Haitians, black Africans and others of our color.'[122]

The debate over Prop. 187 also saw an outpouring by progressive elements, including health workers and teachers, who pledged noncompliance if it passed. When the *Los Angeles Times* endorsed Wilson and hypocritically opposed Prop. 187 in the same issue, Latino reporters revolted and Deputy Editor Frank del Olmo took a self-imposed leave to rethink his future at the *Times*. In an unprecedented move, the *Times* allowed del Olmo to answer its endorsing editorial; he wrote that the governor had offended every Latino with his ugly, bigoted campaign for Prop. 187. The measure had also insulted Asian Americans. 'We can no more forget what Wilson has done in the 1994 campaign than African Americans can forget how segregationist governors like Arkansas' Orval Faubus tried to keep black children from getting a decent education in public schools.'[123]

The Mobilization Against Proposition 187

As the campaign continued, the racism of Prop. 187 galvanized opposition. A September *Los Angeles Times* poll showed that before the anti-187 forces started work, 52 percent of the Latinos supported Prop. 187. By the eve of the 8 Nov. election, opposition to the proposition had become a litmus test for Latino approval. A coalition of Chicano groups against Prop. 187 mobilized in February 1994. A march in Los Angeles drew 6,000, followed by another march on 28 May when about 18,000 trekked up Broadway to City Hall.[124] On 16 October, over 100,000 protestors marched down Avenida César Chávez to City Hall. Many Latinos turned out because the issue of 187 had been personalized and hit home.[125] Critics pointed to the Mexican flags seen on the march, and Harold Ezell criticized the Spanish-language media's support of the march.[126] No doubt many Anglos resented the Mexican nationalist fervor and were angered by the demonstrations and the waving of the Mexican flags. However, did this anger really affect how they voted?

Within the Latino and Chicano community a debate broke out between the coalition Taxpayers Against 187, which included teachers, medical professionals, union activists, and a faction of Latino organizations, headed by Gloria Molina, such as MALDEF, CHIRLA and CARECEN, which were afraid that mass demonstrations would turn off white voters.[127] According to coordinators of the 16 October march, Molina attempted to sabotage the event by urging her followers not to participate. (To her credit, Molina did raise $600,000 to fight Prop. 187.)

The National Coordinating Committee for Citizenship and Civic Participation, also known as *la cordinadora*, played a central role in planning the march. Within this group, One-Stop Immigration raised a major share of the money for the march, which cost over $50,000. Separate from *la cordinadora* was the

Los Angeles Organizing Committee, which included Local 660, the International Garment Workers Union, Justice for Janitors and the California Immigrant Workers Association, among others. (Some of the leaders of the L.A. Committee also belonged to *la cordinadora*.) Within this network, but not part of the governing committee for the march, was a contingent of activists that included Alvaro Maldonado and the Brown Berets, who did effective outreach. A list of 7,000 volunteers signed up on the day of the march for the No on 187 campaign. On the eve of the election a concert was held at East Los Angeles College where 10,000 protested Proposition 187 and waved US flags.[128]

The massive student walkouts against Prop. 187 caught most observers by surprise. Gloria Molina, concerned about the reaction of the archetypal Reseda housewife, was worried that the image of truant students charging down streets to protest Prop. 187 would generate a backlash; she actively pressured students to go back to school. According to Robert Alaniz, Molina's aide, 'It [walking out] reinforces the idea by some that California is being invaded.'[129] Opponents of Prop. 187 were heartened during the last days of the campaign as polls showed that support for the proposition had declined, and they seemed afraid that demonstrations might upset this momentum.

There is no doubt that the 16 October march had a profound impact on the students. They reacted with a militancy reminiscent of the 1960s. However, in the 1960s a general climate of support for student activism existed. Civil rights struggles, the Vietnam War protests and the War on Poverty programs conditioned students for the big 1968 walkouts. Also, the process then was accelerated by the work of leaders like Lincoln High teacher Sal Castro. The Prop. 187 walkouts were more spontaneous, and their leaders were not only Chicanos but also Central Americans.

Walkouts took place at Huntington Park, Bell, South Gate, Los Angeles, Marshall and Fremont high schools. Police were called out in Van Nuys as students took the main street; 200 officers were on tactical alert. 'Police used pepper spray on several unruly students...' In the Valley, thousands of students walked out at Pacoima, Maclay, Mulholland, Fulton, Sepulveda and Van Nuys middle schools. Thousands of high school students walked out in Woodland Hills, Van Nuys, Grant, North Hollywood, Chatsworth, Kennedy, Monroe, Grant, San Fernando, Birmingham and Reseda, among others.[130] Altogether, it is estimated that 10,000 (an estimate on the low side) walked out of thirty-nine schools.[131] District officials cooperated with Chicano activists, and teach-ins were held at those schools where the students did not walk out.[132] Authorities were shaken and the National Guard was put on alert for possible violence at these events.[133]

The dramatic participation of students from the San Fernando Valley shocked many Angelenos. Although Latinos were a majority of the school population there – 60 percent of Valley students were Latino – they had been taken for granted.[134] But their discontent came naturally, since they were on the front lines. Many were bused even within the Valley. Often alienated from other students, they heard the anti-immigrant remarks, and their teachers were more outspoken about their own biases. Moreover, the Valley's Latino population had grown so rapidly that a sense of place had never really developed.

Meanwhile, elected officials, among them Molina and Alatorre, told students to stay in school. Juan José Gutiérrez of One Stop, a principal organizer of the 16 October march, advised students to stay in school and persuaded school authorities to have more on-campus assemblies. Students were also channeled into the Los Angeles County Organizing Committee to Defeat Proposition 187 and the Taxpayers group.[135]

A Field Poll just over a month before the election showed Latinos in California sharply divided over Proposition 187: Latinos opposed the measure by 48 to 44 percent, while white voters favored it by 60 to 17 percent. A *Los Angeles Times* poll reported that Californians favored Prop. 187 by 2 to 1, with Latinos 52 to 42 percent in favor.[136] On 8 November California overwhelmingly passed Prop. 187.[137] Only the San Francisco Bay Area voted against the measure, by 70 percent to 30 percent.[138] Angelenos voted for Prop. 187 by a 12-point margin; the Valley voted 61 percent for Prop. 187. Exit polls showed Latinos opposing the proposition 77 percent to 23 percent statewide.[139] Some 53 percent of Asians voted against Prop. 187, as did a like proportion of African Americans.[140] Interestingly, 53 percent of those aged eighteen to twenty-nine in the general population voted against it, and 68 percent of those over sixty-five voted for it. The older the voter, the more he or she was likely to vote yes. Republicans voted 78 percent in favor, versus 36 percent of the Democrats.[141] The most important 1994 electoral issue was immigration, according to 50 percent of the voters, even more important than crime. Middle-class white Americans had spoken; 80 percent of those who voted were white.[142]

The position of the Catholic Church on 187 was a positive one. Before the election Cardinal Mahoney said that the measure would undermine 'clear moral principles', stopping just shy of calling it a mortal sin. He said that Prop. 187 would tear families apart.[143] The victory of Prop. 187 was a blow to the moral authority of the Catholic Church, however. White Catholics voted 58 percent to 42 percent for Prop. 187. Many priests recognized that there was racial bias associated with 187.[144] Many of the Protestant churches remained silent on the issue.[145]

As expected, legal challenges were filed the day after the election.[146] Initially many municipalities joined the suit, but local officials were intimidated by threats of recall.[147] Vigilantes calling themselves 'loyal citizens' asked Mexican-looking people for their green cards. CHIRLA was flooded with complaints, as were other social service agencies.[148] The pro–Prop. 187 forces pushed forward.[149]

As a result of the passage of Prop. 187, many in the immigrant community feared to seek health care.[150] One of Governor Wilson's first acts after his re-election was to order health clinics not to give prenatal care to undocumented mothers. The results of this decree were predictable. There was the tragic case of twelve-year-old Julio Cano, who died of acute advanced leukemia and a secondary infection because his parents were afraid to take him to a public clinic for treatment and were saving up to take him to a private clinic. The treatment might not have made a difference, but the tragedy was that it might have. Julio was a brilliant student who had tutored members of his family.[151]

Where will the struggle against Prop. 187 and the whole assault on immigrant rights go from here? The students are the key to this. They were morally outraged at the injustice of Prop. 187, and they acted, only to be cautioned by Latino politicos and community leaders. Defeat confirmed in their minds that Californians are racist – and that conclusion is now part of their historical memory. Moreover, the vast majority of the protestors are documented residents who will be able to vote soon. What direction their militancy takes will in great part depend on their future political education. With a view to influencing that future, many of the university MEChAs are beginning to link up with high school and middle school Chicano student associations.[152] In another response to Prop. 187, Chicano and Latino organizations have begun the work of speeding up the naturalization of noncitizens. Despite the sound and fury over Proposition 187, it is clear that Mexicans and other Latinos are here in California to stay.

A Balance Sheet

As many observers have noted, the 1994 California elections reflected the national trend toward meaner – indeed, neo-fascist – politics that pointed to a grim future for people of color and all poor or working-class residents. In California, the reason for the right-wing sweep would certainly include the massive financial support for Republican candidates and causes; the rampant white racism that scapegoated immigrants, welfare recipients, youth in the barrios and ghettoes, and other vulnerable groups; and the fact that Democrats did not address Latino issues or campaign seriously in Latino areas.

Rather than recognizing the power of these forces, the media attempted to portray an apathetic Latino community that did not care enough even to come out against Prop. 187. They reported that only about 8 percent of voters in Los Angeles were Latino, out of an eligible pool of 14 percent (7 percent of L.A. voters in 1992 were Latino, and 9 percent in 1990). The Southwest Voter Research Institute corrected this claim, reporting that its exit polls showed that Latinos turned out 10.2 to 11.4 percent of the vote. An institute sampling of 40 precincts in L.A. showed a 45 to 52 percent Latino turnout. (Southwest Institute director Antonio González notes that Latinos had 300,000 more registered voters than in 1990; the institute spent some $100,000 on voter registration.) That number takes on more meaning when we recall that white voters turned out in unusually high numbers, and that two-thirds of California's Latinos were noncitizens or not old enough to vote. Poverty and lack of education also had an adverse impact on voting patterns.

Because of Prop. 187, the Latino vote was very loyal to the Democratic Party. Some 67 percent of Latinos voted for Diane Feinstein versus 22 percent for Michael Huffington; considering her history of immigrant bashing and lack of attention to Latinos, this was amazing.[153] Despite mid October polls showing a tight race, Feinstein ignored the Latino vote, just as she had done in her 1990 gubernatorial bid, contending that her outreach and voter registration was through the Democratic Party apparatus. In contrast, Jennifer Grossman, spokeswoman for Huffington, said, 'We are reaching out to Latinos as shopkeepers, entrepreneurs, educators, members of the community.'[154]

Statewide, 72 percent of Latinos voted for Brown and 23 percent for Wilson (who had received 40 percent of Latino votes in 1990). Wilson's making illegal immigration the cornerstone of his political resurrection thus seems to have alienated many Latinos who might otherwise have voted for him.[155] He followed the Nixon strategy and targeted Latino professionals and small-business owners, seeking to convince those who had supported him in 1990 to stay with him. According to Wilson's aides, the Latino middle class made up more than one-third of the Latino population statewide. But Wilson never lived down his television spots that depicted Mexicans rushing across the border while the narrator announced ominously, 'Every day they keep coming.'[156]

In other races, Chicanos suffered both losses and gains. The defeat of state Senator Art Torres for insurance commissioner dealt a vital blow to Chicano interests. He would have been the first Latino to hold statewide office since 1876. Torres, who had more potential than any other Chicano politician, lost to Republican Chuck Quakenbush by a mere five percentage points, receiving 3.2 million votes. He was supported by consumer advocate Ralph Nader and had been head of the Senate Insurance Committee since 1992. In contrast, Quakenbush had relatively little experience and was heavily indebted to the insurance industry, which contributed just under $2 million to Quakenbush's campaign.[157]

At the same time, Latinos had their victories. In the state Senate, Richard G. Polanco won in the 22nd District, Hilda Solis in the 24th, Charles Calderón in the 30th, and Rubén Ayala in the 32nd. In the state Assembly, Antonio Villaraigosa won in the 45th, Louis Caldera in the 46th, Diane Martínez in the 49th, Martha Escutía in the 50th, Martin Gallegos in the 57th, Grace Napolitano in the 58th and Joe Baca in the 62nd.[158]

Ultimately, however, pundits blamed Latinos for the fall of Assembly Speaker Willie Brown and the defeat of Democratic candidate for governor Kathleen Brown. In a November 1994 *California Journal* article, the editors speculated whether Latinos had cost Brown his speakership. Latinos made up 46 percent to 65 percent of Assembly Districts 28, 30 and 69 (formerly held by Rusty Areias, Jim Costa and Tom Umberg, respectively, who ran for other offices). The 28th was 46 percent Latino and the 69th was 65 percent. The Democratic candidates lost by narrow margins, so it was speculated that those defeats resulted from the low Latino turnout. This analysis is shallow because it failed, for example, to take into account tense Euroamerican–Latino relations in the 69th Assembly District in Orange County.[159] Nor did it consider the funds contributed by special interests to key Assembly races in the last month of the elections. The California term-limit initiative, which had passed in 1991, gave these special interests additional clout, since it meant that voters would often be unfamiliar with a candidate's record. Moreover, local elections had difficulty attracting money because of the excessive demands of the gubernatorial and senatorial races. Republicans raised $3.5 million for Assembly races alone.

Gun lobbyists made it possible to increase the number of pro-gun representatives in the Assembly from 37 to 46.[160] The tobacco industry reportedly spent $20 million pushing Proposition 188, which would have overturned local anti-smoking ordinances. The insurance lobby turned out in force, pouring millions into the defeat of Proposition 186, the single-payer health insurance initiative.

What really went wrong? It is evident that Kathleen Brown's campaign was thrown together hastily and filled with internal dissension. According to sources working in the campaign, the Brown operation was not part of any long-range Democratic Party strategy. Registration, the key to political success, was expensive and reactive. The Democratic Party was stingy with its money. According to Bob Mulholland, adviser to the Democratic Party, it cost the party $3 to $5 for every new registered voter, and up to $12 to send the voter to the polls. According to Richard Maullin, a pollster with L.A.-based Fairbank, Maullin and Associates, it is doubtful that either party would develop long-term registration programs. To her credit, Brown did target the Latino community during the campaign, but it was a case of too little, too late and the Latino Vote Project, aimed at registering Latinos in East Los Angeles and the Central Valley, fell far short.[161]

Then there was the strategy for defeating Prop. 187 that targeted 'the Reseda housewife' or 'the Fullerton elderly couple', according to L.A. Supervisor Gloria Molina. This strategy recognized that the Latino community could not by itself change the outcome – so it simply ignored Latinos. Hence, with no planning at higher levels the campaign was caught off balance when, as Rep. Xavier Becerra pointed out, the governor pounded out last-minute ads for

Prop. 187, wrapping himself around the issue. The Democrats just did not have the money or the will to counter these ads or to entice Latinos to vote. Roberto Lovato, director of CARECEN, noted that the Democratic Party committed resources to defeat Prop. 187 but never delivered them – at least not in Lovato's Pico-Union district.

After the election, the Chicano/Latino community was left to regroup and reconstruct. Claremont political scientist Harry Pachon of the Tomás Rivera Center estimated that there were at least 2 million Latinos in California who could qualify for citizenship.[162] The process of gaining citizenship, however, is an arduous one that takes resources. As Mulholland pointed out, it takes money to register voters and get them to the polls – and that does not include the cost of political education. Meanwhile, the Democratic Party had lost much of its moral authority among Chicano and Latino communities, where it had become overwhelmingly evident that immigrant bashing was not just insensitive, but a deadly threat.

In 1995 Republicans gained control of the California legislature, which then enacted legislation that would facilitate passage of an initiative to break up the Los Angeles Unified School District. With a breakup of the district likely, those who had previously opposed the idea began a scramble to create their own districts. The splintering of the LAUSD will undoubtedly have a profound impact on Latinos. Smaller districts will not only produce white rule in areas outside the inner city, but also intensify Latino–African American tensions – tensions that were somewhat ameliorated by the need for Blacks and Latinos to form coalitions within the mammoth LAUSD.

Notes

1. Timothy Williams, 'Valley Crime Fell Last Year, But Residents' Fears Soared', *Los Angeles Times*, 1 Jan. 1994. The Valley comprises 266 square miles and has 1.2 million people – almost half the land area of Los Angeles and a third of the population. If it were an incorporated city it would be the nation's sixth most populous city. Calvin Sims, 'Clearing San Fernando Valley's Image', *New York Times*, 31 Jan. 1994.

2. Mike Comeaux, 'Stereotype of Valley Rebutted', *Daily News*, 1 Aug. 1993; Comeaux, 'District 7 Problems Stem from Poverty', *Daily News*, 14 Dec. 1992. The rise of immigrant populations was a statewide trend; Comeaux, 'English Not Home Language for 1/3 of State', *Daily News*, 18 April 1993.

3. Jim Tranquada, 'Valley's Image as "Lily-White Suburbia" a Myth, UCLA Study Says', *Daily News*, 13 Oct. 1993, cited the UCLA Urban Planning study by Diane Foray and Jim Gilbert, 'Beyond Suburbia: The Changing Face of the San Fernando Valley'.

4. The high apartment-house vacancy factor attracted Latinos, who often crowded as many as ten people to an apartment. Developers and corporate apartment complex managers were not as 'selective' as homeowners, who up until the 1960s actively discriminated in selling to Mexicans and Blacks.

5. Julie Sheer, 'Wealth in the Valley', *Los Angeles Times*, 11 July 1993.

6. Alan C. Miller, 'Outcry against Immigration Is Loud in Valley', *Los Angeles Times*, 1 Aug. 1993.

7. Alan C. Miller, 'Citizenship Curb Backed by Beilenson', *Los Angeles Times*, 2 April 1992. Beilenson called for a change in the 14th Amendment to deny citizenship to children of undocumented residents. Beilenson does not have a history as a conservative. He received a respectable 83 in 1990 from the Americans for Democratic Action, while the conservative American Conservative Union gave him an 8 for his voting record.

8. Miller, 'Outcry'.

9. Of the 641,000 students in the Los Angeles Unified School District, 280,000 were classified as Limited English Speaking, 44% spoke a language other than English at home (90% of whom spoke Spanish). The teachers were overwhelmingly white; only around 10% were Latino.

10. The NAACP supported the new councilmanic map; MALDEF opposed it. Richard Simon, 'City Council Approves Redistricting Plan', *Los Angeles Times*, 30 May 1992.

11. Beth Schuster, 'School Board Divided Between Black, Latino', *Daily News*, 25 Sept. 1992; the school population was 64.4% Latino, 14.8% Black, 13.1% white and 5.2% Asian.

12. José Luis Sierra, 'Junta de Educación tendrá otro distrito', *La Opinión*, 8 July 1992.

13. John Schwada, 'Council Chooses Sides for School Remap Battle', *Los Angeles Times*, 17 June 1992; John Schwada, 'School Board Remap Plan Received Preliminary OK', *Los Angeles Times*, 24 June 1992.

14. Richard Simon, 'Latinos Draw Remap Plan to Boost Clout on School Board', *Los Angeles Times*, 24 March 1992. Especially disappointing was an editorial by progressive Board of Education member Julie Kornstein ('Stop the District – We Want Off', *Los Angeles Times*, 20 August 1992).

15. Bill Boyarsky, 'Redistricting and Deep Rifts in L.A. Politics', *Los Angeles Times*, 8 July 1992.

16. John Schwada, 'Foes of School Board Remapping Get Help', *Los Angeles Times*, 20 June 1992.

17. Henry Chu, 'Latina President on the Defensive in New District', *Los Angeles Times*, 12 July 1992; Randall C. Archibold, 'Grass-roots Activist Powered L.A. School Redistrict Plan', *Daily News*, 2 Aug. 1992; Marlene Baker, 'Latino Group Condemns Attack on Remapping Plan', *Los Angeles Times*, 28 June 1992. Chicanos and Latinos throughout the city had similar complaints: only 29.2% of the students in magnet schools were Latinos. Sandy Banks and Stephanie Chavez, 'L.A. Unified Breakup Drive Stirs Suspicions', *Los Angeles Times*, 18 May 1993. Julie Kornstein's Valley District had over three times as many magnet students as the new Latino district, although parts of it ran through the Valley. Latinos from the Northeast Valley and the Eastside also shared class interests: Kimberly Kindy, 'District's Magnet-Center Plan Slammed', *Daily News*, 19 April 1994. Valley leaders ignored poverty in the Valley. Of the 308 public schools receiving Chapter 1 and antipoverty funding, 47 were in the Valley. This was an 80% increase over 1990, when there were 26. Consuelo García, principal of Telfair School noted that 'Poverty is our No. 1 enemy, our No. 1 target.'

18. John Schwada, 'Zarovslasky Says Latest Census Data Upholds Remapping Vote', *Los Angeles Times*, 1 Oct. 1992; Alejandro Balotta, 'Gran aumento en la población de California para año 2000', *La Opinión*, 23 Sept. 1992.

19. Linda Jones of the Valley Chapter of the Black American Political Association and Cecilia Mansfield, new president of the 31st District PTSA, threatened to sue if the Alatorre plan were accepted: John Schwada, 'Valley School Redistricting Triggers Suit', *Los Angeles Times*, 7 July 1992.

20. Henry Chu, 'Initiative Drive to Remap School Board Begins', *Los Angeles Times*, 12 Nov. 1992; Chu, 'School Board Fight on Hold', *Los Angeles Times*, 30 Dec. 1992. By December, CAUSE had postponed its initiative drive and supported the statewide school voucher initiative, which would have given parents tax-funded vouchers to send their children to a school of their choice.

21. 'Nuevo paso en la disputa Rodríguez vs. el LAUSD', *La Opinión*, 8 July 1992; Marcelo M. Zuviría, 'LAUSD debrá distribuir los fondos por igual', *La Opinión*, 15 Aug. 1992; Pablo Comesaña Amado, 'Aplazan la votación sobre caso Rodríguez vs. LAUSD', *La Opinión*, 21 Feb. 1992; Henry Chu, 'Veteran Teachers Fear Forced Transfers', *Los Angeles Times*, 12 Jan. 1992; Barry Siegel, 'Parents Get a Lesson in Equality', *Los Angeles Times*, 13 April 1992. The United Teachers of Los Angeles opposed Rodríguez because teachers did not want equalization if it meant commuting to less desirable areas.

22. Roberti's political survival depended on the Valley voter. He was mentioned as a candidate for Ed Edelman's supervisoral district, state attorney general and state treasurer: David

Bloom, 'Roberti Leans Toward Running for State Office', *Daily News*, 8 Aug. 1993. Roberti could not run for the state senate in 1994 because of term limits; George Skelton, 'Roberti's Old School Approach', *Los Angeles Times*, 4 Feb. 1993; John Jacobs, 'Roberti Prepares for End of His Era', *Daily News*, 10 Sept. 1993; Mike Comeaux, 'Roberti Expected to Announce Candidacy for California Treasurer', *Daily News*, 23 Sept. 1993.

23. The amount of political mileage that Roberti got out of the issue was incredible: he was in the news daily for almost a year.

24. During the budget deliberations Hayden had written, 'The original idealism of many legislators has become exhausted, replaced by a single party: Incumbent Survival." Hayden's words in retrospect seemed prophetic. Tom Hayden, 'The Budget Is on Time, But at What Cost?', *Los Angeles Times*, 4 July 1993. Mike Comeaux, 'Support Grows to Split L.A. Unified', *Daily News*, 10 Jan. 1993

25. Comeaux, 'Support Grows'.

26. Bill Boyarsky, 'Split from School District Seen as Unifying Valley', *Los Angeles Times*, 4 April 1993. Boyarsky interviewed Black businessmen in Pacoima who said that the breakup was not a racial issue. It is clear that even among Blacks and Chicanos there was an inner-city bias.

27. Stephanie Chavez and Henry Chu, 'Activists Oppose Breakup of L.A. Schools', *Los Angeles Times*, 26 Jan. 1993. Citywide there had been tensions between Blacks and Chicanos during October 1992 over who would replace Bill Anton as superintendent of the LAUSD. Rubén Zacarias and Sid Thompson, a Brown and a Black, both eminently qualified, vied for the job. NEWS for America lobbied for Zacarias. Councilman Alatorre summed up the tensions: 'This is about recognition of the changing reality of the city.' James Johnson, director of the UCLA Center for the Study of Urban Power, said, 'Blacks have had their political day in the sun and the numbers are on the side of Latinos and they want their day to shine … It's going to be a painful experience because there is a natural skepticism [with regard to] coalitions': Stephanie Chavez, 'School Battle Is Rehearsal for Latinos', *Los Angeles Times*, 5 Oct. 1993. The board selected Thompson. Chicano leaders were frustrated because this rejection followed the failure of Sheriff Lee Baca to be selected Los Angeles chief of police.

28. Sandy Harrison, 'Breakup of LAUSD in Trouble', *Daily News*, 11 July 1993; Henry Chu, 'Brown Vows to Call in Votes Against Breakup', *Los Angeles Times*, 14 Aug. 1993.

29. Henry Chu, 'Racial Balance Issue May Block Valley District', *Los Angeles Times*, 2 Aug. 1993. There was the continuing debate over how the schools should be run. The business community wanted to restructure the schools, not necessarily to break them up. However, business leaders did not want to make a dollar commitment. Bill Boyarsky, 'The Business of Revolution in Schools', *Los Angeles Times*, 22 June 1990. In July 1993, the RAND Corporation released a study, *Newcomers in American Schools: Meeting the Educational Needs of Immigrant Youth*, which reported that shortages of funds, bilingual teachers and instructional materials meant that big-city schools were failing immigrant children: Lorraine McDonnell and Paul Hill, 'Study Faults Immigrants' Education', *Los Angeles Times*, 28 July 1993. For all its faults, the Board of Education had maintained a commitment to bilingual education; would this commitment be guaranteed under multiple districts?

30. Jeanne Mariani, 'For LAUSD, It's Make-or-Break Year', *Daily News*, 5 Sept. 1993; Anne Burke, 'Latinos Gird for Valley Secession', *Daily News*, 9 Aug. 1992; Douglas Lasken, 'The "Official" Culture Shifts and the Endangered List Grows Larger', *Los Angeles Times*, 28 June 1993, reported that 60% of the San Fernando Valley favored the breakup, along with 42% of Latinos.

31. Sandy Harrison, 'State's Top Educator Attacks Vouchers', *Daily News*, 8 Sept. 1993; George Skelton, 'Getting the Jump on the Voucher Issue', *Los Angeles Times*, 16 Sept. 1993; Skelton, 'Real Lessons Behind Debate on Prop. 174', *Los Angeles Times*, 27 Sept. 1993; Ralph Frammolino, 'Foes Launch Drive Against Voucher Plan', *Los Angeles Times*, 8 Sept. 1993, called voucher proponents 'snakeoil' peddlers; Bill Boyarsky, 'Voucher Issue Cuts Across Traditional Lines', *Los Angeles Times*, 12 Sept. 1993.

32. James Flanigan, 'School Choice Campaign Goes Beyond the Election', *Los Angeles Times*, 24 Oct. 1993; Dan Morain, 'School Vouchers Initiative Too Costly, Wilson Says', *Los Angeles Times*, 6 Oct. 1993; Henry Chu, 'Will $2,600 Purchase a Private School Education?', *Los Angeles Times*, 30 Oct. 1993.

33. Mike Comeaux, 'Voucher Backers See Hopes Fade', *Daily News*, 25 Oct. 1993; Bill Stall, 'Levies Fees Used to Offset Prop. 13', *Los Angeles Times*, 11 Oct. 1993; Jerry Gillam and Glenn F.

Bunting, 'Lawmakers' Trip to D.C. Raises Questions', *Los Angeles Times*, 26 Feb. 1992; Werner Hirsh, 'Culprit of State's Problems Is Prop. 13', *Daily News*, 24 Oct. 1993; Bill Stall and Ralph Frammolino, 'Perception of Inequality Clouds State Tax System', *Los Angeles Times*, 12 Oct. 1993. The voucher fight was also intertwined with immigrant bashing, Sergio Muñoz, 'The Divisiveness of Half Truths', *Los Angeles Times*, 12 Nov. 1992: 80% of Latinos were in the workforce and only 6% on welfare; Peter H. King, 'The View from the Other Side', *Los Angeles Times*, 19 Sept. 1993.

34. Comeaux, 'District 7 Problems'.

35. Jack Cheevers, 'Candidates Tiptoe Around Race Issue in the 7th District', *Los Angeles Times*, 21 March 1993.

36. Marc Litchman, 'Alarcon's Victory in the 7th District Was No Safe Bet after All', *Los Angeles Times*, 27 June 1993.

37. Richard Simon and Sharon Bernstein, 'Valley Voters, Low Minority Turnout Propelled Riordan', *Los Angeles Times*, 10 June 1993.

38. 'Bradley: The Last Flourish of Los Angeles as One City', *Los Angeles Times*, 27 Sept. 1992. The San Fernando Valley would 'force the candidates to look at Valley issues', said Richard Close of the Sherman Oaks Homeowners Association; Rick Orlov, "'93 Election Could Reshape L.A.', *Daily News*, 16 Nov. 1992.

39. James Rainey, 'History May Take Kinder View Regarding Mayor Bradley Era', *Los Angeles Times*, 27 June 1993. Rick Orov, 'Bradley Views His Tenure as "Greatest Experience"', *Daily News*, 27 June 1993. Bradley was criticized in the aftermath of the Rodney King uprisings for calling in Peter Ueberroth, a former Orange County travel agent of 1984 Olympics fame and later baseball commissioner. As urban planner David Díaz put it, Bradley called in his 'white knight' to save the city, Díaz, 'Another Failure of Black Regime Politics: Political Inertia and Corporate Power in Los Angeles', Presented for California Studies Conference V, 'Reassembling California', 4–6 February 1993, Sacramento, Calif.

40. José Luis Sierra, '¿Se Queda o no Bradley?: Los lideres latinos se preparan para la ocasión', *La Opinión*, 24 Sept. 1992.

41. Frank Clifford and Richard Simon, 'Molina Wrestles with Running for Mayor', *Los Angeles Times*, 11 Oct. 1992. Richard Simon and James Rainey, 'Molina Says She Won't Enter Race for Mayor', *Los Angeles Times*, 18 Nov. 1992; Pablo Comesaña Amado y José Luis Sierra, 'Molina no será contendiente a la Alcaldía', *La Opinión*, 18 Nov. 1992.

42. James Rainey, 'Alatorre Won't Join Race for L.A. Mayor', *Los Angeles Times*, 30 Nov. 1992.

43. The former ambassador alienated some Chicano activists over his association with NEWS for America, his seeming support of Chief Daryl Gates, his efforts to recall Bradley, and his participation in Sheriff Sherman Block's committee to review the Sheriff's Department, José Luis Sierra', Julian Nava planea hacer campaña nacional', *La Opinión*, 7 Jan. 1993.

44. Marc Lacy, 'Campaign Spending Little Time in Latino Enclaves', *Los Angeles Times*, 2 March 1993.

45. 'Schools Issue Muscles into Mayoral Race', *Los Angeles Times*, 21 Jan. 1993.

46. Frank Clifford, 'Immigrant Rights Heats Up Mayoral Debate', *Los Angeles Times*, 6 Dec. 1992: Riordan skirted the immigrant issue and focused on crime; María del Pilar Marrero, 'El candidato de la Alcaldía Tom Houston atribuye a inmigrants las penurias de L.A.', *La Opinión*, 15 Dec. 1992; Frank Clifford, 'Houston Calls for Deporting Illegals in 2 Deadly Gangs', *Los Angeles Times*, 15 Jan. 1993. The street vendor controversy continued after the mayoral campaign: James Rainey, 'Vendors Cheer as Legislation Wins Final OK', *Los Angeles Times*, 5 Jan. 1994.

47. George Ramos, 'Taking Issue with Giving the Vote to Non-Citizens', *Los Angeles Times*, 4 Jan. 1993; José Luis Sierra, 'Politicos latinos criticán con dureza la postura electoral de Tom Houston', *La Opinión*, 18 Jan. 1993; María del Pilar Marrero, 'Obreros latinos rechazan ideas de Tom Houston sobre "ilegales"', *La Opinión*, 8 Jan. 1993.

48. Bill Boyarsky, "'More Cops": Candidates' Simplistic Cure for L.A. Woes', *Los Angeles Times*, 11 April 1993.

49. Patrick McGreevy, 'Valley Key to Outcome of Tax, Mayor Vote', *Daily News*, 22 April 1993; however, the voters turned down a tax to pay for more police officers.

50. Rick Orlov and Patrick McGreevy, 'Riordan, Woo Dive Back into Campaign', *Daily News*, 22 April 1993; Richard Lee Colvin, 'Area Is Riordan Country, Times Exit Poll Finds', *Los Angeles Times Valley Section*, 22 April 1993; 'What They Spent', *Daily News*, 22 April 1993; Richard Simon

and Rich Connell, 'Exit Poll Indicates Tight Race, Divided Electorate', *Los Angeles Times*, 22 April 1993. Woo received only 13% of the white vote compared with 45% for Riordan; 58% of the voting age population is non-white, but two-thirds of the votes were cast by whites. 18% of the voters were Black, while only 8% were Latino. Riordan took 65% of the conservative vote. Woo split the liberal vote with other candidates.

51. Adela de la Torre, 'Whose Vision Equals Greater L.A.?' *Los Angeles Times*, 22 April 1993; Sherry Bebitch Jeffe, 'It's Time for the Candidates to Campaign Like a Mayor', *Los Angeles Times*, 25 April 1993.

52. Rich Orlov and Mike Comeaux, 'Mayor Candidates Make Economic Pitches', *Daily News*, 23 April 1993.

53. Sherry Bebitch Jeffe, 'A Lack of Moral Vision Undermines the Mayoral Race as a City Looks for New Leadership', *Los Angeles Times*, 18 April 1993; Bill Boyarsky, 'Riordan on Criminal Justice and the LAPD', *Los Angeles Times*, 26 May 1993. Riordan had been the architect of the defeat of state Chief Justice Rose Bird. He told Boyarsky that he had not opposed Bird because of her anti–death penalty decisions, but because 'she is one reason why some businesses would not come into the state.' Forgotten was that Justice Cruz Reynoso was also a victim of the campaign to defeat Rose Bird.

54. Leticia García-Irigoyen, 'Richard Alatorre preside Comision de Transporte', *La Opinión*, 28 Jan. 1993.

55. Bill Boyarsky, 'The MTA: New Mecca for Lobbyists', *Los Angeles Times*, 3 Sept. 1993; Mark Katches, 'Lobbyists Swarming to MTA', *Daily News*, 28 June 1993. The MTA planned to spend $163 billion over the next 30 years. At a time when Sacramento was slashing funds the MTA was considering $428 million in transit spending. The MTA had 885 more lobbyists than City Hall, and 1,029 more than were registered with the county supervisors. They were an important source of campaign funding and perks for MTA board members.

56. 'Alatorre Named Head of Transit Agency', *Los Angeles Times*, 25 June 1993.

57. Julian Nava, 'Voting Power Up for Grabs', *Los Angeles Times*, Valley Edition, 30 May 1993.

58. Sherry Bebitch Jeffe, 'Mayoral Race Gets Down to Class Warfare', *Los Angeles Times*, 16 May 1993.

59. Marlene Adler Marks, 'The Valley Joins Los Angeles', *Los Angeles Times*, 11 June 1993; Richard Simon and Rich Connell, 'Exit Poll Indicates Tight Race, Divided Electorate', *Los Angeles Times*, 22 April 1993; interestingly, the Westside Jewish vote went 63% to 41% for Woo, while the Valley Jewish community vote went 59% for Riordan.

60. Richard Simon and Sharon Bernstein, 'Valley Voters, Low Minority Turnout Propelled Riordan', *Los Angeles Times*, 10 June 1993.

61. John Schwada, 'Valley Will Gain Clout at City Hall, Experts Say', *Los Angeles Times*, 10 June 1993. Joel Wachs cooed, 'The Valley played a critical role in his campaign, and Dick Riordan understands that.' Under Bradley the Valley's influence was minimal. Wachs said that the Valley was different. 'There's a feeling in the Valley of concern about a breakdown of values in our city, there's a pride in community and sense of the importance of personal responsibility. I don't like to call them old-fashioned values. Rather, they are the values that I learned from my parents'; John Schwada, 'Fielder Nominated for CRA Board over Walters' Complaints', *Los Angeles Times*, 10 Aug. 1993. Fielder had served on the Board of Education from 1977 to 1981 and in Congress from 1981 to 1987. Ultraconservative, she had been a founder of the Bus Stop Movement. Riordan, by appointing her, paid homage to Valley interests.

62. Mark Petracca, 'LA's Season of Mayoral Discontent', *Daily News*, 10 June 1993; Joseph Cerrell, 'Riordan Prepares for Brave New Steps', *Daily News*, 10 June 1993; Rosa Marín, the executive director of the Latino Business Association, said: 'We're ecstatic. He has an understanding of economics. He has a very keen awareness of the problems that business experiences … We really need someone to revitalize the Los Angeles economy who is a business person. We don't need a politician.' Like her business community counterparts, Marín said little about worker rights.

63. Bill Boyarsky, 'Sale of the Central Library Could Be Costly to Affordable Housing', *Los Angeles Times*, 29 Aug. 1993. Philip Morris Capital Corp would buy the library and lease it back to the city, getting a huge tax break under a federal law designed to encourage investors to preserve historic structures.

64. Rich Connell, 'Riordan Finds Appointees in Affluent Areas', *Los Angeles Times*, 9 Sept. 1993.

65. In many ways Riordan was an enigma, and his election caught many Angelenos by surprise. Riordan, in fairness, was not just another millionaire who bought an election: see Bill Boyarsky, 'Riordan Personality, Policy Will Intertwine as He Shapes L.A.'s Future', *Los Angeles Times*, 8 Aug. 1993; see Virginia Postrel, 'If Angelenos Are Apolitical, That's a Plus', *Los Angeles Times*, 10 June 1993; Faye Fiore and Frank Clifford, 'Mystery Mayor', *Los Angeles Times Magazine*, 11 July 1993, pp. 18, 20–25, 34; Jill Stewart, 'Multimillionaire Attorney Richard Riordan Is the City's Pre-eminent Political Donor and Behind-the-Scenes Player. So Why Is he Running for Mayor?', *LA Weekly*, 4 Dec. 1992, p. 19: Stewart provides an analysis of Riordan's business dealings with the city, politicians, organizations and Michael Milken; Bill Boyarsky, 'Mayor Riordan Coaxes 1,000 Flowers to Bloom in an Arid City Hall', *Los Angeles Times*, 19 Sept. 1993. Riordan, like Vice President Al Gore, was an admirer of David Osborne and Ted Graebler's *Reinventing Government*.

66. Frank Clifford, 'Redistricting May Pit Blacks Against Latinos', *Los Angeles Times*, 18 Feb. 1992; Jim Tranquada, 'L.A. Latinos on Brink of Political Power Surge', *Daily News*, 16 May 1993.

67. Raphael J. Sonenshein, 'The Los Angeles Brand of Biracial Coalition Politics', *Los Angeles Times*, 16 April 1989. Councilwoman Walters represented a district with about 250,000 people. In 1991, she won election by a mere 6,251 votes.

68. Miles Corwin, 'L.A.'s Loss: "Black Flight"', *Los Angeles Times*, 1, Aug. 1992.

69. José Luis Sierra, 'Latinos de Los Angeles esperan lograr el poder político que exigén sus números', *La Opinión*, 21 March 1993; James Rainey, 'Through the Eyes of His City', *Los Angeles Times*, 27 June 1993, points out that Bradley was a Black mayor in a white city. When Bradley came into office, 17% of the commissioners were women, 6% were Black, 9% Latino and 1% Asian. Twenty years later half were women, a quarter were Black, 17% were Latino, and 12.5% Asian. The Latino population doubled during this period.

70. Sierra, 'Latinos de Los Angeles'.

71. Robert A. Rosenblatt, 'Blacks Dominate Postal Service, Latino Charges', *Los Angeles Times*, 3 Aug. 1994. Dr Tirso del Junco, vice-chair of the US Postal Service Board of Governors, chair of the California Republican Party and a Regent of the University of California, pitted Latinos against Blacks. Ironically, as a regent, he was in anti-affirmative action. Del Junco stated that L.A. Latinos comprised 15% of the Postal Service – whereas they were 34.7% of the city's workforce, 'while black employees account for 62% of the postal workers and are 9.6% of the local labor force.' While these statistics may be correct, it must be considered that the Black community made inroads into government employment at a period when other jobs were more attractive to white workers. At the same time, the surge in the Latino population came in the last two decades, and the challenge is for more Latinos to be hired as postal employees in the future. It would be unrealistic and against workers' rights to think in terms of immediate displacement. And why didn't del Junco mention the areas where white Americans are overrepresented?

72. Clifford, 'Redistricting'.

73. Ibid.

74. Richard Simon, 'City Council Backs Redistricting Plan', *Los Angeles Times*, 22 May 1992.

75. Mike Davis, 'For a City Adrift, Look to Community Government', *Los Angeles Times*, 4 Oct. 1992. The Black community suffered during the Bradley administration. As Bradley's political ambitions grew, he turned to other sectors of the city for campaign funding, and his interests changed. During the 1970s, Bradley was successful in attracting federal funding for community organizations and development, and the Community Redevelopment Agency became his main economic program to revitalize downtown Los Angeles. However, the 1980s saw a loss of 70,000 jobs due to plant closures and the drying up of federal funds. Many of the community organizations had grown dependent on federal money and collapsed when the flow of funds ended. (The city received $315 million in federal funds in 1979, declining to $156 million in 1992 – a drop of 75% when adjusted for inflation). Proposition 13 cut 15% of the city's budget. Bradley seemed oblivious to these changes and relied on the business community for advice, and on the CRA to provide jobs. As conditions worsened in South Central, criticisms of Bradley were restrained even among Black activists. It was not that the Black community had grown complacent, but having a Black mayor robbed Black leadership of its ability to complain about the mounting problems and the diminishing power of Blacks in South Central L.A. Many Black leaders just did not want to

rock the boat – it might cost 'Tom' the governorship – or his re-election. In the 9th CD, Rita Walters's predecessor, Gilbert Lindsay, shamelessly courted corporate money by favoring developers. He supported Bradley's dream of a Downtown skyline while housing and conditions in the streets of South Central deteriorated. Meanwhile, it cannot be denied that, in terms of the political game, Black politicians were fantastically successful. Bradley and many of his Black supporters did become political and economic players. Through the civil service network of employment, it created a middle-class base of support although one that was threatened by the dismantling of city government; Frank Clifford et al., 'Column One: Leaders Feel for L.A.', Los Angeles Times, 30 Aug. 1992.

76. Jaime Olivares, 'Poder político latino depende cada vez más de inmigrantes que se hacen ciudadanos', La Opinión, 8 March 1993.

77. Antonio H. Rodríguez and Carlos A. Chávez, 'The Rift Is Exposed: Let's Bridge It', Los Angeles Times, 24 July 1992.

78. State Sen. Art Torres (D-Los Angeles) sounded a similar note at the First African Methodist Episcopal Church. Steve Proffitt, 'Antonio Hernández. Working for the Latino Cause with Soft-Spoken Determination', Los Angeles Times, 13 Dec. 1992: Hernández broke with the Leadership Conference when it supported employer sanctions. MALDEF persuaded the NAACP to support its position on sanctions, which was a major coup; José Luis Sierra, 'Los conflictos interétmicos hacen crecer temor en LA', La Opinión, 15 March 1993.

79. Xandra Kayden, 'Political Paralysis – Los Angeles City Fathers Wanted It This Way', Los Angeles Times, 12 May 1991; H. Erik Schockman, 'Is Los Angeles Governable?', Daily News, 4 Nov. 1992; Davis, 'For a City Adrift'.

80. Marc Lacey, 'Council Stalls on Nomination of Activist', Los Angeles Times, 18 Aug. 1993.

81. Rick Orlov, 'Hermosillo Rejected for Fire Post', Daily News, 21 Aug. 1993.

82. Marc Lacey and Richard Simon, City Council Rejects Hermosillo, 9–5', Los Angeles Times, 21 Aug. 1993.

83. Bill Boyarsky, 'Battle over Hermosillo: It's Just the Start', Los Angeles Times, 25 Aug. 1993.

84. Lacey, 'Council Stalls on Nomination'.

85. Lacey and Simon, 'City Council Rejects Hermosillo'; Marc Lacey and Lisa Richardson, 'Nomination Is But Latest Fight for Hermosillo', Los Angeles Times, 20 Aug. 1993.

86. Hermosillo's influence is apparent from several examples: On 3 September 1993, a group of Chicano activists from the Valley picketed Katz's Panorama City office over his switch on the LAUSD breakup. Some of them carried signs reading, 'Can you smell the Refried Beans?' The protestors did not have a history of divisiveness, and in fact worked in coalitions, Paul Hefner, 'Katz Criticized for Stance on Breakup', Daily News, 4 Sept. 1993. Hermosillo also gained visibility by supporting the UCLA Hunger Strike. During the Chiapas uprising, he went there with a delegation led by Dr Jorge Mancillas, which was critical of the Mexican government. In retrospect, the immigration issue was drawing important lines in the Chicano community. For instance, many criticized Hermosillo for being a Republican – but they agreed with him when he supported immigrant rights at a time when the Democratic Party leadership was either leading the bashing or being silent. With that said, few condoned the use of any pejorative term toward any group.

87. Pete Wilson, 'Federal Action Needed to Gain Secure Borders', Daily News, 15 August 1993; Sebastian Rotella, 'Wilson Calls for Mexico to Help Deter Illegal Crossers', Los Angeles Times, 12 Aug. 1993; Rich Orlov, 'Wilson Calls for State Text of ID Card', Daily News, 10 Sept. 1993; Sandy Harrison, 'Wilson's Approval Rating Up, Illegal Immigration Stance Cited for Rise', Daily News, 20 Aug. 1993; Mark P. Petracca, 'Playing Illegal Immigration Card Could Be Gov. Wilson's Last Stand', Daily News, 15 Aug. 1993.

88. Jerry Gillan and John Schwada, 'Governor Tells Critics to "Kiss My Rear End"', Los Angeles Times, 19 Aug. 1993; Daniel M. Weintraub, 'Wilson Tears into Brown on Issue of Illegal Immigration', Los Angeles Times, 5 Oct. 1993; Tom Umberg, 'Bill Targets Employers of Illegal Aliens', Daily News, 22 Sept. 1993.

89. Sally Streff Buzbee, 'Reno Gets Firsthand Look at Busy Border Crossing', Daily News, 18 Aug. 1993; Patrick J. McDonnell, 'Californians Gauge Effect of Immigration Reform', Los Angeles Times, 28 July 1993.

90. Peter Larsen, 'Brown: Tie NAFTA to Alien Issue', Daily News, 26 July 1993; see also, Juanita Darling, 'How Far Will Mexico Go for Free Trade Pact?' Los Angeles Times, 21 Aug. 1993.

Jim Tranquada, 'Brown Steps Up Calls for Reform of Immigration', *Daily News*, 1 Sept. 1993. Before a subcommittee of the House Committee on Operations, Brown called for the enforcement of employer sanctions. Bill Stall, 'Brown Adds Voice to Immigration Debate', *Los Angeles Times*, 30 Sept. 1993.

91. Tim Weiner, 'Administration Weighs Options to Crack Down on Illegal Immigration', *Daily News*, 14 July 1993.

92. The Washington, D.C.–based Urban Institute concluded that the L.A. County report figures were as much as $140 million too high and that undocumented workers paid much more in taxes than stated; Greg Miller, 'Costs of Illegal Immigration Are Inflated, Study Says', *Los Angeles Times*, 3 Sept. 1993. See also Rebecca L. Clark and Jeffrey S. Passell, 'Immigrants: A Cost or Benefit? Studies Are Deceptive', *New York Times*, 3 Sept. 1993; Vlae Kershner, 'Calculating the Cost of Immigration', *San Francisco Chronicle*, 23 June 1993; and Joe Cobb, 'Chapter 12', *The Heritage Foundation Candidates' Briefing Book* (1994), p. 239, a good but decidedly conservative study.

93. Quoted in 'Immigrants Pay Their Way', *Daily News*, 28 July 1993; Mark Katches, 'Some New Citizens Fault Illegal Aliens', *Daily News*, 28 Aug. 1993. Jacqueline Cardenas, a Salvadoran and one of the 50,000 naturalized annually in L.A., said, 'I feel it [being American] even in my blood and my veins. From now on, I'm eating hamburgers. Forget about pupusas [a Salvadoran dish].' Cardenas added that she had a problem with illegal immigrants, who were draining government resources or committing crimes. People like Cardenases always somehow find a way to justify racism. Tony Bizjak, 'Longtime Immigrants Don't Fill Welfare Rolls, Report Finds', *Daily News*, 13 July 1993, found that among immigrants who had been in California at least a decade only 3.8% were on welfare, versus 4.1% for residents born in the United States and who had lived in California for at least five years. The report was requested by Sen. Art Torres. James Flanigan, 'Blaming Immigrants Won't Solve Economic Woes', *Los Angeles Times*, 15 Aug. 1993.

94. Joel Kotkin, 'What Happened to the Ideal of Citizenship?', *Los Angeles Times*, 11 July 1993; 'FAIR Poll Finds Californians Want Tougher Border Restrictions', *Mexico-United States Report* (June 1989), p. 4.

95. Patrick Buchanan, 'GOP Is Caught Napping on Immigration', *Los Angeles Times*, 11 July 1993.

96. Blanche Petrich, 'México no es cárcel, dice Solana', *La Opinión*, 3 Sept. 1993.

97. 'Demanda Pete Wilson usar el TLC como arma de presión contra indocumentados', *La Jornada*, 11 Aug. 1993. Throughout Latin America this was viewed as another example of the Ugly American.

98. Quoted in Frank del Olmo, 'Wilson Risks His Latino Support', *Los Angeles Times*, 23 Aug. 1993; Peter Skerry, 'Why Some of L.A.'s Latino Leaders Take a Walk on Immigration', *Los Angeles Times*, 22 Aug. 1993.

99. Jaime Olivares, 'Crece controversia sobre indocumentados', *La Opinión*, 25 Aug. 1993; María Luisa Arredondo, 'Wilson respalda las medidas para combatir la inmigración ilegal', *La Opinión*, 25 Aug. 1993; Flanigan, 'Blaming Immigrants Won't Solve Economic Woes'.

100. Mark Katches, 'Latinos Blast Wilson for Stance on Illegals', *Daily News*, 18 Aug. 1993. Roger Lindo, 'En Koreatown, Xavier Becerra condena la ola anti-inmigrante', *La Opinión*, 3 Sept. 1993.

101. Larry B. Stammer, 'Mahoney Blasts Politicians for Their Stance on Immigrants', *Los Angeles Times*, 9 Oct. 1993; Robert Scheer, 'A Consistent Pre-Life Stand on Immigrants', *Los Angeles Times*, 21 Oct. 1993; Pat Karlak, 'Mahoney Fires Heated Blast at Anti-Immigrant Politics', *Daily News*, 10 Oct. 1993.

102. Bill Boyarsky, 'Archdiocese Is Organizing Catholics to Lobby for Illegal Immigrants', *Los Angeles Times*, 3 Oct. 1993; Robert Scheer, 'Roger Mahoney', interview, *Los Angeles Times*, 26 Dec. 1993; Mark Katches, 'Mahoney Says Illegal Aliens Entitled to Basic Benefits', *Daily News*, 11 Dec. 1993: 'But when individuals seek to further embody this rhetoric in social policy, then the evil of this rhetoric becomes institutionalized. It is given life. It is what we call social sin.' Social sin, according to Mahoney, is akin to what happened in Nazi Germany.

103. Patrick J. McDonnell, 'Brown Backs Tenets on Rights of Immigrants', *Los Angeles Times*, 20 Feb. 1994.

104. Jerry Gillam, 'Latino Caucus Gains Clout in Legislature as Population Shifts', *Los Angeles Times*, 29 Nov. 1993; George Ramos, 'A House Divided over Illegal Immigration', *Los Angeles Times*,

27 Sept. 1993; Rick Orlov, 'Latino Coalition Warns Candidates to Heed Message', *Daily News*, 22 Dec. 1993.

105. See David Gutiérrez, *Walls and Mirrors: Mexican Americans, Mexican Immigrants, and the Politics of Ethnicity* (Berkeley, Calif.: University of California Press, 1994).

106. Richard Simon and Peter J. McDonnell, 'Immigrant Initiative Tops Signature Goal', *Los Angeles Times*, 17 May 1994.

107. Glen F. Bunting, 'Wilson Backs Immigration Initiative', *Los Angeles Times*, 27 May 1994; quote in Daniel M. Weintraub, 'Wilson Sues US over Immigrants' "Invasion"', *Los Angeles Times*, 23 Sept. 1994. Daniel M. Weintraub, 'No More Mr Moderate', *Los Angeles Times Magazine*, 25 Sept. 1994, pp. 12–18, 40–46.

108. Daniel M. Weintraub, 'Experts Say Suit over Immigrant Costs Will Fail', *Los Angeles Times*, 29 April 1994.

109. Clarence Page, 'Outrage over Immigrants Is a Political Sham', *Los Angeles Times*, 13 Sept. 1994; see Michael Fix and Jeffrey S. Passel, senior fellows at the Urban Institute, 'Clearing Up the Myths and Misperceptions', *Los Angeles Times*, 1 Aug, 1994; they show that working-age immigrants are substantially less likely to use welfare than are natives. Fix and Passel, 'Balancing the Ledger on Jobs, Taxes', *Los Angeles Times*, 2 Aug. 1994; Fix and Passel, 'Who's on the Dole; It's Not the Illegal Immigrants', *Los Angeles Times*, 2 Aug. 1994. The report showed that nearly 50% of welfare was spent on residents over 65.

110. Peter Copelan, 'Study Says Immigrants Productive', *Daily News*, 24 May 1994. An Urban Institute study showed that immigrants paid $30 billion more in taxes than the cost of the benefits they received; Diana Griego Erwin, '"Saving Our State" Would Cost It, Too', *Daily News*, 20 Sept. 1994.

111. Nicholas K. Geranios, 'State Population Projected to Hit 47.9 million by 2020', *Daily News*, 21 April 1994.

112. As recently as 1950, Germany was the largest source of new immigrants. By 2050 the Latino population is predicted to rise, from 10% to 20% of the US population; Asians 3% to 10%; Blacks from 12% to 14%; whites are projected to decline from 74% to 52%. Ben Wattenburg, 'Immigration: Let's Begin with the Facts', *Daily News*, 21 April 1994.

113. Robert Scheer, 'Prop. 187 Is a Search for Scapegoats', *Los Angeles Times*, 27 Oct. 1994; Patrick J. Buchanan, in 'What Will America Be in 2050?' *Los Angeles Times*, 28 Oct. 1994, wrote that a nonwhite majority would become a reality if Prop. 187 was not passed; Stephen Hayward, 'Prop. 187's Misleading Appeal', *Daily News*, 4 Sept. 1994; Lindsey Grant and Leon F. Bouvier, 'Issue Is Overpopulation', *Los Angeles Times*, 10 Aug. 1994.

114. Alexander Cockburn, 'In Honor of Charlatans and Racists', *Los Angeles Times*, 3 Nov. 1994; Paul Feldman, 'Dispute Flares over Planned Radio Spots for Prop. 187', *Los Angeles Times*, 27 Oct. 1994; Gebe Martinez and Doreen Carvajal, 'Proposition 187 Creators Come Under Scrutiny', *Los Angeles Times*, 4 Sept. 1994; Richard D. Lamm and Robert Hardway, 'Prop. 187 Opposition Has Origins in Racism', *Daily News*, 22 Nov. 1994.

115. Cathleen Decker, 'Voters Back Service Cuts for Illegal Immigrants', *Los Angeles Times*, 29 May 1994; George Shelton, 'Bashing the System, Not the People', *Los Angeles Times*, 2 May 1994. A fall 1992 poll by the *Times* showed that 77% believed immigration was a major problem, and that 81% of whites thought that immigrants took more than they gave; 75% of Latinos believed that immigration was a major problem, but 61% believed they contributed more than they received.

116. Richard B. Peiser, 'California Votes No on Future', *Los Angeles Times*, 23 June 1994.

117. John Jacobs, 'Low Turnout Would Favor SOS Initiative', *Daily News*, 16 June 1994.

118. 'Feinstein's TV Attack on Immigration', *Los Angeles Times*, 10 July 1994.

119. Patrick J. McDonnell and Dave Lesher, 'Clinton, Feinstein Declare Opposition to Prop. 187', *Los Angeles Times*, 22 Oct. 1994; Beth Schuster, 'Prop. 187 Called Costly to Schools', *Los Angeles Times*, 21 Sept. 1994.

120. Beth Shuster, '10,000 Teachers Would Lose Jobs Under Prop. 187, District Says', *Los Angeles Times*, 22 Oct. 1994. The response of the proponents was like that of the *Daily News* columnist who wrote: 'There's plenty to disapprove of in Proposition 187, and I'm going to vote for it anyway.' Linda Seebach, 'Continuing Disregard for US Law Is Endangering Freedom for Everyone', *Daily News*, 30 Oct. 1994.

121. Kevin Ross, in 'Is Black–Latino Friction a Voting-Booth Issue?' *Los Angeles Times*, 24 Oct. 1994; María Puente, 'Prop. 187 Heightens Black-Hispanic Tensions', *USA Today*, 4 Nov. 1994.

122. John W. Mack, in 'Is Black–Latino Friction a Voting Booth Issue?' *Los Angeles Times*, 24 Oct. 1994.

123. Frank del Olmo, 'A Dissenting Vote on the Endorsement of Pete Wilson', *Los Angeles Times*, 31 Oct. 1994; 'Pete Wilson for Governor: On the Balance the Best Choice', *Los Angeles Times*, 30 Oct. 1994; Paul Hefner, 'Plan to Back Wilson Angers Times Staffers', *Los Angeles Times*, 29 Oct. 1994.

124. Patrick J. McDonnell, 'Marchers Assail Bias Against Immigrants', *Los Angeles Times*, 29 May 1994; McDonnell, 'March Just 1st Step, Latino Leaders Vow', *Los Angeles Times*, 4 June 1994. In this march, the Central American Resource Center, MALDEF, CIWA, One-Stop and the Coalition for Human Rights participated. It was advertised by the Spanish-language media – television, print and radio.

125. Antonio Rodriguez and Carlos A. Chavez, 'Latinos Unite in Self-Defense on Prop. 187', *Los Angeles Times*, 21 Oct. 1994.

126. Mike Comeaux, 'Proposition 187 Galvanizes Latinos', *Daily News*, 18 Oct. 1994; Carl Shusterman, 'Make It "SOS" for Snake-Oil Salesmen', *Los Angeles Times*, 15 Sept. 1994.

127. Patrick J. McDonnell and Chip Johnson, '70,000 March Through L.A. Against Prop. 187', *Los Angeles Times*, 17 Oct. 1994. Many of the Euroamericans in the Taxpayers' group were overcautious, with a philosophy of 'We're keeping the Brown faces in the background.' The appearance of marches and students walking out of school upset their little tea party, which was divorced from reality. Indeed, if there had been no march nor Mexican flags, Prop. 187 would still have passed. Patrick J. McDonnell, 'Foes of Prop. 187 Toeing a Difficult Line', *Los Angeles Times*, 26 Sept. 1994.

128. Robert J. Lopez, '7,000 Attend Protest Denouncing Proposition 187', *Los Angeles Times*, 31 Oct. 1994.

129. Kimberly Kindy, 'Molina: Walkouts Should End', *Daily News*, 4 Nov. 1994.

130. Terri Hardy, 'Students Stage Walkout over Prop. 187', *Daily News*, 15 Oct. 1994; Beth Shuster and Chip Johnson, 'Students at 2 Pacoima Schools Protest Prop. 187', *Los Angeles Times*, 21 Oct. 1994; Marni McEntee, 'Walkout Staged at Valley School', *Daily News*, 20 Oct. 1994; Kimberly Kindy, 'Racial Tensions Rise as Prop. 187 Debate Spills into Schools', *Daily News*, 27 Oct. 1994; Marc Lacey and Henry Chu, 'LAPD Calls Alert for Student Rallies', *Los Angeles Times*, 29 Oct. 1994; Kimberly Kindy and Pat Karlak, 'Students Walk Out in Protest', *Daily News*, 28 Oct. 1994; Peter Larsen, 'Thousands Fill Streets; Police on Tactical Alert', *Daily News*, 29 Oct. 1994; Jocelyn Stewart and Beth Shuster, 'Thousands of Students Stage Anti-187 Walkout', *Los Angeles Times*, 29 Oct. 1994.

131. Paul Hefner and Terri Hardy, '10,000 Students March off 39 Campuses', *Daily News*, 3 Nov. 1994.

132. Beth Shuster, 'Teachers, Students Debate Prop. 187', *Los Angeles Times*, 25 Oct. 1994; Amy Pyle and Simon Romero, 'Measure Fuels a New Latino Campus Activism', *Los Angeles Times*, 25 Oct. 1994; 'Prop. 187 Controversies in Schools Heat Up', *Los Angeles Times*, 1 Nov. 1994.

133. Sandy Harrison, 'National Guard on Alert for Protests', *Daily News*, 29 Oct. 1994; Betty Kwong, 'Prop. 187 Polarizes Valley Students', *Daily News*, 30 Oct. 1994; Robin Abcarian, 'A Lesson in Empathy Taught by Children', *Los Angeles Times*, 2 Nov. 1994.

134. 'Our Own Melting Pot', *Los Angeles Times*, 20 Nov. 1994.

135. Kimberly Kindy, 'Schools Defend Roles in 187 Protests', *Daily News*, 3 Oct. 1994.

136. End Mendel, 'Voters Still Favor Prop. 187 but Field Poll Finds Latinos Split on Issue', *San Diego Union-Tribune*, 27 Sept. 1994. Howard Breuer, 'Support by Minorities Gives Prop. 187 Unexpected Boost', *Daily News*, 3 Oct. 1994. Paul Feldman, 'Times Poll: Prop. 187 Is Still Favored Almost 2 to 1', *Los Angeles Times*, 15 Oct. 1994.

137. Howard Breuer, 'Voters Approve Prop. 187, Lawsuits to Follow', *Daily News*, 9 Nov. 1994.

138. David Ferrell and Robert J. Lopez, 'California Waits to See What Prop. 187 Will Really Mean', *Los Angeles Times*, 10 Nov. 1994.

139. David E. Hayes-Bautista and Gregory Rodriguez, 'A Rude Awakening for Latinos', *Los Angeles Times*, 11 Nov. 1994; Patrick J. McDonnell, 'State's Diversity Doesn't Reach Voting Booth', *Los Angeles Times*, 11 Nov. 1994.

140. 'Times Poll: A Look at the Electorate', *Los Angeles Times*, 10 Nov. 1994.

141. Ibid.

142. Hugo Martin, 'Immigration Was No. 1 Issue, Local Voters Say', *Los Angeles Times*, 10 Nov. 1994.

143. Ted Rohrlich, 'Mahoney Says Prop. 187 Poses Threat to Moral Principles', *Los Angeles Times*, 9 Oct. 1994; John Dart, '187 Shows Clergy's Weak Influence on Electorate', *Los Angeles Times*, 19 Nov. 1994.

144. Maria Puente and Gale Holland, '"Deep Vein" of Anger in California', *USA Today*, 11 Nov. 1994.

145. John Dart, 'Prop. 187 May Show Clergy's Political Role Is Dwindling', *Los Angeles Times*, 20 Nov. 1994.

146. Herman Schwartz, 'The Constitutional Issue Behind Proposition 187', *Los Angeles Times*, 9 Oct. 1994. The 1982 Pryor case was being debated months before the vote; the City Council and the Board of Education joined suits, but the supervisors held off, Carla Rivera and Paul Feldman, 'County Declines to Join Prop. 187 Challenges', *Los Angeles Times*, 11 Nov. 1994; Mary Hernandez, 'The Courts and Proposition 187', and Eugene Volokh, 'The Courts and Proposition 187', *Daily News*, 20 Nov. 1994.

147. Howard Breuer, 'Outcry Quells Prop. 187 Challenges', *Daily News*, 28 Nov. 1994.

148. Anne Burke, 'Civil Rights Complaints Reported', *Daily News*, 19 Nov. 1994; Mark Katches, 'Some New American Citizens Worried About Initiative's OK', *Daily News*, 11 Nov. 1994.

149. Beth Shuster, 'Valley 187 Activist Shifts Passion to Implementation', *Los Angeles Times*, 15 Nov. 1994. Over three-fourths of people supporting Prop. 187 said they did so because they were sending a message. Only 34% said that they expected to stop immigrants from using facilities. Only 32% said they thought that they would save millions of dollars. Only 2% expected to throw children out of school. James O. Goldsborough, 'A Garbled Message: Just What Did the Prop. 187 Vote Say?' *San Diego Union-Tribune*, 21 Nov. 1994.

150. Paul Feldman, 'Prop. 187 Sponsors Blame Foes for Illegal Immigrants' Fears over Seeking Health Care', *Los Angeles Times*, 26 Nov. 1994.

151. Rubén Martínez, 'The Nightmare Is Coming True', *Los Angeles Times*, 28 Nov. 1994; Lee Romney, 'Boy in Prop. 187 Controversy Mourned', *Los Angeles Times*, 29 Nov. 1994. Prop. 187 added to fears among Latino AIDS patients, who had the daunting task of dealing with cultural and religious stigmas against homosexuality. Even before Prop. 187, gay and heterosexual Latinos and Latinas were afraid to seek information about AIDS for fear of being deported. Lucille Renwick, 'A Different Front in the War on AIDS', *Los Angeles Times*, 28 Oct. 1992.

152. Not all Republicans supported Prop. 187. Former cabinet secretaries Jack Kemp and William Bennett criticized the proposition and the 'ugly antipathy toward all immigrants'.

153. Efrain Hernandez, Jr and Richard Simon, 'Despite Gains, Latino Voters Still Lack Clout', *Los Angeles Times*, 4 Dec. 1994.

154. Elizabeth Lopez and Eric Wahlgren, 'The Latino Vote', *California Journal*, 1 Nov. 1994.

155. 'California: 187 Voters Had Message to Send', *Los Angeles Times*, 22 Nov. 1994; Scripps Howard, 'Proposition's Legacy May Be Voting Shift Among State's Hispanics', *Arizona Republic*, 10 Nov. 1994; John Marelius, 'Election 1994: California Governor', *San Diego Union-Tribune*, 9 Nov. 1994.

156. Lopez and Wahlgren, 'Latino Vote'.

157. Rick Olguin, 'Torres Now on the Outside Looking In', *Los Angeles Times*, 21 Nov. 1994; 'Insurance Commissioner', *California Journal*, 14 Nov. 1994; George Ramos, 'For Latinos, Let Election Setbacks Be Call for Action', *Los Angeles Times*, 14 Nov. 1994.

158. Mary Helen Berg, 'Democratic Wins in Central City Ease Party's Woes', *Los Angeles Times*, 13 Nov. 1994.

159. Marcos Breton, 'Prop. 187 Failed to Move Latino "Sleeping Giant" to Polls', *Sacramento Bee*, 13 Nov. 1994.

160. Mark Gladstone and Dan Morain, 'Last-Minute GOP Donations Tipped Key Assembly Races', *Los Angeles Times*, 17 Nov. 1994; Dan Walters, 'Money Players Also Win and Lose', *San Diego Union-Tribune*, 15 Nov. 1994. The California Correction Peace Officers Association contributed heavily to Wilson's 1990 campaign, and received dividends in the form of additional prison construction, higher salaries and hiring of more guards. Lagain contributed heavily to Wilson in 1994.

161. Lopez and Wahlgren, 'Latino Vote'.

162. Hernández and Simon, 'Despite Gains, Latino Voters Still Lack Clout'.

8

Mexican/Latino Labor in L.A.: Working in a Meaner and Leaner World

In the 1980s near consensus existed that Los Angeles was the miracle city, a world-class place with plenty of resources. In 1989, the *Wall Street Journal* wrote, 'Cheap labor and ready capital are making the region [Southern California] as commercially fertile as the Far East.' The *Economist* noted that 'Los Angeles is the only big city in the industrial world that is still growing rapidly.'[1] L.A. had a diversified economy based on aerospace, defense contracts, television and film production, bio-tech, manufacturing and banking. Its garment industry grew by 60 percent in the 1980s. L.A. could lose 75,000 jobs in traditional heavy industry and still thrive, with economic growth exceeding population growth.[2] L.A. had one-tenth of the nation's defense contracts, and many predicted that it would soon surpass New York as the US financial center. One half of California's 5,462 millionaires lived there, some of them so affluent they could buy a 3,000-square-foot mansion, tear it down, and build a 10,000-square-foot mansion in its place.[3] The only things that seemed to be holding Los Angeles back were its poor public schools and runaway real estate prices.

Nevertheless, ominous notes crept into these glowing reports. In 1989, Los Angeles was called 'a mecca of culture and economic energy', but also 'a wilderness of crime and poverty'. The loss of 'semiskilled manual jobs that for years supported the city's blue-collar middle class – black and white' was taking a heavy toll.[4] As these contradictions emerged, observers saw Los Angeles becoming more like its image in the film *Blade Runner* – a city on the edge of total wipe-out.[5] Former Mayor Tom Bradley's solution was to ignore the problems; Mayor Richard Riordan's solution has been to hold garage sales – privatize everything to pay for city government: 'Everything Must Go. Here's an airport, here's a public library!'[6]

Economist Richard Rothstein tells the story of a General Motors executive who showed United Auto Workers leader Walter Reuther through one of GM's modernized plants. The executive said: 'You know, Walter, this machine does the work of four men and it doesn't pay any union dues!' Reuther replied, 'Yes, but how many cars does it buy?' Restructuring in Los Angeles raises the same question: industrial jobs paying good wages and benefits are traded in for jobs where workers, like the machine, can not buy what they produce.[7] This restructuring was part of the globalization of the economy, which meant that capital became more mobile to exploit both markets and labor outside national borders. The result was plant shutdowns in the United States, resulting in deindustrialization. Intensified global economic competition has also required eliminating or weakening laws, standards and institutions such as unions that protected workers' rights. On the ideological front, the old Fordist idea that every person has the right to a job with a decent wage had to be discredited and abandoned.[8]

Part of this deconstruction of the House of Labor was a push to reduce all labor to a casual, temporary and deskilled status and to force unskilled US workers to compete with low-wage workers in the Third World.[9] Thousands of minimum-wage workers lived on the edge while state policymakers debated whether it would hurt the economy to raise the minimum wage. In effect, workers subsidized California's corporations. This was necessary, according to conservatives, to maintain a 'business-friendly' climate and keep the US competitive.[10]

During the Reagan-Bush years, conservatives asserted that 'there are no civic, no social obligations, only private ones.'[11] In this laissez-faire climate, poverty had climbed to a 27-year high by 1991,[12] with 35.7 million people living below the poverty line – the highest number since 1964, the year that Lyndon Johnson launched the War on Poverty.[13] But now it was much harder to climb out of poverty. According to Michigan economist Gary Solon, 'A child whose father is in the bottom 5 percent of earners, for instance, has only 1 chance in 20 of making it into the top 20 percent of families ... The same child has a 1-in-4 chance of rising above the median wealth and a 2-in-5 chance of staying poor or near poor.'[14] Meanwhile, the gap between workers and corporate executives widened. In the mid 1970s CEOs earned 34 times as much as the average worker: this figure had grown to 110 times by the late 1980s. In Japan, CEOs earned an average of 17 times as much as the average worker; in Germany, 21 times.[15]

In Los Angeles, restructuring the economy did not happen overnight. By the 1981–82 recession, deindustrialization was well under way. Automobile production and the manufacture of civilian durable goods had been sources of middle-income employment in L.A. since the 1930s, and represented economic stepping-stones for working-class people, both Euroamerican and people of color. As heavy industry moved out of L.A. during the late 1970s and 1980s, dramatic increases in defense jobs at first took up the slack during the Reagan-

Bush military buildup. At the same time, capital went on the offensive in private industry, reorganizing production, closing – or threatening to close – plants, lowering wages and demanding 'giveback' contracts. Business leaders were convinced that workers dared not strike during a recession.

For Los Angeles, restructuring meant more service jobs, which had increased dramatically since the 1960s. But unlike manufacturing, the service sector was unable to boost productivity by using new technologies to make similar gains in efficiency.[16] The new kinds of jobs available were for salespeople, waiters, cashiers, nursing aids, secretaries, practical nurses and repair personnel, occupations that were difficult to unionize.[17] Consequently they were low paying, with nearly 60 percent of the new net employment since 1979 hovering at the poverty level.[18]

Restructuring had severe human consequences in Los Angeles. Layoffs produced a human toll of wife-beating, child abuse and desertions. The recession especially hurt women with few job skills; the median salary of female heads-of-household under the age of thirty fell 32 percent in real dollars from 1973 to 1990.[19] In Los Angeles County, Euroamericans made up 17 percent of those living in poverty; Latinos, 56.8 percent; Blacks, 15.5 percent; and Asians, 9.5 percent.[20] US-born Latinos earned 78 cents of every white male's dollar; US-born Latinas earned 47 cents; and immigrant Latinas, 30 cents.[21] As well-paying union jobs became scarcer, street vendors could be seen selling oranges and other produce, often with their entire families, earning $5 for a six- to eight-hour day. As one observer put it, they did not have enough money even to die.[22]

Local government's solution to a lack of jobs was to cut the number of public jobs. The idea that regulation and high taxes were driving businesses out of California became a staple of popular journalism. After the Rodney King uprising, the private sector volunteered to solve the city's problems: it would rebuild Los Angeles without the commitment of public funds.[23] But this widely publicized effort delivered fewer than 5,000 jobs (see Chapter 10). Rebuild L.A.'s leaders cheered General Motors when it pledged to shift $15 million worth of contracts for its Hughes subsidiary to inner-city suppliers, but said nothing when General Motors shut down its Van Nuys assembly plant less than a month later, cutting nearly 3,000 jobs – two-thirds of them held by Blacks and Latinos.[24]

Business-friendly politicians like Governor Wilson promoted solutions such as enterprise zones, which gave tax breaks to businesses if they would relocate to or add jobs in designated areas. Los Angeles had five enterprise zones: Watts, Central City, the Eastside, Wilmington-San Pedro, and Pacoima. City officials claimed that between 1987 and 1990 these zones created 159 jobs in Watts; 212 in Pacoima; 220 in Central City; 157 in the Eastside; and 89 in Wilmington-San Pedro – a pathetic number considering the need and the costs to workers and taxpayers.[25]

In 1986, the Los Angeles Basin held 15 percent of the nation's military jobs and 5.6 percent of its total jobs. By 1991, L.A.'s dependence on the defense industry had become painfully evident. Lockheed, Northrop and McDonnell Douglas in Los Angeles, Orange, Ventura, Riverside and San Bernardino counties accounted for 420,000 or 7 percent of the region's 6.2 million jobs. As this and other industries laid off workers, 208,400 jobs were lost in 1991 alone.[26] The federal government's effort to rescue the beleaguered savings and loan industry worsened the plight of workers by diverting funds from social programs to bail out the rich.[27]

The problem was not only unemployment. According to a 1989 UCLA Urban Planning report, 75 percent of the poor in Los Angeles were spending half their income on rent.[28] By mid 1986, the median house in Los Angeles cost $152,000; three years later, that price had climbed to $369,000.[29] As the economy worsened, displaced workers and mental patients turned out of hospitals and halfway houses filled the streets. In 1993, the Labor/Community Strategy Center estimated that 150,000 people in Los Angeles were homeless during any given year and 70,000 on any given night.[30]

The hardest hit were the children. A Stanford University study found homeless children in L.A. to be reasonably healthy and resilient but subject to depression, disobedience and chronic illness.[31] Poverty among Latino children grew 29.3 percent in the 1980s according to the Children's Defense Fund, the highest rate among the so-called minority groups.

Chicano Workers and the Labor Movement

Not every Chicano or Latino in Los Angeles is an oppressed worker. Many are white-collar workers – managers, professionals and business people. Latinos made real gains nationally during the 1960s in closing the gap between themselves and white workers, but after 1973, these gains began to erode.[32] In Los Angeles, the working-age Chicano population increased by 50 percent, from 292,000 to 473,000, during the 1970s.[33] Simultaneously, the nation's commitment to education waned, with 41 percent of Latinos nationally not graduating from high school, versus 20 percent of African Americans and 15 percent of Euroamericans.[34]

The 1992 Census suggests that more Latinos were entering the professional and technical fields; it also suggests that a gap was developing between these new professionals and business people, on the one hand, and Latino laborers and service workers on the other.

Despite these gains, poverty remained high among Latinos. Over 50 percent of the Mexicanas in the workforce earned under $10,000 a year. Close to 50 percent of the Mexican households with an absent father lived in poverty, and

37.3 percent of Mexican-origin workers who did not have a high school education lived in poverty, versus 16.7 percent of non-Latinos. An indication that not much would change is the fact that while the Euroamerican population increased its college enrollment during the 1980s, from 31.8 percent to 39.4 percent, and the percentage of African Americans with college educations increased from 27.6 percent to 33 percent, college enrollment among Latinos declined from 29.8 percent to 29 percent.[35]

LATINOS IN THE WORKFORCE, 1992
(Percent)

Employment Category	Mexicans		Puerto Ricans		Cubans		Central/ S. Americans		Other Latinos		Non- Latinos	
	M	F	M	F	M	F	M	F	M	F	M	F
Managers	9.3	14.0	10.9	20.8	21.3	26.6	13.8	14.9	18.3	23.1	28.6	29.7
Professional/ Technical	14.0	39.3	23.1	47.9	25.1	48.5	16.7	30.4	20.2	44.6	21.9	45.6
Service	16.6	24.6	22.4	17.7	12.4	13.1	22.2	35.5	15.2	21.5	9.0	15.4
Farming/ Forestry	10.9	2.8	2.2	-	3.5	-	2.8	0.3	2.0	0.4	3.7	0.9
Precision Production	20.1	3.1	18.0	2.6	14.7	1.9	17.8	3.2	22.4	1.7	18.8	1.9
Operators/ Laborers	29.9	16.2	23.5	11.2	22.9	9.9	27.1	15.1	21.7	8.7	18.0	6.5
Labor Force Participation	80.5	51.6	70.3	44.7	72.2	51.7	86.0	57.1	77.4	57.9	75.2	58.0
Earning Less than $10,000	35.3	53.5	23.6	33.5	24.9	37.4	31.1	45.9	24.1	38.5	22.3	38.5

SOURCE: Jesús M. Garcia, 'The Hispanic Population in the United States', US Census, P20-465RV, March 1992. Statistics are for workers aged sixteen and over.

At the same time, few Latinos could be found in executive positions. A report by the Hispanic Association on Corporate Responsibility covering Southern California–based aerospace companies found no Latinos among the top 537 executives and only six Latinos in senior positions. In *Fortune* 500 corporations, 81 of 11,881 executives – less than 1 percent – were Latinos.[36] The lack of diversity meant that 'the [low] numbers for Latinos, African-Americans, Asian-Americans and Native Americans in high management positions ultimately reflect a pattern of exclusion that is becoming glaringly obvious as the nation's population itself grows increasingly diverse.'[37]

Despite the poverty, it is questionable whether Chicanos or Latinos could be said to belong to an underclass. Absent was that sense of hopelessness and permanency that is associated with being a member of an underclass. According to David Hayes-Bautista, Latinos in Los Angeles had a higher labor force participation rate (80.2 percent, versus whites' 73.9 percent and Blacks' 64.2 percent), a higher life expectancy and a lower infant mortality rate than the general population. They were poor not because they did not work, but because they lagged in education and were not paid decent wages, averaging only 9.1 years of education, versus 13.4 for whites and 12.6 for Asian Americans and Blacks.[38]

It is also probably true that most Latinos are from working-class families; their parents or grandparents worked as farmworkers, miners, railroad hands, factory workers or housekeepers. Even most Mexicans and Central Americans with a college education are first generation, just one step out of the barrio. Despite this closeness to their working-class roots, they know little about the struggles of Chicano workers, past or present.

One explanation for this gap in consciousness is that American education has long dismissed labor history as unimportant – or even subversive. Outside the pages of La Opinión and Spanish-language television, few members of the Fourth Estate bother to report the day-to-day struggle of Latinos to unionize. (They aren't very interested in the struggles of non-Latino workers either.) Indeed, it would be impossible to find out very much about this movement of immigrant workers if one had to rely solely on L.A.'s English-language print media.

Dramatic labor movements in Los Angeles during the 1980s and 1990s featured the immigrant worker as protagonist. The power of labor had declined radically in Los Angeles, with the proportion of unionized workers in the county dropping from 25 percent in the 1950s to 15.5 percent in 1993.[39] At a time when union membership was declining, wages falling and prices rising, the political consciousness of immigrant workers rose, and they flocked to union locals that were on the verge of collapse. The militancy of immigrants kindled the dying embers of the union movement, and their resolve to provide a decent living for their families sparked a prairie fire as they took to the streets. When the time came, they breathed new life into the labor movement in Los Angeles.

The obstacles were almost insurmountable: in Los Angeles County Latinos in 1990 made up 55 percent of the population under age twenty, compared with 23 percent of Anglos, 14 percent of Blacks, and 8 percent of Asians.[40] The youth and citizenship status of the immigrants meant that most did not vote. This handicap was compounded by the historical antipathy of organized labor toward immigrants and the myth that immigrants were too vulnerable to organize. Added to this was the fact that L.A.'s print media (especially the Los Angeles Times) and the electronic media were openly hostile to labor. The mounting anti-immigrant hysteria also contributed to robbing immigrants of sympathetic public opinion.

Finally, in very real terms the government conspired against all workers. The United States continues to have the most regressive labor laws of any industrialized nation – for example, unlike other OECD countries, it did not ban the permanent replacement of striking workers. Throughout the 1980s the memory of Ronald Reagan firing 11,400 traffic controllers, decertifying PATCO and replacing its members with scabs haunted the union movement.[41] And PATCO was not the only example: in Clifton-Morenci, Arizona Phelps-Dodge Co. replaced strikers and in the process changed the workforce from 70 percent Latino to 70 percent Euroamerican. A government study of seven unions found that strikes dropped by 50 percent during 1980–87, and that the number of strikers replaced had jumped 300 percent. The National Labor Relations Board and the federal courts also sided with management, which spent as much as a billion dollars a year on union-busting.[42] Despite these obstacles, for Latinos and Chicanos alike unions were their only hope; in purely economic terms, union workers earned 52 percent more than non-union workers and they usually had health care benefits.[43]

Given these repressive conditions, organization among immigrant workers in Los Angeles is that much more impressive an achievement. 'What makes the [labor] movement in L.A. different from the rest of the country is that most unions have finally accepted the large number of immigrants from Mexico and Latin America as a fact of life. This is a big change because unions often saw immigrants as a barrier to organizing', according to María Elena Durazo, president of Local 11, Hotel and Restaurant Employees Union. 'Not long ago, my own union wasted $100,000 in legal fees trying to avoid having union meetings translated into Spanish. But now the attitude is: "What do we have to do to attract them?"' Eric Mann, director of the Labor/Community Strategy Center, draws the proper conclusion: 'The challenge to unions is to reconstruct a social-justice movement for the 1990s, in which labor begins by thinking about the whole society rather than just the needs of its members.'[44]

María Elena Durazo was the highest-ranking Chicana in the Los Angeles labor movement. The daughter of immigrants, she graduated from St. Mary's University and held a law degree. She began her activism as a member of CASA (Center for Autonomous Social Action), an organization dating back to the 1960s that was committed to the defense of the foreign-born. Durazo was part of a student group centered around Magdalena Mora, a brilliant, dedicated UC Berkeley student from Mexico who unfortunately died very young of cancer. CASA members dreamed of organizing immigrant workers.[45]

After working for the International Ladies Garment Workers Union (IL-GWU), Durazo was hired in 1983 as a worker representative for Local 11. She learned that the culture of the union – its whole style of work – was not conducive to serving workers' needs. For example, it closed its offices at 4:00 p.m. and refused to hold meetings in Spanish. The rank and file sued the union to change the situation, which led to a struggle for control of Local 11. Durazo's group won election in the Local 11 in 1987; however, the international responded by putting the local into trusteeship. Another election, held in 1989, again made Durazo president.[46]

Soon afterwards, the Los Angeles hotel industry moved toward restructuring, which meant an attack on working conditions and on workers' health and pension benefits.[47] Local 11 had 13,000 members and a master contract with twenty Los Angeles hotels (Hyatt did not sign the agreement, but used it as a guideline for its agreement with Local 11). Significantly, a clause in the industry's contract noted that if concessions were given to other hotels, they would automatically apply to the signers. This explained why Hyatt management broke the peace and moved to change the terms of the master contract.

A bitter conflict between the union and four Hyatt hotels began in the spring of 1989. After twenty-five weeks, only the Hyatt at the International Airport had settled. The strike at Hyatt's three other hotels – the Sunset, the Wilshire and the Regency – intensified as the Hyatt owners pulled out all stops to break the union. Durazo charged that Hyatt and the other hotels were in collusion – that they had selected the Hyatt hotels to lead in breaking the contract and the union.[48] Indeed, it was not an accident that Hyatt had been chosen to test the waters. The vast majority of the 600 workers at the Hyatt Regency, Hyatt on Sunset and Hyatt Wilshire were people of color and new immigrants who had been working without a contract. Some 60 percent were Latino; 15 percent were Asian immigrants; and 10 percent were African Americans. The bosses' strategy was to weaken long-established industry standards and impose regressive and inhospitable working conditions. The industry-wide contract required preset schedules; Hyatt wanted to stagger the schedules, working its employees for ten days straight so as not to have to pay overtime.[49] The goal was to set a new standard so the industry could cut wages and put workers at the mercy of ambitious managers.[50]

On 1 May 1991, Hyatt pressured the workers by taking away medical benefits and giving them an inferior plan that could cost them thousands of dollars if they were hospitalized. Management refused to restore the health benefits until the workers agreed to the ten-day work schedule, which Hyatt demanded in the name of 'management flexibility'. Hyatt also wanted to fire employees with no right to appeal unfair terminations. The union responded by aggressively by picketing the hotels, with luminaries such as César Chávez appearing at rallies.[51] Some Angelenos complained that the militancy of Local 11 was doing irreparable damage to Los Angeles's tourist trade, an $8 billion industry. Because of the recession, hotel vacancies hovered at 30 percent, and some major hotels were on the verge of bankruptcy. Critics of the union ignored the fact that the hotel industry was using the recession as an excuse to break unions and take away workers' rights.

Local 11 won a brief victory, signing a contract with Hyatt in 1991. In December of that year, however, Hyatt sold its Wilshire property to the Koreana Hotel Co. The Koreana owners immediately fired 175 employees and dumped the contract with the Hotel and Restaurant Employees. The new management offered to hire some of the workers back, but only if they agreed to work without a contract. The average salary under the contract had been $6.70 per hour; Koreana offered $5.20 and announced that it had no legal obligation to honor the old contract. (The NLRB later found that the South Korean owners violated fair labor standards legislation.)[52]

In March 1992, Local 11 produced a video, 'Los Angeles: City on the Edge', on the future of tourism in Los Angeles and sent it to convention planners throughout the US. The video depicted Los Angeles on the edge of disastrous confrontation,[53] an analysis that caused a major uproar among business leaders. The mayor's office responded by accusing the local of attempting to foment class warfare; it had not, of course, made any response to the union-busting tactics of the Koreana Hotel Company.

A month later, the Los Angeles Hotel Employer's Council announced a wage freeze, demanded that over 5,000 workers pay more for medical coverage, and refused to acknowledge their job security. Eric Mann of the Labor/Community Strategy Center argued in favor of an aggressive city strategy on behalf of the hotel workers: 'Tourism is one industry that can't relocate, so it is a perfect candidate for local government intervention to support a high-wage economy as part of a true rebuilding L.A. strategy.'[54] Local 11 immediately launched a campaign of militant actions, including demonstrations before the City Council and civil disobedience. The LAPD arrested union leaders in front of the Biltmore Hotel, detaining a total of thirty-five people. The main opposition to the workers came from the Bonaventure, the downtown Hilton, the Sheraton Town House, the Beverly Hilton and Century Plaza.[55]

Meanwhile, Local 11 had taken on Canter's Deli, one of the oldest Jewish delis in Los Angeles as well as L.A.'s largest unionized restaurant. What angered Canter workers was the owners' withdrawal from the union's health and pension plans. Rogelio Vásquez, a dishwasher at Canter's, put the workers' goals simply: 'We want the [union's] medical plan, [the union's] pension, better salary and respect at work.' Local 11 represented 125 of the 150 Canter's workers. They claimed that management had threatened them, attempted to bribe them and racially intimidate them; and that Alan Canter, the company's vice-president, called them 'dirty Mexicans'.[56] Almost daily confrontations began in 1990, with workers carrying signs reading 'Today's Special – Racism on Rye'. Union officials took special care not to allow the job actions to degenerate into a Jewish–Latino confrontation by involving progressive Jews at rallies. This labor dispute dragged on without any resolution.

Throughout the 1990s María Elena Durazo maintained a high profile. The hotel industry was constantly reorganizing and selling properties to new owners seeking to start from scratch. When Korean investors purchased the Hyatt Wilshire, organizers reached out to local Korean groups and progressive people such as attorney Angela Oh. The Asian Pacific Labor Alliance also pressured the new owners for a settlement. After ten months of boycotts and protests to the Korean consul, with personages such as state Senator Diane Watson, Councilman Mike Hernández and Police Chief Willie Williams supporting the workers by refusing to cross the picket line, the owners accepted a contract in early 1992.[57] Durazo employed these same tactics successfully again in 1994 against the Hanjin corporation after it purchased the downtown Hilton, pressuring the new owners to ratify the contract.[58]

Durazo's persistent message was that 'immigrants are more and more the future of L.A.' She planned for this future, as she prepared for an all-out organizing campaign to put the hotel industry on the defensive. Meetings were held with cells of workers from hotels with and without contracts. The union's goal was to get a living wage for L.A.'s 50,000 hotel employees. Workers organized a peaceful guerrilla army that confronted the industry in a disciplined and unexpected manner, with leafleting, human billboards, flying pickets, delegations to city offices and mass civil disobedience.[59] Along with other local union leaders Durazo was instrumental in getting the California union movement to oppose Proposition 187, the anti-immigration initiative, in 1994. In part because of this political education work, union members voted for the anti-immigrant proposition by a smaller margin than the general white population.[60]

Take Back the Streets: Local 399, 'Justice for Janitors'

One of labor's biggest success stories in Los Angeles has been the national Justice for Janitors campaign, in which Local 399 of the Service Employees International Union (SEIU) played a major part.[61] The janitors, mostly Central Americans and Mexicans, clean L.A.'s office buildings at night for a number of janitorial service companies. The Local 399 organizers had no illusions about the National Labor Relations Board and devised a comprehensive strategy of direct actions, legal tactics, public pressure, aggressive worker organizing, community support and corporate strategies.

In the early 1980s, the standard union contract of janitors called for pay of more than $7.00 per hour plus family health insurance and other benefits. Building owners and managers used four key factors in their campaign to break the union. First, they took advantage of the biggest building boom in the city's history, which allowed them to experiment with small, nonunion cleaning companies in isolated areas of the city. This provided the small companies with a chance to establish reputations in the local markets. Second, many of the larger nonunion companies were bankrolled by key owners in the L.A. real-estate industry in order to undermine union standards and break the union's control of the L.A. market. Third, the 1980s brought L.A.'s largest influx of new immigrants in its history with hundreds of thousands of Asian and Latino immigrants looking for work. Fourth, Local 399 had lost touch with workers and the changing dynamics of L.A.'s real-estate industry. Its efforts to defend workers were misguided and ineffective. As a result, Local 399's membership plunged 77 percent, and by 1987 only 1,500 janitors remained unionized.

During the late 1980s, Local 399 decided to wage a new campaign and hired a largely bilingual staff with organizers such as Jono Shaffer, the organizing coordinator and a graduate of the University of California, Santa Cruz, who almost totally incorporated Latino culture into union organizing methods. Shaffer was complemented by Berta Northey, a fourteen-year rank-and-file member of the union. Despite illness, Northey stayed dedicated to the campaign from day one. She provided a historical memory, a testimony to the principle that workers must never let the union become dormant again, for she had lived through the lean years of the 1980s as a janitor in the Arco Towers on Flower Street in Downtown Los Angeles. Northey and Rocio Saenz were the first organizers assigned to Century City. Saenz, who eventually became a lead organizer, was from Mexico City. A former college student, she came to Los Angeles unable to speak English, for the express purpose of organizing undocumented workers. She felt a special indignation when she heard about new workers having to give a month's pay to a contractor and then cleaning the equivalent of twenty houses a night.[62]

Another outstanding organizer was Salvadoran Ana Navarette, who, along with Patricia Recino and other rank-and-file members, formed an exceptional cadre of militant workers in bright red T-shirts. They were noisy and fearless. Navarette had been active in the Salvadoran liberation struggle and Recino was a product of the Chicano student movement, active in various social justice organizations since her teens. According to one official, the union created excitement by appealing to a sense of dignity among the workers, who cleaned lawyers' offices for $30 a night while the lawyers made $300 an hour. Another said, 'With chants of "¡Sí se puede!" ('It can be done!') they call public attention to injustices.'[63]

Local 399 defied the recession, battling commercial real estate owners fearlessly. Its ranks swelled from 30 percent to 90 percent of those who cleaned Los Angeles high-rises from Downtown to Century City. The Justice for Janitors campaign avoided conventional union strategies, such as government-supervised elections. It also did not strike, fearing permanent replacements of its desperately poor members, but instead went directly to the streets. Its greatest weapon was to make it financially dangerous for the subcontractors not to go union. The Janitors knew that survival meant continual organizing. They fought their biggest battle at Century City, where the contractor was International Service System, Inc. (ISS), the world's largest commercial cleaning contractor. On 15 May 1990, one hundred and fifty armed officers confronted a group of peacefully demonstrating janitors and their supporters. Knowing full well that most of the demonstrators spoke only Spanish, the LAPD gave the order to disperse in English.[64] The police riot that followed resulted in forty arrests and sixteen injuries, with two women having miscarriages as a result of being beaten.

The brutality of the LAPD brought attention to the strike and sent home the message that there would be no peace until a contract was signed. Angelenos were horrified at seeing protestors mercilessly clubbed to the ground by L.A.'s finest.[65] It was clear to everyone that the authorities wanted to teach immigrant workers a lesson: the Century City police attack was as vicious as the Rodney King beatings a year later. The Janitors filed suit against the LAPD and in September 1993, they settled for $2.35 million, though many observers believed that the settlement was far too low.[66] Throughout this period, Local 399 pressed its well-planned campaign, constantly sending community delegations to contractors and office management firms to press demands for a contract. In the end, ISS agreed to a contract for 500 of its 700 janitorial employees.

In April 1995, Justice for Janitors reached the pinnacle of its L.A. organizing campaign. Up to that time, its gains had been confined to the Century City and Downtown areas. Now it got the contract extended to suburban markets, where janitors' salaries jumped from $4.25 an hour to $6.80 plus medical benefits. Eight years after starting its campaign, Local 399 gained control of every single major office market in Los Angeles County.

In the process, the entire culture of Local 399 was transformed, from a sleepy union hall with no desire to wage war to the very symbol of a new union built through militancy, organizing and direct action. Not coincidentally, the militancy of today is built on unions with high percentages of immigrant membership, just as the initial militancy of the labor movement was created by immigrants in days past.

Unfortunately, conflicts developed in Local 399 that threatened many of the gains the union had made. SEIU had taken the desperately poor Latino immigrant janitors and turned them into a militant army. However, victory had its price. Discontent developed, especially in the local's building service division, with what some workers perceived as a lack of representation and followup on grievances on the part of the Local 399 leadership. Eight thousand janitors and 12,000 healthcare workers at Kaiser Permanente of Southern California made up the bulk of the 25,000 members of the local, with the rest working in related industries. Some friction was understandable, considering the division of the workers into different units and industries; in this case, the discontent appears to have come from the healthcare workers as a significant portion of the local's revenues went into expansion of the union and its facilities. Some complained that more resources should be spent on maintenance of existing contracts and fighting speedup of the workforce at Kaiser than on drives to sign up more members.

The reformistas, as the dissidents called themselves, spread their movement to the janitors. According to some in the opposing camp, at this point there were legitimate grievances against the local's leadership, symbolized by the locked door in the union's office anteroom that separated members from their representatives. In the midst of the struggle to expand the union, the leadership had certainly become more centralized and bureaucratized. The reformistas also claimed that the structure had become top-heavy with Euroamericans, allowing little upward mobility for the Latino and Mexican rank and file.

The dissidents began an all-out drive during the spring of 1995 on behalf of a 21-strong alternative slate called the Multiracial Alliance. The Alliance was mostly Latino, but also included whites and African Americans. This campaign was successful in the June 1995 local elections; by a vote of 1300 to 1100, the dissidents won twenty-one of twenty-five contested positions, including the vice-presidency. The fight continued after the dissidents took office on 13 July and demanded control over hiring, the tearing down of the anteroom wall, grievance committee control over firing, and supervision of union staff and the expenditure of union funds. Local President Jim Zellers blocked the new board's directives.

The struggle then expanded to include the right to fire some union officials and many of the organizers who had played major roles in developing the Justice of Janitors strategy, among them Jono Schaffer, Rocio Saenz and Patricia Recino. Zellers, according to some sources in his camp, aggravated the situation by refusing to try to work with the reformistas. As president, he had considerable power and the backing of the International. Instead, Zellers accused the reformistas of using promises of patronage to win the election; a partisan of Zellers charged that César A. Olivia Sánchez, a leader of the reformistas, could not speak enough English to conduct contract negotiations. The reformistas responded by complaining about the white leadership.

The intensity of the struggle caught many supporters of Local 399 by surprise. Although they could sympathize with the need to democratize the union, the attempt of the reformistas to fire all twenty-three members of the local's transition committee seemed extreme. Moreover, many Chicanos and Latinos resented the blanket use of the race card, especially because many of those they wanted to oust were Latinas and Latinos. They also knew that many of the white organizers such as Jono Schaffer were by no means racist, and that the criticisms of him and others were more about issues of personality and style of leadership than any actual or perceived racism. Moreover, their personal contributions to the successes of Justice for Janitors could not be denied or ignored.

As in similar struggles within progressive movements, there is plenty of blame to go around. There is no doubt that there are some opportunists within the ranks of the reformistas. On the other hand, Zellers should have handled the situation by taking assertive steps to deal with the problems raised by Local 399's rapid expansion, rather than taking the membership's support for granted. It was necessary to improve communication with the rank and file, to tear down walls rather than build them to suit the convenience of the bureaucracy. Meanwhile, layoffs and increased pressure for janitors to work more rapidly called for more attention to the problems of the current membership. (Local 399 had also absorbed the bulk of 5,200 layoffs by Los Angeles County.) Zellers should also have provided more leadership training for Latino workers, incorporating rank-and-file members into the leadership.

No doubt the reformistas did achieve victory through a fair election. But with leadership comes responsibility. Winning an election did not give the reformistas the right to destroy the infrastructure that had been built by all the members, not just the reformistas or the Zellers supporters. They should have taken more care to ensure a smooth transition, especially since management would try to exploit the situation. Both sides contributed to a breakdown in governance, resulting in the International's throwing the local into trusteeship.

As of this writing, Local 399 remains in trusteeship, and a degree of normalcy has returned to the local. The SEIU remains a key organization for immigrant workers, as the fastest growing union in the US and the largest in California, where it represents 300,000 workers. To sustain that growth, the leadership must keep peace by increasing the participation of all its diverse sectors. The truth is that the unions need the immigrant as much as the immigrant needs the unions. The percentage of union workers in the workforce has fallen from 35.5 percent in 1945 to 15.5 percent currently, and to just 10.9 percent of the private sector workforce.[67]

Meanwhile, the militancy of the Justice for Janitors movement set the tone for other workers in Los Angeles such as teacher's aides. Problems in the relationship between the Los Angeles Unified School District (LAUSD) and the union representing teaching assistants went beyond normal wage and benefit disputes. They reflected the historical pattern of Anglo–Mexican relations, in which Euroamericans almost always expected to get Mexican labor on the cheap.

A high number of the students in the mammoth LAUSD come from Spanish-speaking homes. Most of the teachers speak only English. Thus, much of the instruction in math, reading, English and science was left to teaching assistants, who spoke Spanish, while the teacher spent time with the English-speaking students. In 1989, the Board of Education refused to give the aides job security and benefits. This treatment was patently racist (and sexist) and resembled the treatment of all teachers before World War II, when women subsidized education by accepting sub-par wages. The public attitude then was that women could afford to work for nothing because it was a family's second salary. But for Los Angeles teaching assistants today, mostly women and about 70 percent Latina, working is not a luxury. More often than not they are the sole support of their families, with few other options open to them because they do not have job security and can be discharged at the whim of the principal. Ultimately, the conflict was settled before a strike crippled the system and hurt non-English-speaking students.[68]

No Other Choice: The Drywallers

A major labor struggle in recent Los Angeles history has been that of the drywallers, a particularly exploited group of construction workers. For sixty hours a week, they lugged around 100-pound, 4 x 6 slabs of sheetrock. They worked under the hot sun and were paid little by contractors, who often shortchanged them. However, although their working conditions were oppressive, few predicted the revolt of the drywallers.

In October 1991 drywall hanger Jesús Gómez complained to a drywall contractor that his weekly check was $60 short. The contractor turned his back and refused to discuss the matter. Gómez began to talk to other drywallers, planting the seed for collective action. Over the months Gómez built an impressive network of support in Southern California, from the International Brotherhood of Carpenters to community organizations such as la Hermandad Mexicana Nacional, Los Amigos of Orange County, the League of Latin American Citizens (LULAC) and the California Immigrant Workers Association (CIWA).

Among the drywallers, the core group came from El Maguey, northwest of Mexico City, and Gómez built the organization around these family networks. Many of the drywallers had arrived in the 1960s and 1970s, and by the late 1970s, dozens of cousins and brothers had immigrated to do this work.[69] They had done well in the early 1980s, but when the bottom fell out of the housing market in the latter part of the decade developers and contractors cut wages to the point that drywallers earned only $300 for a 60-hour week. Families lived in cramped quarters in poor neighborhoods, and their children went to overcrowded schools.[70] The bosses did not believe that the drywallers would strike, because of the economic recession and the construction slump – but they were wrong.

In 1992, a core of a few hundred drywallers issued demands to contractors, who ignored them. The drywallers did not want to affiliate with the Carpenters Union, because they would then have come under the NRLB and an injunction would have limited their tactics. Driven to the wall, in June 1992, 1,800 drywallers walked off their jobs from San Diego to Ventura County.[71] Contractors repeatedly used their political influence to mobilize local government against the strikers. Club-swinging police officers beat and arrested 300 drywallers, then called in the Immigration and Naturalization Service to deport them. Enroute to a rally held for them by Local 399, the drywallers were chased onto the 101 freeway by LAPD, who beat them and arrested sixty-eight.[72] Four hundred drywallers and their supporters protested the arrests in front of the LAPD's Parker Center, calling attention to the brutality.[73] In Palmdale, sheriff's deputies arrested workers and kept them handcuffed in the broiling sun.[74]

Sympathy for the drywallers on the part of other labor organizations made it possible for them to raise some $400,000 for bail and other organizing activities. The strike victory was a community effort, with supporters such as María Incarnación Sándoval (known as 'Adelita') having been beaten by police alongside the workers. The drywallers enjoyed support from the Coalition for Humane Immigrant Rights of Los Angeles (CHIRLA), CARECEN, MALDEF and other groups that furnished legal assistance. The drywallers also received important assistance from the California Immigrant Workers Association (CIWA), whose attorneys instructed workers on their rights – not only as workers but also as undocumented immigrants. The AFL/CIO had organized the CIWA in 1989; it now had 6,000 members. Basically, CIWA was organized to inform immigrant workers of their rights, with a staff of three attorneys, led by Miguel Caballero, and organizers guided by Joel Ochoa and led by premier community organizer José de Paz. Twenty-one AFL/CIO-affiliated unions and six California central labor councils provided funding. Local unions such as the International Ladies Garment Workers Union (ILGWU) and the SEIU played a major role in setting it up.[75] (Unfortunately, CIWA was de-funded by the labor movement in 1994; the de Paz brothers, José and Hector, have kept it alive through volunteers.)

Finally, forty-three contractors in five counties signed a contract with the drywallers, though none in San Diego County.[76] The contract was described by labor leaders as on the cutting edge. Kent Wong of the UCLA Center of Labor Research and Education said, 'Because a majority of the union offices are in Washington, D.C., attention from the national unions toward Latino and immigrant workers on the West Coast has been slow.'[77] Now it looked as though this might change.

New problems developed after the victory. The drywallers had won their first raise in ten years, putting them slightly above their 1982 pay rate, and had gained partial employer payment of health insurance. But they had to pay half the costs of that insurance themselves, which lowered their actual take-home pay. The drywallers had also made other concessions, such as accepting scabs as equal members of the union. This became a sore spot because of the construction slump; drywallers who had struggled and suffered were infuriated when scabs were hired before them.

A half-dozen disgruntled former negotiators left the Carpenters Union, which the drywallers had joined after all, and joined the Painters' Union. One of the defectors was Antonio Hernández, a leader of the Maguey group. They criticized the Carpenters for failing to enforce the contract, accusing the union of not caring as long as it continued to collect dues.[78] The split undoubtedly weakened the drywallers, who nevertheless have continued to press for better wages and working conditions. A very real problem remained with the Carpenters Union, which failed to understand or incorporate the drywallers into its union culture.

The Church and the Workers

The importance of the Catholic Church to the Chicano/Latino labor community has always been great. Before becoming Archbishop of Los Angeles, Roger Mahoney had the reputation of being pro-labor, and many thus expected him to speak out for justice in the tradition of Pope Leo XIII. Latinos also believed that Mahoney had a close relationship with the farmworkers. The Church's conflict with the grave-diggers who worked for the Los Angeles Diocese ended that illusion. In the mid 1980s, this largely Latino workforce demanded the right to have union representation after a colleague died and they belatedly learned that their life insurance policies had been cancelled. (They were told that the insurance had been cancelled as part of austerity measures to pay for the Pope's September 1987 visit.)

Of the 140 grave-diggers, 120 at ten Catholic cemeteries signed cards authorizing the Amalgamated Clothing and Textile Workers Union to represent them. The union then presented the cards to Archbishop Mahoney, who refused to recognize the union as the the workers' bargaining agent. In a hearing before the NLRB, the Archdiocese argued that the labor laws did not protect the grave-diggers because they were religious workers. The NLRB regional director found for the Church, and the union prepared to appeal the decision. The archbishop agreed to new elections, which he then sabotaged by dividing the workers and refusing to recognize the vote.

In 1989 Mahoney allowed the cemetery workers to hold yet another election. Despite considerable arm-twisting by the archbishop, workers voted 66 to 62 in favor of the union; however, Mahoney refused to recognize the results of the vote. More elections and appeals took place until relations between the prelate and the Los Angeles labor community were so strained that Mahoney

cancelled his traditional Labor Day breakfast in 1990.[79] Whether Mahoney intended it or not, his actions gave comfort to those in the business community
who were anti-labor, signalling that free-market tactics were permissible even
if they meant beating down workers.

Plant Shutdowns and Community Strategies

Slowly but surely, heavy industry in Los Angeles has dwindled, eliminating an
important economic option for thousands of residents who either could not,
or did not, want to go to college. One example was the shutdown in September 1990 of the Oscar Meyer Foods plant in Vernon. At that time southeastern
Los Angeles had only recently regained some stability after a series of industrial exits in the mid 1970s – General Motors from South Gate, Uniroyal and
B.F. Goodrich from Commerce, and Bethlehem Steel from Vernon. In Long
Beach, the old Bemis Co., a *Fortune* 500 conglomerate, went out of business,
throwing 150 workers out in the street.[80] As always, workers were blamed for
not being productive enough, or for being too greedy.

Oscar Meyer was once a pacesetter in the meat-packing industry, paying
good wages and benefits. That abruptly changed when the packing house and
its subsidiary, Louis Rich, were gobbled up in the mid 1980s by the largest food
and beverage conglomerate in the country, Philip Morris. Oscar Mayer soon
cut labor costs, largely through technological innovations that enabled plants
to operate economically seven days a week. It also shifted the bulk of its production to more modern facilities in the Midwest. Other savings were extracted
the old-fashioned way – by cutting jobs and wages. Still, most analysts believed
that Oscar Meyer would maintain its profitable, though technologically back-
ward, Vernon facility. Most of its workers had been there for fifteen years or
more. Sixty-five percent belonged to Local 770 of the United Food and Commercial Workers International Union; 75 percent were Latino. But Oscar Meyer
did close, and its exodus was devastating, eliminating 537 union jobs.

A new exodus of plants ravaged the area. Alcoa Aluminum left in 1994,
eliminating 440 more jobs (Alcoa had employed 1,149 workers in 1990). Meanwhile, Aluminum Forge of Santa Ana and International Metals of Torrance
left, resulting in the loss of another 2,000 jobs. Losses like these encouraged
plants like Farmer Johns, which employed 1,000, to take the offensive and cut
back on wages and benefits.

One of the most ingenious strategies for resisting plant closures during the
1980s was devised by GM Van Nuys workers. Los Angeles was once known as
the Detroit of the West, with 15,000 autoworkers producing a half-million cars
a year.[81] In the 1970s, the automakers began to dismantle their California op-

erations; the Ford factory geared down as did the General Motors plant in South Gate. By 1982, Van Nuys workers saw the handwriting on the wall and knew it was only a matter of time before GM would shut down that plant, too. Organizers like Mark Masaoka, formerly at the Ford Plant in Pico Rivera, and Eric Mann, who had worked at GM South Gate, began a fight-back movement with the support of United Auto Local 645 President Pete Beltrán.[82] Pete Beltrán had lived in San Fernando since he was four years old. He had begun working at GM's Van Nuys plant after graduating from San Fernando High School in 1958. Twenty years later, he had been elected president of his union local. The plant and surrounding community were his home.

When Beltrán spoke out against the Van Nuys plant shutdown, he sparked the Campaign to Keep GM Van Nuys Open. His fledgling group built a coalition of over one hundred community and religious organizations whose representatives met with General Motors President F. James McDonald in January 1984. The executive told them that the Van Nuys plant was on the hit list. Beltrán and his campaign responded that if GM shut down the Van Nuys facility, the community would boycott GM products in Los Angeles. Their labor/community strategy was successful, and the Van Nuys plant was kept open while other plants closed.

The UAW's West Coast Regional Director, Bruce Lee, sided with management in its plans to reorganize production, however, and by late 1985 he was pushing the 'team concept', which organized the labor process with workers as interchangeable parts, thus reducing the number of workers needed. Beltrán told the workers that they should not vote for the team concept plan unless GM gave them a guarantee that it would keep the plant open for ten years. In 1986 the workers approved the team concept by a narrow margin of 53 percent to 47 percent.[83]

In the summer of 1991 General Motors announced that it would close the Van Nuys plant. It put 2,600 workers on the streets (already down from 5,200 ten years before). Fifty percent of the plant's workers were Latino. UAW officials acted as if they were outraged, but refused to adopt the successful fight-back tactics of the Save GM Van Nuys Campaign. They diverted suggestions of a boycott, kept militant leaders such as Eric Mann from speaking to workers, and only went through the motions of resistance.[84]

The fact is that GM wore the workers down. Its representatives, with the support of UAW leaders and the press, persuaded workers that the best way to save the plant was to cooperate.[85] GM workers had to sell their houses and move to other states where GM transferred them; those who didn't transfer collected severance pay for a year. The community was left with a worsening economic situation as other businesses also closed.[86]

Accompanying deindustrialization like the GM and Oscar Meyer closures was capital's deconstruction of workers' consciousness, via attempts to control interpretations of events. The US corporate community – and even foreign competitors – spread the idea that the recession was the workers' fault. Yoshio Sakurauchi, speaker of the Japanese House of Representatives, responded to the question of the US trade deficit with Japan by asserting that American workers were to blame for their problems because they were lazy.[87]

Indeed, some blame must be placed at the feet of union leadership. In the 1990 election, Pete Beltrán ran once more for the presidency. He had considerable support and a good chance of winning. However, regional president Bruce Lee cooperated with management to play on worker fears. Lee told the workers just before the election that he and incumbent Jerry Shrieves had reached an agreement with GM to convert the plant into a flex plant, which would build interchangeable units, thus keeping it open. GM officially announced, 'We cannot confirm or deny his [Lee's] statement.' Even the respected labor columnist Harry Bernstein played on worker's fears, in effect supporting Lee. In response Beltrán said: 'My concern is for the rights of the workers not corporate executives who recently helped themselves to major increases in retirement pay.' Out of fear for their jobs, Van Nuys workers elected Shrieves.[88]

The impact of deindustrialization on the San Fernando Valley closely resembled that of the South Gate area: a once thriving community was destroyed, its industrial base wiped out.[89] GM said that it was moving production to a newer factory in Quebec, and that relocation was the reason for eliminating what had admittedly been a productive and profitable plant. Aside from reducing the tax base, closure of these plants had a ripple effect, with hundreds of small businesses going broke.[90]

L.A. County Workers

Competition among workers, power struggles within their union, and local political wars combined to create a difficult situation for Los Angeles County employees in 1991–92. Of the unions representing some 80,000 county workers, SEIU Local 660 was by far the largest, with a membership of over 40,000 and the most militant. Unfortunately, a split developed in the union between the rank and file and the union's governing board. Tensions escalated in March 1992 when the governing board of Local 660, by a vote of 21 to 11, removed Gilbert Cedillo as acting general manager; that same board had appointed him in July 1991. A lawyer, Cedillo had, like María Elena Durazo, come out of the 1960s student movement and been active in CASA. He had strong backing from progressives of all colors as a result of his militant leadership during the successful 'Rolling Thunder' demonstrations against cutbacks in workers' health benefits.[91]

Cedillo's supporters responded by holding a membership meeting in mass at which he was re-elected general manager by a vote of 3,643 to 952. The board refused to recognize Cedillo on the grounds that the local's bylaws empowered the board to appoint the general manager. Cedillo countered that the board had ignored the democratic process and that the membership had the right to override the board.[92] Tensions were so strong that in July the International put Local 660 into trusteeship. In September 1992 Cedillo again won election with 67 percent of the vote.[93] The union remained in receivership until February 1993, when Cedillo, along with a newly elected board and four executive officers, was installed for a three-year term.[94]

Cedillo's election undermined the influence over Local 660's Board of Directors by Ophelia McFadden, president of Local 434 and an African American. An International vice-president, McFadden was part of the old guard of the union movement and a player in regional politics. In an effort to reassert her influence, she cast the Local 660 struggle in racial terms and gained support among African American and white workers. Unfortunately some of the Euroamerican union activists also played a negative role by playing Blacks and Latinos off against each other, increasing racial tensions.

McFadden could by no means be considered a hack, however. She had organic ties to the civil rights establishment of Los Angeles, and she had been part of the struggle that had forged a strong Black presence in politics and in civil service employment. In 1988 she had served as a California delegate for Jesse Jackson's presidential bid and was active in the Democratic Party. Known as a strong advocate for African American interests, McFadden mostly represented licensed vocational nurses and custodians. To further complicate the situation, Cedillo had been appointed several weeks after Gloria Molina was elected a county supervisor. Local 660 had strongly supported her opponent, Art Torres, and had donated thousands of dollars to his campaign. Molina was not surprisingly angry because of this support and was openly hostile to Cedillo.

All this occurred within the context of the hiring situation at the Martin Luther King Hospital and a struggle there going back several years. A county hospital, it had opened its doors in 1972 when the surrounding area was mostly inhabited by African Americans. Proposition 13 and several Deukmejian budgets had devastated the facility. Then, as the Latino community in that area grew, tensions over jobs and hospital services developed. African Americans held 71 percent of the jobs at the hospital compared with 12 percent held by Latinos. The lack of promotions of both Blacks and Latinos to supervisoral positions aggravated competition for middle-management jobs. McFadden's local represented the mostly Black workers at the King Hospital. In many ways the hospital was a symbol for Black Americans in Los Angeles.

Chicano complaints against the county about hiring practices at the hospital dated back to the mid 1980s. The SEIU unions had attempted to respond to pressure from Latino activists by filing a race and sex wage-discrimination complaint before the Equal Employment Opportunity Commission (EEOC) in 1985. The suit was joined by the NAACP and the California chapter of the National Organization for Women. Among other things it called for a study of wage discrimination. This action was opposed by Raul Nuñez, president of the Los Angeles County Chicano Employee Association, and by a coalition of a dozen Chicano groups, who argued that the complaint shifted the focus away from Latinos and Native Americans, who were the most discriminated-against groups in the county workforce.[95]

Tension between the African American and Latino communities came to a head in 1988 with the release of a controversial and long-awaited report by the county's Office of Affirmative Action Compliance, which showed that the county had failed to meet its affirmative action goals. Black employees criticized in particular the conclusion that Latinos were badly underrepresented in county work because in proving the underrepresentation of Latinos, the report seemed to imply that Black employees were overrepresented. Clyde Johnson, president of the 6,000-member Black Employees Association, countered that the Latino numbers were inflated. Nuñez's answer was to step up efforts to persuade the EEOC to investigate charges that the county Department of Health Services (which funded King Hospital) had engaged in 'systemic discrimination' against Latinos. Tough rhetoric on both sides polarized the camps. The Filipino-American Employees Association had also claimed discrimination, and the county report showed that the number of Native Americans, Asians and women lagged as well. The size of the Latino and Black groups, however, gave the impression that it was a Latino–Black conflict, an impression reinforced by the fact they were also the most vocal.[96]

In 1990, the EEOC concluded that the county hospital system, and King Hospital in particular, had discriminated against Latinos and should implement a more aggressive affirmative action policy.[97] In the spring of 1992, an agreement was reached between the county and the EEOC. According to that settlement, Martin Luther King Hospital and the Department of Health Services agreed that if one-third of the qualified job applicants were Latino, then one-third of the new hires had to be Latino. Nuñez criticized the settlement; the problem of poor recruitment of Chicanos remained, Nuñez felt.[98] The agreement also angered many African American employees at the King Hospital.[99]

Cedillo had tried to find the high ground in this complex situation, seeking to balance worker rights with community needs. For years he had helped to build strong multiracial coalitions made up of progressives who wanted more militant unionism, and he was not directly involved in the King Hospital conflict. His victory in September 1992 signified that the overwhelming majority of county workers wanted an end to the tensions at King Hospital. In fact, Cedillo could not have won that election without the support of Black county workers.

Cedillo's victory energized the county workers. On 31 August 1993, Local 660 along with 12 other county unions organized a gigantic march and rally at which Jesse Jackson spoke. County workers voted to strike if planned cutbacks, including a 8.25 percent wage reduction, were implemented. This action drove the county supervisors to the bargaining table and forced them to re-examine priorities and the availability of funds.[100]

Street Vendors and Day Workers

Chicanos and Latinos worked as metal finishers, in construction, and as garment workers. They were the gardeners, the busboys and the cooks at most of L.A.'s coffee houses and cafes. Increasingly Latinos were reduced to the status of casual laborers. Many became domestic workers and/or house cleaners in thousands of homes. Latinas from Pico-Union, South Central and Boyle Heights would take two or three buses to the Westside and the Valley, working for as little as $80 to $125 a week.[101] Indeed, contrary to the stereotype of stay-at-home Mexican and Latina housewives, participation within the labor force by Latinas was higher than that of other women; 61 percent of Mexican American women nationally between the ages of twenty-five and fifty-four worked outside the home, most of them without union protection.[102]

As the L.A. economy became leaner and meaner, a growing number of immigrants turned to street vending. While street vendors had always been part of the city, and of the urban economy in Mexico and Central America, their numbers grew during the late 1980s and early 1990s, and as they did, so did the reaction of Euroamericans against the vendors. *Daily News* columnist Linda Seebach reported on a meeting where the street vendor representative, Angelina Garza, made what Seebach called reasonable proposals. The audience responded angrily: 'I don't think illegal aliens should be here in the United States. I don't think they have any rights.' When Garza reminded the speakers that their own ancestors had been immigrants, a member of the audience yelled, 'Legal', which is not historically true, since many European immigrants did not in fact have papers. Seebach asked whether street vending was not preferable to welfare.[103]

For a time the vendors had an association, headed by Dora Alicía Alarcón; its officers were mostly Mexican and Central American women. They often worked ten hours to earn $20, but considered street vending honest and dignified work. The city for its part fined street vendors and had the power to give them 180 days in jail, treating them the same as drunk drivers. In 1986, police arrested Alarcón, and confiscated her merchandise. The next day she borrowed $5 and was back in business again.[104]

A large number of Mexicans and Latinos also worked as day laborers. They filled the street corners at intersections such as Lankershim and Strathern, Reseda and Parthenia, and others throughout the city. Sixty to seventy men from Mexico, El Salvador and Guatemala would wait together for jobs. In good times, they earned as much as $300 a week; in bad times they went hungry.[105] Homeowner associations and business owners complained about the day laborers, pressuring authorities to get rid of them.[106] A favorite sport of some Angelenos was to taunt the day workers by driving up as though intending to hire, then speeding away when a group rushed to the car. Los Angeles politicos such as Supervisor Yvonne Braithwaite Burke and Councilwoman Laura Chick courted Anglo prejudices by calling day laborers 'loiterers'.[107]

Workers at the Back of the Bus

Essential to these and other workers was transportation. Yet the debate over transit in Los Angeles rarely addressed the transit system's efficiency and cost from the point of view of workers. Interest in mass transit had waned as the ridership became mostly Latino and Black. Since the destruction of the Yellow and Red streetcar lines, the middle-class professional had been the patron targetted by transit planners. The idea of rail transportation was resurrected, and tremendous subsidies were given to the 400-mile Metrolink system, designed to serve suburban professionals. Meanwhile, the regional bus system, which carried 1.3 million passengers and served the working class, received much less support.[108] Bus rides were subsidized at the rate of $1.17 a ride, whereas the yuppies riding Metrolink received a staggering $38.00 subsidy per ride in 1993. The rail lobbyists protected the interests of the rail riders, with no one representing the poor.[109]

Public transportation was consolidated under the Metropolitan Transit Authority, a politically powerful agency that let hundreds of millions of dollars in contracts yearly. It in turn traded patronage with politicians and concentrated on serving the needs of the middle class. In the summer of 1994, the Metropolitan Transit Authority increased the bus fare to $1.35 and did away with monthly bus passes. US District Judge Terry Hatter ordered that the new 25-cent fare increase be stayed.[110] One of the reasons for the increase was the heavy funding for rail lines, which had created a $126 million budget deficit.[111] The multi-ethnic Labor/Community Strategy Center organized a Bus Riders Union to respond to the rate hikes. Along with the NAACP Legal Defense and Education Fund, it filed a suit, *Bus Riders Union* v. *Metropolitan Transportation Authority*, based on the US Supreme Court's 1954 ruling against the separate-but-equal doctrine in *Brown* v. *Board of Education*. By the MTA's own figures, there were 350,000 bus riders compared to 27,000 train riders. Forty-seven percent of the MTA bus riders were Latino; 23 percent, African American; 19 percent, white; 8 percent, Asian; and 1.2 percent, Native American. Most were young and working-class. Not surprisingly, bus fares were raised again after the suit against the MTA was settled in 1995. However, the Bus Riders Union continued to serve as a public watchdog on the MTA.[112]

Workers and Environmental Racism

State budget cutbacks and the Republican Party's anti-worker bias have contributed to a decline in worker safety, especially for Latinos and Chicanos.[113] A *Los Angeles Times* series in September 1993 described widespread safety problems facing Latino workers. According to the reporters, nearly one half the 875,000 manufacturing jobs in Los Angeles were held by Mexican (actually, Latino) workers; in 1991–92, twenty-one workers died as a result of fatal accidents.[114] The article described the feelings of worthlessness and hopelessness among maimed workers, the lack of attention to their needs, and their fear of losing a job. Half a dozen employers did not even take the injured employee to emergency care.

With the lack of union representation, preventive inspection checks plummeted during the 1980s. Republican administrations felt that inspection made government unfriendly to business. In 1990, Cal/OSHA inspected only 4 percent of all factories in Los Angeles, as compared to 10 percent in San Francisco and 16 percent in Sacramento.[115] Latino workers, especially Mexicans and Central Americans, were also exposed to dangerous toxins, a risk that many ignored out of desperation. Ninety-five percent of the plastic workers were exposed to highly toxic plastics. Latinos were also heavily represented in the 400 plants known to use lead. Poor hygiene and ventilation were common, and enforcement of safety standards remained lenient.[116]

Poisoning of the environment has been a serious problem for all workers and entire communities in Los Angeles County. L.A.'s famous smog problem is only the best-known example. Three-fifths of all Blacks and Latinos live in communities of uncontrolled waste, as do half of all Native Americans and Asians, according to a 1993 report. As in other parts of the United States, progress against this intolerable situation has been slowed by the perception of a conflict between jobs and a clean environment. Metal-plating, furniture manufacturing, electronics and garment and janitorial work need to be cleaned up, not eliminated; such jobs remain essential to many people's survival. Too often the conflict has been defined in either-or terms, with many claiming that too much environmental regulation would lead to industry moving out.[117]

The Mothers of East Los Angeles grappled with this problem when they opposed the installation of a gas pipeline in their neighborhood. They also marched against a proposed toxic waste incinerator in Vernon. The Mothers of East L.A. joined Concerned Citizens of South-Central Los Angeles, a largely African American group, in drawing attention to environmental racism. In the San Fernando Valley, Latinos together with Blacks and Euroamericans protested the expansion and efforts to extend the life of the López Canyon landfill for another five years after 1996.[118]

The Labor/Community Strategy Center recognized that Los Angeles needed both clean air and jobs, and it has worked to build coalitions among Mexicans, other Latinos, and the Black, Asian and Euroamerican communities toward this end. Still business interests have insisted that regulation means fewer jobs, alleging a loss of 550,000 jobs since 1990. A recent Southern California Edison study discredited this myth, finding that California had actually lost 160 companies and 21,800 jobs because of environmental regulations; only 9 percent of the firms studied cited government regulations as their reason for leaving. Nevertheless, business continues to propagate this myth.[119]

In 1991, the Labor/Community Strategy Center published a pioneering study of the politics of L.A.'s air pollution, *L.A.'s Lethal Air: New Strategies for Policy, Organizing, and Action*.[120] Led by civil rights activists, the Center worked for environmental justice alongside grassroots organizations such as the Mothers and Concerned Citizens. It acted as a watchdog, monitoring and protesting the activities of the Air Quality Management District and the oil refineries.

The work of the multiracial Southwest Organizing Project (SWOP) has also been of special importance to Latinos. Based in New Mexico, SWOP has been a trendsetter, involving key 1960s Chicano activists. It did groundbreaking work in popularizing the concept of environmental racism on the basis of a 1987 report by the United Church of Christ Commission for Racial Justice, 'Toxic Wastes and Race in the United States', which argued that minority communities, because they were poor and powerless, were targeted disproportionately by contaminating and undesirable industries. SWOP also challenged the environmental establishment known as 'the Big Ten' traditional environmental organizations. Controlled by white middle-class professionals, their interests often diverge from those of minority communities. SWOP also initiated the Southwest Network for Environmental and Economic Justice, a regional body that linked environmental and economic struggles.[121]

A Few Last Words on Chicanos and Unions

For Chicanos, unions are especially important because the majority of them are unskilled workers. They are vulnerable and poor, not because they fail to work but because they are paid too little – and they are paid too little because they do not have collective power. Despite the gains of service workers unions like the Justice for Janitors campaign, the question remains: How can immigrant workers reap the fruits of their sacrifices? Would new immigration laws ultimately exclude them from the workplace? Mexican immigrants in the past could always rely on the need for their labor to override Euroamerican racial nativism. Now, with the globalization of labor, capital can exploit this labor in the workers' home country – at much lower cost. Moreover, the fall of the socialist bloc in Eastern Europe has made available a huge new pool of highly skilled workers.

Further, the immigrant workers' successes threaten to be a double-edged sword. As wages and working conditions improve, service sector jobs would become more attractive to second-generation Latinos, Blacks, Asians and even whites. Pressure will surely increase from racist groups such as the Federation for American Immigration Reform (FAIR) to divide the labor rank and file. The lack of jobs in heavy industry and the growing globalization of the production process will also contribute to making service jobs more attractive to desperate workers of all colors.

Despite the increased visibility of Chicano and Latino labor organizers, they are still not in positions of power within the County Labor Council, which is still controlled by craft unions. Under Mayor Bradley, the Labor Council was allied with the pro-growth sector of the city elite. The service employee unions locals did not control the Labor Council, but they did eat at its table; they began to care what the labor leadership, which once excluded Latino labor leaders, thought of them. Chicano union officials out of necessity grew closer to Chicano elected officials, who, for the most part, delivered a pro-labor vote. As this relationship grows closer in the future, reenforced by ethnic ties, there will be a tendency to put economic goals ahead of the important role that trade unions can play in holding a political party in check or representing the needs of the Latinio community. Labor leadership, like any institution, has its own self-interest; the myth of 'labor brotherhood' can become a cover for the interests of the leadership.

Finally, much of the Latino trade union leadership has roots in the community, both in the US and in Latin America. Many of today's leaders took part in the student struggles of the 1960s and 1970s, in the defense of immigrants, and in the campaigns to organize farmworkers. In addition, many immigrants have histories of union participation in their own countries. The commitment of these leaders is real. However, the interests of the community and those of organized labor are not always congruent. True, workers are part of the community. However, the workers' leadership must define labor interests through involvement in the larger community, keeping this larger context in mind when negotiating contracts or in any other struggle.

Notes

1. 'America Learns to Love L.A.', *Economist*, 24 Dec. 1988, p. 81; see also Paul Ong et al., *The Widening Divide: Income Inequality and Poverty in Los Angeles* (Los Angeles: School of Architecture and Urban Planning, UCLA, 1989).

2. W. Soja, 'The New Economic Order: Where the First World and Third Worlds Meet', *LA Weekly*, 24 Feb. 1989, p. 21. In the 1970s New York lost 330,000 manufacturing jobs and Los Angeles added 225,800. Economic Planning and Developmental Program, 'A Status Report on Southern California's Regional Economy: Profile of an Economic Transition', *Southern California Association of Governments*, 2nd edn (August 1984), p. 2; Mike Davis, 'Chinatown, Part Two?: The "Internationalization" of Downtown Los Angeles', *New Left Review* no. 164 (July/August 1987), pp. 66–87.

3. Eric Mann and Watchdog Organizing Committee, *L.A.'s Lethal Air* (Los Angeles: Labor/Community Strategy Center, 1991), p. 9; Frederick Ross, 'The City of the Future Is a Troubling Place if It's to Be Los Angeles', *Wall Street Journal*, 12 June 1989; 'America learns to love L.A.', pp. 81–2; J. Eugene Grisby III, 'Coping with Ethnic Diversity as Los Angeles Strives to Become a World-Class City' (School of Architecture and Urban Planning, UCLA, April 1989), pp. 4, 17–19; Stephanie Grace, 'Life in L.A.: More Pay, More Newcomers', *Los Angeles Times*, 31 July 1992.

4. Tracy Wilkinson, 'L.A.'s Turn as Urban Laboratory', *Los Angeles Times*, 1 Dec. 1991; Ross, 'The City of the Future'; Harry Anderson, 'Economic Workhorse', *Los Angeles Times* 21 Aug. 1989.

5. Don Parson, 'Many Histories: Postmodern Politics in Los Angeles', *Science as Culture*, vol. 2, no. 12, pt. 3, pp. 411–25, an excellent article by one of the best observers of Los Angeles.

6. Steven P. Erie, 'Balancing a Budget at the Expense of L.A.'s Future', *Los Angeles Times*, 23 May 1993. Erie provides an excellent synthesis of the history of the building of Los Angeles's infrastructure.

7. Richard Rothstein', *L.A. Weekly*, 13 Dec. 1991, p. 22.

8. Harry Bernstein, 'Closing the Wage Gap: Job Equality', *Los Angeles Times*, 8 April 1993; Paul Wallich and Elizabeth Corcoran, 'The Discreet Disappearance of the Bourgeoisie', *Scientific American*, Feb. 1992, p. 111.

9. James Risen, 'History May Judge Reaganomics Very Harshly', *Los Angeles Times*, 8 Nov. 1992; also see Mark Lacter, 'Low Inflation Is Result of Stale Economy, Not Politics', *Daily News*, 16 Sept. 1992; 'No se recupera la economía de California, según estudio de UCLA', *La Opinión*, 18 Dec. 1991; Howard Gleckman, 'What Reaganomics Did for Us – Or to Us', *Business Week*, 4 May 1992, pp. 15–16.

10. Russ Britt, 'Is the Minimum Wage Too Low?', *Daily News*, 23 May 1993; James Risen, 'Lifting Workers Out of Poverty Proves Difficult', *Los Angeles Times*, 3 Sept. 1993; Wallich and Corcoran, 'Discreet Disappearance', p. 111; Mark Bousian, 'Plan to Boost Minimum Wage Taking Some Hits', *Los Angeles Times*, 26 Oct. 1993. Actually, 'the average American manufacturing worker produces more goods per hour than a worker in any other major industrial country in the world. Yet, the American worker earns less in wages and benefits per hour than a worker in any other major full industrialized nation, except Japan where the wages are almost the same as in the United States and the United Kingdom, where workers get about 10% less.' While the American worker in 1992 earned $16.17 an hour, a German worker earned the equivalent of $25.94 per hour. Harry Bernstein, 'Pay of US Workers Doesn't Match Output', *Los Angeles Times*, 27 April 1993; Teresa Watanabe, 'Americans Lazy? Not So, Says Japanese Study', *Los Angeles Times*, 4 Feb. 1992. The Japan Productivity Center wrote that Japanese workers in 1990 worked 2,044 hours, 95 hours more than Americans, but Americans worked more than Germans and French workers. US productivity was still the highest in the world. Walter Russell Mead, 'Picking Up the Pieces After the Free-market '80s', *Los Angeles Times*, 12 Jan. 1992.

11. David Rieff, 'Victims All?' *Harper's* (Oct. 1991), p. 53.

12. James Risen, 'Number of Poor In America Hits a 27-Year High', *Los Angeles Times*, 4 Sept. 1992. Robert R. Brischetto and Paul A. Leonard, *Falling Through the Safety Net: Latinos and the Declining Effectiveness of Anti-Poverty Programs in the 1980s*; Southwest Voter Research Institute, *Public Policy Report 1*, 1988.

13. 'Children Now' ranked Los Angeles last of ten cities in the quality of life of its children. California ranked 42nd out of 50 states in proportion of children without health care. Claire

Spiegel, 'Number of State Children in Extreme Poverty Soars', *Los Angeles Times*, 21 June 1991; Robert Pear, 'Ranks of America's Poorest Soar', *Daily News*, 4 Sept. 1992; 'Según el Gobierno, el 14.2% de la gente vivía en la pobreza en 1991', *La Opinión*, 4 Sept. 1992. Bertha del Rivero, 'El índice de desempleo de California se dispara', *La Opinión*, 7 March 1992; Jason DeParle, 'Poverty Rate Rose Sharply Last Year as Incomes Slipped', *Los Angeles Times*, 27 Sept. 1991; Michael Harrington, 'The Snare of Poverty', *Los Angeles Times*, 1 June 1986. Harrington noted that the Economic Recovery Tax Act of 1981 taxed people just above the poverty line, and called the Democrats co-conspirators. Jaime Olivares, 'Los hispanos, grupo étnico más pobre', *La Opinión*, 21 Jan. 1992.

14. Sylvia Nassar, 'Rich and Poor Likely to Remain So', *New York Times*, 18 May 1992.

15. Karen Tumulty, 'CEO Pay Raises Rise to Level of Campaign Issue', *Los Angeles Times*, 31 Dec. 1991; Richard Rothstein, 'Los salarios de los ejecutivos', *La Opinión*, 22 Feb. 1992. The top ten CEOs in California earned a total of $92.6 million in 1992, with Millard S. Crexler of Gap Inc., earning $41,862,955. The top 100 earned a total of $212.98 million, enough money to pay 1,000 school teachers for six years. Kathy M. Kristof, 'Spotlight on the Top', *Los Angeles Times*, 23 May 1993. The CEO compensation ran almost twice the rate of increase of the average factory worker.

16. 'Service Jobs Dominate the US Economy ...' *Los Angeles Times*, 31 May 1992.

17. Bill Sing, 'Skills May Fall Short of State's Labor Needs, Study Says', *Los Angeles Times*, 17 May 1989. 'The greatest number of new jobs – 22.9 million – will be for retail sales personnel such as maids, waiters and waitresses and top executives.' Bruce Horowitz, 'Booming Demand for Workers in Service Industry Reflects Economy's Evolution', *Los Angeles Times*, 19 Sept. 1985.

18. Rebecca Morales and Frank Bonilla, eds, 'Restructuring and the New Inequality', in *Latinos in a Changing US Economy* (Newbury Park, Calif.: Sage Publications, 1993), p. 7.

19. Janet Rae-Dupree, 'Census Figures Reflect South Bay's Economic Problems', *Los Angeles Times*, 6 Sept. 1992; Jesús Sánchez, 'State's Long-Term Jobless Corps Grows 50% in Year', *Los Angeles Times*, 8 Sept. 1991; Mary Ballesteros, 'La economía de los latinos está rezagada, según cifras del censo', *La Opinión*, 18 Aug. 1992.

20. Shawn Hubler, ''80s Failed to End Economic Disparity, Census Shows', *Los Angeles Times*, 17 Aug. 1992.

21. Sam Fulwood III, 'Latino Child Poverty Swells, Study Says', *Los Angeles Times*, 27 Aug. 1991; Jill Steward, 'Poverty Gap Growing in L.A., Report Finds', *Los Angeles Times*, 20 June 1989.

22. Carlos E. Alcibar, 'Las duras alternativas de la pobreza en la gran ciudad', *La Opinión*, 2 Feb. 1993; 'Aumenta el desempleo en al condado; baja en el estado', *La Opinión*, 9 Jan. 1993; 'El desempleo nacional es del 7.1% y el estatal, del 7.7%', *La Opinión*, 11 Jan. 1992; Mike Hernández, 'Help Los Angeles by Legalizing Street Vendors', *Los Angeles Times*, 29 Sept. 1993.

23. Denise Gellene, '2% of Firms Have Left State since 1980, Report Says', *Los Angeles Times*, 19 Oct. 1992; Peter V. Ueubberoth, 'Business as Usual: Recipe for Failure', *Los Angeles Times*, 9 June 1993.

24. Eric Mann et al., *Reconstructing Los Angeles from the Bottom Up* (Los Angeles: Labor/Community Strategy Center, 1993).

25. Richard Rothstein, 'La inversión pública y el desarrollo económico', *La Opinión*, 27 Aug. 1992; Ralph Frammolino, 'Enterprise Zones Fall Short of Promises', *Los Angeles Times*, 14 June 1992.

26. Stephen S. Cohen, 'L.A. Is the Hole in the Bucket', *Los Angeles Times*, 8 March 1993; Robert Reinhold, 'Test for Peace Dividend: Boom or Bust in California', *New York Times*, 3 July 1990; Russ Britt, 'County Loses 208,400 Jobs in 1991', *Daily News*, 4 April 1991.

27. Bernard Sanders, 'Now They Want to Add Insult to Injury', *Los Angeles Times*, 11 June 1992; Richard Rothstein, 'Ten Ways to End the Recession – and Why the Right-Wing [and some Center and Left] Plans Won't Work', *L.A. Weekly*, 13 Dec. 1991; Robert A. Rosenblatt and Paul Houston, 'Massive Fraud Blamed for 40% of S&L Failures', *Los Angeles Times*, 19 July 1990.

28. Jill Steward, 'Poverty Gap Growing in L.A., Report Finds', *Los Angeles Times*, 20 June 1989.

29. Robert Reinhold, 'Test for Peace Dividend'; Frank Clifford, 'USC Study Criticizes L.A.'s Investment in Downtown', *Los Angeles Times*, 29 Jan. 1992. The report, by USC's School of Urban and Regional Planning, criticized the building of L.A.'s skyline and the crumbling of its commercial core.

30. Labor/Community Strategy Center, 1993, p. 32.

31. Anne C. Roark, 'Homeless Children Found to Cope Well – At a Price', *Los Angeles Times*,

19 Nov. 1991.

32. Martin Conroy, Hugh M. Daley and Raul Hinajosa Ojeda, 'The Changing Economic Positions of Latinos in the US Labor Market Since 1939', in Morales and Bonilla, pp. 34, 39.

33. Rebecca Morales and Paul M. Ong, 'The Illusion of Progress: Latinos in Los Angeles', in Morales and Bonilla, p. 63.

34. Robert A. Rosenblatt, 'A Shortage of Skills?' Los Angeles Times, 1 June 1993.

35. Tamara Henry, 'Latino Dropout Rate Put at 35%', Daily News, 17 Sept. 1992. Rebecca Morales and Frank Bonilla, 'Restructuring and the New Inequality', pp. 11–12; Sam Fulwood III, 'Latino, Non-Latino Income Gap Widens', Los Angeles Times, 17 Aug. 1990. According to the Center of Budget and Policy Priority, 28% of the Latino households were in the poorest fifth of the population and 11% in the richest one fifth. In 1979, the typical Latino household earned 71% of the Anglo average; in 1988, it earned 66%. Donna K. H. Walters, 'Latinas Gaining on Latinos in Management, Survey Finds', Los Angeles Times, 1 April 1994. A Southwest Voter Registration Institute study found that there were 670,000 Latina professionals versus 660,000 Latino professionals nationally; this was up from a combined total of 430,000 in 1974. Latinas were 50.9% of the top category in 1990 versus 49.5% for Latinos. The survey reported that Latinas heavily outnumbered the number of Hispanic males in professions. In spite of these gains, the group as a whole showed that only one of every twenty-two executives and managers was Hispanic.

36. Hispanic Association on Corporate Responsibility, quoted in Amy Harmon, 'Study Finds Few Latinos in Top Jobs, Los Angeles Times, 5 March 1993.

37. Leo Rennert, 'Minorities in the US Ranked Lower Than 30 Nations in Quality of Life', Daily News, 18 May 1993.

38. David Hayes-Bautista in Manuel Jiménez, 'Scholar Challenges Latino Stereotypes', Nuestro Tiempo, 18 March 1993.

39. Patrick Lee, 'To Live and Prosper in L.A.', Los Angeles Times, 1 Feb. 1993; Edward Soja, 'The New Economic Order', L.A. Weekly, 24 Feb. 1989, pp. 21–4. Don Lee, 'Unions Face Unsettling Times in Valley' Los Angeles Times, 8 June 1993; in 1970, women made up 34% of organized workers, in 1992, 39%. Their presence changed the labor culture, with priorities such as child care becoming more important to labor. Nationally, Latinos made up 11% of unionized workers.

40. Rosenblatt, 'A Shortage of Skills?'

41. Harry Bernstein, 'Put Teeth Back in Worker's Right to Strike', Los Angeles Times, 15 July 1993; Bob Baker, 'Workers Fear Losing Jobs to Replacements in Strikes', Los Angeles Times, 7 June 1990; Jane Slaughter, 'What Went Wrong at Caterpillar?', Labor Notes, May 1991; Richard Rothstein, 'Con los sindicatos se aumenta produccion', La Opinión, 23 Jan. 1992. In 1970 31% of American workers were in unions, 37% of Germans were in unions, 31% of Swiss, and 32% of Canadians; by 1987, the US share had dropped to 17%, the German had jumped to 43%, the Swiss to 33%, and the Canadian to 36%.

42. Bob Baker, 'Union Buster Turns to "A Labor of Love"', Los Angeles Times, 5 Sept. 1993.

43. 'Exigen se prohíbia reeplazo permanente de huelguistas', Los Angeles Times, 31 March 1991.

44. Paul Ruggins, 'California's Unions Set Agenda to Secure Labor's Future in America', Los Angeles Times, 6 Sept. 1992.

45. Marita Hernández, 'Latina Leads Takeover of Union from Anglo Male', Los Angeles Times, 6 May 1989; Raiz Fuerte que no se arranca (Los Angeles: Editorial Prensa Sembradora, 1981). Magdalena Mora, 1952–1982, was a member of CASA, a student leader, union organizer and writer for Sin Fronteras.

46. Steve Proffitt, 'Maria Elena Durazo', Los Angeles Times, 27 Sept. 1992.

47. 'LLR: Voices: Local 11 takes on L.A.', and 'Building on Diversity: The New Unionism', Labor Research Review, vol. 20 (1993), pp. 21–3; Marcelo M. Zuviría, 'Durazo se re-elige como presidenta de Local 11', La Opinión, 12 Dec. 1991.

48. Bob Baker, 'Union, Hyatt Hotels Still at Odds', Los Angeles Times, 23 July 1991.

49. Ibid.; Nancy River Brooks, 'Hyatt Touch Leaves Labor Touchy', Los Angeles Times, 27 Sept. 1990.

50. Pamphlet by Local 11, 'Beware of the Real Hyatt Touch … And the Pritzger Hand Behind It'; the Marmon Group was an umbrella for the Hyatt operations, 'Investor Pritzger May Make an Offer for Pan Am', Los Angeles Times, 25 June 1991.

51. Marcelo M. Zuviría, 'Empleados de hoteles realizan una protesta; César Chávez se les une', *La Opinión*, 27 June 1991; Brooks, 'Hyatt Touch'.

52. Leticia Garcia-Irigoyen, '75 empleados son despedidos por los dueños del hotel Hyatt', *La Opinión*, 31 Dec. 1991; Ashley Dunn, 'Hotel's New Owners Cited for Labor Violations', *Los Angeles Times*, 10 May 1992.

53. Jerry Brown, 'L.A. Hotel Employees Issue Video Highlighting Dark Side of City, Los Angeles, California', *Travel Weekly*, 4 May 1992; María Elena Durazo to community leaders, 10 March 1992; *Los Angeles: City on the Edge*, pamphlet, March 1992.

54. Eric Mann, 'Video Age Reaches Union Bargaining', *Los Angeles Times*, 26 June 1992.

55. Jesús Hernández Cuellar and José Ubaldo, 'Arrestan a empleados de hoteles y restaurantes durante una protesta', *La Opinión*, 24 April 1992. Soon afterwards a contract was signed; Monica Limón España, 'Sindicalistas toman medidas legales contra el lujoso hotel Beverly Rodeo', *La Opinión*, 19 Dec. 1992.

56. Mathis Chazon, 'Workers' Beef Has Both Sides Simmering at Deli', *Los Angeles Times*, 11 Feb. 1991; Mathis Chazanon, 'Union Calls Rally at Canter's Deli Mark Year of Picketing', *Los Angeles Times*, 16 Oct. 1991; Laureen Lazarovici and Ruben Martínez, 'In a Pickle: Latino-Jewish Relations on Line in Center's Labor Dispute', *LA Weekly*, 13 Sept. 1991.

57. Jake Doherty, 'Hotel Labor Pact: Room for Everyone', *Los Angeles Times*, 1 Nov. 1992.

58. K. Connie Kang, 'Korean Groups Back Workers', *Los Angeles Times*, 18 Nov. 1994; Kang, 'L.A. Hilton Owner Will Keep Service Workers', 10 Jan. 1995.

59. Mike Davis, 'Trying to Build a Union Movement in Los Angeles', *Los Angeles Times*, 20 March 1994.

60. Stuart Silverstein, 'Unions Do a U-Turn on Immigrant Worker Issue', *Los Angeles Times*, 3 Nov. 1994.

61. 'Building on Diversity: New Unionism', *Labor Research Review 20* (Chicago: Midwest Center for Labor Research, 1993). The SEIU was more sensitive to the issue of immigrants and the need for diversity in its locals than were other international unions.

62. Dave Gardetta, 'True Grit: Clocking Time with Janitors Organizer Rocío Saenz', *LA Weekly*, 30 July 1993, p. 17.

63. Sonia Nazario, 'For Militant Union, It's a War', *Los Angeles Times*, 19 Aug. 1993.

64. Sonia Nazario, 'Janitors Settle Suit Involving Clash in 1990', *Los Angeles Times*, 4 Sept. 1993.

65. Rodolfo Acuña, 'America Retreats on Labor Laws', *Los Angeles Times*, 16 July 1990.

66. Bob Baker, 'Tentative Accord OK'd to End Janitor's Strike', *Los Angeles Times*, 26 June 1990.

67. Diane E. Lewis, 'Labor's Quiet Crusader: Sweeney Sees a Wave of Revolt Putting Him at AFL-CIO Helm', *Boston Globe*, 3 Sept. 1995; 'Official Business: Officers Suspended, Trustee to Run Janitors' Union Local', *Los Angeles Times*, 15 Sept. 1995; Stuart Silverstein and Josh Meyer, 'Fastest Growing Union Hits Obstacles in L.A.', *Los Angeles Times*, 19 Sept. 1995.

68. Elaine Woo, 'Teaching Assistants Seek Union Status', *Los Angeles Times*, 6 Nov. 1989.

69. José de Paz, 'Organizing Ourselves: Drywallers' Strike Holds Lesson for the Future of Labor Organizing', in 'Building on Diversity: The New Unionism', *Labor Research Review*, vol. 20 (1993), pp. 25–8; Leticia Garcia-Irogoyen, 'Liberacion a 47 Obreros de construccion arrestados en Orange en una protesta', *La Opinión*, 8 July 1992.

70. Mike Clements, 'Drywallers' Strike Nails Down a Principle', *Los Angeles Times*, 6 Nov. 1992; Mara Cone and Eric Young, 'Falling Wages, Lack of Jobs Spark Rare Labor Movement', *Los Angeles Times*, 7 Sept. 1992.

71. Leonel Sanchez, 'Drywallers Strike: Confrontations Multiply', *San Diego-Union Tribune*, 23 Aug. 1992.

72. María del Pilar Marrero, 'Protesta acaba en la 101 y con 68 arrestos', *La Opinión*, 24 July 1992; Eric Malnic and David Reyes, '68 Drywaller Workers Seized as Protest Blocks Freeway', *Los Angeles Times*, 24 July 1992.

73. María del Pilar Marrero, 'Protestan ante el Centro Parker 400 constructores', *La Opinión*, 29 July 1992; Kathleen Murray, 'Drywallers File Complaints over Pay, Labor Practices', *Los Angeles Times*, 29 July 1992; Frank Valmaña, 'Constructores denuncian a empleadores ante la NLRB', *La Opinión*, 30 July 1992.

74. Denis Walcott, 'Palmdale Picketing Uneventful', *Daily News, Antelope Valley*, 17 Sept. 1992; Blaine Halley, 'Drywall Strikers Return to Palmdale Day After Arrests', *Los Angeles Times*, 17 Sept. 1992.

75. Mike Davis, 'Trying to Build a Union Movement'.

76. Arthur Jones, 'The Pain and Sacrifice of Birthing a Union', *Labor Notes*, Jan. 1993.

77. Dan McAullife, 'Drywaller Pact Gives Employers' "Safety Value"', *The Press-Enterprise*, 12 Nov. 1992.

78. Michael Flagg, 'Feuding Sours Success of O.C. Drywall Strike', *Los Angeles Times*, 31 May 1993.

79. Henry Weinstein, 'Archdiocese Labor Policy Assailed', *Los Angeles Times*, 17 March 1989; Bob Baker, 'Mahoney and Union Agree on New Vote to Settle 3-1/2 Year Feud', *Los Angeles Times*, 4 Sept. 1991.

80. Tim Waters, 'Paper-Bag Workers Sacked; Bemis Bag Is Packing It In', *Los Angeles Times*, 11 Dec. 1986; Hay Hebert, 'Economic Threat to L.A. Seen in Declining Industrial Plants', *Los Angeles Times*, 5 Dec. 1982. Brick buildings near the L.A. river comprised 35–40% of the city's industrial stock. Most of the buildings were built before 1950 and have not been refitted for present earthquake standards. The Economic Development Corp. of Los Angeles County had been funded to revive the industrial sector. By the end of the decade, there was little talk of reviving heavy industry in L.A.

81. Bob Baker, 'LA's Booming Auto Industry Now a Memory', *Los Angeles Times*, 20 July 1991.

82. Henry Weinstein, 'Boycott by UAW of GM Threatened', *Los Angeles Times*, 15 May 1983; Henry Weinstein, 'Drive on to Save GM Plant', *Los Angeles Times*, 28 Feb. 1983. The automakers took their cue from the massive wage cutbacks at Chrysler. Its restructuring was ordered by Jimmy Carter's administration as a condition for government bailout of that company. Eventually, 57,000 workers were permanently laid off. This began a brutal social policy that gave capital maximum flexibility and which encouraged corporations to abandon a commitment to US workers.

83. Eric Mann, *Taking on General Motors: A Case Study of the UAW Campaign to Keep GM Van Nuys Open* (Los Angeles: UCLA, 1987), pp. 219–50.

84. James F. Peltz, 'General Motors Plant in Van Nuys to Close', *Los Angeles Times*, 20 July 1991; Francisco Robles, 'Descontento los obreros hispanos de la planta de GM', *La Opinión*, 26 July 1991; Robles, 'Analizan solución para los futuros desempleados de la GM en Van Nuys', *La Opinión*, 9 Aug. 1991; Eric Mann, 'Workers and Community Take on G.M.', *Nation*, pp. 161–3; Rodolfo Acuña, 'The Man Behind the Battle at GM Van Nuys', *Los Angeles Herald-Examiner*, 2 June 1989.

85. Eric Mann, 'UAW Backs the Wrong Team', *Nation*, 14 Feb. 1987, pp. 171–5.

86. Tom Furlong and Ralph Vatabedian, 'Squabble at UAW', *Los Angeles Times*, 24 Sept. 1991; 'GM to Lay Off 1,600, Plans to Close More Auto Plants', *Los Angeles Times*, 22 Dec. 1989; Lisa Pope, 'GM Plant – End of the Line', *Daily News*, 16 Aug. 1992; Ralph Nader, 'Protecting the Bloat at Top', *Los Angeles Times*, 25 Dec. 1991. At the time of intense global competition, GM executives received $1 billion in bonuses; Ross Perot was bought out at nearly $750 million. Donald Woulat, 'Troubled GM Will Eliminate 74,000 Jobs, Shutdown 21 Factories', *Los Angeles Times*, 19 Dec. 1991; Mary Williams Walsh, 'Socialized Medicine Cuts Canada's Cost – and Care', *Los Angeles Times*, 9 April 1990. Canada's health system was a major reason GM shifted production there. It saved over $500 a worker in health care premiums monthly. Canada had close to 170,000 auto workers in contrast to Los Angeles, which had none.

87. Teresa Watanabe, 'Japan Hedges Commitments on US Cars', *Los Angeles Times*, 21 Jan. 1992; John Price, 'Workers Are Put Second in Japan', *Labor Notes*, June 1992, pp. J4–J5; Jane Slaughter, 'Blaming Japan Will Get US Nowhere', *Labor Notes*, June 1992, pp. J6–J7.

88. Harry Bernstein, 'Ray of Hope for Van Nuys UAW', *Los Angeles Times*, 19 June 1990; Marcelo M. Zuviría, 'Ratifican el cierre de la planta GM en Van Nuys', *La Opinión*, 18 Dec. 1991.

89. See Mike Davis, 'The New Industrial Peonage', *Heritage*, Summer 1991, pp. 7–12; Marcelo M. Zuviría, 'Cierre de la GM deja un sabor amargo de boca a desempleados', *La Opinión*, 21 July 1991.

90. Russ Britt, 'Locale Cited as Reason for Demise', *Daily News*, 16 Aug. 1992. GM had paid the Department of Water and Power $5 million a year for electricity. It was the city's 20th largest consumer of water. The city also lost $1 million in tax revenues, even though the plant had gotten millions of dollars in tax breaks under Proposition 13. GM left at a period when the market for

industrial property was at its lowest point, and so there was little hope that the GM property would be put to productive use.

91. 'SEIU Takes Control of L.A. County Local Because of Internal Political Fighting', *Daily Labor Report*, 23 July 1992.

92. Eric Malnic, 'County Workers Local Is Seized, Officers Ousted', *Los Angeles Times*, 21 July 1992.

93. Hector Tobar, 'Vote Ends Struggle for Control of County Union', *Los Angeles Times*, 1992.

94. 'SEIU Lifts Trusteeship of Local in Los Angeles, Swears in New Board', *Daily Labor Report*, 11 Feb. 1993.

95. 'Complaint Alleging County Job Bias Files; Latinos, Indian "Opt Out" of Action by Service Employees Union', *Los Angeles Times*, 30 April 1985.

96. Victor Merina, 'County Jobs Pit Blacks Against Latino Workers', *Los Angeles Times*, 29 Feb. 1988; Victor Merina, 'Supervisors Support Latinos in Clash over Hiring Goals', *Los Angeles Times*, 13 July 1988.

97. Jonathan Tilove. 'It's Latino vs. Black in L.A.', *Plain Dealer*, 19 Dec. 1993.

98. Richard Simon and Claire Spiegel, 'County Ok's Plan to Settle Charges of Job Bias Against Latinos', *Los Angeles Times*, 12 March 1992.

99. Jonathan Tilove, 'Latinos Claim Black Prejudice at Hospital', *The Times-Picayune*, 19 Dec. 1993.

100. David Bloom, 'County Union Votes to Strike over Pay Cuts', *Daily News*, 1 Sept. 1993; Xochitl Rita Ybarra, 'The Longest Day', *660 Voice*, Oct. 1993; Carla Rivera, 'County's Tentative Accord with Major Unions Avoids Severe Cuts', *Los Angeles Times*, 11 Sept. 1993.

101. Tracy Wilkinson, 'Column One', *Los Angeles Times*, 12 Feb. 1992.

102. 'Work Picture Varies for Hispanic Women', *Dayton Daily News*, 21 Feb. 1994.

103. Linda Seebach, 'Vendors Spice Up City Streets – And Heat Up a Debate', *Daily News*, 19 Sept. 1993.

104. 'Return to Vendor', *LA Weekly*, 13 Sept. 1991.

105. Bruce Kelley, 'El Mosco', *Los Angeles Times Magazine*, 18 March 1990, pp. 11–18, 38, 42; Marcelo M. Zuviría, 'Arrestan a la presidenta de los vendedores ambulantes de L.A.', *La Opinión*, 14 Feb. 1992.

106. Don Schultz, president of the Van Nuys Homeowners Association, "Toiling over the Problem of Day Laborers', *Los Angeles Times*, 8 Aug. 1993; María del Pilar Marrero, 'Protestan ley que prohibe solicitar trabajo en público', *La Opinión*, 25 July 1991.

107. Caitlin Rother, 'Day Laborers Fight "Loiterer" Image', *Daily News*, 4 Oct. 1993; Ashley Dunn, 'Blue-Collar Anxiety Visits Day-Labor Sites', *Los Angeles Times*, 24 Feb. 1992. After an 18-month recession, white workers began to appear at sites ready to work for $5 an hour.

108. Ryan Snyder and Antonio Villaraigosa, 'Community on the Backs of the Poor', *Los Angeles Times*, 27 Nov. 1992; Bob Sippchen, 'Living Close to the Edge', *Los Angeles Times*, 27 June 1993; Mark Katches, 'MTA Panel on Lobbying to Set Strategy, Recommend Cuts', *Daily News*, 16 Sept. 1993.

109. Eric Mann, 'Invest in Buses – For the Poor', *Los Angeles Times*, 24 Aug. 1993. At one time Los Angeles had one of the most extensive publicly financed electric-streetcar systems in urban America. Big Red trolleys connected the country's numerous communities; yellow cars carried passengers on city streets. But in the late 1930s, city elites conspired with General Motors, the Southern California Auto Club and tire and oil companies to buy up the transportation network and replace the electric trolleys with motorized buses. The US Justice Department filed conspiracy charges against the perpetrators. They were found guilty but fined only $1. By 1963, Big Red was dead and the regional transportation system was in chaos. Shortly thereafter the RTD was created to pull together the numerous financially strained private lines and to meet regional transit needs. County Supervisor Pete Schabarum was not satisfied with the arrangement and sought to privatize transportation. He chaired the LACTC, which he used for political purposes, using his power to force the RTD to do his bidding by withholding funds. Schabarum was especially irked by the RTD drivers and mechanics getting raises. He used his political clout to grab prime routes from the RTD for private companies. His manipulation was facilitated by Mayor Bradley, who was worried over the prospect that service would be interrupted. It was clearly Schabarum's strategy to create two classes of transportation, one in the suburbs and the other in the overcrowded inner city. His intent

was to eventually kill the transit workers union. Meanwhile, Latinos had little representation on the board of RTD. Rodolfo Acuña, 'The Real Victims of the L.A. Transit "Peace Pact"', *Los Angeles Herald Examiner*, 22 Dec. 1988.

110. Janet Gilmore and David Bloom, 'Judge Postpones MTA Fare Hike', *Daily News*, 2 Sept. 1994.

111. Bill Boyarsky, 'Responses to Court Shows MTA's Hypocrisy', *Los Angeles Times*, 4 Sept. 1994. The MTA was also a major source of patronage. Alatorre said that he opposed the increases, but according to *Times* commentator Bill Boyarsky, he 'muscled through a $123-million appropriation earlier in the year for his pet project, a proposed Blue Line rail extension from Downtown Los Angeles through his district to Pasadena.' Some $50 million came from discretionary funds that could have been used for bus transportation. However, in fairness, Alatorre was not the only member on the board who promoted his pet projects. John Hurst and Ronald Taylor, 'RTD Finds Itself on Rocky Road with Contractor', *Los Angeles Times*, 26 Dec. 1990; David Parish, 'Metro Rail', *Daily News*, 23 Jan. 1994.

Because of a lack of space, this book does not extensively cover the Community Redevelopment Agency (CRA), which along with the MTA has been a government within a government. At the time of this writing, it was spreading its influence into the San Fernando Valley, where it wants to redevelop abandoned property devastated by the January 1994 Northridge earthquake. *Los Angeles Times* reporters Margaret Holub and Charles F. Elsesser, Jr, reported in 1988 that the Community Redevelopment Agency took money away from the general fund by diverting taxes to the agency. Homeowners paid for lights, sidewalks and sewers, whereas downtown business avoided these costs. 'Tax increment financing' allowed downtown property tax money to be used to build the downtown area, which in 1977 declared a blighted area. Future revenues were diverted to the downtown area for its exclusive use. Many of the CRA projects were questionable, such as financing the troubled Stock Exchange for $1.5 million, financing a night club on Spring Street and a glitzy Bunker Hill YMCA to serve yuppies who could not afford the California Club. This when the homeless swarmed the downtown area and the Park and Recreation Department cut 75% from recreation programs and proposed firing 350 workers. Margaret Holub and Charles F. Elsesser, Jr., 'The CRA: Powerful, Unexamined Agency', *Los Angeles Times*, 16 Aug. 1988; Frank Clifford, 'City Council Rejects Plan to Take over CRA', *Los Angeles Times*, 28 June 1989; Tom Epstein, 'L.A. County's Road to Recreational Apartheid', *Los Angeles Times*, 1 July 1991.

112. Eric Mann and Lisa Duran, 'Don't Spend Transit Dollars Fighting Poor', *Los Angeles Times*, 11 Sept. 1994.

113. David Freed, 'Molina to Ask Factory Checkups Be Restored', *Los Angeles Times*, 11 Sept. 1991.

114. David Freed, 'The Dangers of Life on the Line', *Los Angeles Times*, 5 Sept. 1993; Ruth Rosen, 'Casualties of Unbridled Capitalism', *Los Angeles Times*, 15 Sept. 1991.

115. David Freed, 'Revived Cal/OSHA Fails to Inspect Most Factories', *Los Angeles Times*, 7 Sept. 1993.

116. David Freed, 'Few Safeguards Protect Workers from Poison', *Los Angeles Times*, 6 Sept. 1993.

117. 'Toxic Wastes and Race in the United States', in 'Building on Diversity: The New Unionism', *Labor Research Review*, vol. 20 (1993), p. 33; Lauree Lazarovich, 'Air Battles', *LA Weekly*, 6 Dec. 1991.

118. Liz Mullen, 'Katz Threatens Suit if L.A. Extends Landfill's Operation', *Los Angeles Business Journal*, 10 Oct. 1994.

119. Joel Schwartz, 'Business Flight: Myths and Realities: Coalition for Clear Air', *Los Angeles Times*, 7 July 1992.

120. Mann et al., *L.A.'s Lethal Air.*

121. Valerie Menard, 'Green Injustice: Who's Winning the Race for Environmental Dollars?' *Hispanic*, vol. 7, no. 10 (Nov. 1994).

9

Chicanas in Los Angeles

All the major issues addressed in this book so far – the negation of the Mexican presence in Los Angeles history and in the city's contemporary reality, struggles for political power, the restructuring of the economy, and immigration policy – have specific meaning for Chicanas and other Latinas, making it necessary to addresss these issues in their gendered particulars. This chapter will map some of those particulars, beginning with the problem of the social invisibility of Chicanas, the accompanying dearth of analysis of Chicana lives, and the absence of a political vision that includes them.

Although they are half of the Chicana people in Los Angeles, Chicanas have been made almost invisible as subjects. When people talk about Chicano immigrants, or workers, or gang members, the image that dominates is of a man, with women somewhere in the background, their faces unnoticed even by those to whom they are introduced. The reasons for this lack of visibility combine racism and sexism. As sociologist Joan Moore has observed, to think about Chicanos in terms of families, in terms of women and children as well as men, humanizes them – and it is not in the interest of those in power, or those who derive their sense of power from identification with the powerful, to do so. The invisibility of female identity thus encourages a racist dehumanization of the whole Chicano community.

This tendency is encouraged by widespread lack of data and a related gender-conscious analysis. For example, when the *Los Angeles Times* writes that L.A. Latinos are poorer than poor Blacks, Asians and Anglos, many readers automatically think of Chicano and Mexican males. In reality, the statement refers to entire families, which of course contain within them gender differences in access to resources.[1] Failure to recognize this plural reality helps society excuse its unequal treatment of Chicanas and other Latinas (along with women in general) and rationalize its habit of ignoring the needs of women and children.

The lack of visibility of Chicanas and Latinas and how issues affect them has effects in Los Angeles that are not unique to that city, of course, but are significant to the understanding of any social formation. For instance, the local trade union movement has been held back by a lack of any real strategy based on recognizing the situation of women workers and by an organizational culture that doesn't involve Latinas and Chicanas in decision making. Many of the white male and female leaders of these unions are decent people, committed to the organization of Mexican and Central American workers. But they are prisoners of their own unions' history and culture. The attitudes of many of the older organizers do not enable them to think about the various forms culture can take: they tend to believe that learning Spanish and reaching out to Latina community organizations is enough.

As a new generation emerges, pressure to address gender issues is increasing. In an attempt to increase that consciousness, students at the University of California, Los Angeles, insisted that the Chicano Studies department rename itself Chicano/Chicana Studies. Chicano Studies programs on other campuses have also adopted the new name, sometimes after a long struggle against traditionalists who insisted that the term *Chicano* – which refers to the male in Spanish – was generic for women as well. This interpretation is, however, being challenged in practice – for example, at high schools where *gritos* or calls for 'Chicano Power' are now being accompanied by 'Chicana Power'.

It is the resistance to such changes that has made terminology more than a symbolic issue, and an example of how gender issues – in addition to those of class and race – are inseparable from culture. Social struggles in contemporary Los Angeles show us clearly how the reverse is also true: class, race and culture are inseparable from gender issues.

Chicana Identity

Chicana gender identity and consciousness are constructed from life experience. From childhood, parents sanction inequality. For instance, when I was growing up, my mother would warn my sister that if she did not learn 'woman's' work, she would have a hard time finding and holding a husband. Then she warned *me* not to marry a *gringa* because the woman would leave me the first time I fooled around, whereas Mexican women were ideal because *eran aguantadoras*, they put up with problems (a myth at least symbolically exploded by Lorena Bobbitt).

Many of these attitudes are changing, as more Chicanas get a high school and even college education. As they encounter new ideas and experiences outside the home, they have lowered their threshold of tolerance for burdens that had once seemed inevitable and have formed new attitudes towards traditional (a code word for patriarchal) values and practices. Moreover, a personal paycheck and the vote have heightened the Chicanas' sense of gender and have encouraged them to question subservient roles. Other factors include the decline of the Church's moral authority, the impact of civil rights struggles throughout society, and the emergence of new role models.[2]

Changes in the Chicano community's beliefs about gender roles are often apparent in subtle rather than obvious ways. And traditional sexism is of course still alive. At a recent conference on Proposition 187 at Riverside, California, which is about sixty miles east of Los Angeles, one of the male participants remarked that it was a good thing that the conference had not been held in L.A. because if it had it would have collapsed. He obviously referred to the fact that, although the majority of the participants were Chicanas, the panelists were overwhelmingly male, and at Riverside the gender issue had been ignored for the good of the cause. In a nutshell this comment expressed the ambivalence of many male Chicanos about sexism: the idea of women's rights is accepted up to a point – after which it is maliciously labeled white feminism or lesbianism.

It is true that such a conference would not have been held in Los Angeles without some debate about gender balance. An understanding of the need for Chicana participation exists today that was absent from the Chicano Movement twenty years ago. The reasons why this expression has become so forceful in Los Angeles itself are complex. The source of feminist consciousness is not be found solely in universities, where female students maintain and/or express their identification as Chicanas. Nor is it mainly a product of gang culture, where female gang members also refer to themselves as Chicanas. In great measure this form of identification has been created by the arts community of Los Angeles, where cultural centers and bookstores have served as forums for Chicana artists, poets, musicians and an occasional filmmaker. Interaction is common between Los Angeles–based artists and those from other parts of the country. The works of Chicana artists generally reflect struggle and are often imbued with the spirit of social protest. Art and literature demand a perspective, which is at the heart of the power of Chicana art. Conflict between aesthetic and political priorities has not been a serious problem in the Chicana universe, which seems to have rejected the idea that serious art should be apolitical.[3] The issue of identity is very important to these women, especially lesbian writers and artists, who have struggled for their space within the community and refuse to concede their identity to the homophobia that is still too prevalent.

As part of identity, sexuality is still controversial in the Chicana universe, which after all is part of Mexican and Latino culture. Still, changes have taken place, though homophobia is very much alive in the Chicana/o community. Growth of racial and feminist consciousness among Chicanas has helped create a separate space where Chicana lesbians can express themselves openly. During the 1980s, the issue of lesbianism was taken out of the closet both in the United States and Mexico, with Chicana lesbians fighting for recognition as a legitmate part of the community. Debate over feminist and lesbian issues continued within the National Association for Chicano Studies throughout the decade and came to flashpoint at the 1990 NACS conference in Albuquerque.[4] This struggle and others raised the consciousness of many Chicanas (and Chicanos) who had themselves been in an intellectual closet with regard to sexuality. They began to see the contradictions involved in struggling against racism and class inequality while at the same time creating an 'other' within their own feminist universe, and to recognize that the time had come to admit their sins of omission.[5]

Chicana Power?

In terms of political and economic empowerment, nowhere have Chicanas made greater strides than in Los Angeles: some of the most powerful members of the L.A. Latino community are Chicanas. In part, this can be attributed to 'the Molina factor'. Easily the most powerful Chicano/a politico, Gloria Molina represents 1.9 million people and is one of five supervisors overseeing Los Angeles County's $13 billion budget. In 1985, *Ms.* magazine named her 'Woman of the Year', and her influence has not diminished since then.

Elsewhere Marta Escutia, Grace Napolitano, Diane Martínez and Hilda Solis all sit in the state Assembly, a majority of the Latinos/as in that house, while Lucille Roybal-Allard sits in the US Congress. Vicky Castro and Leticia Quesada serve on the Los Angeles Board of Education. All are proven fundraisers, with strong constituencies and media presence. Their number is surely impressive, although, as in the case of the male Chicano officeholders, their voting records and the quality of their leadership are open to criticism. Napolitano and Escutia, for example, have at times taken less than progressive positions, playing the law-and-order card with a heavy hand. And it was still uncertain in mid 1995 whether Latina legislators would defend affirmative action. Despite such limitations, these female politicians have had a positive impact on the lives of working-class Latinas. Aside from the obvious benefit of having them as role models, Latinas in politics have been fairly consistent on gender issues like reproductive rights and domestic violence.

Almost all the Latina powerbrokers are of Mexican extraction. Linda Griego, who ran for mayor of Los Angeles in 1993, is at this writing the head of Rebuild L.A. (RLA). Even more influential is Monica Lozano, publisher of *La Opinión*, the oldest Spanish-language newspaper in Los Angeles, with a circulation 108,000 daily. (Indeed, *La Opinión* has a larger readership than most Mexico City newspapers.) Vilma Martínez, the former head of the Mexican American

Legal Defense and Education Fund (MALDEF), and its present director, Antonia Hernández, have both been leading contenders for appointment to the federal bench and remain major figures in the civil rights establishment. María Elena Durazo, president of Local 11 of the Hotel Employee and Restaurant Employees, and Vivién Bonzo, owner of La Golondrina restaurant, are also among this group. Others like Dr Cynthia Telles, a psychiatry professor and director of the Spanish-Speaking Psychological Program at the University of California, Los Angeles, serve as important advisors to the Latina political network. Telles is an example of a woman from an upper-middle-class background who uses her skills to serve the community. Her father, Raymond Telles, was mayor of El Paso in 1957 and was later named ambassador to Costa Rica by John F. Kennedy and head of the Equal Employment Opportunity Commission by Richard Nixon. As one reporter put it, Cynthia Telles would rather focus on the have-nots 'than spend her days listening to the woes of Angst-ridden yuppies ...'[6]

Chicanas and Latinas: A Socioeconomic Profile

Chicanas and other Latinas are generally younger, poorer and less educated than their Euroamerican, Asian and Black counterparts. According to the 1990 Census, some 53 percent of Latinos and Latinas in Los Angeles were foreign-born, compared with 16 percent of Euroamericans. Just over 50 percent of Latinas aged sixteen and over were employed, compared with 52.6 percent of Black females and just under 55 percent of white women; and 6.3 percent of Latinas/os twenty-five or older held a bachelor of arts degree compared with just under 10 percent of Blacks, and 30.5 percent of white women. Their homes were crowded, with 4.14 people per household compared with 2.27 for Euroamericans, 3.34 for Asians, and 2.72 for African Americans. The median age of Latinas was 25.1 years, compared with 30.8 for Black women, 32.3 for Asian and Pacific Islander females, and 38.8 for Euroamerian women. Close to 34 percent of Latino families fit this profile: a female head of household with no husband present and with related children under eighteen living in poverty.

When it comes to employment, Latinas know that, contrary to popular belief, Los Angeles *does* have a thriving manufacturing sector: deindustrialization and restructuring in L.A.'s case have meant the elimination of high-wage manufacturing jobs, but the low-wage manufacturing sector has grown, based largely on the labor of Latinos/as, and especially of immigrants. They have in effect subsidized the garment and electronics factories in Los Angeles, many of which would otherwise have moved abroad. Their low-paid labor has thus maintained employment for white males and others in management and engineering jobs. Mexicanas and Latinas are concentrated in key industries in Los

Angeles. In 1968, there were fewer than 20 electronics firms in L.A. By the mid 1980s there were 486, the largest concentration in the United States. An estimated 100,000 Latinas, many of them undocumented immigrants, were employed in electronics as assemblers, solderers and other positions in the mid 1980s in Southern California.[7] Exposure to toxic chemicals in these factories makes the work not only hard but dangerous.[8]

Latinas also work in the garment industry, which is the sixth largest manufacturing sector in the nation. This industry takes on additional importance in L.A. Women have always dominated the garment workforce, which since at least the 1920s has been a majority Mexicana. This industry shrank by 25 percent nationwide during 1975–85, while in Los Angeles it expanded by 20 percent, from 62,000 workers to an estimated 75,000. Few garment workers receive health insurance or paid holidays. Like electronics, the garment industry relies on subcontracting to cut costs, in this case, through work at home. (It is estimated that 20 to 30 percent of the work in the garment industry is done by homeworkers.[9]) About 43 percent of women in the California garment industry work in shops of less than 50 employees. They face various cost-cutting strategies such as hiring outside cutting services and by paying by piecework, although in California piecework and homework are supposedly illegal. In Los Angeles, subcontractors are commonly used to achieve superprofits. Fifty percent of subcontractors are Asian (particularly Korean) and a smaller percentage Jewish. There are over 100,000 non-union apparel manufacturing workers in Southern California, the largest concentration of unorganized garment workers in the world.[10]

The service sector saw its highest rate of increase in 1960s and 1970s. There have been relatively few studies on the role of women in L.A.'s service sector, which includes cooking, cleaning and caring for children. Wages are low. The bulk of cleaning crews for office buildings, food preparation, shampooing, manicuring, and banquet services are Latinas. Forty-five percent of Central American families who migrated to California within the previous five years were employed in service industries in 1980s.[11]

Immigrant Women

Close to one-half of the Latino immigrants since 1960 have been women.[12] They provide a large, motivated, inexpensive workforce for service and manufacturing jobs, supporting an expanding export-oriented economy.[13] Their role is essential to keeping wages at levels acceptable to capital and allowing it to replace troublesome workers. They assume the assigned role of a transnational workforce, which since World War II has been increasingly integrated into the world economy. As accurately characterized by Elizabeth Martínez and Ed McCaughan, this workforce is stateless, defenseless, isolated from the rest of the working class and comprised of individual workers who can be deported.[14]

About half the new arrivals worked in manufacturing, while 10 percent went into service jobs. Although Mexicanas have supplied needed labor for the restructuring of the Los Angeles economy, many of them have been unable to get more education and increase their skills in order to move into higher paying jobs. Moreover, according to UCLA urban planners Rebecca Morales and Paul Ong, 'Older Mexican females and better educated Mexican females are not likely to fare better than younger and less educated Mexican females. The fact that wages of Mexican immigrant females are compressed suggests they confront an unyielding wage floor.'[15] Wages were not correlated with either educational attainment or years of labor market experience – in contrast to the experience of recent female immigrants from Europe. According to Morales and Ong, 'Without concerted efforts to change the outcome, most Mexicanas will remain trapped in low-wage jobs.' As Morales and Ong observe, the creation of a permanent class of impoverished Latinas is an avoidable outcome – but current social and economic policies make it inevitable.[16] These woman face incredible odds in the United States. Many of them, especially Mexicanas, come from more traditional rural areas, and their roles as women are transformed by the breakdown of the extended family and the socialization and other care it provided.[17]

It should be emphasized that not all immigrant Latina workers are Mexican. Political and economic factors have also influenced the migration of Salvadorans and other Central Americans, an immigration increased markedly by outbreak of civil war in El Salvador in 1979 and continuous US intervention in Central America during the 1980s: an estimated 500,000 migrated in the 1980s from El Salvador alone. Over 89 percent of Salvadoran refugees, and 95 percent of the immigrants (those arriving before 1980) lived in family-based households. Labor force participation among Salvadoran males was 74 percent for refugees in 1988; for Salvadoran females it was 66.7 percent, much higher than the 52 percent recorded for other Latinas. Salvadoran female refugees also had the highest unemployment, 16.7 percent. Aside from economic deprivation, these refugees suffered from the experiences of government oppression and civil war–induced trauma.[18] Guatemalans differed from Salvadorans; the later have generally concentrated in areas such as Pico-Union, whereas Guatemalans are dispersed throughout Los Angeles. The Salvadorans and other Central Americans did not benefit from the kinds of government assistance that were made available to the Vietnamese and the early waves of Cuban refugees, or for that matter to the latest wave of Eastern Europeans.[19]

Central Americans may have lacked material resources, but they brought with them community organizing and leadership skills, especially the Salvadorans. They had among them a large number of students and professionals who organized an impressive network of support groups, which up until the armistice in El Salvador concentrated on supporting the guerrillas. After the armistice, these organizations turned to providing social and political services in the US. Because of the war and the disruption of traditional family patterns, Central American women have become more socially conscious and are often the main providers for the family. In the Los Angeles area, Central American, and especially Salvadoran, women are noted for their militancy.

Within this historical context, the struggle of these groups for survival and human rights takes on heroic proportions. Many children, especially females, grow up translating for parents and providing the day care that society has refused to offer. In 1990, the *Los Angeles Times* reported on this phenomenon. It highlighted Adriana Anguiano, age seven, who translated for her parents. Her mother and father did not speak English, a skill whose aquisition takes the investment of time and money that immigrants often do not have. They came from Jalisco; they were poor. The mother worked, and the family lived in a small one-bedroom apartment with three children. Adriana answered the phone and passed along job leads to her parents. Candida Fernández, principal of San Fernando Elementary School, reported that children were sometimes pulled out of school to serve as translators – an experience that could be overwhelming for a small child who had to negotiate financial transactions or translate unpleasant medical reports.[20]

There are other problems that Mexican and Latino women and their families must deal with. In order to exist on the pittance that they earn they must often sublet portions of their one-bedroom apartments. In 1992, Lupita Compean, my wife, overheard a Salvadoran mother of three children tell a friend that she was exhausted. She and her husband, a day laborer, had to rent the living room to four men, and she was always rushing home to make sure that her three children were safe. They did not know the boarders well. She had a thirteen-year-old daughter and would awake constantly during the night to see if her daughter had gone to the bathroom and returned safely.

In other cases, immigrant Latinas have formed networks to help each other survive. Libertad Rivera, twenty-eight, from Tepic, Nayarit in Mexico, worked for the Coalition for Humane Immigration Rights of Los Angeles (CHIRLA), educating and uniting domestic servants. Every morning she would board a bus bound for Beverly Hills or other points west of Downtown L.A. These busses carried domestic workers, the vast majority of whom were Latinas, most without documents. Libertad would chat with the occupants – the maids and the nannies. The object was not to organize them – forming a union would be unrealistic – but to advise them on the minimum wage laws and their rights as workers. The goal was to establish a mutual support network – a sort of co-op. These women worked off the books, and had no health insurance, disability compensation or other benefits. They had few employment options and were loathe to call attention to abusive employers.[21]

Libertad and her partner, Rosa Campos, distributed yellow booklets for maids to use in keeping track of their hours. The booklet listed referrals to attorneys (in California, domestic workers who only babysit are not covered by the state minimum wage laws). For example, it is useful for the maids to know that an employer can not legally deduct more than $7 a day for food and $20 weekly for a room. In 1980, 27,000 officially worked as maids, which most experts believe is far below the actual numbers. Some are paid as little as $100 a week to clean, cook, wash and iron for as many as ten adults and children. In lieu of pay, employers promise to obtain documents for workers. Some Latinas have formed co-op cleaning services in order to cope: generally, their plight has been ignored even by progressives and unions.

Others work to help immigrant women make adjustments to a foreign environment. For example, Silvia Esqueda worked for a small stipend, providing house meetings for immigrant women to learn survival skills and health education. The Promotoras Comunitarias program, for which Silvia works, is sponsored by Planned Parenthood because Latinas are the group least likely to receive adequate prenatal care; one-third of L.A.'s Latinas receive no prenatal care during their first trimester of pregnancy. The need for such education is pressing, because 64 percent of the live births to unmarried women under twenty in California are to Latinas and almost half of all births in Los Angles County are to Latinas. The state's lack of concern stands in start contrast to the 'family values' rhetoric of politicians: in 1988, Governor Deukmejian cut $20 million in prenatal care programs for pregnant woman.[22]

AIDS education is also vital. In the US 18 percent of all teenagers infected with HIV are Latinos, while in L.A. 38 percent of the babies and children infected with AIDS are Latino, more than double the Latino share of adult AIDS cases. Many of these children have contracted the virus from their mothers.[23] Dr Eunice Diaz, assistant professor of family medicine at the University of Southern California and a member of the National Commission on AIDS, argues that 'we must educate our women. We must empower them to be assertive in protecting themselves.'[24] The fact is that fear of deportation keeps many undocumented Latinas away from health-care services.

Health care is of great concern, not only to immigrant women but other Latinas. Some 70 percent of all women who die of cervical cancer had never had a Pap smear test. The rate is even higher among undocumented immigrant women: many Latinas feel uncomfortable about the test. Cancer rates per 100,000 women in Los Angeles are 9.5 for whites, 21.7 for Latinas, 17 for Blacks, 12.4 for Chinese women, and 6.6 for Japanese women. The cervical cancer rate per 100,000 is 3.0 for whites, 5.5 for Latinas, 6.6 for Blacks, 4.6 for Chinese women and 3.0 for Japanese women.[25]

Immigrant women are even more vulnerable to sexual harassment and rape than other women, and many cases go unreported because the women fear deportation. A particular problem is sexual abuse by employers.[26] The case of an INS officer who was tried for the sexual assault of six Latinas is also indicative of the problems faced by Latina immigrants. The officer, John E. Riley, was stopped only when a young Salvadoran woman came forward to press charges. He had sex with the women after threatening that he would have them deported, but he was convicted on only one count of false imprisonment and given a three-year sentence. Many of the jurors later said that they believed Riley had committed the rapes but could not be certain beyond reasonable doubt. Six of the women testified. They were afraid and, according to the jurors, they did not make a full case because of that fear. (Was this because they had accents and were women of color?) Riley was found guilty of holding one of the victims in his car against her will; however, that same jury absolved him of kidnaping the woman. The Central American Refugee Center was the sole voice in the Latino community to strongly condemn this travesty.[27]

As in the case of other kinds of victimization, Chicanas have banded together, organizing impressive support networks. One such example is Las Mujeres in the San Fernando Valley, which offers support to battered wives. This Van Nuys–based organization offers counseling to Spanish-speaking women who have been beaten by their husbands or boyfriends – an important service given that domestic violence injures more women than car accidents, muggings and rapes combined. Latinas, especially immigrants, have fewer resources and are more vulnerable than other women; and abusers know it. The problem is further compounded by fear that their husbands will kidnap the children and take them to Mexico or Central America, where family networks and indifference will shield him. Moreover, many of the women are devout Roman Catholics who fear divorce. Las Mujeres was founded by a collective of women, among them Virginia Baldioli, therapist Sandra Baca, and Chicano Studies instructor Claudia Cuevas. According to Cuevas, 'the women easily realize when others are in danger, but they close their eyes to their own situation.'[28]

The inclusion of gender as a factor in the study of immigration tells us a lot about US society. Professor Lourdes Arguelles and Anne M. Rivero point out that gender roles, sexual abuse and oppression based on sexual orientation are often an overlooked factor in transnational migration, and they are factors that drive victims to escape from this type of oppression.[29] Often women come to the United States to escape an abusive marriage, incest or rape; others because of harassment as lesbians. Many researchers avoid these causes of migration because they subvert the image of the idyllic traditional Mexican family, forgetting that Mexicans, like Euroamericans and like other people of color, have sexists and homophobes among them. In the United States, aside from the fear of being deported, they have to put up with the 'impact of the violence and cope with the physical, emotional, and spiritual impacts of gender and sexual abuse and the stresses of migration and resettlement.'[30]

Canada has for some time been grappling with whether the United Nations' definition of a refugee fits battered women and lesbians. According to the UN, a refugee is someone who has 'a well-founded fear of persecution' on the basis of his or her race, religion, nationality, political opinion or membership in a particular social group. Should this definition be extended to include oppression because of a person's gender or sexual orientation? Canada has developed guidelines to include gender persecution. There appears to be a similar movement in the United States, where there is a growing consciousness that deporting battered women back to their home countries and abusive households places them in grave danger.[31]

The Glass Ceiling: Chicana Professionals

As noted, Latinos/as in general made advances during the 1960s and 1970s; the 1980s and 1990s have, however, not been the decades of the Latina. Today's immigrants and minority groups face much higher barriers to economic progress than did immigrants in previous decades. Despite some exceptions, Latinas in general have not moved into the upper echelons of the professions.

The term *glass ceiling* entered America's public conversation less than a decade ago when the *Wall Street Journal's* 'Corporate Woman' column identified a puzzling new phenomenon. 'There seemed to be an invisible – but impenetrable – barrier between women and the executive suite, preventing them from reaching the highest levels of the business world regardless of their accomplishments and merits.' The phrase caught on, defined as invisible, artificial barriers to women's upward mobility: in the *Fortune* 1000 corporations, 97 percent of the senior managers were white males; and 95 percent of senior-level female managers were white. Public discussion led to appointment of the Glass Ceiling Commission by President Bush and congressional leaders under the 1991 Civil Rights Act, and public hearings were held around the country. Testimony before the commission emphasized perceptions, societal barriers, governmental barriers, and a lack of women and minorities in middle management as reasons for their scarcity in top positions. In 1990 only 370,000 women had earned the advanced degrees essential for climbing the corporate ladder.[32]

What the Glass Ceiling Commission's report showed was that Latinas (and women and minorities in general) were not succeeding in private industry; most female and minority professionals and managers work in the public sector and in the 'third sector' – non-government agencies in health, social welfare, and education; legal services, professional services, membership organizations and associations, and libraries and museums. Some 90 percent of Black female professionals, and 83 percent of white and Latina women work in the government or the third sector. Women in general are more likely to work in services, finance, insurance and real estate; 75 percent are employed in those industries, compared with 56 percent of white males. The highest percentage of Latino and Latina managers is found in beverages, soaps and cosmetics and building materials and motor vehicles and parts.

Between 1980 and 1990 the proportion of Latinas\os with bachelor's degrees increased from 7.7 percent to 10 percent. Unfortunately, the scarcity of bilingual education discouraged acquisition of one of the assets that business valued – literacy in Spanish. The commission reported that only 4 percent of Latino\a high school students had gained bilingual capability by taking minimum requirements in high school. This is despite the fact that a corporate executive is quoted by the commission as saying, 'I am desperate to find Hispanics who are Spanish literate. It is so important that I am sending Anglos to school to learn to speak Spanish.'

The report went on to note that gender differences in employment stem largely from the roles that women – all women regardless of color or ethnicity – are expected to play in society. In the minds of many white male managers, business is not where women of any race or ethnicity were meant to be and certainly not as the peers of white men. Latinas were said by the report to be carrying a double burden of resistance. The glass ceiling thus originates in the perceptions of white males that they as a group were losing the corporate game, losing control, and losing opportunity.

One could conclude from reading the commission's report that the government was interested in the lot of women and minorities, and that something would be done. This conclusion might have been tenable if the Republican Party of George Bush and Bob Dole was not at the same time pushing to limit, if not eliminate, affirmative action. The matter becomes further confused by the hoopla of Latinos themselves. The Southwest Voter Research Institute reported that in 1994 Latinas should outnumber their male counterparts in top job categories by 50.5 to 49.5 percent, a prediction seconded by *Hispanic Business*. It reported that the number of Latinos employed in professional and managerial categories had fallen, following the trend among Black males. Some Latinas bought into this game, greeting the report with enthusiasm – even though the actual gains were paltry if measured by the gains made by white women or the status of white men.

Given the obstacles to advancement, credit should be given to Latina network groups, which have worked hard with Latina students, encouraging them to go to college and to persevere in the face of discrimination. Organizations like the National Network of Hispanic Women in Los Angeles, which was founded in 1980, have reached out to college-age students and taught them survival techniques.[33] They have made headway, despite the glass ceiling. Latinas made their greatest inroads in mathematics and computer science, where their numbers grew 470 percent from 1980 to 1990, while the number of Latino men and women combined grew only 170 percent in this category. Although Latinos in general were 10 percent of the national workforce, they held only 1 of every 22 executive and managerial jobs.[34] And in the *Fortune* 1000 companies, 86 percent of the Latino senior executives were male.[35]

OCCUPATION BY GENDER AND NATIVE-BORN
RACIAL/ETHNIC GROUP IN CALIFORNIA

Industry/Gender	White, Non-Latino	Mexican American	African American
Manufacturing			
Male	77.0	.7	1.6
Female	19.7	.3	.8
Transportation			
Male	68.8	.9	2.7
Female	25.3	.4	2.1
Wholesale Trade			
Male	69.8	.7	1.7
Female	26.1	.5	1.2
Retail Trade			
Male	54.3	1.2	3.1
Female	37.8	1.1	2.5
Business Services			
Male	65.4	1.1	1.8
Female	30.1	.4	1.3
Financial Services			
Male	49.4	.7	1.5
Female	44.9	1.0	2.4
Professions			
Male	40.0	.4	2.3
Female	52.4	1.0	3.9
Total			
Male	60.1	.8	2.1
Female	34.4	.7	2.1

SOURCE: *California Affirmative Action Sourcebook.* Tomás Rivera Center, April 1995, p. 8.

Patricia Gándara and Leiani Osugi have recently published an illuminating study on Chicana professionals, complementing with the Glass Ceiling Commission's report.[36] They found that even though female enrollments 'have risen dramatically over the last two decades, society's image of women's roles remains blurry and confused, and many young women fall victim to stereotyped notions of their own potential.'[37] And, they point out, African American women and Latinas remain fixed at the bottom of the opportunity ladder at a time when programs geared towards dismantling racial and ethnic bias are being themselves dismantled. Latina gains can be measured in relation to those of their male counterparts, where they closed the gap between 1976 and 1981. For example, in 1989 they accounted for 11 percent of all the women in the UC senior class, 53 percent of the Latino first-year class and 53 percent of graduating Latinos. In 1983, they had accounted for only 4 percent of of the women in the UC senior class.[38]

FEMALE ENROLLMENT AT THE UNIVERSITY OF CALIFORNIA

	Number of Women	Percent	Number of Latinas	Latinas as a Percent of All Women Enrolled	Latinas as a Percent of All Latinos Enrolled
1983					
Senior Class	9,373	47	471	4.0	44
Master's	5,471		221	4.2	52
Ph.D.	1,248	34	52	5.0	43
Law	943	42	98	10.0	42
Medical	1,773	38	133	7.5	30
1989					
Senior Class	15,076	49	1,662	11	53
Master's	4,486	55	320	6.6	52
Ph.D.	1,921	39	90	4.6	41
Law	932	43	106	11.0	45
Medical	2,285	50	175	7.6	40

SOURCE: Patricia Gándara and Leiani Osugi, 'Educationally Ambitious Chicanas', *Thought & Action* (Fall 1994), p. 10.

California data showed that Latinas are more heavily drawn to the humanities and psychology. Only a fraction of 1 percent of all Ph.D.'s at the University of California were awarded to Latinas in the late 1970s, and barely 4/10ths of 1 percent were awarded to Latinas nationwide. Although the authors scoured the country for Chicana Ph.D.'s, they could not find one Chicana Ph.D. in engineering, physical science, or mathematics. Nor could they find a single Chicana surgeon.

Gándara and Osugi also surveyed Chicanas who had received their J.D., M.D. or Ph.D. degrees, using first-generation and second-generation data to compare the two groups. The respondents were from working-class families, and their parents had less than a high school education. In both groups, 65 to 75 percent of the mothers were wage-earners who contributed to the support of the household. Among the first generation, only 30 percent of the females had a mentor from outside the family, compared with 60 percent of the males. All of the women were good or outstanding students throughout their pre-college years, but despite this fact they received less encouragement than their male counterparts. For example, they often had to fight to get into college-track courses in high school.

Among the second-generation Chicana graduates, 70 percent attended mixed schools or mostly white schools, as had 75 percent of the first-generation students. They cited socialization by middle-class students who talked about going to college as an important factor in their decision to attend. Only one-fourth of this group had a mentor outside the family. Gándara and Osugi concluded that the Chicanas who succeeded had disproportionately attended integrated schools and had extensive contact with non-minority peers. Unfortunately, the second generation was not as heavily recruited by colleges as the first generation had been. [39]

Despite the correlation between expanded educational opportunity and school integration, segregation of Chicanas, as of all Latinos, is increasing across the nation. In 1972/73, 56.6 percent of Latinos attended schools that were predominantly minority; by 1991/92, this proportion had reached 73.4 percent. (By contrast, the proportion of Blacks attending predominantly minority schools increased only slightly during the same period, from 63.6 percent to 66 percent.) At California State University, Northridge, Latino students rarely come from schools that are not predominantly minority (meaning Latino). The exceptions have usually attended a private or a magnet school, or have been bused.

The Barrio

The first chapter noted the class differences among Chicanas and Latinas and the complex relationships between the different classes. As more Chicanas enter the middle class, they will tend see their interests as different from those of the working class. For example, although education in an integrated environment has many benefits, in all probability it does erect differences between many middle-class Latinos and so-called barrio youth.

Chicanas must also contend with the influence of the dominant society, which makes objects of those who fit its concept of beauty. In college, many of the more assimilated Latinas are heavily recruited by sororities. Beer companies regularly use Latinas to promote their drug of choice. At the same time, television often prefers Chicanas to Chicano males as news anchors because they are more acceptable to white male viewers. The tendency to separate the so-called beautiful people from the 'other' is common. These news anchors and models are both the victims and beneficiaries of the sexism in society: even when they are highly qualified, like Linda Alvárez of KCBS-TV, they are kept in their place, objectified and packaged as a commodity. *Machismo* is common among all races, and as Elizabeth Martínez points out, is not some weird Mexican phenomenon: it is a 'form of male supremacist ideology serving capital accumulation.'[40]

In a similar way, *cholas* are mystified as dependents of male gang members – a modern version of the old gang moll. This image has retarded actual study of female gang members, who contrary to the stereotype have motivations different from those of their male counterparts. In reality there have always been female cliques – young girls who hung around with street boys, some even joining in getting drunk or high and in gang-fighting. More commonly they hung around social or car clubs, which are different from gangs. The *Pachucas* of the 1940s were not gang members but part of the zoot-suit experience. In that respect they were rebels; they had not yet developed into gangs. The phenomenon of *cholas* affiliating with street gangs is recent; even as late as the 1970s it was considered unlady-like, un-Mexican. The dialectics of multiple marginality apply to those now active in gangs: they are associated with serious alcohol or drug abuse, and some gangbanging occurs.[41]

Joan Moore is one of the few Euroamerican sociologists to seriously study *cholas* and *tecatas*, women heroin users.[42] She writes that the *tecatas* frequently come from broken homes: 'There were higher proportions of girls' homes with no workers (up to 24 percent in the more recent cliques) and fewer fathers and more mothers worked.' Occasionally fathers departed, but the families were not desperately poor. According to Moore, there is no proof that gangs are purely the products of immigration or of poverty.

Gangs are in fact the barrio children whose lives are most intensely affected by marginality; they are also more at risk to join gangs as the economy worsens. Moore found that not all of the female gangs are alike – some are female auxiliaries of male gangs, while others are independent. One finding is particularly interesting: Moore challenges the commonly held belief that *tecatas* are turned on to drugs soley by their boyfriends or husbands. According to Moore, gender is important when it comes to differences in deviant behavior in general and substance abuse in particular. 'The strength of traditional gender norms probably helps account for the fact that Hispanic women have low rates of substance abuse.'[43] The use of heroin among Chicanas is unusual. Gender is defined, and deviance is produced, through social interaction, and traditional gender values label women harshly in the barrio, defining street females in highly pejorative terms that tend to isolate them. Because of such a harsh stigma, there is little interest in tracing specific drug-related behaviors to families of origin. The convenient assumption is that husbands or boyfriends are responsible. While this maybe true in some cases, Moore contends that the emphasis on boyfriends neglects the role of the family and adolescent peer groups, and suggests that both the family and society must be studied to understand the causes of the *tecatas'* isolation.

In this context, the failure of the experts to recognize the difference between male and female gang members and male and female drug users victimizes the females in both groups. According to stereotypes, *tecatas* are in gangs and addiction is gang-related. In the process, the female becomes faceless, since society finds it more acceptable for a boy to be on the street than a girl, who, without doubt must be a bad girl, a social judgement that further isolates her.[44]

The vast majority of *tecatas* in fact came from families some of whose members had been arrested. One quarter of all tecatas had fathers who were addicts; 14 percent had mothers who were addicted. Many came from violent homes where they saw fathers beat their mothers. About a third had been victims of sexual abuse.[45] Almost half the *tecatas* had themselves been in prison, an unusually high figure even for gang women. Almost all the non-*tecatas* reared their children, versus only half the *tecatas*. Most of the mothers who had been in gangs underplayed gang activities and did not want their children to join gangs – but even so, they did see positive sides to gangs such as teaching loyalty, self-esteem and survival tactics.[46]

Moore notes that researchers have ignored the Chicana *chola* and *tecata* and that the media have purposely dehumanized gang members by not pointing out the positive effects of gangs on the lives of their members. For example, male gang members will acknowledge females as part of a family, a concept that is completely absent in the media treatment of Chicano gangs. To include girls in the portrait of the gang would be to humanize it; and 'it might also challenge simplified and comfortable notions about women ...' The stereotype of gang criminality defines the gang members as 'them' – as safely not like other kids.[47]

Constructing a Historical Memory

Despite the growing consciousness among Chicanas, they do not share a common historical memory. Establishing enough moral authority in the community to restructure conferences is certainly an achievement, but can Chicanas build a consciousness of the past and forge a vision of the future? Part of the problem is that it is difficult to change the culture of institutions. For example, Chicanas have become active within the rank and file of the labor movement, and their work has brought about changes in individual attitudes. However, because so little written history is available about past struggles and Chicanas' participation in them, Chicanas during the 1980s had to struggle against the same assumptions about gender, race and class that were prevalent among white male and female chauvinist organizers in the 1930s, when the great International Ladies Garment Workers Union organizer Rose Pesotta encountered opposition to her work in organizing Mexican women garment workers. Pesotta wrote that when she announced she would organize Mexican women in L.A.'s 150 dress factories, which employed some 2,000 workers, about 75 percent of them Mexican women, the reaction was:

> [They] felt pessimistic – 'Mexican women could never be organized.' The skeptics reminded me that Los Angeles garment manufacturers preferred Mexicans to others because they would 'work for a pittance and could endure any sort of treatment.' I contended that Mexican dressmakers were normal human beings, who simply needed honest and intelligent guidance. I had worked with them the previous spring and we got along well.[48]

The stereotype that Mexican women are unorganizable still lingers in the 1990s in Los Angeles. One of the reasons is obvious. Chicanas and others are denied knowledge of their history, and of their heroines. They are the victims of scholarly neglect and racist assumptions, which up until recently went unchallenged. For those reasons, an analysis of Chicanas and Latinas in Los Angeles is difficult. The paucity of sources on this highly important subject often makes it difficult to place gender into an analytical framework. Even a simple time-line of the activities of Chicanas either in the US generally or Los Angeles in particular does not exist.[49]

The history of the general Chicano population in Los Angeles has been pieced together and defined by Chicano male historians.[50] This work, although it helps us to understand the past, does not define gender issues. Two excellent works have been written by Vicky Ruiz, who wrote about Chicanas in the canneries during the 1930s, and Mary Pardo, who compared Chicana leadership in Monterey Park and East Los Angeles. The work of Rebecca Morales is also notable in defining Latinas in the present economic life of the region. These studies, however, explain specific periods or events but do not define the universe of Chicanas in Los Angeles.

History is, of course, usually written by scholars who are trained in the methods of academia. The tendency is for theory to eclipse 'antiquarian' methods necessary for the construction of an authentic historical memory. In this case, Chicana history is reduced to counting the number of Chicanas in the workforce. Academic questions are quantified and successes and failures defined by numbers. There was one Chicana officeholder in 1982; in 1990 there were five, and that is a 500 percent increase. Missing is the element of struggle, which enables us to evaluate the results of Chicana leadership rather than simply count numbers.

A related danger is that we may see the cure for sexsim soley in terms of having more Chicanas in significant political and economic positions. The tendency among some Chicana/o scholars has been to deny that Chicanas have been victims, insisting instead that they have been participants and that they have overcome despite overwhelming odds. There are aspects of this argument that are true, of course: there are single mothers and working-class families whose children make it through college. However, as heroic as the Chicano/a struggle is, Chicanas are still victims. Racism, sexism and poverty still victimize them, and their successes are not products of the system. Yes, Chicanos in general and Chicanas in particular have survived the past two decades of economic restructuring – but at a price. Having more Chicanas make it as politicians and business executives does not mean that climbing the class ladder can be the solution for everyone. And because some Chicanas do not have the aptitude for college does not mean that they do not merit a decent wage, job security and healthcare. Indeed, it is a tribute to the Chicana sense of struggle that many of them are still optimistic about the future: but this optimism is, again, a determination to succeed in the face of the system – not because of it. Truth be told, it is just as hard for a working-class Chicanita to become another Gloria Molina as it is for a young African American male tossing a basketball around to become a star in the National Basketball Association; and just as likely.

Notes

1. Patrick J. McConnell and Carla Rivera, 'Latinos Poorer Than Other Groups But Have Drive to Succeed, Study Says', *Los Angeles Times*, 12 Feb. 1993; McConnell and Rivera, 'Economic Woes and Immigrants', *Los Angeles Times*, 17 Sept. 1993.

2. Sarah Deutsch, 'Gender, Labor History, and Chicano/a Ethnic Identity', *Frontiers*, vol. 14, no. 2 (1994), pp. 1–9.

3. Lilly Wei, 'The Power of Feminist Art: The American Movement of the 1970s, History and Impact', *Art in America* (Jan. 1995), pp. 36–7.

4. Deena J. Gonzalez, 'Malinche as Lesbian: A Reconfiguration of 500 Years of Resistance', in Gloria J. Romero and Lourdes Arguelles, eds, 'Culture & Conflict in the Academy: Testimonies from a War Zone', *California Sociologist: A Journal of Sociology and Social Work*, vol. 14, nos 1–2 (Winter/Summer 1991), pp. 93.

5. Paula Gliddings, *When and Where I Enter: The Impact of Black Women on Race and Sex in America* (New York: Bantam Books, 1984), p. 304; David James Rose, 'Coming Out, Standing Out: Hispanic American Gays and Lesbians', *Hispanic* (June 1994), p. 44.

6. Elizabeth Mehren, 'Coming into Her Own: Cynthia Ann Telles Inherited a Zeal for Public Service', *Los Angeles Times*, 13 April 1992.

7. Kristine M. Zentgraf, 'Gender, Immigration, and Economic Restructuring in Los Angeles', in Marta López-Garza, 'Immigration and Economic Restructuring: The Metamorphosis of Southern California', *California Sociologist* (Summer 1989), pp. 124–5; Rebecca Morales and Paul Ong, 'Immigrant Women in Los Angeles', *Economic and Industrial Democracy*, vol. 12, no. 1 (Feb. 1991), pp. 65–81; Benjamin Mark Cole, 'Do Immigrants Underpin L.A. Business World?' *Los Angeles Busi-*

ness Journal, 27 May 1991.

8. McConnell and Rivera, 'Latinos Poorer Than Other Groups'; McConnell and Rivera, 'Economic Woes and Immigrants'.

9. Cole, 'Do Immigrants Underpin L.A. Business World?'

10. Zentgraf, 'Gender, Immigration, and Economic Restructuring', pp. 125–7.

11. Ibid., pp. 128–9.

12. Martin Carnoy, Hugh M. Daley and Raul Hinojosa Ojeda, 'The Changing Economic Position of Latinos in the US Labor Market Since 1939', in Rebecca Morales and Frank Bonilla, eds, *Latinos in a Changing US Economy: Comparative Perspectives in Growing Inequality* (Newbury Park, Calif.: Sage Publications, 1993), pp. 28–35.

13. Zentgraf, 'Gender, Immigration, and Economic Restructuring', pp. 113–14. Héctor L. Delgado, *New Immigrants, Old Unions: Organizing Undocumented Workers in Los Angeles* (Philadelphia: Temple University Press, 1993) is an interesting work on Mexican immigrant workers.

14. Elizabeth Martínez and Ed McCaughan, 'Chicanas and Mexicanas Within a Transnational Working Class', in Adelaida R. Del Castillo, ed., *Between Borders: Essays on Mexicana/Chicana History* (Los Angeles: Floricanto Press, 1990), pp. 31–52.

15. Rebecca Morales and Paul Ong, 'The Illusion of Progress: Latinos in Los Angeles', in Morales and Bonilla, pp. 69–70.

16. Rebecca Morales and Paul Ong, 'Immigrant Women in Los Angeles', *Economic and Industrial Democracy*, vol. 12, no. 1 (February 1991), pp. 65–81; Cole, 'Do Immigrants Underpin L.A. Business World?'.

17. Two interesting books on the Mexican American and Latino/a family are Norma Williams, *The Mexican American Family: Tradition and Change* (Dix Hills, N.Y.: General Hall, 1990), and Ruth E. Zambrano, ed., *Understanding Latino Families: Scholarship, Policy, and Practice* (Thousand Oaks, Calif.: Sage, 1995).

18. Claudia Dorrington, 'Central American Refugees in Los Angeles: Adjustment of Children and Families', in Zambrana, ed., *Understanding Latino Families*, p. 111.

19. Claudia Dorrington, Ruth E. Zambrano, and Georges Sabagh, 'Salvadorans in the United States: Immigrants and Refugees Demographic and Socio-Economic Profiles', *California Sociologist* (Summer 1989), pp. 137–60.

20. Michael Quintanilla, 'The Littlest Interpreters: Some Bilingual Children Must Grow Up Fast', *Los Angeles Times*, 1 March 1990.

21. Tracy Wilkinson, 'Column One: To Protect Those Who Must Service', *Los Angeles Times*, 12 Feb. 1992.

22. Claire Spiegel, 'Prenatal Care in L.A. Worsening, Report Concludes', *Los Angeles Times*, 12 July 1988.

23. Jill L. Sherer. 'Neighbor to Neighbor: Community Health Workers Educate Their Own', *Hospitals & Health Networks*, 20 Oct. 1994, p. 52.

24. Victor F. Zonana, 'A Latina Response to AIDS', *Los Angeles Times*, 6 March 1990.

25. Shari Roan, '4,600 Deaths a Simple Yearly Test Might Prevent', *Los Angeles Times*, 4 Oct. 1994.

26. Sebastian Rotella, 'Abuses Hound Latino Immigrants', *Los Angeles Times*, 30 Dec. 1991.

27. Sebastian Rotella, 'INS Agent to Stand Trial in Rape of Latinas', *Los Angeles Times*, 31 Jan. 1991; Michael Connelly, 'Jury Acquits INS Officer in Rapes', *Los Angeles Times*, 28 Feb. 1992; 'Rights Group Accuses Border Patrol of Widespread Abuse', *Legal Intelligencer*, 16 April 1995.

28. Maryann Hammers, 'Abused Women Find Solace in Each Other – And in Spanish', *Los Angeles Times*, 30 Jan. 1992; 'Helping Hands: Reaching Out to End Abuse', *Star Tribune*, 30 Oct. 1994.

29. Lourdes Arguelles and Anne M. Rivero, 'Gender/Sexual Orientation, Violence and Transnational Migration: Conversations with Some Latinas We Think We Know', *Urban Sociology*, vol. 22, nos 3–4 (1993), pp. 259.

30. Argueles and Rivero, 'Gender/Sexual Orientation', p. 265.

31. Mary Williams Walsh, 'Battered Women as Refugees', *Los Angeles Times*, 23 Feb. 1993.

32. 'For Business: Making Full Use of the Nation's Human Capital: Fact-Finding Report of the Federal Glass Ceiling Commission Released by the Department of Labor Department', 16 March 1995, in *Daily Labor Report*, 17 March 1995, Special Supplement Dir. No. 52, Washington, D.C.

33. Carol Klieman, 'Hispanics Find Models', *Chicago Tribune*, 15 Sept. 1989.

34. Donna K. H. Walters, 'Latinas Gaining on Latinos in Management, Survey Finds', *Los Angeles Times*, 1 April 1994.

35. 'For Business'; *California Affirmative Action Sourcebook*, Tomás Rivera Center, April 1995, p. 4.

36. Patricia Gándara and Leiani Osugi, 'Educationally Ambitious Chicanas', *Thought & Action* (Fall 1994), p. 7–35.

37. Ibid., p. 7.

38. Ibid., p. 8.

39. Ibid., pp. 23–33.

40. Martínez and McCaughan, *Chicanas and Mexicanas*, p. 52.

41. James Diego Vigil, *Barrio Gangs: Street Life and Identity in Southern California* (Austin, Tex.: University of Texas Press, 1988), pp. 100–102.

42. The latter is a pejorative term in Latin America and Mexico that generally refers to Indians or lower-class people of mixed race.

43. Joan Moore, 'The *Chola* Life Course: Chicana Heroin Users and the Barrio Gang', *The International Journal of the Addictions*, vol. 29, no. 9 (1994), p. 1115.

44. Ibid., p. 1118.

45. Ibid., p. 1120.

46. ibid., pp. 1115–26.

47. Joan Moore, *Going Down to the Barrio: Homeboys and Homegirls in Change* (Philadelphia: Temple University Press, 1991), pp. 86, 88–9, 136–9; Dan Weikel, 'War on Crack Targets Minorities over Whites', *Los Angeles Times*, 21 May 1995.

48. Rose Pesotta, *Bread upon the Waters* (New York: Dodd, Mead, 1944), pp. 20–21; John Lassett and Mary Tyler, *The ILGWU in Los Angeles, 1907–1988* (Inglewood, Calif.: Ten Star Press, 1989) gives an overview of the ILGWU in Los Angeles. Unfortunately, the book does not include an in-depth analysis of white chauvinism by either the International or the white rank and file toward Latinas/os.

49. In a sense this is how I attempted to define Chicano history in my book, *Occupied America: A History of Chicanos*, 3d edn (New York: Harper & Row, 1988), which attempted to periodize Chicano history. Different editions defined the history of Chicanos generally – flawed by the sources available at the time of publication as well as by my own lack of consciousness. Elizabeth Martínez in her *500 Years of Chicano History in Pictures* and Juan Gómez-Quiñones in his *Chicano Politics: Reality & Promise 1940–1990* also establish this chronology.

50. Antonio Ríos Bustamante, Pedro Castillo, Richard Griswold del Castillo, Alberto Camarillo, Ricardo Romo, and George Sánchez. I attempted to add to this definition in *A Community Under Siege. A Chronicle of Chicanos East of the Los Angeles River, 1945–1975* by piecing together, using community newspapers, that definition of a Chicano community in postwar East Los Angeles.

1 0

México Lindo and NAFTA

In 1990, at least one out of three Angelenos was of Mexican descent. It is therefore natural that – aside from economic and historical links – Mexico has occupied a very special place in the *corazón*, the heart of *Nuestra Señora de Los Angeles*. This sense of connection has, however, been marred by an uneven relationship between the two countries, including a history of border conflict and of racism towards Mexicans living north of the Río Bravo. Even the Mexican dictator Porfirio Díaz, so friendly to US investors, once said, 'Pobre México, tan lejos de Díos y tan cerca a los Estados Unidos' ('Poor Mexico, so far from God and so close to the United States'). That powerful northern neighbor overshadowed *México Lindo* – Beautiful Mexico, as the song says, setting the tone for the relationship between the two peoples, both within and outside of the United States.

Mexico did not have an easy time in the 1980s. Dr Jesús Chavarría, publisher of *Hispanic Business*, noted that in 1986 an earthquake cost the country approximately \$4 billion in damages, a drop in oil prices cost another \$6 to \$8 billion, and the foreign debt had leaped approximately \$100 billion since 1981.[1] As the economic crisis deepened, the Mexican government began dealing differently with the Mexican diaspora. From the Revolution of 1910 to World War II, Mexican consuls had been active in defending the rights of Mexicans in the United States. This changed during the presidency of Miguel Alemán – with both the public and private sectors often displaying indifference and even an antipathy to Mexicans living abroad. It changed again as the Chicanos in the US formed national organizations and the civil rights movement gave importance to the 'other' – and a small but increasingly affluent middle class developed, including a number of elected and appointed officials.[2] President Luis Echeverría and Raza Unida Party leader José Angel Gutiérrez met in the early 1970s and, as a result, the Mexican government sponsored a scholarship program for Chicanos to study in Mexico.

Such informality, however, gave way to intensive efforts by the administration of Carlos Salinas de Gortari to recruit Latino political and business leaders in the US to promote Mexican interests. This alliance proved especially valuable during Mexico's campaign for passage of the North American Free Trade Agreement (NAFTA).

As part of that campaign, the Mexican government wined and dined Chicano leaders and presented them with the Aguila Azteca award and other honors.[3] It also contributed to US research on Mexico by endowing various universities – for example, giving over $130,000 to endow the Luis Leal Chair in Chicano Studies at the University of California, Santa Barbara, and contributing substantial funds to the University of California's Mexus program.

For their part, Chicanos and Chicanas have always been concerned about Mexico's image and have often been defensive about any criticism of *México Lindo*, no matter how valid. They have of course hated the outright racism of a Jesse Helms, but have sometimes also found themselves defending the poverty of Tijuana and putting all the blame on the United States (which certainly deserved much of their criticism, given that through the International Monetary Fund and World Bank, it had subverted the economic development of the motherland).[4]

Some Chicanos have also been sensitive to accusations of being disloyal to the United States, often exaggerating their American patriotism to counter any such charges. Indeed, the demand for bilingual education has been seen by many Euroamericans as a form of disloyalty or separatism. The political commentator Eric Sevareid reflects this suspicion: 'I believe that if we come to have a second language which coincides with a territorial section of the country, as for example the Southwest, we could have a separatist movement similar to that in Quebec.'[5]

Caught in the middle, some Chicanos have been reluctant both to criticize Mexico, lest they encourage Mexico-bashing, and to praise Mexico, lest they be considered unpatriotic. However, the Chicano Movement, and later the movement against US intervention in Central America, built a core of people who developed an interest in human rights issues as they related to Mexico. This created two poles of thought: on the one hand, Chicano business executives still thinking in terms of *México Lindo*, and on the other those activists supporting insurgencies within the country such as that of the Zapatistas in Chiapas.

Criticism of Mexico – no matter how painful – is necessary: '*México Lindo*' refers to a people and the land they live in, not necessarily to their government. It would be intellectually dishonest for Chicano scholars, for instance, to absolve the Partido Revolucionario Institucional (PRI) of responsibility for the mass exodus of Mexicans, especially from the presidency of Miguel Alemán to the present, when the PRI's corruption and mismanagement have played, and continue to play, a major role in Mexico's economic instability.

The PRI's *Pocho*-Bashing

In the spring of 1988 the California Democratic Party passed a resolution ask-ing the US government to pressure Mexico to respect human rights and to give Mexican citizens who reside outside the country the right to vote. The plat-form resolution, proposed by the Chicano caucus, also asked 'the North American government to intervene in the Mexican presidential elections of July of this year.' Sergio Muñoz, then executive editor of *La Opinión*, who re-ported the event, quoted Dr Jorge Bustamante, a well-known Mexican aca-demic and president of El Colegio de la Frontera Norte, as noting in reply that the Mexican election was an internal affair of the Mexican government.

La Opinión then published three articles by Bustamante attacking supporters of the Democratic Party resolution. Bustamante's articles also ran in *La Jornada* and *El Excélsior*, two well-read Mexico City newspapers.[6] The harshness of his attack destroyed Chicano illusions about a special relationship with Mexico: 'Just because Chicanos have Spanish surnames, that does not give them the cre-dentials to understand what is happening in Mexico.' According to Bus-tamante, Chicanos would not be in solidarity 'with the interests of the majority of Mexicans' if they criticized Mexican affairs (which many readers interpreted as a reference to the PRI). Bustamante went on to scold Chicanos, telling them that when they proposed solutions to Mexico's problems, such as the California Democratic Party resolution, 'they think like any other *gringo*.' He hit below the belt when he reminded Chicanos that they were citizens of a nation that has historically been Mexico's worst enemy. Bustamante, a strong supporter of the rights of Mexican immigrants, had to be aware that many Mexicans emi-grate to the US because of the Mexican government's mismanagement of the country's economy, and that many Chicano leaders and organizations had for years criticized the violation of the human rights of Mexicans. Bustamante had served as an adviser on Chicano affairs to every Mexican president since Luis Echevarría, often serving as the messenger to Chicanos on behalf of the ruling party's elite and as the key broker between Chicano intellectuals and the gov-ernment.[7] As a master rhetorician, Bustamante turned his defense of Mexican sovereignty into a defense of the PRI: any criticism of the PRI was an attack on the Mexican people. He urged Chicanos to take their Mexican identity out of 'the closet', thus playing blatantly on Chicano nationalism.[8]

Bustamante's articles went unnoticed by monolingual Anglos in Los Ange-les. But *La Opinión*, along with the Spanish-language radio and electronic me-dia, formed an internal network that increasingly identified with issues affecting the business community (as well as the immigrant community). In the case of Proposition 187, the paper served as a voice for the Latino peoples in Los Angeles. Though far from progressive, this network was nevertheless the only vehicle for reporting on Chicanos and Latinos in L.A. – an especially important factor after the *Los Angeles Times* turned radically to the right, censoring the content and form of Chicano and other Latino demands. It was also the only vehicle that expressed the interaction of Chicano–Mexican relations.

For its part, the Mexican government, largely through the intercession of spokespeople like Bustamante, fully understood the value of the US Spanish-language media and worked to advance its interests through those channels. It was here, out of sight of the Anglo population, that Bustamante could place so much importance on such an insignificant incident. Indeed, the attention was in a certain way flattering, given that the US government totally ignored what Chicanos thought or said. In the larger context, the PRI was concerned in the late 1980s and early 1990s about the support that the Partido de la Revolución Democratica (PRD) and its candidate Cuahtémoc Cárdenas had among Chicanos and Mexicans in the United States, especially in Los Angeles, where Joe Sánchez, one of the authors of the California Democratic Party resolution, was a major contributor to the PRD.

México Lindo in the New World Order

Chicanos and Mexicanos in the United States actively protested the official results of the 1988 election in Mexico, which designated Carlos Salinas de Gortari as the new president instead of Cuahtémoc Cárdenas. Like many, perhaps most, people in Mexico, Chicanos believed that Salinas had won thanks to widespread fraud. Supporters of the Partido de Acción Nacional (PAN) were also angry and disgruntled.[9]

Salinas proceeded to implement his neoliberal program for resolving Mexico's acute economic problems, one that bore a chilling resemblance to the 'positivist' program of dictator Porfirio Díaz.[10] Foreign investment played a key role in Salinas's vision for Mexico, along with attempts to entice back Mexican capital that had left the country. To make Mexico more attractive to capital, Salinas moved toward deregulation of the economy and privatization of state-owned enterprises, thus abandoning any pretense of loyalty to the objectives of the Mexican Revolution for which his party was named. Conditions improved for the rich, as indicated by the leap in the number of Mexican billionaires from four to twenty-four, while the gap broadened between rich and poor.[11] Nevertheless, many Latinos in the US – like the rest of the population – believed Salinas was a smart man doing a good job. A *Los Angeles Times* poll in 1991 showed 51 percent of those polled approved of Salinas's performance in office.[12]

After the 1982 economic crisis, the Mexican government had increasingly aligned its foreign and economic policies. It showed a willingness to condemn Manuel Noreiga even before President Bush's invasion of Panama, and it offered to increase oil exports to the US during 'Operation Desert Storm'. At the request of US officials, it deported 658 Chinese immigrants aboard ships off Baja California, helping prevent them from reaching US shores. Such actions, and the high cost of economic growth, troubled many Mexicanos in the US. The Mexican Consulate in Los Angeles was frequently picketed by supporters of the PRD and human rights activists. Chicano involvement in political issues affecting Mexico would accelerate as the debate about the North American Free Trade Agreement heated up.[13]

The North American Free Trade Agreement

In 1986 Mexico joined GATT (the General Agreement on Tariffs and Trade), the international body committed to expanding by eliminating import quotas and licenses and slashing tariffs. Mexico eagerly promoted NAFTA, which called for the creation of a regional trading bloc of Canada, the US, and Mexico as a way of breaking down trade barriers. The downside, however, was that NAFTA shifted power from government to the corporate sector, limiting government's capacity to define and achieve national development goals.[14]

Although NAFTA was in the making during the 1980s, the debate over its ratification did not begin in earnest until 1991.[15] The Bush administration gained a tremendous edge by railroading Congress into putting the NAFTA negotiations on the 'fast track'. In effect, 'fast track' meant that congressional debate and criticism of the treaty would be limited. The Bush administration also adopted the position that critics of NAFTA were enemies of Mexico: this line further inhibited debate on whether the agreement served the interests of working-class people on either side of the border.

Chicano organizations such as the National Council of La Raza (NCLR) bought into Bush's feigned concern for *México Lindo* and supported the agreement. NCLR ranked the interests of the Latino business community high among its concerns: NAFTA, according to its rationale, would give an export-market advantage to Latino-owned businesses in the US. Unfortunately, the NCLR responded to Bush's request to 'Trust me' without fully considering the needs of working-class Latinos.

In addition to self-interest, nationalism played a role in the Chicano business community's support of NAFTA. Salinas billed free trade with the US and Canada as the key to Mexico's future, and packaged the agreement in a mystic nationalism that pretended to defend Mexican national sovereignty. Questions about effects on the environment, human rights, political reform, and Mexican workers and the indigenous populations were swept under the rug.

The debate over NAFTA marked a new stage in Chicano–Mexican relations. The Mexican government, with the approval of the Bush administration, actively lobbied the Chicano community for support. Like the Republican Party in the US, the PRI focused on the Chicano middle class, which was economically and socially compatible with the Mexican government and its own upper-middle-class business community. They were quite flattered to be meeting the Mexican president and dining with cabinet ministers – something that did not happen in the United States.[16]

The National Council of La Raza and other Chicano and Latino organization naturally expected more influence as a reward for their support of the Bush administration. The White House had actively courted Chicano support for the passage of 'fast track' authorization in Congress, and Chicano organizations delivered. Immediately after passage of the 'fast track bill', Chicano leaders announced that the doors to the White House were finally open to Chicanos. This optimistic tone quickly changed, however, as the ardor of the Bush administration chilled: according to Washington-based Latino lobbyists, Bush shut Latino organizations out of the free-trade negotiations.[17]

Even the NCLR felt the ingratitude of the Bush administration. The council had planned to celebrate its new-found influence at its July convention in Houston, and invited Commerce Secretary Robert Mosbacher to be the keynote speaker. Also at the convention, the NCLR fully expected to receive the Census Bureau's Foresight Award for distinguished service for its contribution to boosting Latino participation during the 1990 Census.[18] In the end, Mosbacher did not even show up, sending a flunky in his place, nor did NCLR get the Foresight Award at the convention.

La Opinión's executive editor, Sergio Muñoz, also supported NAFTA. He wrote: 'Now that a free-trade agreement between Mexico, the United States and Canada is in the works, questions about our common future are being raised. One of the most interesting is, can there be a common North American identity among the three countries …?' His answer was yes. Muñoz's conclusion was in many ways naive, however. Muñoz came to the United States as an adult with an education and social background not shared by most Mexican immigrants. According to him, 'An obsessive fixation with historical episodes, intolerable racism and extreme nationalism are some obstacles that stand in the way of a healthy common identity.' He encouraged Chicanos to forget about the past, to recognize that the Euroamerican has changed, and to realize that Chicano malcontents were the only thing standing in the way of cooperation.[19] Muñoz symbolized the euphoria and even pandering surrounding NAFTA: his vision of México Lindo reflected the interests of the ruling party, to which he had close ties.[20]

Meanwhile, Salinas lobbied heavily for NAFTA's passage, even meeting with California Governor Pete Wilson, a long-time Mexico-basher. Wilson believed that Mexican dollars were acceptable, but that Mexicans were not. Wilson remained true to this position, attacking those who opposed NAFTA while denouncing laws that gave undocumented workers rights to public assistance.[21]

El Financiero's Jorge Carrasco Araizaga wrote that Salinas was attempting to sell NAFTA by associating it with the Asian export-oriented model of development. According to Carrasco, Salinas wanted to provide Mexican industry with a North American market of 360 million people, a market that had seen increased competition from abroad, especially from Japan.[22] Salinas estimated that US companies could invest some $300 billion in Mexico to help them compete with their Asian rivals. The growth of the 'Asian Tigers' depended on foreign trade surpluses to finance further investment and export drives. To achieve this virtuous cycle, the Asian countries used a number of tools: administered currencies, tariff and regulatory barriers, targeted investment strategies, and close cooperation between government and major corporate combines. In the case of Mexico, the lack of a trade surplus would leave it with insufficient capital to develop internally; it would be more and more dependent on the United States for investment.

What separated Mexico from the Asian model was the participation in Asia of a strong state with the capacity to control the process of economic growth. The lack of a strong government limited Mexico's ability to stimulate savings and direct investment into productive industries for the future. It was possible to sell off state-owned properties to the private sector, but how would these resources then contribute to economic growth? The accumulation of surpluses and national investment was essential. Mexico had to invest in education and health to create a more productive workforce, among other projects (but efforts to do so were being scuttled by IMF and World Bank austerity programs). Would NAFTA enable Mexico to alter these trends, producing a trade surplus and encouraging investment?

The agreement was more advantageous to the United States than to Mexico. The Mexican market was more concentrated, and US industry much more diversified. The US would in fact use NAFTA as leverage to extract better conditions from other, more important, trading partners. NAFTA would certainly help the US in its GATT negotiations, and it would surely help in negotiations with the rest of Latin America.[23] Mexico, on the other hand, would be tied to the United States, although it had the advantage of being close to US markets.[24]

During this period Salinas pushed through changes in Mexico's constitution that made Mexico even more business-friendly. The most controversial was changing Article 27, the legal basis for the nation's *ejidos*, communal lands, by making it possible for *ejido* members to sell or mortgage their land – thus burying the Mexican Revolution. As one Mexican scholar put it, 'the death of the Mexican Revolution at least deserved a formal farewell.'[25] Blass Padilla, a small farmer in the state of Morelos, said of the changes in the famous Article 27: 'My father left me this *ejido* that was won by force of arms. It is something that I won't sell. It is part of my patrimony that my fathers left to me and I'll leave it to my children.' Another farmer said: 'The people will sell their land because they are tired of living in poverty and with the money they receive for their property they think they'll live well. It's all a trap. The government is sneaky ... very sneaky ...'[26]

From the government's perspective, the reform of Article 27 was necessary to end government subsidies to agriculture – surely an IMF demand. In theory, everyone from the *ejido* owner to the *latifundista* would get richer: the revised Article 27 would allow the producer more 'flexibility'. It would give the producer more power to make decisions, and, according to the *técnicos*, treat the farmer like an adult. The question was, could the *ejido* tradition be broken without a mass exodus to the city? In reality, breaking the *ejido* structure would still leave the small farmer vulnerable to the whims of local *caciques*, bosses. It would not attack poverty and an unjust judicial system. This reform had to occur before development could take place.[27]

During the NAFTA debate, the Mexican government used the *México Lindo* card blatantly on the issue of the environment. Criticism that NAFTA would encourage more damage to the environment because Mexico lacked effective environmental policies was, according to NAFTA spokespersons, Mexico-bashing. Nevertheless, the prospect of NAFTA did prod Mexican officials into making a show of doing something about industrial contamination. The Secretaria de Desarrollo Urbano y Ecología (SEDUE) was formed to deal with the smog in Mexico City, among other projects.[28] But SEDUE's capabilites were limited. In 1991, its budget was about 2 percent of the US Environmental Protection Agency budget (at a time when the Mexican government was paying millions in public relations fees to build support for a free trade agreement). Regulation had been further curtailed by the IMF's insistence on cutting social costs to meet budget targets.[29]

The *Los Angeles Times* ran a four-part series on Mexico's environment during the third week of November 1991. Part of the series dealt with conditions along the border, where US corporations had set up plants in Mexico to save on wages, which were 13 percent of US levels, and to avoid US environmental standards.[30] One subject was David Finegood, a furniture maker who had frequently been cited by the L.A. Air Quality Management District for leaving solvent-soaked rags in barrels, spewing emissions into the air, and causing an accident that resulted in the evacuation of 2,000 people. Finegood moved his 600-worker furniture plants from Compton and Carson to Tijuana, where he found a business-friendly city whose people, according to anthropologist Laura Durazo, 'simply accept that this is part of Tijuana's progress.' Finegood paid his Mexican workers $43 a week versus $330 in the United States, and he did not have to worry about regulations or fines. Altogether, the 2,000 *maquiladoras*, whether owned by small firms like Finegood's or *Fortune* 500 companies, massively polluted the water supply along the border, creating life-threatening hazards in an area where 6 million Mexicans lived.[31] Pressured by his desire to secure passage of NAFTA, Salinas took some steps to ameliorate the situation, at least on paper; actual enforcement of environmental regulations remained weak.[32]

By the end of 1991, momentum in favor of NAFTA had slowed down. This political turn unsettled Salinas, who wanted confirmation of the accord before the end of his term in 1994.[33] One problem he faced was the US election cycle: the United States was entering a presidential election year, and many of Bush's advisers thought the administration should wait on NAFTA until 1993. In Canada the opposition party had won the election, partly by emphasizing its opposition to NAFTA.[34] Bush, however, seemed intent on going forward, and in the end Bush, Salinas and Chrétien reaffirmed their support for NAFTA.[35]

In the US, the debate over NAFTA eventually split the Chicano community into ideological camps. Opposition to NAFTA was led by union activists, environmentalists and human rights groups.[36] Their campaigns were ineffective, however, and often bordered on racism. US labor in general was mainly concerned about NAFTA's impact on jobs and wages.[37] Indeed, US workers had reason to be leery of NAFTA. Since 1985, for example, GM in the US had reported only marginal profits. Its workforce stood at 600,000 in 1985, plummeting to 400,000 by 1991. CEO Robert Stempel shut down twenty-one plants, laying off 74,000 workers in December 1991 alone. During this same period, the GM plant at Reynosa, Mexico, hired 3,000 new workers to assemble Delco stereos. Delco paid $7 a day, while US workers took home $17 an hour.[38] Mexican workers were in fact among the lowest paid in the world. In 1991 hourly compensation for manufacturing labor stood at $2.03, compared with an average of $4.10 an hour in the four Asian tigers – Hong Kong, Korea, Singapore and Taiwan. In the US, the average was $15.33 an hour. UCLA economist Edward E. Leamer predicted that 'over several years this commitment to free trade will reduce real annual income wages for low-skilled work in the US by about $1,000, while annual earnings for high-skilled work could rise as much as $6,000.'

Despite the low wage rates, there were other factors that made Mexico less attractive to North American investors, among them an inadequate highway system, decrepit railroads, tangled bureaucracy, government corruption, a telephone system that did not work and unreliable labor. 'Although President Carlos Salinas de Gortari has engineered economic reforms and radically improved the country's business climate, Mexico has many problems to solve before it can live up to the image Perot tried to give it … Transportation costs, potential delays at the border and … higher inventory storage costs in Mexico', could contribute to US businesses moving back – or, more likely, concentrating investment in the zone along the border so as to take advantage of US infrastructure.[39]

For many US workers, global production was just a fancy word for lost jobs, and Mexico was one of the places the jobs went. Professor Wayne Cornelius criticized opponents of NAFTA for playing to 'nativist' fears. Even though Cornelius was a cheerleader for the Mexican government's position, his point was well taken.[40] Still, more progressive labor leaders were forced by NAFTA to reconsider a strategy that at times consisted of little more than scapegoating Mexican workers as the 'other' for labor's failure to respond to the crisis.[41] The majority of American labor leaders, however, did not seem to understand that the main issue was not jobs. Over a decade, economists estimated that the United States would lose at most 50,000 jobs a year to Mexico, a small number in relation to over 100 million existing jobs.[42] More fundamental was the kind of jobs lost, and the loss of power.

The goal of NAFTA was to give corporations total flexibility, 'from the workplace to the world market.' NAFTA encompassed creation of a market even larger than the European Community; Mexico was just a beginning. In pounding out the agreement, everything was negotiable except the free movement of workers: 'The goal is to bring Mexican and Canadian laws and economic policies in line with the US vision of deregulation. The agreement is about opening Mexico and Canada to US investment.'[43] NAFTA initiated a policy of 'harmonization' to eventually bring social programs, labor laws and environmental protection into line.[44] In this scheme Mexican workers would be the most vulnerable, forced to work in a 'flexible' workforce, doing many different jobs, subject to speedup, deskilling, and constant pressure to find more ways to do the process with fewer people. The result would be a two-tier workforce, with subcontracting of work more frequent. This restructuring of Mexican labor would in turn force Canadian and US workers to compete.[45]

In the face of pressure to regard Mexican workers as nothing more than unwanted competition, some voices in the labor movement called for international cooperation. Baldemar Velásquez, president of the Farm Labor Organizing Committee, based in Ohio, argued that 'It is to our advantage to help the Mexican people increase their wages, to minimize the differential between us and them.'[46] According to Juanita Darling, the L.A. Times Mexico City correspondent, 'Farm workers, telephone operators and electricians are reaching out to counterparts across the continent in search of common solutions to problems with common employers. The contacts involved only a small part of the North American labor movement, at times dissidents or independent unions. But their significance is growing as autos are assembled from parts made on three continents and a North American trade agreement seems imminent.'[47]

Recognizing the threat of such international labor cooperation, Mexico's rulers have responded in often draconian fashion. In Cuaututlán, Mexico, in January 1990, tensions escalated between Ford and its workers when management recruited thugs to suppress worker militancy, resulting in the death of a worker. Ford then fired about 800 Democratic Movement supporters. By 1992 the Mexican government and Ford demanded that the workers cut organizational ties with US and Canadian trade unionists.[48] Leaders of the Ford Workers Democratic Movement were told that 'this conflict has hurt the government's image outside the country.' Volkswagen sought wider flexibility in subcontracting many of its operations, which the Independent Automotive Industrial Workers opposed.[49] In the summer of 1993, a Mexican court upheld VW's right to discharge 14,000 workers who had protested a contract negotiated by government-sponsored leadership.[50]

Supposedly, under NAFTA Canada would supply natural resources, the US would provide the investment capital and Mexico the cheap labor. Mexico, in this scheme, would have to keep wages down. Indeed, real wages had fallen 60 percent over the past ten years. A 1991 Mexican poll showed that 72 percent of Mexicans were favorably disposed to the United States. Among respondents, NAFTA was most popular among the well-to-do, with 83 percent favoring it. It was less popular among the poor, some 51 percent of whom favored it, with 17 percent opposed. (In 1992 another survey, by the Mexican Public Opinion Institute, showed that some 70 percent of Mexicans said that they did not approve of the agreement.)[51] Many Mexicans were worried about NAFTA's affect on Mexican sovereignty. The fears were realistic: in 1991, a confidential memo from US Ambassador John D. Negroponte to Assistant Secretary of State Bernard Aronson observed that, despite the fact that Mexico conducted 60 percent to 70 percent of its trade with the United States, Mexico's vote at international forums was often antagonistic to US interests. The memo suggested that the free-trade agreement would bring Mexico into line.[52]

Opposition to NAFTA Mounts

By 1992, the prospects of NAFTA passing in the US did not look good. It was an election year; moreover, the recession made more and more people worry about possible effects on employment. Bush had made a strategic blunder in not pushing the program through in the summer of 1991, so that it was not until the spring of 1992 that pro-NAFTA activity was anywhere near being organized.[53]

The longer NAFTA came under public scrutiny, the more time the uncoordinated opposition had to mobilize their constituencies, allowing the slow, often cumbersome network-building that bonded disparate human rights and labor groups on both sides of the border to work.[54] Groups such as the L.A. Fair Trade Coalition met regularly, planning activities, and Ross Perot's campaign against NAFTA helped in a way, although Perot's emotional appeal to nativism scared many anti-NAFTA activists.

During this period, Salinas tied the fate of his administration to passage of the agreement. The Mexican government worked hard to win the confidence of the international businesss community, reducing inflation from 159 percent in 1987 to 18.8 percent in 1991, and cutting import tariffs that had once reached 200 percent to an average of 9 percent. It also balanced the federal budget and liberalized regulations limiting foreign investment.[55] These measures, however, had the effect of ballooning the trade deficit, which cut dangerously into Mexico's reserves. The only way to close the gap was to attract more foreign capital, and that could only be done by making more concessions. Thus Mexico became a hostage to NAFTA.[56] Carlos Castañeda described the dilemma faced by Mexicans in assessing NAFTA: 'It would take a free, well-informed debate in a highly educated society to point out the half-truths and unacknowledged trade-offs in the argument for the agreement.' This debate, according to Castañeda, had not taken place in Mexico (nor had it in the United States). Mexicans wanted to believe that NAFTA would solve their economic problems after a decade of stagnation. Even so, according to Castañeda, Mexican business leaders were having second thoughts about NAFTA; some of them were starting to realize that 'an abysmally unequal partnership is in store'.[57]

To help ensure NAFTA's passage, Salinas continued to lobby the US Latino community. In July 1992, the Mexican government announced that it would fund joint ventures in Mexico between US Latinos and Mexican nationals.[58] Mexico set aside an initial $20 million for this purpose, a reward for Latinos who had rallied around the original agreement: the program further increased support for NAFTA in the Latino business community.

Such steps were one reason Orange County Republican Supervisor Gaddi Vásquez was a staunch NAFTA supporter: 'We know the language and we know the system.' With regard to employment, Vasquez declared, 'I prefer losing them [jobs] to Mexico and Latin America [than to Asia].'[59] A La Opinion/Univision poll, taken between 9 and 12 August, showed that 61 percent of Latinos surveyed supported NAFTA, versus 36 percent of Blacks and 44 percent of whites; 25 percent of Latinos, 39 percent of whites and 57 percent of African Americans opposed NAFTA.[60]

Chicano activist Javier Rodríguez described the effect of the Mexican government's campaign: 'The Mexican government has done a masterful job of marketing the free-trade agreement in our community, appealing to patriotism and solidarity to help our mother country make a leap into the First World.'[61] By this time, a split had developed among US Latinos along class lines. A Latina business consultant representing a coalition of fifty business leaders told reporters at a news conference, 'If we stand behind this [NAFTA] we are going to be the beneficiaries.' Long Beach Chicano Studies Professor Adela de la Torre wrote in the Los Angeles Times, '... astute corporate investors – both American and others – view the next four years as the window of opportunity for entering the relatively immature Mexican consumer market with fewer competitors.'[62] In the working-class community of Bell, activists were less enthusiastic.

On the other hand, Rep. Esteban Torres continued to voice his opposition to NAFTA: 'Latino business leaders are mistaken. They have been courted and wooed to believe that they will be [important] participants in this process. But by and large this [NAFTA] is designed to impact and affect large-scale, multinational industry.'[63]

Clinton's Campaign for NAFTA

In November 1992 NAFTA became Bill Clinton's headache. Weeks before the election, Salinas had said that the agreement he had signed was the final version. After Clinton was elected, word slowly leaked out that Salinas was willing to make concessions – an opportune change of course because Salinas's backing of the Bush administration had muddied the waters. In addition, brokers such as Texas Governor Ann Richards stepped forward to play a role in building a relationship between Clinton and Salinas.[64]

An indication of how far Mexico was willing to go was expressed by Jorge Bustamante in a mid-December article in *La Opinión* entitled 'El TLC en el nuevo contexto político de Estados Unidos' ('NAFTA in the New US Political Context'). Bustamante commented on a telephone conversation between Clinton and Salinas in which the former raised concerns about NAFTA's environmental impact and the displacement of US workers.[65] By the spring of 1993, the pendulum seemed to be swinging the other way and passage of NAFTA seemed probable.[66] The new president put his prestige behind its passage. There was considerable jockeying among the different Latino groups as to who would get Clinton's ear. It had been twelve years since any Latino group other than Cuban Americans had had a clear line to the presidency. Up to this point, MALDEF and NCLR were clearly the leading brokers in the Chicano community. The Southwest Voter Registration and Education Project (SVREP) did not have national visibility, although it had clout within the Chicano community based on its work in Texas.

Antonio González of SVREP, who obtained funding for early conferences on NAFTA, moved in late 1992 to push a Latino consensus program. Using the SVREP's Southwest Voter Research Institute (SVRI), a National Latino Strategy Session on NAFTA was held in El Paso on 25 November 1992, and a Latino Summit in Washington, D.C. on 12 and 13 March 1993. González's apparent change of position on NAFTA, which he had once privately opposed, angered many Los Angeles unionists (although he had the support of the Washington-based Labor Council for Latin American Advancement). He gave NAFTA conditional support based on a side deal with Clinton, in which Clinton would provide a border region infrastructure for basic services like sanitation, and

Latino priority in job-training programs and environmental cleanup projects. There were also vague references to the harmonization of labor standards upwards, and the funding of social programs. Clinton would also create a North American Development Bank to invest $10.3 billion in border infrastructure (similar to but not the same as that proposed by the Texas IAF Network, 'Vision for Border Investment Plan', in January 1993).[67] González's leverage relied on his ability, or that of the organizations associated with the plan, to deliver Latino congressional votes for NAFTA. He in turn relied on Clinton's ability to deliver on the side deals. According to González and others, Clinton agreed to the terms.

To signal his new position publically, González co-authored with Supervisor Gloria Molina an article in the *Los Angeles Times*, 'NAFTA Needs a Boost, Not Burial' in May 1993, in which they charged that 'killing NAFTA is both bad public policy and socially irresponsible.' This was a 180-degree shift from González's previous position that NAFTA was a reality and that therefore Latinos should make the best of it. Now González was a cheerleader for the accord. He and Molina reasoned that trade with Mexico favored the United States, so jobs were created in the US (which was true, but for whom?). To justify their new position, they overstated the case that the rejection of NAFTA would contribute to 'Mexican poverty due to underdevelopment' and claimed that the best plan to date was the Latino Consensus Plan.[68]

This article caused considerable debate among Chicano labor activists, who remembered that just over a year earlier González had strategized with them on how to defeat NAFTA. They felt betrayed by González, who had solid leftist credentials. His conversion was, however, predictable. It resulted from an unspoken but very real rivalry among the national Chicano organizations for the ear of the new US president (which now meant the Mexican president as well). During the Bush-Reagan years the National Council of La Raza had been the most successful of these centrist organizations. The election of Clinton changed the game. The national Chicano organizations could sustain the nationalism of '*México Lindo*' while urging support for a Democratic president in order to gain patronage – with NAFTA as the wedge issue. González was almost fanatical in his allegiance to SVREP and to the legacy of its founder, the late Willie Velásquez, a man of extraordinary vision. During the struggles over California redistricting, there had been tension between SVREP and MALDEF, with SVREP criticized for not delivering on its commitments. MALDEF was the most prominent Latino organization in California, and González was sensitive to comparisons. Through the Southwest Voter Research Institute, he brought in grants for work in Central America and Mexico, and sponsored seminars throughout the region to give SVREP more visibility.

NAFTA became his vehicle for pushing SVREP into the national spotlight. González took the opportunity, shifting his position as the occasion demanded.

SVREP was also said to be in the Molina camp, since González had close ties with Molina (he was married to her chief aide), and she played a major role in González's switch to a pro-NAFTA position. For her part, Molina instinctively played the political game of accumulating chips: this time the stakes were high and meant increased access to Clinton. Rep. Esteban Torres would also be leaning toward NAFTA – not surprising, since TELACU had been Torres's brainchild, and the NAFTA North American Development Bank was just a more ambitious version of TELACU.

All this maneuvering led to an interesting realignment. Rep. Marty Martínez came out against NAFTA, but he carefully let it be known that he would reconsider if the president needed his vote. Of the Latino elected officials in Los Angeles, only City Council members Richard Alatorre and Richard Alarcón remained anti-NAFTA, while politicos assumed to be Alatorre partisans – such as Assemblyman Richard Polanco – joined the pro-NAFTA forces.

Meanwhile, even the White House staff was divided over Clinton's NAFTA strategy. Public opposition to the agreement had solidified surprisingly, but by the end of September Clinton's all-out campaign was well under way, focusing on a series of high-profile appearances by the president. Although the struggle to pass NAFTA was eclipsed by the fight over the health care package, Clinton supporters focused on seventy-five members of Congress who were neutral or who had announced their opposition to the agreement.[69]

To bring this group on board, Clinton modified the agreement to satisfy their constituencies. For example, the Iowa firms of Maytag and Amana would have to pay tariffs on their exports to Mexico for ten years, while General Electric and Whirlpool, which manufactured in Mexico, would get immediate access to the Mexican market. Uncommitted legislators would have lunch with Bill, while Hilary would say nice things in a speech about another recalcitrant legislator. As late as 10 October 1993, the seventeen Latino members of the House of Representatives resisted the Clinton administration's argument that they should be natural allies because NAFTA 'would create a huge common market helping Latinos on both sides of the border.' Considerable pressure was applied to the Latino lawmakers, and other inducements were made available: Rep. Esteban Torres (D-La Puente) reversed his previous anti-NAFTA stance for a promise of $450 million to fund the North American Development Bank.[70] Torres's defection to the pro-NAFTA bloc was bound to undermine the unity of the Latino legislators.[71] Meanwhile, Richard Gephardt admitted that the approval of NAFTA was inevitable – an admission that was perhaps premature, since the White House was having a hard time collecting the votes.[72]

On 18 November 1993, the House passed the NAFTA treaty on a vote of 234 to 200; 102 Democrats voted for NAFTA, and 156 voted against it.[73] As expected, the Senate voted for the accord. The Latino vote in the House of Representatives, which was essentially Chicano, included two Chicanos against it,

Henry González and Marty Martinez. The Cuban American representatives voted against NAFTA because they did not like Mexico's amicable relationship with Cuba. The ultimate impact of the NAFTA struggle on the relationship between labor and Clinton remains unclear, since despite their opposition to NAFTA the unions lacked political options.[74] One point was clear, however: in this struggle national Chicano organizations had abandoned the class interests of most working-class Latinos.[75]

Congressional approval of NAFTA locked in the status quo in Mexico and gave the PRI a tremendous, but temporary, boost – temporary because NAFTA was bound to cause dislocation in Mexico.[76] Ramón Eduardo Ruiz, the leading Chicano scholar on Mexican history on both sides of the border, described the *Porfiriato*, which passed similar laws 100 years ago:

> On the agrarian questions, the Liberals of Juárez and Díaz thought alike. Their tonic for agriculture was to 'privatize' the land. Rhetoric about preference for small farmers aside, they prized efficiency and productivity, though that helped concentrate the lands in the hands of a minority. This attitude was hardly novel, dating back from the dismantling of colonial legislation safeguarding the Indian ejido from rapacious hacendados and rancheros. The land rulings of the Reforma merely confirmed this trend. By 1900, the hacendados, their numbers fortified by foreigners, were a bulwark of the Porfiriato.[77]

NAFTA promised to have a similar impact on the Mexican political economy of the 1990s.

The North American Development Bank

During the NAFTA debate, many Chicano leaders aligned themselves with the Southwest Voter Registration and Education Project's 'Latino Consensus', which played an effective role in winning the approval of NAFTA.[78] The Latino Consensus supporting NAFTA, while strengthening Latino negotiating power with the Clinton administration, also aligned Latino leaders with elite interests.[79] Examination of the North American Development Bank (NADbank) provides a good measure of what they got in return for their votes.

Aside from González, Torres and Molina, the other major figure in establishing NADbank was Dr Raúl Hinojosa-Ojeda, a UCLA professor of urban planning and a visiting scholar at the Inter-American Development Bank in Washington, D.C. Like Antonio González, he had leftist credentials. Hinojosa was the mastermind behind the NADbank project, and promoted it tirelessly, traveling throughout the Southwest. Hinojosa seems to have sincerely convinced himself that the bank was the salvation of Mexicans on both sides of the border, and that it would also help build a power base for Chicanos.[80] The bank's aim was to speed financing of environmental infrastructure and economic development projects along the 2,000-mile US–Mexico border. Water supply and waste disposal projects were expected to take top priority. Unlike the Inter-American Development Bank, NADbank emphasized binational public- and private-sector partnerships. Its projects would have to be certified by the Border Environment Cooperation Commission, a binational group. The capitalization of NADbank was set at $3 billion, with Mexico and the US pledging to contribute half of the $450 million of paid-in capital and half of the $2.55 billion in callable capital. (This amount was much less than the original $10 billion touted by González.) Financing would concentrate on an area 100 kilometers deep on both sides of the border, but the bank could use 10 percent of its capital to finance 'domestic' economic adjustment to NAFTA in communities away from the border. The bank was supposed to open its doors in October 1994, with operations split between Los Angeles and San Antonio.[81]

In a June 1994 article, Hinojosa laid out his vision for NADbank: 'The task of building a pattern of equitable and sustainable development in North America will face two major challenges: wide income, productivity, and infrastructure gaps, both within and between countries; and in both countries, a lack of institutional structure to manage uneven development.'[82] The US and Mexico were obviously unequal, their intersection – the border. 'NAFTA is the most ambitious attempt to integrate a highly developed economy with a developing economy.'[83] Because of the nature of the intersection, there was a 'panorama of uneven development' leading to the failure of institutions, including markets as well as governments, 'to direct long-term investments towards equitable and sustainable development.'[84] Hinojosa became a White House consultant on NADbank as well as a leading voice in the NAFTA debate.[85] Working with a network of Latino professional organizations that anticipated a boom, Hinojosa began to build support for NADbank. González held a series of workshops through the Southwest to engage Latino leadership.[86] Along with the Latino lobby, Secretary of the Treasury Lloyd Bentsen played a key role: 'NADbank's job is to deliver financing at a lower cost with longer maturities than would otherwise be available.'[87]

Mexican officials had been concerned that NADbank would duplicate the work of the Inter-American Development Bank and the World Bank; they were also keenly familiar with US-domination of international financial institutions. Their doubts on NADbank were resolved when Bentsen had a talk with his friend and hunting buddy Pedro Aspe Armella, who happened to be finance minister in the Salinas government. They reached an agreement 'under which the US and Mexico would each have three seats on the bank's board and all capital contributions will be ponied up on a 50-50 basis.' Salinas overcame his reservations when it became clear that supporting NADbank was necessary to get passage of NAFTA.[88]

A fundamental weakness was that the bank depended on Congressional willingness to continue appropriations.[89] In the initial stages of establishing the bank, a dispute arose between Latino leaders and the US Treasury, which wanted to place control in the hands of the Border Environmental Cooperation Commission (BECC), diluting so-called Latino control of NADbank. The relationship between NADbank and the commission had not been spelled out in the heat of the NAFTA debate. Again, in a way reminiscent of the war on poverty, the administration seemed inclined to dilute the influence of the advisory councils.[90] Given this history, Latino leaders feared that NADbank would simply end up as a check-writing agency for the BECC, which would be a betrayal of the original agreement. According to Mary Chaves, a senior Treasury official, Mexico and the United States agreed to let the BECC coordinate the projects. This commission – not the NADbank – would identify needs and arrange financing, and the bank would serve only as one source of funds. This arrangement would seriously undercut Latino plans to use NADbank to build an independent political and social power structure, similar to the role TELACU had played in Los Angeles.[91]

Chiapas: Portent of Things to Come?

The profound changes promised by NAFTA, and those that had already taken place in preparation for it, brought about a response that rocked Mexico. On 1 January 1994, the day that NAFTA was to be implemented, a rebellion took place in the southern Mexican state of Chiapas, with rebels citing the passage of NAFTA and the changes in Article 27 of the Constitution as their reasons for continuing the tradition of Emiliano Zapata. NAFTA would permit the influx of cheap Midwestern corn into Mexico, which would destroy the livelihood of small Mayan farmers. In this and other ways NAFTA underscored the inequality that existed in Mexico.[92] The revolt confirmed the fact that the Mexico had not escaped its history, and that the tradition and symbolism of Zapata's rebellion of eighty years before was very much alive.

After a period of brutal military repression, peace negotiations began between the government and the Ejercito Zapatista de Liberación Nacional (EZLN) – largely because Salinas needed to reassure foreign investors.[93] Observers recognized that any solution would have to be a political and not a military one, because rebel grievances were rooted in serious, longstanding social injustices. The PRI had exercised a semi-feudal power over Chiapas, ruling the Indians through *caciques*.[94]

The Chiapas uprising launched a series of extraordinary, historic events in Mexico continuing through 1994 and into 1995. They included the unprecedented assassination of a presidential candidate, followed by a massive cover-up and subsequent scandal involving charges of conspiracy at the highest level; the August 1994 election of current President Ernesto Zedillo, accompanied by new charges of fraud and manipulation; the collapse of the economy, including massive devaluation of the peso, with signs that reliance on foreign investment was a major cause; and the disgrace of Carlos Salinas de Gortari. Divisions within the PRI have become evident, and the party's tight, sixty-year-old grip on power has weakened, with the Mexican military gaining more power.

Where Mexico will go from here, and how Mexicans or Chicanos in Los Angeles and other parts of the United States will be affected, is hard to predict. But any simplistic concept of the homeland as '*Mexico Lindo*' has surely been dealt mortal blows.

Notes

1. Jesús Chavarría, 'Bashing *México Lindo*', *Hispanic Business* (Sept. 1986), p. 4; Alexander Cockburn, 'The Crisis Is Over and the Banks Won Big', *Los Angeles Times*, 17 Aug. 1992. Latin America's external debt was $430 billion; Mexico's was on its way to $120 billion.

2. Rodolfo O. de la Garza, 'US Foreign Policy and the Mexican–American Political Agenda', in Mohammed E. Ahrari, ed., *Ethnic Groups and US Foreign Policy* (New York: Greenwood Press, 1987), pp. 101–14. The author is one of the few Chicano scholars who has studied the phenomenon in a systematic way; de la Garza, 'Chicano–Mexican Relations: Framework for Research', *Social Science Quarterly*, vol. 63, no. 2 (March 1982), pp. 115–30; de La Garza, 'Demythologizing Chicano–Mexican Relations', in Susan Kaufman Purcell, ed., *Mexico–United States Relations* (New York: Academy of Political Science, 1981), pp. 88–96.

3. Carlos Ramos, 'Tres Mexicoamericansos condecorados en México', *La Opinión*, 12 Dec. 1991: the recipients were Antonia Hernández, Blandina 'Bambi' Cárdenas and Professor Luis Leal.

4. John M. Broder and Dan Williams, 'Mexico Feuding with Lenders as Cash Needs Rise', *Los Angeles Times*, 12 May 1986. By 1986 the debt had grown to $99 billion; commercial bankers held nearly 75 percent of this debt and were playing hardball. Unlike its policy with regard to two other large debtors, Poland and Egypt, the United States, via the IMF and the World Bank, squeezed Mexico until it became more friendly to multinational business.

5. De la Garza, 'Chicano–Mexican Relations', pp. 116; de la Garza, 'Demythologizing Chicano–Mexican Relations'; de la Garza, 'US Foreign Policy and the Mexican–American Political Agenda'.

6. Jorge Bustamante, 'Intervencionism de chicanos', *La Opinión*, 1 June 1988.

7. Rodolfo Acuña, 'Chicanos and Mexicans: A Heated Controversy', *La Opinión*, 8 June 1988. In *La Opinión*'s 24 June issue, Jorge Bustamante, in a piece titled *Chicanos y Mexicanos: Un debate*, answered my reply to his article *Intervencionismo de Chicanos*.

8. Rodolfo Acuña, 'Segunda refutación a Bustamante', *La Opinión*, 1 July 1988; Jorge Bustamante, 'Chicanos y Mexicanos', *La Opinión*, 10 July 1988.

9. Tom Berry, ed., *Mexico: A Country Guide* (Albuquerque, N.M.: The Inter-Hemisphere Education Resource Center, 1992). Berry's is probably the best book on contemporary Mexican politics; Enrique Krause, 'El Titanic de la izquierda', *La Opinión*, 20 Oct. 1991. A 1989 Los Angeles poll indicated that only one out of four Mexicans believed that Salinas had won the election honestly, Marjorie Miller, 'Mexicans Ambivalent About US, Poll Finds', *Nuestro Tiempo*, 14 Sept. 1989.

10. Berry, *Mexico*, p. 79; Reimundo Reynoso, 'México anuncia medida para protegar a mexicanos que viven en Estados Unidos', *La Opinión*, 22 Feb. 1992; Jorge G. Castañeda, 'Again, People Are Mexico's No. 1 Export', *Los Angeles Times*, 24 March 1992.

11. Berry, *Mexico*, p. 96: one-sixth of Mexicans in poverty are concentrated in the states of Hidalgo, Oaxaca, Chiapas and Guerrero.

12. Richard Boudreaux, 'Mexicans Favor Trade Pact', *Los Angeles Times*, 22 Oct. 1991.

13. Sebastian Rotella, 'Mexico to Send Back Chinese Held at Sea', *Los Angeles Times*, 15 July 1993; 'Oposición mexicana acusa al Gobierno de ceder ante EU', *La Opinión*, 20 June 1992. After the NAFTA negotiations got under way, accusations were made by Central Americans that Mexican government was cracking down on refugees, a charge denied by Mexican officials. In 1993, some 130,000 Central Americans were ejected from Mexico. Many of them had been stranded on way to the United States and reduced to working in brothels in bordertowns such as Tecun Uman.

14. Berry, *Mexico*, pp. 111–13; James Gerstenzang, 'Agreement on Dumping Breaks GATT Logjam', *Los Angeles Times*, 13 Dec. 1993.

15. Mary Williams Walsh, 'Canadians Still Divided over Pact with US', *Los Angeles Times*, 4 Feb. 1990; the impact of the free trade agreement signed with Canada caused considerable debate. The Canadian Labor Congress monitored plant closings, and reported that Canada lost 72,000 jobs during the first year of the US–Canada free trade agreement, 1989; Marie Claire Acosta, 'The Democratization Process in Mexico: A Human Rights Issue', *RESIST* (Jan. 1991), pp. 3–6: the author is co-founder of the Mexican Commission for the Defense and Promotion of Human Rights. Bill Richardson, 'Free Trade with Mexico, Sí!', *Washington Post*, 22 March 1991: Richardson is a congressman from New Mexico of Mexican origin; Carlos Ramos, 'Demanda que al negociar se trate sobre migración y el efecto que tendrá en los trabajadores hispanos', *La Opinión*, 21 April 1991, reported a demand by Antonia Hernández of MALDEF that the impact on Mexican workers in the US be considered.

16. 'Segunda Reunión de Líderes Hispanos', *La Paloma*, San Antonio, April–May 1992. Hispanic leaders including Raul Yzaguirre held a press conference with Mexican President Salinas.

17. Sergio Muñoz, '"Free" Farm Trade: A Trilateral Hot Potato', *Los Angeles Times*, 30 May 1991, pointed out that any agreement must be carefully balanced to avoid human disaster. He pointed to the 'eloquent' silence of César Chávez on NAFTA (one of the reasons for César's silence was that the Mexican president gave medical benefits to UFW members and families). According to Muñoz, in the US, 3 million people cultivate 250 to 359 million acres of land, whereas in Mexico 20 million cultivate 45 million acres. Although some are modern, capitalist farmers, many still use nineteenth-century tools. If noncompetitive farmers are displaced by US agricultural imports, what would Mexico – and the US – do with 20 million landless campesinos? Surely this would mean increased flight to the US; Esteban E. Torres, 'Our Back Door Will Need Double Locks', *Los Angeles Times*, 7 June 1991.

18. Henrick Rehbinder, 'La Raza firma acuerdo de intercambio con México', *La Opinión*, 17 July 1991; Yzaguirre announced a cultural exchange program with Mexico at the convention.

19. Muñoz expressed these opinions before the passage of Proposition 187: Sergio Muñoz, 'Yes, Mexico Is North American, Too', *Los Angeles Times*, 14 Aug. 1991; Lorenzo Meyer, 'El Gobierno mexicano y sus dos solidaridades', *La Opinión*, 21 Aug. 1991: Meyer notes that the Mexican government has chosen orthodox capitalism as the solution.

20. Marjorie Miller and Juanita Darling, 'Mexico Shift to Free Trade Fosters Hope', *Nuestro Tiempo*, 7 Nov. 1991. In an article for *Nuestro Tiempo*, *Los Angeles Times* reporters Marjorie Miller and Juanita Darling sum up what consumers thought of Mexico's substitution policy, which consisted of Mexico's manufacturing replicas of foreign goods: 'Mexico's best was mediocre.' Indeed, for *pochos*, this was the problem with Mexicans, always thinking themselves mediocre, as if the needs of Mexico could be cured by buying US breakfast cereals, listening to Japanese stereos, and having a Big Mac for lunch.

21. Patrick McConnell, 'Salinas Lobbies for Trade Pact', *Los Angeles Times*, 29 Sept. 1991; Pete Wilson, 'El Tratado de Libre Comercio beneficiará a California', *La Opinión*, 17 Oct. 1991.

22. Gabriel Székely, 'California and Mexico: Facing the Pacific Rim', in Lowenthal and Burgess, p. 126: Székely noted that investors outside North America were watching with interest. If the agreement included a strict 'rules of origin' provision to limit participation of investors from Third World countries, particularly the Far East, they would lose interest in investing in Mexico.

23. 'Latinoamérica siente alivio por apoyo de Clinton a TLC', *La Opinión*, 28 Feb. 1993.

24. Jorge Carrasco Araizaga, 'México, el TLC y el modelo asiático de desarrollo', *La Opinión*, 21 Aug. 1992; Adolfo Aguilar Zinser, 'El Tratado de Libre Comercio y el nuevo orden mundial', *La*

Opinión, 22 Aug. 1992.

25. Carlos Ramos, 'Salinas propone cambios en el ejido', *La Opinión,* 8 Nov. 1991; 'Salinas anuncia reestructuracion profunda en el campo mexicano', *La Opinión,* 16 Nov. 1991. The question was who would pay the social costs for the restructuring of rural Mexico. Sergio Aguayo Quezada, 'La Revolución Mexicana y el Tratado de Libre Comercio', *La Opinión,* Aug. 18, 1992.

26. Carlos Ramos, 'Campesinos venderán sus parcelos en los ejidos', *La Opinión,* 25 Nov. 1991.

27. Luis Rubio, '¿Producura el campo con las reforms de artículo 27?', *La Opinión,* 25 Nov. 1991.

28. 'Es alarmante la contaminación atmosférica en la capital mexicana', *La Opinión,* 6 Dec. 1991; 'México como un socio de los Estados Unidos: ¿dictadura perfecta or democracia imperfecta?' *La Opinión,* 18 Oct. 1993.

29. Juanita Darling, Larry B. Stammer and Judy Pasternak, 'Can Mexico Clean Up Its Act?', *Los Angeles Times,* 17 Nov. 1991.

30. Judy Pasternak, 'Firms Find Haven from US Environmental Rules', *Los Angeles Times,* 19 Nov. 1991.

31. Patrick J. McDonnell, 'Foreign-Owned Companies Add to Mexico's Pollution', *Los Angeles Times,* 18 Nov. 1991; Patrick Lee and Chris Kraul, 'Uniqueness of *Maquiladoras* Could Fade', *Los Angeles Times,* 19 Nov. 1993.

32. Karen Tumulty, 'Free-Trade Talks Raise Questions That Alarm Environmentalists', *Los Angeles Times,* 17 Nov. 1991.

33. Raymundo Riva Palacio, 'Salinas Holds His Breath: Will Treaty Be Put on Hold?' *Los Angeles Times,* 11 Dec. 1991.

34. William A. Orme, Jr, 'A Presidential Election Year Is No Time to Talk Mexico Free Trade', *Los Angeles Times,* 15 Dec. 1991; 'Salinas pide pronto aprobación de TLC', *La Opinión,* 14 Dec. 1991; Marjorie Miller, 'Mexico Worries US May Stall Trade Pact', *Los Angeles Times,* 12 Dec. 1991.

35. Adolfo Aguilar Zinser, 'TLC: Ina coversacion no intuitiva de fin de año', *La Opinión,* 15 Dec. 1991; for Cuahtémoc Cárdenas, approval of NAFTA had to be made conditional on political and economic reforms, see Salvador Salado Guerrero, 'Partidos políticos mexicanos opinan sobre el TLC', *Union Hispana,* 17 Dec. 1991.

36. Patrick McDonnell, 'Doubts Voiced About US–Mexico Plan', *Los Angeles Times,* 24 Sept. 1991; Patrick McConnell, 'Environmental Fears Voiced on Free Trade Plan', *Los Angeles Times,* 14 Sept. 1991; Juan José Gutierrez, 'Derechos humanos y libre comercio', *La Opinión,* 8 May 1992; Bob Howard, 'US Latinos Speak Up on Free Trade Accord', *Nuestro Tiempo,* 7 Nov. 1991; Steve Proffit, 'Interview: Arturo Rodríguez', *Los Angeles Times,* 26 Sept. 1993: the United Farm Workers had no position on NAFTA. Claire Conrad, '"Free Trade": Economic Development, or 1990s-Style Colonialism for Mexico?' *Voces Unidas,* Southwest Organizing Project (Third Quarter 1991); in THE same issue, Elizabeth Martínez, 'EPA's Institutional Racism Exposed'.

37. *AFL-CIO Legislative Fact Sheet,* 1 March 1991. The concerns of the US labor movement were real: NAFTA increased the incentives for companies to move south to take advantage of Mexico's weaker unions, lower wages, and limited environmental and safety and health regulation. NAFTA-inspired plant migration would surely increase downward pressure on wages in the United States, especially affecting workers in small agricultural, textiles and electronics plants employing deskilled labor whose jobs could easily be moved. NAFTA thus gave employers an advantage in labor disputes: submit or we'll leave. And once NAFTA was signed, it would be nearly irreversible – increasing pressure on other Latin American countries to follow suit or lose US trade and investment, John Anner, 'Trading Away Labor Rights', *Minority Trends Letter* (Summer 1991), pp. 4–5.

38. John Weiner, 'General Motors Grows in Mexico', *Texas Observer,* 28 Feb. 1992, p. 23. At the same time that the Delco dispute was taking place, US automakers announced that they were putting Mexican expansion plans on the back burner. In essence, they claimed that the automakers were reducing their commitment to manufacturing in Mexico because of declining sales and Japanese competition. In 1991 the Japanese reportedly increased their market share from 28 percent to 31 percent. The article predicted that unless the US economy turned around, US firms would have to cut production. What this indicated was the dependent nature of the Mexican economy. John Watling, 'US Big Three Put Mexico on Hold', *El Financiero International,* 27 Jan. 1992.

39. Karen Pennar, 'The US and Mexico: A Close Look at Costs of Free Trade', *Business Week,* 4 May 1992, p. 22; Ted Robberson, 'In Mexico, Only the Labor Is Cheap', *Washington Post Weekly*

Edition, 11–17 Oct. 1993, p. 17.

40. Wayne Cornelius, 'The Scare Stories Don't Wash', *Los Angeles Times*, 28 Feb. 1992.

41. Juanita Darling, 'Crossing Labor's Borders', *Los Angeles Times*, 7 Sept. 1992. Kim Moody and Mary McGinn, in a *Labor Notes* book titled *Unions and Free Trade: Solidarity and Competition*, wrote: 'The North American Free Trade Agreement is not about commerce of nations. This agreement binds the United States, Canada, and Mexico in economic union and was more about corporate profits than about trade. It was about letting private business reorganize the North American economy without the checks and balances once provided by unions, social movements, or governments. The North American Free Trade Agreement (NAFTA) would roll back a hundred years of controls and restrictions that were placed on private business in the interests of the majority of people (Detroit: Labor Notes, 1992), p. 1.

42. Alexander Cockburn, 'A Foretaste of Free Trade's Real Price', *Los Angeles Times*, Sept. 28, 1992. This article also reports on Bush's visit to the United Nations: 'To the surprise of the international delegates mustered in the General Assembly building, Bush launched a vigorous attack on part of his own government, the US Agency for International Development, which operates under the aegis of the State Department and whose mandate is the furnishing of technical assistance to poor nations. Bush called USAID a "weapon in the Cold War" that had outlived its function and must now be forged into an instrument fostering "mutually productive economic relationships"', which subsidized US manufacturers to move to Central America to take advantage of workers paid $5.00 a day. These companies get low-interest US loans; about 200 are scattered in the Caribbean, Honduras and El Salvador, mostly in the apparel and electronics industries. In El Salvador the investigative reporters asked USAID official John Sullivan about threat of union labor; he responded cynically that workers with known union tendencies were blacklisted. The work of the USAID had lowered wages in Central America, not raised them.

43. Moody and McGinn, *Unions and Free Trade*, pp.4–5.

44. Ibid., pp. 4–5; Maribel Hastings, 'El Gobierno presenta alegatos contra fallo judicial adverso al tratado de Libre Comercio', *La Opinión*, 25 Aug. 1993.

45. Moody and McGinn, *Unions and Free Trade*, pp. 25–6; John Cavanaugh and John Gershman, 'Free Trade Fiasco', *Progressive* (Feb. 1992), pp. 32–3; special Issue on NAFTA and Free Trade Economics, *Resource Center Bulletin* (Spring 1993).

46. Juanita Darling, 'Closing Labor's Borders', *Los Angeles Times*, 7 Sept. 1992.

47. Ibid.; Alexander Cockburn, 'When Jobs Go South – A True Parable', *Los Angeles Times*, July 27, 1993. Cockburn describes job flight from the Salinas Valley to Irapauto, Mexico, displacing Mexican Green Giant workers. Local 912 in Watsonville gave financial help to the Frente Autentico de Trabajadores in Irapauto to organize workers there.

48. Matt Witt, 'Ford Demands That Mexican Workers Cut Ties to US, Canadian Unionists', *Labor Notes* (Feb. 1992), p. 15.

49. Alberto Aziz, 'Hipotesis sobre la huelga de la Volkswagen', *La Opinión*, 30 Aug. 1992; Richard Rothstein, 'El éxito del NAFTA depende del aumento salarial en México', *La Opinión*, 1 April 1993.

50. Richard Rothstein, 'Continental Drift: NAFTA and Its Aftershocks', *American Prospect* (Winter 1993), p. 69.

51. A *Los Angeles Times* poll in 1989 showed that Mexicans were ambivalent about the United States. According to this poll, one-third of Mexicans believed that they would never leave Mexico, and another third said that they did not want to live in the United States. Apparently, it is not the dream of every Mexican to emigrate to the US. Drugs and discrimination were seen as the biggest drawbacks to life in the United States. On the other hand, 6 percent said that they would probably migrate *al norte* in the next year, which would translate into 5 million if those intentions became a reality. For this group, money was the main attraction. It was on this reluctance to leave Mexico that the Mexican government attempted to sell NAFTA to the Mexican public: if NAFTA was a success they wouldn't have to leave the motherland. Marjorie Miller, 'Mexicans Ambivalent About US, Poll Finds', *Nuestro Tiempo*, 14 Sept. 1989; Richard Boudrezus, 'Mexicans Favor Trade Pact', *Los Angeles Times*, 22 Oct. 1991; 'El 70 percent de mexicanos no quiere el TLC', *La Opinión*, 8 Oct. 1992.

52. Rodolfo Acuña, 'Latinos Ask, with Friends Like These...' *Los Angeles Times*, 26 May 1991; 'The Negroponte Cable', International Reports, IBC USA Publications, Inc., 22 May 1991.

53. The Canadian Government sponsored a conference entitled 'US/Mexico/Canada Free

Trade Agreement: Its Impact on California' in association with the University of Southern California's Jesse Unruh Institute of Politics on 23 January 1992. In Los Angeles, the L.A. Coalition for Fair Trade and Economic Justice held a caucus meeting at the event. The coalition comprised Latino union activists and other progressives, led by Peter Olney, then of Local 399. It represented a progressive agenda, but it did not receive sufficient support from the labor Internationals, whose anti-NAFTA strategy remained ineffective. The Fair Trade Campaign attempted to build a grass-roots movement with limited success. Craig Merrilees and Don Wiener, to Rudy Acuña, 15 June 1992; Andrew Le Page, 'Free-Trade Pact Targeted by Protesters', *Los Angeles Times*, 23 Oct. 1992; Cristina Lee, 'Union Caravan Drives to Stop Free Trade Pact', *Los Angeles Times*, 24 Sept. 1992; Paul Schmitt, 'Teamster Chief Blasts Trade Pact as "Phony Deal"', *Sacramento Bee*, 15 Sept. 1992; Pat Donner, 'In Heartland Races, Trade Agreement with Mexico Is Proving to Be Unpopular', *Wall Street Journal*, 27 Oct. 1992; José Luis Sierra, 'Anuncian inicio de campaña estal de oposición al TLC', *La Opinión*, 18 June 1992.

54. William Langewiesche, 'The Border', *Atlantic* (June 1992), pp 91–105; Daniel R. Cavazos, 'Los latinos del suroeste y el Tratado de Libre Commercio', *La Opinión*, 22 June 1992.

55. Juanita Darling, 'Mexico Pinning Its Hopes on Free Trade Agreement', *Los Angeles Times*, 4 July 1992.

56. Jorge Castañeda, 'Peligro el TLC', *La Opinión*, 28 June 1992; Luis Rubio, 'El problema ecológico y el Trado de Libre Comercio', *La Opinión*, 10 June 1992.

57. Jorge Castañeda, 'Mexico Jumps in with Eyes Shut', *Los Angeles Times*, 13 Oct. 1992.

58. Jesús Sánchez, 'Mexico to Fund Latino Ventures', *Los Angeles Times*, 23 July 1992.

59. Henrik Rehbinder, 'Los latinos son los que mas se beneficiarán del TLC, dicen', *La Opinión*, 20 Aug. 1992.

60. Maribel Hastings, 'Los electores estadounidenses están divididos en partes iguales respecto al TLC', *La Opinión*, 14 Aug. 1992; Adonis E. Hoffman, 'The Black–Latino Alliance Withers', *Los Angeles Times*, 18 Oct. 1993. The Congressional Black Caucus opposed NAFTA because members feared its international consequences and its impact on Caribbean nations.

61. Javier Rodríguez, 'Latinos Are Selling Out on Free Trade', *Los Angeles Times*, 3 Aug. 1992.

62. See Adela de la Torre, 'Getting a Piece of the Mexican Rock', *Los Angeles Times*, 11 Aug. 1993; for a pro–Mexican government point of view, Aliza Chelminsky, 'Mexican Pact Means More Jobs for All', *Los Angeles Times*, 12 Aug. 1992.

63. Jesus Sanchez, 'US Latinos Divided over Free Trade Pact', *Los Angeles Times*, 18 Aug. 1992; Raul Hinojosa-Ojeda, 'The Impact of a North American Free Trade Agreement on California: A Summary of Key Research Findings' (Los Angeles: Lewis Center for Regional Policy Studies, UCLA, September 1992); Hinojosa concluded that the impact would not be a bad as predicted.

64. Adolfo Aguilar Zinser, 'El TLC, el salinismo y la Administración Clinton', *La Opinión*, 3 Dec. 1992.

65. *La Opinión*, 13 Dec. 1992.

66. 'Clinton apoya el TLC, pero con acuerdos paralelos', *La Opinión*, 24 March 1993; Blanche Petrich, 'Gephardt fué a México y habló con Salinas ayer', *La Opinión*, 24 March 1993; Jaime Olivares, 'Coalición latina presentar ocho recomendaciones', *La Opinión*, 24 March 1993.

67. 'Latino Consensus Position on NAFTA', Latino Summit on NAFTA, 12–13 March 1993, Washington, D.C.; James Gerstenzang, 'Clinton Presses for NAFTA, Blasts Fear-Mongering', *Los Angeles Times*, 21 Oct. 1993.

68. See Harley Shaiken, 'The "Sticker Price" Doesn't Add Up', *Los Angeles Times*, 20 Sept. 1993. Shaiken noted that predictions of new US jobs as a result of NAFTA didn't add up, mostly because of blind optimism about the ability of Mexican consumers to buy US goods.

69. James Gerstenzang, 'Clinton Maps Uphill Battle for Trade Pact', *Los Angeles Times*, 13 Sept. 1993.

70. Risen and Gertenzang, 7 Nov. 1993.

71. Clifford Krauss, 'Latino Lawmakers Resisting NAFTA', *Daily News*, 12 Oct. 1993.

72. 'Aprobar el TLC "es inevitable"', dice Gephardt', *La Opinión*, 18 Oct. 1993.

73. James Gerstenzang and Paul Richter, 'Fight over NAFTA Moves to Congressional Districts', *Los Angeles Times*, 15 Nov. 1993; James Gerstenzang and Michael Ross, 'House Passes NAFTA, 234–200', *Los Angeles Times*, 18 Nov. 1993.

74. Kevin Phillips, 'The Vote Was Just a Taste – Now the Tough Part Lies Ahead', *Los Angeles*

Times, 21 Nov. 1993. Phillips put the NAFTA victory in perspective. Surely the accord would increase tensions among the three signers, and labor would seriously challenge Clinton in 1996. According to Phillips, it would have been better for Clinton if he had lost the vote.

75. Harry Bernstein, 'Pro-Union Label Won't Fit Clinton', *Los Angeles Times*, 1 Sept. 1993; Bernstein, 'Post NAFTA, Don't Discount Union Strength', *Los Angeles Times*, 21 Nov. 1993; Guy Molyneux, 'Labor and Democrats Vital Link for Clinton', *Los Angeles Times*, 5 Dec. 1993. The truth was that labor leaders came out of the NAFTA fight angry, but Clinton knew that they had no place to go. In the end, the unions grumbled but returned to backing Democrats who had abandoned labor to support Clinton on NAFTA.

76. Harley Shaiken, 'Watch Mexico Dig in Its Heels', *Los Angeles Times*, 16 Nov. 1993.

77. Ramón Eduardo Ruiz, *Triumphs and Tragedy: A History of the Mexican People* (New York: Norton, 1992), p. 305.

78. George Ramos, 'An Emotional Tug of War for Mexicans Living in the United States', *Los Angeles Times*, 22 Nov. 1993.

79. Rodolfo Acuña, 'Chiapas polariza a los chicanos', *La Opinión*, 14 Jan. 1994.

80. NADbank was the brainchild of Albert Fishlow, Sherman Robinson and Raul Hinojosa-Ojeda, 'Proposal for a North American Regional Development Bank and Adjustment Fund', in *North American Free Trade: Proceedings of a Conference* (Dallas, Tex: Federal Reserve Bank of Dallas, 1991). Hinojosa's model was not without controversy: William Spriggs and Robert Wright, Letter to the Editor, *New Republic*, vol. 209, no. 22 (29 Nov. 1993), p. 6., assert that Hinojosa's co-modeler was Robert McCleery and refer to a dispute between their figures and those of Hinojosa's.

81. William H. Carlile, 'Prop. 187 Puts Mexico Ties at Risk, Banker Says', *Arizona Republic*, 24 Nov. 1994; Suzanne Bilello, 'NAFTA Costs 1,200 Jobs Statewide', *Newsday*, 8 Nov. 1994; Susan Ferriss, 'NAFTA Coming into Focus', *San Francisco Examiner*, 19 June 1994.

82. Raul Hinojosa-Ojeda, 'The North American Development Bank: Forging New Directions in Regional Integration Policy', *Journal of the American Planning Association*, vol. 60, no. 3, p. 301.

83. Ibid.

84. Hinojosa makes the point that Mexico has spent more on infrastructure border development than on the rest of the debt-ridden country. According to Hinojosa, this development was hampered by the lack of a legal framework for collection of taxes and issuance of bonds, as well as a lack of forums for democratic participation. His plan was naturally the alternative.

85. *San Francisco Examiner*, 19 June 1994; Janine Friend, 'US, Mexico to Run Development Bank to Fund Border Cleanup, Infrastructure', *The Bond Buyer*, 26 May 1994.

86. During my many conversations with Antonio while he was building the so-called 'Latino Consensus', he couched his position in terms of 'grassroots' support. However, the support came primarily from groups interested in the accumulation of capital and whose interests NAFTA served. The creation of the NADbank was a brilliant ploy to consolidate this coalition.

87. *The Bond Buyer*, 26 May 1994.

88. Lucy Conger, 'Can NAFTA Reinvent Development Banking?', *Institutional Investor* (March 1994). Clinton confided to a group of congressmen that the new bank was the best of all the deals he had made to get passage of the agreement.

89. Diane Linquist, 'NADbank to Be Fiscal Tool to Smooth NAFTA's Path', *San Diego Union-Tribune*, 25 May 1994.

90. 'Post-NAFTA: Hispanics' Ire Raised over NADbank', *The Hotline*, 2 March 1994.

91. David LaGesse, 'Clinton May Shun NADbank', *Dallas Morning News*, 28 Feb. 1994.

92. Anita Snow, 'Rebels Retain Hold on 3 Towns, Battle for 4th in South Mexico', *Daily News*, 4 Jan. 1994; Juanita Darling, 'Mexican Revolt in 2nd Day: 65 Dead', *Los Angeles Times*, 3 Jan. 1994; Victor Perera, 'Can Mexico's Ruling Political Party Save the State, and Itself, from Balkanization?' *Los Angeles Times*, 27 March 1994. Subcomandante Marcos captured the imagination of many Mexicans; Patrick J. McDonnell, '*Campesinos*' Struggle over Land Rights Is Widespread', *Los Angeles Times*, 5 Jan. 1994.

93. Tracy Wilkinson, 'Mexico Steps Up Bid for Truce with Zapatista Rebels', *Los Angeles Times*, 12 Jan. 1994; Juanita Darling, 'Mexican Rebels Ready to Reject Peace Offer', *Los Angeles Times*, 18 March 1994.

94. Denise Dresser, 'A Painful Jolt for the Body Politic', *Los Angeles Times*, 12 Jan. 1994; Juanita Darling, 'With Chiapas Cease-Fire, Political Fallout Begins', *Los Angeles Times*, 14 Jan. 1994.

11

Troubled Angels

Bill Clinton won his 1992 campaign for the presidency by focusing on voters' most pressing concern, as indicated by the reminder on his campaign headquarters wall: 'It's the economy, stupid.' Two years later, with the economy improved, crime had apparently become the voters' top concern. In California, the right's law-and-order campaign paid off with the passage of Proposition 184, the so called 'Three Strikes' initiative, with 72 percent of the vote in November 1994. This law mandated sentences of twenty-five years to life for three-time felons. It seemed to matter little to Californians that the legislature had already passed a Three Strikes bill in March that had taken effect on 1 July.[1] Opportunistic politicians, having found a winning theme, kept on the attack.

The fear of crime was in great part a product of hysterical TV coverage, which equated crime with gangs and portrayed Mexicans, like Blacks, as universally gang members or drug dealers. In Los Angeles, the dimensions of this fear were expressed in a 1992 article by Los Angeles Police Commissioner Bert Beockmann and Mayor Richard Riordan, who wrote that the 'fear of crime, violence in the home and public places, the tyrannical messages of graffiti, the presence of gangs, and the weakening of local government's infrastructure ...'[2] contributed to a clamor for more police. They suggested that the only way people would feel safe was to have a police officer on every corner: 'Crime, and the fear it creates, is one of the primary reasons the city is losing its business. During the next year, it is estimated that the city will lose up to 31,000 tourism jobs because of the recent [Rodney King] riots.'[3] Beockmann and Riordan thus combined the potent themes of economic insecurity and fear of crime for maximum political advantage.

'Three Strikes' was not the only strategy they pursued. In March 1993, City Attorney James K. Hahn sought to score political points by asking for a court order to declare a 'free-fire' zone in the San Fernando Valley, where 500 unnamed members of the Blythe Street Gang would be forbidden to associate with friends in public and to wear specific kinds of clothes and jewelry.[4] The order would also forbid gang members to stop in any one place for more than five minutes, with undesirables totally banished from the Blythe Street zone in Van Nuys; an 8 p.m. curfew would be placed on Latino youth under the age of eighteen.[5]

Another territorial solution to the crime problem was to build gates that separated the rich from the poor. Many of the rich lived in gated communities with guards and community social clubs, while the poor had their streets barricaded and apartment complexes gated by both fences and police. In Northridge's gated estates on the northern part of Tampa Avenue, for example, 5,000-square-foot homes might house as few as one to three people, while just three miles south on Tampa, the Bryant-Vanalden apartment complex was also gated, with permanently closed roads. There one to four families lived in 800-square-foot apartments.[6]

Gang Violence

Whatever the proposed solution to crime, however, there was widespread agreement on the equation of crime with gangs. Countywide an estimated 450 to 500 gangs operated on the streets of Los Angeles: by the 1990s, there were 60,000 Latino gang members in Los Angeles and about 35,000 Black gang members. Black and Latino gangs differed, with Latino gangs being more territorial than their Black counterparts.[7] In both neighborhoods most residents were frustrated by the gang problem. Many parents sent their children on one-and-a-half-hour bus rides to suburban schools because they were less crowded and thus safer. Latinos and Chicanos even moved to unfriendly places like Thousand Oaks or Malibu, where they lived on the margins of society, to get their children away from the commotion of barrios like Pico-Union.[8]

Gang violence reached its peak during the early 1990s. Reflecting the savage capitalism of society in the Reagan era, there appeared to be no rules: drive-by shootings were a common occurrence and took a toll on innocent bystanders. In this context 'La Eme' – also known as 'M' – short for the Mexican Mafia, moved into the vacuum. On 18 September 1993, over a thousand gang members attended an *Eme*-sponsored gang summit on the doorstep of the Police Academy in Elysian Park to end barrio warfare. *Eme* dictated a truce, changing the way barrio gang war would be conducted. It halted drive-by shootings, and called for fights to be conducted face-to-face between the participants, thus limiting the danger to innocent bystanders. The message seemed to be, 'If you have to take care of business ... at least do it with respect, do it with honor and dignity.'[9]

Eme's intervention sent shock waves through the community. Some, tired of gang violence, saw it 'as a ray of light' in a seemingly endless tunnel of fear and violence.[10] Others doubted *Eme*'s motives. The *Eme*, formed in the late 1950s in the state penitentiary system, achieved its greatest influence in the late 1970s. According to sociologist Joan Moore, the *Eme* used 'extreme' violence in pursuit of power and economic control. During the decade, they waged a war against *Nuestra Familia*, made up of inmates largely outside the L.A. area. At first the *Eme* comprised primarily state-raised inmates, but gradually incorporating other cliques until it finally controlled the underground economy of the prisons.[11] *Eme* grew as the prison population expanded, thriving because of that system. Its core association numbered about 400 to 600. The lack of rehabilitation and abandonment of state-raised youth encouraged the expansion of this prison organization, affecting even the lives of nongroup members whose exposure to prison life then influenced street behavior and gang codes outside prison.

Those who questioned the *Eme*'s motives in calling the summit charged it had intervened only because violence was interfering with the drug trade. Others, cautioning against the spread of organized crime in the barrios, called for a rejection of *Eme*. Another school of thought, made up of some gang experts, questioned whether *Eme* really was a major player in the barrio narcotics traffic, which in Los Angeles is much less organized than on the East Coast.

The only groups not joining the truce were the Maravilla gangs in unincorporated East L.A. The other gangs fell into line because the *Eme* dominated the prisons, and it was clear that they could make dissidents pay a high price for their dissent.[12] In the San Fernando Valley seventy-five Latino street gangs maintained a five-month peace pact, partly because of the *Eme*'s intervention, but mostly because of the work of volunteers like William 'Blinky' Rodríguez, a former champion kick-boxer who established the Peace Treaty Council in October 1993. Rodríguez is credited with negotiating a two-year truce in the Valley between rival Chicano gangs that resulted in a 70 percent drop in gang-related homicides during this period. Rodríguez got involved with youth when his fifteen-year-old son, 'Sonny', was killed in a drive-by shooting. But sustaining projects like gang truces remains difficult, because by themselves they don't provide social and economic alternatives to gang life. Gangs in fact proliferated as the recession deepened in the early 1990s: in 1985 there had been 45,000 gang members, but by 1991 there were reported to be nearly 100,000 gang members, a number that may reflect the favorite anti-gang strategy of the LAPD and the Sheriff's Department: 'rounding up suspects', then fingerprinting them and identifying them as gang members. Anyone who 'looked like' a gang member or 'hung around' gang members would be picked up by the authorities and tagged as a gang member. This strategy has the advantage of justifying a larger police budget, but at the same time is cheaper and less complicated than actually doing something about the social conditions that produce gangs. As Omar Vásquez, a member of Vineland Boys 13, put it: 'In a lot of poor areas I guess people don't want to put money into the schools.'[13]

Much of the racial tension in the community was gang-related. In the West-side's Venice Oakwood district, violence between two Latino gangs and an African American gang spread to the Mar Vista housing projects, and thirty people were shot in a square-mile radius; Latino gangsters were suspected of fire-bombing three units in the project. According to the Housing Authority Police, the Black–Brown gang confrontations were part of a large-scale plot by the *Eme* to control West Coast narcotics. Before this outbreak, the Westside gangs had co-existed. There were also Black–Brown tensions between gangs in the Aliso Village Housing Projects of East L.A., where seven Latino gangs and one Black gang claimed turf. *L.A. Times* journalist Jesse Katz reported that the *Eme* in Riverside had ordered Latino gangs to sever ties with Black gang members.[14] Here as elsewhere, *Eme* moved into a void left by society. Some barrio residents saw it as a result of the failure of the system to provide security. The reality was that gang youth had no role models, and *Eme* filled the void, assuming a moral authority that US institutions, Euroamerican and Chicano politicos, and even church leaders, did not have.[15]

While much gang activity was irrational, the hysteria about gang activity was even more so. California historian Kevin Starr of the University of Southern California described its grip on Euroangelenos: 'A downtown banker, otherwise the perfect paradigm of bottom-line skepticism, calmly reported that he had inside information that 20,000 gang members – a tight, disciplined army – were prepared to move into the Westside following the verdict in the Rodney King civil-rights trial. The city bristled with scores of rumors like this one, most of them catastrophic, most of them in one way or another serving Los Angeles' deepest, most fearful image of itself: a city at the end of its history.'[16]

In such a climate, few Angelenos bothered to ask themselves why so many youth had joined gangs. San Fernando football coach Tom Hernández gave a partial explanation: 'Kids are basically the same, but everything else has changed in 20 or 30 years ... Some of these kids know they could get shot down on the street. That never entered my mind at age 18 or 19. It seems to me that it's just very tough today to be a teenager.'[17] The growth of gang violence and crime in general was a socioeconomic phenomenon. It was exacerbated by the dramatic growth in population and measures such as Proposition 13, which had crippled the ability of local government to raise revenue for social services just when the need for such services began to increase dramatically.[18] As a result, youth programs were drastically cut or eliminated.[19] Gang violence prevention programs, such as the work of Father Patrick Boyle in Aliso Village and the Pico Garden housing projects, were also cut back. Father Boyle had worked with eight gangs and had achieved some success;[20] his project indicated that something could be done if only the city had the will to do it.

But in reality, gangs are 'fundamentally irrelevant to the level of criminal violence' in society, according to UCLA sociology professor Jack Katz. Nevertheless, it remains convenient to believe that crime is mainly a gang problem. Katz concluded that the LAPD's current anti-gang policy of mass arrests has led to the needless violation of the rights of young minority males and females, in effect identifying them publically as criminals and thus encouraging them to act accordingly. While Katz did not advocate sending out social workers to hug offenders, he did argue for limiting the use of prison to the really violent and for getting the guns out of the hands of youth. Early identification of (actual) gang members is vital – or would be if jobs were available and if the city offered adequate social services.[21]

The Death of a Tagger

The widespread tendency to blame all crime on impoverished youth was brutally demonstrated by the public reaction to the killing of a tagger.[22] There were an estimated 30,000 taggers in L.A. county by 1993.[23] Unlike gang members, individual taggers were generally peaceful, acting out individual identification rather that of the group. Nevertheless, public reaction to tagging has been hysterical. For example, Gerald Silver, a member of the National Graffiti Information Network and an Encino homeowner activist, wrote: 'There is the brazenness of it. They have gone on private property and taken enormous walls, and they have put these ugly graphics up. There are symbols, tags, anti-social comments.' Said Silver, 'I don't consider them "taggers." That's kind of innocuous. These are crooks, vandals who are destroying public property – more important – they are destroying the heart of a community.'[24] (It did not occur to Silver and his ilk that billboards legally pollute poor neighborhoods, pushing alcohol and tobacco. Indeed, billboards are the rich man's graffiti.)

Most Angelenos did not differentiate between gang members and taggers. In 1995, many cheered the vigilante action of 35-year-old William Masters II, who shot and killed an unarmed eighteen-year-old tagger named César Rene Arce and wounded his companion. Masters became an instant celebrity and was praised for protecting the community. A city councilwoman from nearby Simi Valley went so far as to propose giving Masters a commendation from that city. It did not dawn on them that there was something strange about William Masters II wanting to take long, solitary walks through the Sun Valley barrio after midnight.[25] On one such walk Masters stumbled on two taggers, who confronted him when he flamboyantly jotted down their license plate number. Next, according to Masters, the taggers tried to rob him – and in self-defense he killed the unarmed Arce by shooting him in the back. He then shot the second youth, David Hillo, who was supposedly holding a screwdriver. Masters – a former marine – said that he felt in 'imminent danger', even though he was armed, and even though Hillo was ten to thirty feet away.

Arce and Hillo did not have serious police records and were not known to be violent. In contrast, Masters had a previous conviction in Texas for carrying a gun into a federal court. He was also a failed actor and playwright who wanted to make it in the movies. His shooting of Arce and Hillo was stagily reminiscent of the vigilante 'heroism' exemplified by Charles Bronson in *Death Wish* or Robert De Niro in *Taxi Driver*. It would have been surprising if the commercial value of his story had escaped Masters. He also talked like a predator, bragging to the media: 'I chose to arm myself [at an early age]. I knew eventually, at some point in my life, I would eventually use it [the gun].' Adding that he was a marine and prepared to take the enemy with him, Masters next concluded, 'This situation is what everyone lives in fear of – a couple of skinhead Mexicans robbing you at 1 a.m. with a screwdriver.' The reasonable person would surely ask why he singled out Mexicans. Wouldn't white taggers also scare him? Masters's characterization of the taggers as Mexicans proved what many Latino leaders had been saying about the mood of white Los Angeles. Yet Latino elected officials remained quiet in the face of such racist remarks: apparently the widespread support for Masters made them afraid to speak out.

Masters even went so far as to blame Arce's mother for his death: 'She murdered her son by being an irresponsible, uncaring parent', referring to stereotypes of Mexican mothers on welfare, with too many kids to care about their children's well-being. Masters seemed to have lived for the day when he would kill a tagger, preferably a dark-skinned one. Even his sardonic statement that his only fear was that he would become an Aryan Brother pinup betrayed his cynicism.

District Attorney Gil Garcetti refused to prosecute Masters. It made little difference to the D.A. that the prisons were full of young men of color who had much better claims of having killed in self-defense. Garcetti failed to explain how Masters was in 'imminent danger', why Masters was carrying a concealed weapon, and why he believed Masters's version of events and not Hillo's. Garcetti's blatant prejudice in the high-profile Masters case further eroded the Latino community's respect for the justice system. Many felt that if Masters had been a Mexican who had killed a white youth, the district attorney would not have been quick to drop the charges. And more important, Garcetti's refusal to prosecute in practical terms amounted to a declaration of open season on Mexicans.

Many Euroangelenos – and unfortunately even some Latinos – were so gripped by anti-gang hysteria that they celebrated Masters as an urban hero. A seventeen-year-old friend of Arce's provided a succinct and more accurate summation of Masters: 'He's no hero. A hero saves lives. He took one.'

A Final Solution

As of 1993 Angelenos had not reached the extremes of Río de Janeiro, where street kids have been hunted down and murdered. Instead, California's 'final solution' is to build prisons. In 1995, for the first time, California would spend more on prisons than on its two university systems, the University of California and the California State Universities.[26] California has spent $5 billion to expand its prisons from 23,534 to 61, 983 beds; the number of inmates increased from 23,511 to 119,668 by Deccember 1993. Although most Latino politicians knew better, in public they have generally accepted the proposition that the state's social decay can be ended by passing tougher laws and building more and bigger prisons.

By the year 2000, the total prison population in California is expected to be almost double the 1990 figure. According to the L.A. Sheriff's Department, Latinos were a majority of the inmates in county jails by the early 1990s, and they were fast becoming a majority of the state prison population.[27] Latinos will probably comprise 50 percent of all new inmates by 2000.

This is predictable, since most Latinos are poor and the Latino population is relatively young – two factors associated with crime. Another reason for the increasing Latino incarceration rate is the dependence of Latinos on an underground economy, largely fueled in California by the drug trade. The government's War on Drugs has disproportionately targeted young Latinos and African Americans.[28] And penalties for using the drugs of choice among minorities carry heavier sentences than those used by the white middle class, a factor also resulting in a high rate of incarceration for Latinos and Blacks. Then these youth are held in detention centers, which are breeding grounds for gangs: 'Parental controls are weakened both by the obvious impotence of the parents against the system, and by the ever-increasing amount of control exerted by the system.'[29] Being incarcerated together increased solidarity among Chicanos and introduced them to organized criminal behavior, building a core of state-raised kids whose reality was in fact not the barrio but the institution.

Mandatory sentences also played a role in the institutionalization of the poor, which included many Latinos. Even judges were angered by the unfairness of the mandatory sentencing requirements passed by the state legislature. The public seemed convinced that harsher punishment would make criminals think twice about committing crimes, even though a number of studies indicate that mandatory sentences are ineffective in curbing crime.[30]

By the mid 1990s, hysteria about crime had built to the point that California Governor Pete Wilson saw it as a major political opportunity and began pushing his 'Three Strikes' bill. Wilson signed the law in front of seventeen TV cameras, dismissing arguments that the 'Three Strikes' law would cost taxpayers heavily. According to Wilson, the increased prison population would save taxpayers money because prisoners would not have the opportunity to commit crimes. An additional 84,000 inmates, he said, would save the state $16.8 billion in social benefits, since each inmate committed an average of $200,000 in crimes.[31] The only problem with this argument was the total lack of evidence supporting it.

Anti-crime proposals at the state and federal levels included everything but the spending of money for intervention programs. The public sense was that problems such as drugs could be solved by putting the burden of saying 'no' on a poor teenagers who wanted the 'good life'. The state spent $3,900 a year to educate a child and roughly $30,000 a year to keep an adult behind bars. Something was seriously wrong with the public's perception of reality – or even of its own long-term interests.[32]

The Children's Advocacy Institute reported that 'slow strangulation of public resources for children's education, health and welfare' was taking place as the state diverted funds to prisons. California's school districts were already spending $1,000 per child less than the national average. Given California's neglect, the Three Strikes law would cost an estimated $2 billion a year more by 2000 and $5.7 billion annually in thirty years. The money would have to come from still more cuts in education, given the limitations of Proposition 13 and other budget realities.[33]

Although crime was a problem, crime rates were no higher than they had been a decade earlier. According to the Department of Justice, there were 3,500 crimes for every 100,000 Californians in 1992 – down from 4,000 in 1980. There was just over a 1 percent chance of being a victim of a violent crime in any given year, and 1/100 of 1 percent of being a murder victim.[34] Yet hysteria raged on mindlessly, serving to justify abuse by police agencies.

The Gangs in Tan and Blue

In the days before a Los Angeles deputy sheriff's projectile killed Chicano journalist Rubén Salazar during the 29 August 1970 Chicano Moratorium, he was working on a series called 'What Progress in Thirty Years of Police–Community Relations?'[35] The series had been inspired by the shooting deaths of Guillermo Sánchez, twenty-two, and Beltrán Sánchez, twenty-three, known as the Sánchez cousins. They were killed by five Los Angeles Police Department officers and two San Leandro officers who broke into a room where the two men were visiting with friends. The police shouted 'freeze' in English, and gunned down the cousins. Officers called it a case of mistaken identity – but Rubén Salazar thought otherwise and began an investigation. To this day, many Chicanos are convinced that as a result of his police exposés Salazar was stalked and deliberately murdered. The fact that the deputies involved in

Salazar's murder were never prosecuted gives credence to this belief.

Throughout the 1970s and 1980s police authorities spied on community organizations, attempting to frustrate efforts for social change. As a result in 1978 the American Civil Liberties Union filed *The Committee Against Police Abuse* v. *Los Angeles Police Department* on behalf of 141 plaintiffs, including individuals and groups. The legal discovery process revealed extensive police spying. In one case, a police officer lived with a plaintiff for seven years and had a child with her so as to spy on her friends. Surveillance of Left groups such as the California State University, Northridge chapter of the Movimiento Estudiantil Chicanos de Aztlán (MEChA) and the Chicano Studies Department at that institution was common. At least two LAPD officers, Augie Moreno and José Ramírez, infiltrated MEChA and took Chicano Studies classes. The Police Department's Intelligence Division (PDID) even turned over files on individuals to the Western Goals Foundation, an ultra-right wing group.

The city spent millions of dollars in tax funds to defend the PDID, which police tried to portray as an anti-terrorist unit. As part of the final settlement, the PDID was officially dissolved in January 1983.[36] But its clone, the Criminal Intelligence Division, continued functioning until July 1992, when Chief Willie L. Williams ordered the offices of that division closed and its files sealed, amid allegations that the unit had continued the PDID's work of spying on politicians and community organizations.[37]

Only occasionally did the media report police abuse; even rarer was the politician who criticized law enforcement agencies. It was just not good politics to be perceived as 'soft on crime'. The unwillingness to prosecute errant police officers placed an unfair burden on the relatives of their victims, who were forced to live with the stigma that came with public perception that their beloved had committed a crime. To get a measure of justice, families were forced to hire lawyers and go to civil court to clear their reputations, an expensive and time-consuming process. And although a family might succeed in clearing the name of their dead son or daughter, the system remained unchanged. And the officer who had used deadly force was not even deterred from doing so again: officers knew that the chance of being prosecuted was slight and, even if they were indicted, the costs of defense would be assumed by taxpayers. Furthermore, while on trial they still collected their salaries and if punitive damages were eventually awarded, taxpayers would again pay the bill.

Even so, many complaints were filed and lawsuits were pursued. In 1992 the City of Los Angeles paid $18.9 million in settlements, judgements and misconduct cases, exceeding the $13 million paid in 1991 and $7 million in 1990. This was more than 10 percent of the city's $140 million budget shortfall in that year.[38] These settlements mapped only a small of part of the mountain of police abuse that marked both the LAPD and the L.A. County Sheriff's Department.[39]

The Los Angeles County Sheriff's Department

For most people, especially those outside Los Angeles, the sheriff's deputies are probably less known for their brutality than the LAPD – but they deserve a similar reputation. In May 1992, President George Bush's Justice Department rated the Los Angeles Sheriff's Department second highest in its brutality in the US for its annual average of thirty-four complaints for violations of civil rights.[40]

The Los Angeles Sheriff's Department patrols most of the unincorporated areas and incorporated municipalities in the county that are outside the City of Los Angeles, and has therefore often escaped close scrutiny from the L.A. press and other media. Its best-known activity was for many years the appearance of Eugene Bizcailuz, scion of an old California family, who rode a horse in Pasadena's Rose Parade. The department itself has deliberately kept a low profile, but its history includes longstanding abuse of Mexicans and Chicanos. In 1942, Captain Ed Durán Ayres, chief of the Sheriff's Bureau of International Relations, presented a report to a grand jury stating that Mexicans had an innate desire to kill, or at least to let blood; such characteristics were supposedly inherited from their Indian and Mexican pasts. The Ayres report, used in evidence during the infamous Sleepy Lagoon Case described in Chapter 6, helped to convict those defendants. It also served to justify a massive dragnet involving the sheriff's deputies, the LAPD and the California Highway Patrol that netted over 600 suspected gang members in August 1943.

In 1946, a deputy shot and killed thirteen-year-old Eugene Montenegro while he climbed out of a window, allegedly with a knife in his hand. The district attorney dismissed the murder as 'justifiable homicide.' This set a pattern for postwar treatment of Chicanos by sheriff's deputies. During the 1950s, Sheriff Eugene Bizcailuz used the supposed gang menace as an excuse to declare a curfew for gang members. In that climate, City Councilman (later Supervisor) Kenneth Hahn began building his career by attacking the Mexican gang menace.

In 1964, the L.A. County Relations Commission released a report critical of the sheriff's department and other police agencies. The community had protested the rash of county jail beatings, such in January 1966 when seven deputies beat three Chicano inmates. As usual, the district attorney dropped the case against the deputies, on the grounds that they had not been told of their right to have an attorney present at the time of their confessions. Nothing came of the commission's report; nor did law-and-order politicos protest this use of the Supreme Court's recent *Miranda* ruling to let lawbreakers go free.

On 23 May 1966, over a hundred East L.A. residents confronted officers when they tried to make an arrest. Eventually, twenty-five officers arrived to back up the pair, and two shots were fired to disperse the crowd. Sheriff Peter

Pitchess accused the Council of Mexican American Affairs of inciting the community because it documented brutality cases. The American Civil Liberties Union's East Los Angeles Police Practices Center recorded seventy-six complaints against the sheriff's department from September 1966 to July 1968.

Tensions between the sheriff's deputies and the Chicano community were strained on the eve of the 1970 Chicano Moratorium against the Vietnam War; twenty-two people were arrested in front of the Belvedere substation for protesting the death of six inmates under mysterious circumstances at this facility in a five-month period. On 29 August 1970, sheriff's deputies led the offensive against the 30,000 demonstrators peacefully protesting the Vietnam War. In the wake of that attack, which left three Chicanos dead, including Rubén Salazar, Sheriff Pitchess's defense was, 'Don't forget these deputies were in combat.' The sheriff's department intended to keep a tight lid on the Chicano community, and it took advantage of the occasion of the 16th of September parade that year to beat marchers.

In 1972 Gerald F. Uelmen, dean of the Santa Clara University School of Law, conducted a study that found only 1 of 82 deputy-involved shootings in the preceding two years had been ruled outside of policy, that is, contrary to deparmental guidelines on the use of force. (Even the LAPD had found that 34 of 258 police shootings had been out of policy.)[41] Given their impunity, it is hardly surprising to find the sheriff's deputies were involved in so many instances of flagrant abuse. Take the 1978 case of Gordon Castillo Hall, sixteen. In Duarte, an L.A. county town northeast of Downtown L.A., a gang member shot at postal officer Jesse Ortiz and his two stepbrothers, Victor and Daniel Lara, killing Ortiz. L.A. sheriff's deputies raided a party near the shooting, arrested Castillo Hall, and dragged him in front of a makeshift lineup with squad cars shining their lights in his face. The Laras, contradicting an earlier description of the murderer, identified Castillo Hall, although he was much smaller than the earlier suspect. At the trial Castillo Hall was represented by incompetent counsel who did not investigate properly and did not call witnesses to prove that Castillo Hall had not been at the scene of the crime. Hall's attorney further failed to challenge 'expert' witnesses, who testified that Castillo Hall had been a gang member and that Chicano gang members had a greater propensity to violence than Black or white gang members.[42]

Castillo Hall's mother, Bertha, had sold her home to pay for the incompetent trial lawyer. After her son was convicted, she approached the now legendary lawyer Ricardo Cruz to represent her son. The Committee to Free Gordon Castillo Hall was formed and raised over $60,000 for legal expenses. Meanwhile, many Duarte residents knew that Castillo Hall had not murdered Ortiz, and the Laras told authorities that they had made a mistake in identifying Hall as the shooter. Investigating deputies recommended that the case be reopened. However, the judge refused to grant such a motion, and District Attorney John Van de Kamp, then running for state attorney general, stone-walled. Finally, a sympathetic state Supreme Court (many of whose members were later removed precisely because their fairness) arranged for a state referee to hear the new evidence. The referee recommended reopening the case, citing as reasons an overzealous district attorney, trial errors and incompetent defense counsel.[43] In June 1993, a Los Angeles jury finally awarded Castillo Hall $4.4 million in damages. They held that sheriff's deputies and the district attorney's office had violated his civil rights 'when they put him – a shirtless and hand-cuffed sixteen-year-old – in that nighttime lineup.'[44] The story did not end there, however. County attorney John Daly, wanting to wear down Castillo Hall, recommended that the county appeal the verdict. It did, but later agreed to a settlement. As of this writing the county has still not paid Castillo Hall.[45]

Another infamous case is that of Jildardo Plasencia. In 1980, the Plasencias hosted a family New Year's Eve party in their Willowbrook home. The women and girls were in the house, the men and boys in a converted rumpus room in the garage. At about 9 p.m. Jildardo fired two guns and a shotgun into the air to celebrate the approaching New Year. The firing of guns into the air on New Year's was of course illegal. Sheriff's deputies, however, had been instructed at roll call that day to call for backup in such incidents and to go in with flashing lights. But deputies David Anderson and Sandra Jones did neither.

According to the deputies, they encountered two men. The first immediately put up his hands. The other, Jildardo, allegedly stood in the garage doorway and pointed a gun at Jones, who shot and killed him. In the next three or four seconds, the deputies fired nine times, seven times through the partially opened garage door. Inside, three men, two teenagers and three small boys crouched in terror. When the shooting stopped, Jildardo lay dead with an unloaded revolver in his hand; Juan Santoyo, eighteen, was wounded in the leg; and three-year-old Jilardo, Jr had also been hit.

An investigation subsequently cleared the deputies of any wrongdoing. Although they were mistaken, they had acted 'reasonably' according to investigators. Witnesses were said to corroborate the officers' version of events. The coroner's report, based on a blood-splatter test, supposedly proved that Jildardo had pointed the gun at Jones. The district attorney refused to prosecute the officers or investigate further.

Six years later, Stella Plasencia, her five children, and Santoyo received a judgement of just under $1.4 million. Attorney Samuel Paz, cofounder of the People's College of Law, had refuted the original findings. He found that the coroner's report had misquoted witnesses, and Jildardo had not been standing in the doorway but was sitting in the rear of the garage when he was shot and killed. The officers had blindly shot into the garage. However, even with this new evidence the district attorney declined to prosecute.[46]

When Sherman Block replaced Peter Pitchess as Los Angeles County Sheriff in 1982, his authority was much more encompassing than that of LAPD Chief Gates, which was enormous. Block answered only to the district attorney and the Board of Supervisors, which amounted to carte blanche. Moreover, he was an elected official who had amassed political chips by supporting incumbents and candidates in unincorporated areas throughout Los Angeles County. Block, who was a Jewish American, also had a strong constituency within that community. Like Gates, Block refused to discipline errant deputies within his force of over 7,900 officers. He also refused to share with the public information on internal discipline within the department, further shielding his officers.

The *Daily News* reported in 1990 that of fifty-six persons shot under questionable circumstances since 1985, 89 percent were minorities. Of twenty-two Sheriff's Department shootings during this same period, the district attorney failed to prosecute a single case as excessive force, although lawsuits nearly doubled and the county paid out $8.5 million to settle suits during the three-year period ending in September 1989. Beth Barrett and David Parish of the *Daily News* ran a multipage story of deputy misdeeds in October 1990. The reporters found that Deputy Paul J. Archambault was involved in two controversial shootings in the previous three years. One of these shootings had cost the county $520,000 (the other featured in one of the largest police brutality lawsuits in Southern California history). In both cases, officers involved had planted a gun and a police baton on suspects after deputies had shot them. The department spokesperson refused to tell reporters if the cases involving Archambault had been investigated or whether disciplinary action had been taken.

The first shooting occurred on a night in March 1987, when deputies went to East Los Angeles looking for Pascual Solis. Reportedly, Solis had hit his pregnant wife. Deputies said that they had been warned Solis might be on PCP. According to the deputy, Solis ripped the baton from his hands and threatened hi, apparently under the influence of drugs. Archambault said he drew his gun after Solis raised the baton in a motion to hit him, pouring all six rounds into Solis. He then reloaded his gun and shot four more bullets into the suspect. An autopsy stated that Solis was not under the influence of PCP and witnesses said that Solis had never grabbed the deputy's baton. Solis was crouching, not standing, when the deputy shouted at him not to move and began shooting. After firing six rounds, according to a witness, another deputy asked if Solis was moving, whereupon Archambault said 'yes' and fired four more rounds into him. A pathologist's findings were consistent with the witness's testimony.[47]

The reporters found that since 1985 at least fifty-six persons had been shot under highly questionable circumstances; forty-nine of them were minorities; thirty-one were not armed; and not one of the fifty-six had fired at a deputy.[48] According to the reporters, in five and a half years no charges had been filed against on-duty deputies. The Sheriff's Department assigned the investigation of shooting cases to its own homicide detectives, and the District Attorney's office had the authority to prosecute or not. (Even the LAPD had a special officer and team to investigate officers involved in shootings; this team provides reports to the Police Commission, the DA's office and higher LAPD officers.) Only a fraction of the cases involving misconduct by sheriff's deputies were even written up.[49] Evaluation of deputies was oral, and no written record was ever produced.[50] The Golden Rule among the deputies was a code of silence.

In 1992 the two *Daily News* investigative reporters studied the county jail system, which had been the focus of periodic protests. Block claimed that his deputies did an 'outstanding' job under difficult circumstances, but Parrish and Barrett discovered evidence to the contrary: 'County taxpayers have paid more than $11.1 million in the past five years alone in neglect, beating or wrongful death cases involving jail inmates – many of the victims had been arrested for seemingly minor offenses such as unpaid traffic tickets or drunk driving.'[51] During the 1980s, poor or indifferent medical care led to at least fourteen deaths.[52]

The racial breakdown of the L.A. County jail inmates by the early 1990s was 46 percent Latino, 34 percent African American, 18 percent white, and 2 percent other. Former deputy Steven Gordon described the attitude of many deputies as a plantation mentality: racism was rampant and deputies went unpunished for burning a Klu Klux Klan cross in front of African American prisoners' cells. Inmates were subjected to 'flashlight therapy' (hitting them with a flashlight). In one case, after a gang clash an inmate was forced to crawl through a gauntlet of baton-swinging deputies.[53]

Inside the jails, deputies enjoyed an impunity comparable to that enjoyed by deputies on patrol outside. Between 1985 and 1990, only eight of the eighty-nine deputies disciplined for using excessive force in the jails were fired; of the remaining eighty-one, ten received a reprimand and seventy-one, suspensions. In 61 percent of the suspensions for using excessive force in the jail, the deputies received five or less days; in 18 percent, fifteen or more days. Two deputies resigned before any discipline was imposed.[54]

Deputies also were accused of fomenting racial tension between Blacks and Latinos in jail. At the 8,300-inmate Saugus facility (the 'Peter J. Pitchess Honor Ranch'), there were frequent fights between Blacks and Latinos. On 2 October 1993 2,600 inmates rioted, and it took fifty-four deputies to restore order; there were more than fifty fights in all in the overcrowded facility during 1993.[55]

Meanwhile, tensions between Latinos and the sheriff increased as a grand jury found insufficient evidence to prosecute deputies in the killing of David Angel Ortiz on 18 August 1991, and Arturo Jiménez on 3 August 1991.[56] Father Juan Santillan led the community in calling attention to these and other killings, demanding that the police violence stop.[57] Deputy José Belmares had shot fifteen-year-old David Ortiz in the back in late August after a high-speed chase in Artesia. Ortiz and another teenager had been seen driving a stolen car, and had tried to get away. A witness said that after Ortiz finally stopped, the officer apparently shot him in the back without provocation. Belmares replied that he thought that the boy was reaching for a gun. The deputy did not summon paramedics, handcuffing the youth first. Dr Irving Roots testified that the Ortiz could have survived if he had been given prompt medical attention.[58]

Arturo Jiménez was shot by Deputy Jason Mann in the Ramona Gardens Housing Project, a murder that touched off an outbreak with over 300 residents taking part: seventy-five deputies were called in to quell the rebellion. According to the Sheriff's Department, Mann had never been subject to official disciplinary action. In fact, he had been transferred with four other deputies from the Lynwood station, where allegations were made that he belonged to a neo-Nazi group called the Vikings, a charge that Mann denied. In October, US District Judge Terry J. Hatter, Jr confirmed the existence of a 'neo-Nazi, white supremacist gang' of deputies called the Vikings at Lynnwood and found evidence of racial hostility towards African Americans and Latinos.[59] Deputies claimed that the Vikings were a harmless social group.

Community protest over the murder of Jiménez and other killings pressured the Board of Supervisors to commission an investigation of the department by Special Counsel James G. Kolts, a retired Superior Court judge. The Kolts report was modeled after the Christopher Commission probe of the LAPD (see below).[60] A team of thirty attorneys and volunteers examined 124 civil suits and 800 internal investigations, along with training and disciplinary procedures. Kolts reported that one deputy had at least twenty-seven excessive force and harassment complaints against him. Another was the subject of seven internal investigations; the report identified a total of sixty-two problem officers.[61] It described a department where discipline and oversight had broken down, and supervisors routinely tolerated abuse of prisoners and suspects, particularly Latinos and Blacks. Discrimination against gays and lesbians was also widespread.[62] The report criticized the department for the lack of Latino and Spanish-speaking officers in general at its Firestone station, and called for civilian participation in the review of the sheriff: 'The sheriff has no real boss. He is not appointed by the Board of Supervisors, and he is not supervised by them … we know of no major metropolitan police department in the United States which is not subject to some civilian oversight – except the Los Angeles County Sheriff's Department.'

Kolts was a 67-year-old grandfather, a registered Republican, and a fervent supporter of the death penalty who, according to one colleague, was a real law-and-order guy. Even so, Kolts was appalled by what he found.[63] However, he was not shocked enough to urge real control over the Sheriff's Department. His plan to control Block did not call for civilian oversight. In essence, he proposed that a retired judge to review complaints. If the judge were unsatisfied, a 'relevant captain' would reinvestigate. The entire process would remain in-house, which defeated the purpose of civilian oversight. To be effective, the oversight authority would have to have investigative powers along with the power to discipline, and its staff would have to be professional and competent.[64]

The Board of Supervisors moved slowly on the Kolts report. Not much could be done without Block's agreement unless the board was willing to challenge Block politically in a way that the supervisors were unwilling to consider.[65] Block had his own political machine, which cut into most of the supervisors' districts. City Council members and mayors of small towns like Bellflower, San Dimas, Lakewood, La Cañada and Paramount were beholden to Block, who endorsed them at election time and helped them sell tickets to their fund-raising banquets. On occasion Block fixed the officials' 'problems'. All of the supervisors tread softly, with Supervisor Kenny Hahn calling Block 'the most intelligent sheriff in America'.[66]

In January 1993, supporters of reform on the Board of Supervisors finally voted to appoint an outside panel of retired judges to review the department. This was a compromise agreed to by Kolts and Block. Supervisor Gloria Molina claimed that this was the best that could be achieved at the time. Representatives of the Coalition of Sheriff's Accountability, made up of minority groups and the American Civil Liberties Union, were disappointed. Psychology professor Gloria Romero, who along with Attorney Sam Paz had been among the Chicano leaders most active on this issue, condemned the compromise: 'There is nothing civilian about this review. It is a facade.' Block had insisted that the ombudsman, the retired judges and the auditor could only raise questions about his actions, but could not issue orders themselves or reverse any of his decisions. Despite this setback, Romero, Paz and Father Santillan worked tirelessly to keep the issue of police brutality before the county supervisors, pressure that was necessary even to achieve the minor gains of the Kolts reforms.[67]

Supervisor Yvonne Brathwaite Burke questioned the composition of the panel, pointing out that it was 'a terrible mistake' to restrict membership to a judicial group dominated by white males. Indeed, of the eighty-seven retired Superior Court and appellate judges in the county, 96.5 percent were male; 94.2 percent were Anglo. Only Brathwaite Burke and Molina were willing to question the predominance of white males on the review commission; they were joined by none of the liberal white males on the board. Supervisor Ed Edleman announced that he would support a compromise only if it were approved by Block.[68] Both Edleman and Supervisor Mike Antonovich gave Block free rein, allowing him to exclude Kolts from the panel of judges who would review the most serious unresolved cases of excessive force.[69]

The Gang in Blue and Rodney King

For years the Los Angeles Police Department has been known for abusive conduct, especially towards Blacks and Latinos. Daryl Gates, its chief during the infamous beating of Rodney King, epitomized the LAPD attitude with a comment during a 1986 case. Six LAPD officers had crashed into the home of Jesse Lárez, purportedly searching for a weapon hidden by Lárez's son Edward. Officers smashed windows, pulled his daughter, Diane, onto the floor by her hair, destroyed household items, and broke the senior Lárez's nose in their search for a weapon they never found.[70] Much later, in October 1988, federal district court jurors awarded the Lárez family $90,503 in damages. Upon hearing the federal jury's verdict against his officers, Gates told reporters that Lárez was 'probably lucky' that they only broke his nose, adding, 'How much is a broken nose worth?'

US District Judge Robert M. Takasugi was incensed by Gates's remarks, and allowed them to be entered into the record during the second phase of the trial, which sought to determine if Gates had condoned the tactics used by his officers. The jury agreed, and ordered Gates to pay more than $170,000 in punitive damages. The Los Angeles City Council voted to pay the judgement against the chief, with a council member remarking that Gates's comments had been made 'in the scope of his employment'.

As the council's actions suggest, the LAPD has historically been a political force in the city of Los Angeles, with the chief insulated from political control and equivalent in power to the mayor. The chief broke unions, kept secret files on people, and at one time protected notorious madams. Because of resulting scandals, Mayor Fletcher Bowron replaced his old chief with William H. Parker, who in the early 1950s converted the LAPD from an inefficient and unreliable organization into a national model of a military-like police department.[71] In the 1950s the TV series *Dragnet* helped promote the image of the department as being thoroughly objective and fair, an image that the *Hunter* TV series continues today; Parker had his own television program called *The Thin Blue Line*. TV and movie studios found it useful to promote the LAPD, whose cooperation was essential in filming action scenes, and in giving producers a clean bill of ideological health during the McCarthy years. In reality, the department's image of itself was of an occupying army, and its *modus operandi* was to brutally beat a suspect, then charge him or her with drunkenness and resisting arrest. The local media, especially the *Los Angeles Times*, glorified Chief Parker, who built a legacy of departmental arrogance that made the Watts outbreaks and the Rodney King beating inevitable.[72] The next three chiefs, Tom Reddin, Ed Davis and Daryl Gates, were all Parker clones.

Addressing a Chamber of Commerce group in 1970, then Assistant Chief Gates characterized radical movements as nothing less that 'a revolution against the free-enterprise system'. He urged businessmen to support law enforcement's efforts to suppress radicalism. In 1990, Gates declared that casual drug users 'ought to be taken out and shot.'[73] On another occasion, he denounced Salvadorans as 'drunks', and gang members as the 'new barbarians'. Gates's public pronouncements and style of leadership clearly set the tone for the department and encouraged his officers to believe themselves the 'thin blue line' defending 'American' civilization.

Along with politicos, for many years the media turned the other way when it came to the excesses of Gates and the LAPD. This willful ignorance slowly began to change in after a 1979 incident. Two LAPD officers responded to a call after an African American woman, Eulia Love, threatened a gas company serviceman who came to disconnect her utilities, and forced him to leave her property. When Love brandished a kitchen knife, the officers shot and killed her. Although the Police Commission charged the officers with serious errors of judgement, Gates ruled the shooting in line with departmental policy. The Herald-Examiner took up the story, while the Los Angeles Times attempted to bury it. The Committee Against Police Abuse (CAPA) kept the story alive, launching what would become an era of piecemeal scrutiny of the LAPD in the press. This scrutiny unsettled Gates, who, in the Parker tradition, was not accustomed to being questioned. Gates's growing paranoia contributed to a siege mentality among his officers. As the 1980s went on, the chief seemed to become more aggressive, intimidating the media and politicians alike. In the process, a small crew of officers began to think that they were the law.[74]

Despite public criticism, Gates refused to give an inch, and was backed by the D.A.'s office, which conspired with Gates to cover up police abuse: John Van de Kamp refused even to release statistical data about police misconduct.[75] Complaints against the LAPD escalated from 972 in 1980 to 1,826 in 1990.[76]

In 1990, the year before the Rodney King incident, the LAPD broke up a Justice for Janitors protest and brutally beat peaceful demonstrators; two women lost their unborn babies. (See Chapter 8.) This police attack was also videotaped. However, the media chose to give the attack on the janitors only limited coverage, perhaps because they saw the janitors as 'illegal aliens' who did not have the right to organize. In the case of the janitors, the Latino community kept its anger within channels defined and controlled by the system. What made the King beating different was the outpouring of moral outrage in the Black community; without that, nothing much would have happened, and the King case would eventually have been forgotten. But the message from the Black community this time would be, No justice, no peace.[77]

Even before the acquittal of the LAPD officers who beat Rodney King, the African American community was outraged by the fatal shooting of fifteen-year-old Latasha Harlins by Korean grocer Soon Ja Du, in March 1991 in a dispute over a bottle of orange juice. Even more outrageous was the decision of

Judge Joyce Karlin to grant probation to Soon Ja Da, fining her only $500 and ordering her to perform 400 hours of community service.

On 3 March 1991, not long after the shooting of Latasha Harlins, 25-year-old Rodney King was out on the town with friends, drinking and driving. On parole for second-degree robbery, King panicked and exited the freeway when a Highway Patrol car attempted to pull him over. The CHP gave chase through city streets, joined by the LAPD. When King finally stopped, more than two dozen police converged on him: twenty-one from the LAPD, four from the CHP, and two from the LA Unified School District. What happened next is probably the best-known event in recent Los Angeles history. King was repeatedly beaten by LAPD officers, who hit him with their batons a total of fifty-six times. The beating was so vicious that King's tooth filings were literally knocked out of his mouth. Before and after arresting King, they made racist remarks over the police radio; the official recordings preserve their words in all their hatred and contempt. But something made this different from many similar incidents over the years: a tenant in the apartment building overlooking the scene videotaped the beating and gave the tape to a local television station.

In July, a commission headed by Warren Christopher, a well-known L.A. lawyer and political player, produced a 228-page report on the beating that criticized the Los Angeles Police Department and its leadership. It identified a 'problem group of dozens of officers who used excessive force regularly'; it found racist and sexist messages on police computers, and a 'siege mentality' that alienated the police from the community. It called the LAPD's disciplinary and complaint system inadequate. Finally, it recommended that Gates retire and that his successor be limited to two five-year terms.[78]

Gates stonewalled the Christopher Commission, refusing to resign. The mayor and the City Council finally took the initiative and put the reforms on the June 1992 ballot as Charter Amendment F, which passed; the campaign for the amendment was led by Christopher and among Latino politicos was supported by Mike Hernández, Art Torres and Gloria Molina, as well as by activists such as Gloria Romero and Sam Paz.[79] Cracks started to appear within the previously monolithic police department, with Gates purging some of his closest friends on the force because they had cooperated with the Christopher Commission.

Throughout the tumult, the majority of the members of the Los Angeles City Council supported Chief Gates, excusing the King affair as an aberration rather than an example of the LAPD's standard operating procedure. Councilman Richard Alatorre, for example, attacked critics of the chief, and declared that he was waiting for the evidence to come in. The Christopher Commission report *was* the evidence – but still the council did nothing.[80]

Elected Latino officials created a moral crisis by remaining largely silent about the King incident. Their timidity emboldened some Latino leaders to support Gates, perhaps hoping for a political payoff by doing so. In refusing to judge when judgement was clearly required, these leaders undercut their own civil rights tradition. Calling the LAPD's brutality problem 'systemic' – which was true – did not excuse them from withholding moral censure of Daryl Gates's record as police chief. The situation was all the more tragic because the Latino officials knew better: both the LAPD and the L.A. County Sheriff's Department had a history of using nightsticks on Chicanos. But not enough public pressure came from Latino communities to make the politicians speak out.

Los Angeles is a very segregated city, with most of its residents keeping to their own communities. Chicanos and Latinos are no different than other Angelenos; they have incorporated much of the separateness of the dominant culture. Just as the Black community was largely silent after police attacked the Justice for Janitors demonstration at Century City, and for the most part did not participate in the movement against US intervention in Central America in the 1980s, most Latinos and Chicanos looked at the King beating as 'an African American thing'. Moreover, there was open hostility in the Latino community towards Mayor Bradley, clouding the real issue of how Daryl Gates and Sherman Block ran their departments. In addition, the Chicano and African American communities had competing candidates to succeed Gates as the next police chief.

Meanwhile, the trial of the four officers was transferred to Simi Valley in Ventura County, a white, conservative area where many police officers lived.[81] The jury, all-white except for one Latina, found officers Theodore J. Briseño, Laurence M. Powell, probationary officer Timothy E. Wind, and Sgt Stacey C. Koon not guilty on 29 April 1992.[82] Anger at this verdict swept Los Angeles. Two thousand people gathered at the First African Methodist Episcopal Church to protest the verdict, but anger in the streets soon turned to violence. Mayor Bradley called for a curfew; the National Guard was deployed; and calm did not return until the weekend. The city came to a standstill from 29 April to 2 May.[83]

During five days of unrest, ten African American and Latino men died at the hands of officers from the Sheriff's Department, the National Guard, and the Los Angeles, Compton and Pasadena police departments: a total of forty-five people died in connection with the uprising; 5,633 were arrested. A RAND Corporation analysis determined that 51 percent of those charged with various crimes from 29 April to 2 May were Latino and 36 percent were Black. Latino males aged eighteen to twenty-four accounted for 30 percent of the eventual arrests; Anglo males accounted for 11 percent. Many were picked up on curfew and/or looting violations. Blacks accounted for 47 percent of the arrests on weapon charges, Latinos 39 percent and Anglos 12 percent.[84] (While the statistics were not limited to uprising cases, they reflected widespread Latino involvement in the unrest.)

Many of the Latino arrests were not directly connected to the outbreak, but reflected the LAPD's strategy of working with the INS to spread a reign of terror among Latinos by turning over those arrested to La Migra for investigation as 'illegals'. *La Opinión* reported that some 1,888 undocumented workers were picked up during the outbreaks.[85] Labor Secretary Lyn Martin bragged that 30 percent of those arrested for looting were 'illegal aliens', a claim that investigation did not substantiate. The LAPD entered apartments under the pretext of looking for goods stolen by looters and also made sweeps of labor sites where undocumented workers waited to get work.[86]

Except for crowd pictures of looters, the media generally ignored Latinos during the outbreaks.[87] Latino reporters at the *Los Angeles Times*, according to my sources, had a showdown with their assignment editors after the uprising, complaining about their assignments as well as the paper's coverage.[88]

According to a poll taken soon after the outbreak, Californians were not as polarized by the King verdict as one might imagine: 74 percent were very or somewhat sympathetic with African American anger at the verdicts; only 15 percent were not sympathetic at all; 35 percent blamed the uprising on the breakdown of moral authority in the inner city, while 33 percent blamed it on the lack of economic opportunity, and 12 percent blamed it on racism. A majority of 51 percent said that future outbreaks could be prevented through more moral leadership.[89] But there appeared to be a lack of consensus as to what was meant by 'moral leadership', and the entire poll seemed more upbeat than reality suggested. How much Angelenos were changed by the Rodney King uprising, as it came to be known, is open to conjecture. A UCLA survey six months afterward found that public confidence in government remained low. It also found very little evidence of positive change. Negative ethnic stereotypes seemed firmly in place. Indeed, even before the uprising, residents felt such despair that 'there was little room', said the survey, 'to further shift opinion in a negative direction.' The survey found no renewed commitment to addressing poverty, racial inequality or prejudice, making a future uprising inevitable. Most respondents believed that poverty, for example, resulted from societal and individual shortcomings: 45.1 percent of non-Blacks rated Blacks as lower in intelligence, while 44.6 percent of non-Latinos rated Latinos as less intelligent, and 63.4 percent rated Blacks as more likely to prefer living on welfare to working, versus the 52.2 percent of non-Latinos who believed that Latinos were more likely to prefer living on welfare.[90]

When the LAPD officers were retried in Los Angeles on federal charges, Sgt Stacy Koon and Officer Laurence Powell were found guilty. The other two officers were acquitted. US District Judge John G. Davies outraged everyone by sentencing those convicted to a paltry two and half years in jail,[91] but this time no mass protest followed.

The trial of the defendants in the beating of Reginald Denny, a white truck driver who was pulled from his vehicle in South Central L.A. and beaten during the outbreak, took place in a charged atmosphere. Three Black men, Damien Williams, Antoine Williams and Henry Watson, were accused of beating Denny and eleven others during the outbreak. From the perspective of many African Americans, the defendants were themselves victims and the charges should have been dropped. At the same time, almost everyone realized that Denny had done nothing to deserve the vicious beating he had received, but had simply been in the wrong place at the wrong time. Some pointed out that Latinos and Asians had also been brutalized by Denny's attackers.[92] Fidel López, one of these victims, testified at the Denny trial later; he was upset with the relatively moderate verdicts, since, he said, 'They tried to kill me.'[93] *L.A. Times* writer Tina Daunt reported that 'as Lopez lay bloody and unconscious on the pavement, his face and genitals were spray-painted' and he was robbed of $2,800. But it's also important to note that Rev. Bennie Newton, an African American, saved López by throwing himself on top of him during the attack.[94]

The difference between the treatment of the white police officers and the Denny defendants made genuine dialogue about the verdicts impossible. First, the court granted the motion on behalf of the four police officers for a change of venue, which led to their being judged by an all-white jury (the one Latina on the Simi Valley jury was subjected to incredible peer group pressure). In contrast, the Denny defendants were not judged by their peers. The jury did not have a Black majority, and the judge was certainly not Black.[95] There was also an obvious difference in the charges. The most serious charge against the officers was assault, which carried a maximum sentence of seven and a half years. The Denny defendants were charged with attempted murder, which carries a life sentence (with the possibility of parole). Moreover, the bail for the officers was $5,000 to $30,000, whereas the bail for the Denny defendants ranged from $250,000 to $580,000. Finally, the quality of the prosecution differed in the two cases. The prosecution seemed much better prepared in the case of the Denny defendants.[96] In the end, however, the Black defendants won a symbolic victory with the acquittal of Damien Williams on the attempted murder charge; he was, however, sentenced to ten years on other charges.[97]

The verdicts in the trial for the attack on Denny revealed the problems that arise as inner-city diversity increases. Many of the Black–Latino tensions in this period developed out of the changed demographic character of South Central L.A. as the neighborhood approached 50 percent Latino (see Chapter 6). Many Blacks resented the arrival of so many Latinos in South Central; they were changing many of its traditionally Black institutions. As one of my students commented, 'Jefferson High School is over 90 percent Latino, but the Black students and alumni want to treat it as if it was still Black.' The adjustment was difficult, with many Blacks themselves saying that they felt like the whites who had fled the neighborhoods as the Black community moved in.[98] They resented their Mexican and Latino neighbors hanging clothes on their fences, or seeing a favorite restaurant replaced by a Salvadoran restaurant with a sign reading 'I love El Salvador.'[99] Even the sound of the street changed with Mexican music blaring away and people speaking an unfamiliar language.[100] In addition to cultural rivalry, widespread poverty forced both Black and Brown to compete for limited resources. Tensions were natural, and those with influence in the respective communities clearly had a responsbility to try to keep competition within bounds. Black and Brown leaders needed to educate their constituencies on the difference between revolutionary acts and lumpen behavior, and to refuse to see each other as the enemy. Instead, tensions between Blacks and Latinos were heightened by squabbling among community powerbrokers as they competed for the resources promised in the wake of the King uprisings.

But for all the fanfare about Rebuild L.A., the city's response to the root causes of the King uprising, the private sector did not come through on projections of $6 billion in new private investment in the area. A year after the outbreak, the *Daily News* reported that despite government promises, the scars of the uprisings remained. Of the 1,112 buildings that had to be demolished, permits to rebuild or repair them had been issued for only 176. Unemployment had risen from 9 percent to 10.4 percent in Los Angeles County by March 1993, and homicides from 228 to 244. Hundreds of Korean businesses had reopened, but more than two-thirds of those destroyed or damaged did not. Of an estimated 850 Latino businesses affected by the outbreak, most were unable to start up again. RLA claimed to have secured $500 million in private investment for the next five years. However, those commitments were like pledges for public radio; they could not be counted until they were paid. When the project ended on 30 June 1993, RLA had spent $2.9 million, or 70 percent, of the funds on salaries and administration, and only $533,000 on programs and services.[101] Eighteen months after the outbreak, jobs were still hard to come by.

Bradley's decision to appoint a private task force rather than tackle the job from City Hall came under increasing criticism,[102] as did the RLA's strategy of trickle-down economics. The Labor/Community Strategy Center published an alternative plan, *Reconstructing Los Angeles from the Bottom Up*. It called for a strengthening of democratic institutions like trade unions instead of depending on corporate solutions. Manuel Pastor, Jr of Occidental College also produced a study for the Tomás Rivera Center, suggesting that the impact of the outbreak continued to plague the city and that any recovery was contingent on improving Latino economic well-being. It warned that tensions between Blacks and Latinos might worsen because of competition for increasingly scarce resources. In the end most outside observers agreed that RLA's high-profile, eighty-person board was mostly show and that it had promised much more than it could deliver.[103]

Latino elected officials cooperated with the Rebuild L.A. effort. Supervisor

Gloria Molina and a coalition of Latino leaders fanned out from Pacoima to Pomona to win support for the plan they wanted to present to the RLA. Molina acknowledged that she was not optimistic that fundamental economic and social changes would take place, and admitted that lip service was being given to cleaning up the rubble in South Central. Council members Richard Alatorre and Mike Hernández also participated in the process, while residents of Pico-Union marched for peace.[104]

These efforts were soon caught up in political maneuvering. A group called La Alianza demanded that Xavier Hermosillo and Lee Baca be appointed to the RLA board, to counteract board member Rev. Danny Bakewell.[105] Bradley had announced that 80 percent of the clean-up contracts would be given to minority contractors, which many Blacks interpreted as African Americans. Rev. Bakewell of the Brotherhood Crusade checked worksites to see that Blacks were there, stopping the work at one site because he found Latinos working on the project. This caused a strong negative reaction from Latinos.[106] L.A. Times columnist Bill Boyarsky summed it up: 'It was one of the saddest and most troubling sights I'd witnessed since the riots – struggling African-American contractors against poor Latino construction workers, the bleak side of the new L.A.'

Amidst the frustration of attempts to secure public and private investment, many community groups were initially attracted by a US Justice Department program to consolidate social services delivery called Operation Weed and Seed. Its strategy was to 'weed out' crime from targeted neighborhoods, then to 'seed' the targeted areas with crime and drug prevention programs and increased resources for human services agencies.[107] Critics charged that the system was fraught with potential for abuse such as police spying, and the Labor/Community Strategy Center launched a county-wide fight against Weed and Seed. In the end, the city adopted the program to get $19 million in post-outbreak money, changing the name of the program and allegedly allowing local control.[108]

Meanwhile, the implementation of the Christopher Commission report on police conduct went slowly. Richard Riordan was elected mayor, and he took office with a tremendous political debt to the Police Protective League. During the campaign, his two arrests for drunk driving came up, and the League came to his defense. Riordan had opposed Charter Amendment F for reform of the police, and had been a close friend of Gates. Now it was up to him to name a new Police Commission that, under the city charter, would control the department.[109] Riordan appointed a Police Commission consisting of Herbert F. Boeckman II, a San Fernando car dealer and supporter of Pat Robertson's campaign for president in 1988; Rabbi Gary Greenbaum, a supporter of Charter Amendment F; Eugene Hernández, Jr, an unknown in the Latino community other than that he was a Republican and a graduate of Harvard Law School;

attorney Diedre Hill, daughter of a Black Assemblywoman; and Art Maddox, a senior account manager for Xerox.[110] The city's budgetary crisis seemed to be the standard reason given for their not doing anything about the Christopher Commission recommendations.[111]

The Fires to Come

In the aftermath of the King outbreak, Randy Holland produced a thought-provoking documentary called *The Fire This Time*, a film so controversial that even public television in Los Angeles refused to air it. Critics called it polemical, angry and disturbing – and it was. It was also the first time that the King outbreak had been put into a historical perspective. *The Fire This Time* traced the profileration of gangs and the resulting despair in South Central to the destruction of organic mainstays like the Black Panther Party and the Watts Writers' Workshop by the LAPD, political and cultural organizations that could have counteracted the deterioration of the community and the subsequent takeover by drugs and gangs. The centerpiece of the Holland argument was 'If a community is strong and groups are together, they can fight those things. But if they're in disarray and fighting each other, they can't come together and question policy and authority.'[112]

Few will deny Holland's assertion that South Central is worse off today than in 1965. Since the mid 1970s, the area has lost an estimated 200,000 jobs and its main industry now appears to be liquor stores. In a search for answers, Holland looked for a copy of a massive federal 25-year Master Plan to restore South Central and other urban centers commissioned by President Lyndon Johnson and published two years after the Watts Riots. Holland's search led him to the city archives where 'there's a file card there but you can't find the plan.'[113]

Without a doubt, a link exists between the Watts Riots of 1965, which also originated in South Central Los Angeles, and the Rodney King outbreak. Following the 1965 uprising, Governor Edmund G. Brown, Sr appointed the now famous McCone Commission, which included a young attorney by the name of Warren Christopher. The McCone Report itself contained, as one critic put it, 'little information that an intelligent college undergraduate could not have unearthed during 2 weeks of research.' It did, however, publicize the urban problems underlying the disturbances, and it remains one of the most highly quoted documents on urban riots.

As a Commission, we are seriously concerned that the existing breach, if allowed to persist, could in time split our society irretrievably. So serious and so explosive is the situation that, unless it is checked, the August riots may seem by comparison to be only a curtain-raiser for what could blow up one day in the future.[114]

The McCone Report recommended establishing an office of inspector general made up of civilians and LAPD officers to handle civilian complaints against officers, operating outside the regular LAPD chain of command. The office would report directly to the chief.

In 1968, Illinois Governor Otto Kerner chaired the eleven-member interracial National Advisory Commission on Civil Disorders. This commission asked three basic questions: What happened? Why did the urban riots happen? And what can be done to prevent them from happening again? It concluded: 'Race prejudice has shaped our history decisively; it now threatens to affect our future. White racism is essentially responsible for the explosive mixture which has been accumulating in our cities since the end of World War. II.'[115] Twenty-five years later, the Milton S. Eisenhower Foundation reported that 'Overall, in spite of some gains since the 1960s but especially because of the federal disinvestment of the 1980s, the famous prophesy of the Kerner Commission, of two separate societies, one Black, one White – separate and unequal – is more relevant today than in 1968, and more complex, with the emergence of multiracial disparities and growing income segregation.'[116]

The report continued, 'America found money to fight the Persian Gulf War, and it found the hundreds of billions of dollars needed to bail out the failed, deregulated savings and loan industry. America can find the money for a true strategy of child investment, youth investment and community reconstruction', adding that there had to be the right kind of leadership, and that it thought Bill Clinton was that leader.

But only an incorrigible optimist would conclude that Clinton will do anything about racism and the causes of urban unrest. Closer to the truth are the words of Dr Kenneth B. Clark, a renowned psychologist who appeared before the 1968 Kerner Commission and referred in his testimony to the reports of earlier commissions:

> I read the report ... of the 1919 riot in Chicago, and it is as if I were reading the report of the investigating committee on the Harlem riot of '43, the report of the McCone Commission on the Watts riot. I must again in candor say to you members of this Commission – it is a kind of Alice in Wonderland – with the same moving picture reshown over and over again, the same analysis, the same recommendations, and the same inaction.[117]

The logical conclusion to the history of inaction pointed out by Kenneth Clark is that someone should begin work on the sequel to *The Fire This Time*.

Notes

1. Gail Diane Cox, 'Voters Tough on Criminals', *National Law Journal*, 21 Nov. 1994; Daniel B. Wood, 'State Ballot Initiatives Place Hot-Issue Decisions in Laps of Electorate', *Christian Science Monitor*, 3 Nov. 1994.

2. Bert Beockman and Richard Riordan, 'L.A. Can Win the Battle of Fear and Crime', *Daily News*, 15 Nov. 1992.

3. Ibid.

4. Paul Hoffman and Mark Silverstein, 'Safe Streets Don't Require Lifting Rights', *Los Angeles Times*, 11 March 1993; Richard Lee Colvin and Jocelyn Y. Stewart, 'Life on the Street', *Los Angeles Times*, 24 Feb. 1992; Richard Lee Colvin and Jocelyn Y. Stewart, 'Gang Rules Valley's "Worst Block"', *Los Angeles Times*, 24 Feb. 1992: 4,000 people lived on this strip; 63 percent of the housing units were considered overcrowded, in contrast to 20 percent in Mission Hills, Panorama City, Sepulveda, and 28 percent in Los Angeles County as a whole. The block is 96 percent Latino; 90 percent of crime went unreported.

5. Sam Fulwood III, 'Federal Study Finds Violent Crime Hits Hardest at Nation's Latino Population', *Los Angeles Times*, 15 Jan. 1990.

6. Tracey Kaplan and Gabe Fuentes, 'Permanent Street Barricade in Valley Urged', *Los Angeles Times*, 15 Nov. 1989; 'Protestan en Pico-Union', *La Opinión*, 8 Aug. 1991. Activists with the Coalition Against a Police State burned some barricades in Pico-Union, which were supposed to keep drug dealers out and which also in effect imprisoned residents. Anne Burke, 'Fenced Community Reduces Crime, But Not Without Cost', *Daily News*, 31 Oct. 1993. Similar circumstances exist in the twenty-one city-run housing projects, with 31,000 tenants.

7. Jesse Katz, 'Latino Gang Carnage Is Part of an Invisible War', *Los Angeles Times*, 12 July 1992; José Luis Sierra, '1991 estableció nuevo récord de criminalidad', *La Opinión*, 24 Jan. 1992. Ramparts, the busiest precinct, had 139 homicides; there were 1,039 homicides, 39,458 robberies and 47,443 assaults in the city as a whole. The symbolism of Latino and Chicano gang members differed from those of Black gangs, which, although smaller in number, received much more media attention. The Crips and the Bloods, for instance, couch their rhetoric more in terms of victimization, tracing their roots back to the Black Power movement. 'Their message is steeped in themes of rebellion, brutality and community control', which incidentally ingratiated them with white radicals. Some Latino gang members saw themselves as defenders of the barrio, and, according to one source, had a more fatalistic vision, 'play now and pay later, what goes around comes around'; 'It is all part of the price for choosing *la vida loca*, they say, the crazy life.' Katz, *Los Angeles Times*, 12 July 1992.

Memo Muñoz, 'Lack of Opportunity Contributes to Latino Gang Problem', *Nuestro Tiempo*, 30 Jan. 1992, reported that according to James Diego Vigil, USC anthropologist, the cause of gangs is rooted in the disparity in the income of Chicanos and Anglos. He blames this on racism and inferior education. It is a vicious circle, in which people's earning power is limited, and they live in rundown neighborhoods where rents are cheap. Parents working long hours and family break-ups lead to lack of supervision. Peer pressure plays a major role in the recruitment of gang members. TV programs, films and videos indirectly promote gangs. Vigil estimated that 4 to 10 percent of Latino youth get involved in gangs. In Los Angeles, there were Chicano, Mexican and Central American gangs. Father Gregory Boyle of Dolores Mission said gang members have trouble coping with boredom and despair in their lives, drop out of school and start hanging out on the streets. In another work, gang experts Joan Moore and James Diego Vigil wrote: 'By the middle of 1989, Los Angeles law enforcement counted a total of 770 gangs in the metropolitan area. Although the Crips and Bloods (both black) received most of the media attention, Latino gangs were actually more numerous, accounting for 56 percent of the total number of gangs in the Los Angeles metropolitan area': Joan Moore and James Diego Vigil, 'Barrios In Transition', in Joan Moore and Raquel Pinderhughes, eds, *In the Barrios: Latinos and the Underclass Debate* (New York: Russell Sage Foundation, 1993), p. 42; Sylvester Monroe, 'Life in the 'Hood', *Time*, 15 June 1992, pp. 37–8; James Diego Vigil, *Barrio Gangs: Street Life and Identity in Southern California* (Austin, Tex.: University of Texas Press, 1988).

8. Psyche Pasqual, 'In Search of Peace', *Los Angeles Times*, 21 Oct. 1992; Marilyn Anita Dal-

rymple, 'Delinquency Hits Families Emotionally', *Daily News*, 27 June 1993. There was a tendency to want to shift the entire blame for delinquency to parents. The California legislature even passed a Street Terrorism Enforcement and Prevention Act under which parents could be jailed and fined if their children broke the law.

9. Robert J. Lopez and Jesse Katz, 'Mexican Mafia Tells Gangs to Halt Drive-Bys', *Los Angeles Times*, 26 Sept. 1993. There had been a previous meeting in July which 300 gang members attended. There was some speculation by reporters that these meetings were an outgrowth of Black–Chicano tensions in the prisons and that the *Eme* was strengthening its base through racial alliances. This meeting was not the first; another was held in Santa Ana in Orange County with 500 in attendance. The word was that those who broke the truce would be treated in the prisons like child molesters; Jesse Katz, 'Reputed Mexican-Mafia Leader Dies in State Prison at 64', *Los Angeles Times*, 10 Nov. 1993.

10. Antonio Rodríguez, Javier Rodríguez and Jaime Rodríguez, 'Mexican Mafia Is Only Filling a Void', *Los Angeles Times*, 4 Oct. 1993.

11. Moore, *Homeboys*, pp. 114–15.

12. Jesse Katz and Robert Lopez, 'Police Question Mexican Mafia's Impact on Gangs', *Los Angeles Times*, 28 Sept. 1993: according to police Sgt Wes McBride, 'The Mexican Mafia is a business, street gangs are a lifestyle – and there's a big difference.'

13. Richard Lee Colvin, 'Valley Gangs' Peace Is Strained But Holding', *Los Angeles Times*, 26 Dec. 1993; Patrick McGreevy and Jaxon Van Derbeken, 'Latino Gang Truce Cited for Drop in Valley Killings', *Daily News*, 7 April 1994.

14. Jesse Katz, 'Clashes Between Latino, Black Gangs Increase', *Los Angeles Times*, 26 Dec. 1993; José Luis Sierra, 'Tratan de conseguir una tregua entre las pandillas latinas y negras de L.A.', *La Opinión*, 25 Aug. 1992; Pablo Comesaña Amado, 'Promueven la armonia racial en Los Angeles', *La Opinión*, 26 June 1992.

15. Ron Harris, 'Hand of Punishment Falls Heavily on Black Youths', *Los Angeles Times*, 24 Aug. 1993. In 1985 white males comprised 53 percent of those detained in juvenile facilities nationally, and Blacks, 33 percent; Latinos, 12 percent; and others, 2 percent. In 1991, whites comprised 35 percent; Blacks, 44 percen; Latino, 18 percent; and other, 3 percent.

16. Kevin Starr, 'L.A.'s History of Mixing Rumor with Reality', *Los Angeles Times*, 18 April 1993.

17. Jesse Katz, 'A Community's Mission of Peace', *Nuestro Tiempo*, 1 July 1993; Louis Sahagun, 'Coalition Opens Drive to Reclaim Park, Neighborhoods as Havens', *Nuestro Tiempo*, 28 March 1991: in February 1991 a coalition of community-based groups including the United Neighborhood Organization and Community Youth Gang Services reclaimed the park and neighborhood as safe havens for community.

18. See also Paul Lieberman and Jim Herron Zamora, 'ACLU Challenges Law Banning Gangs from San Fernando Park', *Los Angeles Times*, 18 Dec. 1991. The ACLU filed suit to overturn a city ordinance that fined gang members $250 for going to Las Palmas Park; Jim Herron Zamora, 'Suit over Park Ban on Gangs Causes Dismay', *Los Angeles Times*, 18 Dec. 1991: 'The people who filed the lawsuit should try living here for a while, then they'll get the picture.' Supporters of the ordinance charged that the gangs were denying innocent people the use of the park. The Las Palmas Park ban was eventually allowed to expire.

19. Joan Moore, *Homeboys: Gangs, Drugs, and Prison in the Barrios of Los Angeles* (Philadelphia: Temple University Press, 1978), pp. 129–48; José Fuentes Salinas, 'La pandillas, problemas del crecimiento urbano', *La Opinión*, 24 Jan. 1993.

20. Jesse Katz, 'Painfully, the Priest of the Projects Leaves the Gangs He Loves', *Nuestro Tiempo*, 6 Aug. 1992.

21. Jack Katz, 'Gangs Aren't the Cause of Crime', *Los Angeles Times*, 31 May 1992. According to Katz, the key factors are these: 1) crimes are disproportionately committed by young males; 2) young males prefer to commit crime collectively, whereas older males strike alone; and 3) youth violence is often senseless, more for excitement than financial gain.

22. Los Angeles appears to have three types of painters: the individual tagger who puts his *placa*, or personal sign on the wall; the crew, whose members work in groups and spray the sign of the crew on the wall; and the graffiti artists, who work in crews, but go beyond the desire of the individual tagger or crew to be noticed, and who weave a theme into their symbols.

23. Jaxon Van Derbeken, Beth Laski and Betsy Bates, 'Violence Infiltrates Social Scene', *Daily News*, 28 Feb. 1993; Jaxon Van Derbeken, 'Complex Dynamics Shape Local Graffiti Phenomenon', *Daily News*, 28 Feb. 1993. Taggers are not necessarily gang members. According to one source there were 422 active crews in Los Angeles County, who drew graffiti on anything that stood or moved in L.A. The city spent $3.5 million in 1992 to clean up graffiti, the RTD another $1.1 million.

24. Van Derbeken, 'Complex Dynamics'.

25. Sun Valley is in the northeast San Fernando Valley.

26. Fox Butterfield, 'Prison-Building Binge in California Casts Shadow on Higher Education', *New York Times*, 12 April 1995.

27. Mary Ballesteros, 'Sube el nivel de crímenes en el condado angelino', *La Opinión*, 30 Jan. 1992; James Austin and Aaron David McVey, 'The 1989 NCCD Prison Population Forecast: The Impact of the War on Drugs', *NCCD FOCUS* (National Council on Crime and Delinquency), Dec. 1989.

28. See Rodolfo Acuña, 'Life Behind Bars Is No Way to Build Character', *Los Angeles Times*, 12 Feb. 1990.

29. Joan Moore, *Homeboys*, p. 104.

30. Jim Newton, 'Judge Denounces Mandatory Sentencing Law', *Los Angeles Times*, 19 Dec. 1992; Joan Petersilia, 'Building More Jail Cells Will Not Make Us Safer', *Los Angeles Times*, 4 Oct. 1992.

31. Dan Morain, 'Wilson Adviser Says "3 Strikes" Will Save Money', *Los Angeles Times*, 7 April 1994.

32. Robert Bryce, 'Pay Now or Later: The Exploding Prison Budget', *Texas Observer*, 16 Oct. 1992, pp. 8–9; Judge Stephen Reinhardt, 'The Trickle Down of Judicial Racism', *Harper's* (Aug. 1992), pp. 15–17. 'While California has rushed to improve its ability to punish convicts, it has dramatically scaled back its rehabilitation programs. Parole failure rates nearly doubled during the past 10 years.' The breakdown of moral authority was also important and could not be explained away by blaming the loss of so-called family values. The savings & loan scandals and the greed and corruption of the 1980s broke down respect for the system and with it parental authority. Political corruption of those espousing family values eroded their moral authority. Take the case of state senator Alan Robbins, who was convicted of public corruption. The *Daily News* on 20 October 1993, carried the article 'Attorney Labels Robbins a "Prostitute"; He Agrees': 'The more you were able to raise, the more clout you had in your career. My name was always near the top of the [funds] list, so I had more staff and more assistance from the leadership when I needed it.'

33. John Jacobs, 'Schools Are Big Losers Under "3 Strikes" Plan', *Daily News*, 14 March 1994; Anne Burke, '"3 Strikes" Impact Unclear', *Daily News*, 11 April 1994; Jonathan Freedman, 'Help Children, Families Must Start Before Birth', *Los Angeles Times*, 27 Sept. 1993; Mark Gladstone and Daniel M. Weintraub, 'Hate Is Abandoning Its Children, Advocacy Group Says', *Los Angeles Times*, 8 March 1994; Dan Morain, 'Costs to Soar Under "3 Strikes" Plan, Study Says', *Los Angeles Times*, 1 March 1994.

34. Dan Walters, 'Crime Frenzy Fed by Misunderstanding', *Daily News*, 11 April 1994; Susan Estrich, 'Everyone Is Tough on Crime – But Avoids the Real Issues', *Los Angeles Times*, 6 March 1994: according to Estrich, 'The political debate on crime is not about cutting crime: It's about politics.'

35. See Rodolfo Acuña, *Occupied America*, 3d edn (New York: Harper & Row, 1988), p. 346.

36. See Acuña, *Occupied America*, 3d edn, pp. 400–401; 'Standards and Procedures for the Anti-Terrorist Division', Supplemental Draft, 18 Jan. 1984; David Freed, 'State Won't File Charges in L.A. Police Spying Case', *Los Angeles Times*, 17 Oct. 1985; Paul Hoffman and Robert Newman, 'The Police Spying Settlement', *Los Angeles Lawyer* (May 1984), pp. 19–25; James Mann, 'Deep Throat: An Institutional Analysis', *Atlantic* (May 1992), pp. 106–112.

37. Richard Serrano, 'Charges of Spying Close LAPD Unit', *Los Angeles Times*, 10 July 1992; Mike Rothmiller and Ivan G. Goldman, *L.A. Secret Police: Inside the LAPD Elite Spy Network* (New York: Pocket Books, 1992); Daniel S. Levy, 'We Have to Start Talking to Each Other', *Time*, 11 May 1992, pp. 37–40.

38. Patrick McGreevy, 'City OKs Brutality Settlements', *Daily News*, 10 Dec. 1992.

39. Ted Rohrlich and Victor Merina, 'Racial Disparities Seen in Complaints to LAPD', *Los Angeles Times*, 19 May 1991; Carol A. Watson, 'Police Abuses Laid Bare, But Solutions Fall Short',

Los Angeles Times, 11 July 1991; Mary Ballesteros, '200 integrantes de MEChA acusan de abuso policial a la Division Foothill', *La Opinión*, 12 Nov. 1992.

40. Robert L. Jackson, 'Sheriff's Dept. No. 2 on US Brutality List', *Los Angeles Times*, 20 May 1992.

41. David Parrish and Beth Barrett, 'Investigation of Deputies Called an Illusion', *Daily News*, 7 Oct. 1990.

42. Michael Seilar and Ted Thackrey, Jr, 'Convicted Killer Who Denied Crime Is Freed', *Los Angeles Times*, 3 July 1981; Henry Mendoza, 'For Gordon Hall, First Steps Taken in Freedom Are Frightening', *Los Angeles Times*, 5 July 1981.

43. See Acuña, *Occupied America*, 3rd edn, p. 400.

44. Vicki Torres, 'Man Wrongfully Convicted Wins $4.4 Million in Suit', *Los Angeles Times*, 26 June 1993.

45. 'Time for County to Drop Appeal', *San Gabriel Valley Tribune*, 9 July 1993. Meanwhile, Richard Cruz died in the summer of 1993 at the age of fifty. As a law student Cruz had been the leader of the *Católicos por La Raza* demonstration at St Basil's Cathedral, protesting the indifference of the Catholic Church. When he graduated from law school, he had to fight the state bar for admittance. In the 1970s he successfully fought the county's policy of forced sterilization of indigent and undocumented patients at the USC-County Hospital.

46. See Rodolfo Acuña, 'Police Brutality Still Alive and Threatening', *Los Angeles Herald-Examiner*, 20 March 1987.

47. David Parrish and Beth Barrett, 'Deputy Accused of Firing at Men on Ground, Planting Weapons', *Daily News*, 7 Oct. 1990.

48. Parrish and Beth Barrett, 'Investigation of Deputies'.

49. David Parrish and Beth Barrett, 'The Sheriff's Shootings: Minorities are a Majority', *Daily News*, 7 Oct. 1990.

50. Parrish and Barrett, 'Investigation of Deputies'.

51. David Parrish and Beth Barrett, 'Breaking the Rules can Invite Trouble', *Daily News*, 5 July 1992; Parrish and Barrett, 'Behind Bars, A Harsh World', *Daily News* 5 July 1992.

52. Beth Barrett and David Parrish, 'The Threat to Inmates' Health', *Daily News*, 6 July 1992.

53. David Parrish and Beth Barrett, 'Abuses Ignored, Covered up as Code of Silence Endures', *Daily News*, 7 July 1992.

54. David Parrish and Beth Barrett, 'Deputies Seldom Fired, Prosecuted for Excessive Force', *Daily News*, 7 July 1992.

55. Rocky Jamarillo Rushing, 'Pitchess Jail Complex Called "Recipe for Riot"', *Daily News*, 16 Jan. 1994.

56. Pablo Comesaña Amado, 'Gran Jurado dice que no hay pruebas para procesar a unos agentes del Sheriff', *La Opinión*, 21 Dec. 1991; Leticia García-Irogoyen, 'Departamento de Justicia investiga muertes a manos de agentes del Sheriffato', *La Opinión*, 8 Feb. 1992; 'Comité del Senado pretende exigir documentos al Sheriff', *La Opinión*, 10 Jan. 1992.

57. Stephen Braun, 'Deputies' Credibility Took a Beating at Latino Project', *Los Angeles Times*, 20 Dec. 1991.

58. Michele Fuetschi, 'Deputies Shot Teenager in Back, Lawyer Charges', *Los Angeles Times*, 3 Aug. 1991.

59. Hector Tobar, 'Deputies in "Neo-Nazi" Gang', *Los Angeles Times*, 12 Oct. 1991.

60. Sheryl Stolberg and Frank Clifford, 'Kolts Starts Deputies Probe in Christopher's Shadow', *Los Angeles Times*, 22 Dec. 1991; Maribel Hastings, 'El Sheriff debe indicar en 60 días qué recomendaciones de expertos adoptaría', *La Opinión*, 16 Aug. 1991; Richard Simon, 'Three Supervisors Call for Inquiry into Sheriff's Dept.', *Los Angeles Times*, 11 Dec. 1991; Francisco Robles, 'Activistas denuncian inactividad de grupo asesor del Sheriff', *La Opinión*, 10 Dec. 1991.

61. Victor Merina, '62 "Problem Officers" Found in Department', *Los Angeles Times*, 21 July 1992.

62. Hector Tovar and Kenneth Reich, 'Probe Finds Pattern of Excess Force, Brutality by Deputies', *Los Angeles Times*, 21 July 1992.

63. Hector Tovar, 'Sheriff's Probe Transformed Kolts' Views', *Los Angeles Times*, 27 July 1992.

64. Jerome H. Skolnick, 'Oversight, But Not by Other Cops', *Los Angeles Times*, 29 July 1992.

65. Kenneth Reich and Frederick M. Muir, 'Block's Cooperation Key to Reform Measures',

Los Angeles Times, 21 July 1992.

66. Bill Boyarsky, 'Stacking Up Support for Sheriff Block', *Los Angeles Times*, 13 Sept. 1991.

67. Amy Pyle, 'Political Fallout Likely to Turn Up Heat on Incumbents', *Los Angeles Times*, 22 July 1992.

68. Kenneth Reich, 'Block, Kolts Propose Conduct Review Panel', *Los Angeles Times*, 5 Jan. 1993; Reich, 'Supervisors Vote for Panel to Review Sheriff's Dept.' *Los Angeles Times*, 6 Jan. 1993.

69. David Bloom, 'Block Bars Kolts from Brutality Panel', *Daily News*, 4 Aug. 1993.

70. Carol McGraw and Henry Weinstein, 'Two Juries Deliver Verdicts After Abuses by L.A. Deputies, Police', *Los Angeles Times*, 2 April 1991; Joe Domanik, 'Safer Streets Are Priceless: Less Painful Enforcement Would Be, Too', *Los Angeles Times*, 26 Feb. 1990; 'Gates's Reply', *Los Angeles Times*, 22 Dec. 1988.

71. Martin J. Schiesl, 'Behind the Badge: The Police and Social Discontent in Los Angeles since 1950', in Lein and Martin J. Schiesl, eds, *20th-Century Los Angeles: Power, Promotion, and Social Conflict* (Claremont, Calif.: Regina Books, 1990), pp. 153–94, quote on p. 154.

72. David Shaw, 'Chief Parker Molded Image – Then Came the '60s', *Los Angeles Times*, 25 May 1992.

73. Richard A. Serrano, 'Little Support for Gates's Comment', *Los Angeles Times*, 7 Sept. 1990.

74. Shaw, 26 May 1992.

75. Cynthia Anderson, *Police Abuse in Los Angeles*. Latino Community Justice Center, Report Number 1, April 1989, pp. 1–2; Jesús Hernández C., 'Protestan contra supuestos abusos de la Policía', *La Opinión*, 29 April 1989.

76. Dean E. Murphy, 'Complaints Against L.A. Police Up 70 percent in '91', *Los Angeles Times*, 17 Oct. 1991.

77. David R. Díaz, 'Another Failure of Black Regime Politics: Political Inertia and Corporate Power in Los Angeles', Presented to The Center for California Studies, California Studies Conference V, Reassembling California, 4–6 Feb. 1993, Sacramento. Díaz blamed the riots in part on Bradley's corporate-centered urban policy, which pumped millions of dollars into Downtown while the rest of the city deteriorated.

78. 'What the Christopher Commission Found', *Los Angeles Times*, 10 July 1991; Bill Boyarsky, 'Task That Remains for Commission', *Los Angeles Times*, 10 July 1991; Sheryl Stolberg, 'Investigation was an Eye-Opener for Christopher, Arguelles', *Los Angeles Times*, 10 July 1991.

79. Marcelo M. Zuviría, 'Líderes latinos piden favorable para la reforma del departamento de Policía', *La Opinión*, 31 May 1992; Louis Sahagun, 'New Latino Group Stirs Up Campaign for Police Reform', *Los Angeles Times*, 30 April 1992: Citizens for Law Enforcement and Reform (CLEAR) campaigned for more City Hall control over police; Gloria Romero of the Los Angeles Police Commission's Hispanic Advisory Council was campaign coordinator for Latinos for Charter Amendment F. La Ley, a group of Latino police officers, came out against 'F', Louis Sahagun, 'Latino Campaign Eludes 2 Camps in Charter Vote', *Los Angeles Times*, 23 April 1992.

80. See Rodolfo Acuña, 'Blind Before, How Can They Lead Us Now?' *Los Angeles Times*, 17 July 1991; *L.A. Times*, special issue on the outbreaks: 'Understanding the Riots: Images of Chaos', *Los Angeles Times*, 12 May 1992, pp. 35–43.

81. Patrick McGreevy, '83 Percent of LAPD Officers Live Outside City', *Daily News*, 29 March 1994.

82. Laurie Levenson, 'Justice in Court Doesn't Mean Social Justice', *Los Angeles Times*, 30 April 1992; George Ramos and Tracy Wilkinson, 'Unrest Widens Rift in Diverse Latino Population', *Los Angeles Times*, 8 May 1992.

83. *Los Angeles Times*, 12 May 1992; Jim Hoagland, 'Las causas latent de los disturbios de L.A.', *La Opinión*, 14 May 1992.

84. Paul Lieberman, '51 Percent of Riot Arrests Were Latinos, Study Says', *Los Angeles Times*, 18 June 1992. In all 2,852 Latinos were arrested, 2,619 males and 233 females; 2,037 Blacks, 1,756 males and 281 females; 601 Anglos, 471 males and 130 females; and 143 others. 2,361 were arrested for civil disturbance, primarily curfew, 426 for traffic violations, 244 for drug violations, 1,964 for property (primarily looting) and 570 for violent crimes: 'Looting and Fires Ravage L.A.: 24 Dead, 572 Injured; 1,000 Blazes Reported', *Los Angeles Times*, 1 May 1992; David Shaw, 'Gates Hammered by Media over LAPD Riot Response', *Los Angeles Times*, 28 May 1992, Gates was accused of indecisive action; Gates responded that he had not wanted to appear to be overreacting.

85. 'Pretexto para perseguir', *La Opinión*, 6 May 1992; Richard Martínez, 'Violencia y derechos civiles', *La Opinión*, 25 May 1992; Letcia García-Irogoyen, 'El Sheriff de Orange aresta y el INS puede deportar a 88 obreros de la construccion', *La Opinión*, 4 July 1992; María del Pilar Marrero, 'Acusan al LAPD de violar ordenanzas de la ciudad', *La Opinión*, 20 May 1992.

86. Neils Franzen and Frank Acosta, 'Immigrants' Roundup Was a Dirty Trick', *Los Angeles Times*, 11 May 1992; Jack Anderson, 'Abusos a indocumentados', *La Opinión*, 20 May 1992; María del Pilar Marrero and José Luis Sierra, 'Acusan al INS de redadas en el área de Pico-Union', *La Opinión*, 5 May 1992; Neils Franzen, 'Los inmigrants latinos y los disturbios', *La Opinión*, 19 May 1992; Michael A. Heller, 'Bad News', *Hispanic* (Nov. 1992), p. 20. The *Los Angeles Times* had fifty-six stories on Latinos during this period, of which twenty-six were negative: 'Quite often racial and ethnic issues are in black and white and you find Latinos don't exist' p. 24.

87. Louisa Ollague sheds considerable light on the neglect of Latinos in the *Los Angeles Times* and even *La Opinión*, Louisa B. Ollague, 'Media, Politics and Latinos: Latinos and the Los Angeles Uprising' (Thesis, Wellesly College, 1993). According to Ollague, *La Opinión* tended to feature Latinos as leaders, good samaritans and as other victims, while the *Times* cast Latinos as mostly leaders, lawbreakers, property or assault and emotional victims (p. 69).

88. David Shaw wrote a critical analysis of the 'riots' and concluded that the *Times* emphasized political aspects of the upheaval, whereas the *Daily News* stressed the pattern of force. Sources at the *Times*, according to Shaw, tended to be critical of the *Daily News*, which was, according to the sources, out to get Gates, David Shaw, 'Story of King Beating Put L.A. Media in Spotlight', *Los Angeles Times*, 27 May 1992; David Shaw, 'TV Added More Heat Than Insight to King Saga', *Los Angeles Times*, 27 May 1992.

89. George Skelton, 'Moral Leadership Needed in Inner Cities, Voters Say', *Los Angeles Times*, 23 May 1992.

90. Amy Wallace, 'Riots Changed Few Attitudes, Poll Finds', *Los Angeles Times*, 3 Sept. 1992; 'Money and Power, *Los Angeles Times*, 18 Nov. 1992.

91. Davies regarded the case as 'atypical'. According to the judge, Koon and Powell were good family men who had served meritoriously. He showed no sympathy for King, insisting that King had brought much of the beating on himself, Ron Harris, 'A Black-and-White Answer to the Question of Who's Really to Blame', *Los Angeles Times*, 7 Aug. 1993; Mike Davis, 'A Verdict After Years of Trouble', *Los Angeles Times*, 18 April 1993. Davis points out that they threw Koon and Powell into jail, and let Gates go: the foot soldier is always tried and the generals go free.

92. Xandra Kayden and John W. Mack, 'A City on Edge Again: Justice Versus Mercy', *Los Angeles Times*, 10 Oct. 1993; Charles L. Linder, 'The Denny Verdicts: A Temporary Safety Valve', *Los Angeles Times*, 24 Oct. 1993; Peter Larsen, 'Race Relations: L.A.'s Great Divide', *Daily News*, 24 Oct. 1993.

93. Amy Wallace and John Hurst, 'Veredictores dejan sabor amargo para "victima"', *Nuestro Tiempo*, 21 Oct. 1993.

94. Tina Daunt, 'Fund Drive Begins for L.A. Riot Victim', *Los Angeles Times*, 11 Nov. 1993.

95. Raphael J. Sonenshein, 'Which Way Now?' *Daily News*, 24 Oct. 1993; Jim McGoldrick, 'Separating Myth, Truth in Denny Case', *Daily News*, 24 Oct. 1993.

96. William Hamilton, 'Many, a Contrast in Black and White', *Washington Post*, 25 Feb. 1993; Paul Hefner, 'Black Leaders Say Fairness of Verdict, Entire System in Doubt', *Daily News*, 13 Oct. 1993; Charles L. Linder, 'The Denny Trial's Confusion: Is It Reality or Is It Tape?' *Los Angeles Times*, 19 Sept. 1993.

97. Edward J. Boyer and John L. Mitchell, 'Attempted Murder Acquittal, Deadlock Winds Up Denny Trial', *Los Angeles Times*, 21 Oct. 1993; Edward J. Boyer and Andrea Ford, 'Williams Given Maximum 10 Years in Denny Beating', *Los Angeles Times*, 8 Dec. 1993.

98. Charisse Jones, 'Arrival of Latinos Spurs Black Self-Examination', *Los Angeles Times*, 18 Feb. 1992.

99. Charisse Jones, 'Old Memories Confront New Realities in South L.A.', *Los Angeles Times*, 17 Feb. 1992.

100. Hector Tobar, 'Black, Latinos Coexist in a Peace Tempered by Fear', *Los Angeles Times*, 19 Feb. 1992; Alejandro Morelos, 'El racism en las escuelas de L.A. es violento y cíclico: ¿hay solución?', *La Opinión*, 19 May 1992.

101. Paul Felderman, 'RLA Funds to Run Out Before Planned', *Los Angeles Times*, 2 Nov. 1993.

102. The *Los Angeles Times* ran a series entitled 'Understanding the Riots'; the 15 May 1992 article was 'The Path to Recovery'. The articles in general were optimistic, ignoring the real problem of L.A., which was the gap between rich and poor; David R. Díaz, 'Out of Touch and Out of Mind: L.A.'s Leadership After the Insurrection', National Association for Chicano Studies, San Jose, Calif., 25–27 March 1993; Manuel Jiménez and Henry Weinstein, 'Latino Leaders: Little Rebuilding of Riot-Torn Areas', *Nuestro Tiempo*, 5 Nov. 1992.

103. See also Lorenzo Muñoz, 'Los Angeles: The Dilemma of Political Incorporation in a Multi-Ethnic City' (Honors Thesis, University of California, Berkeley, 1993); and Manuel Pastor, *Latinos and the Los Angeles Uprising: The Economic Context* (Claremont, Calif.: Tomás Rivera Center, 1993); Roger Lindo, 'Hacen público estudio sobre los latinos y los motines de LA', *La Opinión*, 16 March 1993; Roger Lindo, José Luis Sierra and Pablo Comesaña Amado, 'No se ha dado ayuda por disturbios', *La Opinión*, 29 Oct. 1992; Manuel Pastor, Jr, 'Rebuild with the Working Poor', *Los Angeles Times*, 5 March 1993; Carla Rivera, 'Study Calls for Aid to Latinos as Key to Rebuilding City', *Los Angeles Times*, 16 March 1993.

104. Alejandro Morelos, 'Realizan doe breves marchas por la paz residentes de Pico-Union', *La Opinión*, 17 June 1992.

105. Henry Weinstein, 'Tensions Escalate Between Leaders of Blacks, Latinos', *Los Angeles Times*, 11 July 1992; Leilani Albano, 'Lost Between Black and White', *diatribe* (Oct. 1992); Antonio H. Rodríguez and Carlos E. Chávez, 'The Rift Is Exposed; Let's Bridge It', *Los Angeles Times*, 24 July 1992.

106. Henry Weinstein, 'Minority Firms to Be Part of Rebuilding', *Los Angeles Times*, 16 June 1992; Mary Ballesteros, 'Emleados de limpieza protestan ante el Comité de Reconstrucción de LA', *La Opinión*, 19 Dec. 1992; Danny Bakewell, 'Who Is It That Cries for Us?' *Los Angeles Times*, 8 July 1992; Xavier Hermosillo, 'Latinos Defend Right of All to Work', *Los Angeles Times*, 9 July 1992.

107. *A Call to Reject the Federal Weed and Seed Program in Los Angeles*, The Urban Strategies Group, Labor/Community Strategy Center (September 1992), p. 3.

108. Patrick McGreevy, '"Weed and Seed" Program Renamed', *Daily News*, 21 Nov. 1992.

109. Bill Boyarsky, 'Law Enforcement and New Reality of L.A. Politics', *Los Angeles Times*, 8 Sept. 1993; Boyarsky, 'Riordan Borrows a Page from Reagan Era', *Los Angeles Times*, 17 Oct. 1993; Boyarsky, 'New Face of Police Union: Friendly – and Formidable', *Los Angeles Times*, 22 Sept. 1993.

110. John Schwada, 'Riordan Appoints Diverse Police Panel', *Los Angeles Times*, 10 July 1993.

111. Patrick McGreevy, 'Panel Urged to Take Steps to Implement LAPD Reforms', *Daily News*, 8 Sept. 1993; Mike Salcido, *The People's Right to Know: Excessive Force: Blood on The Hands of the Legislature* (Los Angeles: Community Service Organization, 1992). The report pointed out that the Peace Officers Research Association of California contributed $117,000 to state legislators; the California Highway Patrol, $150,000 to Diane Feinstein's campaign for governor; and the California prison guards union contributed $1,800,000 to campaigns, of which $760,000 went directly to Gov. Wilson's campaign; see also Mike Davis, 'The Uncritical Eye: Has the LAPD Really Changed?' *Los Angeles Times*, 9 May 1993; Pablo Comesaña Amado, 'Niega el LAPD malos tratos a albañiles en un protesta', *La Opinión*, 20 Jan. 1993.

112. Peter Stack, 'Fire Sheds Light on Roots of Los Angeles Riots', *Los Angeles Times*, 16 Sept. 1994; Randy Holland, 'Counterpunch: We Haven't Seen It All', *Los Angeles Times*, 11 July 1994; Holland, 'What About the Plan?' *Los Angeles Times*, 22 May 1994.

113. Holland, 'Voices What About the Plan?'; Robert Levine, 'Why L.A. Was "On Fire This Time"', *Los Angeles Times*, 28 April 1994.

114. Caswell A. Evans, Jr, 'Public Health Impact of the 1992 Los Angeles Civil Unrest', *Public Health Reports*, May 1993.

115. Quoted in '25 Years Later: Is White Racism Still Dividing America into Black and White Races – Separate and Unequal?', *Jet*, 31 May 1993, p. 12.

116. Quoted in '25 Years Later', p. 12.

117. Ibid.

1 2

The Stairway to the Good Life

For many Mexicans and other Latinos in Los Angeles, the public schools have been their main hope of rising above a destiny severely limited by class and race: education was 'the stairway to heaven'. In the 1970s the restructuring of the city's economy, especially the decline of heavy industry, made education seem even more crucial: manual labor jobs were disappearing, and business was demanding a more educated workforce. In reality, society had either to invest in the public schools and educate Latinos and other Angelenos, or spend more money on police, prisons, welfare, housing subsidies, health care and security systems.

Chicanos and other Latinos now found two new barriers on that stairway. The first was the decline of funding for education in California, which had once been a national leader in per pupil spending on education. A major blow fell with the passage of Proposition 13, the so-called tax reform measure, in 1978. By rolling back property tax rates and requiring a two-thirds majority vote for tax increases, Proposition 13 slashed the local tax base for education and other social services. This, combined with budget cutbacks by Republican governors George Deukmejian and Pete Wilson during the 1980s and early 1990s, accelerated California's fall to forty-fifth place in the US in per pupil spending by 1993. Because the state government was unable to compensate completely for Proposition 13's cuts in local property taxes, the Los Angeles Unified School District (LAUSD) found itself facing a $50 million deficit by the early 1990s.[1]

Latinos supported the schools by voting for bond issues, and local school board elections generated as much interest among registered voters in Latino communities as did statewide contests. (It can generally be said that the LAUSD Board of Education was the most progressive elected agency in the city.)[2] Unfortunately, Latinos (and other communities of color) did not have controlling votes, and thus they did not set the agenda for public education.

At the same time, the white voting majority did not want to pay for the education that restructuring the workforce would require, because that would mean educating 'the other' – in the American tradition, 'other than white'. In 1992 Latinos accounted for over 63 percent of the pupils in the Los Angeles Unified School District and close to 70 percent of those in elementary schools (twenty years before, only 22 percent of Los Angeles students were Latino).[3] Many of the Latino students badly needed more educational resources. Some 200,000 of 625,000 students were Limited English Placement (LEP) students, and this number was growing by 10 percent a year. The gap in reading scores between Latino and white students in California was marked. In 1987, Latino third graders averaged scores of 500 in the California Assessment Program (CAP) math and reading tests, compared with 614 for whites. By the eighth grade the gap was 414 to 567. Latino high school seniors performed at the ninth-grade level in reading. Statewide, their high school dropout rate was double that of white students; 54 percent of the 19,381 high school students dropping out of the LAUSD in 1987/88 were Latinos.[4] Overall, Latinos in the late 1980s had a 40 percent high school dropout rate, lower than the 46 percent among African Americans, but much higher than the rate among Anglos.[5] Nor were high dropout rates closely related to increased immigration of Latinos, legal or undocumented. As much as Euroangelenos wanted to scapegoat the immigrant, a 1992 report by the Department of Education, *Are Hispanic Dropout Rates Related to Migration?*, found that the high Latino dropout rate would continue even if immigration slowed down.[6]

There was, however, a correlation between students' SAT scores and parental educational level and income: 'Parents of California seniors with average SAT scores of 600 to 649 had average income of $54,000 in 1985, while parents of those with average scores of 350 to 399 had average income of $39,000.' Studies also showed that the mother's education indicated how well students would score on the California Assessment Program reading scores. Students whose mother had graduated from high school averaged a score of 277, while those whose parents had not averaged 188.[7] In California, 42 percent of Latino high school seniors' parents had not graduated from high school, compared with only 3 percent of whites. Moreover, 64 percent of Mexican immigrants had eight years or less of schooling, compared with 13 percent of Koreans and 18 percent of Filipinos.

Language was another problem. Most English as a Second Language (ESL) and bilingual programs were grossly understaffed and underfunded. In the LAUSD monolingual teachers were often deployed as bilingual teachers – 2,000 bilingual teachers a year were needed to meet the demand.[8] The growing anti-immigrant hysteria generated a backlash against bilingual education, which had been mandated by Title VII of the Elementary and Secondary School Act of 1968 and sustained by the US Supreme Court in *Lau v. Nichols* (1973). Much of the language problem was due to Euroamerican biases towards other languages. An old joke portrays this attitude well: in the US, if you speak three languages you're trilingual; two languages, bilingual; one language and you're American. Speaking only English has often been the litmus test for feeling American and being thought American.

As in the case of most immigrant groups, the transition of Latinos into higher education has been slow. European ethnics in the 1940 Census averaged about the same educational level as Mexicans do today – less than tenth grade. Only after massive government spending programs in the 1940s and 1950s such as the G.I. Bill, federal aid to education, low tuitions at public colleges and universities, flexible admission standards, government subsidies for homebuyers, and government loans did their median level of education completed rise to today's median of 12.9 years.[9]

This recent history shows that it takes several generations to raise the educational level of a group – but it can certainly be done if society is committed to that goal. Euramericans have conveniently forgotten how much lower their educational status was when they were new immigrants – and how much government aid was involved in helping them raise it.[10] But instead of studying the role of class and race in producing differences in educational success, 'experts' such as Charles Murray and Richard Herrnstein have focused on the so-called testing gap. They and other Bell Curvers conveniently neglected the fact that most tests are based on vocabulary and that therefore first-generation, and even second-generation, students are handicapped in this respect. IQ tests thus do not measure intelligence or motivation but class background and the educational advantages that accrue from it.[11] (The current SAT scores of Mexicans and other minorities compare favorably with those of Anglos in the post–World War II period.)

Comparison of the lives of minority and majority students shows how absurd the focus on IQ and other tests is. A 1993 *Los Angeles Times* article contrasted the differences between experiencing school in Pico-Union and in Palo Alto (near Stanford University):

> Ten-year-old Yuri de Paz wakes up each morning in a cramped Pico-Union apartment she shares with eight other family members, and walks to school through a Los Angeles neighborhood that is so dangerous that police have barricaded it to keep drug dealers out ... More than 400 miles away, in the Northern California town of Palo Alto, 9-year-old Patrick McKowan eats a homemade pancake breakfast, then sets off for his campus along quiet streets with names such as Oberlin, Yale and Princeton.[12]

Yuri attended Leo Politi Elementary, which had an enrollment of 850 students, 94 percent of whom were Latino, 4 percent Asian American, 1 percent Black and 1 percent white. The average class size was 32, and the average spent

per student was $3,900. Patrick attended Escondido Elementary, with an enroll-
ment of 367 students, 57 percent of whom were white, 21 percent Asian American, 13 percent Latino, 7 percent Black and 2 percent American Indian. The
average class size was 27, and the average spent per pupil $4,800. 'Yuri's teacher
hopes to raise her academic standing so that she is only half a year behind
grade level; Patrick's teacher says measurable skills are not as important as
making him a "lifelong learner".' The average price of houses on Patrick's
block was $749,000.[13]

Latino schools in the 1990s were more apt to be overcrowded, older and,
because of the lack of classrooms, more frequently used all year round. Inner-
city school buildings in Los Angeles were usually deteriorating and hence less
desirable places to teach. More experienced teachers therefore gravitated to the
newer Valley and Westside schools. It should be noted that overcrowding in
barrio schools was not necessarily the fault of the district. Until 1984, districts
were forbidden to build schools in minority neighborhoods lest they contribute
to de facto segregation. The state in 1990 was $5 billion behind in school con-
struction, and it would have cost $400 to $500 million to reduce class size statewide by one pupil.[14] That same year, 50,000 mostly Latino students were bused
to schools in other parts of the district. According to economist Richard Rothstein, 'It is the refusal of California's taxpayers and political leaders to finance
needed construction ... that robs many Mexican-origin students of equal educational opportunity.'[15]

Residential segregation has an important impact on the quality of education
available to Latinos and other minorities, and Los Angeles has been becoming
increasingly segregated, with Mexicans and other Latinos more segregated in
1990 than they had been in 1950. In 1992, a National Association of School
Boards report showed that Latinos were the most segregated ethnic group in
the United States.[16] Aside from being separate, the public schools were unequal. The United Teachers of Los Angeles opposed MALDEF's efforts to
equalize school funding within the district and filed a motion to intervene in
Rodríguez v. *Los Angeles Unified School District* (see Chapter 7). The *Rodríguez*
case would have compelled individual school budgets to reflect teacher salaries
now paid by the district. This change would have been important because average teachers' salaries were often much higher at all-white suburban schools
than they were in the inner city. This method of measuring per-school spending discriminated against minority and poor students and resulted in unequal
opportunity. UTLA claimed that the Rodríguez case would cause tremendous
dislocation of teachers and interfere with the collective bargaining process.[17]
On the other hand, there was popular discontent among minorities and the
public in general with the LAUSD and the growing power of teachers' union.[18]
UTLA even drew criticisms from other service employees unions, which
claimed it was not willing to take its fair share of the pending budget cuts.[19]

The teaching profession continued to be dominated by white men and women. A 1991 survey by the National Education Association found that 86.5 percent of all public school teachers were white, the same percentage as twenty years earlier. Nationally, 8 percent of teachers were Black and 3 percent Latino.[20] In Los Angeles, the schools were 63 percent Latino, but only 12 percent of teachers were Latino; the actual number was somewhat smaller because the classification 'Hispanic' was often loosely used. Teachers of Mexican and Central American origin were 6 to 8 percent of the total.[21] Many non-Latino teachers resented Latino teachers, in part because their language skills earned bilingual teachers a $5,000 a year bonus.

The Attack on Bilingual Education

One of the first salvos in today's war on 'alien cultures' was fired in 1987 when Governor George Deukmejian vetoed extension of the native-language instruction requirement of the state's education code, which allocated state funding for bilingual programs. This meant that districts wanting to fund bilingual education could use only whatever federal funds were available. Conservatives justified their hostility to bilingual education by claiming that 'structured immersion' was the best way for students to learn English, and that bilingual education would lead to separatism. But bilingual education was originally intended to prevent students from falling behind in academic subjects taught in English while they were learning the language. (A maintenance component has usually been built in to make sure that students' Spanish-language vocabulary does not remain at an elementary level.[22]) Where funded properly, bilingual education worked well.[23]

Opposition to bilingual education (read: Mexicans) was well organized and a key component of the 'English-Only' movement.[24] In 1987, 74 percent of the United Teachers of Los Angeles voted against bilingual education, and in the summer of 1988 voted overwhelmingly to adopt the immersion method to teach English to the limited-English speaking. This was a return to the traditional 'sink-or-swim' philosophy, which had long crippled the education of Latino students and which devalued any language other than English. Consistent with this position, former UTLA President Wayne Johnson helped organize the Learning English Advocates Drive organization (LEAD) and its attack on bilingual education. LEAD was born in Sun Valley, once a lower working-class white San Fernando Valley community, now rapidly changing to Latino, and was financed by the US English and English First groups. In 1989 LEAD petitioned the UTLA to oppose bonuses for 4,000 bilingual teachers and again called for a return to the immersion program; the petition was expected to be approved by over 70 percent of the teachers.[25] Tensions eased somewhat after the election was postponed because Chicano activists the next year supported a teachers' strike for higher wages.

The crisis in bilingual education did not develop overnight. School officials should have and could have planned for the changes in student demographics taking place throughout the district. Instead of targeting recruitment and training of Spanish-speaking teachers from Los Angeles, they instead sent recruiters to Mexico and Spain to hire teachers. The reality was that nationwide fewer Latinos were entering the teaching profession. In 1977, 3,050 Latino college graduates received teaching certificates; eight years later, the number had declined to 2,533.

Instead of focusing on recruiting and training Chicano and Central American teachers, the LAUSD concentrated on developing magnet schools designed to attract white students, who were leaving the district in droves. These schools were better funded, and their teachers were rigorously screened to ensure their competence. Only 4 percent of the 30,000 students in magnet schools in 1990 spoke limited English, compared with 35 percent of students in the regular schools. Bilingual instruction was given in only thirteen magnet school classrooms. Peter Roos of the Multicultural Education Training and Advocacy Center sued the LAUSD in the public interest, claiming that the magnet schools reserved 30 to 40 percent of their seats for Euroamericans, who made up only 15 percent of students in the LAUSD. The LAUSD of course denied that any favoritism existed, and its administrators noted that tens of thousands of students were on the waiting list to attend the magnet schools. The suit demanded that the children of immigrants be identified and given education available to other students, and as a result of this pressure, the LAUSD finally opened a bilingual magnet school.[26]

Many Latino students were immigrants needing role models to provide guidance.[27] Their parents believed in discipline and hard work, and Mexican and Latino parents, in general, were concerned about the education of their children. A February 1992 poll taken by La Opinión and Univisión suggested that Latinos were more concerned about education (39 percent) than unemployment and the recession (32 percent). But passage of Proposition 187 in 1994 dealt a devastating blow to these expectations. Fortunately, despite widespread hysteria over spending public money to educate immigrant children, most responsible educators saw the need to invest funds in educating this critical mass of students.[28]

Rightwingers on Campus and the Lupe Song

The education stairway to heaven was blocked for Chicanos by racist and reactionary politics not only at the primary- and secondary-school level but also in higher education. By the late 1980s, college campuses had become a battleground where groups such as the National Association of Scholars (NAS) and other conservative scholars used phrases like 'equality versus quality' in education to mask their opposition to making traditionally Eurocentric Academia more inclusive of other perspectives.[29] For example, the Massachusetts Association of Scholars, a 150-member affiliate of the NAS, in 1984 released an 80-page study that condemned affirmative action and diversity seminars, and called multiculturalism 'antagonistic to the traditions of Western Civilization.'[30]

Across the nation the NAS argued that academic freedom and American institutions were under siege by 'tenured radicals', imposing so-called political correctness (PC) in place of academic freedom. According to them, there was a conspiracy of liberals, Latinos, African Americans, radicals and homosexual professors to take over the Academy – an evil empire of sorts.[31] These radicals, in their demands for greater diversity, were politicizing the university and trying to use new standards of political correctness to silence anyone who disagreed with them.[32]

The NAS argued that it was upholding 'truth, reason, morality, and artistic excellence' in the face of barbarism. In reality it was *their* truth, *their* reason, *their* morality, and *their* idea of artistic excellence that they used to exclude the 'other'. Far from libertarian, in essence they did what they accused the Left of doing: politicizing knowledge and imposing their own standards of political correctness, enforced by ultraconservative boards of regents and politicians.

The attack on multiculturalism was soon broadened to include the question of whether there should be ethnic studies classes. Because of their lack of knowledge of ethnic studies, conservative scholars assumed that there was a community of interests between Chicano Studies professors, multiculturalists, and 'PCers'. In actuality, most ethnic studies professors were wary of multiculturalism, suspecting that it meant integrating curricula at the expense of hiring minority faculty.[33] And only the most politically naive person, or the most opportunistic, would defend the proposition that radicals, Chicanos, Blacks, gays, and women, in whatever combination, agreed on a strategy and had decision-making power on university campuses to impose it.

Those being labelled 'PCers' called for collegiality – a university climate that did not tolerate words like *greaser*, *wetback*, *queer*, *bitch*, *kike* and *nigger*. They argued that these words shouldn't be used by students, not because they were politically incorrect but because no one had the right to insult anyone else. By any objective standard, the far right's attack on diversity was political – not scholarly. Indeed, the assault by the NAS and its gaggle of professors was much more of a threat to academic freedom and campus peace than telling people they shouldn't be racists, sexists, anti-Semites or homophobes.[34]

The kind of role that the NAS and its allies would play with regard to Chicanos on California campuses became all too clear during a notorious incident concerning fraternities holding 'theme parties' depicting Mexicans as well as African Americans in grossly racist ways – for example, portraying Mexican heroes as bandits and thieves. The fraternities mirrored a larger campus racism: the film school at the University of California, Los Angeles, for example, even showed a student film called *Animal Attraction,* which featured a Mexican woman having sex with a donkey.

The most serious incident occurred in 1992. A song to 'Lupe' was found in the Theta Xi education manual for new members by a UCLA student, who turned it over to the Chicano student newspaper *La Gente,* which in turn published it.[35] After reading the song, Chicanos were up in arms over verses such as these about an eight-year-old Mexican girl:

> Twas down in Cunt Valley, where Red Rivers flow
> Where cocksuckers flourish, and maidenheads grow,
> Twas there I met Lupe, the girl I adore
> My hot fucking, cocksucking Mexican whore
>
> ...
>
> She'll fuck you, she'll suck you, she'll tickle your nuts
> And if you're not careful, she'll suck out your guts,
> She'll wrap her legs round you, till you think you'll die
> I'd rather eat Lupe than sweet cherry pie [36]

The Theta Xi chapter president responded that the song had absolutely 'no effect on my view of women. We teach etiquette here. We teach respect for women.' Ana Rojas, coordinator of La Raza women, replied, 'These are college men. The politicians, the lawyers, the doctors and the teachers of our future. They don't acknowledge women ... we're all whores.'

In November 1991 Theta Xi members had been sanctioned by the UCLA student government for painting sexist slogans such as 'cheap chicks for sale' on Winnebagos bound for a football game at Stanford. Members were required to take gender-related workshops, observe a five-week suspension of social activities, and perform community service. (Chancellor Charles Young was generally reluctant to discipline fraternities himself because many powerful alumni protected them.)

MEChA, joined by community leaders and other Chicano off-campus student groups, pressured the university to do something about Theta Xi and the Lupe song. Supervisor Gloria Molina, City Council members Richard Alatorre and Mike Hernández, and mayoral candidate Julian Nava all sent messages supporting a demand to discipline Theta Xi. In the end, the fraternity was suspended for three weeks.[37] However, university officials quickly caved in and lifted the suspension when the fraternity threatened to sue them for violation of their free speech rights.

Meanwhile, the Lupe affair also reared its ugly head at California State University, Northridge. CSUN had a new president, Dr Brenda Wilson, a Black educator from the Midwest. A conflict between Chicanos on campus and the Zeta Beta Tau fraternity developed when the ZBT got clearance to hold a party dedicated to 'Lupe'. Campus Activities Director Tom Piernak warned ZBT officers that holding the party might cause an incident. The ZBT officers, according to Piernak, responded arrogantly that it was their First Amendment right to call the party anything they wanted, and to express their 'solidarity with their brothers at UCLA.'[38] They held the party.

On 27 October 1992, more than 200 *Mechistas* packed an Associated Student Government meeting, supported by the Black Student Union president, Strong Queers United in Stopping Heterosexism, and others, urging that the ZBT be disciplined. President Wilson urged that students follow due process in seeking the expulsion of the ZBT, and admitted that she was shocked by the level of racism she had found in California. MEChA held a press conference at which ZBT members in the audience almost provoked a fistfight. That weekend over 500 Chicano students marched on the ZBT house.[39] The fraternity was suspended for fourteen months.

In spring 1993, ZBT was reinstated at CSUN after it had filed a lawsuit against the university. CSU General Counsel Fernando Gómez recommended that the university settle with ZBT to avoid further legal costs. Complicating matters was the fact that ZBT had originally been a Jewish fraternity, formed because Jews were excluded from other fraternities. (A ZBT supporter, Dr Jody Meyers of Religious Studies, expressed disappointment that the values of ZBT had been betrayed.) Chicanos did not want the incident to further anti-Jewish sentiment, and the Anti-Defamation League and the campus Hillel group were asked to join the Chicanos in solidarity against racism, which they did.

Meanwhile, *Los Angeles Times* reporter Sam Enríquez revealed that CSUN had agreed to pay all ZBT's legal expenses and to pay for its full-page ads in the *Sundial* apologizing to the Chicano community for the incident. MEChA was never supposed to be told about the deal, nor were Chicano students supposed to learn about the involvement in the case of David Horowitz, a former radical turned reactionary.

According to Sharon Bernstein, a *Los Angeles Times* reporter, Horowitz had recruited a national network of rightwing lawyers to his Individual Rights Project to defend fraternities and other campus conservatives. He had recently intervened at Occidental College in favor of Alpha Tau Omega, forcing the college to drop a disciplinary action against fraternities there. Horowitz ran the $700,000-a-year Center for the Study of Popular Culture in Los Angeles, funded by the conservative Olin and Bradley foundations and the Scaife Trusts. It published the journal *Heterodoxy*, with San Diego Attorney John Howard as Horowitz's co-publisher and co-editor.

In the Northridge case, John Howard called Jeff Berns, the attorney repre-senting ZBT, who was about to give up the case, to offer the resources needed to continue fighting. Horowitz and his cabal were also active at Chico State, where they defended students who had ridiculed Malcolm X; at UC San Diego, where a student was allegedly failed by a professor for not agreeing with her feminist approach; and at Marietta College in Ohio, where a campus newspa-per called a gay student a 'deviant'.[40]

Stepping Stones to Survival

For Chicanos and other Latino students – as well as working-class students in general – California's two-year community colleges have long been the main ports of entry into higher education because of their open admissions policy. Ideally students transferred after two years to a four-year institution to com-plete their education. The state's community colleges did not, however, neces-sarily offer a supportive environment for Latinos. For example, only 5 percent of the faculty at the community colleges was Latino.[41] A committee reviewing the state's plan for higher education pointed out that in 1986 only 4,468 Blacks and Latinos were among the 27,761 students transferring from a community college to a University of California campus.[42]

In the last decade, surveys and studies have consistently shown that Mexican Americans were more likely to be from a disadvantaged background than any other group. Latinos in 1993 were twice as likely as the general population to be first-generation college students, and the least likely to have been identified for a college preparatory track. They had the lowest average family incomes, yet were the least likely to borrow money for college. They were the most likely to try to work their way through school, hence the burden of rising tui-tions and cuts in financial aid has fallen disproportionately on them.[43] More-over, attending community college was not the panacea described by rightwing educators. In the early 1990s, of the 150,000 Latinos annually taking commu-nity college courses that met university requirements, less than 900 transferred to a University of California campus and about 3,600 to a California State Uni-versity campus. In the fall of 1990, 368,000 students attended twenty CSU cam-puses. Asian American students formed 12.5 percent of that total; Mexican Americans, 9.3 percent; Blacks, 6 percent; and Filipino and other Hispanic, 3.3 percent.[44]

Built to provide mass education, the California State University system cam-puses have been another important educational resource for Chicanos. The CSU system's mission is supposed to be different from that of the University of California system, emphasizing teaching instead of research. It was intended to be a working-class college system, open to children of working-class people.

But in the late 1980s and early 1990s, annual student fees increased over 100 percent, and were projected to climb to $2,500.

The percentages were in fact worse when it came to faculty. In 1989 'Hispanics' comprised 529 (4.33 percent) of the CSU's 12,230 tenured, probationary and lecture faculty, with less than 2 percent of the tenured faculty being of Mexican descent. Statistics were regularly padded with Spaniards and Portuguese listed as 'Hispanics'. Temporary lecturers made up a significant portion of this group.

Prospects for reforming the CSU system did not improve with the arrival of controversial chancellor W. Ann Reynolds in 1982. Playing to faculty pretensions, she deemphasized the teaching mission of CSU and indicated that one day it would be granting doctorates, a prospect that seduced faculty and public alike. A key point in Reynolds's plan for CSU was to raise entrance requirements to force high schools to upgrade the quality of the education their graduates received. If the system was not adequately educating students, the reason lay in their being unprepared when they first arrived on campus. Critics charged she was attempting to undermine the California Master Plan for Postsecondary Education, which separated the missions of the UC and CSU systems.[45] Reynolds had excellent relations with the *Los Angeles Times* as well as Latino leaders and organizations like MALDEF, and was therefore shielded from criticism. In addition, the Mexican American community shared her professed concern about the lack of academic preparation of public school students, although they did not blame the public schools alone for this failure, nor did they absolve the CSU system, which after all trained 86 percent of the state's teachers.

Reynolds also postured as the champion of affirmative action – but the CSU's failure to integrate minority staff, faculty and students into the Academy and to provide a quality experience for its own students cast doubt on her sincerity. Dr Kenneth Washington, vice-chancellor for educational services at the Los Angeles Community Colleges, questioned the logic of the CSU's efforts to enact admission policies identical to those of the University of California, fearing that the CSU was abandoning its teaching mission, and that the results would be devastating for minority students.[46]

Many suspected that the CSU's raising of entrance requirements and its spiraling tuition were surreptitious efforts to squeeze Blacks and Chicanos out of the system.[47] The Mexican American community was concerned about the growing funding gap between white and minority students. Even in higher education, less instructional money was spent per minority student than per Euromerican student. The CSU recommendation that more minorities attend community college to make up deficiencies in academic preparation threatened to widen the gap between Mexicans and whites. Indeed, the community colleges received about a third as much per student as the CSU; they had more part-time teachers, greater faculty loads, and fewer professors with doctorates. Increased community college attendance by minorities would result in increased racial segregation, with the community college students becoming darker as a group and the CSU students lighter. The downward push would also increase competition between Chicanos and Blacks for CSU admission. The net effect would be to exclude just the kind of disadvantaged student the CSU was designed to serve and once sought to recruit.

In response to this threat, MEChA chapters in Southern California planned demonstrations and other protests. Unfortunately, divisions developed among Chicano student activists over issues of ideology, personality, and region (Southern versus Northern California). A series of controversies pitted MEChA and others against the League for Revolutionary Struggle (LRS), one of the organizations in the Marxist-Leninist party-building movement. This struggle led to a serious split in MEChA that ended the common front being built against Reynolds's policies – or at least made that struggle ineffective. Her control over the CSU grew tighter, which meant even greater exclusion of Chicanos from faculty and administrative posts. (We should note that the recent history of the Chicano student movement in California, including its internal conflicts, remains to be told.)

In 1989, the entire CSU system had only one Mexican American president and that was at its smallest campus, Bakersfield. (A Spaniard and a Cuban American were later named to head other campuses, appointments that, according to CSU officials, met the CSU's 'Hispanic quota'.) At one campus, qualified Chicanos were passed over in favor of a 'white jock from the South'. Bill Stacy, who became president of a new CSU campus at San Marcos, had been the president of Southeast Missouri State University, and had no experience of California or the Southwest generally.[48] With the exception of Trini Melcher, an accounting professor, Stacy initially ignored Chicano faculty with strong roots in the community.

Reynolds's tenure saw the numbers of 'Hispanic' faculty increase from 3.42 percent in 1986 all the way to 3.98 percent in 1989. Six key administrative vacancies had occurred in the CSU system since 1983, and each time Latino candidates were ignored. Tomas Arciniega, president for seven years at California State University, Bakersfield, applied for the presidency of California State University, Fullerton. The large Latino population in Orange County made him a natural candidate, but Arciniega was passed over in favor of Milton Gordon, vice-president for four years at tiny Sonoma State University in Northern California, which did not have a large Latino community. CSU Fullerton professors apparently felt too threatened by the prospect of a Chicano president. (In 1987, Fullerton had twenty-three 'Hispanic' professors, a number that had fallen to nineteen by 1989.) Insiders said that a coalition of liberal and conservative professors derailed Arciniega's appointment in the name of faculty autonomy, just as it had systematically excluded Chicano faculty. Gordon, an African American, was a perfect out for them – in backing his candidacy they could not so easily be accused of racism.

W. Ann Reynolds was ousted as CSU chancellor in 1990 because she had engineered pay hikes of 21 to 43 percent for herself and other top administrators at a closed session of the system's Board of Trustees.[49] Soon after her fall from grace, she took over as chancellor of the City University of New York – the premier working-class college system in the nation – after selling herself as the affirmative action candidate. CUNY's mission was to educate the poor, and two-thirds of its students were Black and Latino. As she had done in California, Reynolds changed this mission drastically.[50]

The charade continued even after Reynolds left. At Fresno State University qualified Chicano candidates for president did not make it to the final cut. Meanwhile, the Fresno State selection process was partially reopened to include a Latino candidate, and to show that it was not racist, CSU Fresno appointed a Chicano vice-president. At San Jose State, the campus presidency opened up in 1992. Arciniega was again a finalist. This time objections came from the San Jose State Alumni Association, which pressured CSU to abort its search, saying that the search had resulted in an 'affirmative action pool and a political correctness pool'. The Alumni Association claimed that the finalists, which included three women, one Mexican American, one Black and one Asian, were not qualified to run a campus the size of San Jose.[51] In the end, the alumni and contributors won out: a white male was appointed as interim president.[52]

What happened at Fullerton, Fresno and San Jose exposed the weakness of the so-called Hispanic Caucus in the state legislature. As a group, they had little power within the Democratic Party; the caucus was taken into account only after key decisions had already been made. The CSU chancellor knew that the caucus lacked muscle and could therefore ride out any ripples that it made. Moreover, only one of the CSU Trustees, Ralph Pesqueira of San Diego, was a Latino, and he didn't seem to want to acknowledge that he was Mexican. The Trustees were all people who contributed to the governor's campaign; and the last two governors, Deukmejian and Wilson, were conservative Republicans who were basically anti-Mexican.

None of the eighteen or so academic vice-presidents named from 1985 to 1990 was Mexican American, and less than half a dozen academic deans were Chicano. It was from this pool that future CSU presidents would be selected. In an August 1991 report, The Latino Issues Forum had written:

It is no secret that the California State University is dominated and run by white men. It is no secret that the CSU has failed to fully integrate any of its university campuses. But it should be no secret that the foundation upon which the university was constructed and the continued maintenance, both the physical upkeep of the grounds and the tax-based support from the state for the twenty campuses, is done increasingly by people of color.[53]

The CSU Trustees had appointed Barry Minitz, a business whiz kid, to succeed Ann Reynolds as chancellor. Minitz was a smoother Reynolds and even less of a scholar who followed Reynolds's cynical policies. Under Minitz two more presidents with Spanish surnames were appointed (the Spaniard and the Cuban mentioned above, neither of whom had ties to the Mexican community). Indeed, the 'Hispanic' illusion was working against Chicanos at this point.

Minitz did not move to make the CSU a research institution as Reynolds had done; instead there was talk of creating a two-tier system, hiring instructors with Master of Arts degrees for less money than those with doctorates. The result would be to lower the quality of the education available to working-class students, many of whom were from communities of color. Minitz also kept the lid on faculty salaries and raised student fees.[54] In September 1993, Minitz announced that presidential salaries were 21 percent less than at comparable institutions and suggested that they be raised: meanwhile, tuition rates increased.[55]

The University of California System

The University of California is a semi-autonomous system reserved for the brightest and best students in California, drawing from the top 12.5 percent of high school graduates. It is a governmental agency that is not responsible to the legislature but to its own Board of Regents. Almost totally committed to the corporate interests that lavish funds on it and its faculty, UC has tremendous political power, influencing even the judicial system. Unlike the CSU, the 'UC has constitutional independence to make most decisions.'[56]

In 1993, the California State University system received over 90 percent of its budget from the state, $1.4 billion. The University of California received *less than* 30 percent, or $1.6 billion, of its budget from taxpayers. In 1993, the University of California's annual budget was approximately $6 billion (some observers estimate its budget at closer to $10 billion), but its 166,000 students were less than half the CSU student population.[57] (The community colleges, with a much larger enrollment than either the UC or CSU, received even less public funding.) The annual salary at UC ranged from $43,000 for associate professors to over $100,000 for distinguished and experienced faculty. The more experienced UC professors often taught a total of four classes a year on a quarter system, with two quarters on and one off. Most didn't bother to teach undergraduates.[58] According to an audit committee of the legislature, UC administrators were living 'palatially' and 'regally'. Indeed, a scandal concerning the $425,000-a-year income of UC President David Gardner, as well as excessive benefits, surrounded his retirement in 1992.[59]

The following year, the University of California let it be known that the new budget threatened its academic reputation. The system faced a $243 million shortfall in its 1993/94 budget as the state tried to find ways to make up a deficit of several billion dollars. Legislative analyst Elizabeth Hill suggested that UC faculty teach six courses instead of the standard five a year to help meet the crisis. Instead, the UC raised the salaries of its top administrators.[60] The proposal to increase the teaching load was a viable option. Some of the full professors were not even teaching five courses, but four, and many lab scientists taught even less. According to UC Riverside professor David Glidden, 'Teaching assistants carry more of the burden of instruction... Faculty advancements at research universities are based on quantity of publication more than quality of research. Since most faculty don't have the time to assess specialized research in areas they themselves know little of, quantity of publications reigns supreme.' Glidden called UC professors' offices 'desktop factories' in which the professors churned out the work, paying less and less attention to their classes.[61]

Chicano groups criticized the UC for its lack of progress on affirmative action. The UC responded by commissioning yet another three-year study on Latinos, which examined the factors that affected admission, retention and graduation of Latino students and recommended strategies to increase Latino enrollment and graduation rates.[62] Meanwhile, at UCLA during the 1989/90 school year there were only two Latinos at the level of assistant chancellor and above.[63] In 1991, 3.2 percent of the UC faculty was listed as Hispanic; and only 3.4 percent of the doctoral candidates were Latino.[64]

Under the California Master Plan for Higher Education, UC supposedly admitted the top 12.5 percent of high school graduates and the CSU the top 33.3 percent. At UCLA the permanent faculty was 86 percent white, while the percentage of white students had fallen from 70 to 44 percent in a decade. The Latino student population, which included Mexican Americans, had risen from 6.5 percent to 16.6 percent, and Blacks from 5 percent to 6.3 percent. Asians outnumbered Anglos, 36.9 to 34.2 percent.[65]

While academically competitive with white students, minority students lacked the financial support available to mainstream students. The vast majority of Central American and Chicano students were working class and the first generation of their families to attend college. Books were rare in their homes, with the possible exception of an encyclopedia that their parents had bought at an inflated price. Indeed, Chicanos and Central Americans were from socioeconomic backgrounds other than their classmates. In 1988, the average parental income of white undergraduates was $58,230; for Asian Americans it was

$46,885, and for African Americans it was $40,393. For Latinos, the figure was $36,494, and this average included the incomes of some wealthy Latin Americans.[66] Some 38 percent of all undergraduates required financial aid at UCLA. About 65 percent of the minority students received some kind of aid, indicating that they were the ones most adversely affected by rising tuition costs. Moreover, the worsening economy made it more difficult for students to get part-time employment.

El Centro César Chávez

In the 1980s deteriorating economic conditions polarized society, making many minority students more aware of the problems of their particular group. In Los Angeles the 'Lupe' incidents at UCLA and CSUN, and later Proposition 187, politicized many students who were normally uncomfortable emphasizing their ethnic identities. The decline of military industries and businesses made majors in those fields less attractive; by the 1990s many turned back to the social sciences and humanities. All this contributed to a revival of interest in Chicano studies among students of Mexican descent. In the community, dances like the *quebradita* became popular among youth, and the *danzantes* became a permanent fixture at the *fiestas patrias* and protest marches.

The call for Chicano Studies dated back to the Plan of Santa Barbara in the spring of 1969. In recent years there has been pressure to add a Meso-American perspective that would include the history and culture of Central America.[67] The largest of the Chicano Studies departments was created at California State University, Northridge, with twenty-two positions. Chicano Research Centers were also established at major research universities. The National Association for Chicano Studies (NACS) has grown to some 2,000 members, and holds annual conventions; it has also developed a strong Chicana caucus including a lesbian caucus. Within NACS there were varied ideological perspectives and views on the nature of Chicano Studies; debate ranged from whether Chicano Studies should follow the lead of the traditional disciplines or forge its own identity.[68] The debate differed, however, from that in the African American community over Afrocentrism. Chicano/a Studies was driven by the goal of inclusion as an equal partner in the Academy, which meant autonomy in the development of the curriculum and management of the discipline.

The struggle for Chicano Studies did not proceed smoothly. Nativist scholars claimed that Chicano Studies was not a legitimate field of study and that its existence therefore threatened academic standards.[69] Within this context, a truly historic struggle took place at UCLA in 1993.[70] The struggle for a Chicano Studies department at UCLA began in 1989 when first-year Chicano students protested the inaction of Chancellor Charles Young after the film department premiered a student film showing a Mexican woman having intercourse with a donkey.[71] Demonstrations and unsuccessful negotiations produced a feeling of powerlessness and desperation among the students. Tempers flared when a faculty committee proposed suspending the Chicano Studies program, citing the administration's lack of support for the major as indicated by its having spent only a few thousand dollars a year since 1969.

For three years, students drew up proposals, lobbied faculty, held conferences and went through the system in an attempt to win establishment of a core Chicano Studies department. In a core department the professors would have tenure within that department, in contrast to the interdepartmental program favored by administrators.[72] Students wanted a core department because they believed it would offer more autonomy in hiring faculty and developing curricula. To win support in their struggle against the UCLA administration they reached out to the community, and a support committee, headed by Vivién Bonzo of La Golondrina restaurant, was formed.

When Chancellor Young finally announced his decision not to create a core department on the eve of César Chávez's funeral in 1993, and to cut back Chicano library funds, students immediately mobilized the community.[73] Chicano *politicos* and community leaders petitioned Young. By this time, Chicano faculty and the student community were badly divided. Many Chicano faculty members were ambivalent, with some clearly looking at Chicano Studies as a danger to their own aspirations.

The Concerned Students of Color (CSC), a recently formed coalition, held a rally on 11 May that ended in the takeover of the faculty center. The administration supported the arrest of ninety-nine students, eighty-three of whom were jailed and strip-searched. The overreaction by the administration created martyrs of the arrested students and galvanized support for a core Chicano Studies department.[74]

The United Community/Labor Alliance met at La Golondrina restaurant soon after the arrests. Final exams would be starting within three weeks, and normally this meant that all campus activism died; the administration was relying on the traditional impact of the academic calendar. Moreover, how long could rallies and marches hold public attention?

Marcos Aguilar and his wife, Minnie Ferguson, both UCLA students, had been leaders in the movement to win full departmental status for Chicano Studies at UCLA since 1989. It was they, among others, who developed the first proposals, changing the name of the proposed department from Chicano Studies to Chicana(o) Studies. Over the years, Marcos and Minnie, along with Bonnie Díaz, had become highly controversial. Marcos, for instance, had become alienated from MEChA; also many faculty members considered him abrasive and insolent for not taking their guidance. No doubt, however, the single-mindedness of Marcos and Minnie kept the issue alive.

Marcos and Minnie proposed the strategy of a fast to the students, many of whom rejected the idea. Even sympathetic faculty members feared for the lives of the students and spoke against it. But in the end, no one could offer a viable alternative. Dr Jorge Mancillas of the UCLA Medical School, who had first opposed the hunger strike, personally joined the fast. UCLA student Joaquín Ochoa also joined. Marcos was a member of the Grupo Danzante Cuauhtemoc (Cuauhtemoc Dance Group), as were UCLA students Laura Balvina, Cindy Montañez, and Cindy's sister Norma, a sixteen-year-old San Fernando High junior.[75] The leader of the *danzantes*, Paztel Mireles, also fasted, as did Arturo Díaz, a nonstudent member of the *danzantes* from Mexico. The last Chicano student in the group of hunger strikers was María Lara, who throughout the fourteen-day strike was one of its most vocal members. Most strategy sessions during the hunger strike were open only to actual participants, select faculty members and invitees.

The strikers and their supporters were housed in a tent city set up in the quad immediately to the west of Campbell Hall, the administration building. At any given period during the hunger strike there were 100 to 200 campers. Ceremonial events were staged throughout the day and evening, revolving around indigenous ceremonies, often led by Professor Laura Medina. Those fasting were monitored by Chicano medical doctors. Prof. Gina Váldez, a visiting professor at UCLA, coordinated medical attention. Kathy Ochoa, a staff member at the Chicano Research Center, coordinated a cadre of Chicanas who handled the press and public relations.

The students selected Dr Leo Estrada of the School of Architecture and Urban Planning to head the negotiation team. Attending meetings were Dr David Hayes-Bautista and Dr Cynthia Telles, director of the Chicano mental health unit. Dr Juan Gómez Quiñones served as an adviser and took part in later negotiations.[76] A team of lawyers worked feverishly behind the scenes, headed by Chicano attorney Jorge González. From the community, Vivién Bonzo, the head of the Alianza, took a leading role, as did Juan José Gutiérrez of One Stop Immigration. MEChA leader Milo Alvárez also played a key role during the negotiations. Chicano actor James Edward Olmos attracted the press,[77] and also tried to bring the different factions of the faculty together, since the lack of faculty unity was a problem delaying resolution of the struggle. Local 399, Justice for Janitors, actively supported the strike, as did most Chicano students and organizations from the Brown Berets to the Mothers of East Los Angeles, as well as the Third World Coalition, which included Native Americans, Asians, African Americans and whites.

For the most part, Chicano politicos supported the strike. State Senators Art Torres and Tom Hayden were permanent fixtures, with Hayden participating in student strategy sessions into the early morning. Meanwhile, the hunger strikers became more resolute with every passing day, willing to starve to death if they did not get what their community needed. Chancellor Young ignored the danger.[78] One of the highlights of the entire strike was the sixteen-mile march in the rain from Olvera Street to UCLA on 5 June. Two hundred marchers started the trek, which picked up momentum after it passed La Brea, and a gigantic rally took place on the UCLA campus. During the next week, the hunger strikers entered a euphoric state. They became more determined than ever to win all their demands – a department or nothing. A delegation of elected officials led by the retired but much respected former Congressman Edward R. Roybal, his daughter Rep. Lucille Roybal-Allard and Congressman Xavier Becerra visited the strikers and also met with university officials to make clear their concern for the lives of the students. Reports began to filter in that some 20,000 high school students were getting ready to walk out in support of the UCLA hunger strike. Authorities saw another Rodney King scenario in the making. Security around the compound tightened after fraternity members and others hostile to Chicano activism were seen surveying the camp.

At this point, several leaders of the faculty senate attempted to negotiate a compromise. But Young would not budge even if it meant putting the whole city at risk. Around-the-clock negotiations took place, attended by the hunger strikers in wheelchairs. Finally the administration agreed to establish a center that in practice would have the same autonomy as a department. It also agreed to reinstate cuts in the budgets of the ethnic and gender studies centers. But Young still refused to drop charges against those arrested at the 11 May demonstration. It was not until 13 June that the administration finally agreed not to press this point on the condition that restitution would be made.[79] Students had won the César Chávez Center for Interdisciplinary Instruction in Chicano and Chicana Studies, el Centro César Chávez. The administration agreed to the hiring of seven full-time core appointments in the following three years.

The hunger strike was one of the most dramatic episodes of the Chicano student movement in recent history. For outsiders, one of its most controversial aspects was its *indigenismo* or indigenousness, which often verged on a spirituality unfamiliar to many. Chicana activist-intellectual Elizabeth Martínez wrote about this aspect of the struggle: 'By its very nature a hunger strike is a spiritual affirmation of moral authority through willingness to sacrifice...For self-defined Leftists, the affirmation of spirituality corrects a long-standing tendency to neglect or deny a genuine human need that the Right has consistently exploited. Today's reevaluation of past Marxist and socialist strategies needs to include taking a hard look at this error.' She recognized that *indigenismo* can be manipulated to encourage patriarchy and cultism. But those tendencies are not exclusive to *indigenismo*. They are all too present in leftist or progressive groups, as well as in mainstream society.[80] The challenge is to go beyond the structural imperfections of the Chicano movement in the past to create a new vision for the future.

Indigenismo and nationalism were strong in Southern California for several reasons. This is the most segregated part of the state, where racism against Chicanos has been most intense. Alienation has driven students to search for an identity and an alternative vision, a void that *indigenismo* has filled. Indeed, indigenism was strong among Chicano students during this period – largely because of the failure of both society and the left to attract them.[81] There was also the fact that the end of a century approached: the history of Mexico tells us that a great interest in indigenous culture and values marked the end of the last century in that country.

Affirmative Action:
From the Trenches of California's Race War

Even as Chicanos celebrated the UCLA victory, reactionary forces across the nation were setting out a deadly agenda. In California it first sounded in Proposition 187, whose target was not merely Latinos and other immigrants. Proposition 187 was designed to light a prairie fire that would remake the American political landscape. None other than Patrick Buchanan himself sounded the call to arms in January 1995: 'America should be listening for drums along the racial frontier.' Buchanan went on to ridicule the idea that Latinos had a history of civil rights struggle: 'Hispanics were never enslaved in America for 300 years. Nor were they victims of 100 years of racial discrimination.' Seconds later he threatened that the California Civil Rights Initiative (CCRI), a proposal to abolish state affirmative action programs, would make Proposition 187 'look like a pillow fight in a sorority house'. Buchanan warned that 'words like "racist" ... have lost their power to intimidate. No one is cowed anymore. Already, clones of the CCRI are being readied in other states.' The issue of affirmative action would probably be on the Republican platform in 1996. In Orwellian fashion Buchanan then softened his threats by saying that the initiative would go a long way toward making America, the Land of the Free, a color-blind society.[82]

The attack on affirmative action formed part of the New Right's deconstruction of civil rights. From the beginning these extremists attempted to control political discourse and to redefine the meaning of the past. They effectively used people of color like Supreme Court Justice Clarence Thomas, Sacramento businessman and UC Regent Ward Connerly and the opportunist Linda Chávez as fronts.[83] They also effectively broadcast the idea that unqualified minorities were getting special treatment, costing white Americans jobs and admission to college. This message played to white male frustration, and resentment over scholarships for minority students and legislative redistricting, in the context of a recession that has reduced opportunities for all. Affirmative action was a time bomb, as one source put it, ready to detonate in the 'middle of the American political marketplace'.[84]

Affirmative action grew out of the Civil Rights Act of 1964. President Lyndon B. Johnson formally advocated it as a way of enabling people hobbled by generations of bias to compete for jobs, university admissions and government contracts. Thirty years ago Johnson realized that two separate Americas existed, and that it made sense to reconstruct the country so as to prevent the growing polarization. However, just as the civil rights movement had made sense to northerners when voting rights applied only to the South, the idea of affirmative action ceased to be popular when minorities began to compete with white middle-class interests.

The Republican Party hammered away on this theme, falsely labelling affirmative action as quotas, reverse racism and preferential treatment of unqualified minorities. The fact was that more than half the students entering UC Berkeley, for example, were admitted solely on the basis of high school grades and their scores on standardized tests. The percentage of minority students admitted had not increased that much. Beneath the surface lay the problem that Asians were outperforming whites, who, while seeking to preserve their advantages over Blacks and Latinos, complained that Berkeley was becoming an Asian university.[85]

The assault on affirmative action was part of the new Republican majority's taking aim at Clinton. It was the ultimate wedge issue, gathering strength from a slow-growth economy. Stagnant middle-class incomes and corporate downsizing made the white middle-class nervous: who gets fired next? The New Right brilliantly defined the debate in terms of a conflict between two cherished American principles: the belief that all Americans deserve equal opportunities and the idea that hard work and merit, not race, religion, gender or birthright, should determine who prospers.

Because economic restructuring has hit California hard, and because it has fifty-four electoral votes, the state has become the nation's affirmative action battlefield. Assemblyman Bernie Richter (R-Chico) introduced a bill to end affirmative action, but it failed to get the necessary two-thirds majority. What became more of a threat was a referendum authored by Tom Wood, executive director of the California Association of Scholars, and Glynn Custred, an anthropology professor at California State University, Hayward. Masters of double-speak, they insidiously called their measure the California Civil Rights Initiative (CCRI). They had for three years tried to put a measure on the ballot banning 'state-sanctioned preferential treatment based on race or gender'. The New Right's victory in passing Proposition 187 now catapulted affirmative action into center stage. The authors of the CCRI themselves admitted the ties between Proposition 187 and their own initiative.[86]

Initially, the anti–affirmative action initiative appeared to have a guaranteed place on the 26 March 1996 primary ballot. White voters made up 78 percent of the California electorate in November 1994. It was not certain whether the Asian community would support the initiative; it had split on Proposition 187, which affected them. Many observers saw white women as the key group in this struggle: would they vote to preserve affirmative action programs (which included them), or vote along racial lines? There was little public opposition, with key leaders of the Democratic Party running for cover. Bill Press, chair of the California Democratic Party and a long-time liberal, admitted that his party simply couldn't oppose the initiative. If affirmative action was being used to discriminate against white males, Democrats had to fix it.[87] Lieutenant Governor Gray Davis retreated as well: 'There aren't any sacred cows. We should reexamine every program.' But Davis said nothing about the fact that some 12 percent of admissions to elite colleges were the result of preferences given to the unqualified children of alumni.[88] At a later stage, Clinton took a 'mend it, don't end it' position, which was hardly surprising given his history of strategic retreats. The clearest voice in defense of affirmative action was that of the former Speaker of the California Assembly, Willie Brown, who asserted that the CCRI was an attempt 'to maintain white America in total control' and denounced the measure as racist.'[89] In contrast the Latino Caucus of the state legislature offered little leadership.

Even though it lacked serious opposition from liberals, the campaign for the CCRI unexpectedly ran into problems during the fall of 1995. The campaign had collected 200,000 signatures, but 694,000 were needed by 21 February 1996 to ensure a place on the ballot. This meant that proponents would need to use professional petition-circulators, at a cost of over $1 million. Perhaps more significant, some supporters were losing faith in the right's initiative strategy because the courts had ruled key parts of previous conservative initiatives unconstitutional. In November 1995, for example, federal Judge Mariana Pfaelzer struck down much of Proposition 187, the anti-immigration initiative. At this writing, the CCRI campaign was trying to reorganize and to get financing for an intensive signature-gathering drive. But the struggle over affirmative action promises to continue even if the CCRI fails to qualify for the ballot.

The fact was that affirmative action had been considerably modified by the courts since 1964. In the 1970s, the *Griggs* v. *Duke Power* decision established that employment policies that tend to concentrate nonwhite workers in low-paying jobs did not necessarily violate federal civil rights law. In a five-to-four decision in 1978 the US Supreme Court ruled in *Regents* v. *Bakke* that quotas were unconstitutional and decided in favor of white plaintiff Allan Bakke. Indeed, although California State University's admissions process made race a consideration, other criteria included whether the applicant was a first-generation college student, economically deprived, or physically handicapped.[90] And it was simply a myth that unqualified women and minorities were being hired in large numbers. The New Right knew this, but to gain political advantage they exaggerated the occasional abuses that come with any large-scale program.

The truth is that the campaign to do away with affirmative action has nothing to do with the truth. White American veterans have been the principal beneficiaries of preferential hiring and educational assistance programs. California's largely white, aging middle class amassed equities through cheap housing and government financing of housing tracts that openly discriminated against minorities. There is also the preferential treatment of older, white middle-class homeowners over young, first-time buyers with regard to property tax assessments. The allegation of William Bennett, a former secretary of education, that affirmative action had led to damaging forms of resegregation was intellectually dishonest. Integration is not simply a state of mind; it includes equality of opportunity, which can be achieved only through socioeconomic parity.

The aggressiveness of the campaign against affirmative action left people of color little choice but to take to the streets. It was doubtful whether Chicano politicos would be able to hold the line internally in 1996 as they had in the case of Proposition 187. Indeed, cracks appeared when local politicians convinced Chicano and Latino students to return to class after walking out on the eve of the 1994 election. The question was whether, in view of the trouncing that the Latino community took on Proposition 187, Chicano politicos would have the moral authority to control the situation in 1996. At some point the defensiveness of 'Please don't take affirmative action away from us!' would have to give way to a more active approach.

Among many Latinos it was not really affirmative action that they were fighting for, it was the idea of equal opportunity. Rejection of that value would represent a return to the past, a decline in the power of civil rights forces and a faltering commitment to the concept of equality on the part of Democrats. Latinos could not buy the excuse that the Democratic Party was 'caught between angry white males and the party's traditional liberal base.' Nor could they accept the racism and tyranny of the majority of voters – who happened to be a minority of the population – and the excuse that they were 'frustrated' by bad times.[91]

If successful, the anti–affirmative action campaign would take a brutal toll in Los Angeles. Because the city is home to so many people of color, here is where the blow could fall with horrendous impact. In 1967, for example, California State University, Northridge (then San Fernando State College) had all of 7 Chicano students. In 1969 it had some 50; today it has over 3,500. That growth could never have happened without affirmative action. A whole Chicano professional class and professional societies would not have emerged in Los Angeles without it. The same is true of many areas but for reasons of sheer numbers, the example of Los Angeles stands out most starkly.

The campaign to kill affirmative action also promises to expose the fault-lines within the Democratic Party in Los Angeles; politicians will have to take sides.[92] Republicans will continue to gain if no serious challenge to their agenda is presented. To many, the sharp lurch to the right on the American political scene represents an embryonic stage of neofascism, one that must be confronted. Black and Chicano workers have been the biggest losers in the economic restructuring of the United States, including Los Angeles.[93] They cannot afford to lose anymore, to sacrifice yet another generation to the intellectual ovens of ignorance.[94]

Notes

1. William Trombley and Larry Gordon, 'State's Per Pupil Spending Would Decline Under Deukmejian's Budget', Los Angeles Times, 26 Jan. 1990.

2. See Richard Rothstein, 'In Search of the American Dream: Obstacles to Latino Educational Achievement', in Abraham F. Lowenthal and Katrina Burgess, eds, The California–Mexico Connection (Stanford, Calif.: Stanford University Press, 1993), pp. 176–95; María del Pilar Marrero, 'Hispanos dan calificaciones mediocres a escuelas públicas', La Opinión, 17 May 1991.

3. Alejandro Morelos, 'Baja representación hispana en Distrito angelino de escuelas', La Opinión, 7 Nov. 1992; Latinos were the most underrepresented workers in the LAUSD, comprising about 12 percent of the workforce.

4. Rothstein, 'In Search of the American Dream', pp. 176–8; Elaine Woo, 'L.A. Confronts Dropout Crisis Among Latinos', Nuestro Tiempo, 31 Aug. 1989; Elizabeth Shogren, 'College Aspirations Have Increased but Stats Haven't', Los Angeles Times, 24 Nov. 1993.

5. Elaine Woo, 'School Dropouts: New Data May Provide Elusive Clues', Los Angeles Times, 11 Sept. 1988.

6. Esmeralda Barnes, 'Study Shows High Latino Dropout Rate Linked to Immigration Patterns', Black Issues in Higher Education, 28 Jan. 1993, p. 35; Woo, 'L.A. Confronts Dropout Crisis.'

7. Rothstein, 'In Search of the American Dream', pp. 181–2; Rothstein, 'When Johnny's Whole Family Can't Read', Business Week, 20 July 1992, pp. 68–9; Ronald Grover and Eric Schine, 'The Other Fault Lines Slicing Through California's Future', Business Week, 20 July 1992, p. 67.

8. Rothstein, 'In Search of the American Dream', pp. 184–7; Rothstein, 'Inmigración y cambio de actitudes hacia la educación', La Opinión, 9 Jan. 1992; Teresa Puente, 'Más enseñanza bilingue', La Opinión, 28 Jan. 1992; Sam Enríquez, 'Faculty Can't Fill Bilingual Needs of State', Los Angeles Times, 17 Oct. 1990. An additional 20,000 bilingual teachers will be needed in the next ten years; in 1989, 415 college students graduated with bilingual credentials in California; Sandy Banks, 'Schools Are Frustrated by Bilingual Class Demands', Los Angeles Times, 21 Nov. 1989; Stephanie Chavez, 'L.A. Schools Challenged on Bilingual Programs', Los Angeles Times, 17 Sept. 1993.

9. David E. Hayes-Bautista et al., The Burden of Support: Young Latinos in an Aging Society (Stanford, Calif.: Stanford University Press, 1988), p. 81.

10. Rothstein, 'In Search of the American Dream', pp. 178–9; Jean Meryl, 'Latinos Lagging on Every School Level, Study Finds', Los Angeles Times, 25 Jan. 1991.

11. James Powell, 'New Ideas About Smarts Stand Logic on Its Head', Washington Times, 31 Oct. 1994.

12. Sandy Banks and Stephanie Chavez, 'Yuri and Patrick: 2 Faces of State's Troubled Schools', Los Angeles Times, 30 October 1993.

13. Ibid.

14. William Trombley, 'No Simple Answer to Class Size Problem', Los Angeles Times, 26 Aug. 1990; Maribel Hastings, 'Educación y poder posible solución a problemas hispanos', La Opinión, 9 Dec. 1991.

15. Rothstein, 'In Search of the American Dream', p. 180.

16. Vincent Thomas, 'Estudio nacional revela que los latinos son los estudiantes más segregados', *La Opinión*, 10 Jan. 1992.

17. Update, *United Teachers of Los Angeles Flyer*, 20 Nov. 1991; 'Community Response', *League of United Latin American Citizens, Northeast Los Angeles Council*, Dec. 1991; Nancy Folbre, 'Remembering the Alamo Heights', *Texas Observer*, 13 Nov. 1992, pp. 1, 6–9; Michael Kennedy, 'Texas School Districts Learn Price of Sharing the Wealth', *Los Angeles Times*, 17 Sept. 1991; Alejandro Morelos, 'UTLA se opone a los cambios de alumnos', *La Opinión*, 9 March 1992; Pablo Comesaña Amado, 'Maldef demanda apoyo para fondos escolares', *La Opinión*, 4 Dec. 1991; Lew Hollman, 'Let's Put an End to Unequal Schooling', *Los Angeles Times*, 27 Dec. 1991; Pablo Comesaña Amado, 'MALDEF demanda apoyo para los fondos escolares', *La Opinión*, 4 Dec. 1991.

18. María del Pilar Marrero, 'Hispanos dan calificaciones mediocres a escuelas publicas', *La Opinión*, 17 May 1991. In a Univisión and *La Opinión* poll, 71 percent of Latinos surveyed said they would pay more taxes to support schools. Latinos have a history of supporting bond issues and improvement of education.

19. Charisse Jones, '4 Labor Groups Form Alliance to Counter L.A. Teachers Union', *Los Angeles Times*, 20 June 1992.

20. Stephanie Grace, 'White Men, Women Dominate Teaching Corps', *Los Angeles Times*, 7 July 1992.

21. Lydia Ramos, 'Big Challenge Awaits Anton', *Nuestro Tiempo*, 30 Aug. 1989. Bill Anton became the first Mexican American superintendent of the LAUSD in 1989, William C. Velásquez, 'Bilingual Education Programs Cut Nearly 40 percent'; News Release, Southwest Voter Registration Education Project, undated; Maribel Hastings, 'Desproporción en la nación entre maestros y alumnos latinos, reitera un estudio', *La Opinión*, 27 Oct. 1993. Nationally, 11.8 percent of students were Latino, but only 3.7 percent of teachers. In California 36 percent of the students and 7.5 percent of teachers were Latino.

22. Lee May, 'Latinos Assail Bilingual Education Plans', *Los Angeles Times*, 25 Jan. 1986.

23. Daniel M Weintraub, 'School Funding Defines Lines of State Budget Battle', *Los Angeles Times*, 27 Aug. 1992; Joseph Berger, 'School Programs Assailed as Bilingual Bureaucracy', *New York Times*, 4 Jan. 1993; 'Whose Language?' *New York Times*, 4 Jan. 1993.

24. Bill Billiter, 'Bilingual Education Battle Heats Up in the Legislature', *Los Angeles Times*, 11 June 1986; Lee May, 'English-Only Foes Line Up Behind US Education Bill', *Los Angeles Times*, 11 June 1986; May, 'Less English Urged in Bilingual Teaching', *Los Angeles Times*, 18 June 1986; 'English-Only Threats', *MALDEF*, April 1986, p. 4.

25. See Rodolfo Acuña, 'Teachers Without Eyes', *Los Angeles Herald-Examiner*, 4 March 1988, and 'The Cancer in the Ranks of L.A. Teachers', *Los Angeles Herald-Examiner*, 3 March 1989; Sam Enriquez, 'Bilingual Foes Force a Vote on Bonus Pay', *Los Angeles Times*, 28 Feb. 1989. There were LEAD chapters in Los Angeles, San Diego, San Francisco and Orange counties; the organization claimed 20,000 members; Sam Enríquez, 'L.A. Parents Protest Teachers' Bid to Halt Bilingual Program', *Los Angeles Times*, 19 April 1989.

26. Sam Enríquez, 'Magnet Schools Deter Immigrant Pupils', *Los Angeles Times*, 15 October 1990. While the LAUSD is overwhelmingly Latino, there is considerable resistance to Latinos assuming leadership of the district. A contributing factor is the vehement opposition of many Blacks to undocumented parents voting in school board elections and the fact that Black teachers have acquired an equity within the system, since there are proportionately more Black teachers than Black students. When Anton resigned and the board named Sid Thompson as interim superintendent over Rubén Zacarias, Chicanos were up in arms. There was no doubt that Thompson was well qualified, but not better qualified than Zacarias. Beth Shuster, '4 on School Board Support Thompson', *Daily News*, 30 Sept. 1992.

27. Carmen Ramos Chandler, 'Plan to Charge Illegal Aliens Higher Tuition Fuels Argument', *Daily News*, 20 Aug. 1992; Henry Muñoz Villalta, 'La educación y los latinos', *La Opinión*, 28 Aug. 1992; Pablo Comesaña Amado, 'Jaime Escalante se despidió de sus alumnos y colaboradores', *La Opinión*, 8 Aug. 1991. Without a doubt the best-known teacher among Chicanos was Sal Castro, whose work focused on motivating a broad range of Chicano and Latino students: many Chicanos have long waited for 'The Sal Castro Story.' A teacher in Los Angeles schools for thirty years, Castro had urged his students to pressure school administrators to stand and deliver. In 1963, Castro

got into trouble when he encouraged Chicano students at Belmont High School to take over student government. Although a majority, Chicanos did not hold a single student-body office, so Castro urged the Chicano students to hold a convention and nominate a slate of candidates. To conceal its strategy from school administrators, the Tortilla Movement, as Castro called it, became TM. Taking their cue from John F. Kennedy, who spoke to Mexican American audiences in Spanish, TM candidates concluded their speeches in Spanish. When student-body elections rolled around, TM candidates swept all offices except that of president. This campaign earned Castro a quick transfer to Lincoln High. Nearly 30 years later, Castro was still pushing his Tortilla Movement, Rodolfo Acuña, 'He Oughta Be in Movies', *Los Angeles Times*, 28 April 1990.

28. Henrik Rehbinder, 'Educación preocupa más que desempleo y recesión a hispanos del sur de California', *La Opinión*, 18 Feb. 1992.

29. 'The Latin-Americanization of the Universities', *National Review*, 24 May 1993, p. 18. This is an important editorial from an ultraconservative journal, reporting on the NAS convention in San Francisco; John Leo, 'Separatism Won't Solve Anything', *US News & World Report*, 19 April 1993.

30. Alice Dembner, 'Diversity Run Amok at UMass-Amherst, Teachers Say', *Boston Globe*, 10 Nov. 1994.

31. These are neither poor nor defenseless scholars who just want to search for the truth. They are part of a well-funded campaign to oppose 'political correctness' and multiculturalism. The purpose is to solidify conservative control of the Academy. The irony is that these archconservatives have adopted the liberal jargon of the sixties in their campaign, accusing the PCers and multiculturalists of being 'neo-McCarthyites'. Their efforts are supported by conservative and right-wing foundations and think tanks with links to the national media; Daniel Reich, 'The Overlooked Problem of Multiculturalism', *Los Angeles Times*, 14 Feb. 1993; '"Political Correctness" Statement of AAUP Committee is Criticized', *California Academic Review* (Fall 1991); John L. Rosenfeld, '"Political Correctness" in the Classroom', *California Academic Review* (Fall 1991); John Ellis, 'Political Correctness and Reason', *California Academic Review* (Fall 1991). NAS's precursor, the Coalition for Democracy, was founded in 1982. By the spring of 1986, its president, Professor Stephen Balch, wrote in its ultraconservative magazine, *Society*, about the 'politicization of scholarship'. With New York University Dean Herbert L. London, Balch co-authored an article in *Commentary* entitled 'The Tenured Left'. That year the Coalition became the NAS, receiving money from the Heritage, Smith-Richardson and Olin foundations, among others; Louis Menand, 'English at Queens College Grad Center of CCNY', *Harper's* (Dec. 1991), pp. 47–56. The Baltimore-based National Institute Against Prejudice and Violence estimated that 20 to 25 percent of students experienced some form of ethnic or religious prejudice, and pointed out that faculty diversity has not kept up with student diversity; 'The Campus Right', *Texas Observer*, 31 May 1991, pp. 6–7.

32. See Carol Iannone, 'PC with a Human Face', *Commentary*, vol. 95, no. 6, p. 44. Iannone incorrectly labels the PCers members of the hard Left.

33. Dinesh D'Souza, 'A New Moral Majority Dictates an "Illiberal Education"', *Los Angeles Times*, 14 April 1991.

34. Mona Charen, 'Last Gasps of Political Correctness', *Daily News*, 6 Dec. 1993.

35. It should be made clear that not all Chicanos supported MEChA and other activist organizations. Indeed, many Chicanos and other Latinos were joining professional organizations and the Greek system and did not take part in demonstrations, Jeffrey C. Alexander and Steven Jay Sherwood, 'American Dream at a Turning Point', *Los Angeles Times*, 15 Sept. 1991.

36. Theta Xi Songbook, quoted in Kelly Besser and Heather Skinazi, 'A Theta Xi Education', *together*, 28 Sept. 1992, p. 3.

37. María del Pilar Marrero, 'Exigen más acciones antirracistas en UCLA', *La Opinión*, 29 Oct. 1992.

38. Thomas E. Piernack, Director, Office of Campus Activities, to Dave Wagner, President, Zeta Beta Tau, 12 October 1992: 'The blatant insensitivity on your fraternity's part and the ignorance of your leadership as to why this is a serious issue astounded me. Your actions merit serious sanctions from the University and National organization as well as public apology to women, the Chicano community, and to your fellow fraternities who will unfortunately share in the questions of organizational character.' Piernack went on: 'At one point your Vice President Harris Barton challenged me on two issues other than your right to be in"solidarity" with Theta Xi at UCLA.'

Considering this and other communications to ZBT, it cannot be doubted that they intended to insult, and knew what the issues were.

39. Sam Enríquez, 'CSUN Official May Suspend Fraternity on Racism Issue', *Los Angeles Times*, 22 Oct. 1992; Mary Ballesteros, 'MEChA se enfrenta a uno grupo que hizo un presunta ofensa a la mujer mexicana', *La Opinión*, 22 Oct. 1992.

40. Sharon Bernstein, 'Network of Rightists Recruited by Activist', *Los Angeles Times*, 12 April 1993. The Inter-Fraternity Council, whose rules, regulations and standards of conduct they pledged to uphold, found the ZBT's actions objectionable and suspended the ZBT's charter. The administration settled the case without consulting with the IFC, thus undermining the IFC and in effect telling ZBT and other organizations that they need not obey regulations.

41. *Latino Leadership of the California Community Colleges*, n.d., p. 2.

42. Larry Gordon and Douglas Huit, 'Report Assails UC, College on Minorities', *Los Angeles Times*, 31 March 1989; Stephen R. Barnett, 'Who Gets In? A Troubling Policy', *Los Angeles Times*, 11 June 1992.

43. Commission on Hispanic Underrepresentation, *Hispanics and Higher Education: A CSU Imperative*, Office of the Chancellor, The California State University, Sept. 1984; *Hispanics and Higher Education: A CSU Imperative, Final Report*, Commission on Hispanic Underrepresentation, Office of the Chancellor, The California State University, June 1985, p. 41; Robert O. Bess to the Commission on Hispanic Underrepresentation, 25 Jan. 1985; Commission on Hispanic Representation, Sept. 1984, p. 4; 'College Admissions: Latinos Face Obstacles in California', *Daily Report Card*, 22 April 1993; Lisa Lapin, 'For Latinos, College Still a Distant Land', *Sacramento Bee*, 18 April 1993.

44. James Michael Brodie, 'Black–Latino Tensions Flare over Cal State Hiring Practices', *Black Issues in Higher Education*, 23 April 1992, pp. 6–7.

45. On 12 January 1985, in a letter to the editor of the *Los Angeles Times*, 'Cal State Plan Makes Assumptions', I criticized a 15 Dec. 1984 letter by Reynolds thanking the *Times* for its 19 Nov. editorial support, 'Cal State: Quality with Equality'. The letter criticized trickle-down education – and the proposition that requiring more solid subjects would improve high school training: 'This assumption reflects a total ignorance of history, a retreat from the 1960s commitment to equal access to the state system for minority students, and a return to hypocritical racist policies that have traditionally excluded minorities from higher education.' The letter charged that there had been some success with a more open admissions policy that had been won through considerable struggle. 'Now Chancellor Reynolds, a newcomer to California with no previous track record with Latinos, says the system wants to correct "the disparity between the proportion of minorities, especially Hispanics, who enroll in the state's universities ..."' The letter objected to the assumption that the high schools would change because the CSU willed it. Where were the funds going to come from? It pointed out that only 40 Mexican American students had been recruited to CSUN in 1985, with priority given to the recruitment of Vietnamese students. As a result of the letter, the Academic Senate Executive Committee, four white males and a white female, wrote a letter to the *Times* on 22 January 1985. Essentially, the Academic Senate rubber-stamped the chancellor's policies. Its degree of naiveté was displayed in the following passage: 'The State Legislature, Governor Deukmejian, and Superintendent of Public Instruction have taken the same view as Chancellor Reynolds and the Trustees by requiring more rigorous high school graduation standards for *all* California high school students.' Then the letter gave examples of the 'ongoing efforts' to increase representation – but if Chicanos did not meet the requirements they could always go to a community college. Acuña to Claudia Hampton, 16 Jan. 1985; Acuña to John W. Bedell, Acting Assoc. Vice Chancellor, 1 Feb. 1985; Bedell to Acuña, 23 Jan. 1985.

46. Commission on Hispanic Underrepresentation, *Hispanics and Higher Education: A CSU Imperative*; Tomas A. Arciniega was the chair of the commission.

47. Roberto Rodríguez, 'Financial Woes Hamper Latino Recruitment and Retention Efforts', *Black Issues in Higher Education*, 29 Jan. 1993. An American Council on Education study stressed that more Latinos were attending school part-time because of financial woes in 1990; Larry Gordon, 'Financial Aid Requests at Universities', *Los Angeles Times*, 20 Jan. 1992.

48. See Rodolfo Acuña, 'Creating Another White-Male Institution', *Los Angeles Herald-Examiner*, 6 Oct. 1989.

49. Ralph Frammolino, 'Trustees Are Urging Pay Hikes for CSU Presidents', *Los Angeles Times*, 15 Sept. 1993. Reynolds, a daughter of a missionary who served on a Native American reservation,

had an air to her: she could easily be visualized wearing wellington boots and holding a swagger stick. Even her friends described her as imperious. She was nevertheless an accomplished self-promoter who has almost always landed on her feet.

50. Billy Tashman and Robert Neuwirth, 'CUNY Under Siege', *Village Voice*, 19 May 1992. New York state spent $7,653 per student for its university system, and $6,927 for CUNY, compared with Yale, which spent $74,000 per student.

51. *Latino Issues Forum*, 1991, appendix.

52. Michelle Guido and Alan Gathright, 'Finalists Outrage Alumni at SJS', *San Jose Mercury News*, 11 March 1992.

53. *Latino Issues Forum*, 1991, p. 19.

54. 'Suben cuotas y bajan sueldos en el sistema académico de UCLA', *La Opinión*, 20 March 1993.

55. Frammolino, 'Trustees Are Urging Pay Hikes for CSU Presidents'.

56. Larry Gordon, 'UC Regents Pressured to Change Elite Image', *Los Angeles Times*, 6 July 1992; Peter Schrag, 'Is There a Need to Break Up UC System?' *Daily News*, 16 March 1994. Schrag pointed out that undergraduate education receives only a small portion of the budget, and that large amounts go to subsidize the privatized professional schools within UC. The author estimated that less than $370 million went to undergraduate education, about 4 percent of the $9.5 billion UC budget. UC was deceptive, claiming that student fees paid for only 35 percent of students' undergraduate education when the proportion was closer to 86 percent.

57. Assembly Bill No. 111, 11 January 1993, pp. 262, 271, 281.

58. Larry Gordon, 'UC Adopts Policy to Place More Emphasis on Teaching', *Los Angeles Times*, 17 July 1992.

59. William Trombley and Larry Gordon, 'Spending by UC Officials Raises Questions', *Los Angeles Times*, 26 Aug. 1992. Expenses paid out of public funds included $2,628 for a wedding reception.

60. Carmen Ramos Chandler, 'Cuts Threaten UC's Academic Integrity', *Daily News*, 17 May 1993; Charles Hornberger, 'Stalled State Budget Leaves Funding for UC in Danger of New Cutbacks', *Daily Nexus*, 1 July 1991; 'UCSB Raises', *Santa Barbara News-Press*, 1 July 1992. During this budget crisis, UCSB gave eighteen administrators raises averaging $6,026: the administrators called the raises well deserved.

61. David Glidden, 'The Incredible Shrinking Course Load at Pricey UC', *Los Angeles Times*, 22 March 1992; Jeff Smith, 'Those Who Teach Get the Least', *Los Angeles Times*, 28 Aug. 1992; Ralph Frammolino, 'UC Chief Rejects"Teaching Only" Campuses', *Los Angeles Times*, 25 Sept. 1993. The California Policy Center in San Jose urged some campuses to concentrate more on teaching.

62. 'El sistema UC efectuará una investigación sobre latinos', *La Opinión*, 19 June 1992.

63. UC Office of the President, *Admissions & Outreach Services, FCPER2 Statistical Summary*, April 1990; Teresa Puente, 'Profesores Latinos', *La Opinión*, 3 Aug. 1991; 'Ligero aumento en la proporción de profesores universitarios hispanos', *La Opinión*, 21 Jan. 1992.

64. Latino Issues Forum, *A Statistical Analysis of the Status of Chicanos of California*, September 1991, pp. 2, 4. One of the major barriers to Chicanos in the UC system was the faculty governance process; it was based on a hierarchy made up almost entirely of white males whose academic communities were thoroughly Eurocentric, elitist and racist. Within this system there was an innate bias against applied research or any knowledge that was 'popular' – as they termed it.

65. Larry Gordon and David Treadwell, 'On Race Relations, Colleges Are Learning Hard Lessons', *Los Angeles Times*, 4 Jan. 1992.

66. Auris Jarasunas, 'Wealthier Minorities Entering UC, Study Says', *Daily Bruin News*, 24 May 1990.

67. Refugio I. Rochin and Adaljiza Sosa-Riddell, 'Chicano Studies in a Pluralistic Society', Chicano Studies Program, University of California, Davis, Nov. 1991, p. 3. In 1972 there were only twenty-nine programs at four-year colleges, but by the early 1990s there were hundreds of Chicano Studies programs.

68. Rodolfo Acuña, 'Chicano Studies: A Public Trust', in *Chicano Studies: Critical Connection Between Research and Community*, The National Association for Chicano Studies, March 1992, pp. 3–13; Gilberto García, 'Beyond the Adelita Image: Women Scholars in the National Association for Chicano Studies, 1974–1990', unpublished MS.

69. Rallies and protests were held throughout the Southwest and Midwest for Chicano Studies. My rejection for a post in Chicano Studies at the University of California, Santa Barbara led to a lawsuit, *Acuña v. The Regents of the University of California et al.*, which among other things called attention to the fact that UC Santa Barbara's Chicano Studies Department only had three and a half positions after nearly twenty-five years of existence. The crux of the case was the 'disparate impact' of UC policies on the hiring of Chicano scholars – that is, that UC systematically discriminated against Chicanos; less than 3 percent of the professors were of Mexican descent. (According to the *Latino Issues Forum*, the University of California is increasing the numbers of its Latino faculty at the rate of 1/11th of 1 percent a year). As of December 1995, *Acuña v. UC Regents* was still in the courts. UC had at that time spent $4 million defending the case. Documents recovered in discovery showed that one of the members of the ad hoc (secret) committee was a former member of the Central Intelligence Agency and that the faculty senate committee attempted to put history professor Otis Graham in charge of the secret committee (Graham sat on the executive board of the reactionary Federation for American Immigration Reform). Thousands marched on 1 February 1992, taking over State Street in Santa Barbara in a 'Take Back Your History' protest. The first national Chicano teleconference was held in November 1993 involving over 900 high school students bused into the University of Southern California from local high schools with over forty universities hooking in on television via satellite. The theme was once more 'Take Back Your History!' Jocelyn Y. Stewart, 'Conference Urges Study of Chicano History', *Nuestro Tiempo*, 17 Dec. 1992.

70. José Luis Sierra, 'Senado de UCLA decidera creacion de instituto para estudios chicanos', *La Opinión*, 19 April 1991; Ray Davis, 'Grab Education, My Children', *CrossRoads* (May 1992), pp. 2–6; Elizabeth Martínez, 'New Twists on the Multiculturalism Front', *CrossRoads* (May 1992), pp. 7–9; Robin Templeton, 'Taking Back the University', *CrossRoads* (May 1992), pp. 10–13; George Martinez and Al Robles, 'Chicano Youth Shake Up the Valley, *CrossRoads* (May 1992), pp. 20–23; 'Secret Committee Vetoes Chicano Historian', *CrossRoads* (May 1992), p. 21.

71. Juan Gómez Quiñones, 'UCLA's Donkey Show', *Eastside Sun*, 29 June 1989.

72. George Ramos, 'Plan Unveiled for UCLA Department of Chicano Studies', *Los Angeles Times*, 29 Jan. 1992. MEChA and Chicano professors generated the proposal. Throughout the three-year struggle, Young expressed his disapproval of ethnic studies departments, José Luis Sierra, 'Propondrán departamento de Estudios Chicanos para la UCLA', *La Opinión*, 28 Jan. 1992.

73. Larry Gordon, 'UCLA Rejects Plan to Elevate Chicano Studies to Department', *Los Angeles Times*, 29 April 1993.

74. Dawn B. Mablon, 'Students Rally for Library, Programs', *Daily Bruin*, 12 May 1993; Scott Burgess, 'Police Arrest 85 on Counts of Vandalism', *Daily Bruin*, 12 May 1993; Larry Gordon and Marina Dundjerski, 'UCLA Chief Stands Firm on Chicano Studies Issue', *Los Angeles Times*, 15 May 1993. Sen. Torres persuaded legislative subcommittee to hold up $838,000 on UCLA Law School construction. Young had been insultingly arrogant with a group of legislators, claiming that he would not yield to political pressure, although he routinely gave in to the pressure of wealthy alumni, Ruben Navarrette, Jr, 'Outrage of Latino Elite: Good Sign for 21st Century', *Los Angeles Times*, 16 May 1993; Andrea L. Rich, 'Pro: Debate Is on Method, Not Goal', *Los Angeles Times*, 18 May 1993; Adela de la Torre, 'Con: Departmental Status Is Critical', *Los Angeles Times*, 18 May 1993.

75. Josh Meyer, 'Unlikely Activist Joins Hunger Strike', *Los Angeles Times*, 2 June 1993.

76. David E. Hayes-Bautista, Edward James Olmos and Gregory Rodriguez, 'A Wake-Up Call at Death's Door: Chicano Studies Are Our Future', *Los Angeles Times*, 2 June 1993; 'Back to the '60s?, *Daily News*, 8 June 1993.

77. Richard Stayton, 'The Ballad of Edward James Olmos', *LA Style* (March 1990), pp. 146–8, 176.

78. Tom Hayden, 'The Mission of UCLA's Hunger Strike', *Daily News*, 14 June 1993; Larry Gordon and Bernice Hirabay Ashi, 'Chancellor Holds Firm Amid Protest', *Los Angeles Times*, 2 June 1993.

79. Sergio Muñoz, 'Media, Beware: L.A.'s Invisible Majority Is Giving Up Its Silence', *Los Angeles Times*, 6 June 1993; Larry Gordon and Sonia Nazario, 'Fasters, UCLA Officials Meet to Defuse Protest', *Los Angeles Times*, 6 June 1993; Carmen Ramos Chandler, 'Hunger Strikers Feasting on Success', *Daily News*, 13 June 1993; Rubén Martínez, ' ... the Emergence of L.A.'s True Identity', *Los Angeles Times*, 9 June 1993; Larry Gordon, 'UCLA Strikers End Fast; Compromise Reached', *Los*

Angeles Times, 8 June 1993.

80. Elizabeth Martínez, 'Seeds of a New Movimiento', reprinted from *Z Magazine* in the Chicana (o)/ Latina (o) student newspaper *Venceremos*, University of Utah, Fall 1993.

81. A gnawing question remained after the hunger strike: Was Chicano Studies worth dying for? Historically, however, people have died for less – oil, for example. During the hunger strike students said they were willing to die for principle. In ten years the UCLA hunger strike will be studied by whites, Blacks and Chicanos. Some will call it a millennarian movement; others will call it nationalism; and others, altruism. When all is said and done, the reality is that there would be no autonomous Chicano Studies program at UCLA without that sacrifice. The UCLA hunger strike students represented the best in the Chicano community – students who've gotten a university education and who still care about others. See Rodolfo Acuña interview, 'A Chicano Activist-Scholar on the Hunger Strike and the Future', *Los Angeles Times*, 22 June 1993.

82. Patrick J. Buchanan, 'The Racism of Affirmative Action', *Pittsburgh Post-Gazette*, 23 Jan. 1995.

83. 'Higher Ed In Calif.: An End to Affirmative Action', *Daily Report Card*, 6 Feb. 1995. About 13 percent of the students were Latinos, which included South Americans and even Spaniards; 5.5 percent were African Americans. Less than 3 percent of the professors were Chicanos. Connerly, who had introduced a resolution to abolish affirmative action at the University of California, has said that he wants to be known by the quality of his work. Although he was hardly a household name in the civil rights movement or in the Black community, he has become a leader in trying to abolish racial preferences. According to him, affirmative action was dead, and he was going to negotiate burial rites. But what moral authority did he have to arrange such a funeral?

84. Steven V. Roberts, et al., 'Affirmative Action on the Edge', *US News & World Report*, vol. 118, no. 6 (Feb. 1995), p. 32 (printout). A *Wall Street Journal/NBC News* survey found that two out of three Americans, including half of those who had voted for Clinton, opposed affirmative action. The *Los Angeles Times* found that 73 percent of Californians backed the initiative.

85. Mandalit Del Barco, 'UC Scrutinizes Affirmative Action Policies', *All Things Considered*, National Public Radio, 8 Feb. 1995.

86. 'Living by the Numbers', *San Francisco Chronicle*, 12 Dec. 1995; Ed Mendel, 'Bill to End Affirmative Action Programs Killed', *San Diego Union-Tribune*, 11 Aug. 1994.

87. Peter Brown, 'Clinton's Dilemma', *San Francisco Examiner*, 5 Feb. 1995; William Claibone, 'Catching the Tidal Wave on Affirmative Action', *Washington Post National Weekly Edition*, 13–19 Feb. 1995, p. 31. Jerry Roberts, 'Democrats Must Face Tough Issues of Race', *San Francisco Chronicle*, 5 Feb. 1995.

88. Joe Klein, 'The End of Affirmative Action', *Newsweek*, 13 Feb. 1995.

89. Steven V. Roberts et al., 'Affirmative Action on the Edge', *US News & World Report*, vol. 118, no. 6 (Feb. 1995); Dave Lesher, 'Willie Brown Fervently Defends Affirmative Action', *Los Angeles Times*, 15 Feb 1995.

90. 'Living by the Numbers', *San Francisco Chronicle*, 12 Feb. 1995.

91. Nicholas Mills, 'About Affirmative Action: Mean Times in California', *Newsday*, 12 Jan. 1995.

92. Carl Irving, 'The Pendulum Swings, and Could Knock the Democrats Flat', *San Francisco Chronicle*, 8 Feb. 1995; Jerry Roberts, 'Democrats Must Face Tough Issues of Race', *San Francisco Chronicle*, 5 Feb. 1995.

93. Ira Eisenberg, '"The Anxious Class" vs. Racial Quotas', *Daily News*, 26 Jan. 1995.

94. 'Advocates Comment on California Civil Rights Initiative': guests, Thomas Woods, co-author of the California Civil Rights Initiative, and Elizabeth Schroeder, ACLU of Southern California, *Inside Politics*, Cable News Service, 10 Jan. 1995.

Conclusion

Chicanos: Claiming

a Future in Los Angeles

Much of this book has been devoted to what can be called the struggle by people of Mexican origin in Los Angeles (and often other Latinos sharing space with them) to replace a politics of exclusion with the politics of inclusion. Whether the immediate issue is economics or education, in the end it is framed by that set of opposites. At this writing, the future looks quite bleak for a politics of inclusion in which the voice of the working-class Chicano majority will be heard. But there are small lights suggesting a path to potential change in power relations. Despite all the barriers, Chicanos and other Latinos have been carving out their place in Los Angeles as a potential political force.

This is true in one very literal sense. In 1994, Chicanos were the fastest-growing group of homebuyers in Los Angeles County's hard-hit real estate market. They accounted for nine of the top surnames listed as homebuyers in the county, with García leading the list. The recession and deflated home values gave them a window of opportunity, as did a slowing down of domestic migration to Los Angeles. Ironically, earthquakes worked in favor of Chicanos and Latinos. The market's high prices in 1989 had prevented them from buying homes. Since then the number of Latinos buying homes has climbed by 40 percent. Government oversight regarding discriminatory lending practices (which many Angelenos wanted to eliminate) assisted the process, as did Latino cultural patterns, whereby two or three families cooperatively bought a home in spaces that others had abandoned.[1] Permanent residents facilitate the development of a political base.

There is also the fact that from 1989 through 1992, 2.6 million former undocumented residents were granted permanent US residence. Most lived in California, and over half of them lived in Los Angeles. Nearly 500,000 were eligible to become citizens in 1994, another 880,00 in 1995, and more than a million in 1996. The overwhelming majority of them will be of voting age before the turn of the century.[2]

How those thousands of new citizens will evolve politically, how they will vote, is a question of growing importance. Many come to the US with a radical consciousness because of struggles in their homelands – especially Mexicans and Central Americans. But conservative forces have been at work among Latinos in Los Angeles, and they have had success in recent years. In the 1980s, many of the 'New Hispanics' *se hicieron pendejos*, 'made fools of themselves', by adopting the politics of Ronald Reagan, George Deukmejian and George Bush.[3] Reagan created racial resentment with his image of the 'welfare queen', vetoed the 1988 Civil Rights bill, resisted extension of the Voting Rights Act, and tried to protect tax subsidies for private white schools that excluded Blacks. Many Latinos still supported Reagan, who remained popular til the end, attracting a high proportion of Chicano and other Latino votes.

In California, Republican governors George Deukmejian and Pete Wilson lured many Latino influence peddlers into their fold.[4] The term *Hispanic*, with its European pretensions, lifted the 'Hispanics' from the 'immigrant masses'. Few of these Latino brokers bothered to question the racial or class politics of their adopted party, ignoring the widening gap between rich and poor. It is ironic that many of the Educational Opportunities babies of the 1960s and 1970, like white World War II veterans, forgot that they had been given a helping hand by programs like the G.I. Bill and EOP. Like the rest of society they spoke less about class-based politics and more about the economic concerns of the individual. They made it because they had worked for it, they said. Many, like Richard Rodríguez, even expressed resentment of the helping hand.[5] It became much more popular to pick up *Hispanic Business* and read about the '100 Influentials' or the Hispanic 500 Corporations than to read about Chicanos as victims or exploited workers. Our 'Hispanics' saw no contradiction in demanding entitlements for themselves and their families while supporting conservative plans to end government aid to others.

We can only hope that fewer of our people will *hacerse pendejos* in the next, crucial, period of time, as Chicanos and Latinos build their political base in Los Angeles and elsewhere in the United States. In this era of vicious attacks on immigrant rights, on workers' rights, on the rights of women and all people of color, Chicano politics will be the scene of ideological controversies and sharp divisions over strategy. But there remains one fact that all Latinos and the dominant society need to remember: Neither riots, fires, earthquakes, police harassment or Proposition 187 can drive *mexicanos* and other Latinos out of Los Angeles. That is because they have no other place to go – this is and has been their home, and they will not be driven away. So perhaps, if people remember that, the days of 'anything but Mexican' are numbered.

Notes

1. Stephanie O'Neill, 'Latino Home Buyers Are the Fastest-Growing Group in the Los Angeles County Real Estate Market', *Los Angeles Times*, 4 Dec. 1994.

2. Ellis Cose, 'The Lesser of Two Evils', *Newsweek*, 21 June 1993, p. 29.

3. *Los Angeles Times*, 28 July 1991.

4. See my *Occupied America: A History of Chicanos*, 3d edn (New York: Harper & Row, 1988); Chapters 10 and 11 contain a discussion of the formation of a Chicano broker class.

5. David Laute, '"Class War" Is Poor Politics', *Los Angeles Times*, 24 Oct. 1990; Fred Risen, 'Fed Says '80s Boom Mostly Aided the Rich', *Los Angeles Times*, 7 Jan. 1992.

Index

affirmative action: attacks on by New Right 308; need for 309; initiative against 133, 310–11

African Americans: 1990 Census in L.A. 2; and Bradley regime 169 n75; and immigration 157; and LAUSD 313 n26; political competition with Latinos 60 n9, 73, 127–30, 149–50; political mobilization 47, 129, 149; in workforce 221

Aguilar, Marcos 305

AIDS crisis 35

Alarcón, Richard 144

Alatorre, Richard 50, 105 n21; base of support 51–2, 58; City Council race 58; Eastside machine 57, 75; and Olvera Street 24, 26, 27; political style 51–2, 58, 72, 85 n35; and reapportionment 55–6, 59

alcoholism 31–2

Alianza Hispano-Americana 34

Almárez, Carlos 13

Alvárez, Gloria 13

American G.I. Forum 31, 44

América Tropical (Siquieros) 23, 26

Anglo-Americans: population decline in L.A. 5, 48, 156

anti-immigration hysteria 121–22, 154–8

Antonovich, Mike 115

Arciniega, Tomas 300–301

Asian Americans 131–3; 1990 Census in L.A. 2; labor 109; lack of representation 49

assimilation 2, 8–10

August 29 (Valenzuela) 13

Baca, Jim 103

Baca, Joe 97

Baca, Judith 13

Bakewell, Danny 278

barrios, use of urban space in 11–12

Becerra, Xavier 76–7, 99

Bell Gardens 3

Beltrán, Pete 193–4

Benavidez, Max 13

Berman, Howard 98, 117

Bielenson, Anthony 124

bilingual education 290–91, 293–4

Block, Sherman 75, 266–7,

Bonzo, Vivién 24, 27–8, 213, 306

Border Patrol 116

Boxer, Barbara 102

Boyle Heights 5, 6, 38, 50, 65–6

Boyle, Patrick 258

Bracero Program 112

Bradley, Tom 25, 30, 58, 129, 167 n39, 169 n75, 175, 277

Braithwaite Burke, Yvonne 270

Brown, Jerry 55

Brown, Kathleen 125, 163

Brown, Willie 55, 58, 66, 71, 83 n12, 95, 163

Bush, George 22, 82, 100, 101–2, 236, 252 n42

Bustamante, Jorge 233–4, 243

Calderón, Charles 75, 76

Calderón v. City of Los Angeles 50

California Civil Rights Initiative (CCRI) 133, 309–11

California Democratic Council (CDC) 48, 50, 61 n25

California Immigrant Workers Association 190

California State University system 298–302, 315 n45: CSU Fresno 301; CSU Fullerton 300; CSU Northridge 10, 304; CSU San Jose 301

Californios for Fair Representation (CFR) 54–5, 57

THE HAYMARKET SERIES

Related Titles

IT'S NOT ABOUT A SALARY: Rap, Race and Resistance in Los Angeles
by Brian Cross, with additional text by Reagan Kelly and T-Lov

CITY OF QUARTZ: Excavating the Future in Los Angeles
by Mike Davis

PRISONERS OF THE AMERICAN DREAM: Politics and Economy in the
History of the US Working Class *by Mike Davis*

NO CRYSTAL STAIR: African-Americans in the City of Angels
by Lynell George

ROLL DOWN YOUR WINDOW: Stories from a Forgotten America
by Juan González

RACE, POLITICS, AND ECONOMIC DEVELOPMENT: Community Perspectives
edited by James Jennings

BEYOND BLACK AND WHITE: Rethinking Race in American Politics and Society
by Manning Marable

THE OTHER SIDE: Los Angeles from Both Sides of the Border
by Rubén Martínez

YOUTH, IDENTITY, POWER: The Chicano Movement
by Carlos Muñoz, Jr.

FIRE IN THE HEARTH: The Radical Politics of Place in America
The Year Left 4